Transformative Impact of Digital Technologies on Artistic Production:

Photography and Visuality

Murat Han Er
https://orcid.org/0000-0002-3896-2796
Ataturk University, Turkey

Basri Gençcelep
Ataturk University, Turkey

IGI Global
Scientific Publishing
Publishing Tomorrow's Research Today

Vice President of Editorial Melissa Wagner
Director of Acquisitions Mikaela Felty
Director of Book Development Jocelynn Hessler
Production Manager Mike Brehm
Cover Design Jose Rosado

Published in the United States of America by
IGI Global Scientific Publishing
701 East Chocolate Avenue
Hershey, PA, 17033, USA
Tel: 717-533-8845 | Fax: 717-533-7115
Website: https://www.igi-global.com E-mail: cust@igi-global.com

Library of Congress Cataloging-in-Publication Data

Names: Er, Murat Han, 1981- editor | Gençcelep, Basri, 1980- editor
Title: Transformative impact of digital technologies on artistic production : photography and visuality / edited by Murat Er, Basri Gençcelep.
Description: Hershey, PA : IGI Global Scientific Publishing, [2026] | Includes bibliographical references and index. | Summary: "This book examines the transformative effects of digital technologies on artistic production, with a particular focus on photography and visuality, from a multifaceted perspective. At its core, this study explores how digitalization has reshaped artistic production processes in technical, aesthetic, and conceptual dimensions, transformed traditional approaches, and paved the way for new forms of expression"-- Provided by publisher.
Identifiers: LCCN 2025023217 (print) | LCCN 2025023218 (ebook) | ISBN 9798337322308 hardcover | ISBN 9798337322315 paperback | ISBN 9798337322322 ebook
Subjects: LCSH: Technology and the arts
Classification: LCC NX180.T4 T73 2026 (print) | LCC NX180.T4 (ebook)
LC record available at https://lccn.loc.gov/2025023217
LC ebook record available at https://lccn.loc.gov/2025023218

British Cataloguing in Publication Data
A Cataloguing in Publication record for this book is available from the British Library.

Table of Contents

Detailed Table of Contents

This article examines the impact of digital technologies on artistic production, focusing particularly on the reinterpretation of the concept of "ready-made" in the context of photography. Digitalization has fundamentally transformed both the creative processes and production tools of photographers and artists, reshaping traditional artistic practices. While ready-made is traditionally understood as an element of an artwork, as pioneered by Duchamp, in the digital age, this concept has expanded to include elements such as digital image banks, 3D modeling, and visuals created using artificial intelligence. The article emphasizes that the use of ready-made in the digital environment, while increasing the possibilities of artistic expression, also brings with it discussions of originality, creativity, and ethics, as in the first examples of ready-made. Additionally, it discusses how photography and art can create more innovative visual narratives with the unlimited resources available on digital platforms and the contributions of this process to meaning production in art.

Michael Christopher Brown's 90 Miles project challenges foundations of documentary photography by employing artificial intelligence to generate images rather than capturing them through a camera. This project disrupts traditional notions of photographic truth, blurring the line between reality and fiction, and forcing a reassessment of what constitutes a documentary image. By replacing the indexical relationship between photograph and subject with machine-generated interpretations, 90 Miles raises critical questions about authorship and the role of human intervention in visual storytelling. This paper examines 90 Miles through a critical lens, exploring how AI-generated imagery reconfigures the ethics and aesthetics of documentary photography. By situating 90 Miles within debates on

The close relationship between photography and technology has also shaped its interaction with other related disciplines. Historically, continuous technical transformations have significantly influenced the language, visual structure, and image quality of photography. The relationship between archaeology and photography is based on a utilitarian expectation of documentation. Artists have subjected archaeological objects or ancient artifacts to a kind of visible and effective transformation through digital photography. The objects seen in photographs are already works of art, but there have also been artists who have worked directly with found photographs. In addition to this utilitarianism, a creative aspect has also emerged, strengthened by artistic desire.

Digital transformation creates a radical shift in the representation of gender in the practice of photography, allowing the de-gendering of photographic language. Digital technologies contribute to the polyphony of the gaze towards the subject of the photograph by enabling the creation of a visual production process independent of the gender and identity of the artist. In this context, digital artists emphasizing the fact that gender is a social construction tend to develop a genderless photographic language with tools that reshape identity and the body. By focusing on the work of artists, this study explores the potential of digital technologies to both increase visibility and create a space of resistance against algorithmic exclusion. By widening and deepening the boundaries of photography, digitalization opens up a space that transcends gender norms and allows for a move beyond traditional representations.

Photography has undergone a significant evolution from its analog roots film and darkrooms to today's digital and automated methods. One of the most impactful changes is the incorporation of artificial intelligence (AI) in image production,

Foreword

We are living at the very center of an era in which digital technologies are transforming artistic production. Since the invention of photography, each technical leap has redefined not only our ways of seeing but also our aesthetic criteria and ethical responsibilities. This book approaches that transformation through both historical continuity and contemporary plurality, opening the relationship between photography and new media to discussion on theoretical and practical planes.

Building from ready-made and other avant-garde experiments, the chapters reconsider the meaning of "material" and "method" today, in the context of digital image banks, 3D modeling, and AI-assisted production. In doing so, concepts such as "originality," "creativity," and "ethics" cease to be merely the terms of a historical debate and become living questions renegotiated within the current production ecosystem. The tension between photography's archival function and artistic imagination is read alongside circulation, re-production, and shifts of context; issues of source transparency, economies of attribution, and co-authorship are brought into view.

Throughout the book, ruptures and continuities intertwine: conceptual strategies inherited from Dada gain new layers of meaning through the technical possibilities of the digital age, while the aesthetic and political consequences of technical innovation are examined through concrete examples. The theoretical framework addresses the production, circulation, and reception of images from the perspectives of data–aesthetics relations, copyright regimes, and the sharing of decision-making. In parallel, practice-oriented contributions present contemporary methods—from digital negatives to archive-based narratives, from algorithmic montage to exhibition design—together with the possibilities and pitfalls of production processes.

The chapters interlock like parts of a whole: they establish the core debate by examining their subjects through both historical origins and contemporary practices; they deepen the ethical and legal questions raised by visual circulation in digital environments; and they invite readers to rethink the notion of the "original image" in the age of AI. Case studies drawn from artistic practice demonstrate the creative potential of methods and tools, while strategies of display and spatialization propose a balanced model between audience experience and ethical visibility.

Beyond offering a technical inventory, the book forges a shared language across disciplines. Bringing conceptual clarity into dialogue with practical know-how, the texts create a platform for artists, photographers, designers, curators, and scholars alike. In so doing, the book opens doors to new collaborations and inquiries across production, research, and practice.

H. Ozan Bilgiseren
Mimar Sinan Fine Arts University, Turkey

Preface

INTRODUCTION

In a period when digitalization has radically transformed visual culture, production processes, and audience experience, this book offers a comprehensive framework for rethinking the conceptual, aesthetic, and ethical horizons of photography and the visual arts. From artificial intelligence to algorithmic visualization, from data aesthetics to augmented/virtual reality, these tools not only generate new modes of expression but also put long-established notions such as "reality," "originality," "authorship," and "evidence" up for negotiation. Bringing together conceptual debates with concrete artist/case studies, this volume examines the impact of digital transformation on artistic practice, visual narratives, and the public imagination.

Today, the circulation of images has reached an unprecedented level in terms of speed and scale. Social networks, online archives, platforms embedded in production–consumption cycles, and AI-assisted tools are reshaping how visual knowledge is produced and verified. The oscillation of photography between document and fiction, the strengthening of post-photography debates, the redefinition of authorship/aura, and the need for ethical labeling are among the most prominent issues in this context. By relating these transformations to both historical backgrounds and contemporary examples, the book proposes an interdisciplinary reading.

CHAPTER OVERVIEW

Chapter 1: New Possibilities for Photography in the Digital Age in the Context of the Dada Movement: Ready-Made, Collage, and Photomontage

This article examines the impact of digital technologies on artistic production, focusing particularly on the reinterpretation of the concept of "ready-made" in the context of photography. Digitalization has fundamentally transformed both the creative processes and production tools of photographers and artists, reshaping traditional artistic practices. While ready-made is traditionally understood as an element of an artwork, as pioneered by Duchamp, in the digital age, this concept has expanded to include elements such as digital image banks, 3D modeling, and visuals created using artificial intelligence. The article emphasizes that the use of ready-made in the digital environment, while increasing the possibilities of artistic expression, also brings with it discussions of originality, creativity, and ethics, as in the first examples of ready-made. Additionally, it discusses how photography and art can create more innovative visual narratives with the unlimited resources available on digital platforms and the contributions of this process to meaning production in art.

Chapter 2: 90 Miles and the AI-Mediated Documentary: Rethinking Reality in the Digital Age

Michael Christopher Brown's 90 Miles project challenges foundations of documentary photography by employing artificial intelligence to generate images rather than capturing them through a camera. This project disrupts traditional notions of photographic truth, blurring the line between reality and fiction, and forcing a reassessment of what constitutes a documentary image. By replacing the indexical relationship between photograph and subject with machine-generated interpretations, 90 Miles raises critical questions about authorship and the role of human intervention in visual storytelling. This paper examines 90 Miles through a critical lens, exploring how AI-generated imagery reconfigures the ethics and aesthetics of documentary photography. By situating 90 Miles within debates on post-photography, this study interrogates how AI redefines the relationship between visual narratives and historical truth.

Chapter 3: Exploring New Meanings in Post-Photography and Digital Art

This chapter examines the transformative impact of digital technologies on photography and visual culture through the lens of post-photography. Drawing on theoretical frameworks from Jean Baudrillard, Hito Steyerl, Lev Manovich, and Joan Fontcuberta, it explores how artificial intelligence, algorithms, and digital manipulation reshape image production, aesthetic norms, and representation. Social media aesthetics, archival politics, and algorithmic decision-making processes are analyzed in connection with contemporary art practices. The chapter presents a critical discussion of artists such as Rafman, Rickard, Fontcuberta, Anadol, and Meyohas, whose works challenge traditional notions of authorship, visuality, and truth. Post-photography is positioned not only as a technical shift but as a cultural paradigm that redefines the relationship between data, identity, and visual experience.

Chapter 4: Reality, Fiction, Propaganda, Fantasy! The Art of Photography

This study maps how photography, from its first exposures to today's platforms, has evolved from a recording device into a narrative system that both documents and constructs reality. Oscillating between fact and fiction, art and reportage, propaganda and fantasy, the medium's digital manipulability intensifies debates over truth, representation, and ethics. Through cases such as Kundera's individual–state–memory triangle, Capa's Falling Soldier, Doisneau's The Kiss at Hôtel de Ville, and Nick Ut's Napalm Girl, the research probes photography's political and aesthetic power. It also examines staged imagery in the work of Jeff Wall and Gregory Crewdson to analyze how cinematic setups shape perception in the networked era. Bringing historical manipulation into dialogue with contemporary practice, the study repositions photography as visual memory requiring renewed ethical, aesthetic, and technical scrutiny.

Chapter 5: The Digital Presentation of Archaeological Data in Photography and Its Artistic Context

The close relationship between photography and technology has also shaped its interaction with other related disciplines. Historically, continuous technical transformations have significantly influenced the language, visual structure, and image quality of photography. The relationship between archaeology and photography is based on a utilitarian expectation of documentation. Artists have subjected archaeological objects or ancient artifacts to a kind of visible and effective transformation through digital photography. The objects seen in photographs are already works of art, but there have also been artists who have worked directly with found photographs. In addition to this utilitarianism, a creative aspect has also emerged, strengthened by artistic desire.

Chapter 6: Paradigm Shift in Photography in the Perspective of Digital Transformation and Gender

Digital transformation creates a radical shift in the representation of gender in the practice of photography, allowing the de-gendering of photographic language. Digital technologies contribute to the polyphony of the gaze towards the subject of the photograph by enabling the creation of a visual production process independent of the gender and identity of the artist. In this context, digital artists emphasizing the fact that gender is a social construction tend to develop a genderless photographic language with tools that reshape identity and the body. By focusing on the work of artists, this study explores the potential of digital technologies to both increase visibility and create a space of resistance against algorithmic exclusion. By widening and deepening the boundaries of photography, digitalization opens up a space that transcends gender norms and allows for a move beyond traditional representations.

Chapter 7: The Perception and Ethical Implications of AI-Generated Images as Press Photography

Photography has undergone a significant evolution from its analog roots film and darkrooms to today's digital and automated methods. One of the most impactful changes is the incorporation of artificial intelligence (AI) in image production, sparking both innovation and debate. This article explores the contentious use of AI-generated hyper-realistic visuals in journalism. It raises ethical concerns about presenting such images as authentic news content, warning of the risk of misleading viewers, damaging trust in the media, and contributing to misinformation. The paper stresses that transparency in labeling AI-generated images is crucial to uphold photojournalistic ethics. It also highlights the urgent need for media literacy to help the public critically evaluate visual content in a digital age shaped by advanced technologies.

Chapter 8: Artificial Intelligence and Artistic Creativity: Redefining the Boundaries of Photography and Visual Expression

Artificial intelligence quickly transforms the landscape of photography and visual representation, seeking creativity and traditional ideas from artists. In this chapter, we will discover how AI technology can help not only roles from generation algorithms to neural networks but also actively create artistic content that redefines the role of human artists. Through tools such as AI-generated images, style transmission, and automated processing, photographers and visual artists are pushing beyond what is possible with visual storytelling. These advancements open new ways of creativity and raise essential questions about originality, aesthetic values, and ethical responsibility. Investigating practical applications and artistic collaboration with AI highlights the opportunities and tensions arising in the interface between technology and ART. Ultimately, AI is not a replacement for creativity, but a redesign of artistry reviews, defining artistic intentions, visual authors, and developing the language of photography in the digital age.

Chapter 9: Digital Images: A New Way of Seeing

This chapter examines the transformative impact of digital technologies on artistic production and visual communication, focusing on photography and digital images. It argues that digital visuality constitutes a new way of seeing and remembering, reshaping aesthetic norms, cultural representation, and collective memory. Drawing on theorists such as McLuhan, Flusser, Manovich, and Mitchell, the chapter explores how digital images function as tools of perception, cultural memory, and social witnessing. Through case studies including AI-generated art, protest imagery like the "Lady in Red," and social media archives, the chapter highlights the dual role of digital images as both aesthetic and mnemonic agents in contemporary culture.

Chapter 10: Reconstructing Aura in the Digital Age: The Search for Authenticity in Artificial Intelligence Art

This article aims to reconsider Walter Benjamin's concept of "aura" in the context of artworks produced with artificial intelligence (AI). Benjamin's claim that art loses its authenticity in the age of mechanical reproduction is revisited through the lens of digital and algorithmic art practices. The study employs a qualitative theoretical analysis, using Refik Anadol's Melting Memories and Machine Hallucinations as case studies. It proposes four contemporary forms of aura: processual, data-based, interactional, and algorithmic. The analysis demonstrates that AI-generated artworks can convey originality not only through their physical form, but also through their processes, cognitive dimensions, and audience interactions. Ultimately, it argues that rather than erasing subjectivity, digital and AI-driven production fosters a multi-layered, interactive aesthetic paradigm where aura persists in new forms.

Chapter 11: Artificial Intelligence and Negative Space: The Artificial Construction of Space in Visual Imagery

This study investigates how artificial intelligence perceives and aesthetically constructs negative space in visual production processes. Rather than being merely a visual element, space functions as a communicative tool for meaning-making and audience engagement. How is this traditionally meaningful aesthetic choice interpreted by AI? To explore this, three models—DALL·E, Stable Diffusion, and Leonardo AI—were tested using identical textual prompts, and their use of space, composition, and figure placement were comparatively analyzed. The findings reveal model-specific approaches to spatial organization, raising the critical question: does AI merely fill space, or can it meaningfully employ it as a compositional strategy?

CONCLUSION

This volume demonstrates that visual production in the digital age cannot be reduced to a merely technical evolution; rather, it constitutes a multilayered transformation interwoven with aesthetics, politics, ethics, and economics. Throughout the book, foundational concepts such as "aura," "authorship," "truth," and "evidence" are revisited; actionable methodological proposals are developed regarding archiving, ethical labeling, and media literacy; and direct contact with production processes is established through artist practices and case analyses. The conceptual bridges built between photography, cinema, graphic design, communication, and new media deepen the discussion on an interdisciplinary plane; thus, the work functions both as a reliable reference for researchers and practitioners in the field and as a guiding map for a broad readership seeking to understand the visual regimes of the digital age.

Murat Han Er
Atatürk University, Turkey

Basri Gençcelep
Atatürk University, Turkey

Chapter 1

New Possibilities for Photography in the Digital Age in the Context of the Dada Movement:
Ready-Made, Collage, and Photomontage

Murat Han Er
http://orcid.org/0000-0002-3896-2796
Atatürk University, Turkey

ABSTRACT

This article examines the impact of digital technologies on artistic production, focusing particularly on the reinterpretation of the concept of "ready-made" in the context of photography. Digitalization has fundamentally transformed both the creative processes and production tools of photographers and artists, reshaping traditional artistic practices. While ready-made is traditionally understood as an element of an artwork, as pioneered by Duchamp, in the digital age, this concept has expanded to include elements such as digital image banks, 3D modeling, and visuals created using artificial intelligence. The article emphasizes that the use of ready-made in the digital environment, while increasing the possibilities of artistic expression, also brings with it discussions of originality, creativity, and ethics, as in the first examples of ready-made. Additionally, it discusses how photography

DOI: 10.4018/979-8-3373-2230-8.ch001

and art can create more innovative visual narratives with the unlimited resources available on digital platforms and the contributions of this process to meaning production in art.

INTRODUCTION

Today, we are being drawn into a completely digital world. Virtual worlds and artificial intelligence are drawing us into this digital world in unimaginable ways. We are facing a system in which all human activities can be carried out through digital worlds. The digital universe is irrevocably transporting humanity into the world it has created. In today's world, where daily routine tasks are carried out using digital tools, many fields such as the military, healthcare, engineering, architecture, art, marketing, and economics are fueled by the digital world. In this world where humanity benefits from the digital pool, we are unknowingly creating the data network of "big markets." This data network is used in many fields such as economics, security, marketing, and even art. In the digital age, artists have also found opportunities to adapt themselves to new applications and take advantage of every opportunity. Artists who see the digital world's vast data pool and succeed in transforming it in the face of digital applications have discovered ways to use the new artistic tools of contemporary art.

The transformative role of the digital world in changing everything, along with the almost incomprehensible role of Contemporary Art, has also transformed the concept of "artwork" and the "Ready-Made" concept, which encompasses this work, in terms of application. Once a physical object, "Ready-Made" has now become an image and writing consisting of 0s and 1s that exist in the digital environment. "Ready-Made," which changed the course of art and art history and is one of the important turning points, is being used by artists in a way that cannot be opposed digitally.

In the digital age, found objects or "Ready-Mades" sometimes consist of images taken from the web, and sometimes of object images 'appropriated' from various media applications. These approaches are the "Ready-Mades" of the digital world, beginning with Dada. Thomas Ruff's use of images of significant events obtained through "appropriation" from the web, or Penelope Umbrico's creation of her work 'Sunset' using over half a million sunset photographs from "Flickr," can be cited as examples of "Ready-Made" in the digital age. Since Ready-Made, collage, photomontage, and appropriation practices are intertwined both theoretically and practically, it would be highly beneficial to examine their historical use during the Dada and Surrealism periods before addressing digital "Ready-Mades."

An Overview of Dada

In the early 20th century, Dada and similar art movements were shaped by the devastating transformations brought about by World War I. Influenced by Freud, Einstein, and the Machine Age, individuals' perceptions of the world changed radically; Joyce's novels and Eliot's poems reflected this modernist break. Movements such as Cubism and Futurism challenged the boundaries of traditional painting and questioned the structure of consciousness; however, it was Dada and Surrealism that most effectively explored the mental depth of the modern individual (Hopkins, 2004, p. 1). With this period, the traditional understanding of art opened the door to thought and mental inquiry.

According to Hopkins, modernist rebellions, particularly Dada and Surrealism, are “avant-garde” movements. Art, which had become synonymous with the bourgeoisie in the 19th century, was ideologically questioned for the first time with Courbet's Realism movement. Courbet represented the first conscious “avant-garde” orientation in art history by combining a socialist agenda with an aesthetic principle. In the 20th century, movements such as Futurism, Constructivism, De Stijl, Dada, and Surrealism rejected the distinction between art and life, integrating social experience into art; these movements differed according to their political contexts (Hopkins, 2004, p. 2).

The most radical movement that deeply influenced artists of the period and today was Dada. Emerging as a rebellion against materialism and the destruction of war, this movement defended a new understanding of art that broke with tradition. The group expressed their despair but also envisioned a new form of art that would dismantle outdated traditions and mental barriers. As Tristan Tzara stated in his 1918 Dada Manifesto, Dada is defined as “a great act of destruction” (Tzara, 1990, cited in Mariens, 2018, p. 240). According to Genç (1983, p. 73), Dada was actually a cry from artists and thinkers who had become aware that the wars and senseless massacres carried out in the name of humanity's most sacred values stemmed from capitalist bourgeois logic and its distorted order, vested interests, and obsession with sharing the world. According to Tzara, “once upon a time, concepts such as honor, country, morality, family, art, religion, freedom, and brotherhood were able to meet people's needs. But now these concepts have been emptied of their meaning, and all that remains is a meaningless set of rules (Antmen, 2010, p. 123).

According to Sanouillet (2017, pp. 359-360), although Dada intersected with other avant-garde movements such as constructivism in Berlin, neo-plasticism in the Netherlands, or futurism in Italy, each national group has preserved its own uniqueness and been able to integrate into a common body. Sanouillet emphasizes that Dada should not be confused with movements such as Futurism, despite structural similarities. Furthermore, Breton (2017, p. 375) states that Cubism is a school of painting, Futurism is a political movement, and Dada is a way of understanding, and that it is malicious to present them as opposites.

A Brief History of Dada

Emerging in 1916 and losing its influence in the early 1920s, Dada was an artistic phenomenon that developed on an international scale (Hopkins, 2004). According to Eroğlu, Dada served an important function in reminding the world that there were people living for completely different ideals, especially outside of fascism and war (Eroğlu, 2015, p. 81). According to Antmen, Dada was a gathering of artists who came together in opposition to the division of the world into camps in the name of new divisions and who sought international solidarity against this meaninglessness (Antmen, 2010, p. 123).

In response to the atrocities of World War I, Dada began in Zurich, Switzerland, and developed as an "anti-art" movement. Influenced by Cubism, Futurism, Constructivism, and Expressionism, Dada encompasses visual arts, literature, poetry, theater, music, and graphic design (Hodge, 2019, p. 38). According to Genç (1983, p. 5), Dada is a phenomenon of total rebellion; it is the challenge of artists who rebelled against the fragmentation of humanity in the name of civilization, mocking the social order they lived in, and opposing capitalist bourgeois society's morality and traditions. According to A. Artun, futurism, which reflected the spirit of the period before World War I, can be said to have aroused excitement about the glorification of modernity through war. Dada, which emerged after the war, expresses the failure of modernity, civilization, and eventually art in the face of the horrors of war (Artun, 2010, p. 116).

According to Hodge (2019, p. 38), Dada was not only anti-war but also anti-bourgeois. The art produced by individual Dadaists did not accept artistic traditions because it was variable, colorful, and absurd. All Dadaists aimed to create shock, cause anger and resentment, and strive to be crude and disrespectful. Marcel Duchamp, Francis Picabia, Tristan Tzara, Hans Arp, Kurt Schwitters, and Raoul Hausmann were among the leading figures of Dada (Hopkins, 2004). According to Hopkins (2004), Dada artists aimed to overturn traditional norms through productions based on irony and provocation in response to a world that pushed the boundaries of reason. Indeed, Dada's absurdity was like a weapon against everything that was used as a justification for war (Genç, 1983, p. 73). Furthermore, the Dadaist revolution represents the purest and most extreme form of the liberating and nihilistic protest sentiment that has existed in Western literature throughout the centuries and across all countries (Sanouillet, 2017, p. 359).

In late 1915, all the elements that would later form the basis of Dadaism were present in Zurich, albeit in a scattered state; it was Hugo Ball who brought these elements together and created a center of activity (Sanouillet, 2017, p. 361). The story of Dada began with the gathering of many artists and writers at the Cabaret Voltaire, a nightclub in Zurich owned by writer Hugo Ball (Hodge, 2019, p. 38). German writer and performance artist Hugo Ball went to Switzerland; in May 1916, Ball and a group of friends opened the Cabaret Voltaire club in Zurich. The club was also the venue for the first Dada performance (McGinity, 2017, p. 411).

Ball's diary mentions that he invited young artists and intellectuals living in Zurich to his cabaret through newspaper advertisements (Sanouillet, 2017, p. 361). Among Ball's first friends at the cabaret were his life partner Emmy Hennings; Tristan Tzara and Marcel Janco; Hans/Jean Arp; and Sophie Taeuber. Within a short time, Richard Huelsenbeck, Walter Serner, Hans Richter, and Viking Eggeling also joined the group (Hopkins, 2004, p. 4). With the inclusion of Huelsenbeck in particular, Cabaret Voltaire took on a much more aggressive tone (Lynton, 2004, p. 124). Cabaret Voltaire offered a heterogeneous program of events ranging from poetry readings in the Expressionist style, which was one of the dominant aesthetic trends of the time, to performances. Initially, the performances had a relatively traditional structure; however, they soon turned into open provocations (Hopkins, 2004, p. 4).

Ball developed a "phonetic" form of poetry that blended meaningless made-up words with primitive linguistic elements (Hopkins, 2004, p. 6). Dada aimed to break down the boundaries of art through the collision of images and sounds triggered by chance in the visual arts and performances (Mariens, 2018, p. 240). According to Genç (1983, p. 5), Dadaist artists expressed their existence through their attitudes and actions and considered their madness a form of art.

Appearing on stage in 1916 wearing a shiny metallic costume and a conical hat, Ball revealed his artistic identity with his poetic manifesto. In these poems, which are devoid of meaning, words serve only a phonetic function (McGinity, 2017, p. 411). According to Lynton (2004, p. 124), Cabaret Voltaire became an open opposition to Western civilization and severed its ties with this world through its stage performances. Ball also defines cabaret as a gesture against the corruption of the era: "Our cabaret is a gesture... it expresses that this disgusting era has not succeeded in stripping us of our respect" (Ball, 1975, cited in Genç, 1983, p. 73). Ball is not only the founder of Dada but also its intellectual forerunner. The movement's primary source is his notebook, as no other Dadaist left behind any records. Furthermore, there is no other figure as organized, determined, and systematic in expressing his ideas as Ball (Genç, 1983, p. 84).

Dada poets and performance artists staged collective performances with "simultaneous poems" that they recited as if they were divine (Hopkins, 2004, p. 6). In addition to poetry and dance, Cabaret Voltaire also featured different artistic productions such as Hans Arp's geometric collages; this diversity reflects the equality between visual and literary production (Hopkins, 2004, p. 7). While Arp assembled colorful papers through random arrangements, Tzara produced poetry using randomly selected words. These methods, such as "Papiers Collés" and object placement, serve as a protest against the rational systems of war (Turani, 1992, p. 602). According to Antmen (2010, p. 123), Tzara's peculiar language structure is a clue to new artistic explorations in terms of its rule-breaking nature. Arp's memoirs, "Dadaland," attracted attention in Dada circles; here he mentions meeting Tzara at "Café Terasse" and writing many of his poems there. For this reason, some sources refer to "Café Terasse" as the birthplace of Dada (Genç, 1983, p. 85).

The Dada group's rejection of art as a limited category and its confrontational approach were shaped more by social and political realities than by aesthetics. The reason the members were in Zurich was Switzerland's neutrality in World War I. The Zurich Dadaists established a direct link between the horrors of war and the corrupt values of pre-war art. Instead of traditional art associated with elite spaces, they created structures using everyday objects and pieces of paper; they also fragmented and reconstructed poetry, transforming it into meaningless piles of sounds. They rejected the professional understanding of art and defined themselves as "cultural saboteurs." However, this attitude did not mean a complete rejection of art, but rather a questioning of its role in serving singular understandings of human nature (Hopkins, 2004, p. 7). In this sense, Dada was the first conceptual movement to raise conscious questions about the function of art and the social role of the artist (Hodge, 2019, p. 38). According to Eroğlu (2015, p. 182), according to Dada, if art is to serve, it must serve humanity; otherwise, it is a meaningless pursuit.

By the summer of 1916, the group abandoned Voltaire's name and adopted the name "Dada," which resembles baby talk (Lynton, 2004, p. 124). The origin of the word "Dada" is unclear, and it is referenced in different ways by different members. Ball and Huelsenbeck came across the word "dada" while flipping through a dictionary and chose it because it meant "fool" (McGinity, 2017, p. 411). Some sources, however, claim that Tzara found the word in the dictionary while specifically looking for a meaningless term (Hodge, 2019, p. 38). Additionally, Ball, in his work *Flight Out of Time*, writes that he suggested the name "Dada" to Tzara, who adopted it. According to Hopkins (2004, pp. 7–8), Huelsenbeck was also part of this process. When all accounts are considered, it appears that the name "Dada" emerged in the circle of Ball, Tzara, and Huelsenbeck. The word 'Dada' means "yes, yes" in Romanian and "wooden horse" or "child's toy" in French. For Germans, this word is associated with childlike innocence, the joy of creation, and the image of infancy. According to Huelsenbeck, this word symbolizes the first sound a child makes; it represents starting from scratch in art and returning to the basics (Hopkins, 2004, p. 8). Furthermore, "Dada" has meaning in some languages but is meaningless in many others (Hodge, 2019, p. 38). Huelsenbeck, in his 1920 article "En avant Dada," emphasizes the striking brevity and suggestive nature of the word (Turani,

1992, p. 602). Ball defines Dada as a universal cultural language, almost a "cultural Esperanto," while Huelsenbeck emphasizes the movement's dimensions of rupture and renewal. These two approaches form the fundamental building blocks of Dada (Hopkins, 2004, p. 9). Huelsenbeck also states that "the Dadaist considers it necessary to fight against art because he has recognized fraud as a moral safety valve within it" (Lewis, 2018, p. 56). Dada has a structure that encompasses everything on both the verbal and philosophical levels but does not represent anything. Therefore, it has demonstrated a conscious variability in what it accepts or rejects (Eroğlu, 2015, p. 183). According to Hopkins (2004, p. 9), the word is an absurd combination of affirmation and negation; it is interpreted as a form of false mysticism; if art is a dead religion, Dada has been born in its place.

Additionally, according to Turani (1992, p. 602), the focus of Dadaism is not on grandeur, permanence, or the artwork itself; rather, it is on doubt, protest, and individual freedom. Art objects may seem contrary to the spirit of Dada, because even the most extreme work of art is constructive. Nevertheless, the fact that Dada inspired important works of art shows that it had an inherent creative aspect. As Gombrich states in "*The Story of Art*," "There is no such thing as art; there are only artists." Dada was also an event created by artists. This event revealed that performances and various activities could also be considered art. Thus, the concept of art expanded to include elements such as cabaret, theater, exhibitions, recitals, marches, music halls, and circuses, and was never again reduced to a narrow meaning (Lynton, 2004, pp. 124–125).

The fact that the movement emerged in different geographical locations at the same time complicates the development of Dada (Hopkins, 2004, p. 9). Dadaist thought emerged almost simultaneously in Zurich and New York, developing similar but different principles before spreading to Europe. Berlin, Hanover, Cologne, and Paris were centers where Dada was strongly embraced; various groups also formed in these cities (McGinity, 2017, p. 410; Hodge, 2019, p. 38). The movement was active in New York between 1915 and 1920, in Berlin between 1918 and 1923, and in Paris between 1919 and 1922 (Genç, 1983, p. 69).

The New York Dada Movement

In 1915, French artists Marcel Duchamp and Francis Picabia moved to New York in search of a new environment more open to new ideas, away from the destructiveness of war (Hopkins, 2004, p. 9). Both artists were well-known figures in France. Although quite different from Zurich, the art scene in New York was also fueled by the same sarcastic, iconoclastic, and nihilistic spirit. Upon arriving in the city in June 1915, Duchamp and Picabia brought together their separately developing tendencies, laying the foundation for a unique movement characterized by Dada (Sanouillet, 2017, p. 367).

However, New York Dada was initially regarded not as an artistic movement but as a state of mind or mental illness stemming from social upheaval. However, when the public realized that it was not merely a game, they began to perceive their own ignorance as cultural backwardness. Americans were aware of the destructive nature of civilization and thus admired the courage of this small group of artists who questioned cultural values (Huelsenbeck, 1975, cited in Genç, 1983, p. 78).

In 1915, Marcel Duchamp developed an "anti-retinal" stance in response to the visual innovations represented by Matisse and Cubism, rejecting art that appealed solely to the eye. This approach was combined with a mocking attitude toward the effects of the machine age on the human mind. Duchamp and Picabia developed a parodic artistic language featuring human/machine hybrids in 1915–1916 as a response to the mechanization of society. The primary example of this approach is Duchamp's unfinished work *"The Bride Stripped Bare by her Bachelors, Even"* (or *The Large Glass*) (Hopkins, 2004, p. 9). Duchamp was influenced by Max Stirner and Henri Poincaré in this work; he later published the sketches, notes, and drafts of the work, revealing the mathematical, alchemical, symbolic, and technological foundations behind it (Graf, 2023, p. 80; Lynton, 2004, p. 133). Despite giving the impression of random decisions, it is clear that the work was meticulously planned with a high degree of consciousness. This meticulous attitude actually stems from Duchamp's past; thanks to his painter brothers and family, he was exposed to art at an early age and had the opportunity to experiment with different artistic forms at a young age (Eroğlu, 2015, p. 194; Cauquelin, 2005, p. 375).

Duchamp expressed his reaction to the relationship between art and craftsmanship by prioritizing ideas over manual skill. This approach led him to transform everyday objects into "ready-made" artworks from 1913 onwards, paving the way for a radical break in modern art (Hopkins, 2004, p. 9). Viewers in New York were astonished by these ready-made objects, which gained the status of art objects solely through the artist's selection. However, Duchamp rejected the influence of traditional painting, which he referred to as "turpentine poisoning," and the tyranny of the commercial art market, developing a new understanding of art production based on "chance" (Sanouillet, 2017, p. 367).

Among Duchamp's most controversial works is the male urinal he submitted to the 1917 New York Society of Independent Artists exhibition. This piece, titled "Fountain," was submitted under the pseudonym "R. Mutt" (Hopkins, 2004, p. 10). The pseudonym Duchamp carefully chose symbolized "Richard," which means 'rich' in French slang (Hodge, 2019, p. 138). The rejection of "*Fountain*" at an exhibition where every participant had the right to exhibit their work in exchange for a membership fee directly reflected the provocative spirit of Dada. At the exhibition, every artist who paid the $6 participation fee could exhibit their work without any stylistic or aesthetic restrictions (Hopkins, 2004, p. 10; Graf, 2023, p. 80). Despite this, the committee found the work both inappropriate and lacking in originality, viewing it as an attack on the nature of art. However, Duchamp argued that art did not have to be made by the artist's hand, that what mattered was the idea (Hodge, 2019, p. 138). Indeed, throughout history, the artist's direct intervention in studio production has not always been individual (Graf, 2023, p. 82). Duchamp himself stated that he was actually among the jury members but chose to submit the work anonymously under the name "R. Mutt," and that this choice was a deliberate provocation (Cauquelin, 2005, p. 81).

The rejection of "Fountain" has been interpreted as a powerful provocation not only against the definition of art but also against the functioning of art institutions (Hopkins, 2004, p. 10). Henri-Pierre Roché supported this approach by stating, "It is not important whether Mr. Mutt produced '*Fountain*' himself; he selected it, gave it a new title and context, thereby imparting a new idea to the object" (Sanouillet, 2017, p. 369). The incident received extensive coverage in the press, and "*Fountain*" found its place in American art yearbooks. Additionally, in a 2004 survey conducted by the BBC among 500 art experts, it was selected as the most important artwork of the 20th century (Graf, 2023, p. 80). However, the original version of the work is lost and can only be seen in a photograph taken by Alfred Stieglitz; all known examples today are copies commissioned by Duchamp in the 1950s and 1960s (Graf, 2023, p. 81).

Like *Fountain*, Picabia's magazine *391* also made Dada's fundamental goals visible. With this publication, Picabia and his circle began to question the concept of the "artwork" and the public began to notice their skepticism toward traditional values such as inspiration and technique (Sanouillet, 2017, p. 370).

However, Duchamp and Picabia were aware of Zurich Dada; yet the "Dada" label did not become widely used in New York until the 1920s. Therefore, their activities between 1915 and 1917 are generally referred to as "proto-Dada." Nevertheless, during this period, an important circle of representatives of the American avant-garde formed around Stieglitz's *291 Gallery* and Arensberg. Key figures in this circle included Man Ray, Arthur Cravan, and Baroness Elsa von Freytag-Loringhoven (Hopkins, 2004, p. 11). According to Genç (1983, pp. 78–79), Stieglitz had a huge impact on Dada; his aesthetic quest that went beyond reflecting reality formed the basis of the New York Dada movement, and the "*291 Gallery*" became known as the birthplace of this movement. Stieglitz organized over 190 events supporting modern art in the United States, most of which were held in small galleries. His main venue, the "291 Gallery," was only 4.5 square meters in size (Roberts, 2012, p. 203). Ultimately, according to Sanouillet, the Dada movement developed in New York through the contributions of artists and intellectuals who gathered around galleries such as Stieglitz's *291* and *Photo-Secession*, as well as publications like *Camera Notes* and *Camera Work*. The *Armory Show* held in 1913 reinforced Stieglitz's modernist claims and marked the beginning of a major artistic transformation for young artists (Sanouillet, 2017, p. 366).

The Berlin Dada Movement

The German Dada movement began as a reaction to expressionism (Artun, p. 112). In 1918, Richard Huelsenbeck's move from Zurich to Berlin brought the Dada movement to the city. Huelsenbeck had developed a more aggressive form in 1917, which he called "Super-Dada." Berlin quickly became the center of this approach, and in the context of the war's defeat and economic collapse, Berlin Dadaists adopted an extremely political stance (Hopkins, 2004, p. 11; McGinity, 2017, p. 411). According to Hopkins (2004, p. 11), the group known as Club Dada was divided into two sub-circles: one with a political orientation, including George Grosz, John Heartfield, and Walter Mehring; and another consisting of anarchist-leaning artists such as Raoul Hausmann, Hannah Höch, and Johannes Baader (Hopkins, 2004, p. 12). Genç (1983, p. 71) defines Berlin Dada as having both political and irrational characteristics.

The Berlin Dada movement directly linked art to workers' actions and political struggles. The movement's pioneer, Raoul Hausmann, was known for his theoretical writings as "Dadazof" and also served as editor of the magazine "Der Dada." This magazine followed a disruptive line with its random texts, poems, photomontages, and content (McGinity, 2017, p. 412). Hausmann began producing satirical photomontages against bourgeois values in 1918, creating works that addressed current political events using clippings from newspapers and photographs. Berlin Dadaists rejected traditional art and, along with Hausmann's phonetic poetry, adopted photomontage as their primary means of expression (Hopkins, 2004, p. 12).

Photomontages were prepared using the "Klebebild" (collage) method, then photographed and reproduced, thus gaining a form suitable for publication in avant-garde magazines (Mariens, 2018, p. 241). Hannah Höch, Hausmann, and Grosz were pioneers of this technique with their absurd and satirical collages made from newspaper images. The artists aimed to construct a new reality at both the social and artistic levels. Some added objects to their collages, while others preferred to use images (McGinity, 2017, p. 411).

Early Berlin Dada photomontages, similar to those of New York Dada, were composed of mechanical images. This technique evolved into the nearly flawless montages masterfully executed by John Heartfield. Heartfield used Surrealist methods to create striking contrasts and produce political critiques (Hopkins, 2004, p. 12). In 1920, Dadaists in Berlin organized the "Erste Internationale Dada-Messe" (First

International Dada Exhibition). The exhibition, held at Otto Burchard's gallery, featured 174 works displayed in two rooms, including a cover designed by Heartfield (McGinity, 2017, p. 413). Additionally, the banners at the Berlin exhibition highlighted Dada's political nature: "Dada is political," "Dada is the conscious subversion of the bourgeois conceptual world," "Down with art" (Artun, p. 112).

The Dada movement spread to other regions of Germany. For example, Hannover, with its calmer and apolitical character, was the place where Kurt Schwitters was active. Although Schwitters established friendly relations with Berlin artists Hausmann and Höch, he was not accepted into the "Club Dada" by Huelsenbeck (Hopkins, 2004, p. 13).

According to Lynton (2004, p. 140), the group considered itself too apolitical, and Hauelsenbeck claimed that it was overly bourgeois. Schwitters developed his unique collage technique, which he called "Merz," by reevaluating urban waste (such as tickets and packaging) within abstract structures (Hopkins, 2004, p. 13).

The term "Merz" is derived from the word 'commercial' and became the general name for the artist's plastic and poetic productions (Cabanne, 2015, p. 382; McGinity, 2017, p. 411). Schwitters sometimes transformed this term into wordplay; for example, "Merzschaf" (a sheep separated from the flock) (Lynton, 2004, p. 141). In the mid-1920s, Schwitters transformed his "Merz" approach into a massive installation project encompassing the rooms of his home, titled "*Merzbau*" (Hopkins, 2004, p. 13). Constructed using plaster, wooden pieces, and various waste materials, this structure served as a personal refuge against the destructiveness of life. The term "Merz" also evoked the German word "Schmerz," meaning "pain" (Lynton, 2004, p. 144).

In Cologne, which offered a more peaceful environment compared to Berlin, Dada developed between 1918 and 1920. Max Ernst and Alfred Grunewald were the leading figures of this movement. The group took shape around the anarchic "Cologne Dada Fair" in April 1920. Although names such as Franz Seiwert and the Hoerle couple, who had strong political leanings, were involved, Max Ernst's aesthetic line left its mark on the group. Ernst's absurd and striking collages defined the apolitical but aesthetically sharp character of Cologne Dada (Hopkins, 2004, pp. 13-14).

Paris Dada Movement

Poets such as Louis Aragon, André Breton, Paul Éluard, and Philippe Soupault played an active role in the Paris Dada group (Turani, 1992, p. 603). In Paris, Dada emerged primarily as a literary movement and aimed to create "scandal for scandal's sake." Dada events were often associated with absurd and provocative actions. For example, Johannes Baader, who was given a certificate by the police stating that he had "no responsibility for breaking the law," became known for major scandals (Genç, 1983, pp. 75-72).

Just as Cologne is culturally situated between Germany and France, Max Ernst also showed a stronger orientation toward Paris than other German Dadaists (Hopkins, 2004, p. 14). Furthermore, according to Turani (1992, p. 603), the Dada movement found its strongest expression in Ernst's personality. Ernst settled permanently in Paris in 1922. Paris Dada was a complex formation due to the variable affiliations of its participants. The movement began in early 1919 with the arrival of Francis Picabia in Paris. Picabia hosted Marcel Duchamp, who had returned to his country. Duchamp gained the admiration of young poets in Paris with his iconoclastic gesture of adding the letters "LHOOQ" and drawing a mustache and beard on a reproduction of the "*Mona Lisa*"; he inspired the group that gathered around the magazine "*Littérature*" (Hopkins, 2004, p. 14).

André Breton, one of the important figures of Dada, developed a unique understanding of Dada that was largely shaped by the influence of others but was intellectually grounded (Hopkins, 2004, p. 15). With Tzara's arrival in Paris in January 1920, Breton's search for intellectual consistency distanced him from both Picabia and Tzara. Like Ball, Breton rejected Tzara's doctrine of "anti-art for anti-art" and viewed his fruitless actions as "sterile agitation" (Sanouillet, 2017, p. 364). During this period, Breton rose to become the leader of the Paris avant-garde. However, Paris Dada was distant from the constructive spirit of Zurich and, compared to Berlin, exhibited a less direct form of opposition (Hopkins, 2004, p. 15). The movement disintegrated in 1922 with the rise of Surrealism and the split between Breton and Tzara (Genç, 1983, p. 75).

When looking at Dadaist artistic methods in general, it can be seen that no particular medium dominated. Everything was acceptable, and "Ready-Made" was mostly used (Hodge, 2019, p. 38). Duchamp created excitement with his "Ready-Mades" (taking everyday objects and repurposing them to create new relationships and transform them into works of art) (Turani, 1992, p. 603). Some artists created collages using waste materials, while others turned to performance art. Dada was an approach that embodied both destructive energy and boundless creativity. Dadaists challenged aesthetic traditions, artistic skill, and the sanctity attributed to artworks; they defined the illogical, worthless, and temporary as art (McGinity, 2017, p. 410).

According to Hopkins (2004, p. 4), Dada and Surrealism emerged as movements based on ideas rather than form, rejecting the notion of art as a sacred or separate entity from life. Therefore, it is misleading to view them as a defined "-ism"; there is no formal homogeneity within them, and literature is as influential as visual art. It is much more appropriate to define Dada as a set of ideas that express certain thought-based attitudes toward life. Sanouillet (2017, p. 359) defines Dada not as a school but as a "vortex" that draws in the innovative currents around it and then transforms them. Similarly, according to Genç (1983, p. 5), Dada is not a school, but an attitude free from rules and not limited by self-defined structures; therefore, it is not easy to analyze its material products with a holistic approach.

According to Eroğlu, Dada emerged in Germany on common ground with Expressionism, but created a unique productivity with an approach opposed to its spirituality-based theories. In this context, Expressionism served as a kind of reflection and testing ground for Dada. Furthermore, Surrealism inherited Dada's artistic legacy (Eroğlu, 2015, p. 181). According to Hopkins, Dada and Surrealism are seen more as intellectual tendencies that shaped modern art than as traditional movements. While Dada followed a destructive and confrontational line, Surrealism, while sharing the same anti-bourgeois spirit, turned toward the unconscious and myth creation. Although they are two distinct art movements, they are often equated with one another. While art historians frequently describe Dada as the precursor to Surrealism, this transition primarily applies to Paris Dada. While Dada aestheticized the chaotic nature of modern life, Surrealism aimed to repair this fragmentation (Hopkins, 2004).

Dada and Surrealism owe much to Cubism, Expressionism, and Futurism in terms of developing new visual forms of expression. For example, the Cubist collage technique laid the groundwork for Dadaists to develop their photomontage method. However, both movements criticized Cubism's approach, which deemed formal innovation alone sufficient for art. Like Futurism, Dada and Surrealism are notable for their efforts to question the accelerated, multi-sensory modern experience (Hopkins, 2004, p. 3). Finally, it should be noted that Dada is not so much a specific art movement as a multidisciplinary movement that had a profound impact on 20th-century art. By engaging in various fields such as painting, theater, poetry, circus, and film, it broke down traditional artistic boundaries, and this approach was revived in the 1950s with the "Neo-Dada" movement (Genç, 1983, p. 4).

PHOTOGRAPH AND "READY-MADE" IN THE CONTEXT OF PHOTOGRAM, COLLAGE / PHOTOMONTAGE AND APPROPRIATION

In 1885, pictorialists transformed both the shooting and developing processes in order to liberate photography from imitation and turn it into a means of artistic expression.In contrast, in 1916, Dadaists used photography to subvert traditional notions of painting and create original images. Surrealists, meanwhile, explored photography's poetic and dreamlike potential, treating flaws such as scratches, burn marks, and halos as aesthetic materials. Over time, some artists began to consciously produce these flaws, pushing the boundaries of photography with techniques such as double exposure, solarization, and overexposure (Couturier, 2012, p. 238).

The Dadaists were united not so much by a common style as by similar intellectual beliefs and recurring artistic strategies. The Dadaists presented the first examples of collage, montage, performance art, assemblage, and ready-made, which became fundamental art forms of the 20th century. According to them, traditional art institutions were inadequate in adapting to technological changes. Photography, on the other hand, blurred the boundaries between art and life by offering the possibility of bringing everyday objects into an artistic context. According to the Dadaists, photography was an expression medium that had not yet been corrupted by artistic traditions (Knierim, 2012, pp. 192-193). In this context, photography experienced some of its most powerful periods during Dada, Bauhaus, and the integrated, multimedia art of the last 30 years (Soulages, 2022, p. 340).

When viewed from the perspective of Surrealism, Surrealism, which emerged in Paris in 1924, was influenced by Freudian theory and turned to exploring the unconscious mind. Photography has held an important place within this movement due to its power to reflect the imaginary and mysterious and its relationship with reality (Lewis, 2018, p. 62). Dadaists were also interested in dreams and the subconscious; Breton, Aragon, Ernst, and Desnos attempted to access subconscious images through hypnosis and sleep (Barnard, 2010, p. 167). Experimentation, chance, unusual arrangements, and contrasts between reality and fantasy are common in surrealist photographs (Lewis, 2018, p. 62). According to Genç (1983, p. 5), most of the artists involved in the Dada art movement were pioneers of a Surrealist understanding from the outset; however, the Dadaists did not accept the spiritual automatism adopted by the Surrealists in their pictorial period. While Dada adopted a conscious fantasy approach, Surrealism emphasized dreamlike and intuitive elements.

According to Mariens, in Surrealist practice, photography was regarded as the visual counterpart of methods used to express unconscious thoughts. Some Surrealist artists directed the camera randomly, recording everything that came into view, thereby attempting to document the traces of the unconscious (Mariens, 2018, p. 251). Photography has been adopted both as a recording device and as an independent art form. In this context, it has become the "medium par excellence," the "most competent tool" for Surrealist expression. According to Susan Sontag, Surrealism "deviates from the natural form of seeing to create a secondary and dramatic reality." The camera, by alienating the familiar through chance, has formed the basis of Surrealist aesthetics (Hopkins, 2004, p. 84).

The Surrealist approach encompasses not only chance-based but also consciously constructed "artistic" photography. One of the most prominent examples in this field is Man Ray's studio-based works and his "rayograph" (photogram) experiments (Hopkins, 2004, p. 85). In 1922, Man Ray published his "rayographs," created using unusual arrangements of everyday objects such as combs and knives, under the title "Les Champs délicieux" (Delicious Fields). Tristan Tzara titled the foreword to this work "La photographie à l'envers" (Photography Upside Down), referring both to the negative imaging technique and the reversal of traditional rules of photographic practice (Mariens, 2018, p. 252).

Dora Maar created disturbing compositions by combining everyday objects in unexpected ways and placing figures in strange positions. Hans Bellmer designed and photographed toy dolls bent into nightmarish shapes (Lewis, 2018, p. 62). Bellmer, who met the Berlin Dadaists, went to Paris in 1924 and came into contact with the Surrealist circle. Bellmer began producing and photographing his own dolls, inspired by a scene of an automaton doll in J. Offenbach's opera *"The Tales of Hoffmann"* and his personal experiences (Mariens, 2018, p. 252).

Techniques such as double exposure and superimposing negatives in photography expanded the expressive possibilities of Surrealism. The images obtained through these processes have a fragmented and dual structure. According to R. Krauss, these practices challenge the idea that photography objectively records reality; they transform the image into an unstable and multi-layered sign system. Surrealist painting spawned many imitators in Europe but left few lasting heirs. Nevertheless, traces of Surrealist influence are strong in 20th-century photographers such as Cartier-Bresson, Brassaï, Brandt, and Kertész (Hopkins, 2004, p. 85). However, this study will focus more on Dadaist approaches than Surrealist influences.

When examining the photographic productions of Dadaist and Surrealist artists, it can be seen that their works are diversified based on the concepts of photogram, photomontage-collage, and ready-made. These works, produced with different artistic approaches and techniques, also encompass the approach of appropriation (removing from context and reclaiming). The free use of these forms of expression, which appear separate but refer to each other, reflects the attitude that forms the basis of Dada. This is because Dada does not limit itself to any structural system that restricts artistic production beyond certain founding principles; on the contrary, it offers a creative space shaped by structurelessness, lawlessness, and opposition.

In particular, the use of daily newspapers or found photographs in photomontage and collage practices relates these methods to the ready-made concept. The fact that the visual material used in such works is "found," that is, taken from a source other than the artist's original production, also aligns these productions with the practice of "appropriation." Despite all these conceptual and formal intertwining, the methods and artistic uses discussed in this section will be addressed under separate headings.

Ready-Made

At the beginning of the 20th century, modern art in Europe became increasingly pluralistic and heterogeneous, with many styles coexisting, from figurative to abstract, political to poetic. These avant-garde movements developed new aesthetic strategies to meet modernism's need for originality and innovation. Innovation became a driving force in the evolution of modern art (Graf, 2023, p. 79). During this process of change, objects that fell outside the traditional understanding of art—snow shovels, urinals, canned soup cans—were used to question the boundaries between art and everyday life. Artists such as Duchamp, Warhol, Oldenburg, Lichtenstein, Morris, and Judd have included these objects in their works, questioning the foundations of art education and perception (Danto, 2016, p. 118).

In 1913, Duchamp developed the "ready-made" approach, which radically changed the direction of modern art, similar to the collages of Picasso and Braque. Ready-mades are works that gain the status of art by being exhibited directly or with the intervention of the artist. The first example of this method, "*Bicycle Wheel*," 1913, opened up the definition and function of art to questioning (Graf, 2023, pp. 79-80). According to Bourdieu, ready-mades enable everyday objects to be taken out of their context and take on new meanings. These objects are abstracted from their conventional functions and acquire different layers of meaning (Bourdieu, 2006, p. 376).

Furthermore, Cauquelin (2005, p. 78) defines ready-made as a form of representation with a fragmented structure that functions within a system of signs rather than as a work of art. Marcel Duchamp explains the term "Ready-Made" as follows:

As early as 1913, I had the unique idea of attaching a bicycle wheel to a kitchen stool and watching it turn... In 1915, I bought a snow shovel from a hardware store in New York and wrote "In case of broken arm" on it. The term "ready-made" came to mind at that moment. I did not adopt ready-mades based on aesthetic taste. This choice was based on a visual indifference that was consistent with a complete lack of pleasure or displeasure at that moment... actually, a complete apathy. The short sentence I wrote on the ready-made when the time came was an important feature. This phrase, like a title, was intended to draw the viewer's thoughts away from describing the object and toward other, more linguistic areas. Sometimes I added a graphic detail related to the presentation: I called this "ready-made aided" to satisfy my penchant for sound repetitions. In addition, I designed a "reciprocal ready-made" to highlight the fundamental conflict between art and ready-mades: the design was to use one of Rembrandt's paintings as an ironing board. I realized very early on the danger of presenting this narrative form indiscriminately. For this reason, I decided to keep the annual production of ready-mades to a very small number (Duchamp, 2017, p. 378). (For this reason, the artist produced only 13 ready-made works in his

40-year artistic career. Graf, 2023, p. 81.) Another feature of the ready-made is its lack of uniqueness... A copy of a ready-made conveys the same message; in fact, almost none of today's ready-mades are original products in the accepted sense of the term. In conclusion, just as the paint tubes used by the artist are manufactured and ready-made, all canvases in the world must be considered "ready-mades aided" (Duchamp, 2017, p. 379).

According to Cauquelin (2005, p. 78), the choice of object in ready-mades is generally random, and Duchamp describes this as a "conservative coincidence." The Dada artist favors not only traditional craftsmanship but also consciously relinquishing control over the production process. This approach is evident in Duchamp's works (Lynton, 2004, p. 124). In this context, the artist is not creative but rather a presenter; the only indication of his presence is the signature accompanying the object. The artist's intervention is limited; the material of the object is external to the artist. The artist's work is concerned with changing the place and time of the object. Thus, the claim to create color and form disappears. In ready-made art, the first producer is industry, while the second producer is the artist who brings this object into an artistic context (Cauquelin, 2005, pp. 77-80). According to Genç (1983, p. 89), Dadaists, in a sense, worked with what was "already there"; they clung to whatever remained from that relentless war whose causes they could not eliminate. This was a metaphysical attitude, a nihilistic worldview. The available design materials were what they had at hand.

Duchamp became the symbolic figure of Dada by exhibiting industrial objects in an artistic context. Duchamp questioned what makes a work of art a work of art. With this approach, he questioned traditional notions of the function and value of art, blurring the boundaries between art and everyday objects (McGinity, 2017, p. 411). Following in his footsteps, Beuys argued that anyone could be an artist approximately 40 years after "Fountain"; Judd suggested that the definition of art could be based on personal expression. Ai Weiwei, on the other hand, emphasized that "*everything is art and everything is political*" (Graf, 2023, p. 84).

Duchamp, as a pioneer of Found Art and Conceptual Art and one of the first creators of Kinetic Art, Optical Art, Installation, and Appropriation approaches, determined the direction of contemporary art. The ready-made approach has deeply influenced movements such as Pop Art, Minimalism, and Arte Povera (Graf, 2023, p. 85). In particular, the Dadaist identity, which draws on everyday experiences, has influenced Pop Art. From the idea of everyday experiences to the idea of everyday ordinary objects, Pop Art will fully emerge (Eroğlu, 2015, p. 184). According to Cauquelin (2005, p. 79), this understanding, in which the artist is positioned as a sign producer rather than an aesthetic talent, has transformed the role definitions of art. With ready-made, the materials used by artists became unlimited means of expression, turning toward conceptual equivalents rather than reality (Cabanne,

2015, p. 380). From the emergence of ready-made to the present day, many artists have used this approach as a method.

When looking at the photographic use of everyday objects, it can be seen that artists turn to everyday objects and shape them with a photographic basis. When considering a directly photographed object, the photographic way of seeing and the way of seeing with the eyes generally lead to similar perceptions in the viewer. According to K. L. Walton (2018, p. 50), objects are mechanically the cause of photographs and the visual experiences of viewers; therefore, we see objects through photographs. Furthermore, according to Walton, the photographer shows the viewer a sign through objects. As in Dada, ready-mades also convey a sign from the artist through objects.

According to Cotton (2020, p. 121), the photographic representation of everyday objects in a frame displays an attitude parallel to Dada's ready-made approach. Cotton defines the content of the use of these everyday ordinary objects as "nothingness" and classifies the selection of objects as "the determination of the ordinary." According to Cotton, such works conceptually transform ordinary objects and produce a meaningful 'thing' from "nothingness." While arousing the viewer's curiosity, the artist encourages us to think about the material elements of the world around us in new ways. These types of photographic approaches are shaped by the artist's attempt to produce art from the material of everyday life by dissolving the boundaries between the artist's studio, the gallery space, and the everyday world. There is also a common research interest in producing works where the artist's technical skill is not immediately apparent. In this process, technical mastery has been replaced by conceptual inquiry; the question "Who made this?" has been replaced by "Why is this object here?" (Cotton, 2020, p. 122).

In contemporary art, artists such as Patrick Tosani, Jean-Luc Moulêne, Maurizio Anzeri, Zoe Leonard, and Sarah Lucas produce works that relate everyday objects to photography. Zoe Leonard, in particular, engages with both the visual representation of the object and the photograph itself, creating a game of meaning with the viewer (Bright, 2011, cited in Er, 2022, p. 61). Leonard attributes her choice of ordinary objects to their lack of drama and their symbolic connotations. For example, her work "For Which It Stands" features 32 postcards that make critical references to American identity. These postcards ironically present ordinary yet symbolic objects such as a "Burger King crown," a "toy gun," and "plastic Native American figures in battle," thereby questioning American values. The symbols are sufficiently clear, even ordinary, but when taken together, they form an effective critique (Frieze, 2025).

Another example can be seen in the works of Maurizio Anzeri, who uses everyday objects or objects loaded with various references. Anzeri collects found portrait photographs from old family albums that do not belong to him. He covers the figures with colored threads and sews them, thus giving new meanings to everyday objects.

Anzeri leaves one eye of the figures open in his thread interventions on found portrait photographs. Through these interventions, Anzeri both preserves the photographs and gives them new identities. The artist establishes an emotional connection with these visuals and names them by characterizing them (Er, 2022, p. 107). Additionally, visual artist and photographer Marystela Camacho also produces her works by combining textile techniques and photography using a similar technique to Anzeri.

In her work "Sod You Gits, 1991," Sarah Lucas presents a double-page photocopy of a British tabloid newspaper as a work of art. By removing this object from its everyday context, she both critiques the sensational and exhibitionist content of the newspaper and transforms it through a feminist lens. The obscene and sexist stories in the newspaper are transformed into an art object that reflects Duchamp's ready-made approach through Lucas' intervention. Thus, not only the function of photography but also the value, status, and representation of the artwork are reconsidered (Bright & Erp, 2019, p. 72). Lucas uses not only newspapers but also ordinary objects such as toilets and cigarettes, which may be considered degrading in everyday life. In his treatment of these objects, the humorous language of English, with its double meanings, comes to the fore. However, Lucas's work is not merely a simple critique. The statement, "A story changes depending on who tells it, how, and where," summarizes his artistic practice (Griffiths, 2006, cited in Cozzi, 2025; Bright & Erp, 2019, p. 72).

Another example is Juan David Laserna Montoya's 2012 series "Advertisement Extraction," which consists of approximately 130 magazine pages sanded down. This sanding process creates a fragile structure and visual ambiguity on the pages. The protest, economic, and advertising-themed images on the magazine pages are detached from their context and transformed into cultural objects. Montoya views these images as a critical interrogation of consumer culture (Laserna Montoya, Tarver & Duganne, 2017).

In an interview with G. M. Tarver and E. Duganne, David Laserna Montoya explains his work as follows. "What I do is go to second-hand bookstores and rummage through piles of old magazines. The artist interacts with the visual sensibility of the pre-digital era by selecting magazines from the 1980s and 1990s. The reproduction and circulation of images draw attention to the use of strategies similar to those found in political protest imagery in advertising. According to him, these images promise prosperity to the consumer while also serving to construct an idea or product. Montoya's approach proposes "active visual intervention" instead of passive consumption. By purifying and repositioning images, their mystery and potential meaning are enhanced (Laserna Montoya, Tarver & Duganne, 2017).

Another artist who adds found objects to his photographs with a completely different approach is Stephen Gill. Gill produces his photographs in his "Outside In" series using traditional analog systems. However, what sets Gill apart is the various objects he throws onto the negative inside his camera during the photography process. These objects can be anything. By combining ready-made objects in his photographs by chance, Gill creates intriguing interpretations.

Art and fashion photographer Nigel Shafran's photographic practice focuses on documenting ordinary objects from everyday life with a poetic and intuitive gaze. Through details such as stains, supermarket shelves, and grass, he makes people's lifestyles and relationships visible. Using natural light and long exposure techniques, he avoids artificial intervention and transforms domestic life into symbolic scenes. Shafran resists the urge to stage photographs; her approach is to remain sensitive to the ordinary subjects of everyday life and to discover our individual characters, relationships, and ways of life through these subjects (Cotton, 2020, p. 137).

Shafran prefers to compile his work in photo books. His book, "The Well," offers a critical look at his career in fashion and portrait photography from a young age; it includes not only visuals but also background narratives (Shashasha, 2025). His other book, "Workbook," contains sketches, notes, drawings, and diary details from his production process between 1984 and 2024. These notebooks are both process documents and aesthetically complete objects. According to D. Chandler, these books reveal Shafran's working principles and his commitment to the material nature of photography. Each is filled with drawings, notes, and everyday objects, and each possesses a certain aesthetic characterized by visual simplicity and clarity, which are characteristic of Shafran's intuitive organizing principles and entire working process, as well as a sense of easy material craftsmanship (Chandler, 2025).

Working across collage, video, sculpture, and performance, Mutu develops a visual narrative language that weaves together themes of gender, race, identity, and violence to create her own mythology. Recurring elements in her work include masked female figures, serpentine extensions, and materials sourced from nature. In her collages, she uses transparent surfaces like "mylar" alongside everyday or culturally charged materials such as vinyl, linoleum, Kenyan soil, feathers, tea, and synthetic hair, thereby deepening both the material and conceptual layers of her work (Wolfe, 2025). In her art, she updates Hannah Höch's feminist collage legacy and Richard Hamilton's Pop Art strategies, combining them with postcolonial criticism (Wolfe, 2025).

James Welling is one of the important figures who effectively repositioned photography as an experimental and material art form within contemporary art. In the 1980s, he broke away from appropriation artists and followed a path that focused on the technical structure and formation process of photography (Cotton, 2020, p. 250). Working with various techniques such as darkroom experiments, photograms, kemigrams, Polaroids, and inkjet prints, Welling aims to trigger "states of being" in the viewer and question the structure of the image. Welling's work proposes a conceptual inquiry not only into the representation of objects but also into the process of image formation and its modes of reception (Marian Goodman Gallery, 2025; Zwirner, 2025). In one work, he dramatized crumpled aluminum foil with light to produce prints the same size as the negative. These works create a three-dimensional effect in two dimensions, offering intense visual experiences through the interplay of light and shadow (Whitney, 2025).

Photogram

Photograms are photographic images created directly on light-sensitive paper without the use of a camera. This method is achieved by placing various objects on light-sensitive surfaces and exposing them to daylight; the areas exposed to light are exposed, while the areas under the objects remain unexposed, thus forming the image. When examining the historical origins of the photogram, it becomes clear that this technique predates the invention of photography by many centuries. The "anthotype" method, which dates back centuries and uses plant extracts, is known to be one of the earliest examples of photogram-based images. Similarly, with the discovery of silver nitrate's sensitivity to light, photogram-based images were also produced on surfaces coated with silver nitrate. Additionally, the cyanotype method, one of the alternative printing techniques used in the early days of photography, can be cited as an example of this field, with botanist Anna Atkins' photogram-based images created from plant specimens. However, when examining the Dada period, which is the focus of this study, it is seen that the photogram technique was adopted by the artists of the period not only as an experimental technique but also as an artistic form of expression.

Additionally, this technique, also known as "camera-less photography," is one of the oldest applications in the history of photography and was developed in the 19th century by pioneers such as Talbot and Bayard to observe the chemical effects of light. In these scientific experiments, which were conducted to study the effects of light on various chemicals, transparent, perforated, or opaque objects were placed on photosensitive paper and exposed to daylight for a period of time, after which the image was fixed (Couturier, 2012, p. 166). Although the images produced by this method originated from the desire to "capture" the physical presence of objects, over time they moved away from scientific objectivity and became visual suggestions that were immaterial, open to interpretation, and aesthetic (Ware, 2019, p. 187). Although camera and negative-based photography applications came to the fore in the 20th century, photograms have retained their importance as an experimental field that questions the conceptual limits of the medium (Batchen, 2016, cited in

Ware, 2019, p. 186). Camera-less photography production is generally divided into three main groups: photogram, luminogram, and chemigram (Ware, 2019, p. 190). Photograms are the most commonly used method (Jäger, 2002 cited in Ware, 2019, p. 190).

From an artistic perspective, according to R. Krauss, photography was first integrated into artistic practice in the 1920s through Russian Constructivists and Dadaists. This approach was soon followed by Surrealists (Krauss, 1999, cited in Preston, 2019, p. 32). Dada and Constructivist artists, in particular, developed "photomontage" techniques by combining newspaper clippings, typography, and drawings, thus pioneering the integration of photography into other media types (Preston, 2019, p. 9).

For Dadaists, photography was a radical tool against bourgeois art. Photograms, produced without a camera and containing aesthetics open to chance, were therefore appealing to them (Lewis, 2018, p. 56). Photograms were widely used by artists such as Christian Schad and Man Ray between the 1920s and 1930s. Structuralist artists Moholy-Nagy and El Lissitzky used similar effects to produce "mechanical images," working with light and materials instead of brushes (Couturier, 2012, p. 166). As with all the art forms they employed, the Dadaists' approach to photography, including photograms, was characterized by a variety of attitudes ranging from disrespect to anarchy (Lewis, 2018, p. 56).

Photograms have become a more selective technique today. Contemporary artists who prefer this method have embraced the aesthetic of the moment when an image is formed or the structure that makes objects appear as if they were "X-rayed." Among the artists working in this field, names such as Sigmar Polke, Adam Fuss, Joan Fontcuberta, and Dieter Roth stand out (Couturier, 2012, p. 166). This orientation toward these techniques began to regain interest in the late 20th century and early 21st century. This revival is linked to artists' desire to return to traditional practices based on light, paper, and chemistry during a period when digital technologies began to significantly shape the definition of photography. This approach emphasizes a labor-intensive and tactile production process (Rexer, 2002, cited in Ware, 2019, p. 189).

Looking at the pioneering Dada examples of photograms, one of the most important names for Dada and photograms is Christian Schad. Schad was an artist associated with the Zurich Dada group who abandoned traditional notions of composition under the influence of Hans Arp (Mariens, 2018, p. 241). In keeping with the spirit of Dada, he produced abstract and subjectless images by placing everyday and seemingly insignificant materials such as newspaper clippings, fabric, and paper fragments on gelatin silver print paper and exposing them to sunlight in front of a window (Ware, 2019, p. 188).

Working with printing-out paper, which reacts very slowly to light, Schad was able to change the position of objects during exposure. The small photograms he produced as a result of this process have a playful language that seeks an abstract artistic truth (Knierim, 2012, p. 193). Tzara used the term "Schadograph" to describe these works, a term that both refers to the artist's name and alludes to the German word "schaden" (to harm), reflecting Dada's chaotic aesthetic. Additionally, "Schadograph" evokes Talbot's early "shadowgraph" method and stands out as one of the creative examples of camera-less photography (Mariens, 2018, p. 241).

Another important name in photogram art is Man Ray, who began his career in painting in New York but turned to photography under the guidance of Stieglitz. After meeting Duchamp, he moved to Paris and became involved in the Dadaist circle (Johnson, et. al., 2012, pp. 531-532).

Man Ray began working with this technique after discovering it by chance in a darkroom. However, this technique is very similar to Schad's early photograms called "Schadographs." Indeed, when one of Schad's works was published in 1920 in Tzara's "*Dada 7" (DADAphone)*, Man Ray had probably seen this work at Tzara's home in Paris. Man Ray produced photograms similar to those made by Talbot, using leaves, flowers, and strings (Roberts, 2012, p. 199). Man Ray's works, produced through long experiments, are called "Rayographs."

Although this technique had been discovered by other artists before him, Man Ray did not hesitate to give it his own name. The term "Rayograph" is derived from the combination of 'Ray' (the first part of his surname) and "photogram." Man Ray describes his discovery in his 1963 book *Self-Portrait*: "I waited a couple of minutes for the image to appear. Thinking the paper was wasted, I mechanically placed a glass funnel, a graduated cylinder, and a thermometer on the wet paper. I turned on the light. An image began to form before my eyes. Man Ray embraced the abstract forms created by this accidental process as a way of producing images (Couturier, 2012, p. 166).

Incidentally, it is said that the name of Man Ray's "Rayograph" technique was suggested by Tzara. Tzara described these images with a poeticism that found them compelling on both the visual and mental planes. Tzara wrote the following about this technique: "When everything we call art has become completely stagnant, a photographer... invented a power far more important than all the constellations designed for our visual pleasure... (Johnson et al., 2012, p. 532). Between 1922 and 1928, Man Ray produced photograms composed of abstract and representational images using everyday objects such as magnifying glasses, wire rolls, and cigarettes. These works incorporate both Dada's found object approach and Surrealism's dreamlike aesthetic (Roberts, 2012, p. 199). According to Couturier (2012, p. 166), this technique emphasizes the power of chance in aesthetic production. Another technique Man Ray discovered by chance is "solarization." This method is achieved by briefly exposing the darkroom light during the developing process, causing a halo of light to form around the images (Hopkins, 2004, p. 85).

László Moholy-Nagy, on the other hand, argued that the photographer's perspective needed to be radically changed. He sought images produced without the use of a camera, including photograms (Mariens, 2018, p. 245). Moholy-Nagy arrived in Berlin in 1920 and met Berlin Dada artists such as Höch and Hausmann. Like them, he was interested in industrial materials and new technologies (Mariens, 2018, p. 243). Invited to the Weimar Bauhaus in 1923, Moholy-Nagy became an instructor for the preparatory program "Vorkurs." There, he explored the creative possibilities of both camera-based and camera-less photography, as well as graphic design, color, and materials (Ware, 2019, p. 188). Moholy-Nagy argued that the photographer's perspective needed to be fundamentally transformed. He also sought to produce images without using a camera, including through photograms (Mariens, 2018, p. 245).

Moholy-Nagy argued that photography should develop its own aesthetic and conceptual language in the evolution of art, viewing this process as "the first and most important issue" for art. According to him, the role of technology and light in artistic production is of fundamental importance. He also pointed out that scientific research is necessary for visual information to be as effective as written language. In his view, "This century belongs to light," and "photography is the first medium to give concrete form to light; of course, transformed and... almost abstract." "Today," writes Moholy-Nagy, "everything is focused on visuality much more strongly than in the past." Again, in his most striking statement: "The illiteracy of the future will be the inability to read photographs" (Phillips, 1989, cited in Mariens, 2018, pp. 243–245).

Another example is August Strindberg. In the 1890s, Strindberg transferred his scientific curiosity to photography and developed camera-less photography techniques. In his method, which he called "celestography," he exposed photographic plates directly to the night sky, aiming to record the traces of nature automatically and without intervention. Strindberg's method ensured that photography became not only a means of producing visual documents but also a tool for investigating truths that transcend perception. These images, composed of stars, clouds, and atmospheric effects, represent an experimental approach to photography that brings together the natural sciences and art. Celestographs offer not only visual appeal but also philosophical insights into nature, perception, and the unknown (Birinci, 2019, pp. 71-72).

Floris Neusüss is one of the important names in photogram. Neusüss, who first exhibited his "expressive and gestural *Körperfotogramm*" (naked, full-body photograms) in 1960, embarked on a lifelong journey of exploring the visual potential of the photogram and became an important historical source in this field (Ware, 2019, p. 189). Neusüss internalized the photogram as follows: "A photogram is like a painting: you have a blank sheet of paper in your hand and you create an image on it step by step. A camera, on the other hand, instantly gives you a copy of something you can already see with your own eyes" (Davies, 2010, cited in Ware, 2019, p. 191).

Stephen McNeill refers to his photogram works as "stephographs" (McNeill, 2025 b). Although photograms are technically similar to traditional photographs, their visual results are completely different. According to McNeill, producing a photogram is like "photographing" an idea; just as a painter completes a painting with the final brushstroke on a blank canvas, images are only completed through a conceptual and intuitive process. In this sense, the photogram is not a representation of reality but a visual projection of the non-existent. This production, based on light and experience, is valuable as an extension of modernist and experimental aesthetic understanding. McNeill's "Valley of the Livet, photogram, 2018" is a photogram work created by exposing a glass bottle with a smartphone flash. McNeill describes the photogram process as follows: "Photograms often require a great deal of patience and often produce surprising results" (McNeill, 2025 a).

In addition to these examples of photograms, photograms are also widely used in alternative photography techniques. Anna Atkins' book, in which she copied images of plants using the "cyanotype" method, is also essentially a 'photogram' technique. There are many artists who produce "photogram"-based works using alternative techniques.

Ruth Brown and Mitch Phillips use the cyanotype method to create works using interesting objects such as ferns, flowers, bamboo, insects, and feathers, particularly employing fabric as a photographic surface. Brown, in particular, creates regional blurriness in plant and leaf images by moving the objects she uses in the "photogram," such as plants, to achieve different exposures (Brown & Phillips, 2025).

It is possible to encounter unique photograms using alternative photographic techniques such as anthotype and cyanotype. In these methods, the use of different surfaces such as fabric instead of photographic paper, as well as the size of the printing surface, further liberates the photogram. It is even possible to transfer the image of a person or more onto a light-sensitive surface.

For example, in 2017, the Richmond Center for the Visual Arts created a "cyanotype photogram" on a 125-square-meter fabric, earning it the title of "The World's Largest Photogram." Additionally, Maria Solaguren-Beascoa organized a large-scale cyanotype wall installation as part of the "Experimental Photo Festival" in 2014. This 22-square-meter work consists of five pieces connected to each other, forming a cyanotype photogram measuring 10 meters by 2.2 meters (Alternative photography, 2025).

Marco Breuer, who works with a very different approach, produces his images by transforming photographic paper through physical and chemical interventions. He disrupts the emulsion through processes such as folding, scratching, and burning;

this process becomes a performative act, almost an action painting (Ware, 2019, p. 206). Breuer's aim is not to record the world or objects around him; rather, he experiments with the chemistry of colored photographic paper to create contemporary, original visuals. This approach is similar to the camera-less experiments of the Dada, Surrealist, and Russian Constructivists. The artist's relationship with paper can be interpreted as an archaeological intervention that excavates the old, as well as a visionary architecture that constructs new structures (Ware, 2019, p. 206).

Collage / Photomontage

Collage is an artistic form of expression that has been used in various periods. This form has reached its current form through the influences and directions of artists and period movements throughout history. When we look at the areas of use of collage in artistic disciplines, we see that it is used in quite different disciplines ranging from painting to sculpture and photography. For this reason, this section will first discuss collage and then its use in photography.

When talking about collage, we first encounter Degas. In 1881, Edgar Degas shocked the art world by presenting a wax sculpture of a ballet student at the Paris Opera, dressed in real fabric and human hair. Although collage is not a new technique, this unconventional realism shook the traditional understanding of materials and opened the door to techniques such as collage in art. Although collage was used alongside poetry in Japan during the 10th-12th centuries, it was the Cubists who first attributed the same expressive power to it as they did to paint. The Cubists, Futurists, and Dadaists, inspired by pioneers such as Degas, turned produced materials into part of the artistic language (Hodge, 2019, p. 183; Cabanne, 2015, p. 380).

Collage derives from the French word "coller," meaning "to stick." It was introduced into fine art in 1912 by Picasso and Braque, 30 years after Degas. These two artists made their works more accessible by incorporating real materials into their canvases, creating a turning point in art history. For example, Picasso's collage "Still Life with Chair Caning" is one of the first examples of this technique. Braque also applied similar methods in his work "Fruit Dish and Glass." According to critic C. Greenberg, collage is a decisive stage not only in the evolution of cubism but also in all modern art (Hodge, 2019, p. 216).

When examining examples of collage in the fine arts, Cabanne (2015, pp. 381-383) historically explains collage examples as follows: Paradoxically, the harsh and uncompromising Juan Gris emerged as a collage virtuoso. In the development of collage, Gris produced rhythmic and rich compositions using material elements (e.g., glued paper, broken mirrors). Collage was also adopted by various artists as it transitioned from Cubism to Futurism. For example, Boccioni encouraged artists to use industrial materials such as wood, cement, and electric lamps in his 1912

Futurist Sculpture Manifesto. However, this idea was not fully realized at the time. Carlo Carrà used collage in structures based entirely on typography and wordplay, while Hans Arp transformed collage into the artwork itself by cutting and pasting pieces of paper. Surrealists also made use of this technique. Man Ray produced collages consisting of abstract patterns, titled "Revolving Door," between 1916 and 1917. Max Ernst's series "*La Femme 100 Têtes*" and "*La Semaine de Bonté*" took collage to a narrative structure, creating disturbing but meaningful conflicts with fragmented images. Kurt Schwitters took collage beyond a mere formal game and turned it into a unique means of expression in modern art. He transformed objects he collected from everyday life (which he called "merz") into artistic compositions, viewing collage as a dynamic process that combines creation and destruction. This approach enhanced collage's spatial expressive power and paved the way for many forms of contemporary art (assemblage, environmental design, sculpture-architecture fusion, happening) (Cabanne, 2015, pp. 381-383).

The term "photomontage" refers to a type of collage created by combining images or photographs obtained from different media. Photomontage is also known as photo-collage. M. Y. Preston approaches photo-collage as "fragmentation." According to Preston, fragmentation and the collage practice associated with it are among the oldest forms of photographic manipulation. Its origins can be traced back to the Cubist aesthetic of fragmentation. Dadaist and Surrealist approaches developed this fragmentation, while in contemporary works, contrasts and discontinuities are more prominent than wholeness (Preston, 2019, p. 20).

As Preston also points out, the origins of photomontages are related to the first manipulation techniques. This method was actually a reinterpretation of earlier technical experiments—particularly compositions created by combining multiple negatives—with a different spirit. Examples include Gustave Le Gray's famous "Marines" series, composed of two separate negatives, and Oscar Rejlander's 1857 work "The Two Ways of Life," created by combining thirty-two negatives (Couturier, 2012, p. 165).

Lady Mary Georgina Caroline Filmer's photomontage works from the 19th century feature a creative approach that combines painting, drawing, and cut-and-paste techniques. These works are related to the Victorian era's popular culture of cartomancy and Disdéri's "carte de visite" format. Filmer's collages are considered precursors to Surrealist collages (Duganne et al., 2020, p. 192). Art critic Plagens compares such practices to early forms of modern social media and collection culture (Plagens, 2010, cited in Duganne et al., 2020, p. 192). Georgina Berkeley's album from 1867–1871 features humorous and symbolic photomontages created by mounting personal photographs onto playing cards. These collages contain humorous references to the class structure of the period, while combining photographs of family and friends with various objects to establish personal yet social contexts (Duganne et al., 2020, p. 192).

According to Couturier (2012, p. 165), the date of the first photomontage remains uncertain. Soulages (2022, p. 320) suggests that two practices can be considered the precursors of photomontage. The first is found in the non-artistic sphere: photographic assemblages used in the late 19th century to create a humorous effect, particularly common in postcards. The second is Cubist collage, which belongs to the artistic domain. Dadaists, especially after the First World War, combined these two approaches and used the term "photomontage" to refer to artistic compositions made entirely or partially from photographs. They employed this form of production as a critical stance at the time. Dadaists positioned themselves as engineers or craftsmen, pushing the artist's individual expression into the background; they interpreted art through technical intervention and reconstruction. In this context, photomontage became a form of incorporating photography into art. Dadaists criticized both art and media images by removing photographs from their original context and giving them new meanings. Furthermore, this technique has blurred the boundaries between the artistic and the non-artistic by bringing together images from many different sources, such as newspapers, dictionaries, catalogs, and posters, in a way that supports the multifaceted nature of photomontage (Soulages, 2022, p. 320).

Photomontage was adopted by Dadaists George Grosz and John Heartfield in 1916, and by Raoul Hausmann, Hannah Höch, and Johannes Baader in 1918. The initial idea behind photomontage was to combine processes of recycling and reconstruction to produce compositions made entirely of pre-existing images (Couturier, 2012, p. 165). Dadaists used photomontage as a tool for political struggle; "Use Photography as a Weapon!" was one of their most famous slogans. Dadaists preferred photomontage to spread their messages through posters, book covers, illustrations, and propaganda materials. It is generally accepted that these artists were the first to use the term "photomontage" (Johnson, et al., 2012, p. 524). Berlin Dadaists created various photomontages with the aim of bringing together the imaginary and the realities of different times (Özel, 2005, p. 287). According to Couturier, Raoul Hausmann and Gustav Klucis viewed photomontage as an approach that rejected the artist and positioned them instead as an engineer. The Dadaists wanted to "construct," "combine," or "assemble" images. This view argues that photomontage is based on an industrial and mechanical understanding of production (Couturier, 2012, p. 165).

Raoul Hausmann used both photographs and words in his photomontages, presenting two types of production. As in his work "Tatlin at Home," his works are often based on formal experiments with artistic connotations rather than political messages. In this work, the steering wheel and machine parts placed on the figure's head reflect a vision of the future where the human body is integrated with machines, while the figure with its pockets turned outward symbolizes the artist's emphasis on poverty. Hausmann preferred abstract narration in his photomontages, completing his works with pictorial elements by painting the backgrounds. This demonstrates that he developed a unique form of expression that combines his artistic and political approaches (Hudson, rev. ed., 1986, cited in Mariens, 2018, p. 243).

George Grosz, on the other hand, added photographic fragments to his watercolor drawings. In Grosz's photomontages, the message conveyed by the seemingly random accumulation of images and text is clear and direct (Soulages, 2022, p. 321; Mariens, 2018, p. 243). Rodchenko experimented with photomontage to translate Mayakovski's “About That” poems into images. Moholy-Nagy used photomontage at the Bauhaus. As in Raoul Ubac's “Le Combat de Penthesilee” (The Battle of Penthesilee), it was sometimes used to enrich his imagery through strange, even absurd associations (Soulages, 2022, p. 321).

On the other hand, in the Soviet Union, under the umbrella of socialism, photomontage was adopted and used for a completely different purpose, “openly for political purposes” (Duganne et al., 2020, p. 192). Soviet experimental artists referred to this type of work as “photomontage” rather than “photocollage.” The word “montage” derives from different sources. In the context of silent cinema, for example, it was used to describe a rapid sequence of images expressing the transition of a place or idea (Mariens, 2018, p. 244). El Lissitzky, on the other hand, used this technique in the Soviet Union in the 1920s as an ideological tool to represent the “New Man,” while in Germany it became a tool of Nazi resistance. This highlights the revolutionary and resistant potential of photomontage (Couturier, 2012, p. 165).

The Surrealists, on the other hand, saw photomontage as a gateway to a more internal quest; for them, it was a technique for visualizing the unconscious. Max Ernst's works represent the aspect of photomontage that connects with the unconscious. Ernst created intense images that triggered “the random collision of meaning” by bringing together incongruous images selected from catalogs or advertising brochures. In Ernst's words, these collages are “the coming together of two irreconcilable realities, through conscious coercion, on a surface unsuitable for this purpose” (Lynton, 2004, pp. 145–146). Another example is the Czech artist and photographer Jaroslav Rössler, who worked in commercial genres such as portrait and advertising photography while also experimenting with Cubist angles and layers in his photomontages (Mariens, 2018, p. 247).

One of the most important figures in collage, Hannah Höch, joined the Dada group in 1917 and gained attention with her photomontages. Höch held a unique position as the only woman in the group and for her work on gender issues (Graf, 2023, p. 89). Using images collected from popular visual culture such as magazines, newspapers, and fashion publications, she celebrated the new female figure while sharply criticizing the army, government, and capital. Her most famous work is the large-scale photomontage titled “Cut with the Kitchen Knife.” This piece was first exhibited at the First International Dada Exhibition in Berlin in 1920 (Duganne et al., 2020, p. 192; Mariens, 2018, p. 243). Höch's photomontages, while containing elements that are visually recognizable, produce multi-layered and open-ended meanings through the combination of these elements. In "Cut with the Kitchen Knife," she addresses the clash between modern female figures and traditional roles, as well as the social duality of women alongside symbols of modernity such as automobiles, machine parts, and electric light bulbs; at the same time, these compositions reflect the hopeful dynamism of avant-garde art (Mariens, 2018, p. 243). Höch's photomontage contains direct and powerful criticism in its historical context—particularly in 1919 Weimar Germany—while these references may remain more ambiguous for today's audience. The work takes a critical stance toward bourgeois aesthetics and the concepts of originality and genius (Duganne et al., 2020, p. 192). As Maud Lavin observes, the work bears traces of the Victorian collage tradition and also points to the rise of mass media imagery (Verlag, 1994, cited in Mariens, 2018, p. 243).

In Höch's work, "*Dada-Review*", while the country is undergoing a major collapse, she satirically criticizes the relaxed image of President Ebert on vacation, creating visual humor with details such as the violet attached to his swimsuit. While reflecting the irrational spirit of Dada, according to G. Clarke, this collage cannot be read directly or interpreted narratively; with its fragmented structure, it reflects the social mood of the period (Höch, 1919, cited in Duganne et al., 2020, p. 191; Clarke, 1997, cited in Duganne et al., 2020, p. 192). In this context, Höch's photomontage functions as a kind of visual code that the viewer must decipher (Duganne et al., 2020, p. 192).

Höch challenged the conservative structure of modern art with her photomontages, which were shaped by feminist and postcolonialist ideas from the early 20th century onwards. In her 1930s series "Ethnographic Museum," she produced disturbing yet critical images by juxtaposing non-Western figures with modern symbols (Mariens, 2018, p. 243). In this sense, Höch is one of the important pioneers of both modern and contemporary art. In addition, his works never go out of style or become outdated (Graf, 2023, p. 88).

One of the artists who stood out with his collages, which created counter-narratives using images already circulating in the mass media, was John Heartfeld (Duganne et al., 2020, p. 191). Heartfield was one of the founders of the Dada movement. He demonstrated his opposition to nationalism in Germany by anglicizing his name. During the period when the Dada movement in Berlin was losing its influence, Heartfield transformed photomontage into a political weapon and developed intense criticism against the tensions in the Weimar Republic (Johnson et al., 2012, p. 524). Heartfield taught himself the technique of photomontage and used it to produce extremely striking political images. He superimposed or placed images obtained with a camera side by side to convey his messages powerfully (Lynton,

2004, p. 138). His 1932 montage titled "Adolf, the Superman..." draws attention to the bourgeois supporters of Nazi leader Hitler. This work combines an X-ray image of a human chest with a photograph of Adolf Hitler, which was very popular at the time (Knierim, 2012, p. 193). Heartfield presented a powerful visual opposition to totalitarian structures with 237 political montages published in the AIZ magazine (Johnson et al., 2012, p. 524).

Robert Rauschenberg, on the other hand, brings photographs together with other objects and various materials, pasting and mixing them to create his "combine paintings." With this approach, painting positions itself between art and life (Soulages, 2022, p. 324). Rauschenberg brings together everyday objects, trash materials, and animal figures in a humorous style, returning them to the Dadaist accessory shop. The object loses its own nature for the sake of a prepared, organized, rationally constructed, and constantly controlled whole (Cabanne, 2015, p. 383).

Soulages (2022, p. 324) suggests that in Rauschenberg's works such as "Odalisque" (1955–58) and "Kite" (1963), photography can be approached in two ways: First, as a material, and second, as an image. The 1981 exhibition "Rauschenberg Photographe" shows that some of the artist's works belong primarily to the purely photographic realm. For example, series such as "Photem Series, 1981" consist solely of pieces where photography is the only medium; "Photem Series n°25" brings together eight photographs selected from different compilations and transferred into a single series to form a composition. In this way, Rauschenberg himself transfers from the world of painting to the world of photography: In this way, he brings them together within what we call art; he questions painting through photography and photography through painting (Soulages, 2022, p. 325).

Chuck Close's "Self-portrait/Composite/Sixteen Parts, 1987" photographs challenge the concept of autonomy. This fragmented and grandiose self-portrait is composed of 16 large (23"x19") black and white Polaroids placed side by side. In this portrait, each eyeglass lens is as large as the viewer's head. As in his other works, size, deformation, and grid structure are important to him. However, here they take on a new function. Size no longer merely emphasizes photographic deformation; it also intensifies the autonomy of the image, as we are confronted with Polaroids rather than prints. The size of each component means enormous detail and resolution (Barbara, 2018, pp. 159-161). When evaluated in the context of photomontage, Close's work presents a visual strategy that dismantles and reconstructs the classical understanding of portraiture. This self-portrait, composed of sixteen large-scale Polaroids, goes beyond the artist's physical image to fragment the structural nature of representation. This fragmentation aligns with the fundamental principle of photomontage, "fragmentation," as each fragment functions both as an autonomous visual element and as a component related to the whole.

The use of Polaroid is reminiscent of the Dadaist approach to direct and instantaneous production. Another example is David Hockney's photo collage work "Pearblossom Highway, 1986, 2," which features irregular intervals and angles. Hockney's images, which when brought together show a highway in the California Desert, littered with trash and road signs and supported on one side by a short cactus, are composed of hundreds of colorful prints. The camera is positioned so that the yellow line of the highway cuts the image vertically and disappears into the blue sky. Additionally, since the images were taken at specific times, there are differences in color, light, sky, and the positioning of objects and lines. Hockney's work consists of photographs taken to document a specific time and place. However, when taken together, they create a fictional space that could never exist in reality (Barbara, 2018, p. 162). This work, in a sense, replaces the photographic "moment" seen from the perspective of the eye with a photomontage, creating the artist's own landscape. In this way, the space, or landscape, is transformed from its existing state into a new form.

Carl Chiarenza's collage photographs, titled "*Untitled Triptych, 1994*," present abstract compositions while also carrying the textural traces of the materials used, creating a complex visual layer. Brightness, wrinkles, and intense contrasts arouse curiosity in the viewer; while trying to identify the materials in the image, the viewer is also confronted with the frustration of not being able to make sense of it. According to Chiarenza, the main issue is that the viewer should see the photograph not as a "window" but as a new field of experience. The role of collage here is to form the starting point of the photograph. However, the distinctiveness of objects disappears in the photograph; a torn piece of paper can turn into a riverbed, a cloud, or another landscape. Thus, the act of recognition and differentiation is consciously problematized (Barbara, 2018, p. 155).

Another example is the artist Raquel van Haver. Van Haver's work focuses on people from all walks of life and from all corners of the world. She is passionate about presenting snapshots of the lives of individuals who are often ignored or marginalized in society. In this vein, she communicates with young men who spend time on the streets in her neighborhood in Southeast Amsterdam, with young groups in London, with teenage gangs in Lagos, Nigeria, and with residents of "favelas" in South America. Van Haver immerses himself in their lives, striving to understand these individuals. He then photographs them. These photographs become the source material for his paintings. The artist uses these visuals to bring together different faces and spaces, creating collage-like compositions featuring people he has encountered during his travels and in his daily life. This approach allows his paintings to be read not only as figurative representations but also as a network of encounters and a space of social memory (Wolfe, 2025). The production process seen in Haver's work highlights the social and narrative aspects of photomontage, such as belonging and representation.

Alma Haser's artistic practice is defined by her contemporary reinterpretation of the portrait tradition. Haser does not merely reproduce portraits; she also critically examines the place of the portrait genre in the history of art and photography. This approach is related to modernist art movements such as Cubism and Surrealism, as well as conceptual art's questioning attitude towards portraiture and its relationship with collage. Haser's "Cosmic Surgery" (2012–2015) series thus offers a multi-layered structure in both aesthetic and intellectual terms. Haser does not merely produce his portraits as photographs; he transforms them into modular origami sculptures, creating new layers of meaning. Each portrait is first photographed, then the origami form created from that image is reintegrated with the portrait and photographed again. This presents the viewer with both a physical and conceptual transformation process. Through this transformation, identity and facial perception are deliberately disrupted; the familiar is alienated. The series suggests that the face is not merely a representation but also a fragile, malleable structure (Preston, 2019, pp. 17-19).

All these examples of artists demonstrate that collage or photomontage has developed new forms of artistic production. Collage, which originated with Degas and Picasso and then reached Ducamp, has evolved into Surrealism and Pop Art, and finally to the present day. This technique is frequently used in the digital realm today, with the addition of various digital image processing programs and new media. Furthermore, this deep-rooted history and contemporary applications indicate that collage will continue to be an indispensable form of expression for future generations of artists.

Appropriation

Appropriation, also known as "appropriation," is an artistic method used in contemporary art, as in Dada, where the boundaries of originality are removed. However, in the context of this study, when we look at the works of Dada, ready-made, collage, and photomontage artists, we see that these practices also contain a large degree of the "appropriation" approach. There is an intertwined relationship between all these approaches.

The term "appropriation" (borrowing from originality or re-acquisition) refers to the re-presentation of an existing work of art, image, or object within another work (Emerling, 2012, cited in Er, 2023, p. 22). As mentioned earlier, the precursors of this strategy include Marcel Duchamp's iconic 1913 "Fountain," the collages and photomontages of Dada artists, and Robert Rauschenberg's "assembly" works created from various magazine advertisements in the 1950s works created from various magazine advertisements, and the Pop Art and Fluxus movements of the early 1960s

(Er, 2023, p. 22). Andy Warhol's striking silkscreen prints featuring multiple images of Hollywood icons such as Campbell's Soup cans, Coca-Cola bottles, and Marilyn Monroe have served as a cornerstone for subsequent generations of artists following the appropriation practice (Warren, Patrick, 2006, cited in Er, 2023, p. 22). With postmodernism, "appropriation" practices have become one of the primary tools for questioning the discourses and myths of modernism. The fundamental aim of "appropriation" is to give a familiar image a new meaning or set of meanings by presenting it in a different context. In this sense, appropriation art opens up concepts such as the originality of the artwork, authenticity, and the artist's literary property (Emerling, 2012, cited in Er, 2023, p. 22).

When considered in the context of photography, it is evident that photography has long been associated with the history of appropriation. In the early examples given above, appropriation was used only as a part of the work, whereas in photography-based works, the work itself consists of appropriation. *John Stezaker,* Barbara Kruger, Richard Prince, *Sherrie Levine,* Cindy Sherman are among the most influential examples of photography-based appropriation.

Furthermore, when considered solely in terms of images, photography can be seen as an act of "taking." Unlike traditional art forms such as painting or drawing, which are more associated with the act of "making," photography works by "appropriating" images from everyday life, capturing the scene in front of the camera, and making it its own. Therefore, reproducibility and transferability are among its fundamental characteristics rather than originality (Duganne et al., 2020, p. 184).

The "appropriation" approach, which emerged with the postmodern process, is a widely used method in photography. Within this approach, artists have created their works by directly using images they have appropriated, mostly without any intervention. Appropriation has emerged as an effective way of reusing images that are available in the public domain, other artists' works, or visuals belonging to broader cultural contexts through borrowing, copying, or stealing (Warren, Patrick, 2006 cited in Er, 2023, p. 23). In the appropriation approach, the aim is often to question the original meaning of a particular work or to place it in a different context. In this context, the concept of the artist's "authorship" also becomes an object of questioning (Smith, 2018, p. 187).

Among the names that actively use the appropriation approach is *John Stezaker*. When looking at Stezaker's work, although the "cutting" and 'combining' methods in collage are clearly evident, what is most important is the use of photographs as "appropriation." Stezaker cuts, shapes, and combines photographs obtained from different times and different media, such as flea markets, to create a new photographic image.

Stezaker's "Mask" series is a striking example of creating something original using found materials. What makes these images interesting is that, despite the fact that none of the elements they contain are contemporary, they appear very contemporary to the viewer. In the "Mask" series, Stezaker takes promotional photographs of film stars from the 1940s and 1950s and places landscape photographs or old postcards over them to mask the faces. In this series, Stezaker cuts out a woman's face and combines it with another image, causing a disruption at both the level of identity and representation. This process is not merely a visual intervention but also reads as a symbolic "death" act. Thus, appropriation not only reworks and transforms images but also their ideological and psychoanalytic backgrounds (Bright & Erp, 2019, p. 182). Additionally, traces of time and space are discernible in these images. Postcards mostly feature North American and European landscapes from the early 20th century, while film stills and studio portraits are mostly British in origin and date from the 1930s to the early 1950s. Stezaker's "new" images are dialectical compositions in which fragments are brought together; these elements, combined in opposition, clearly reveal their incompatibility (Preston, 2019, pp. 23-24).

Sherrie Levine, on the other hand, applied this approach by directly copying the works of famous male artists. A striking example of this is her work "*After Walker Evans: 4*." Here, Levine directly photographed a photograph by Walker Evans, that is, she produced a photograph of a photograph. She has applied the same strategy to famous paintings, criticizing the systematic second-class treatment of female artists in art history. She even produced a bronze urinal sculpture titled "*Fountain*" in 1991, referencing Duchamp's conceptual approach (Bright & Erp, 2019, p. 174). Levine's understanding is completely different from the traditional understanding of photography, both in terms of form and content. What is involved is the transmission of a conceptual idea through the mere appearance of an existing object (which may be an iconic photograph). According to Levine, the practice of photographic appropriation resembles "a re-creative act of collaboration that transforms the masterpiece, which is considered extraordinary, into something organic and constantly renewable" (Leeuwen, 2010, cited in Duganne et al., 2020, p. 194).

Ulla Jokisalo's art combines appropriation with surrealist play in her work since the 1980s. The artist uses found objects such as insects, mirrors, sewing materials, and old-fashioned photographs to transform the photographic surface into three-dimensional, temporary sculptural objects. This approach results in a layered form that encompasses both materiality and visual narrative. In Jokisalo's series titled "Headless Women," animal faces are added to female bodies, drawing inspiration from the world of 19th-century children's fairy tales. These collages create elegant yet unsettling hybrid portraits that question the concept of "mirror-self" on a fairy-tale and symbolic level (Preston, 2019, pp. 25-26).

Carmen Winant's installation "*Body/Index*, 2018" is a large-scale collage work composed of 'found' photographs of female figures. "Body/Index" is a single piece that is modular and can be divided into many separate sections. Winant's works are often quite specific in theme and group an entire project around a single image or type of action (Artworks, 2025). In this work, she brings together images taken from reference books prepared for women to pose, questioning how representation is constructed and what is excluded. When images are detached from their context, they lose their meaning, transforming into visual puzzles that encourage the viewer to question. Winant's strategy reappropriates ordinary images through a feminist critique, drawing attention to historically overlooked women's experiences. The physical circulation history of the photographs adds a tactile and historical layer to the installation. It offers a powerful visual archive critique that raises awareness about women's visibility while questioning who is represented and who is excluded (Bright & Erp, 2019, p. 173).

Stezaker's 1990s landscape images, which bring to mind *Svetlana* Kopystiansky's portrait and landscape compositions, appear distorted at first glance, but upon closer inspection, the reason for this becomes clear. Each work combines a photograph with a postcard. The two are connected in a way that is far from perfect, yet they create a strange continuity. These works vividly demonstrate the difference between how we look at photographs and paintings. The proximity and connection between the two images bring about an identity crisis and reveal our habit of seeing two differences in conflict with each other (Barbara, 2018, p. 162).

THE USE OF CURRENT TOOLS THROUGH IMAGES

In contemporary photography, just as in the Dadaist tradition, ordinary objects and iconic images are not merely regarded as aesthetic references but also as a field for reproduction and critical commentary. Especially the interaction of digital images with social media and other digital platforms enables these images to be detached from their original contexts and re-shaped with new meanings. Artists are reconstructing the physical objects, methods, and theoretical approaches used in Dada and Surrealism through contemporary digital tools. According to Preston (2019, p. 31), contemporary artists now construct form, content, and meaning in multifaceted and flexible ways rather than in fixed structures. Contemporary tools such as digital collage, augmented reality, and artificial intelligence offer the possibility of reinterpreting iconic images by multiplying or transforming them (Gençcelep & Özkemahlı, 2023, pp. 3063-3064). This process enables visual art to break free from its past limitations and become an experimental and critical field of creation.

Digitalization is a concept that has become established in the field of art today, just as it has become part of human life in all areas of society. Thanks to digital applications, which have emerged as a new medium for art with technological innovations, the concept of digitalization has found its place in art and plays a transformative role (Taşçı & Erdem, 2024). In the narrative techniques used in the digital world, Ducham's physical "Fountain" has been replaced by digital coding and software tools. Today, collaging physical objects and cutting and pasting have been replaced by the unlimited possibilities of interactive media. Sherrie Levine's iconic photographs, which she copied as if they were objects and translated into a photographic language, have been transformed into Penelope Umbrico's "Flickr," which uses approximately half a million images as an archive. The boundaries of originality in photography have been redefined in the boundless visual world of the internet age. Michael Wolf, in his series "a series of unfortunate events," transformed Google images that were not physically present and did not belong to him into documentary-style photographic art. **As** in these examples, Robert Shore (Shore, 2023, cited in Preston, 2019, p. 8) has noted that "sharing is a key concept of the digital age and that appropriating others' images is one of the leading post-photographic strategies."

But beyond that, while discussing issues of ownership in photography, we can now see that with AI-powered software, as in the example of Boris Eldagsen, photographs that never actually existed can be transformed into works of art. Sherrie Levine, Penelope Umbrico, and Michael Wolf are clear examples of "appropriation." However, works produced with artificial intelligence (even though artificial intelligence applications take the images they produce from the existing visual network) have gone far beyond "appropriation." It is no longer necessary for the object to exist; artists today do not select, steal, or appropriate objects from the real world. As has been the case throughout art history, it is a fact that today's artists are influenced by the technology and developments of their time in all their artistic approaches. Research on the transformation of thought into text through artificial intelligence and even the transfer of thought into visual form through artificial intelligence, the creation of digital worlds, advancements in robotic technology, and the ways in which social media shapes our understanding and interpretation of the world, and the (relatively) unlimited access to information and visuals will continue to transform future artists and art.

Looking at examples from contemporary artists, Daniel Gordon's work "*Pineapple and Shadow*" demonstrates how he transforms contemporary tools into a form of artistic expression. Danto's (2016, p. 120) statement that "the modern artist perhaps presents the craft object as a work of art by 'appropriating' it" finds its place in these examples.

In this work, Gordon constructs a three-dimensional 'sculpture' using images he usually finds on the internet, then photographs this fiction. The artist's productions mostly contain references to art history traditions and still life symbolism. They imitate reality but also clearly leave traces of Photoshop interventions in the visuals. Gordon re-constructs visuals and media through quotation, sampling, rearrangement, and hybridization (Bright & Erp, 2019, p. 174). In the artist's exhibition titled "Free Transform, 2023," there is a still life measuring twenty-three feet in length. Its ultra-bright background and various subjects (houseplants, bouquets of flowers, fruits, vegetables, lobsters) evoke elements from a giant Colorforms set. The work derives its name from a Photoshop tool that allows for fluid image manipulation; however, digital editing is merely one stage of Gordon's distinctive layering process, which draws on various photographic sources. In Gordon's approach, images are printed, cut out, and rephotographed as collages. Despite their photographic foundations, Gordon's pieces invite visual comparisons (Fateman, 2025).

According to Duganne et al. (2020, p.190), "photography has never been merely a way of depicting the world. Beyond that, it has functioned as a powerful tool for discovering new, sometimes contradictory, and always meaningful ways of envisioning the future." This discovery, as in Gordon's approach, led to the digitalization of collage, which, as Tarı (2025) also points out, reached the "digital collage" format with the encounter of contemporary art with technology. Ceren Bülbün's works can be cited as another example in this context.

In her interview with N. Tarı, Ceren Bülbün explains her artistic production and approach to collage. For Bülbün, the difference between digital and traditional collage is like the difference between analog and digital cameras. The artist believes that digital techniques are used more today due to technological developments, the ability to utilize more sources, and their applicability in the digital environment. According to Bülbün, there is no distinction between traditional and digital in terms of style for a creative and original person. Creativity is very important to her; "if the work is creative, it will be effective even if a traditional technique is used." What matters to Bülbün is "what you love and what you feel when you do it." What draws him to collage is that this method offers unlimited possibilities. According to him, "The collage technique is not bound by specific materials or rules; it is a free technique in terms of materials and expression. What I do is use this freedom to observe and express the concrete and abstract unity of humanity, which is part of nature, with its environment and the cosmos." The artist has a notebook in which she collects images she has found in magazines, newspapers, and on the internet, as well as writings she likes or things she has thought about. She describes this notebook as an "idea book" that shapes her thoughts and outlook on life and helps her bring them together. The artist, who is interested in science, philosophy, and nature, also focuses on these topics in her emotions, thoughts, and collages (Tarı, 2025).

Julianna Foster's photographic production, on the other hand, transforms memory, representation, and time into not only intellectual but also physical and multi-layered forms based on symbolism. This approach challenges the traditional boundaries of photography while inviting us to reconsider the reality of the image. Foster reworks images using different printing techniques, constructs objects, and rephotographs these scenes, creating new landscapes that reveal the tension between the organic and the artificial. This creative process pushes the viewer to question the line between the familiar and the fictional (Foster, 2025).

Foster's "Swell" series, deals with an extraordinary event that allegedly took place in a small coastal town. According to legend, as a northeasterly storm (nor'easter) formed from the remnants of a hurricane in the Atlantic Ocean, several townspeople reported seeing something they had never witnessed before—and have not seen since (Foster, 2025). *Fostter* uses video, fabric, and prints on paper in his work, digitally combining his own models with landscape photographs to offer interpretations of memories shaped by his imagination (Preston, 2019, p. 15).

In his current project, "Geographical Lore," the artist documents geological features in the western United States and combines them with studio representations he has created by hand. This approach aims to make the fine line between nature and human intervention visible while also creating a strong awareness of environmental change and the delicate balance of nature. Blending a critical perspective with a romantic aesthetic, the artist addresses pressing issues of our time, such as climate change, through a poetic language (Foster, 2025). Adopting a process-oriented and cyclical production method, the artist deliberately blurs the boundaries between authenticity and fiction in her images by combining analog and digital techniques. In this way, they invite viewers to rethink their perceptions of the landscapes they encounter and the images of nature stored in their memory. Aiming to take their project to different geographies and deepen it through interdisciplinary research, the artist continues to expand the boundaries of visual narrative (Foster, 2025).

Daisuke Yokota, who uniquely combines analog and digital production techniques, strategically integrates traditional photographic approaches with contemporary technologies. This synthesis unites the past and the present on an aesthetic and conceptual level. As a result, his work displays an experimental approach. Yokota transfers the physical and material structure of analog to digital.

The artist's production process often begins with capturing his subject using a compact digital camera, typically at night and with a flash. The image is saved as a low-resolution JPEG file, which compresses the file into a smaller, lower-quality format. The artist then prints this image and rephotographs it using medium-format film. Each image is reprinted an average of ten times. Deliberate darkroom "mistakes"—dust, scratches, overheated chemicals, light, and in some cases even acid or fire applications—make the artist's physical intervention in the process visible. Yokota's works create a series of disruptive effects that interrupt our ways of seeing and experiencing time. Yokota mentions that he was influenced by experimental sound artist Aphex Twin in this approach; he states that he adapted sound manipulations such as delay, reverb, and echo, particularly in relation to time, to his photographic practice (Preston, 2019, p. 19).

Another artist who sees the difference between digital and traditional works as merely a technical distinction is Meriç Canatan. In an interview with N. Tarı, he explained his approach to production. According to him, while one is shaped by being physically cut and carved, the other undergoes the same process using digital tools. However, at its core, both approaches share a similar intellectual foundation and express themselves within the same framework. Although he prefers traditional-based, and sometimes mixed media methods, his admiration for digital works is also quite evident. Canatan considers these two methods not as rivals, but as complementary forms of creation (Tarı, 2025).

After completing his undergraduate education in Fashion Design, the artist chose to shape his artistic journey around collage and fashion. For him, collage is not merely a technique but also a creative form of expression that integrates with fashion. The artist's creative process is often shaped by an idea or a strong feeling. However, this process can sometimes begin with just a detail that catches her eye at that moment. The visual image becomes one of the fundamental elements that determine the direction of the work, and the artist grants herself freedom without intervening in either the material or the image. She prefers to work with forms and colors that catch her attention rather than relying on inspiration. They select images that exist on the boundary between beauty and ugliness, ones that bring them joy when they look at them (Tarı, 2025). In addition, in an interview with artist Z. S. İlkan, he describes his technique as quite instinctive and reminiscent of his childhood approach. According to him, this process is like a playground where form, color, and stain come together freely, much like in kindergarten. However, within this play, elements that particularly interest him, such as nature, the human body, and various surface textures, become more pronounced. He is most influenced by the unique freedom offered by collage. The power of collage to create its own reality often surprises the artist and leads him in unexpected directions (İlkan, 2025).

Going far beyond photography and collage, another artist, Nick Veasrey, produces works using a very different approach similar to photogram. The artist, who says that working with X-rays is very dangerous, emphasizes that this method requires a high level of attention and safety. To minimize these risks, Veasrey has constructed a specially designed concrete structure. Inside this structure, there are various X-ray machines with different output powers and characteristics, as well as a film developing system. Objects to be X-rayed are carefully placed on the ground or wall; then, the film is positioned beneath or behind the object. As the X-ray beams pass through the object, they create a life-size image on the film. If the object is too large to fit on a single film, the process is repeated using multiple films. The resulting films are then digitized using high-resolution scanners in the final stage. This ensures that both sharpness and detail are maximized. Imaging large and complex objects can sometimes take months; this process, consisting of hundreds of separate films, ultimately results in a unique X-ray composition that offers the viewer extraordinary detail and visual aesthetics (Veasrey, 2025).

CONCLUSION

The possibilities offered by the digital age have transformed ready-made art from material objects into a new form of creation based on digital data. This process has also brought about a transformation that overlaps with the origins of the Dada movement. In particular, the concept of Ready-Made has evolved into a form where digital content, media images, and visual data have become artistic materials, detached from physical objects. Digital Ready-Mades are now shaped by processes such as digital collectivity, sharing, and re-arrangement. The artist's role extends beyond that of the creator of the work, encompassing selective and archival roles as well.

This situation brings with it a radical rethinking of the meaning, circulation, and consumption of art, as once experienced with Dada. New forms of techniques such as appropriation, collage, and photomontage in the digital environment are extensions of Dada's strategies of fragmentation and recontextualization.

Works produced in the digital environment bring individual experience and data flow to the center of art. Thomas Ruff's media images obtained from the internet or Penelope Umbrico's massive visual archives created using Flickr data are contemporary examples of this approach. In this context, these art practices in the digital age are redefined as a critical field that questions the relationship between meaning and context. Digital variations of Ready-Made carry the avant-garde attitude of the past into the present while transforming the artist's relationship with the digital. Thus, the Dadaist spirit continues to live on in the dynamics of contemporary art through new technologies.

REFERENCES

Alternative photography (2025, 4 March). *alternativephotography.com,* Alternative Photographic Processes World of Records https://www.alternativephotography.com/alternative-processes-records/

Antmen, A. (2010). *Sanatçılardan Yazılar ve Açıklamalarla 20. Yüzyıl Batı Sanatında Akımlar.* Sel Yayıncılık.

Artun, A. (2010). *Sanat Manifestoları, Avangard Sanat ve Direniş.* İletişim Yayınları.

Artworks, (2025, 15 May). *artworks.se,* Carmen Winant, https://artworks.se/utstallningar/body-index

Barbara, S. (2018). Belgesel Özerklik ve Fotoğraf Sanatı, S. Walden (Ed.), *Fotoğraf Felsefesi, Doğanın Kalemi Üzerine Denemeler* (pp. 139-166). (A. Yılmaz, Trans.), Espas Yayın

Barnard, M. (2010). *Sanat Tasarım ve Kültür* (Korkmaz, G., Trans.). Ütopya.

Birinci, G. (2019). Fotoğraf Sanatında Fotografik Malzemenin Görsel Bir Dil Olarak Kullanımı. *Uluslararası Sanat Kültür ve İletişim Dergisi, 2*(1), 68–80.

Bourdieu, P. (2006). *Sanatın Kuralları,* Trans. N. K. Sevil, Yapı Kredi Yayınları-1216/57

Breton, A. (2017). İki Dada Bildirisi, E. Batur (Ed.), *Modernizmin Serüveni, Bir "Temel Metinler" Seçkisi 1840-1990* (pp.375-376). (S. Rifat, Trans.), Sel Yayıncılık

Bright, S., & Van Erp, H. (2019). *Photography Decoded.* Tate.

Brown, R., & Phillips, M. (2025, 21 March). *alternativephotography.com,* Cyanotype photograms, https://www.alternativephotography.com/photograms/

Cabanne, P. (2015). Kolajlar, E. Batur (Ed.), *Modernizmin Serüveni, Bir "Temel Metinler" Seçkisi 1840-1990* (pp.380-383). (M. Cansever, Trans.), Sel Yayıncılık

Cauquelin, A. (2005). *Çağdaş Sanat,* (Ö. Avcı, Trans.), Kültür Kitaplığı-20, Dost Kitapevi

Chandler, D. (2025, 23 March). *martinparrfoundation.org,* https://www.martinparrfoundation.org/product/nigel-shafran-workbooks/

Cotton, C. (2020). *The Photograph as Contemporary Art.* Thames & Hudson.

Couturier, E. (2012). *Talk Abaut Contemporary Photography.* Flammarion.

Cozzi, L. (2025, 10 May). *x-traonline.org,* Sod You Gits: Sarah Lucas's Fleet Street Surrealism, https://www.x-traonline.org/article/sod-you-gits-sarah-lucass-fleet -street-surrealism

Danto, A. (2016). *Brillo Kutusu, Post-Tarihsel Perspektiften Görsel Sanatlar* (Kayaş, C., Trans.). Sanat ve Kuram.

Duchamp, M. (2017). Marcel Duchamp ve Ready-Made, E. Batur (Ed.), *Modernizmin Serüveni, Bir "Temel Metinler" Seçkisi 1840-1990* (pp.378-379). (S. Rifat, Trans.), Sel Yayıncılık

Duganne, E., Diack, H., & Weissman, T. (2020). *Global Photography, A Critical History*. Routledge. DOI: 10.4324/9781003085485

Er, M. H. (2022). *XXI. Yüzyıl Çağdaş Fotoğrafta Yaratım Sürecine Bakış* (Bilgiseren, H. O., Ed.). Efe Akademi Yayınları.

Er, M. H. (2023). Portrait Photography and Appropriation. *Contemporary Issues of Communication, 2*(1), 18–32.

Eroğlu, Ö. (2015). *Modern Sanat.* Tekhne Yayınları.

Fateman, J. (2025, 10 May). https://www.danielgordonstudio.com/, Daniel Gordon, https://www.danielgordonstudio.com/press/85=daniel-gordon

Foster, J. (2025, 12 May). *juliannafoster.com,* https://juliannafoster.com/section/325750-Swell.html

Frieze (2025, 03 May). *frieze.com,* Finding the Right Darkness, Zoe Leonard's photographs and sculptures meditate on wonder and loss, https://www.frieze.com/article/finding-right-darkness

Genç, A. (1983). *Dada, Antropi ve Nedensizlik Açısından Dadacı Sanat Hareketlerinin Çözümlemesine İlişkin Bir Yöntem Araştırması.* Dokuz Eylül Üniversitesi, Güzel Sanatlar Fakültesi, Resim Bölümü, Doktora Tezi.

Gençcelep, B., & Özkemahlı, K. K. (2023). "Gerçek Olandan Simülasyona: Fotoğraf Stüdyosu Eğitiminde "Set.A.Light 3D" Örneği", International Academic Social Resources Journal, (e-ISSN: 2636-7637), Vol:8, Issue:51; pp:3062-3071. DOI: DOI: 10.29228/ASRJOURNAL.70969

Graf, M. (2023). *Modern ve Çağdaş Sanat Kafası.* Hayalperest Yayınevi.

Hodge, S. (2019). *Sanatın Kısa Öyküsü* (Öztok, D., Trans.). Hep Kitap Yayın.

Hopkins, D. (2004). *Dada and Surrealism: A Very Short Introduction.* Oxford University Press. DOI: 10.1093/actrade/9780192802545.001.0001

İlkan, Z. S. (2025, 10 May). vogue.com.tr, Meriç Canatan - Interviewed by Zeynep Seren İlkan, https://vogue.com.tr/metropol/12-soruda-meric-canatan

Johnson, W. S., Rice, M., & Williams, C. (2012). A History of Photography, from 1839 to the present, T. Mulligan & D. Wooters (Ed.), The George Eastman House Collection, Taschen

Knierim, F. (2012). Dada, J. Hacking (Ed.), *Photography The Whole Story* (pp.192-195). Thames & Hudson

Laserna Montoya, J. D., Tarver, G. M., & Duganne, E. (2017). Advertisement Extraction: Interview with Juan David Laserna Montoya. *Photographies, 10*(3), 329–345. DOI: 10.1080/17540763.2017.1340735

Lewis, E. (2018). *İzmler, Fotoğrafı Anlamak* (Aydemir, M. M., Trans.). Hayalperest Yayınevi.

Lynton, N. (2004). *Modern Sanatın Öyküsü,* (C. Çapan & S. Öziş, Trans.), Remzi Kitabevi Marian Goodman, Gallery (2025, 20 March). *mariangoodman.com,* https://www.mariangoodman.com/artists/james-welling/

Mariens, M. W. (2018). *Photography A Cultural History*. Laurence King Publishing.

McGinity, L. (2017-a). Dada, S. Farthing (Ed.), *Sanatın Tüm Öyküsü* (pp: 410-411). (G. Aldoğan & F. C. Çulcu, Trans.), Hayalperest Yayınevi

McGinity, L. (2017-c). Sanat Eleştirmeni, S. Farthing (Ed.), *Sanatın Tüm Öyküsü* (pp: 412-413). (G. Aldoğan & F. C. Çulcu, Trans.), Hayalperest Yayınevi McNeill, S. (2025, 3 May-a). *alternativephotography.com,* Photograms – a magical concept, https://www.alternativephotography.com/photograms-cameraless-photography/

McNeill, S. (2025). *stephenmcneill.com,* https://www.stephenmcneill.com/stephen-mcneill/

Özel, Z. (2005). *Fotoğraf Akımları İçinde Gerçekliğin Sunumu, Yeni Düşünceler, Yıl 1, Sayı 1*. Haziran.

Preston, M. Y. (2019). Building Images, Building, A. Leighton Massoni and M. Shindelman (Ed.), *Spaces The Focal Press Companion to The Constructed Image in Contemporary Photography* (pp.7-34). Routledge

Roberts, P. G. (2012). Experimention and Abstraction, J. Hacking (Ed.), *Photography The Whole Story* (pp.196-203). Thames & Hudson

Sanouillet, M. (2017). Dadacılığın Kökenleri: Zürih ve New York, E. Batur (Ed.), *Modernizmin Serüveni, Bir "Temel Metinler" Seçkisi 1840-1990* (pp.359-372). (T. Ilgaz, Trans.), Sel Yayıncılık

Shashasha, (2025, 20 May). *shashasha.co,* https://www.shashasha.co/en/book/the -well

Soulages, F. (2022). *Fotoğrafın Estetiği* (Şansal, D. E., Trans.). Espas Yayıncılık.

Tarı, N. (2025, 5 June). artfulliving.com.tr, Deneyselliği Dijitalle Buluşturan 5 Kolaj Sanatçısı, https://www.artfulliving.com.tr/sanat/deneyselligi-dijitalle-bulusturan-5 -kolaj-sanatcisi-i-14417

Taşcı, F., & Erdem, S. (2024). An analysis on reality and virtuality in art: Virtual space, virtual body and virtual object example. *Art Vision, 30*(52), 58–71. DOI: 10.32547/artvision.1415560

Turani, A. (1992). *Dünya Sanat Tarihi.* Remzi Kitabevi.

Tzara, T. (2017). Dada Hiçbir Anlama Gelmez, E. Batur (Ed.), *Modernizmin Serüveni, Bir "Temel Metinler" Seçkisi 1840-1990* (pp.373-374). (S. Rifat, Trans.), Sel Yayıncılık

Veasrey, N. (2025, 10 March). *nickveasey.com,* N. Veasrey, X-ray Catalogue, 2025, https://catalogue.nickveasey.com/books/mmjz/#p=7

Walton, K. L. (2018) Geçirgen Fotoğraflar: Fotografik Gerçekliğin Doğası Üzerine, S.Walden (Ed.), *Doğanın Kalemi Üzerine Denemeler* (pp.29-67). (H. Yılmaz, Trans.), Espas Yayınları

Ware, K. (2019). Camera-Less: Photographıc Fidelity (And Infidelity), A. Leighton Massoni and M. Shindelman (Ed.), *SpacesThe Focal Press Companion to The Constructed Image in Contemporary Photography* (pp.186-208). Routledge

Whitney (2025, 15 March). *whitney.org,* https://whitney.org/artists/3788

Wolfe, S. (2025, 5 May). magazine.artland.com, 5 Contemporary Collage Artists Adding New Layers, https://magazine.artland.com/5-contemporary-collage-artists/

Zwirner, D. (2025, 10 May). *davidzwirner.com,* https://www.davidzwirner.com/ artists/james-welling

ADDITIONAL READING

Cammaer, G. (2018). Recycling Reality: Found Footage Filmmaking and the Digital Turn. *Found Footage Magazine*, (6), 30–39.

Manovich, L. (2001). The Language of New Media. MIT Press. Foster, H. (1996). The Return of the Real: The Avant-Garde at the End of the Century. MIT Press. Benjamin, W. (2008). The Work of Art in the Age of Mechanical Reproduction. Penguin.

Taylor, B. (2015). *Art Today*. Laurence King Publishing.

Tribe, M., & Jana, R. (2007). *New Media Art. Taschen. Quaranta, D. (2013). Beyond New Media Art. Link Editions. Greene, R. (2004). Internet Art. Thames & Hudson. Shanken, E. A. (2014). Art and Electronic Media.* Phaidon.

KEY TERMS AND DEFINITIONS

Appropriation: The use of pre-existing images or artworks in new creations, raising debates on originality, authorship, and ethics in contemporary art.

Artificial Intelligence in Art: The use of AI tools to generate visual art, transforming creative processes and challenging the notion of artistic authorship and uniqueness.

Collage: A composition made by combining various images, texts, or materials. In digital art, this is often achieved through software and multimedia layering.

Dada Movement: An early 20th-century avant-garde movement questioning traditional aesthetics and meaning in art. It pioneered the concept of ready-made.

Digitalization: The transformation of physical processes into digital formats, revolutionizing how artists create, distribute, and exhibit their work.

New Media Art: Art created with digital technologies such as video, AI, VR, and interactive installations. It integrates technological tools into the artistic process.

Photomontage: The combination of multiple photographs into a single image, often manipulated digitally to create a new visual narrative.

Ready-Made: An object not created by the artist but presented as an artwork. In the digital age, it includes digital images, AI-generated visuals, and stock content.

Chapter 2
90 Miles and the AI-Mediated Documentary:
Rethinking Reality in the Digital Age

Gulay Dogan Bas
http://orcid.org/0000-0003-4721-3321
Istanbul Yeni Yuzyil University, Turkey

ABSTRACT

Michael Christopher Brown's 90 Miles project challenges foundations of documentary photography by employing artificial intelligence to generate images rather than capturing them through a camera. This project disrupts traditional notions of photographic truth, blurring the line between reality and fiction, and forcing a reassessment of what constitutes a documentary image. By replacing the indexical relationship between photograph and subject with machine-generated interpretations, 90 Miles raises critical questions about authorship and the role of human intervention in visual storytelling. This paper examines 90 Miles through a critical lens, exploring how AI-generated imagery reconfigures the ethics and aesthetics of documentary photography. By situating 90 Miles within debates on post-photography, this study interrogates how AI redefines the relationship between visual narratives and historical truth.

INTRODUCTION

Since its inception, photography has occupied a central role in documenting the world, shaping public memory, and negotiating the boundaries between truth and fiction. The documentary tradition in photography—rooted in a commitment to

DOI: 10.4018/979-8-3373-2230-8.ch002

witnessing, recording, and revealing—has historically been invested with a truth-claim grounded in the indexical relationship between image and referent. From early social reform photography to war reportage and ethnographic documentation, the photographic image has served as both evidence and narrative, offering visual testimony of events, people, and places often absent from dominant historical records.

Yet, the documentary genre has never been free from critique. Questions around framing, authorship, power dynamics, and the ethical responsibilities of representation have long complicated the assumed neutrality of the photographic document. As John Tagg have argued, the documentary image is not a transparent window onto reality, but a constructed artifact shaped by institutional practices and ideological frameworks. The critical legacy of documentary photography, therefore, involves a continuous interrogation of what it means to "bear witness" through images.

In the contemporary landscape, the advent of artificial intelligence (AI) has further destabilized the documentary function of photography. Generative AI models—capable of producing hyperrealistic images without a physical referent—raise profound questions about authenticity, evidence, and the ontology of the photographic image. These technologies blur the boundaries between the captured and the created, challenging the viewer's ability to distinguish between documentation and fabrication. While AI-generated images can simulate the aesthetic conventions of documentary photography, their detachment from lived experience and material reality introduces ethical and epistemological concerns, particularly in contexts where visual representation holds evidentiary or testimonial value.

This convergence of documentary photography and AI image generation compels a reexamination of the genre's foundational assumptions. What does it mean to document in an era where images can be synthesized without direct experience? How do issues of authorship, credibility, and historical accountability shift when the indexical trace—the hallmark of traditional photography—is no longer a given? This study aims to explore these tensions by situating the current technological developments within the broader documentary legacy of photography, tracing continuities and ruptures that define our contemporary visual culture.

Methodology

Focusing on photojournalist Michael Christopher Brown's post photography project, 90 Miles (2023), this study discusses the production of images with artificial intelligence through the foundations of documentary photography. This project, which is said to be 'AI reporting-illustration experiment', centers on the forced migration from Cuba to the United States. The project, whose main narrative is the escape of Cubans, is also notable for its visualization of specific historical crises from the 1960s, when Fidel Castro's rule began, to the present day (Artist web page, n.d.).

Because it deconstructs the relationship between visual memory and photography by re-imagining history. The visualization of news reports and interviews using artificial intelligence tools is significant as a turning point in visual storytelling. Drawing on the literature of definitions and theories on documentary photography and post photography, this study examines the relationship between the aesthetics of artificial intelligence and reality through historical comparisons and Brown's work on the foundations of documentary photography such as indexicality, witnessing, authorship and authenticity.

Reportage Illustration, Journalism and Documentary Photography Through History

The roots of reportage illustration trace back to the 19th century, when visual documentation of historical events was largely in the hands of illustrators, engravers, and lithographers. Prior to the invention of photography, illustration was the primary medium through which journalistic and historical events were visually communicated to the public. It was in this period that visual storytelling began to intertwine with journalism, a relationship that would continue to evolve as photography emerged. Illustrators like Honoré Daumier (1808–1879) in France, and Thomas Nast (1840–1902) in the United States, became widely recognized for their critical and political cartoons, which served both as visual reportage and social commentary. Their illustrations were seen as mirrors of political and social realities, reflecting the struggles and triumphs of the times. Daumier's lithographs, for example, provided a satirical and humanizing look at the social issues and political climates of France (Laughton, 1996), while Nast's illustrations in Harper's Weekly depicted significant historical events like the U.S. Civil War and the rise of political corruption (Wei, 2021). In the mid-19th century, the advent of lithography and wood engraving opened up new possibilities for mass distribution, making illustrated stories accessible to wider audiences. These illustrated journals and magazines, such as Harper's Weekly and The Illustrated London News, became crucial for disseminating visual narratives of war, exploration, and social issues. At the time, these illustrations were seen as more reliable than verbal reports, as they were thought to offer an authentic representation of distant events, even though they were heavily stylized and filtered through the perspective of the artist.

The introduction of photography in the mid-19th century revolutionized the visual representation of reality. Photography's potential to capture the world with unprecedented detail and immediacy provided a more direct link to truth, in stark contrast to the artistic interpretations of illustration. The daguerreotype (introduced in the 1839) and later the albumen print allowed photographers to document events with a level of accuracy that illustrators could not match. One of the early milestones of photojournalism was Matthew B. Brady's (1823-1896) documentation of the U.S. Civil War in between 1861 and 1865. Brady's studio, with photographers like Alexander Gardner, George Bernard and Timothy O'Sullivan, captured the scene of war through photographs that were widely distributed in the press. Although the actual battles rarely viewed in these photographs, posed drama of soldiers may have played the trauma of Americans who lost their relatives in the war (Smithsonian American Art Museum, n.d.).

By the early 20th century, photography had firmly established itself as the dominant medium for visual journalism. The photojournalist emerged as a new kind of storyteller—one who operated in the field, capturing spontaneous moments of social, political, and cultural events. Photographers like Henri Cartier-Bresson, Robert Capa and Dorothea Lange became icons of modern reportage in the 1930s and 1940s. Cartier-Bresson's notion of the "decisive moment" (Scott, 2007) revolutionized how photography was practiced, emphasizing the photographer's ability to capture a fleeting moment of significance. Robert Capa's war photography, particularly his images from the Spanish Civil War and World War II, created a visual legacy of the human cost of conflict (Whelan, 1985). The ability of photographers to document events as they unfolded, often in dangerous or volatile situations, made them indispensable in the newsroom. While documentary photography has often been associated with the pursuit of truth, its history reveals a persistent tension between representation and manipulation. From its early days, documentary photography was entangled with subjective framing, aesthetic choices, and institutional agendas that challenged its claim to objectivity. For instance, Jacob Riis's *How the Other Half Lives* (1890), while pioneering in exposing urban poverty, scenes to evoke particular moral reactions from middle-class readers, reinforcing social hierarchies even as it sought reform (Jensen, 2004). Similarly, during the Great Depression, the Farm Security Administration (FSA) project, under Roy Stryker's direction, curated a visual narrative of rural hardship that was carefully edited to fit a national ideological script of resilience and American perseverance. Dorothea Lange's iconic *Migrant Mother* (1936) image, for example, framed to amplify the subject's vulnerability—thus aestheticizing suffering to produce empathy: "... this look appears on the face of more than half the subjects of documentary portraits in the thirties. And again there was a reason. The photographers sought it out" (Stott, 1973, p. 59). The illusion of transparency in documentary photography, then, masks the selective processes behind the lens—choices about what to include, exclude, or stage—casting doubt on its epistemological authority. Allan Sekula (1978) went further to call for a materialist critique of the documentary genre, noting how it often serves institutional powers by constructing visibility according to dominant ideologies rather than revealing hidden truths.

In the post-World War II era, magazines like Life and Look played a crucial role in the rise of photojournalism, offering photo essays that blended personal stories with global events. The ability of photographers to encapsulate complex narratives in a single image made them powerful agents of social change. However, as the medium gained prominence, it was also subject to criticism. The depiction of war and suffering, particularly, raised questions about the ethics of photography. Critics such as Susan Sontag in *On Photography* (2005) questioned whether photographs, especially those of human suffering, could truly represent the complexity of the situations they depicted or whether they reduced them to consumable images. The presumed objectivity of documentary photography has been increasingly challenged in the digital era, as new technologies and distribution platforms have amplified its potential for manipulation. The traditional belief in the photograph as a transparent window into reality has eroded in the face of controversies and critical reassessments. One high-profile example is the work of Steve McCurry, long celebrated for his striking portraits such as *Afghan Girl* (1984). In 2016, McCurry was accused of digitally altering images—removing objects and adjusting compositions in post-production—leading critics to question the ethical boundaries between documentary and art photography (Shaw, 2016). Though McCurry claimed to be a "visual storyteller" rather than a photojournalist, the controversy exposed the tension between aestheticization and truth-telling in contemporary practice.

Additionally, social media platforms have further blurred the lines between documentation and performance. During the Syrian Civil War, numerous images and videos circulated purporting to show the suffering of civilians, but some were later revealed to be misattributed or taken from other contexts. Even authentic images became suspect in an environment where virality often outweighed verification (Meis, 2016). More recently, the emergence of AI-generated and AI-enhanced imagery has deepened this crisis. In 2023, a deepfake image of Pope Francis wearing a white puffer jacket, created using Midjourney, went viral on Twitter before being revealed as synthetic. Though not documentary per se, its visual credibility triggered public confusion and underscored how easily fabricated images can occupy the documentary space (Vincent, 2023).

The relationship between photography and illustration became increasingly complex. Digital tools allowed photographers to manipulate images more easily, which in turn raised questions about the authenticity of visual journalism. The development of photo-editing software like Photoshop and the rise of stock photography meant that what appeared to be an authentic moment could, in fact, be altered or staged. In the 21st century, the role of reportage illustration has evolved to include digital illustrations and AI-generated imagery. In response to the limitations of photographic realism, artists and journalists have incorporated illustrations into their reportage work once more. Both photography and reportage illustration face ongoing ethical challenges, especially regarding issues of representation and bias. The question of who controls the narrative and what images are selected for publication is central to both fields. As visual culture continues to evolve, scholars like Fred Ritchin (2009) have emphasized that the power of images lies in their ability to shape public perceptions, particularly through the framing and editing processes and, with the increasing use of AI and digital tools in both illustration and photography, these ethical considerations are more relevant than ever.

John Tagg (1988) famously argued that photography is not a neutral medium but a social practice embedded in regimes of power and knowledge. In an AI-mediated context where images can be generated without any referent in the real world, the documentary function of photography is radically transformed. The authority once vested in the photographic index—the trace of light from a real object captured by a camera—no longer guarantees authenticity or evidentiary value. The "truth" of the image must now be located elsewhere, often within the metadata, algorithms, or platforms that generate and distribute visual content.

Ariella Azoulay's (2008) conceptualization of photography as a "civil contract" also provides a critical framework for understanding these ethical and political implications. For Azoulay, photography entails a relational obligation between the photographed subject, the photographer, and the spectator. This triangular relationship assumes a shared world and the potential for political recognition. In the context of AI-generated imagery, this civil contract is disrupted: there may be no photographed subject to speak of, no moment of encounter between photographer and witness, and thus no ethical reciprocity. "What was there is never only what is visible in the photograph, but is also contained in the very photographic situation, in which photographer and photographed interact around a camera. That is, a photograph is evidence of the social relations which made it possible" (Azoulay, 2008, p. 119).

Moreover, the proliferation of AI-generated images risks normalizing visual fictions as legitimate records, thereby eroding public trust in photographic evidence. While documentary photography has always been mediated, edited, and framed, it at least operated under the premise of an indexical relationship to the world. As that premise dissolves, new criteria for visual truth and accountability must be established. This shift demands not only technological literacy but also a reevaluation of the social contracts that underpin photographic practice.

In light of these concerns, documentary photography today finds itself at a crossroads. The medium must contend with synthetic visualities that mimic its aesthetic strategies while abandoning its material and ethical commitments.

Post-Photography: Definitions and Theoretical Perspectives

The term *post-photography* has gained prominence in recent decades as scholars and artists seek to articulate the profound transformations in photographic production, circulation, and reception in the digital era. While definitions vary, the concept broadly signifies a departure from traditional photographic paradigms grounded in indexicality, authorship, and materiality. Post-photography marks a condition in which the photograph is no longer primarily valued for its evidentiary function or physical trace, but for its ability to be endlessly manipulated, remixed, and disseminated within networked visual cultures.

Conceptual artist Joan Fontcuberta, a key figure in theorizing post-photography, argues that the digital revolution has displaced photography from its historical role as a guarantor of truth. In his view, post-photography is characterized by the collapse of the medium's indexical relationship to reality, and by the proliferation of images created, altered, or generated without direct human intervention. Fontcuberta emphasizes the role of skepticism, irony, and conceptual play in post-photographic practice, positioning it as a response to the "crisis of credibility" in visual representation (Moreiras, 2017). Scholar Fred Ritchin extends the conversation by addressing how digital technologies have redefined both the image and the image-maker. In *After Photography*, Fred Ritchin (2009) proposes that the digital image is less a "photograph" in the traditional sense than a "flexible" visual artifact—editable, interactive, and embedded with metadata. Beyond digital imagery, post-photography term signals not only a technical shift but also a conceptual and ethical one, requiring new modes of visual literacy and accountability in an age where visual documents are frequently indistinguishable from simulations. The post-photographic condition, images no longer exist as discrete objects but as data flows—interacting with users, platforms, and automated systems in ways that challenge traditional notions of authorship and temporality. Post-photography is not simply about "after photography," but about photography's transformation into a computational and post-human practice.

Lev Manovich, a prominent media theorist and scholar in digital culture, has written extensively on the transformations brought about by computational technologies in the realm of visual media. In his early work, *The Language of New Media* (2008), Manovich explores how digital photography and computational tools have radically altered our understanding of photography, leading to what we now call "post-photography". In traditional photographic theory, a photograph was understood as an indexical representation—it was a trace of the real world, capturing the world as it was at a given moment. The photograph held an inherent connection to the object or scene it depicted. However, Manovich argues that digital photography and image manipulation technologies have severed this direct link. In the digital age, the photograph no longer holds the same "indexical" relationship to reality;

it is a data construct that can be altered, reproduced, or simulated in infinite ways. With the ability to manipulate, distort, or even generate images artificially (through AI, for example), the idea of the photograph as a truthful representation becomes increasingly tenuous. In the context of post-photography, this idea pushes us to question the very nature of a photograph—is it still a document of reality, or has it become something else entirely?

In the context of journalism, post-photographic approaches respond to both the crisis of trust in photographic truth and the growing dominance of algorithmic image production. These practitioners critically interrogate what constitutes evidence, authorship, and realism in an era saturated with digital manipulation and AI-generated content. As defined by Fred Ritchin in *Bending the Frame* (2013, p. 49), post-photographic shift in journalism creates a rhetorical problem: "a consideration of how to persuade with one's imagery." These approaches do not merely document; they construct, critique, and recontextualize visual information.

On the other hand, Geoffrey Batchen (2009) offers an earlier and more nuanced prelude to post-photographic thinking, suggesting that photography has always been a hybrid and unstable medium, shaped by technological, cultural, and institutional forces. Rather than a sudden break, represents an intensification of tendencies already latent within photography's history—particularly its status as a reproducible, mutable, and deeply constructed form of representation.

Yet, in post-photography, the role of software goes beyond editing; it becomes a key player in the creation of images that may never have existed in the "real world." Geoffrey Batchen (1992), who argues that post-photography uncomforts us by reminding how fragile and transient our being and photography, according to Batchen, lives on the vocabulary of conventions, not as a separate entity.

Collectively, these perspectives suggest that post-photography is less a defined genre or movement than a conceptual framework for understanding the changing ontology of images. It invites a critical reassessment of how images function in contemporary culture—how they are made, circulated, read, and trusted. In documentary contexts, this shift presents both possibilities and perils: while post-photographic practices can challenge dominant visual narratives and expand creative agency, they also blur the boundaries between truth and fiction, presence and simulation, visibility and manipulation.

Indexicality, Authorship, Authenticity, and Ethical Paradigms in the visual of AI

While traditional photography is rooted in an indexical relationship with the world—what Roland Barthes (1981) referred to as the "that-has-been" of the photographic image—AI-generated images operate outside of this referential logic. In traditional photography, the camera functions as a mechanical witness; the image bears an existential trace of the real, produced through the physical interaction of light, time, and photosensitive material (even in digital sensors). Conversely, AI-generated images are synthetic constructs: they do not emerge from a referent in the empirical world, but from the statistical recombination of data and patterns learned from existing images.

This ontological shift also raises pressing questions about authorship. In traditional photography, even with the involvement of automated mechanisms, the photographer exercises intentionality—framing, timing, and decision-making—thus maintaining a clear authorial presence. AI-generated photography, particularly through generative adversarial networks (GANs) or text-to-image models, redistributes authorship across multiple agents: the developer of the model, the provider of the dataset, and the user issuing the prompts. The act of creation becomes dispersed, and authorship more collaborative or even ambiguous. This calls for a reevaluation of the auteur paradigm in photographic discourse.

Authenticity, long contested in photography, is further destabilized. While photographic authenticity has never been absolute—given the possibilities of manipulation, staging, or selection—there was nonetheless a belief in a foundational relation to reality. AI images, by lacking a real-world referent, challenge traditional claims to authenticity. Yet, paradoxically, they may still evoke a sense of photographic realism through their aesthetic mimicry. This disjunction produces a new regime of images that feel photographically real while remaining entirely fabricated.

Traditional photography has long been implicated in issues of representation, consent, surveillance, and exploitation. AI-generated images introduce new layers: deepfakes, synthetic identities, and visual misinformation destabilize trust in the image. The use of scraped datasets without consent, especially from marginalized communities, raises issues of data colonialism and visual appropriation. Moreover, AI systems often reproduce and amplify societal biases encoded in their training data, raising urgent concerns about algorithmic ethics and visual justice (Ferrara, 2024). Therefore the ethical paradigms of photographic production and reception must be reexamined.

In sum, AI-generated photography does not merely extend the possibilities of image-making—it demands a fundamental reconsideration of photography's philosophical and cultural frameworks. The image is no longer a trace, but a prediction; not an index, but a hallucination rendered with photographic grammar. Navigating this terrain requires both critical vigilance and conceptual innovation.

RETHINKING DOCUMENTARY AND REIMAGING HISTORY THROUGH 90 MILES

Michael Christopher Brown has emerged as a pivotal figure in contemporary documentary photography, known for his innovative use of technology and introspective approach to storytelling. His work often blurs the lines between traditional photojournalism and conceptual art, challenging viewers to reconsider the nature of photographic truth and representation. Brown's early work, notably during the 2011 Libyan Civil War, marked a departure from conventional photojournalism. Utilizing an iPhone—a tool not traditionally associated with professional photography—he captured intimate and unfiltered moments of conflict. This choice was not merely technical but philosophical, as it allowed him to immerse himself within the events, reducing the barrier between photographer and subject. Brown reflected on this approach, stating that using a smartphone made him less conspicuous, enabling a more authentic engagement with his environment. His publication *Libyan Sugar* (2016) encapsulates this methodology, combining raw imagery with personal journal entries and correspondence. The work offers a candid exploration of the psychological toll of war, both on those directly involved and on the observer. Brown's introspective narrative challenges the notion of the detached photojournalist, emphasizing the subjective nature of witnessing and documenting conflict (Walsh, 2016).

90 Miles is a post-photography AI reporting illustration experiment created by Michael Christopher Brown exploring historical events and realities of Cuban life that have motivated Cubans to cross the 90 miles of ocean separating Havana from Florida. In 2023, Brown ventured into uncharted territory with his project *90 Miles*, employing artificial intelligence to generate images depicting the perilous journey of Cuban migrants across the Florida Straits. This endeavor was born out of ethical and logistical constraints; during his time in Cuba (2014–2016), Brown found it impossible to document these stories without endangering the individuals involved. AI offered a solution, enabling him to visualize narratives based on real accounts without compromising anyone's safety (Artist web page, n.d.).

Brown described *90 Miles* as a continuation of the tradition of reportage illustration, a practice dating back over 150 years. By utilizing AI, he sought to create "photographic looking imagery" that connects audiences with significant stories of our time. The images, while not real in the traditional sense, are grounded in truth, derived from conversations with Cubans and extensive research. The project includes not only Cubans' preparation, escape, crossing and arrival in Miami, also historical events independent from time and space: "This works is based on true stories, but is, of course, not real" (Artist web page, n.d.). The method he has used is to gather AI prompts from years of conversations with Cubans while living in Cuba.

The reason Brown has attempted to this way is not to endanger Cubans who remained in the country. And beyond the migration, Brown's storytelling choice was also to go back to history and reimagine it with AI visualizing. In the project which starts late 50s and beginning of 60s that Fidel Castro came to power. The historical periods Brown concentrated on except escape story is The Mariel boatlift and mass migration, the Frikis who are Cuban punk subculture gets HIV positive blood in order to get state run food and shelter.

The *90 Miles* project has sparked discussions about the evolving nature of documentary photography. Critics have lauded Brown's innovative approach, noting that AI-generated images can offer new avenues for storytelling, especially when traditional methods are fraught with ethical dilemmas. However, concerns have been raised about the potential for such images to blur the line between fact and fiction, challenging viewers' ability to discern reality. Brown acknowledges these complexities, emphasizing that while the images are not real, they are rooted in real stories and experiences. He asserts that the project aims to shed light on narratives that are otherwise inaccessible (Growcoot, 2023). The 90 Miles images mentioned in this study are hosted and sold on the NFT platform OpenSea (2023).

Aesthetically 90 Miles and Visual Clichés of Ideology

In many of Michael Christopher Brown's 90 Miles portraits, the faults of artificial intelligence visual production are visible, especially in the body parts. This contradiction to the anatomical reality of the eyes or the nose reveals the intention to acknowledge and disclose the synthetic nature of the images. This opens up another artistic debate about the ontology of the medium of photography, even though 90 Miles is a reportage illustration. The images in the 90 miles project refer to a pictorial style with dramatic light and color. As in the images "#073 Family Dinner", "#078 Pray" (OpenSea, 2023), the scenes of everyday life such as suffering, coping with poverty, the dinner table, bread and holiness symbols are used in religious references. When talking about the aesthetics of artificial intelligence, it should be noted that image production is synthetic. Therefore, the aesthetics on which these images are based is a hybrid form of the data streams on the Internet, in other words, the photographs in the history of documentary photography. Therefore, for instance, "#339 Storm" (OpenSea, 2023) bears a formal, but not a direct, resemblance to Eugene Smith's Guerda Civil photograph in the Spanish Village photo essay published in Life magazine (Cosgrove, n.d.). Especially in the gaze of the figure in the foreground, there is an imprecise but visual affinity.

One of the most urgent critiques of AI-generated imagery lies in its tendency to reproduce and amplify visual clichés and cultural stereotypes. Because generative AI models are trained on large-scale image datasets scraped from the internet, their outputs often reflect the dominant visual regimes and socio-cultural biases embedded in those datasets (Ferrara, 2024). As a result, AI tends to depict people, places, and historical moments in reductive and often problematic ways. Scholars have pointed out that AI-generated portraits by Stable Diffusion and DALL-E, when prompted with demographic features, encodes biases about different communities. For instance, while "an attractive person" prompt creates a "white ideal" beauty, "a terrorist" prompt generates brown faces with dark hair by Stable Diffusion (Bianchi et. al., 2023). When translated into image generation, this tendency to essentialize identities through patterns in training data results in a feedback loop of cultural flattening. In the domain of image-making, Crawford and Paglen (2021) have analyzed datasets like ImageNet and MIT's Places, showing that the semantic labels used to train AI systems are often ideologically charged. In their essay *Excavating AI* (2021), they argue that the classifications used in machine learning reflect a "visual taxonomy of the world" that is deeply entangled with Western, gendered, and racial biases.

Recent controversies surrounding text-to-image platforms like Midjourney, Stable Diffusion, and DALL·E have demonstrated that media clichés—depicting slums, traditional clothing, or hypersexualized figures, rather than diverse, realistic, or self-determined representations. This has sparked criticism not only from academics but also from communities whose visual identities are being algorithmically simplified or misrepresented.

In the context of 90 Miles imagery, the visual narrative constructs a stark dichotomy between Cuban revolutionaries and Cuban émigrés arriving in the United States. The revolutionaries images (OpenSea, 2023) depicted in green uniforms and caps—clearly marked as ideological subjects—are portrayed as stagnant, passive, and gazing into indeterminate space. Their lack of action or clear direction not only decontextualizes their historical role but also visually strips them of political agency. In contrast, Cuban migrants arriving in Miami (OpenSea, 2023) are shown in dynamic motion—joyfully running towards supermarkets and basking under the U.S. flag, a classic symbol of liberal freedom and capitalist abundance.

This visual juxtaposition is not neutral. It performs an ideological distortion by equating socialism exclusively with authoritarianism and stagnation, while idealizing the U.S. as a site of liberty and material plenitude. Crucially, the imagery omits any reference to the decades-long U.S. embargo, economic sanctions, or the geopolitical pressures that have shaped the Cuban economy and society. By erasing these structural conditions, the photographs create a depoliticized binary that privileges capitalist democracy while discrediting socialist imaginaries.

Although documentary photographs are often seen as objective records, they do not inherently establish causal or explanatory relationships. In this series, the photographic sequencing and framing choices act as a vehicle for ideological projection. The photographer's editorial decisions—what to include, how to frame, and what to juxtapose—are not neutral acts but reflect a particular worldview. Thus, even in the absence of explicit narrative, the photographer functions as an ideological agent whose visual rhetoric reinforces dominant Cold War tropes and neoliberal values. The images are inadvertently emphasize the notion of the United States as a land of salvation. Such portrayals risk simplifying complex socio-political realities and perpetuating stereotypes (Terranova, 2023).

The critique of AI bias in visual production is not only a technical issue but a deeply epistemological and political one: it concerns who gets to define what the world looks like, whose faces are rendered visible, and which ways of being are rendered legible in the algorithmic imagination. Another issue is reimagining history and its connections with memory and simulation. The emergence of AI as a creative and reconstructive tool has opened new avenues for reimagining historical events, figures, and narratives. Through generative models—especially those based on deep learning architectures such as GANs (Generative Adversarial Networks)—artists, researchers, and media producers are now capable of simulating photographic moments that were never captured or reconstructing archival absences. While these methods offer exciting opportunities to fill historical gaps or visualize marginalized perspectives, they also provoke critical ethical, epistemological, and political debates.

One of the most well-known uses of AI in reimagining history is Deep Nostalgia by genealogy site MyHeritage (2021), a tool that animates historical portraits, allowing users to see their ancestors "come to life." This as a novel form of affective connection with the past, on the other hand, such technology could distort historical understanding by producing emotionally compelling but fictional representations. The realism of the animations risks misleading viewers into equating these outputs with verified historical footage, thus destabilizing the boundary between memory and simulation.

In *The Atlas of AI*, Crawford (2021) situates AI within a historical continuity, so that argues AI does not create a groundbreaking new era, it rather amplifies historical patterns. But with AI regime of machines has the technological ability to bring us imagining past, present and future at the same time. Therefore, this new visual production model, in which humans are not producers, is taking shape in humanity's historical and cultural remains. Communicative or artistic uses of AI continue to progress along quite different and rich paths and to open doors to possibilities of imagining. However, representational biases that exist in the selected data sets cannot be ignored.

In 90 Miles, setting aside the question of historical accuracy in the visualization of events such as Fidel Castro's leadership or the Cuban Missile Crisis, the portrayal of the struggle for survival at sea—particularly the depiction of individuals caught in storms or drifting on the ocean—invites critical reflection on the aestheticization of trauma. These images, while visually compelling, risk transforming a harrowing, life-threatening experience into a stylized spectacle. The rendering of such moments through carefully composed frames, color grading, and narrative abstraction may obscure the violence, desperation, and structural conditions underlying these journeys.

By aestheticizing trauma, the project potentially desensitizes viewers to the human cost of forced migration. The ocean, often a symbol of the sublime in visual culture, becomes a backdrop for a dramatized encounter with death, while the material and geopolitical realities are implied only through mood rather than explicit critique. As such, the visual language of the 90 Miles project may elide the asymmetries of power and historical responsibility, prioritizing emotional resonance over political accountability.

Adding another layer to the debate is the project's commercialization through the sale of its AI-generated images as NFTs (Non-Fungible Tokens). The entire 400-image collection was made available on platforms like OpenSea (2023), with pieces offered for sale to collectors. This move has sparked discussions about the commodification of historical narratives and the ethical considerations of profiting from representations of real-life struggles and traumas. Monetizing AI-generated depictions of sensitive historical events may trivialize the lived experiences of those who endured them. The sale of these images as digital assets raises questions about the line between artistic expression and exploitation, particularly when the subjects of the work are communities that have historically been marginalized or misrepresented. It may be argued that the photographs are synthetic and do not refer to any entity, but in a work that claims to be based on historical facts, responsibility is transferred to artificial intelligence, which is known to contain stereotypes, while the ownership of sales creates a contradiction.

CONCLUSION

Michael Christopher Brown's *90 Miles* exemplifies the transformative potential of integrating technology into documentary practice. By leveraging AI, he navigates ethical challenges and expands the boundaries of visual storytelling. His work prompts critical reflection on the role of authenticity in photography and the responsibilities of the documentarian in an era where the lines between reality and simulation are increasingly blurred. Brown's *90 Miles* (2023) exemplifies how AI and synthetic imagery enter the terrain of journalistic storytelling. While Brown's background is in conflict photojournalism, this project fully embraces post-photographic aesthetics by using AI (via Midjourney) to visualize untaken photos of Cuban migration. As such, *90 Miles* demonstrates the tension in post-photographic journalism: between imaginative re-enactment and ethical misrepresentation. It has been criticized for replacing lived realities with AI-generated fiction, raising questions about the place of authorship and historical accountability in synthetic documentary. While Brown insists the images are based on true stories, scholars have raised concerns about the ethics of fictionalizing history and the potential of reinforcing Cold War-era ideologies that cast the U.S. as a liberatory force. Moreover, the sale of 90 Miles as NFTs has been criticized for commodifying historical suffering, raising questions about the project.

When evaluated specifically within the framework of the 90 Miles project, one must consider how the suffering of individuals who risk their lives to cross the ocean is subjected to an aesthetic filter. This visual treatment risks transforming the traumatic and politically charged act of migration into a stylized narrative, potentially distancing viewers from the material and existential realities of those portrayed. Moreover, although the project openly acknowledges that its imagery is not documentary in a traditional sense but rather a visual re-enactment based on real news reports, it still claims a degree of factual grounding. This blurring between fiction and reality raises critical concerns regarding the ethics of representation. Central to this issue is the question of who holds responsibility for the visual representation of Cubans. In the classical documentary sense, Michael Christopher Brown does not occupy the position of a witness, but rather that of a mediator—a role that inherently involves interpretive and selective choices.

Thus, the hybrid nature of this visual narrative complicates conventional notions of authorship. If the images are not direct documents of events but are nonetheless tied to real socio-political conditions, then who should be held accountable for how Cubans are portrayed? In this context, criticism becomes suspended in ambiguity: the line between artistic license and representational responsibility is blurred, leaving the question of authorship—and by extension, critique—unresolved.

Post-photography challenges the fundamental assumptions of journalistic objectivity by acknowledging the constructedness of all visual narratives. The capacity to generate fictional yet believable visual narratives risks displacing the lived experiences of real subjects, further complicating the photographer's (or algorithm's) ethical responsibility toward representation. The integration of AI tools into documentary photography presents both exciting possibilities and significant challenges. As artificial intelligence becomes an inescapable part of our creative and cultural landscapes, it undoubtedly opens new avenues for storytelling—especially in expanding the imaginative boundaries of narrative construction. AI's capacity to visualize the previously unphotographable offers opportunities for speculative forms of documentary that blend memory, fiction, and archival reconstruction.

However, these advantages come with considerable risks. AI-generated imagery tends to gravitate toward homogenization, often reproducing visual clichés embedded in its training data. As a result, instead of offering unique or situated perspectives, AI may replicate dominant visual tropes, reinforcing existing stereotypes or aesthetic norms. This tendency is especially problematic in the context of documentary photography, which has historically been valued for its capacity to challenge dominant narratives and make visible what is otherwise marginalized or overlooked.

While the documentary tradition has itself been critiqued—particularly in post-photographic discourse—for its limited capacity to represent complex realities, the synthetic and hybrid nature of AI-generated visuals intensifies these concerns. If we strip away the photographer's responsibility, their reflective engagement with form and content, and their lived or researched connection to the subject matter, what remains is a hollow simulation. The risk is not merely aesthetic flattening, but a detachment from the political, historical, and ethical dimensions that give documentary work its critical power.

Therefore, while we may enthusiastically explore the new storytelling capacities that AI enables, we must not lose sight of documentary photography's enduring commitment to engaging with real-world conditions. Its strength lies in its ability to bear witness to histories, communities, and truths often excluded from dominant narratives. The challenge ahead is to ensure that AI-assisted practices do not dilute this commitment but instead find ways to deepen and expand it through thoughtful, responsible, and contextually grounded visual storytelling.

REFERENCES

Artist web page. (n.d.). Michael Christopher Brown. https://www.michaelchristopherbrown.com/artificial-intelligence/90-miles

Azoulay, A. (2008). *The civil contract of photography*. Zone Books.

Barthes, R. (1981). *Camera lucida: reflections on photography* (Howard, R., Trans.). Hill & Wang.

Batchen, G. (1992). On post-photography. *Afterimage: The Journal of Media Arts and Cultural Critism*. https://www.researchgate.net/publication/362643203_On_Post-Photography

Batchen, G. (2009). Seeing and saying: a response to "incongruous images". *History and Theory*. https://www.jstor.org/stable/25621436

Bianchi, F., Kalluri, P., Durmus, E., Ladhak, F., Cheng, M., Nozza, D., Hashimoto, T., Jurafsky, D., Zou, J., & Caliskan, A. (2023). Easily accessible text-to-image generation amplifies demographic stereotypes at large scale. *Proceedings of the 2023 ACM Conference on Fairness, Accountability, and Transparency*, 1493–1504. https://dl.acm.org/doi/10.1145/3593013.3594095

Cosgrove, B. (n.d.). *'Spanish village': W. Eugene Smith's landmark photo essay*. https://www.life.com/people/life-behind-the-picture-w-eugene-smiths-guardia-civil-1950/

Crawford, K. (2021). *The atlas of AI*. Yale University Press.

Crawford, K., & Paglen, T. (2021). Excavating ai: The politics of training sets for machine learning. *AI & Society*, *36*, 1105–1116. DOI: 10.1007/s00146-021-01301-1

Ferrara, E. (2024). Fairness and bias in artificial intelligence: A brief survey of sources, impacts, and mitigation strategies. *Sci*, *6*(1), 3. DOI: 10.3390/sci6010003

Growcoot, M. (2023, May 15). *Photojournalist controversially turns to ai to illustrate 'inaccessible' stories*. https://petapixel.com/2023/05/15/photojournalist-controversially-turns-to-ai-to-illustrate-inaccessible-stories/

Jensen, L. (2004). The photographs of Jacob Riis: history in relation to truth. *Constructing the Past*. https://digitalcommons.iwu.edu/constructing/vol5/iss1/6

Laughton, B. (1996). *Honore Daumier*. Yale University Press.

Manovich, L. (2008). *The language of new media*. The MIT Press.

Meis, M. (2016). When is a conflict a crisis? On the aesthetics of the Syrian civil war in a social media context. *Media, War & Conflict, 10*(1), 1–18. DOI: 10.1177/1750635216653903

Moreiras, C. (2017). Joan Fontcuberta: Post-photography and the spectral image of saturation. *Journal of Spanish Cultural Studies, 18*(1), 57–77. Advance online publication. DOI: 10.1080/14636204.2016.1274496

MyHeritage. (2021). https://www.myheritage.com/deep-nostalgia

OpenSea. (2023). *90 miles*. https://opensea.io/collection/90-miles

Ritchin, F. (2009). *After photography*. W.W. Norton & Company.

Ritchin, F. (2013). *Bending the frame: photojournalism, documentary, and the citizen*. Aperture.

Scott, C. (2007). *Street photography*. I.B. Tauris & Co. Ltd. DOI: 10.5040/9780755604210

Sekula, A. (1978). Dismantling Modernism, Reinventing Documentary (Notes on the Politics of Representation). *The Massachusetts Review, 19*(4), 859–883. https://www.jstor.org/stable/25088914

Shaw, M. (2016, May 31). *Steve Mccury's rickshaw*. https://www.readingthepictures.org/2016/05/steve-mccurrys-rickshaw/

Sontag, S. (2005). *On photography*. Rosetta Books Smithsonian American Art Museum (n.d). *Mathew B. Brady*. https://americanart.si.edu/artist/mathew-b-brady-6668

Stott, W. (1973). *Documentary expression and thirties america*. The University of Chicago Press.

Tagg, J. (1988). *The burden of representation: essays on photographies and histories*. Palgrave Macmillan. DOI: 10.1007/978-1-349-19355-4

Terranova, A. (2023, April 26). *How AI imagery is shaking photojournalism*. Blind Magazine. https://www.blind-magazine.com/en/stories/how-ai-imagery-is-shaking-photojournalism

Vincent, J. (2023, March 27). *"The swagged-out pope is an AI fake – and an early glimpse of a new reality*. The Verge. https://www.theverge.com/2023/3/27/23657927/ai-pope-image-fake-midjourney-computer-generated-aesthetic

Walsh, L. (2016, September 10). *Picturing conflict: an interview with Michael Christopher Brown*. https://hyperallergic.com/318407/interview-with-conflict-photographer-michael-christopher-brown/

Wei, S. (2021, Jan 7). *Thomas Nast: the rise and fall of the father of political cartoons*. Illustration History. https://www.illustrationhistory.org/essays/thomas-nast-the-rise-and-fall-of-the-father-of-political-cartoons

Whelan, R. (1985). *Robert Capa: a biography*. Knopf.

ADDITIONAL READING

Cotton, C. (2009). *The photographs as contemporary art*. Thames & Hudson.

Grundberg, A. (2021). *How photography became contemporary art*. Yale University Press. Aperture Magazine (2024). *Image worlds to come: Photography & AI (No.257)*. Aperture.

Hacking, J. (2021). *The photography the whole story*. Thames & Hudson.

Lester, P. M., Martin, S. A., & Smith-Rodden, M. (Eds.). (2022). *Visual ethics: a guide for photographers, journalists, and media makers*. Routledge. DOI: 10.4324/9781003243045

Ritchin, F. (2025). *The synthetic eye: photohraphy transformed in the age of ai*. Thames & Hudson.

Shobeiri, A., & Westgeest, H. (Eds.). (2024). *Virtual photography: artificial intelligence, in-game and extended reality*. Transcript.

Zylinska, J. (2023). *The perception machine: our photographic future between the eye and ai*. The MIT Press. Hirsch, R. (2017). *Seizing the light: a social & aesthetics history of photography*. Routledge. DOI: 10.7551/mitpress/14471.001.0001

KEY TERMS AND DEFINITIONS

AI Mediated Documentary: Refers to a type of documentary photography or storytelling where artificial intelligence is used in the process of creation, narration, or interaction.

NFTs (Non-Fungible Tokens): They are unique digital assets stored on a blockchain that represent ownership or authenticity of items like art, music, videos, or virtual goods.

Photography: A medium which uses a camera to produce and create visual representations.

Post Photography: It is a concept describing how photography evolves beyond its classical form, focusing more on image manipulation, circulation, and data-driven creation than on capturing reality.

Reportage Illustration: It is a form of visual storytelling where an artist creates drawings or illustrations based on direct observation of real events, people, or places, often in journalistic or documentary contexts. It is a mixture of real things and illustrator's perspective.

Representation: of Truth: How reality or facts are depicted, interpreted, or constructed through a medium—such as film, photography, or literature.

Visual Journalism: It is the practice of telling news stories primarily through visual media, such as photography, video, infographics, and illustrations.

Chapter 3

Exploring New Meanings in Post-Photography and Digital Art

Özlem Demircan
http://orcid.org/0000-0002-3041-7160
Faculty of Fine Arts, Department of Photography, Dokuz Eylul University, Turkey

ABSTRACT

This chapter examines the transformative impact of digital technologies on photography and visual culture through the lens of post-photography. Drawing on theoretical frameworks from Jean Baudrillard, Hito Steyerl, Lev Manovich, and Joan Fontcuberta, it explores how artificial intelligence, algorithms, and digital manipulation reshape image production, aesthetic norms, and representation. Social media aesthetics, archival politics, and algorithmic decision-making processes are analyzed in connection with contemporary art practices. The chapter presents a critical discussion of artists such as Rafman, Rickard, Fontcuberta, Anadol, and Meyohas, whose works challenge traditional notions of authorship, visuality, and truth. Post-photography is positioned not only as a technical shift but as a cultural paradigm that redefines the relationship between data, identity, and visual experience.

INTRODUCTION

The rapid rise of digital technologies has fundamentally transformed photographic art and the modes of production, representation, and circulation across all artistic disciplines. This transformation goes beyond the emergence of new technical tools; it has led to a comprehensive restructuring of artistic creation, distribution, and consumption processes. Today, artistic production practices have become increasingly

DOI: 10.4018/979-8-3373-2230-8.ch003

complex and multi-layered, shaped by digital networks, algorithms, and artificial intelligence systems. In this context, the concept of "post-photography" offers a theoretical framework not only for transcending the boundaries of traditional photography but also for rethinking the ontology and aesthetics of artistic production in the digital age.

With the advancement of digital technologies, visual culture has entered an unprecedented period of transformation. The image's meaning, circulation, and perception have undergone radical shifts with digital transformation; consequently, culture has become digitalized. Within this digital culture, screens have assumed a central role and have become foundational to the visual experience. Photography, which shapes the language of screens, was once synonymous with the production of documents and the representation of reality; however, in the digital age, it has been repositioned on entirely new ontological and epistemological grounds.

Since the 1990s, the development of digital imaging technologies has transformed photography from a recording medium into a visual language reconstructed through algorithmic processes. As William J. Mitchell emphasized in his seminal work "The Reconfigured Eye: Visual Truth in the Post-Photographic Era" (Mitchell, 1992), digital photography has moved away from the truth claims of the analog era and has evolved into a new regime of representation based on manipulation, simulation, and reconstruction.

Within this framework, post-photography was introduced to define the structural and conceptual transformations that photography has undergone during the process of digitalization. Joan Fontcuberta defines post-photography not as a means of reflecting reality but as a practice that deconstructs perceptions of reality and blurs the boundaries between fiction and truth. Similarly, André Rouillé draws attention to the emergence of a new visual regime shaped not by photography's documentary function but by the modes of circulation and the speed of image consumption in the digital environment.

On the other hand, post-photography signals a broader and more layered process of transformation that is not limited to digitalization alone. During the 1960s and 1970s, influenced by conceptual art, alternative photographic approaches began to challenge the boundaries of the medium. These tendencies laid the groundwork for new areas of theoretical debate, framing photography not merely as a representational tool but as a mode of critical and conceptual thinking. Geoffrey Batchen (1997) argues that during this period, photography came to be viewed as a form of thought rather than merely a technical apparatus, fundamentally transforming the nature of the photographic medium.

Exhibitions such as "Photography into Sculpture" (1970) and the emergence of postmodern art practices from the 1980s demonstrated that photography could be treated as a construction, installation, and aesthetic intervention strategy. In such practices, photography goes beyond representing reality to become a means of transforming, staging, and rewriting it. Although these tendencies existed before digitalization, they became more visible and widespread with the advent of digital technologies. Therefore, post-photography should not be seen solely as a result of technological rupture but as a conceptual and aesthetic process of evolution.

In this context, Martha Rosler's work, particularly "The Bowery in Two Inadequate Descriptive Systems" (1974-75), critically interrogates the relationship between text and image. Her method deconstructs photography's documentary claim and seeks to reveal the representation's social and ideological dimensions. Such works demonstrate that "post-photography" is not merely an aesthetic strategy but also a critical mode of thinking.

Although photography has long been considered a visual representation of reality, its meaning has eroded technically and conceptually in the digital age. The rise of digitization has radically altered the control over the production, manipulation, and circulation of images, calling into question the documentary value of photography. This study explores how post-photography has created a new artistic and theoretical field in the digital era. Drawing on contemporary theoretical perspectives such as Jean Baudrillard's "theory of simulation", Hito Steyerl's notion of the "poor image", and Lev Manovich's "software aesthetics", this research will reassess the meaning of photography, its production processes, and its relationship with the viewer.

The central problem this study addresses is how the contemporary visual regime, referred to as post-photography, transforms the concepts of reality, representation, and artistic production. This transformation will be examined through a multilayered approach, considering its theoretical, aesthetic, and technological dimensions and offering a critical reading of its impact on visual culture in the digital age.

The effects of artificial intelligence, algorithms, and social media platforms - key components of digital culture- on photography will be analyzed through a multilayered framework. Building on the theoretical foundation, this study will comprehensively analyze digital manipulation techniques, social media aesthetics, and contemporary artistic practices. Based on the findings, the research will offer critical reflections on the current role of "post-photography" in modern art and its conceptual and aesthetic possibilities for the future.

Post-Photography: Reconstructing Visuality in the Digital Age

The influence of the post-medium condition has blurred the boundaries between artistic media, enabling photography to be present everywhere while risking losing its distinctive qualities. Especially with the widespread adoption of digital technologies, the ontological features of photography- such as its modes of representation, tools, manipulation processes, and relationship with reality - have been reopened to critical inquiry (Fontcuberta, 2011; Rouillé, 2005).

Critics argue that new digital imaging technologies have eroded photography's "effect on reality". Rouillé (2005) defines classical photography as a document based on the trace of an object in the world, whereas pre-coded images and circulatory logic nourish post-photography. Thus, a clear distinction emerges between classical photography -produced directly from physical reality- and images constructed through digital data processing.

The weakening of photography's link to reality has also rendered its privileged status as a medium increasingly problematic. As Ariella Azoulay emphasizes in "The Civil Contract of Photography" (2008, p. 26), photography is a visual object and an ethical agreement between the subject and the viewer. However, in the post-photographic condition, this agreement has weakened; images have become decontextualized structures dissolving into algorithmic flows rather than visible expressions of claims to rights. From Azoulay's perspective, the digital era produces a regime of visuality that neutralizes representation and suppresses photography's civic potential. Meanwhile, Roland Barthes' notions of studium and punctum, central to understanding the emotional depth of analog photography in "Camera Lucida" (1981, p. 27), have given way in the digital age to ephemeral, surface-level experiences driven by instant consumption.

Fred Ritchin examines this transformation in depth in "After Photography". For Ritchin, the central question in digital visuality is no longer simply whether an image is real, but why it was produced (Ritchin, 2009). This shift foregrounds intention and ethics in processes of representation. Ritchin further argues that the digital age transforms photography not only technically but also epistemologically and ethically. Unlike the singular and authoritative logic traditionally associated with photographic representation, digital photography accommodates multiple perspectives and offers a mutable, interactive structure. As a result, the viewer becomes an active participant in the production of meaning. This paradigm shift has had a profound impact on documentary photography, displacing the emphasis on truth with a greater concern for context, interpretation, and ethical responsibility.

According to Fontcuberta (2016), the digital age has introduced a photographic logic focused more on constructing than documenting reality. This perspective blurs the distinctions between "taking, making, and constructing" photographs, challenging the objectivity and referential link to the outside world. In this new condition, the boundary between reality and representation has become fragile, and photography increasingly welcomes fiction, intervention, and digital manipulation.

In "La Furia de las Imágenes" (Fontcuberta, 2016, p. 9), Joan Fontcuberta characterizes the digital age's relationship with images through the metaphor of "inflation". He argues that contemporary images have not only proliferated but also lost their intrinsic meaning-transforming into a kind of visual noise that is ubiquitous yet ineffective. Within this climate of visual excess, photography's traditional claim to truth becomes increasingly meaningless, and post-photography emerges as a creative space that reconstructs, interrogates, and, at times, fabricates reality. Fontcuberta contends that photography no longer functions to discover truth but to construct it. He further asserts that contemporary photography has evolved into a practice of imaginative construction rather than mere representation. In this context, post-photography centers not on the accuracy of visual information but on the construction and critical interrogation of visual narratives.

These developments have rendered the concept of post-photography critical in terms of chemical or digital production methods and the cultural and conceptual implications of those methods. Today, images generated by software, algorithms, and artificial intelligence do not merely represent a technical innovation; they also transform ontological assumptions about representation itself. Photography's meaning, function, and epistemological position within digital and post-digital culture must be redefined.

Thus, post-photography signals a technical shift and a multifaceted ontological and aesthetic rupture. Traditional photography's stable and material representation has been replaced by visual practices that are digitally constructed, manipulated, and continuously circulated (Mitchell, 1992; Fontcuberta, 2013). Software-based production processes, digital platforms, and emerging representational strategies have further complexified this transformation. For this reason, theoretical approaches developed to explain post-photography attempt to conceptualize a structural rupture in visual culture.

The transformation of photography's documentary function represents a critical starting point in this process. In the digital era, the image has broken away from direct reference to reality and evolved into a structure shaped by simulation, fiction, and manipulation. Fontcuberta (2013) views this transformation as harboring creative and critical potential. In his "Post-Photographic Manifesto" (2011), he declares that photography has distanced itself from its foundational values and historical relationship with truth, becoming instead a vehicle for the circulation of messages. For Fontcuberta, post-photography is not merely a technical form but a philosophical, aesthetic, and experimental practice.

This process also redefines the artist's position. Rather than focusing on singularity and originality, artistic production increasingly prioritizes meaning-making, collaborative models, and strategic anonymity. Images are defined less by their content than by their modes and velocities of circulation. At the same time, artistic experience is shaped more by principles of sharing, access, and reuse than by ownership.

In this context, Nicolas Bourriaud's concept of relational aesthetics suggests that contemporary art derives meaning not from the production of objects but from social interactions and audience engagement (Bourriaud, 2002). Similarly, in "In Defense of the Poor Image", Hito Steyerl critiques the commodification of high-resolution images and argues that artistic value in the digital age should be measured through circulation and accessibility (Steyerl, 2009). From this perspective, post-photography is not merely a representational strategy but a site where visual economies, power structures, and artistic identities are continuously negotiated and reconfigured.

Steyerl's notion of the poor image has become central to post-photographic practice within this circulation-based visual regime. These images -low-resolution, compressed, and repeatedly copied- often carry alternative forms of knowledge produced outside cultural centers (Steyerl, 2009). As oppositional forms to the fetishization of high definition, poor images facilitate pluralistic and horizontal aesthetic experiences. The poor image has evolved into a technical category and a form of visual resistance through social media, open archives, and digital activism.

Integrating software into aesthetic production has also redefined the role of the artist and the nature of creative practice. Lev Manovich's (2001) concept of software aesthetics emphasizes the increasing dominance of algorithms in visual production. This shift affects the tools used and the nature of the aesthetic experience itself. Interfaces are no longer neutral tools but have become aesthetic environments and, in many cases, content in their own right. Accordingly, the language of visuality is now interwoven with code, as software architectures and user interaction shape the form and meaning of the image.

While the increased accessibility of production tools may democratize content creation, it can also result in a loss of depth and aesthetic quality (Rubinstein & Sluis, 2008). Post-photography is thus not only a form of aesthetic expression but a complex construct shaped by socio-political conditions, technological infrastructures, and cultural shifts. The theoretical frameworks proposed by thinkers such as Mitchell, Fontcuberta, Rouillé, Steyerl, Manovich, and Ritchin allow for a multidimensional analysis of this transformation encompassing technical, conceptual, and political dimensions.

The networked circulation of photography has also radically transformed the viewer experience. Photography has dematerialized, becoming a process-based, screen-bound phenomenon. Visual perception now involves optical engagement and cognitive, cultural, and contextual participation. Images no longer represent moments; they exist as dynamic data flows, constantly reconstructed within digital environments.

Computer-generated images can now be produced without any reference to the physical world, yet they are still perceived within collective memory as photographic. Baudrillard's simulation theory suggests that this points to "hyperreality", in which representation does not merely reflect reality but becomes a reality in itself (Baudrillard, 1994). In this sense, though detached from reference, digital images shape and influence collective memory, constructing -and sometimes distorting- shared perceptions of the real.

As Manovich (2001) notes, meaning in this new visual regime emerges from content, the software infrastructure, algorithmic logic, and the user interface through which the image is produced and encountered. Photography has thus become a multilayered site of interaction rather than a fixed object, and the viewer has shifted from passive observer to active participant—decoding, selecting, and repositioning visual information.

Within this emerging visual paradigm, post-photography has become a dematerialized yet increasingly potent force that redefines both modes of representation and the construction of visual memory.

This holistic perspective reveals that post-photography is not merely a technical or aesthetic phenomenon but a multilayered cultural regime interwoven with political, technological, and epistemological dimensions. Today, post-photography is understood not only as a shift in modes of production and representation but as a paradigmatic transformation in visual culture itself, one that rearticulates visual epistemologies and collective modes of experience.

Artificial Intelligence, Algorithms, and Digital Manipulation

In the digital age, visual production has moved beyond relying solely on human aesthetic intuition; software, algorithms and artificial intelligence (AI) systems have emerged as active agents directly guiding this process. Post-photographic practices embody a multidimensional transformation encompassing technical but also aesthetic, ethical, and political layers (Manovich, 2001; Paglen & Crawford, 2021). Generative AI tools such as Midjourney and DALL·E can construct highly realistic scenes that have never existed in the physical world, effectively reducing the artist's role to a data-driven user interaction (Elkins, 2011).

This shift has radically transformed the notion of representation. AI-generated images are not rooted in the testimony of a witnessing subject but are derived from the statistical processing of data. As such, these visuals offer a probabilistic simulation of non-existent scenes rather than "representing" the world. This blurs the boundaries between reality and fiction in representation even further.

Originality in AI-based production has also become a matter of debate. Since the generated content is derived through recombining existing datasets, it does not stem from a traditional creation process but follows an algorithmic compilation logic. Thus, the boundaries between the artist's creative agency and the generative function of AI systems have become increasingly ambiguous. Art is being reconceptualized not as a personal expression but as a systematic output.

This algorithmic redefinition of creativity raises the question of whether AI can learn aesthetic values. While AI can imitate certain styles, visual trends, or formal structures, its ability to generate art's critical, experimental, and emotional dimensions remains contested.

From an ethical standpoint, these technologies raise significant concerns, including the lack of attribution, copyright violations, manipulative or misleading representations, and distortions in cultural representation. In sensitive contexts of identity, race, gender, and class, AI's deployment of biased datasets has been subject to intense criticism (Crawford, 2021).

Consequently, AI-supported visual production practices demand reconsideration not only on a technical level but also in philosophical, political, and ethical terms.

In this context, delegating creative decisions to software-based systems has redefined fundamental concepts such as creativity, originality, and the responsibility of representation. Mitchell (1992) argues that digital visuality has shifted from representation to simulation. Ritchin (2009) notes that viewers now focus less on an image's factual accuracy and more on the intention behind its creation. This is particularly pressing in domains like documentary and archival practices, where AI-generated imagery intensifies ethical and representational challenges.

Due to their mathematically abstract nature, digital images have become modular, replicable, and easily manipulated (Rubinstein & Sluis, 2008). This technical infrastructure prioritizes accessibility, circulation, and contextual multiplicity over originality. As Manovich (2001) emphasizes, software has become not just a tool but the primary ground where aesthetic decisions are shaped. Accordingly, post-photographic images derive meaning from their representational content and the nature of their production processes and technological frameworks.

In the framework of Baudrillard's (1994) theory of simulation, digital images no longer refer to reality but to their systems of production and coding. Render technologies aim not to capture but to reconstruct the image, leading to a shift from visual representation to constructing artificial and calculated realities. In this sense, photography moves away from its traditional representational role toward the production of hyperreality.

In their work, "Excavating AI", Paglen and Crawford (2021) demonstrate that AI systems function not merely as technical tools but as cultural actors with ideological functions. These systems reproduce social hierarchies through classification, labeling, and norm-setting via visual datasets. For example, datasets such as ImageNet often include images labeled with gendered, racial, or class-based biases. The categorization of a woman's image into a negative category due to assumed moral nonconformity is not just a technical flaw but a political, cultural, and ethical issue.

Aesthetics of Social Media and the Transformation of Representational Forms in Visual Culture

In the post-photographic era, social media has emerged as one of the primary arenas for visual production, circulation, and representation. Platforms like Instagram and TikTok facilitate content creation and construct a visual regime shaped by aesthetic norms, engagement algorithms, and platform design (Leaver, et al., 2020; Gillespie, 2014). In this context, social media aesthetics transforms visual preferences and the digital age's identity and representational strategies.

The mathematical nature of digital images enables their production, duplication, manipulation, and decontextualization. These images now operate as integral data flow components (Rubinstein & Sluis, 2008). Encoding digitized images within Cartesian coordinate systems has shifted the image from an extension of the hand to an extension of the mind, placing it firmly within digital environments (Mitchell, 1992; Manovich, 2001). This transformation deepens the crisis of representation and blurs the boundaries between simulation and reality. Social media images no longer represent reality but construct their systems of reference.

In this regard, meme culture emerges as one of the most characteristic visual languages of the post-photographic era. With their features of anonymity, repetition, irony, and recontextualization, memes rapidly circulate on social media. These structures serve humorous purposes and convey symbolic meanings related to social critique, identity politics, and cultural traumas. The reproducibility of memes exemplifies the collective aesthetic mode of postmodern imagery.

Another dimension of social media aesthetics is the prevalence of algorithmically driven filter bubbles and echo chambers. These digital constructs homogenize users' aesthetic preferences and limit the visibility of alternative representations. Within the post-photographic context, this demonstrates that visuality is produced in formal terms and within political and economic frameworks.

Correspondingly, through the lens of Goffman's (1959) theory of performance and Benjamin's (2008) concept of aura loss, it can be argued that social media users construct identities through visual self-representation. According to Goffman, individuals manage impressions by performing roles in social settings, navigating between front-stage (public) and back-stage (private) behaviors. On platforms such as Instagram and TikTok, the front stage is carefully curated through visual aesthetics, while the backstage remains obscured or is selectively revealed. Selfies, stories, and daily posts function as tools of performative self-presentation (Abidin, 2016), where users embody roles shaped by the demands of the visibility economy. Aesthetic components such as filters, stylized frames, and color schemes are no longer purely personal choices but are increasingly dictated by algorithmic trends and platform norms. In this process, users become agents of aesthetic production, not solely driven by self-expression but by the strategic aim of achieving visibility and engagement.

Algorithms determine which content will be seen and shape users' aesthetic preferences. AI systems process engagement metrics such as likes, comments, and shares to dictate content rankings. Rather than fostering original visual creation, this mechanism prioritizes content optimized for platforms, systematically excluding alternative forms of representation.

Unlike images' archival function in the past, social media visuals contribute to memory formation in immediate, transient, and fluid ways. The digital image no longer serves as a fixed document but functions as a dynamic component that continuously reconstructs memory. Even the most mundane moments of daily life gain visibility through aestheticization, turning sharing into a strategy for remembrance and recognition. Thus, visuals serve not as durable repositories of memory but as transient objects of the attention economy.

Lev Manovich's concept of "database aesthetics" provides a critical framework for understanding the visuality of social media. Contemporary visual culture is built not on linear narratives but on modular, fragmentable, and reassemblable structures. Social media users are no longer passive viewers but active subjects who transform, reconstruct, and narrate images. Each constructs a digital identity through their personal visual data set.

In parallel with postmodern art, social media users reconfigure popular culture images to perform identity. The instrumentalization of the body found in the works of Cindy Sherman and Yasumasa Morimura is rearticulated in the filtered self-portraits of today's social media users. Sherman's identity games have evolved into the aesthetic-political strategies present in the constantly recreated selfies of everyday life.

In the context of Guy Debord's (1994) theory of the society of the spectacle, social media becomes a showcase not of real life but of representations of that life. The spectacle has evolved into a representational regime that replaces social reality. The raw material of this spectacle consists of images, follower counts, and aesthetically coded posts. Social media has become a stage where individuals are compelled to be visible and produce narratives and personas.

Accordingly, social media aesthetics should be understood as a multilayered visual regime that redefines representation, identity, memory, and visibility. This aesthetic cannot be explained solely by individual preferences, as algorithmic structures, cultural norms, and economic strategies shape it. In the post-photographic context, social media has become not only a site for producing visuals but also one where images circulate, are received, and acquire meaning. How users aestheticize their bodies, daily lives, and social relationships should be seen not merely as acts of individual expression but as performative strategies carrying the cultural codes of the digital age.

Additionally, beauty filters, widely used on platforms like Instagram and TikTok, constitute a digital manifestation of body politics. These filters reinforce and obscure normative beauty standards, leading users to objectify themselves in line with these standards. Beauty filters crystallize core post-photographic concerns such as representational shifts, algorithmic mediation, and digital identity construction. Within the framework of Rosalind Gill's (2007) notion of controlled freedom, such digital aesthetic practices offer the illusion of choice while compelling individuals to act by the codes of the visibility economy. Similarly, Sarah Banet-Weiser (2012) emphasizes that the female body in digital culture is constantly reshaped and that visibility politics are governed not solely by personal expression but by structural norms. These digital beauty regimes redefine the political relations between representation and visibility within post-photographic aesthetics. Thus, social media aesthetics evolves into a complex and dynamic representational domain where individual expression and social norms intersect.

These systems operate not only as production technologies but also as structures that shape and legitimize cultural values. This transformation profoundly alters the position of both the artist and the viewer. The artist is no longer a mere image producer but becomes an agent who selects data, manages algorithms, and configures systems. Meanwhile, the viewer transitions from a passive observer to an active participant who transforms, recontextualizes, and regenerates the content.

AI-based production processes intersect deeply with postmodern aesthetic strategies. These systems employ simulation, pastiche, appropriation, and repetition methods to re-create physical reality, cultural memory, visual archives, and fictional worlds. In this regard, Baudrillard's concept of the simulacrum underscores that contemporary visual forms operate not through originality but through reproduction, imitation, and reconfiguration (Baudrillard, 1994). The computational construction of rendered images signifies that physical reality is not represented but simulated.

In conclusion, AI and algorithms are reshaping aesthetic forms and the ethical, epistemological, and political orientations of visual culture. Elkins (2011) emphasizes that this transformation fundamentally reconfigures the artist's creative control; Manovich (2001) highlights the central role of algorithms in aesthetic decision-making; Ritchin (2009) points out that digital images are increasingly assessed by their intent rather than their truth value; and Paglen and Crawford (2021) describe AI systems as mechanisms that reproduce cultural codes and legitimize social norms. This multilayered transformation necessitates evaluating post-photography as an aesthetic development and a cultural-political paradigm.

Artists and Works in Post-Photographic Practices

Today's understanding of post-photography calls for a reconsideration of the image within its broader contextual integrity. As Camila Moreiras argues, the post-photographic image can be understood as a composite of collected, ordered, layered, stored, and discarded information (Moreiras, 2017). Within this framework, the circulation of visual data in cyberspace, the blurring of the boundaries of virtual reality, and the rapid proliferation of digital images on the internet have become central conditions shaping both the content and the modes of production of post-photographic practices.

Artists utilize social media platforms not merely as spaces of expression but as critical grounds where systems of surveillance, technologies of representation, and data policies are conceptually interrogated. At the same time, through the visual representation of archives, they aim to reinterpret past traumas and destructions from today's political and aesthetic perspective. This transformation is not limited to technological advances but has profoundly influenced and reshaped the conceptual framework of art.

In this period when digitalization has transformed modes of representation, perceptions of reality, and the processes of artistic production–circulation–reception, post-photography is positioned as a field that transcends traditional understandings of photography, encompassing critical and conceptual practices (Fontcuberta, 2013). In this context, artists develop new aesthetic strategies by associating image production with the politics of surveillance, identity, memory, and representation.

One of the most commonly employed strategies in this context is appropriation, developed in the digital age. Online platforms, social media, and open-source visual data pools offer artists rich content across material and conceptual dimensions.

For instance, Jon Rafman's project "Nine Eyes of Google Street View" (2008-ongoing) is a striking post-photographic practice that questions the apparent neutrality promised by machine vision and exposes the surveillance strategies of the digital age. Rafman selects hundreds of scenes from the imagery captured by the nine cameras integrated into Google Maps Street View system and re-frames these images on both aesthetic and conceptual levels. The visuals in this project often focus on moments when people interact with their surroundings or with one another. However, these images are devoid of a photographer's gaze or creative intention; instead, they are shaped by an algorithmic and systematic mode of seeing.

By appropriating and recontextualizing Google Street View images, Rafman (2009) highlights the aesthetic, cultural, and representational dimensions of images produced through surveillance technologies. Drawing on strategies associated with appropriation artists such as Sherrie Levine and Richard Prince, he critically engages with the anonymous, reproducible, and mass-circulated visual regimes of the digital age. Because these images are generated not through the gaze or creative intention of a singular subject, but through the operation of automated systems, they destabilize photography's traditional association with authorship, originality, and authority. Thus, Street View images, which at first appear to function as neutral and direct records of reality, are better understood as culturally coded visual texts that demand interpretation. From this perspective, Nine Eyes of Google Street View makes visible the visual power normalized by surveillance technologies while simultaneously subverting practices of visual archiving. In doing so, Rafman's work reflects the fragmented, disordered, and often passive experience of the contemporary subject. His strategy also reveals that the quantitative proliferation of digital images does not necessarily produce deeper perception or understanding; rather, it may generate excessive visibility, distraction, and a weakening of interpretive engagement. In this sense, Rafman's work offers a compelling example of the epistemological ruptures that emerge within post-photographic visual culture.

Similarly, Doug Rickard uses selected images from Google Street View in his series "A New American Picture" (2010) to question the claims of neutrality in machine-generated imagery. This project offers a powerful post-photographic critique of documentary photography's aesthetic and ethical boundaries in the digital age. With a background in American history and sociology, Rickard adopted the Google Street View platform as a form of digital archive. He virtually navigated economically and socially marginalized neighborhoods and re-photographed the scenes he encountered by capturing screenshots (Rickard, 2010).

The A New American Picture project offers a critical perspective on the limits of visual representation and surveillance systems by making the individuals living in America's overlooked rural and urban areas visible. After capturing the scenes as screenshots, Rickard reframed them in panoramic compositions, removing the visual watermarks that denote Google's ownership and aesthetically reinterpreting these machine-generated images. His practice transforms these representations produced by surveillance technologies into a form of counter-surveillance. In doing so, he generates a critical alternative to the all-seeing technological gaze of the digital era at once aesthetically and politically subversive.

Pavel Maria Smejkal's "Fatescapes" (2009-2012) series (Smejkal, 2015) is a significant post-photographic work that explores themes such as visual memory, reality, and historiography from a postmodern perspective. In this project, the artist engages in radical appropriation by digitally reworking iconic documentary images embedded in the collective memory of the 20th century -such as Robert Capa's Falling Soldier or Nick Ut's Napalm Girl. Smejkal digitally erases the figures and events in the foreground of these photographs, rendering only the background landscapes- empty, quiet spaces visible. This strategy simultaneously questions how history can be visually rewritten and highlights how humanity's collective traumas can be rendered invisible.

In this regard, Fatescapes reveals the fragile nature of historical reality and visual representation. The artist deconstructs and transforms Photography -not through physical manipulation but via digital erasure- integrating past visual documents into the present's critical aesthetic strategies. The series is not merely about an aesthetic of loss and absence; it uncovers the layered meanings that echo within these silent spaces and the vulnerability of a visual memory open to reinterpretation.

French artist Isabelle Le Minh produces post-photographic works that question identity, surveillance, and representation in the digital age, drawing from visual history and photographic archives. In her series “After Alphonse Bertillon” (2013), she takes inspiration from the anthropometric portrait systems of Alphonse Bertillon, a pioneer in forensic identification methods in the late 19th century. In this series, Le Minh connects this historical methodology to contemporary forms of digital surveillance, offering a critical reading on visual representation and the traceability of individuals (Le Minh, 2013).

Drawing on Bertillon's systematically archived criminal portraits, Le Minh processes Facebook users' profile photos in a similarly systematic manner. Through this, Le Minh draws a direct analogy between the physiognomic surface analysis of 19th-century criminals and the algorithmic techniques social media platforms employ to recognize, classify, and archive users. Her work highlights new identity production strategies that threaten individual privacy at the intersection of visual representation and digital surveillance technologies.

The artist also visualizes how biometric and digital traces -such as fingerprints, retinal scans, and cookie tracking- enable control over individual identity today. In this sense, After Alphonse Bertillon is a powerful post-photographic project that establishes a critical distance from historical and contemporary visual regimes.

Within post-photographic practices, artists produce critical works around themes such as visual excess, anonymity, and aesthetic repetition. These approaches interrogate the limits of individual representation and the meaning of visual production in the digital age. For instance, Penelope Umbrico's ongoing project “Suns from Flickr” (2006-present) compiles thousands of sunset photographs shared on Flickr to form a collective visual structure rooted in anonymous repetition. Presenting countless versions of the same image emphasizes the erasure of individual perspective and the dissolution of singular expression within algorithmic accumulation. By appropriating publicly available anonymous content, Umbrico formulates an aesthetic critique through this project (Umbrico, 2011).

Similarly, Erik Kessels' installation “24 HRS in Photos” (2011) visualizes the overwhelming nature of digital culture by printing approximately 350,000 images uploaded to social media and photo-sharing platforms within a single day and piling them into a gallery space. Through this massive visual accumulation, Kessels exposes the attention economy of the digital age, the oversaturation of information, and the suffocating sensation associated with the representation of personal experiences. By removing digital images from the online sphere and transferring them into a physical space, Kessels enacts a striking post-photographic intervention that questions the boundaries of privacy and representation (Kessels, 2011).

By appropriating existing visuals, both artists transform them from aesthetic objects into tools for generating critical discourse. These projects make the desensitization caused by visual abundance and repetition in digital culture visible within a critical framework. At the same time, the political and cultural contexts of aesthetic production are brought into question.

Among the post-photographic artists aiming to critique cultural constructs and expose digital mechanisms of power, Trevor Paglen stands out as a prominent figure. In projects such as “Limit Telephotography” (2020) and “Machine Vision” (2019), Paglen unveils the invisible surveillance technologies employed by states, drawing attention to the inherently political nature of visual information. His work, which includes images of NSA spy satellites, geospatial intelligence centers, and secret military operation zones, establishes a form of counter-surveillance aesthetics.

This approach aligns with Michel Foucault’s concept of the panopticon, reinterpreted through the lens of contemporary, networked surveillance technologies. Paglen’s photographs often depict structures from a distance, in dim light, or blurred focus. This aesthetic choice emphasizes the limitations of visibility and the lack of access to information rather than the explanatory power of the image itself. His work does not merely aim to document but serves as an aesthetic-political performance that interrogates the boundaries of representational regimes.

Another artist who critically engages with contemporary panoptic models is Jud Turner. In “Blind Eye Sees All-No Secrets Anymore” (2014), Turner references the NSA’s unlawful surveillance practices by creating a mixed media assemblage composed of lens elements, each symbolizing an eye. The piece visualizes the paradox of transparency in the digital age and the destructive impact of perpetual surveillance on personal privacy. Turner produced 50 miniature versions of the work and sold them, donating part of the proceeds to the Electronic Frontier Foundation (EFF), an international NGO advocating for digital rights and freedoms. In this way, the project transcends aesthetic expression, functioning as an activist post-photographic practice that directly engages in social intervention.

Through the work of these artists, post-photography emerges not merely as a mode of image production but as a critical discursive field that interrogates who produces images, for what purposes, how they circulate, and within which structural frameworks they operate.

The video series "Dark Content" (2015-2018) by Eva & Franco Mattes focuses on visual censorship, algorithmic surveillance, and representations of digital violence through the testimonies of anonymous laborers who moderate content on social media platforms. The artists reframe interviews conducted with moderators working for platforms such as YouTube and Facebook by using avatars and synthetic voices, thereby seeking to make the hidden digital spaces inaccessible to the average user (Mattes & Mattes, 2018). These narratives reveal the limits of representation in visual culture, the decision-making processes of algorithms that determine what is deemed "appropriate," and the psychological toll on moderators themselves. While visualizing these testimonies, the Mattes duo simultaneously anonymizes them, transforming the otherwise invisible and individualized experiences within platform aesthetics into artistic expression.

Dark Content is a powerful post-photographic intervention that questions how photography in the digital age is filtered ethically and aesthetically, what is made visible, and what is erased. At the same time, it offers a politically charged archiving strategy that highlights human labor and its affective burdens within the context of visual overproduction and platform capitalism.

As previously discussed, digital aesthetics demands a re-evaluation of representation not merely in terms of what is shown, but also of how it is produced. Through these tools, and within what contextual codes? For example, Thomas Ruff's "JPEGs" series presents compressed, pixelated digital images in large-scale prints, thereby problematizing the image's materiality and contextual integrity (Ruff, 2009). In this regard, Hito Steyerl's "poor image" concept draws attention to the political potential embedded in low-resolution, widely circulated secondary visuals (Steyerl, 2009). Ruff's works transform these degraded visuals into aesthetic objects, reflecting the processes of knowledge production in the digital age.

Joan Fontcuberta, one of the pioneering figures in the theoretical and artistic formation of the post-photographic paradigm, is renowned for deconstructing the conventional belief that photography inherently represents truth. Fontcuberta's oeuvre is grounded in a critical strategy aimed at systematically undermining the viewer's trust in photographic veracity. His project "Googlegram" (2004-2010) exemplifies this approach in the digital era. By collecting thousands of images retrieved via keyword searches on Google Images and assembling them into mosaics, Fontcuberta reconstructs iconic visuals imbued with political and popular significance (Fontcuberta, 2013).

In this project, the image's content is composed of fragments directly determined by the internet search algorithms; therefore, each Googlegram functions both as an image database and as a narrative that exposes the ideological structure of that database. In this sense, Fontcuberta materializes what Lev Manovich (2001) terms the database's aesthetics. Each mosaic becomes a critical visual text in terms of its content and mode of production.

When considered alongside his earlier projects, such as "Fauna" (1987) and "Sputnik" (1997), Googlegram demonstrates that post-photography is not limited to a technical or digital transformation but involves a profound theoretical reconstruction of reality, representation and visual knowledge production.

Within the post-photographic paradigm, not only the images being represented but also the processes of their production have been transformed, paving the way for new aesthetic and technological paradigms. One of the most radical examples of this transformation lies in production models in which aesthetic decisions are made through artificial intelligence and algorithms. These AI-based practices, where the artist takes on the role of system designer and data becomes narrative, have emerged as defining strategies in the contemporary formation of post-photography.

For example, German artist Mario Klingemann is a pioneer in AI-assisted production processes. He frequently employs Generative Adversarial Networks (GANs) to automatically generate human faces, abstract forms, and digital deformations. Klingemann's approach reframes algorithms involved in production not merely as passive technological tools but as subjective agents shaping aesthetic decisions, thereby challenging traditional assumptions about human authorship and creative agency (Klingemann, 2019).

One of the artist's most striking projects, "Memories of Passersby I", is a continuously evolving digital installation in which artificial intelligence generates new real-life portrait faces. By making the machine's capacity to create visible, the project introduces an aesthetic paradigm where visual decisions are guided by algorithms independent of human intervention.

Klingemann's approach, when considered within the framework of post-photography, reveals that visual production is no longer shaped by the human gaze but by data flows and computational processes. His work represents a new visual regime in which aesthetic control is transferred to algorithmic systems. In this sense, Klingemann opens up new avenues for rethinking the human-machine relationship in artistic production and the nature of contemporary creativity.

Refik Anadol is another pioneering media artist who integrates artificial intelligence, data science, and architectural forms, placing the concept of "data visualization" at the core of artistic creation. His work reflects a post-photographic approach in which visual information is no longer passive content but an active element in constructing aesthetic structures (Anadol, 2021).

His "Machine Hallucinations" series (2021) consists of digital images generated by processing publicly accessible visual archives through AI-driven analysis and reconstruction. These projects transform the algorithmic visual hallucination generation into immersive aesthetic experiences. In works such as "WDCH Dreams"

(2018) and "Unsupervised" (2022). Anadol processes institutional image archives to create data sculptures and spatial installations.

Anadol considers software not merely a technical tool but a creative agent actively participating in aesthetic decision-making. In this context, his work interrogates the algorithmic aesthetics of the digital age through spatial, sensory, and data-driven dimensions. By doing so, Anadol expands post-photography beyond the image, transforming data into a perceptible, experiential, and aestheticized form.

Among contemporary artists who critically explore digital subjectivity, identity representation, and the relationship between being and aesthetics, LaTurbo occupies a distinctive position. As an avatar artist whose practice emphasizes non-physical identity and authorship, Avedon produces work within virtual environments and online exhibition spaces. In this regard, the artist's identity is constructed not as a fixed representation but as a performative process (LaTurbo Avedon, n.d.).

Avedon's approach is closely aligned with Judith Butler's (1990) theory of performative identity. According to Butler, identity is not a fixed or essential structure but a practice continually reconstituted within social, cultural, and linguistic contexts. Similarly, LaTurbo Avedon's works emphasize the instability of digital identity and the permeability of representation within virtual space. By positioning their existence as subject and medium, Avedon offers a critical strategy that blurs the boundaries between subject and tool within the framework of post-photographic visuality.

In LaTurbo Avedon's work, photography is not merely a representational tool but a living form that constructs, sustains, and embodies presence. Avatar aesthetics open a new field of inquiry into how identity is continuously reconstructed in the digital age and how the body is represented within virtual space. In this context, Avedon's works position post-photography as a technological shift and an existential reconstruction process.

Contemporary post-photographic practices are shaped by aesthetics or representation and structures intertwined with data politics. Sarah Meyohas utilizes data as an aesthetic material and a speculative form of representation. In her pioneering project, BitchCoin (Meyohas, 2015), the artist converted her self-portraits into cryptocurrency, interrogating the relationships between art, economy, and value. In "Cloud of Petals" (Meyohas, 2017), she photographed thousands of rose petals and processed them with artificial intelligence, creating a poetic map of digital memory.

On the other hand, Molly Soda is known for her work exploring social media aesthetics and digital identity performances. She examines how platform norms and algorithmic structures shape individual representation through platforms like Tumblr and Instagram. In her eight-hour video piece "Inbox Full" (2016), she reads aloud messages received via social media, exposing the emotional weight of digital visibility. Soda's works offer a critical framework for understanding affect, loneliness, and the politics of visibility in the post-photographic age.

Tabita Rezaire (n.d.) is one of the artists who combines the digital decolonial politics and techno-spiritual practices of the African diaspora with post-photographic methods. Her work critiques the colonization of data and visuality while simultaneously making visible the ethical and political transformations of digital media. In the age of artificial intelligence and big data, visual archives are no longer aesthetic objects they have become powerful political tools.

Within this context, "data colonialism" refers to global structures that restrict access to and control over digital data for specific geographies and communities. The historical and cultural biases embedded in the datasets used to train AI models are not merely technical issues but structural problems that directly affect the justice and representational fairness of visual production. Thus, post-photographic practice is not only an aesthetic or technological form of expression it also operates as a site of political resistance against the inequalities of the digital age.

Post-photography is no longer limited to image-making; it has evolved into a broad artistic field encompassing complex issues such as representation, surveillance, identity, culture, algorithmic production, and data aesthetics. The artists examined in this chapter move beyond a purely technical interpretation of post-photography, instead engaging in a deep and critical interrogation of representation, production methods, and visual regimes. Shaped around themes like reproduction, glitch aesthetics, surveillance mechanisms, data politics, identity construction, and networked culture, these artistic approaches enable a multidimensional analysis of the digital era's cultural, political, and aesthetic structures.

These works transform the image's form and function through appropriation, counter-surveillance, digital deconstruction, algorithmic simulation, and data representation. The image is no longer simply a tool of representation; it becomes a conceptual object-data-driven, AI-constructed, continuously rewritten, and often aimed at revealing what is invisible. Accordingly, the artist's role is redefined-from a fixed producer to a system designer, archival researcher, data interpreter, and political agent.

Post-photography emerges as a contemporary mode of expression that reconsiders visuality not merely as an aesthetic surface but as a conceptual and political terrain shaped by digital technologies and embedded in meaning-making structures.

CONCLUSION

This study has comprehensively examined the multi-layered transformations of the concept of post-photography in the digital age through its aesthetic, technical, cultural, and intellectual dimensions. While photography has long been regarded as the visual representation of reality, this notion has undergone semantic erosion in the digital era. With the influence of simulation, data, algorithms, and artificial intelligence, visual production has experienced a profound transformation-not merely as a technological shift but also in representation, aesthetic norms, and knowledge production processes.

The concept of post-photography defines the evolution of photography from a traditionally "objective document" into a re-constructed, software-based, and computational form of expression in the digital age. The theoretical foundations of this transformation are grounded in Jean Baudrillard's theory of hyperreality, Hito Steyerl's notion of the poor image, Lev Manovich's software aesthetics, and Joan Fontcuberta's post-photographic manifesto. Today, visuality is no longer limited to what is represented but focuses on how these representations are produced and circulated.

Under the shaping influence of digital culture, photography has transformed into a data-driven, networked, algorithmic, and highly reproducible structure. The aesthetic steering power of social media platforms significantly molds the production and consumption of images, leading to a new visual regime based on the economy of attention, where personal representations blend into anonymous content. Filters alter individual appearances and merge with algorithmic aesthetic norms, shaping visibility strategies. In this context, post-photography has become a critical space in which cultural codes, political representations, and aesthetic experiences are fundamentally restructured—not just a technical transformation.

Artists have developed investigative and interventionist visual languages by linking digital environments with surveillance technologies, algorithmic decision-making processes, and data politics. Appropriate counter-surveillance, digital de-construction, algorithmic production, and data representation have become defining strategies within contemporary artistic practices. Artists such as Jon Rafman, Doug Rickard, Isabelle Le Minh, Penelope Umbrico, Trevor Paglen, Eva & Franco Mattes, Joan Fontcuberta, and Mario Klingemann have opened new fields of discourse by critically addressing how visuals are produced, distributed, and perceived-both technologically and socially.

These artists demonstrate that post-photography is not merely a mode of production but also a way of thinking, a critical position, and a means of aesthetic-political expression. As the visuality of the digital era is reconstructed around data, the body, representation, and algorithms, artists become not only witnesses to this transformation but also its active agents. AI- and algorithm-driven production systems do not merely reshape aesthetic forms; they also redefine the ethical and political dimensions of representation. In this regard, artificial intelligence systems are not neutral technical tools but carriers of ideological structures. Especially in the case of text-to-image generators like Stable Diffusion and DALL·E, the role of the creative subject is reduced to algorithmic preferences, making visible the inherently political nature of aesthetic decisions.

Thus, post-photography represents a new mode of image production and a visual regime that critically examines the cultural dynamics, representational crises, and knowledge-production processes of the digital era. The image is no longer merely an aesthetic object but a cultural artifact woven with data, shaped by artificial intelligence, and circulated under algorithmic control. Within this visual regime, artists are redefined as system designers, data interpreters, and political actors, while viewers become not just passive recipients but active agents who interact and construct meaning. Post-photography, a hybrid field in which aesthetic decisions carry political implications, now stands at the center of contemporary art, transforming the operations of visual culture and opening new conceptual possibilities for the future.

REFERENCES

Abidin, C. (2016). Visibility labor: Engaging with influencers' fashion brands and #OOTD advertorial campaigns on Instagram. *Media International Australia, Incorporating Culture & Policy*, *161*(1), 86–100. DOI: 10.1177/1329878X16665177

Anadol, R. (2018). WDCH Dreams [AI-driven immersive projection]. https://refikanadol.com/works/wdch-dreams/

Anadol, R. (2021). Machine Hallucinations - Nature Dreams [AI-generated video installation]. https://refikanadol.com/works/machine-hallucinations-nature-dreams/

Anadol, R. (2022). Unsupervised [AI-generated data sculpture]. https://refikanadol.com/works/unsupervised/

Azoulay, A. (2008). *The civil contract of photography*. Zone Books.

Banet-Weiser, S. (2012). *Authentic: The politics of ambivalence in a brand culture*. New York University Press.

Barthes, R. (1981). *Camera lucida: Reflections on photography* (Howard, R., Trans.). Hill and Wang.

Batchen, G. (1997). *Burning with desire: The conception of photography*. MIT Press.

Baudrillard, J. (1994). *Simulacra and simulation* (Glaser, S. F., Trans.). University of Michigan Press.

Benjamin, W. (2008). *The work of art in the age of its technological reproducibility and other writings on media* (Jennings, M. W., Doherty, B., & Levin, T. Y., Trans.). Harvard University Press. DOI: 10.2307/j.ctv1nzfgns

Bourriaud, N. (2002). *Relational aesthetics* (Pleasance, S., & Woods, F., Trans.). Les Presses du Réel.

Butler, J. (1990). *Gender trouble: Feminism and the subversion of identity*. Routledge.

Crawford, K. (2021). *Atlas of AI: Power, politics, and the planetary costs of artificial intelligence*. Yale University Press.

Debord, G. (1994). *The society of the spectacle* (Nicholson-Smith, D., Trans.). Zone Books.

Elkins, J. (2011). *What photography is*. Routledge. DOI: 10.4324/9780203886489

Fontcuberta, J. (2011). *Post-photographic manifesto* [Post-photographic manifesto]. La Vanguardia. https://www.lavanguardia.com/cultura/20110511/54152218372/por-un-manifiesto-posfotografico.html

Fontcuberta, J. (2013). *The photography of nature & the nature of photography*. Mack.

Fontcuberta, J. (2016). *La furia de las imágenes: Notas sobre la postfotografía*. Galaxia Gutenberg.

Fontcuberta, J. (2004-2010). Googlegrams. https://www.juanmagonzalez.com/fontcuberta/googlegrams.html

Gill, R. (2007). *Gender and the media*. Polity Press.

Gillespie, T. (2014). The relevance of algorithms. In Gillespie, T., Boczkowski, P. J., & Foot, K. A. (Eds.), *Media technologies: Essays on communication, materiality, and society* (pp. 167–194). MIT Press. DOI: 10.7551/mitpress/9042.003.0013

Goffman, E. (1959). *The presentation of self in everyday life*. Anchor Books.

Kessels, E. (2011). 24 HRS in Photos [Installation]. https://www.erikkessels.com/24hrs-in-photos

Klingemann, M. (2019). Memories of Passersby I [AI-generated installation]. https://quasimondo.com/2018/12/29/memories-of-passersby-i/

LaTurbo Avedon. (n.d.). Portfolio. https://www.laturboavedon.com/portfolio

Le Minh, I. (2013). After Alphonse Bertillon. https://isabelleleminh.com/isabelle-le-minh---works/portrait-souffle.html

Leaver, T., Highfield, T., & Abidin, C. (2020). *Instagram: Visual social media cultures*. Polity Press.

Manovich, L. (2001). *The language of new media*. MIT Press.

Mattes, E., & Mattes, F. (2018). Dark Content [Video series]. https://0100101110101101.org/dark-content/

Meyohas, S. (2015). BitchCoin. https://sarahmeyohas.com/bitchcoin

Meyohas, S. (2017). Cloud of Petals. https://sarahmeyohas.com/cloud-of-petals

Mitchell, W. J. (1992). *The Reconfigured Eye: Visual Truth in the Post-Photographic Era*. MIT Press.

Moreiras, C. (2017). Joan Fontcuberta: Post-photography and the spectral image of saturation. *Journal of Spanish Cultural Studies*, *18*(1), 1–18. DOI: 10.1080/14636204.2016.1274496

Paglen, T. (2019). Machine Visions. https://paglen.studio/category/machine-visions

Paglen, T. (2020). Limit Telephotography. https://paglen.studio/2020/04/22/limit-telephotography

Paglen, T., & Crawford, K. (2021). Excavating AI: The politics of images in machine learning training sets. *AI & Society*, *36*, 1105–1116. DOI: 10.1007/s00146-021-01162-8

Rafman, J. (2008-ongoing). Nine eyes of Google Street View. https://9-eyes.com

Rafman, J. (2009, August 12). *Nine Eyes of Google Street View. The Eye of Photography.* https://loeildelaphotographie.com/en/the-eyes-of-google-street-view-by-jon-rafman/

Rezaire, T. (n.d.). Tabita Rezaire. https://tabitarezaire.com

Rickard, D. (2010). *A New American Picture*. White Press.

Ritchin, F. (2009). *After photography*. W. W. Norton & Company.

Rosler, M. (1974-75). The Bowery in two inadequate descriptive systems. https://www.martharosler.net/the-bowery-in-two-inadequate-descriptive-systems

Rouillé, A. (2005). *La photographie: Entre document et art contemporain*. Gallimard.

Rubinstein, D., & Sluis, K. (2008). A life more photographic: Mapping the networked image. *Photographies*, *1*(1), 9–28. DOI: 10.1080/17540760701785842

Ruff, T. (2009). JPEGs [Photographic series]. https://www.thomasruff.com/en/works/jpeg/

Smejkal, P. M. (2015, February 23). Fatescapes. LensCulture. https://www.lensculture.com/projects/80186-fatescapes

Soda, M. (2016). Inbox Full [Video]. Tumblr. https://www.tumblr.com/paddleson/629998391111/inbox-full-by-molly-soda-is-an-eight-hour-long

Steyerl, H. (2009). In defense of the poor image. *e-flux journal*, (10). https://www.e-flux.com/journal/10/61362/in-defense-of-the-poor-image/

Turner, J. (2014). Blind Eye Sees All – No Secrets Anymore [Mixed media sculpture]. https://judturner.com/blind-eye-sees-all/

Umbrico, P. (2011). Suns from Flickr [Online art project]. http://www.penelopeumbrico.net/index.php/project/suns-from-sunsets-from-flickr/

ADDITIONAL READING

Edwards, E. (2019). *Photographs and the practice of history*. Bloomsbury.

Frosh, P. (2019). *The poetics of digital media*. Polity Press.

Gere, C. (2008). *Digital culture*. Reaktion Books.

Hand, M. (2020). *Ubiquitous photography*. Polity Press.

Jurgenson, N. (2019). *The social photo: On photography and social media*. Bloomsbury.

Manovich, L. (2020). *Cultural analytics*. MIT Press. DOI: 10.7551/mitpress/11214.001.0001

Mirzoeff, N. (2015). *How to see the world*. Pelican.

Rubinstein, D. (2020). *Fragmentation of the photographic image in the digital age*. Routledge.

Senft, T. M., & Baym, N. K. (2015). What does the selfie say? Investigating a global phenomenon. *International Journal of Communication*, *9*, 1588–1606.

Zylinska, J. (2017). *Nonhuman photography*. MIT Press. DOI: 10.7551/mitpress/10938.001.0001

Zylinska, J. (2020). *AI art: Machine visions and warped dreams*. Open Humanities Press.

KEY TERMS AND DEFINITIONS

Digital Art: Digital art encompasses artistic practices that employ digital technologies, such as software, algorithms, and artificial intelligence, as creative tools. It reflects a shift from material-based production to computational, interactive, and networked forms of artistic expression (Manovich, 2001).

Digital Culture: The socio-cultural environment shaped by digital technologies, online networks, and algorithmic infrastructures. It encompasses practices of communication, representation, memory, and identity in a context where digital media structures everyday life and artistic production (Gere, 2008; Manovich, 2020).

Digital Manipulation: The alteration, reconstruction, or fabrication of images using digital tools such as Photoshop, AI generators, and algorithmic systems. It challenges conventional notions of authenticity, originality, and truth in photography and visual culture (Ritchin, 2009).

Hyperreality: Hyperreality, a concept popularized by Jean Baudrillard (1994), describes a state in which signs and simulations no longer reflect reality but instead produce a reality of their own. Within visual culture, digital images and simulations construct experiences that blur or replace the "real."

Post-Photography: Post-photography refers to the critical and aesthetic practices that challenge photography's traditional role as a medium of truth and documentation. Emerging with digital technologies, it emphasizes manipulation, circulation, and reconstruction of images rather than their indexical relationship to reality (Fontcuberta, 2016; Mitchell, 1992).

Simulation: Simulation is the process of replicating or constructing representations that imitate reality without necessarily referring to it. In digital culture, simulations are generated through algorithms and software, producing alternative or artificial worlds that may surpass the experience of physical reality (Baudrillard, 1994).

Chapter 4
Reality, Fiction, Propaganda, Fantasy!
The Art of Photography

Ozan Bilgiseren
http://orcid.org/0000-0001-7085-5758
Mimar Sinan Fine Arts University, Turkey

ABSTRACT

This study maps how photography, from its first exposures to today's platforms, has evolved from a recording device into a narrative system that both documents and constructs reality. Oscillating between fact and fiction, art and reportage, propaganda and fantasy, the medium's digital manipulability intensifies debates over truth, representation, and ethics. Through cases such as Kundera's individual–state–memory triangle, Capa's Falling Soldier, Doisneau's The Kiss at Hôtel de Ville, and Nick Ut's Napalm Girl, the research probes photography's political and aesthetic power. It also examines staged imagery in the work of Jeff Wall and Gregory Crewdson to analyze how cinematic setups shape perception in the networked era. Bringing historical manipulation into dialogue with contemporary practice, the study repositions photography as visual memory requiring renewed ethical, aesthetic, and technical scrutiny.

INTRODUCTION

Since the first photographic frame was exposed, photography has become one of the foundational elements of visual culture, serving both as a documentary tool and as a form of aesthetic expression. In modern times, with the evolution of technology, this dual nature has become increasingly complex. Photography's oscillation between

DOI: 10.4018/979-8-3373-2230-8.ch004

reality and fiction, documentation and art, propaganda and fantasy has sparked numerous critical debates. Especially with the advent of the digital age, the manipulability of the photographic image has transformed photography into a narrative medium—one that not only captures what is, but also constructs and reconfigures it. Within this context, the boundaries between documentary photography and artistic expression have become increasingly blurred, bringing issues of truth, representation, and ethical responsibility back to the forefront. This study aims to explore the transformation of photography through a multi-layered perspective, spanning from its historical relationship with manipulation to contemporary artistic practices, from darkrooms to digital platforms, and from the ethical stance of photographers to the viewer's engagement with visual truth. Through critical examples such as Milan Kundera's narrative triangle of individual–state–memory, Robert Capa's "Falling Soldier," Robert Doisneau's "The Kiss at Hôtel de Ville," and Nick Ut's iconic "Napalm Girl," this research interrogates photography's function across both aesthetic and political dimensions. Moreover, by examining the impact of staged imagery through the works of contemporary artists like Jeff Wall and Gregory Crewdson, the perceptual effects of the digital era on audiences are also analyzed. Ultimately, this study invites a reconsideration of photography as both a practice of visual memory and a powerful medium whose forms of transformation must be critically evaluated through ethical, aesthetic, and technical lenses.

RED CARD

Milan Kundera, the Czech-born French novelist and the last existentialist writer, who passed away in July 2023, joined the Communist Party at the age of 18, shortly after the end of World War II (Milan Kundera, 2025). However, he was expelled from the party in 1948 due to accusations of engaging in activities against it. Up until this point, Kundera regarded what he had experienced as a sort of joke. The episode of his expulsion became the subject of his novel *The Joke* (*Žert*) (The Joke, 2025). In 1956, he was reinstated into the Communist Party (Figure: 01).

Figure 1. Czech-born French writer Milan Kundera

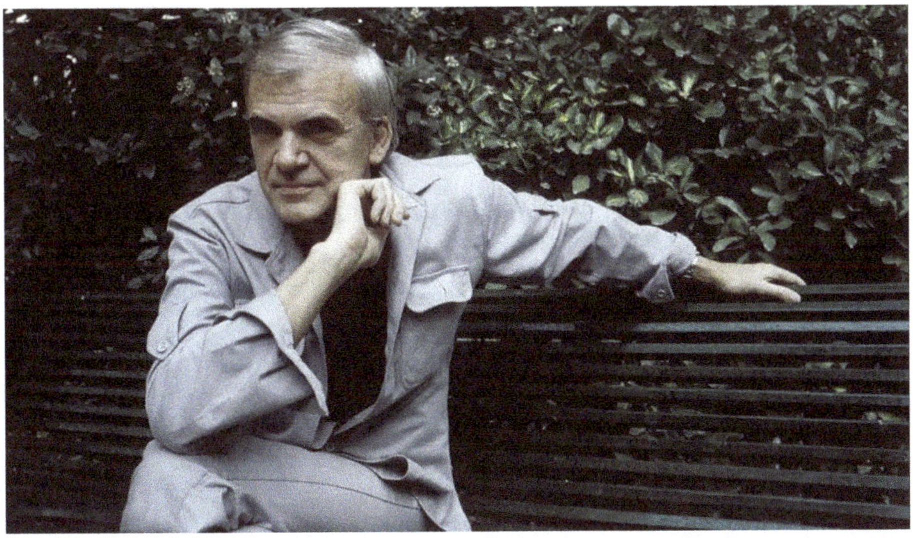

However, in 1970, he was expelled for the second and final time, along with other prominent Czech writers and artists of the era. Following the Soviet invasion in 1968, Kundera was dismissed from his position at the Academy of Music and Performing Arts in Prague. Unable to withstand the political pressures, he emigrated to France in 1975 and acquired French citizenship in 1981. After the publication of *The Book of Laughter and Forgetting* in 1979, the Czechoslovak government stripped him of his Czech citizenship (Figure: 02).

Figure 2. The book cover of Laughter and Forgetting

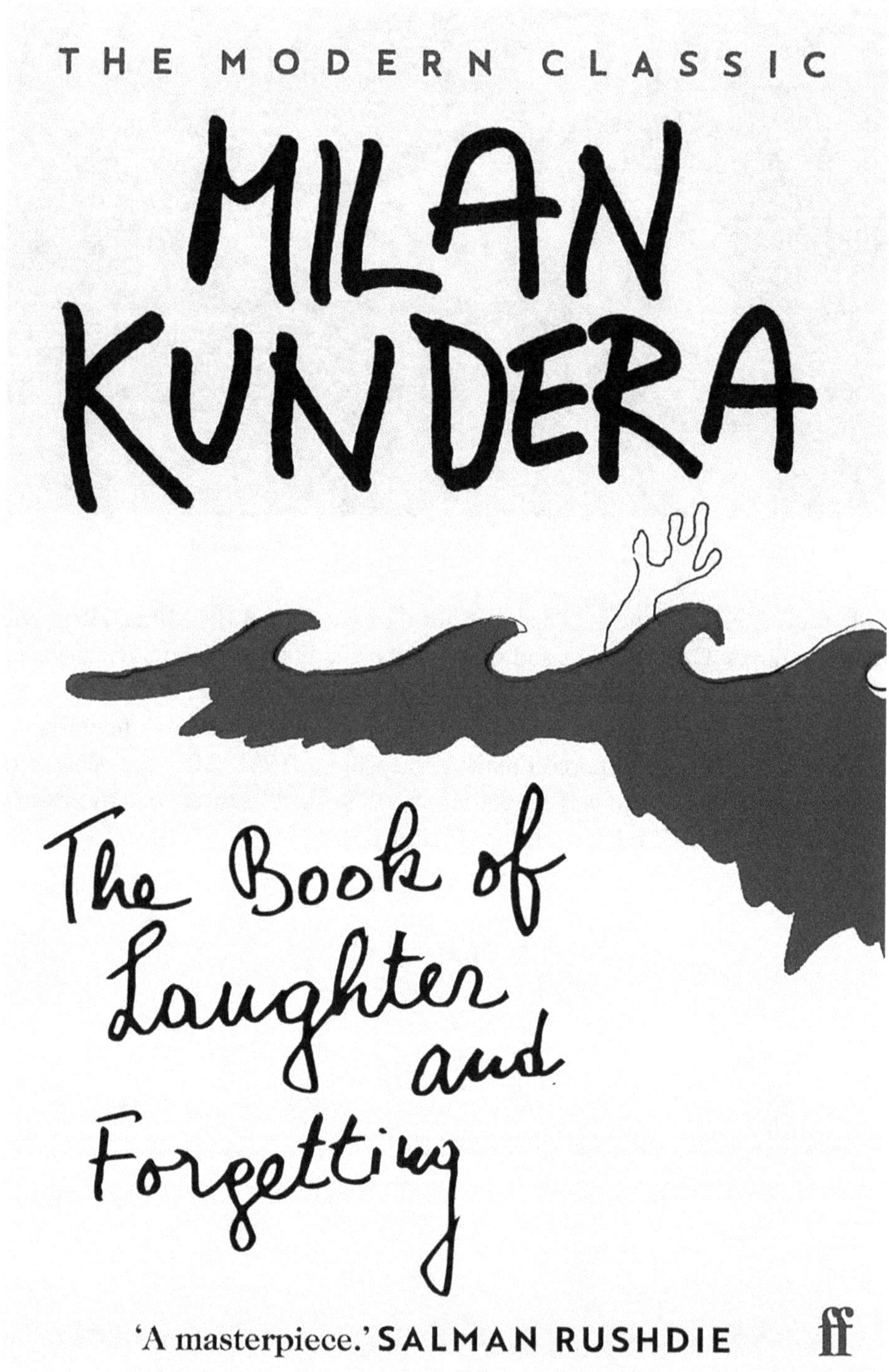

This novel consists of seven chapters—titled *Lost Letters*, *Mama*, *The Angels*, *Lost Letters*, *Litost*, *The Angels*, and *The Border*—which may seem disconnected at first. However, these seemingly independent sections are skillfully held together within a unified narrative structure and a framework of historical reality. In the work, the author frequently illustrates how ideological doctrines distort the concepts of "good" and "evil" under authoritarian regimes, and how the state tends to erase human memory and historical truths. These themes are presented through personal experiences, observations, and dark humor, while simultaneously conveying a profound sense of melancholy (The Book of Laughter and Forgetting, 2025).

When I first picked up *The Book of Laughter and Forgetting* in 1988—not merely as a literary narrative but in search of insights into the history of Bohemia—the Berlin Wall had not yet fallen. At that time, although I was not as deeply engaged in photography as I am today, my experience with the darkroom was rapidly expanding. Perhaps for this reason, I found myself particularly unsettled by a scene described on the very first page of the book: the moment captured in a historical photograph of Communist leaders Vladimír Clementis (1902–1952) and Klement Gottwald (1896–1953), and the subsequent erasure of Clementis from that frame not long after. I was struck by the disturbing nature of this political manipulation of photographic truth. (Figure: 03)

Figure 3. Klement Gottwald (before and after)

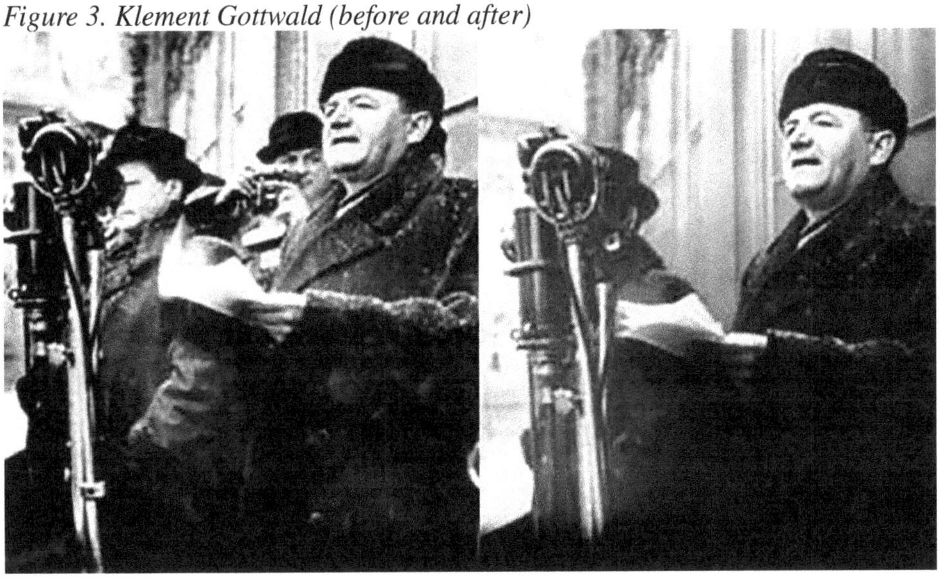

As recounted by Kundera, during the historic speech delivered by Czechoslovakia's first Communist leader, Klement Gottwald, on February 21, 1948, in Prague's

Old Town Square, Clementis placed his fur hat on Gottwald's head to keep him warm. This small but symbolic act was immortalized in one of the most significant photographic records of Bohemian political history. Yet only four years later, Clementis was executed and, worse still, erased from the photograph by darkroom intervention—a form of visual censorship that resembled a political abortion. At the time, I was only nineteen years old, and I found it difficult to comprehend such a drastic manipulation. These were the years—what some might now consider an ancient era—before the invention of Adobe Photoshop, when photography still reigned as the ultimate authority of truth and was regarded as a document of incontrovertible evidence.

Many years later, during the winter of 2020, in the midst of the pandemic, I happened upon *The Book of Laughter and Forgetting* once again, this time while browsing my late mother's library in her summer house. The moment I opened the cover, I was instantly reminded of this episode and felt compelled to investigate the matter more deeply. After all, Milan Kundera—whom I had admired for decades for masterfully interweaving fact and fiction with philosophical insight, and whose works I had read in Turkish translations—was an author whose honesty and commitment to truth I had never questioned. I found myself asking: on what factual basis had Kundera constructed this narrative? Needless to say, in 1988, the internet and web communication as we know them today did not exist, and thus the possibilities for research were significantly limited (Figure: 04).

Figure 4. A photomontage poster from the speech of Klement Gottwald in Old Town Square in Prague on 21st of February 1948 for the 25th anniversary.

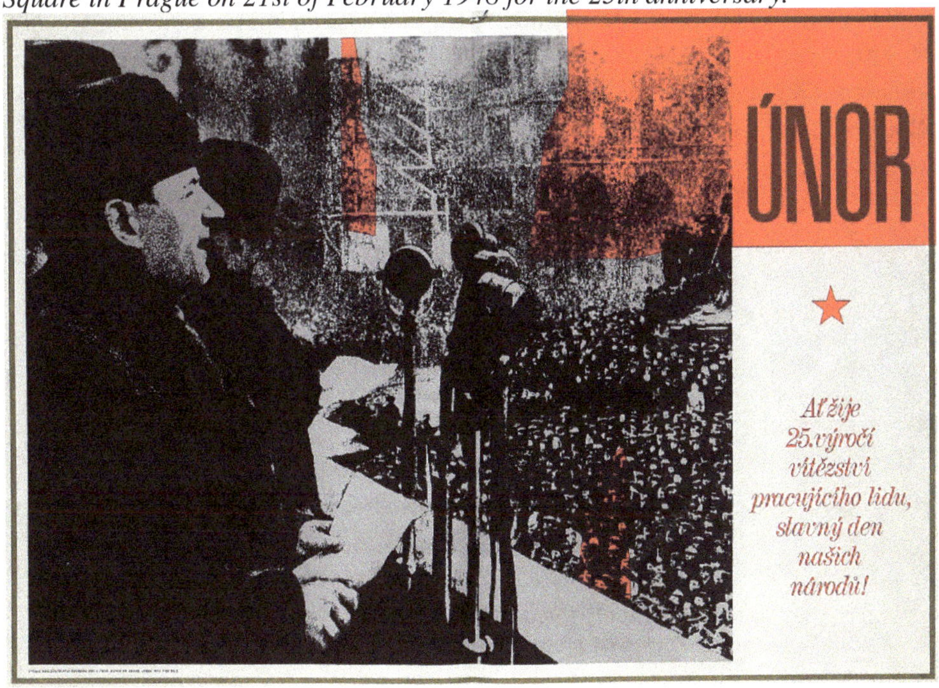

When Vladimír Clementis, a victim of political turmoil in his country, was convicted in 1950 and executed on December 3, 1952, both his physical existence and his image in a historic photograph were erased. In other words, his presence and his photographic representation were eliminated one after another. The photograph in question was taken by Karel Hájek (1900–1978), a journalist, photographer, and typographer (Mcardle, 2025). In April 1939, Hájek was hired as a correspondent for *LIFE* Magazine, and on March 15 of the same year, he captured a historic moment for *LIFE* from a traffic police platform in Wenceslas Square, photographing the arrival of German occupation forces in Prague. These images, however, were not directly credited to him but to the international news agency ČTK. After being arrested and taken to the Gestapo headquarters, Hájek managed to avoid imprisonment by proving he was a *LIFE* correspondent.

During the war, he continued to produce photo-reportages for the Czech weekly *Pestrý týden* ("Colorful Weekly"), which after the war was renamed *Svět v obrazech* ("The World in Pictures") (Pestrý týden, 2025) (Figure: 05). On May 4, 1945, he documented the Prague uprising. In the postwar period, he became the only Czech photojournalist granted access to photograph the Nuremberg trials. His approach during this period was particularly striking: by juxtaposing images of war criminals on trial—visibly marked by fear, anxiety, remorse, and guilt—with archival photographs of their documented wartime actions prior to arrest, he created powerful photo layouts that implicitly dismantled their defenses and made their guilt visually undeniable (Figure: 06). Hájek's perspective was shaped by his own experience as someone who had suffered under the Nazi regime in Czechoslovakia (Norimberk: Zlocin A Soud, 2025).

Figure 5. Page from the Pestrý týden magazine

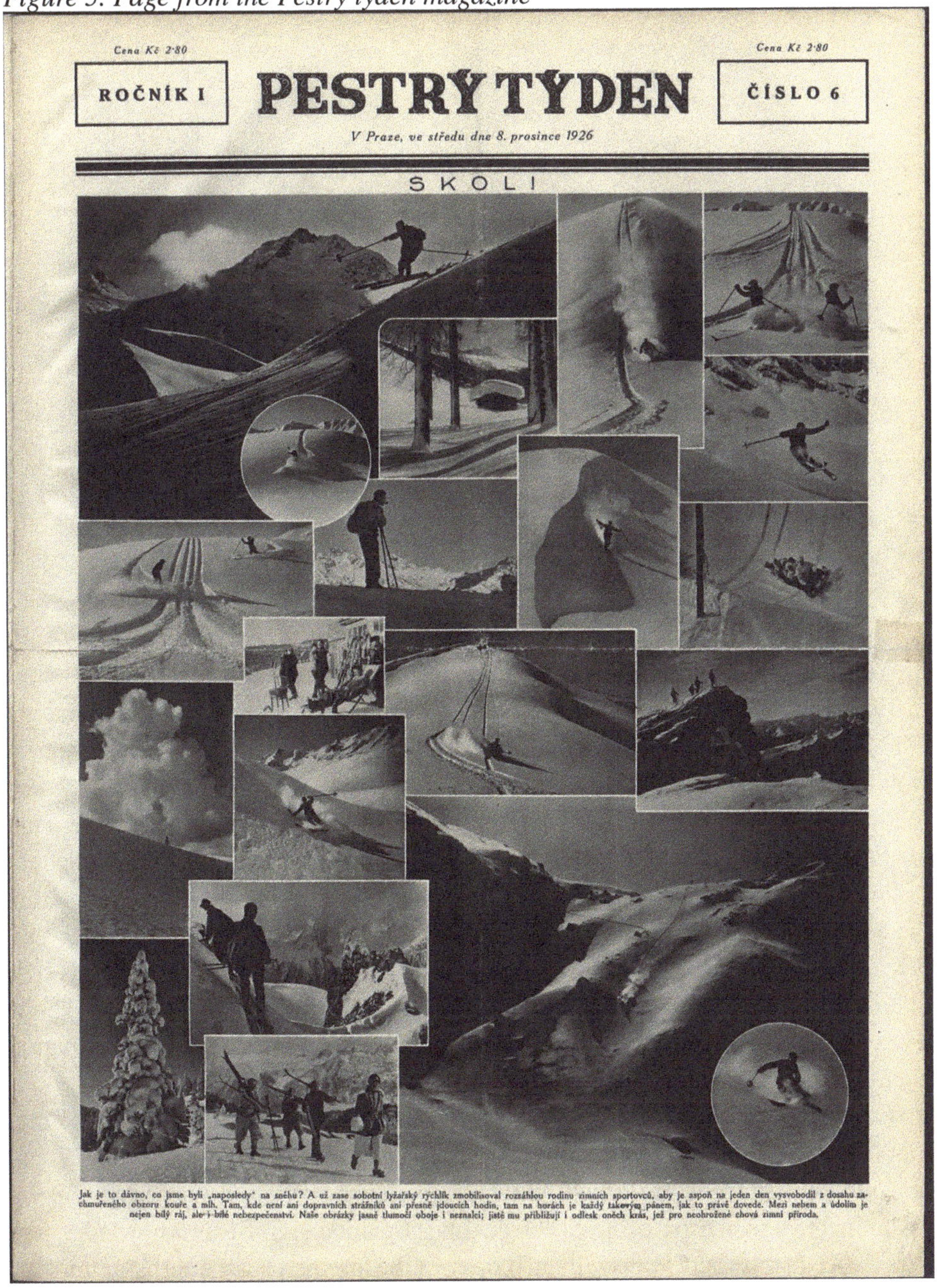

Cena Kč 2·80 Cena Kč 2·80

ROČNÍK I **PESTRÝ TÝDEN** ČÍSLO 6

V Praze, ve středu dne 8. prosince 1926

SKOL!

Jak je to dávno, co jsme byli „naposledy" na sněhu? A už zase sobotní lyžařský rychlík zmobilisoval rozsáhlou rodinu zimních sportovců, aby je aspoň na jeden den vysvobodil z dosahu zachmuřeného obzoru kouře a mlh. Tam, kde není ani dopravních strážníků ani přesně jdoucích hodin, tam na horách je každý takovým pánem, jak to právě dovede. Mezi nebem a údolím je nejen bílý ráj, ale i bílé nebezpečenství. Naše obrázky jasně tlumočí oboje i neznalci; jistě mu přibližují i odlesk oněch krás, jež pro neohrožené chová zimní příroda.

Figure 6. Karel Hájek's powerful photo layouts side by side during Nuremberg trials

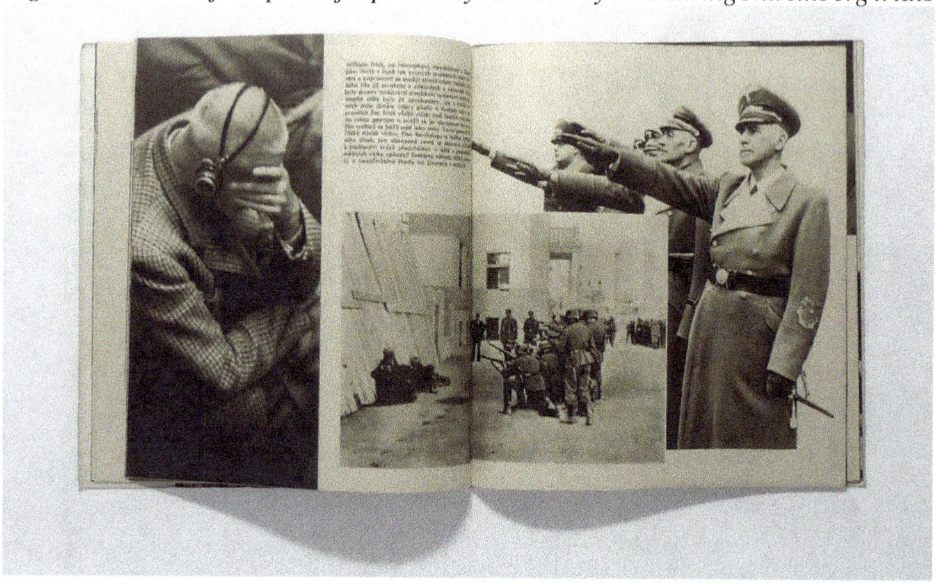

Yet, inevitably, he too would fall victim to political repression in his own country. In 1950, the Ministry of the Interior confiscated Hájek's archive of approximately 80,000 photographic negatives, under the pretext that politically sensitive material would be reviewed and the rest returned. Unfortunately, his repeated efforts in the following years to retrieve the archive proved fruitless. It was not until 1965—following his growing international reputation, an invitation to lecture at the Vienna School of Photography, and the circulation of his solo exhibition in South America—that the Ministry finally returned around 16,000 of his negatives. The following year, the state awarded him the honorary title "Deserving Artist," thus restoring his reputation within the country. Karel Hájek died in 1978 in Prague, Czechoslovakia. Even today, it remains remarkably difficult to access comprehensive information about the photograph in question (Karel Hájek, 2025).

Over the decades, I personally encountered and practiced various forms of manipulation in the darkroom—manipulations that, compared to the ease of the digital era, required immense technical skill and patience—through numerous analog assignments and artistic projects. Over time, I gained significant knowledge and experience in this field. Especially in the age of the internet, I came across numerous historical examples in my research on the history of retouching. It became increasingly clear to me that the erasure of once-prominent political figures from historical records and visual archives—particularly in totalitarian regimes such as those of Hitler and Stalin, and resembling the case of Clementis—was not an exceptional or surprising occurrence. While contemporary equivalents may differ in form, one could argue that the deletion or suppression of news content, personal messages, or images from social media—due to ideological conflicts or the arbitrary censorship of so-called digital overlords—has likewise become normalized, and perhaps even passively accepted.

Returning to the subject of photography, when I was first invited to the People's Republic of China as a guest artist in 2019, I visited the photography books section of a large exhibition and art fair, intending to purchase an encyclopedic volume on *Contemporary Chinese Photography*. I was offered two versions of the same book by the seller: a pristine, shrink-wrapped edition lacking approximately twelve pages, and an alternative copy—used, with a torn cover and inner binding—that was slightly thicker. Curiously, both versions were priced identically. When I inquired about the missing pages in the new edition, I was informed that certain images of Mao Zedong, the founding leader of the Chinese state, had been deemed inappropriate for later printings. (Figure: 07)

Figure 7. Chinese Contemporary book of Photography

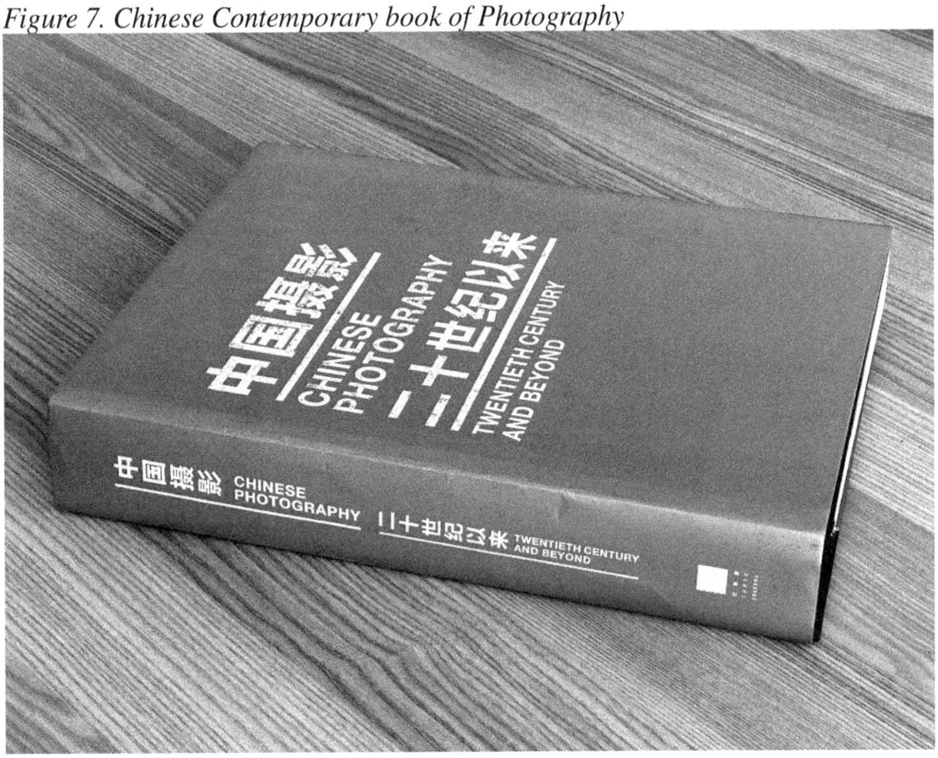

Although I still do not know why these particular photographs—depicting Chairman Mao in everyday outdoor meetings with his comrades—were initially included in what is ostensibly a contemporary art book, nor why they were subsequently removed, I can only assume, somewhat resignedly, that "there must be a reason." The motivations behind such editorial decisions remain unclear to me, but the incident nevertheless offers another poignant reminder of how photographic narratives can be selectively shaped—or erased—by ideological imperatives, even in the realm of art publishing.

ALTERATION, ERASURE

Yet at times, even when individuals are deliberately erased or removed from public memory, life occasionally reintroduces them in unexpected ways—particularly when their historical significance resists disappearance. One of the most notable examples of such a figure is Edward VIII, the former King of the United Kingdom (Edward VIII, 2025). Before the outbreak of the Second World War, Edward's covert sympathies and interactions with the Nazi regime provoked considerable concern and disappointment among both the British political establishment and the royal family. (Figure: 08) However, he became far more widely known for a dramatically different reason: his abdication of the throne for love. Edward achieved global notoriety for renouncing his kingship in order to marry Wallis Simpson, a twice-divorced American woman—a decision that shocked the monarchy and captivated the public imagination.

Figure 8. Edward VIII The Prince of Wales

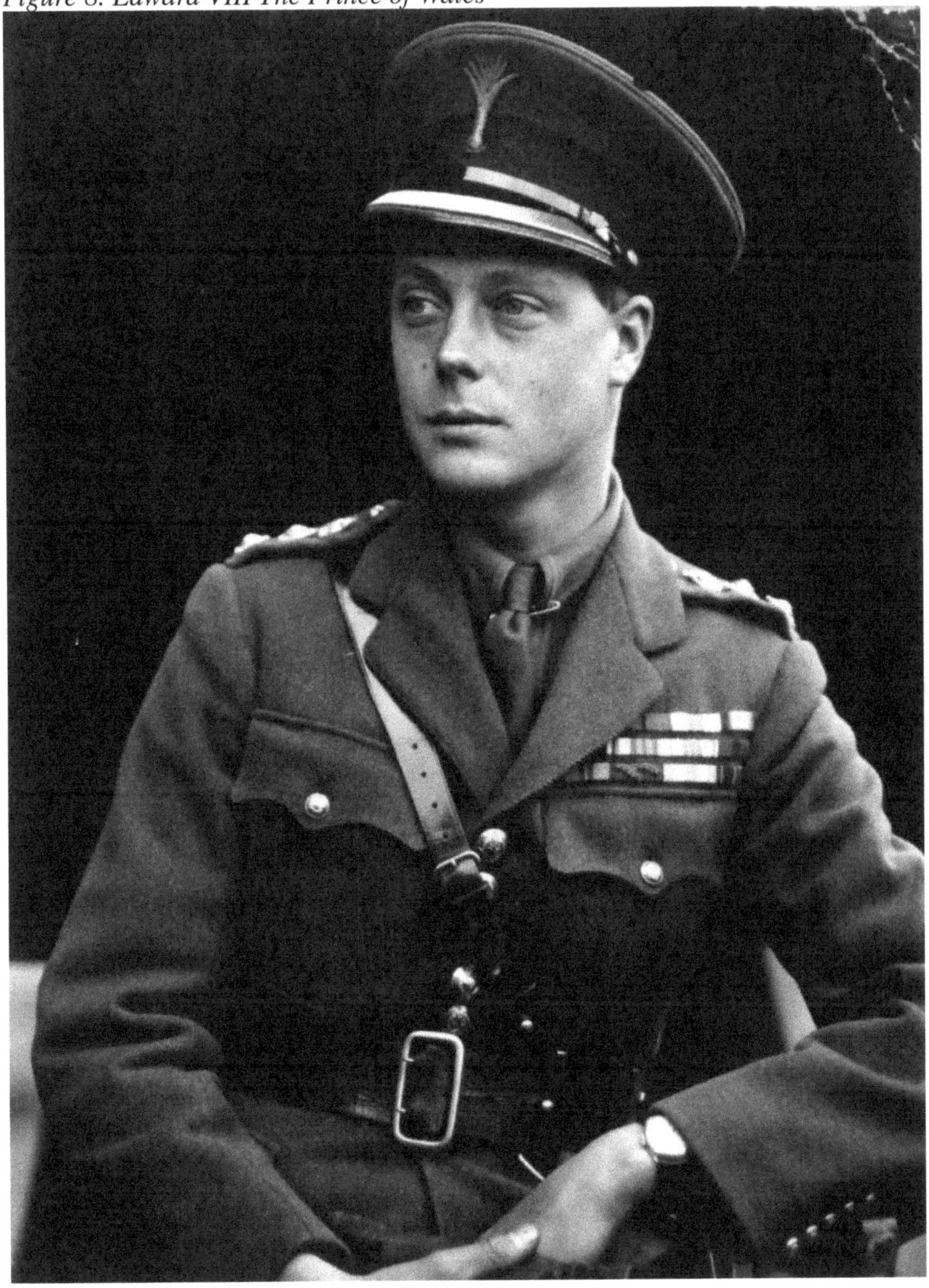

After a reign lasting less than eleven months, Edward relinquished the throne and, in defiance of royal conventions and mounting pressure, married Wallis Simpson. On

September 4, 1936, the couple was received by Mustafa Kemal Atatürk at Dolmabahçe Palace in Istanbul—an event emblematic of the international visibility of their controversial relationship (Şapolyo, 2025). Though their romance left a lasting mark on the cultural memory of the twentieth century, Edward was effectively ostracized by the royal family and forced to build a new life outside of Britain. (Figure: 09) In one symbolic instance, he had once posed alongside the Queen and the Canadian Prime Minister for the press, but following his abdication, his image was retouched and removed from the widely circulated photograph, illustrating the monarchy's desire to excise him from public representation (Restorapic, 2025).

Figure 9. Canadian Prime Minister, Queen and Edward VIII (before and after)

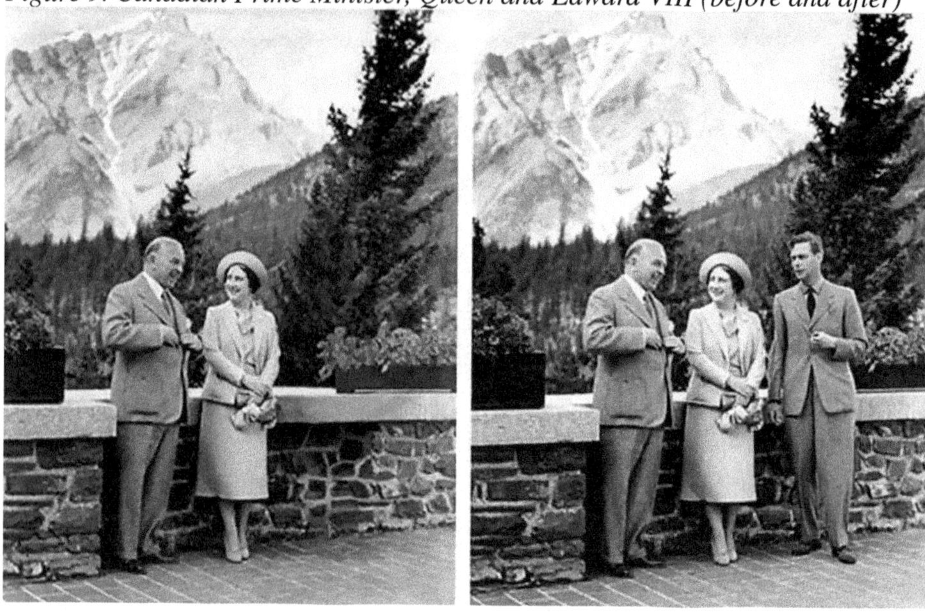

Despite the passage of nearly a century, this legendary love story continues to fascinate. (Figure: 10) It has been the subject of numerous books, films, and documentaries—including one directed by Madonna—which reinterpret the narrative of passion, scandal, and political disruption (W.E., 2025). Frequently featured on magazine covers and in photo-reportages by the major media outlets of their time, Edward and Wallis were captured in a variety of visual styles by many prominent photographers. Among the most celebrated were Henri Cartier-Bresson, Philippe Halsman, and Richard Avedon, each of whom contributed to the visual mythology surrounding this controversial and romanticized couple.

Figure 10. 2011 movie "W.E." directed by Madonna

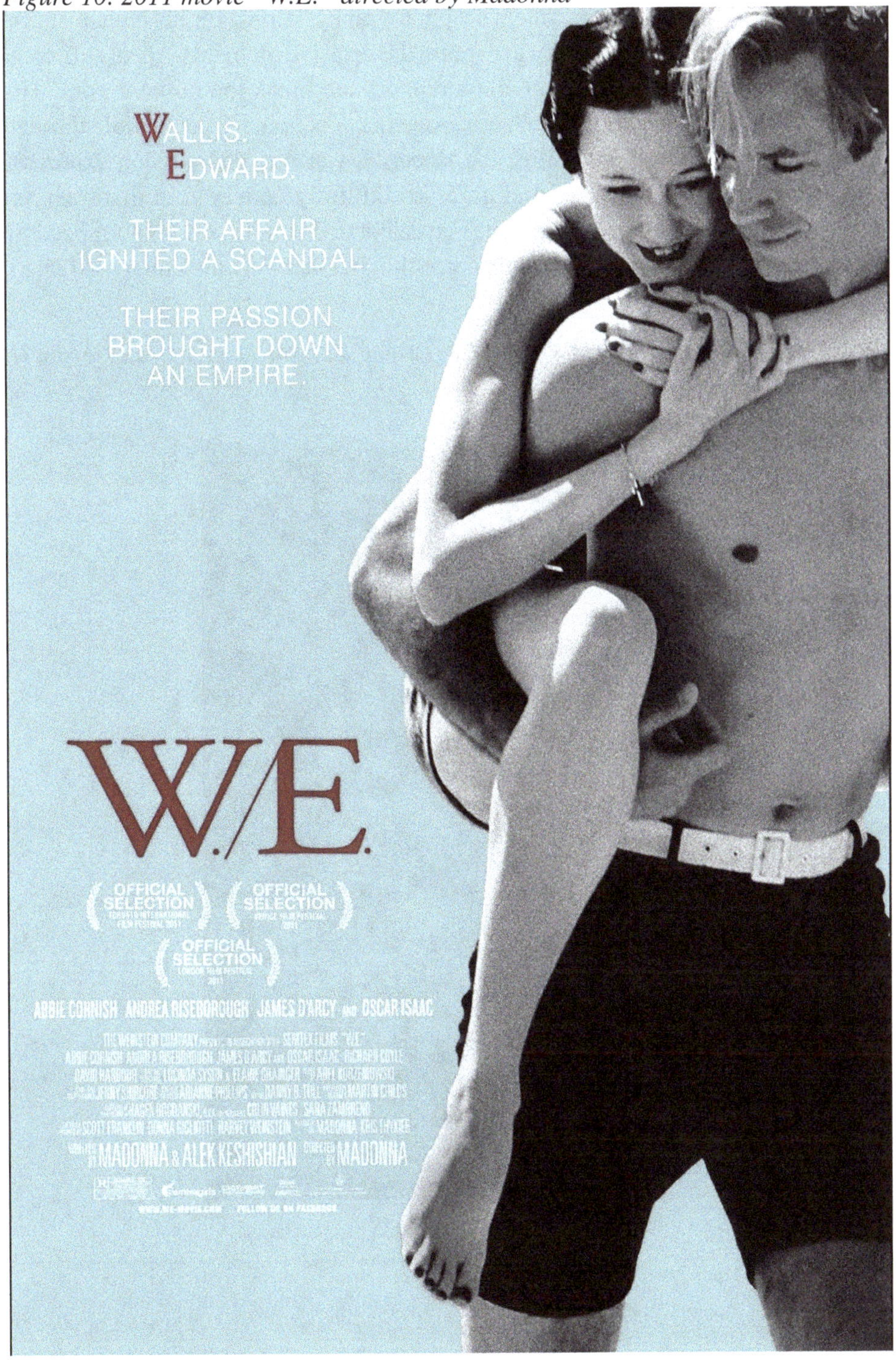

It is immediately evident in the photograph that Henri Cartier-Bresson—the legendary master of direct documentary photography, known for his humanist perspective and extraordinary ability to capture the decisive moment—spent sufficient time with Edward and Wallis to build a rapport and break the initial tension. His success in earning their trust within the space they occupied is perceptible through the lens. (Figure: 11) Beyond this, the sincerity, warmth, and passion expressed in Edward's facial expressions and gaze are skillfully conveyed in this brief yet magical moment captured by Bresson. The celebrated couple was immortalized by the photographer's distinctive visual approach (National Portrait Gallery, 2025, a).

Figure 11. Wallis Duchess of Windsor & Prince Edward Duke of Windsor by H. C. Bresson

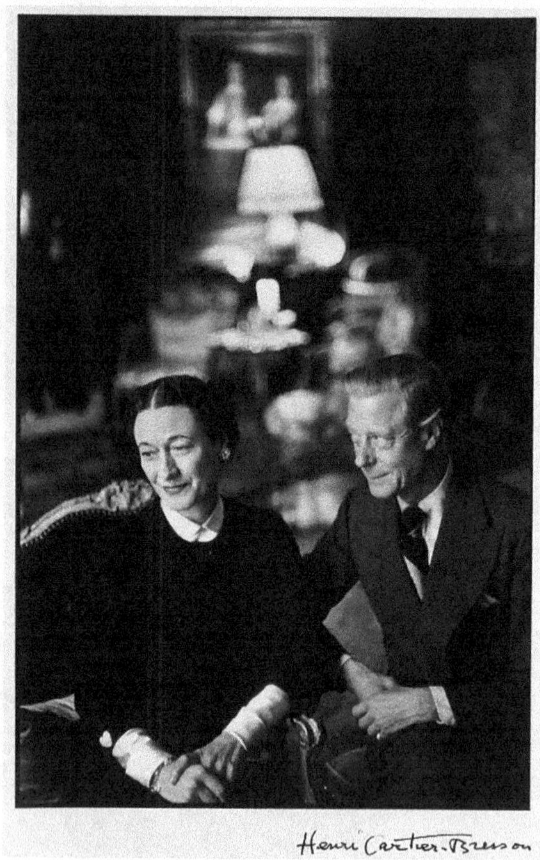

Outside of portraiture, the French artist consistently remained faithful to reality, never compromising its integrity. When photographing cities or landscapes, Bresson was known for his preference for a 50mm lens. This optical discipline, which he maintained throughout his career, earned him a special place in the photographic community. As is widely recognized, the 50mm lens is categorized as a "standard focal length" in 35mm format photography and, though not always the easiest or most pleasurable to work with, remains a valuable tool for producing imagery that closely replicates the proportions perceived by the human eye. Thanks to Bresson's modest style and principled artistic stance, one can imagine that standing in a Parisian street once framed by his lens, the visual proportions—foreground and background architecture—would closely resemble those in his photographs. For this reason, his unwavering commitment to unaltered reality and his uniquely honest and humanist approach secure Henri Cartier-Bresson an unparalleled position in the history of photography.

In May 2016, I had the opportunity to visit a comprehensive exhibition of the renowned American portrait photographer Philippe Halsman at Kunsthal Rotterdam. Over the course of his career, Halsman produced 101 covers for *LIFE* Magazine, working with a remarkable array of celebrities and cultural icons (Life, 2025). He became a major source of inspiration for the generations of visual artists that followed. (Figure: 12) (Figure: 13) (Figure: 14) Particularly notable was Halsman's distinctive, unconventional method developed specifically for studio shoots: a personal technique designed to rapidly break the ice when meeting famous figures for the first time. This approach eventually became his signature and earned him a singular place among portrait photographers.

Figure 12. Philippe Halsman's Exhibition at Kunsthal Rotterdam May 11st 2016 by © Ozan Bilgiseren

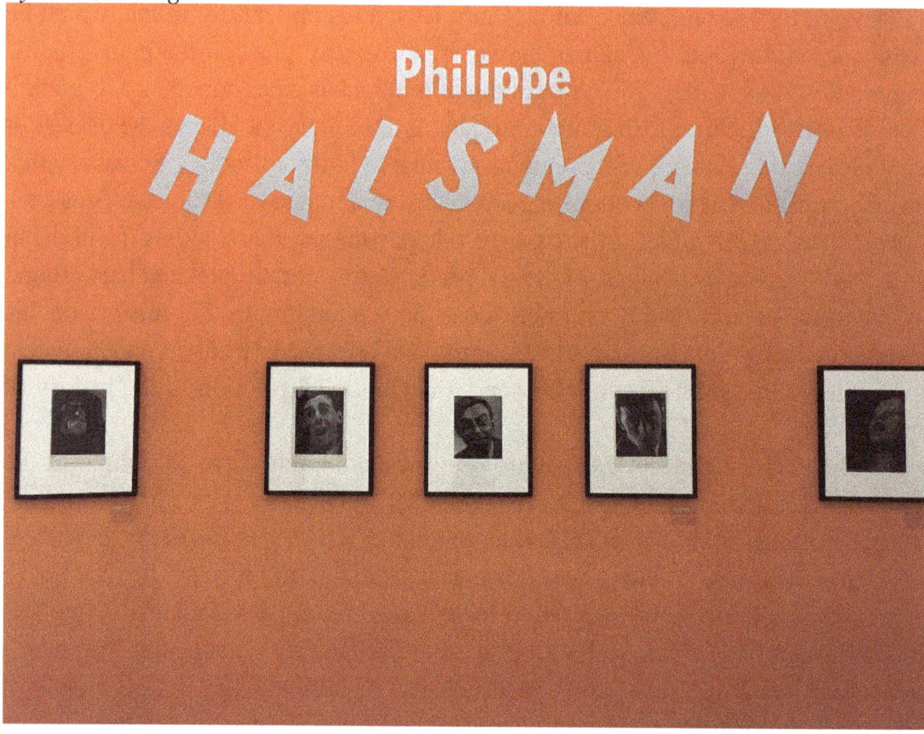

Figure 13. Philippe Halsman's small prints of various portraits at the exhibition - © Ozan Bilgiseren

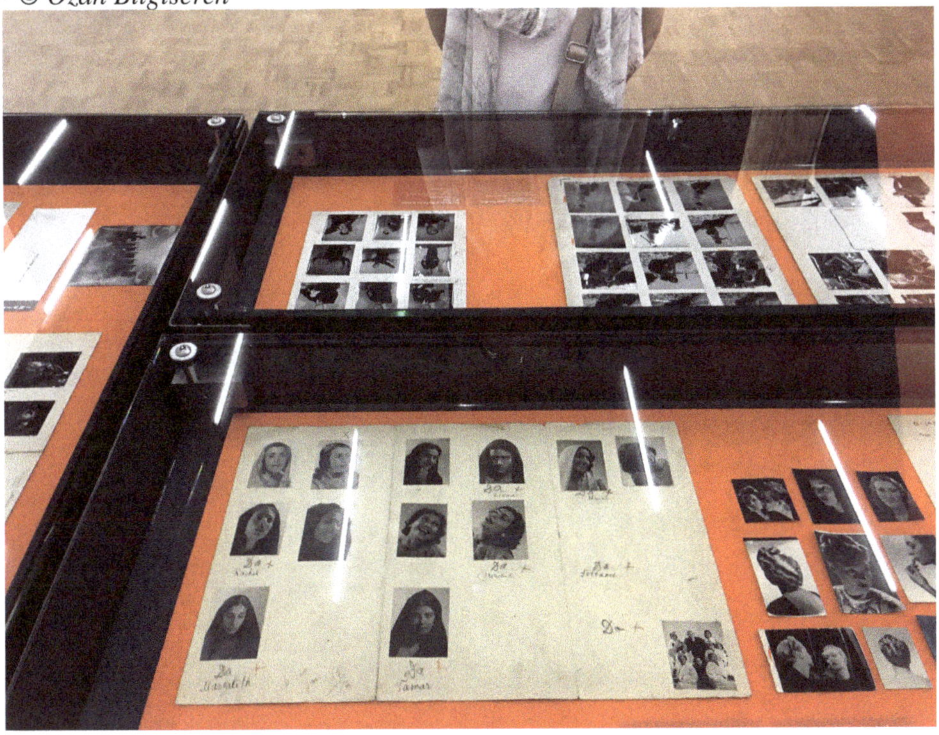

Figure 14. Halsman produced 101 covers for LIFE Magazine - © Ozan Bilgiseren

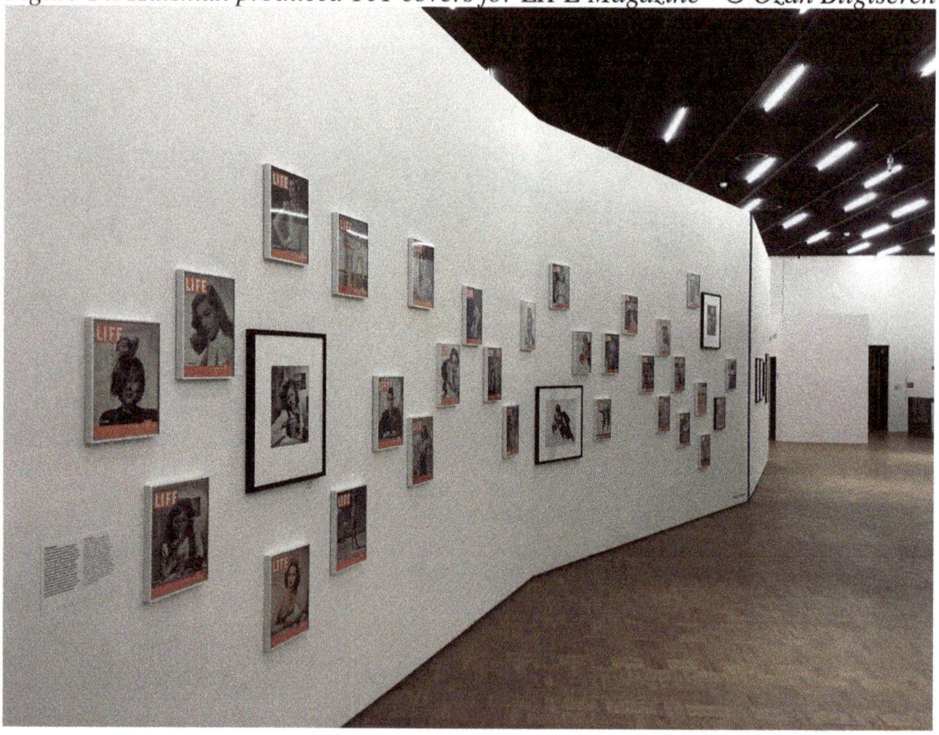

The series titled *Jumpology*, invented by Philippe Halsman, was directly related to his goal of building instant rapport and authentic interaction with celebrities. This playful photographic technique invited famous individuals—including Marilyn Monroe and Princess Grace Kelly of Monaco—to leap repeatedly into the air in front of a neutral backdrop in Halsman's studio (Adams, 2025). The resulting images were strikingly unconventional, as no individual could leap in exactly the same way. Just like a handwritten signature, each subject revealed a unique and deeply personal style of jumping, exposing something intimate and unguarded within themselves (Magnumphotos, 2025).

It is also Halsman who created the unforgettable image known as *Dali Atomicus*, which remains emblematic of surrealist photography (Moma, 2025). Unsurprisingly, Halsman also turned his lens on Edward VIII and the Duchess of Windsor, incorporating them into his imaginative photographic visions. In a particularly memorable portrait taken at their private residence, the couple is seen barefoot, holding hands, and mid-air in a joyful leap. Captured from ground level, the photograph exudes intimacy, spontaneity, and warmth—suggesting a deliberate effort to portray them in a playful and humanizing light, far removed from the constraints of royal formality. (Figure: 15)

Figure 15. Wallis Duchess of Windsor & Prince Edward Duke of Windsor by Hallsman

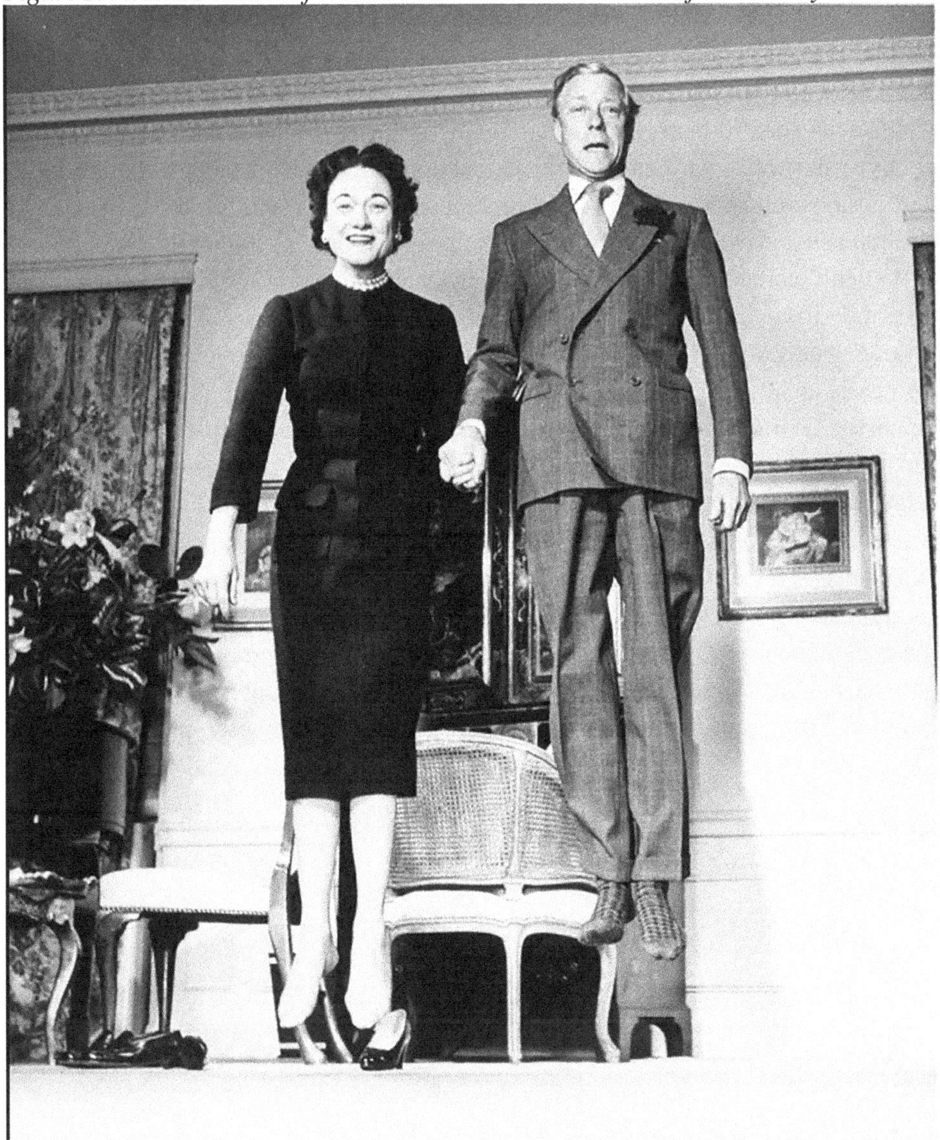

Turning to Richard Avedon, one of the world's most influential fashion and portrait photographers, we find a radically different yet equally impactful artistic trajectory. Avedon's professional ascent began in the realm of commercial and advertising photography, from which he transitioned into the fine arts—an uncommon reverse path that he pursued relentlessly over five decades. His photographic legacy includes not only iconic portraits of actors, presidents, political leaders, athletes, and artists, but also an extensive body of work driven by his fascination with the human face. This interest led him to capture thousands of individuals across a wide social spectrum, ranging from napalm-scarred victims of the Vietnam War to anonymous rural Americans (Pinault Collection, 2025). Using large-format cameras and on-location shoots, Avedon documented these lives with profound simplicity and intensity, affirming his position as a master chronicler of human expression.

When it came to Edward and Wallis, Richard Avedon's approach differed significantly from that of other photographers. In his recollections, Avedon shared the following anecdote: Known for their fondness for dogs, the couple was kept waiting for nearly an hour due to Avedon's delayed arrival. As he set up his equipment and began the session, he offered a fabricated excuse—that he had witnessed a dog being run over on the way, which had delayed him. (Figure: 16) At the precise moment he relayed this story, he pressed the shutter (National Portrait Gallery, 2025, b). The story was entirely fictional. At that time, Avedon harbored a particular perception—perhaps even a bias—regarding the couple. He believed that Edward VIII, despite being the figurehead of what he termed the "Club of Losers," always wore a performative mask of happiness. For Avedon, the emergence of genuine emotion once that mask slipped was an artistic imperative. In this context, introducing a minor deception or emotional provocation during the shoot was, in his view, wholly justified.

Figure 16. Wallis Duchess of Windsor & Prince Edward Duke of Windsor by Avedon

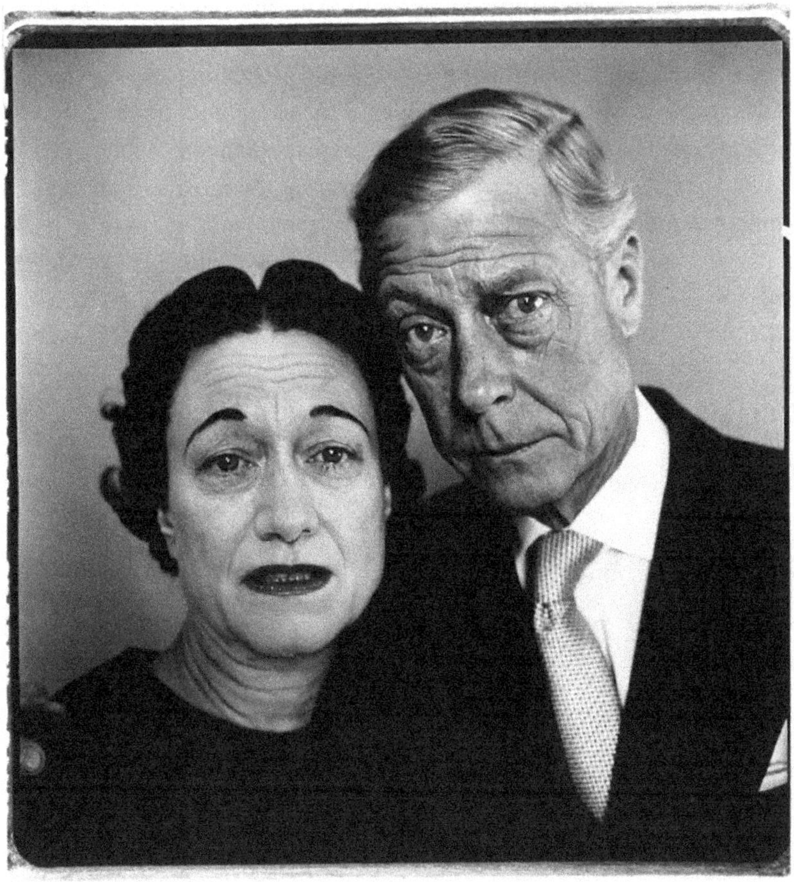

In fact, every photographer seeks to perceive truth through their own subjective lens—through the personalities they photograph and the stylistic approaches they have refined over many years. While these approaches may diverge dramatically, each aims to render "truth" in a way that aligns with the photographer's vision and artistic integrity. One might then ask, "Which truth?" Upon reflection, it is reasonable to accept all three perspectives—Bresson's, Halsman's, and Avedon's—as legitimate interpretations of truth, each filtered through a distinct philosophical and aesthetic lens.

Returning to the pivotal year of 1936—when Edward ascended and abdicated the throne—we find another iconic moment in photographic history. On March 6 of that year, Dorothea Lange, working for the Farm Security Administration (FSA), which had been established to document rural poverty during the Great Depression, was conducting a field assignment in Nipomo, California. While visiting a migrant workers' camp, she encountered a woman with five children and, within ten minutes, captured seven frames using her 4x5 Graflex camera. The woman, Florence Owens Thompson (1903–1983), was thirty-two years old at the time and the mother of seven. (Figure: 17) She was temporarily living in the camp with her children while her husband and two sons were in town seeking spare parts to repair their car. One of the images from that session would later become one of the most iconic photographs of the twentieth century and a defining portrait of the Great Depression. Now widely known as *Migrant Mother*, the image was eventually dubbed the "Mona Lisa of the 1930s" by the Library of Congress and continues to symbolize resilience amid hardship (Mccormack, 2025).

Figure 17. Retouched print of Migrant Mother

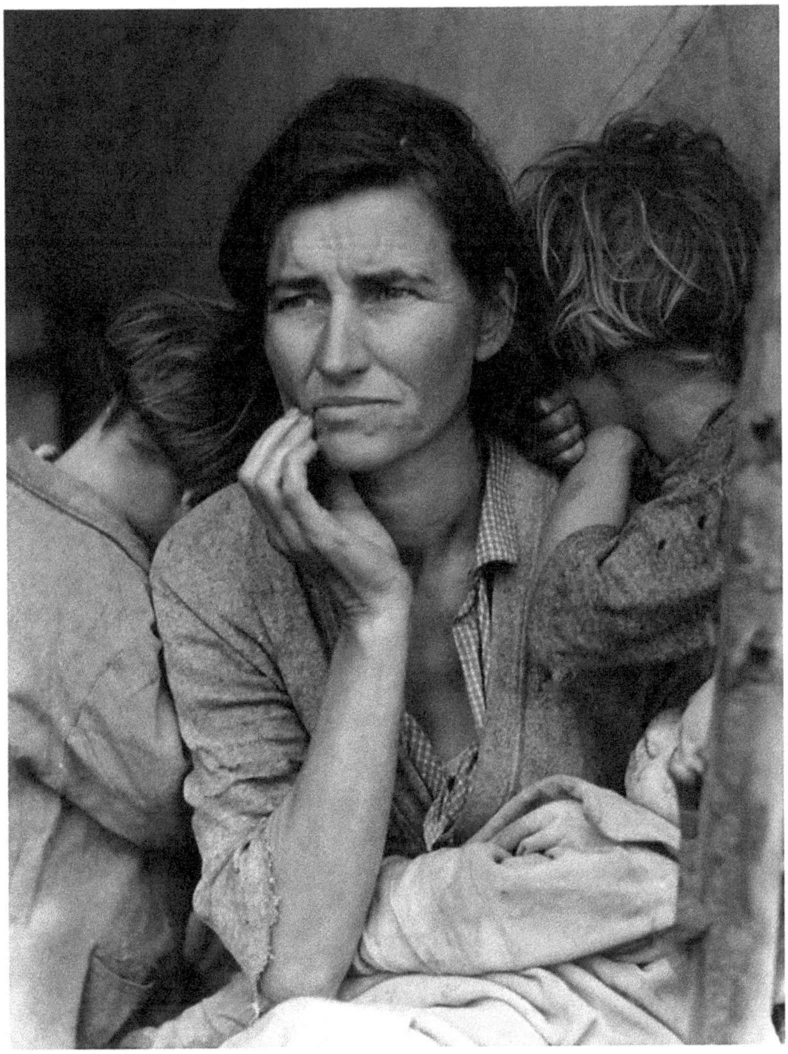

In the late 1960s, the original *Migrant Mother* photograph and thirty-one of Lange's untouched prints were discovered in a trash bin at the San Jose Chamber of Commerce by a man named Bill Hendrie. (Figure: 18) However, it took years before the photographs were brought to public attention (Sothebys, 2025). Following Hendrie's death, the images were rediscovered—this time hidden inside a sofa cabinet during the clearing of his home—and were eventually made public once again by his daughter in the early 2000s.

Figure 18. Original print of Migrant Mother

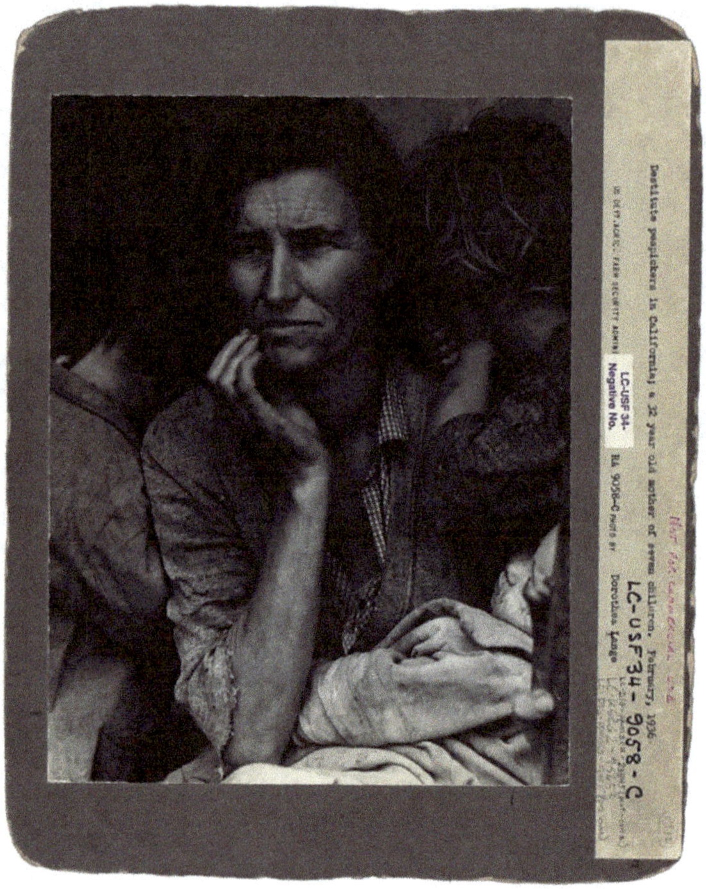

The most conspicuous detail observed in the original print is the woman's right thumb, visible in the lower-right corner of the frame. Considered a distracting element by Dorothea Lange, the thumb was removed through darkroom manipulation. Roy Stryker, Lange's supervisor at the FSA—and himself a respected documentary photographer—was deeply displeased with this intervention. Although such retouching was not entirely uncommon in that era, Stryker believed even this minor alteration compromised the authenticity of the image and, more broadly, jeopardized the integrity of the FSA's extensive documentary projects (Zhang, 2025). As a result, this seemingly insignificant modification was viewed by Stryker as a direct violation of documentary truth under the agency's working principles, and it became a point of considerable contention between the two. (Figure: 19)

Figure 19. Migrant Mother's vesions side by side

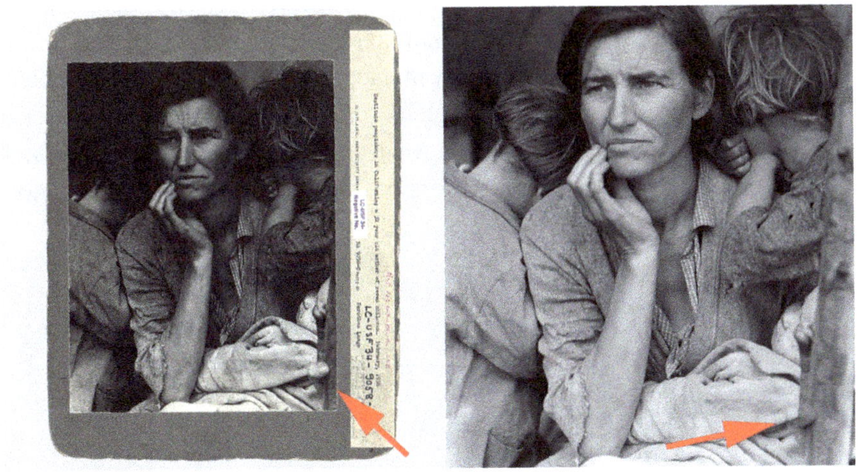

Despite the controversy, the retouched version of *Migrant Mother* is the one that entered the collective memory of the public. In 1998, this altered version was featured on a 32-cent U.S. postage stamp. In the same month, a print bearing Lange's handwritten notes, signature, and annotations was sold at Sotheby's New York for $244,500. Later, in November 2002, another print from Lange's personal archive of *Migrant Mother* was auctioned at Christie's New York for $141,500 (Campany, 2025).

For many years, the identity of the mother in the photograph remained unknown. It was not until more than four decades after the image was taken—in 1978—that the truth began to surface, following a tip received by a local newspaper reporter. In a subsequent interview, the woman, Florence Owens Thompson, stated: "I wish she hadn't taken my picture. I can't get a penny out of it. [Lange] didn't ask my name. She said she wouldn't sell the pictures. She said she'd send me a copy. She never did" (National Gallery of Art, 2025, c).

As the photographic work had been financed by the Resettlement Administration and funded through the federal government, the images were classified as public domain, which meant that photographers such as Lange could not claim copyright or receive royalties. (Figure: 20) Nonetheless, the image significantly elevated Lange's reputation, contributed to her being awarded the prestigious Guggenheim Fellowship in 1941, and served as a key visual inspiration for John Steinbeck's 1939 novel *The Grapes of Wrath* (Gottschalk, 2025). Despite the personal grievances expressed by Thompson, *Migrant Mother* gained immense cultural traction due to its widespread reproduction and circulation across the United States. The photograph came to serve as a powerful symbol of endurance and resilience, evoking emotional responses in ways that words alone could not. It was instrumental in galvanizing public empathy and solidarity during the hardships of the Great Depression, offering a visual representation of maternal strength and national perseverance. Over time, *Migrant Mother* became more than a documentary image; it was canonized as an emblem of collective suffering and fortitude. Through its symbolic weight and evocative composition, the photograph etched itself into American cultural memory as a definitive portrayal of what it means to endure adversity—and what it means to be a mother.

Figure 20. The movie poster "The Grapes of Wrath" (1940)

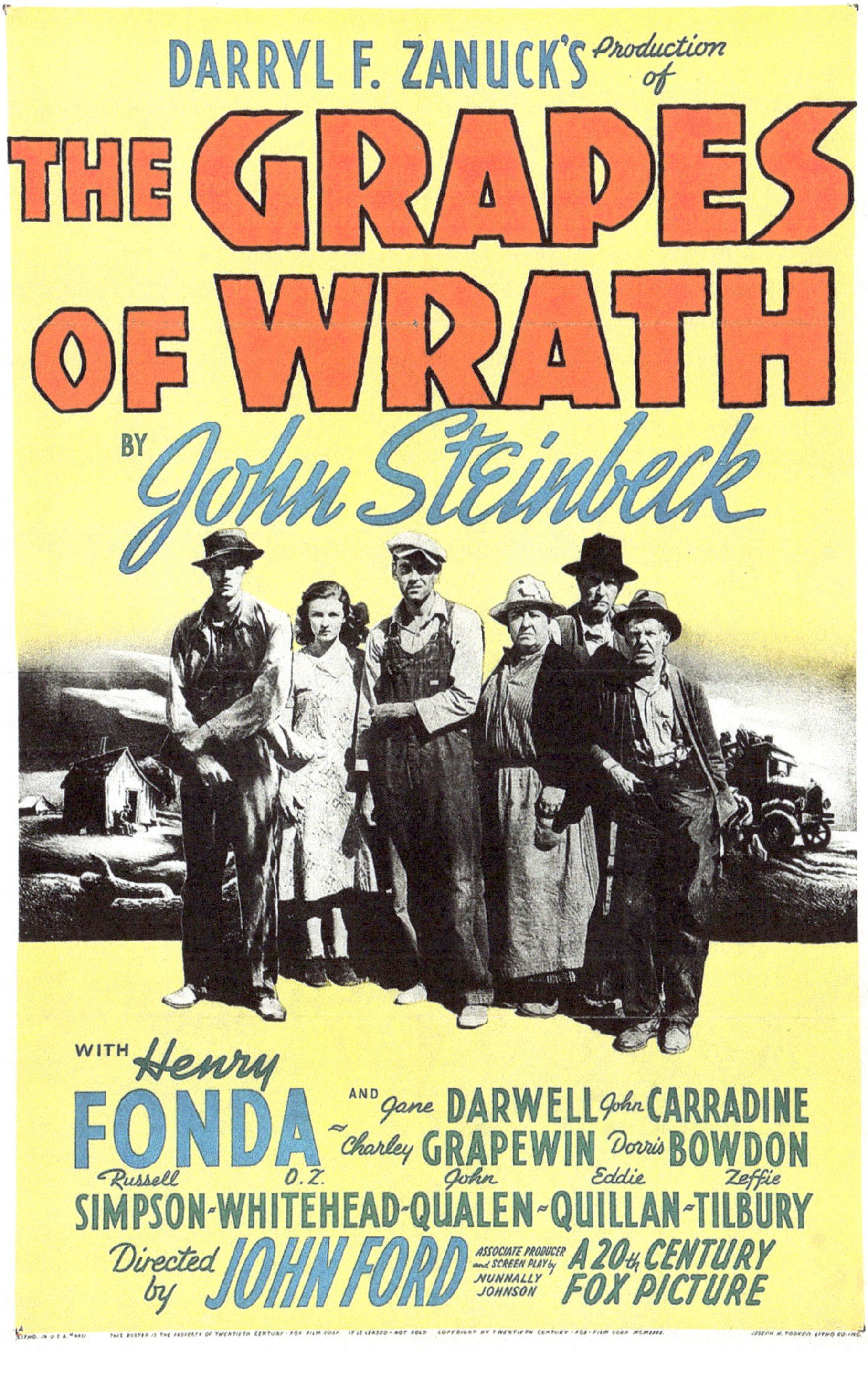

TRUTHS, FALSEHOODS, AND REALITIES

Another iconic photograph that entered the history of global press imagery in the year 1936 is *The Death of a Loyalist Soldier*—also known simply as *Falling Soldier*—a black-and-white image attributed to Robert Capa and captured on Saturday, September 5. The photo was first published in the French news magazine *Vu* on September 23, 1936, and later appeared in the United States in *Life* magazine on July 12, 1937. (Figure: 21) In a 1947 radio interview, Capa provided the following account of how the photograph was taken: "I was there in the trench with about twenty *milicianos* ... I just kind of put my camera above my head and even didn't look and clicked the picture, when they moved over the trench. And that was all. ... That camera which I hold above my head just caught a man at the moment when he was shot. That was probably the best picture I ever took. I never saw the picture in the frame because the camera was far above my head" (BBC, 2025).

Figure 21. "Falling Soldier" by Robert Capa

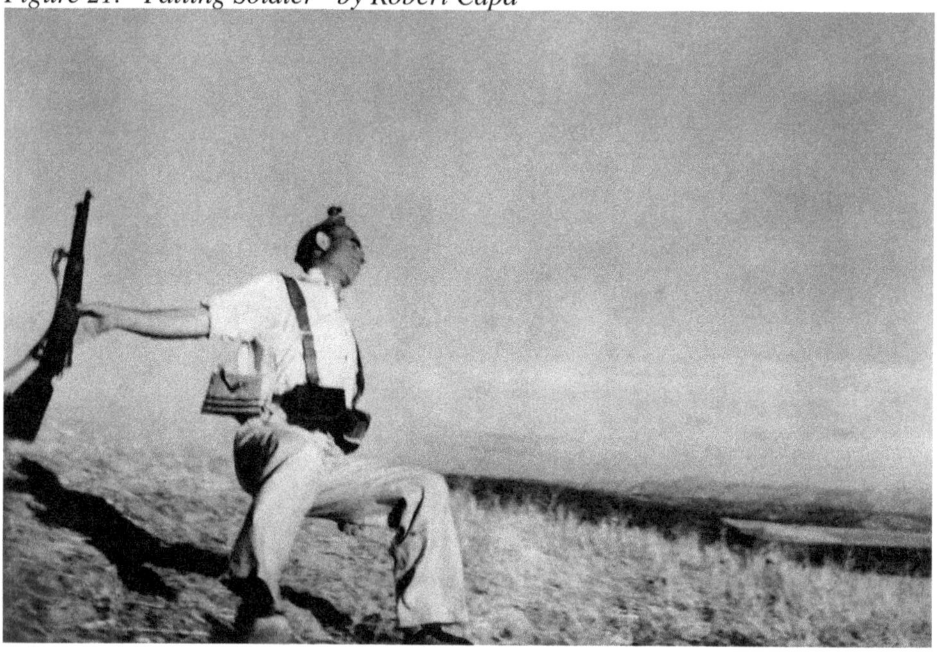

Universally regarded as one of the most powerful war photographs ever taken, the image has also been the subject of enduring controversy regarding its authenticity. Numerous allegations over the years have claimed that the scene was staged by Capa himself. Decades of debate about the precise location of the photograph's capture began to shift in 2007, when the long-lost "Mexican Suitcase"—a collection of Capa's negatives—surfaced at the International Center of Photography in New York (Friswell, 2025). This suitcase, which had been transported to Mexico at the end of the Spanish Civil War, contained hundreds of Capa's original negatives and offered new insights into his work from that period.

Unfortunately, among the contents of the suitcase, the specific negative depicting the alleged moment of death of anarchist militiaman Federico Borrell García (1912–1936) from the Libertarian Youth (FIJL) during the Battle of Cerro Muriano was not found. However, alternative frames from the same session provided enough visual evidence to confirm that the photograph had been taken near the village of Espejo in the province of Córdoba. Despite this partial validation, numerous speculative debates regarding the photo's authenticity and context persist to this day (PBS, 2025).

Following his documentation of the Spanish Civil War, Robert Capa continued to produce extraordinary and seemingly impossible images until his untimely death in Vietnam in 1954 at the age of forty. Beyond his renowned coverage of the D-Day landings during the Second World War—arguably the most perilous military front—Capa also documented the Second Sino-Japanese War, the 1948 Arab-Israeli War, and the First Indochina War. Furthermore, he was among the founding members of Magnum Photos, which would become one of the most prestigious photographic agencies in the world.

In post-World War II Europe—a continent devastated by destruction and economic collapse—revitalizing urban economies and rebuilding key capital cities required fast-generating revenue sources, particularly from tourism. In this context, countries like France and Italy turned to photography, media, and promotional campaigns to rejuvenate public interest and international travel. By the early 1950s, images of the Eiffel Tower, Parisian streets, and sidewalk cafés began to feature prominently in the fashion pages of major global magazines, particularly those published by Condé Nast. The goal was to rebrand these cities as romantic, desirable destinations that could draw tourists and their spending power.

The term "Paris Syndrome," now widely recognized in psychological and cultural studies, describes the profound disillusionment experienced by many tourists—especially those from East Asia—upon confronting the everyday realities of the city, which often diverge sharply from the idealized imagery presented in media and film (Paris syndrome, 2025). This disparity can be traced back to the romanticized representations of Paris that emerged during the 1950s. Among these, one of the most famous and controversial photographs in the history of photography is *Le Baiser de l'Hôtel de Ville* (*The Kiss by the Hôtel de Ville*), captured by Robert Doisneau for *Life* magazine in the spring of 1950. Published on June 12, 1950, as part of a photo essay depicting love in Paris in the springtime, the image became emblematic of romantic Paris. (Figure: 22) However, as revealed by Doisneau's daughter and curator Francine Deroudille in a later interview, the photograph was staged. She explained, "My father's agent submitted a series on 'lovers in Paris' to American publications, and *Life* commissioned the work accordingly," thereby acknowledging the constructed nature of the scene.

Figure 22. "The Kiss by the Hotel de Ville" Robert Doisneau

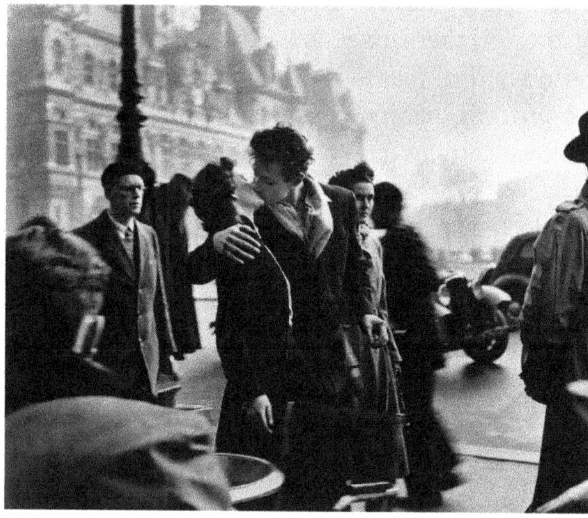

The Kiss by the Hôtel de Ville by Robert Doisneau

To avoid legal complications, Robert Doisneau often chose to work with friends or young models from his close circle in certain photojournalistic or editorial assignments. On an afternoon in March 1950, Doisneau ventured into the streets of Paris with two young models he knew, allowing them to interact naturally and without instruction. The couple strolled hand in hand, flirted, conversed, and kissed while Doisneau followed discreetly, photographing them with his Rolleiflex camera from close range, capturing the scenes with a seemingly candid spontaneity.

The now-iconic image of a tousled-haired young man kissing a slender girl on the lips was captured at the corner of Rue du Renard and Rue de Rivoli, just across from the Hôtel de Ville. For a long time, the identities of the couple remained unknown to the general public, who believed the moment to be spontaneous. An additional element contributing to the photograph's narrative depth is the gaze of the woman in the background, whose expression adds a layer of observational complexity. While the anonymous crowd moves uniformly in the same direction, the lovers appear momentarily frozen in time, immobile within the frame. A man seated at a table in the bottom-left corner allows viewers to project themselves into the scene as though they were café patrons witnessing the event in real time, thereby enhancing the sense of immediacy and immersion. In this almost cinematic tableau, the young couple positioned at the center of the composition seems curiously unnoticed by the surrounding Parisians and passing cars.

The photograph remained largely unnoticed in archives until the early 1980s, when it was rediscovered by a perceptive advertising executive working at the Rapho agency. Eventually, in the mid-1980s, Robert Doisneau granted permission for the image to be reproduced in various poster and postcard formats. As a result, the photograph became one of the most recognizable images of Paris and a global symbol of Parisian romance. Within five years, it had sold 410,000 copies, marking an extraordinary commercial achievement. By 1986, the poster had become a best-seller, adorning the walls and bedrooms of young people around the World (Henley, 2025, a).

The "young woman" in the photograph was Françoise Bornet, a former actress who passed away at the age of 93 during Christmas 2023, and whose identity remained unknown until the 1990s. At the time the photograph was taken, she and her then-real-life boyfriend Jacques Carteaud were both drama students enrolled at the Cours Simon acting school. For their participation in the shoot, they received a modest fee of approximately 500 francs. However, following the photograph's commercial success after 1986, other individuals emerged, seeking recognition and compensation. In 1992, a couple named Jean and Denise Lavergne claimed in *L'Express* magazine that they were the actual subjects in *The Kiss* and intended to pursue legal action for unauthorized use of their likenesses. Consequently, Bornet—who had posed for the image—and the Lavergnes, who asserted that they had, both filed lawsuits against Robert Doisneau and eventually against one another, each asserting their identity as the woman in the photograph and claiming a share in its substantial global revenues (Howard, 2025).

Until that point, the image had been widely celebrated as one of the most distinguished examples of candid street photography—an extraordinary moment captured spontaneously within the natural flow of everyday life. However, faced with mounting legal pressure, Doisneau was compelled to disclose that the photograph had in fact been staged. Having previously seen the young couple passionately kissing at a café, he had approached them and requested they pose for a recreation of the moment. For reasons unknown, no one had publicly questioned the image's authenticity prior to this revelation. According to Francine Deroudille, Doisneau's daughter and curator, this public disclosure "ruined the final years of my father's life."

The strongest piece of evidence submitted by Bornet to the court in support of her claim—that she was indeed the woman in the photograph—was an original, numbered, stamped, and signed print that Doisneau himself had gifted her after the shoot. In 1993, the Paris High Court successively dismissed the lawsuits filed by the individuals asserting authorship claims over the photograph and seeking royalties. No additional compensation was granted to any party for modeling in the image.

Robert Doisneau once reflected on his photographs with the following remark: "As in cabaret performances, I presented little 'Paris' scenes; Paris will always be Paris. It may sound cliché, but at the time it sold well. The photograph of the lovers at the Hôtel de Ville was part of a series I had worked on for a week, and I needed two or three images like that to complete it. But I don't find them disturbing. In essence, nothing is more subjective than objectivity—we do not show the world as it is. The world I tried to show was one in which I would feel comfortable, where people would be kind, where I could find the tenderness I longed to see. My photographs were, in a sense, proof that such a world could exist."

Bornet and her former boyfriend remained together as a couple for only eight or nine months, parting ways shortly after the photograph was taken. Although the image would go on to become one of the most recognized photographs in the world, immortalizing them as lovers bound forever, the two maintained no contact afterward—except for a brief phone call decades later. Bornet continued her career in cinema, advertising, and voice acting, and eventually retired in the South of France.

On April 25, 2005, Françoise Bornet—who never received any royalties from the photograph—placed the original signed silver gelatin print of *The Kiss*, gifted to her by Doisneau shortly after the shoot, up for public auction at the Hôtel de Ville. Her intent was to finance a documentary film production company and support emerging filmmakers. In an interview at the time, she stated: "I now believe this is a photograph that should never have existed, which is why I am letting it go." She then added, with a note of melancholy, "The photograph was staged, but the kiss was real" (Henley, 2025, b).

The photograph was sold at auction for a record-breaking sum of €155,000. Robert Doisneau passed away in 1994, and Françoise Bornet's former partner, Jacques Carteaud, died in 2006. When Françoise Bornet passed away on Christmas Day, December 25, 2023, she left behind a kiss that would endure forever (McIntosh and Schofield, 2025).

"People like my photos because they see in them what they would see if they stopped rushing about, and took the time to enjoy the city." – Robert Doisneau (Kaninsky, 2025).

IN PURSUIT OF LIGHT

Although not a photograph of a kiss, one of the intimate moments in which a man and a woman draw close to one another was captured through the lens of the late Prof. Sabit Kalfagil (1934–2017), a master photographer, academic, and one of the leading figures in Turkish documentary photography. (Figure: 23) Trained originally as an architect, Kalfagil began photographing at the age of twenty-six as a personal hobby. Through his travels across various regions of Anatolia, he introduced Anatolian culture and its people to the world. The photographs he took during these journeys graced the covers of numerous magazines, were used in promotional materials by the Ministry of Culture and Tourism, published in both national and international outlets, exhibited in group and solo shows, and were awarded in competitions.

Figure 23. "Couple" at Samatya circa 1970's by Sabit Kalfagil

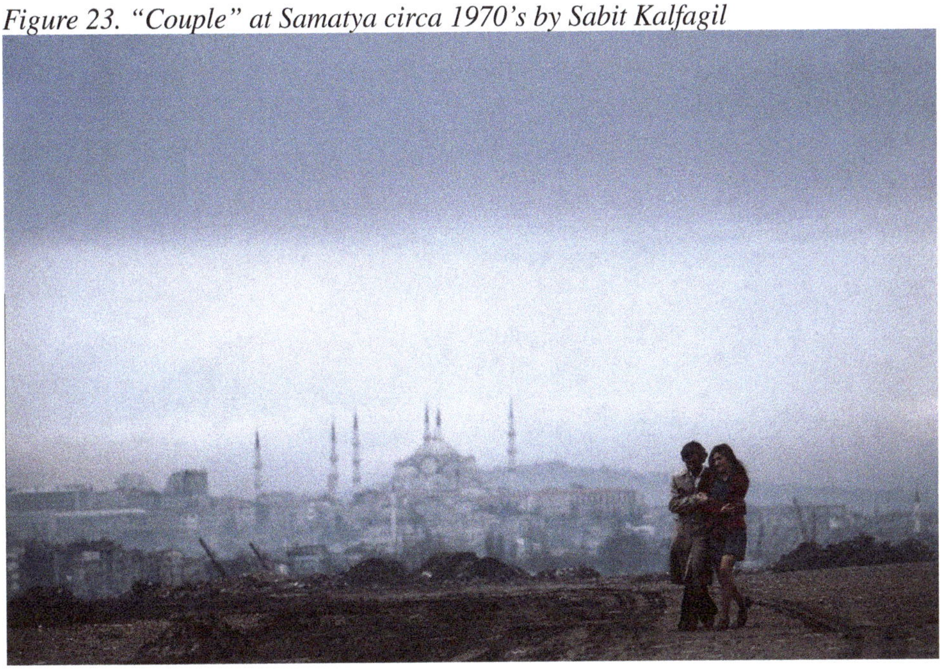

Beyond his artistic contributions, Prof. Sabit Kalfagil played a pivotal role in the institutionalization of photographic education in Turkey. From the late 1970s onward, he significantly contributed to the establishment and academic structuring of the country's first photography department at the Faculty of Fine Arts, Mimar Sinan University. In 1978, he was among the founding members of the Photography Institute at the State Academy of Fine Arts. Similarly, toward the end of the 1990s, he assumed major responsibilities in the foundation of the photography department at the Faculty of Fine Arts, Marmara University.

Opening his first solo exhibitions in 1972 and 1988, Kalfagil served as a distinguished jury member in numerous national photography competitions. In conferences and symposia, he frequently shared his personal insights on documentary photography, particularly emphasizing the effective use of natural daylight in photographic practice. Long before GPS devices and smartphones became widespread, determining the path of the sun in an unfamiliar city or ancient ruin required significant expertise or advance preparation. Anticipating the sun's trajectory at any given date became a matter of both intellectual and practical concern for Kalfagil. In response, he hand-designed a series of transparent, pocket-sized solar diagrams specifically calibrated to Turkey's geographical coordinates. (Figure: 24) On days with favorable atmospheric conditions, photographers could use these tools—combined with a map indicating true north—to accurately predict the sun's path throughout the day. The process simply involved selecting the appropriate seasonal diagram, aligning it over a map on the intended photographic subject, and using the notches and time markers etched into the tool to follow the sun's course from its first to its last visible position (Simurgkitabevi, 2025).

Figure 24. Pocket-sized solar diagrams designed by Prof. Sabit Kalfagil - © Ozan Bilgiseren

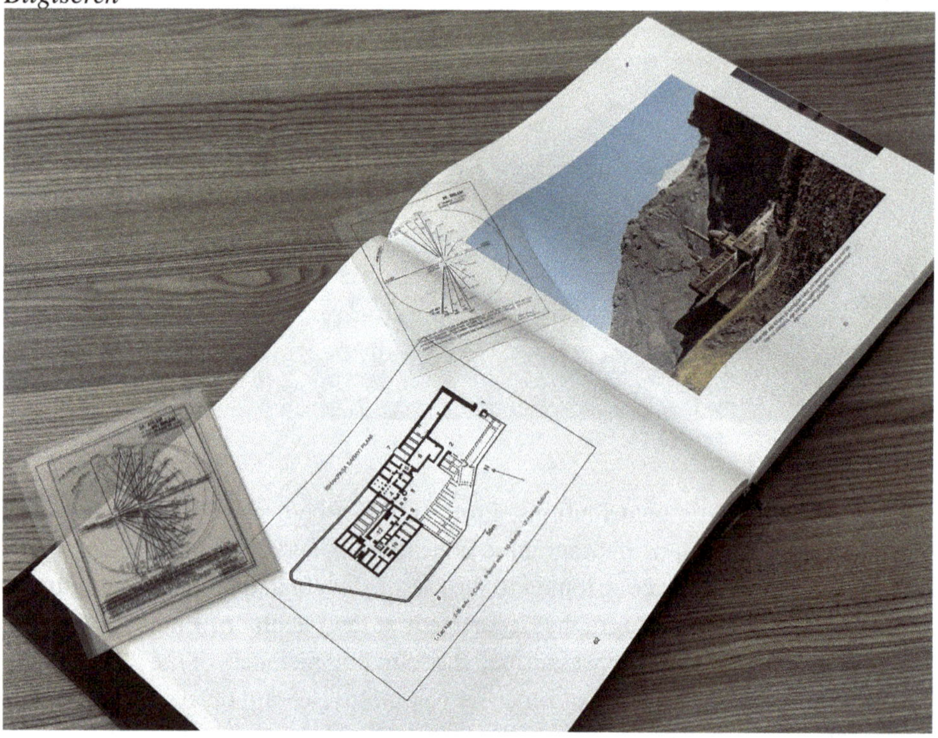

For instance, imagine a photography excursion planned for mid-November—outside the peak tourist season—to the ancient city of Ephesus, where the goal is to photograph the historical Library of Celsus. In such a photographic assignment, knowing in advance the path that light would take across the monumental structure at specific hours of the day would naturally enhance the efficiency and productivity of the travel itinerary. (Figure: 25) After many years of working with slide film, which demanded considerable exposure precision, Kalfagil eventually transitioned—like many of his contemporaries—to digital photography due to its practical advantages. He rephotographed many of the locations he had previously captured on slide film, thus creating a rich and extensive photographic archive. His work was not confined to tourism catalogs, posters, and exhibitions; it also appeared in magazine *"Fotoğraf Dergisi"*, to which he regularly contributed articles, as well as in his authored and edited boks (Fotografdergisi, 2025). In his 1981 publication *Composition in the Art of Photography*, he presented the geometric proportions and structural principles underlying his successful compositions. In subsequent books and magazine contributions, he also shared comparative analyses between his successful and unsuccessful frames, striving to instill a clear understanding of fundamental photographic principles in his readers.

Figure 25. Book titled "Light On Türkiye" by Prof. Sabit Kalfagil - © Ozan Bilgiseren

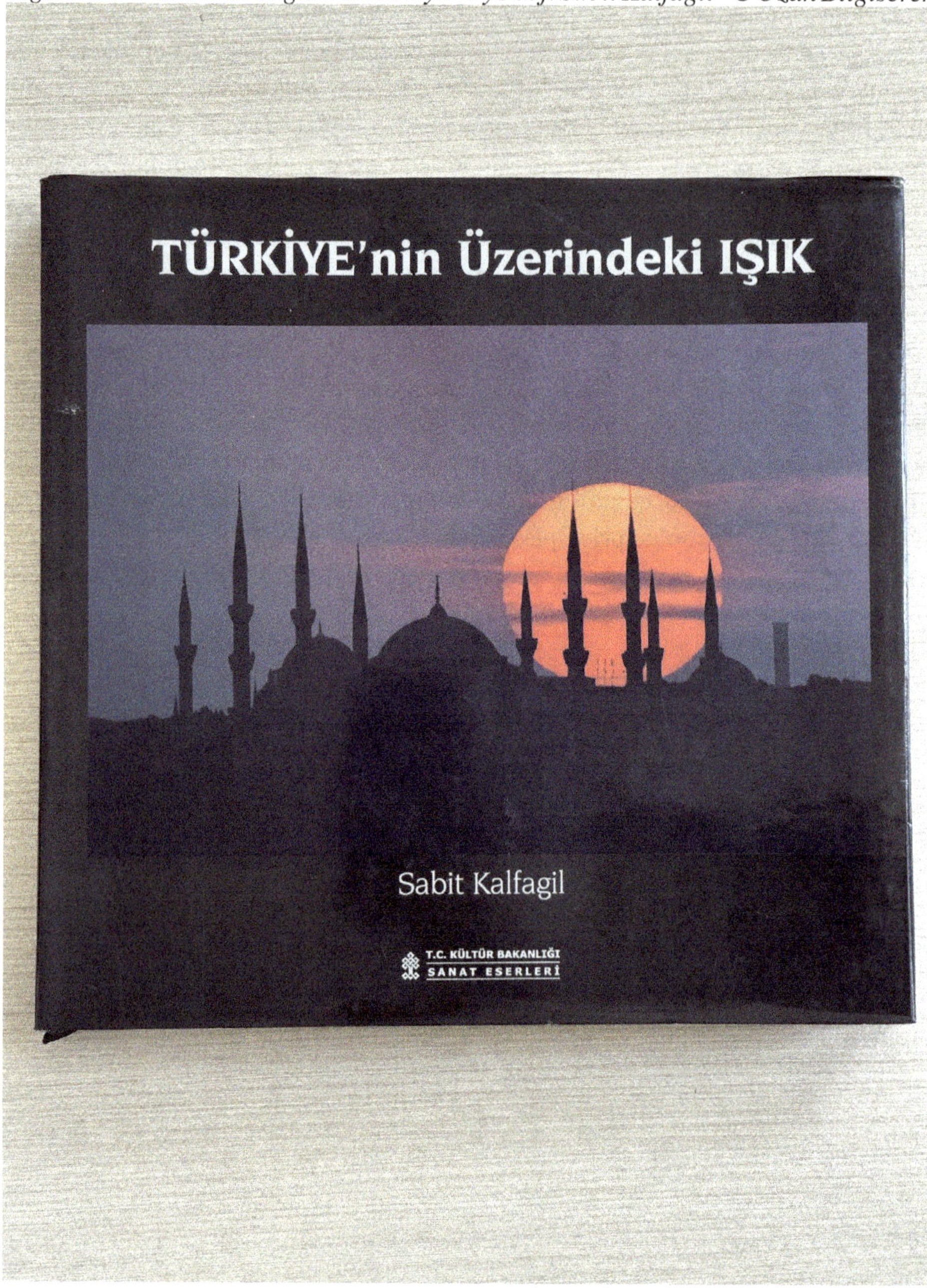

Although he initially embraced digital photography for its economic advantages, Prof. Sabit Kalfagil remained staunchly opposed to digital manipulation. He never compromised the integrity of his documentary discipline, grounded in the ethos of

"Straight Documentary" photography. He did not digitally erase elements within the frame that appeared superfluous, nor did he insert foreign elements from elsewhere into the composition. On the contrary, even when he was visibly frustrated by visual distractions—such as telegraph or telephone wires that disrupted the harmony of a scene—he would still allow them to remain in the frame. Rather than digitally remove them, he employed optical and aesthetic techniques to minimize their visual impact. Both in his life and in his photographic philosophy, he was a candid, honest, and principled individual, as well as a highly respected artist. Perhaps it was for this reason that his presence on juries of photography competitions was perceived as a guarantor of fairness—by participating photographers, organizing institutions, and fellow jurors alike.

Although I never had the opportunity to speak with Sabit Kalfagil directly about the image discussed in this text, regrettably, there is very little information currently available regarding this particular photograph. Even those who knew him closely have provided limited insight. What is known, however, is that the photograph was taken in the 1970s in the Samatya district of Istanbul. In the background, the silhouette of the Sultanahmet Mosque (Blue Mosque), with its six minarets, dominates the skyline—leaving no doubt about its identity (İstanbul Modern, 2025; Karahasan, 2025). For many viewers, this image of a couple, captured in the melancholic atmosphere of an overcast Istanbul spring, evokes strong emotions, nostalgia, and personal memories. It is widely regarded as a sincere and heartfelt image, one that also stands as a poignant visual representation of a lost era—one to which we can never return.

It is quite evident that this photograph by the unquestionably honest Sabit Kalfagil is not a staged composition. Perhaps it is precisely because it was not staged that there is little traceable information about it today. The identity of the couple in the image remains unknown—a rather common circumstance in the context of street photography, travel documentation, or spontaneous souvenir imagery. Still, one might wish that more contextual data were available. Even if Prof. Kalfagil were still alive and I had had the chance to ask him directly, it is likely that I would not have obtained much further detail about the photo. If, hypothetically, I were to capture a contemporary version of this type of image today—pressing the shutter first and seeking permission from the subjects afterward—there would be only a fifty percent chance of success. Given current legal frameworks, particularly those governed by the "Personal Data Protection Law," it would not be surprising if the individuals requested deletion of the image from my device, or even pursued legal action should the photo be used without their explicit consent (GOV, 2025; KVKK, 2025).

In a vast metropolis that is continuously fading, deteriorating, and sacrificing its beauty in countless ways with each passing moment, perhaps the only sustainable method—akin to Robert Doisneau's meticulous practice in the 1950s—is to secure consent in advance. Consequently, one should not be overly critical of the tens of thousands of contemporary influencers who, operating within carefully curated visual communities, replicate similar scenes—albeit in selfie format or in tandem with equally photogenic partners—and derive income from such activities.

At this juncture, I feel compelled to share a personal anecdote. During my first visit to the People's Republic of China in 2019 for a solo exhibition, my wife and I had the opportunity to visit Beijing and Shanghai prior to arriving in Xiamen. On Sunday evening, June 2, 2019, while waiting at a traffic light along the Bund—Shanghai's most famous tourist promenade—just as the sun was setting and the streetlights were coming on, I encountered a picture-perfect couple standing in front of me, facing away toward the Huangpu River. Given the extended duration of the traffic signal due to the dense vehicular and pedestrian flow, the best action I could take in that moment was to instinctively photograph the couple with my phone, capturing 15–20 frames despite the limitations posed by the phone camera's technical quality and the low light. Feeling lucky and sensing the potential for alternative perspectives, I attempted to step back and shift to a telephoto view. (Figure: 26) (Figure: 27) (Figure: 28) But as I turned around, I found myself face-to-face with what appeared to be a small battalion—around 20 to 25 Chinese photographers equipped with long lenses—who instantly conveyed through their expressions, "If only this silly tourist would get out of the way so we could take a proper shot." At that very moment, the light turned green, and my wife and I quietly made our way back to the hotel.

Figure 26. "Couple" at The Bund of Shanghai - © Ozan Bilgiseren

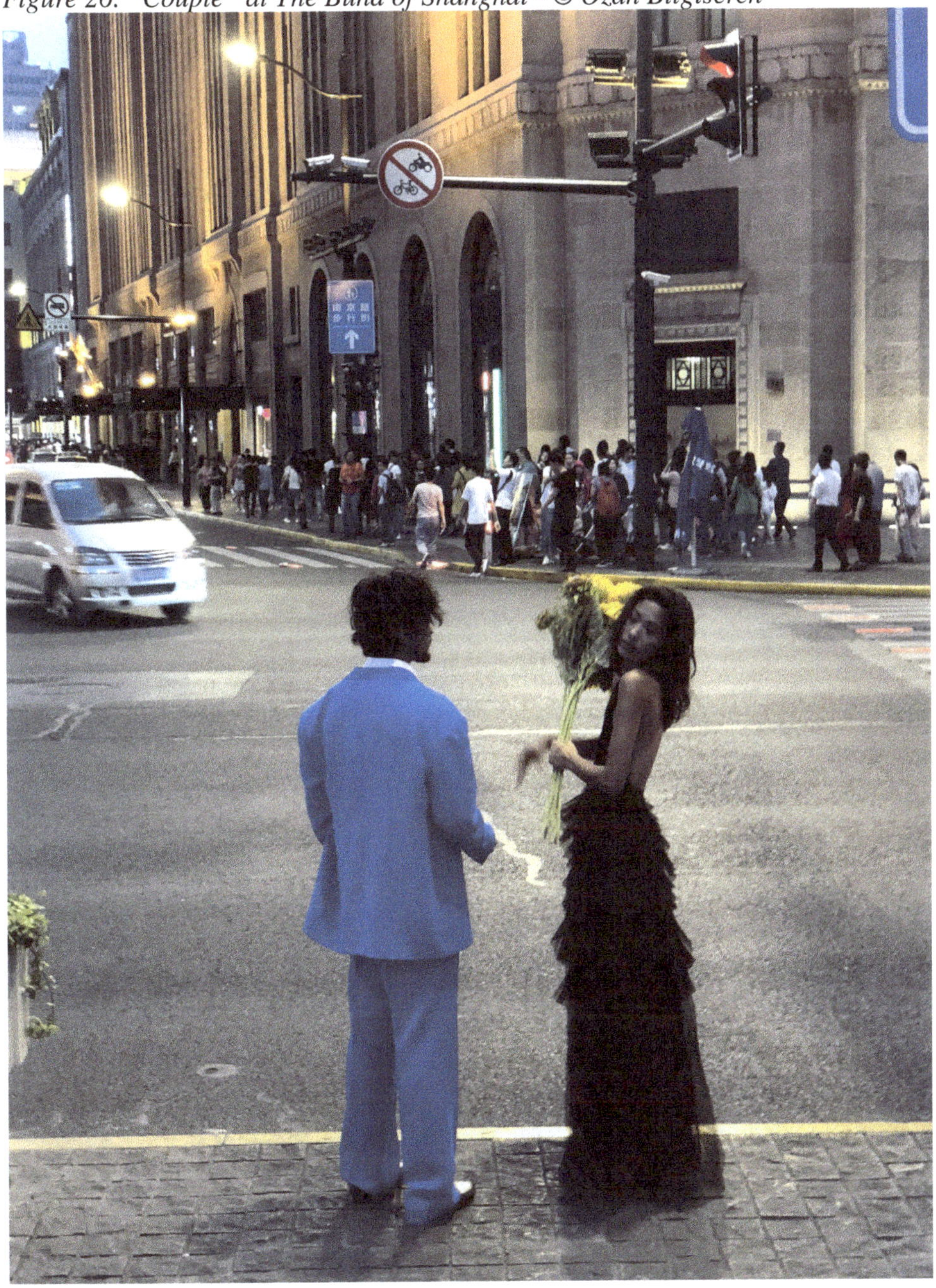

Figure 27. "Couple" at The Bund of Shanghai - © Ozan Bilgiseren

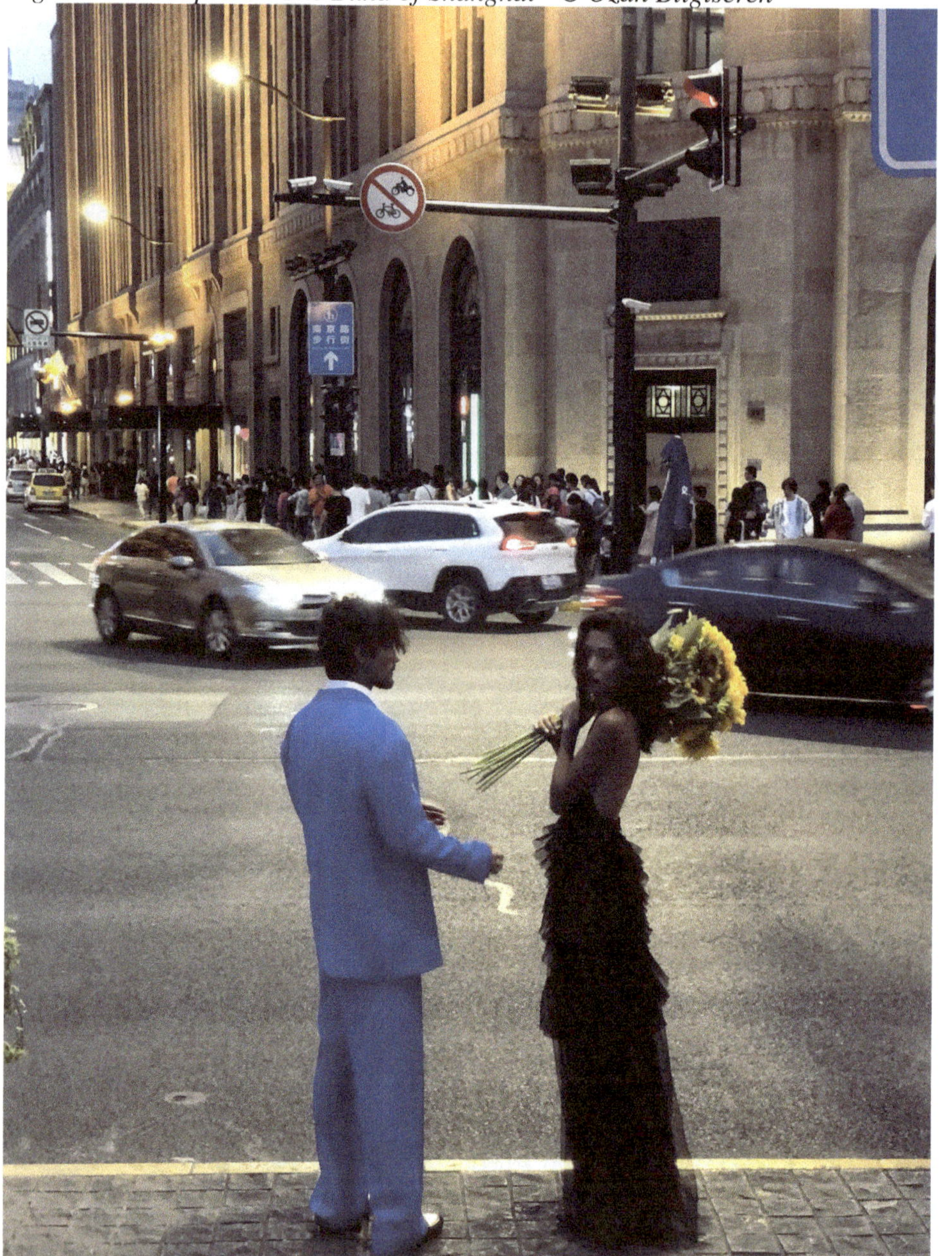

Figure 28. "Couple" at The Bund of Shanghai - © Ozan Bilgiseren

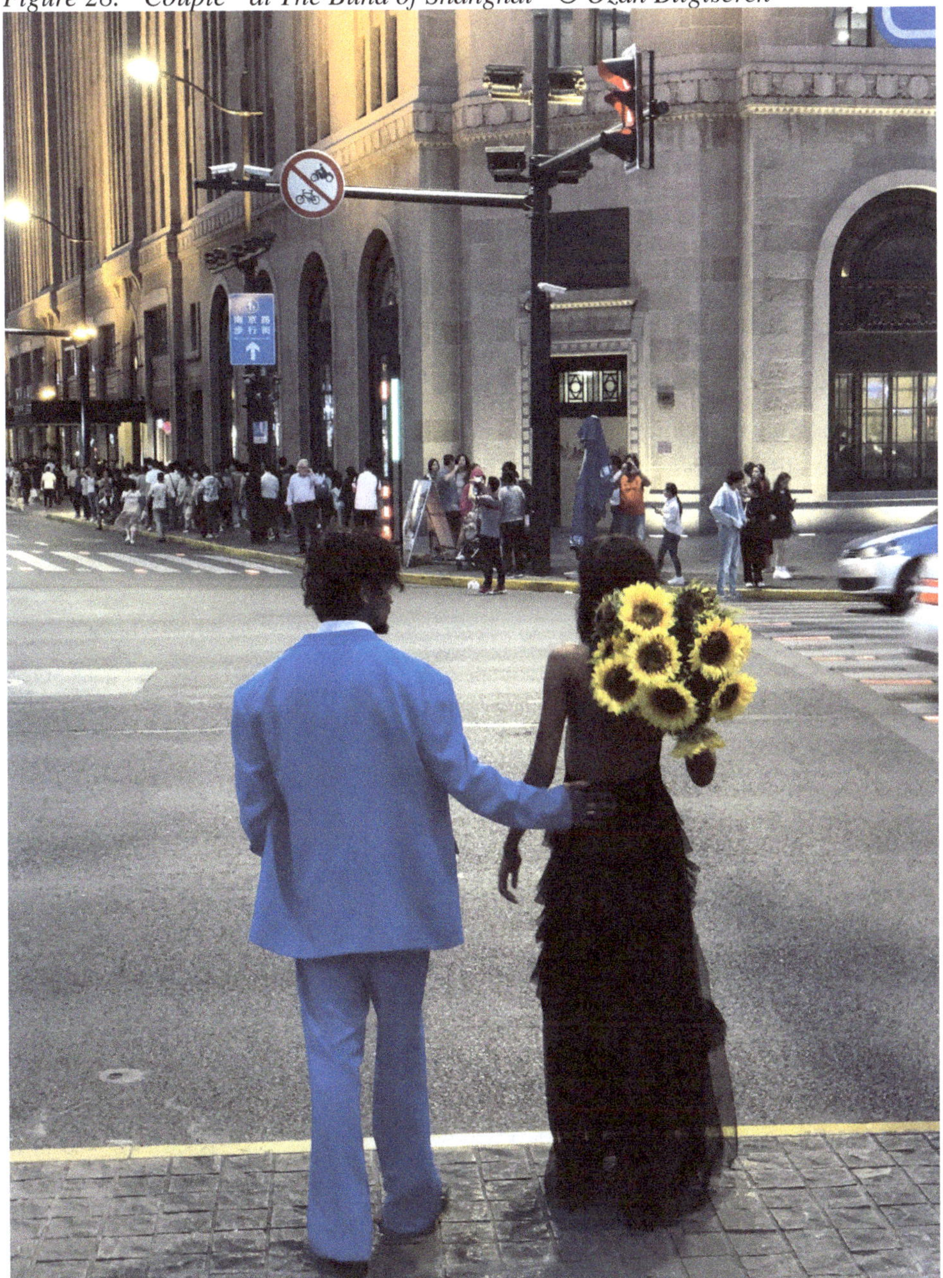

YELLOW CARD

Up to this point, we have examined what people hope to see—or are inclined to believe they are seeing—in a photograph considered to be "well captured" or at least assumed to be so, along with the broader issues associated with such imagery. To delve into the matter from a different angle, one may recall the highly publicized relationship between Princess Diana of Wales and her Egyptian-born partner, Dodi al-Fayed. Nearly three decades ago, their romance not only dominated tabloid headlines but also received widespread coverage in mainstream news outlets. Toward the end of her fractured marriage to Prince Charles—now King of the United Kingdom—Lady Diana became a global focus of attention amid speculation that she was on the verge of marrying Dodi al-Fayed, a wealthy Muslim businessman, although definitive proof of this never emerged. (Figure: 29) As if drawn by blood in the water, the world's top paparazzi closed in like a swarm of sharks. Tragically, these same photographers were ultimately implicated in the events that led to the couple's untimely deaths.

Figure 29. Lady Di & Dodi al-Fayed at the front page

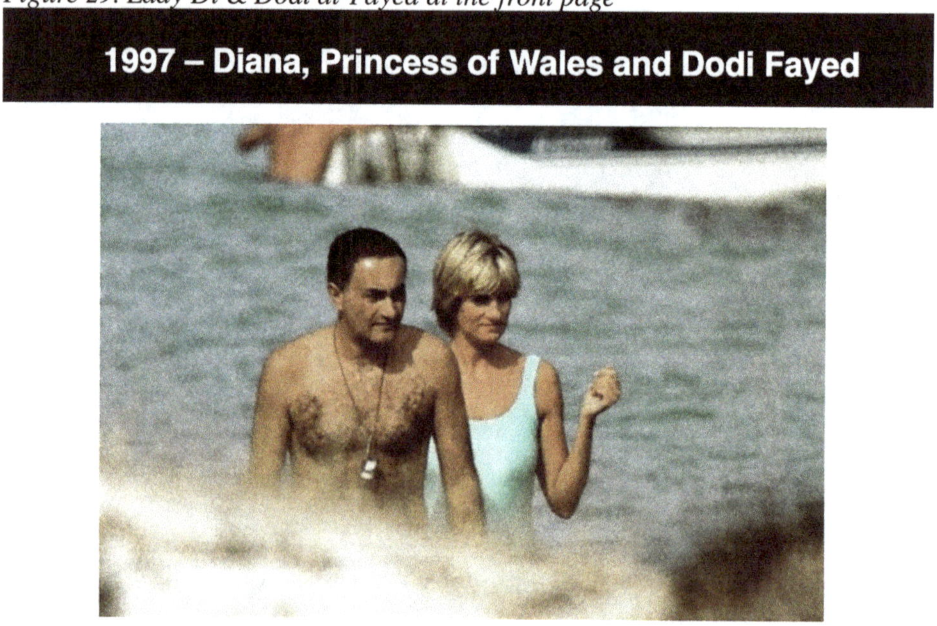

Today, such paparazzi images—once widely circulated—are considerably harder to locate via online searches than they were two decades ago. Likely due to the "right to be forgotten" applied in digital platforms, and perhaps also out of respect or belated remorse for Princess Diana, many of these images appear to have been systematically removed from digital archives. In the few remaining photos, it is still possible to detect traces of Photoshop manipulation dating back to that era. After Diana's death, numerous tabloids and scandal-driven editors were forced to admit that the images—especially those intended for magazine covers or front pages—had been digitally altered using long-focus paparazzi shots. In these manipulated versions, the couple's physical proximity was artificially enhanced to suggest greater intimacy (Serbestiyet, 2025). Such interventions not only amplified public curiosity but also provoked the paparazzi further, distressed members of the royal family, and created a whirlwind of escalation with increasingly damaging consequences. Reflecting on the outrage sparked by the removed thumb in *Migrant Mother* six decades prior highlights how far notions of authenticity have shifted—and how much public attitudes have changed. At this point, it is also worth recalling the subtle yet far-reaching influence that Photoshop—developed in the late 1980s and widely adopted by the early 1990s—has exerted over public perception and collective memory for nearly forty years.

In the early 1990s, as a Fine Arts student enrolled in documentary photography courses taught by Prof. Sabit Kalfagil, we sought to broaden our visual literacy using the limited foreign photography magazines and rare art publications accessible in Istanbul at the time. Occasionally, we would borrow visual arts books, photography monographs, and cinema journals from consular libraries. It was during those years that I first encountered the work of Canadian artist Jeff Wall—whose conceptual and staged photographic work felt strikingly unconventional and provocative in an era still largely dominated by traditional photographic aesthetics. (Figure: 30) Lacking sufficient information about the artist and with little understanding of how his work was received by art collectors and institutions, we often found ourselves engaged in awkward, sometimes shallow debates with fellow academics. Our struggles to conceptually anchor the series we created using darkroom experiments or photographic tricks reflected a broader difficulty in articulating coherent artistic frameworks. Perhaps most importantly, at the time, photography had yet to gain widespread recognition as a legitimate art form in Turkish society or within the country's galleries. Nonetheless, there were exceptions—individuals who, by imitating Western models, managed to attract attention from the art world. At the same time, opportunities for young artists were exceedingly limited. There were few grants, competitions, or scholarships to support emerging talent, and the awards from photography contests, when held, often consisted of little more than a plaque bearing one's name—or, if one was fortunate, a few rolls of film.

Figure 30. "A View from an Apartment" by Jeff Wall / 2004-2005

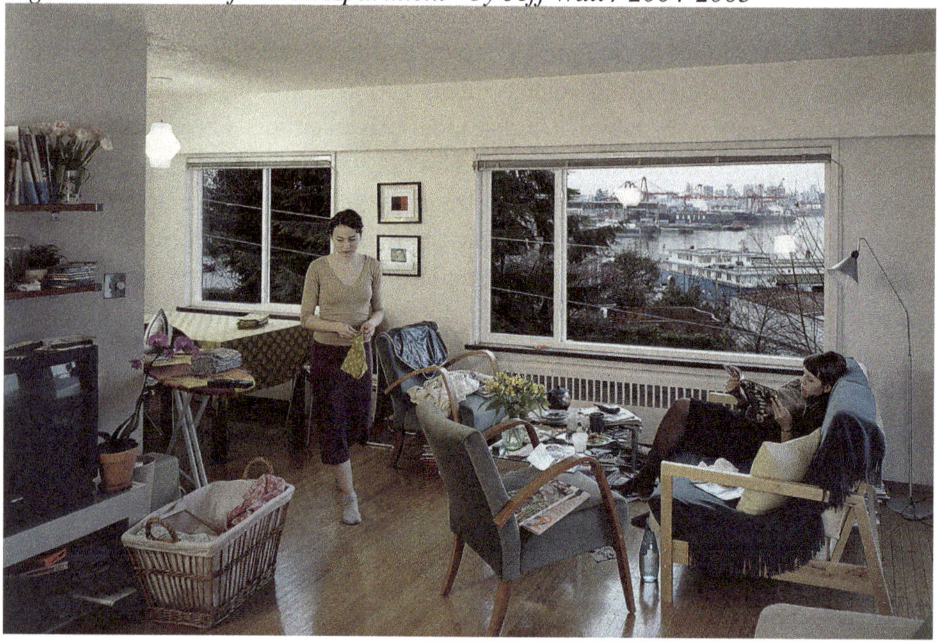

THE FOOTSTEPS OF CHANGE

Returning to Jeff Wall, his renowned works such as *Mimic*, *A View from an Apartment*, and *The Thinker* signaled a transformative shift in photographic art throughout the 1990s, distinguished by their overtly constructed and deliberately staged natüre (Mimic (photograph), 2025). These images boldly confronted viewers with their artificiality, in stark contrast to the principles of traditional documentary photography. (Figure: 31) At the time, the conscious embrace of fiction in photographic practice was difficult for many to accept and posed a direct challenge to established visual norms. (Figure: 32) It would take another 10 to 15 years—and a gradual transitional period—before such cognitive paradigms were more widely dismantled. Meanwhile, technological developments facilitated this shift, often unintentionally, by pushing the boundaries of photographic production. For instance, while the average print size of the most iconic photographs of the 20th century rarely exceeded A3 dimensions, the advent of inkjet printing enabled the production of large-format works, which significantly enhanced the visual impact of contemporary exhibitions. Frames once discarded for rendering the subject too small on an A4 print could now be enlarged to grand proportions, thereby amplifying facial expressions and improving legibility. Today, even a 40×60 cm print is considered modest in many student exhibitions. More importantly, the democratization of digital photography created a more inclusive platform—one that was open to new voices, ideas, and visual experimentation.

Figure 31. "Mimic" by Jeff Wall 1982

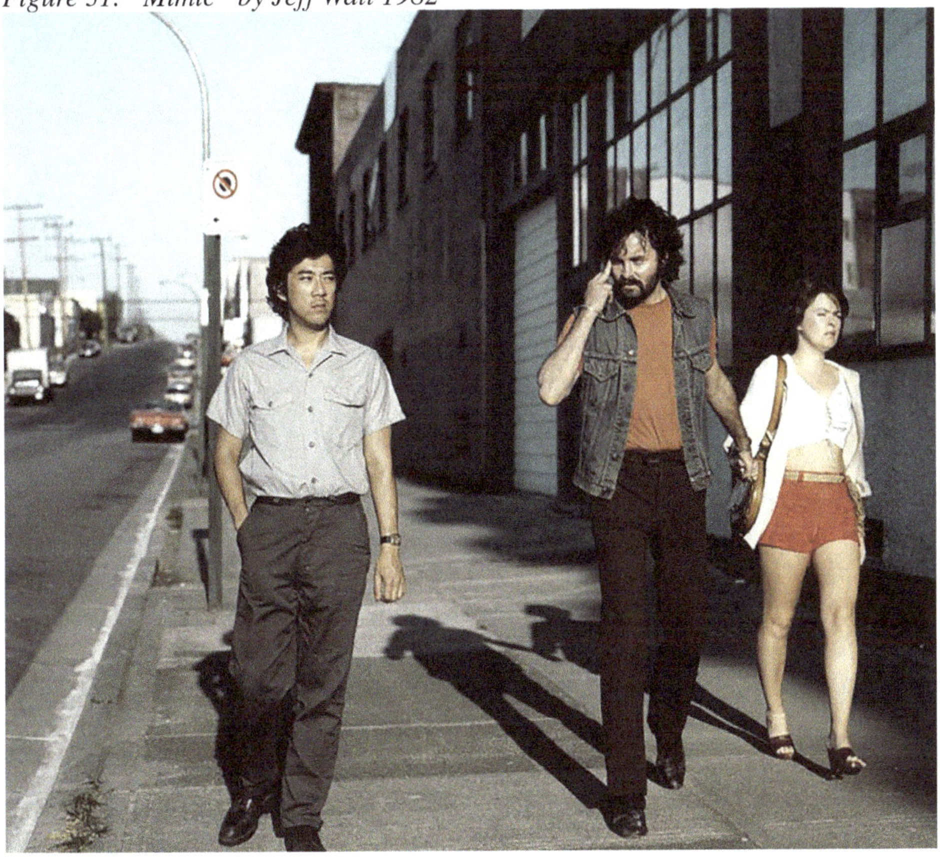

Figure 32. "The Thinker" by Jeff Wall (1986) 1989

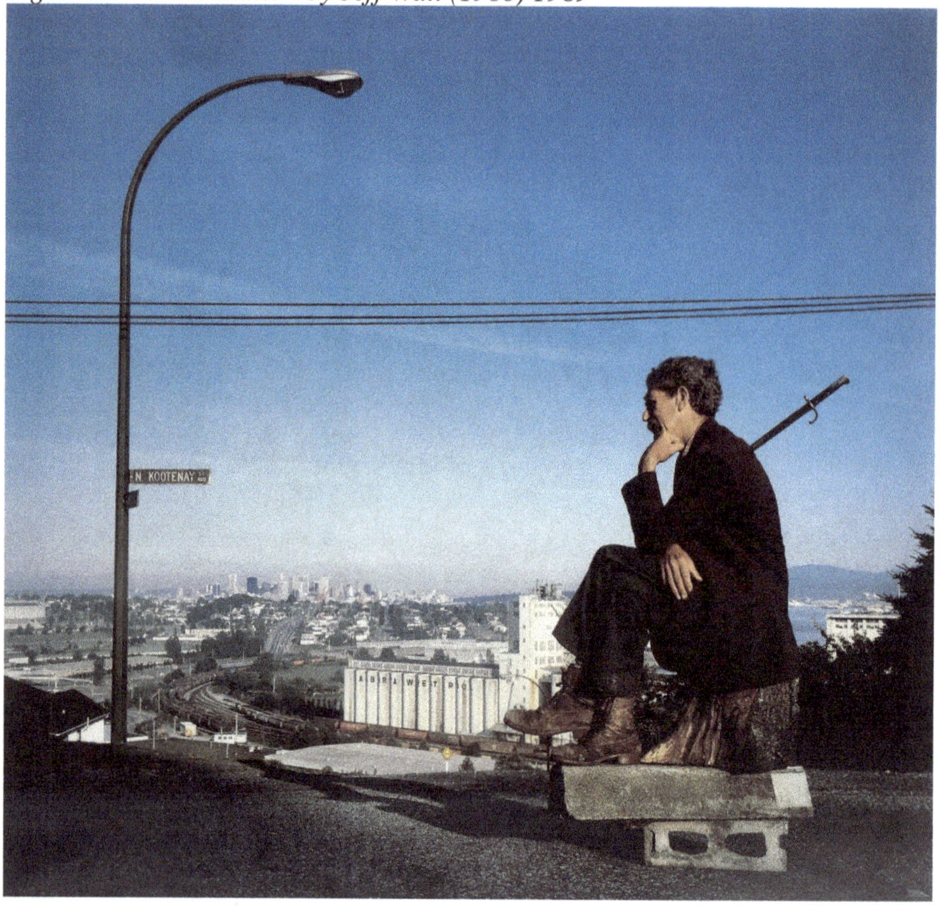

Even so, early pioneers of constructed photography such as Jeff Wall and Gregory Crewdson played a pivotal role in breaking down intellectual barriers and encouraging photography to adopt a cinematic sensibility. As a student some 35 years ago, I found myself simultaneously frustrated by the overwhelming fictionalization of photography and fatigued by the repetitive critiques I received in documentary photography projects. Capturing images that were both aesthetically compelling and aligned with notions of "truth," "honesty," and "reality" was not impossible—but in my opinion, such endeavors rarely reflected the full complexity of lived experience. Furthermore, I was increasingly troubled by the ethical implications of documentary photography, particularly when the subjects portrayed were depicted in moments of social or economic vulnerability. Often, such individuals were unintentionally exploited in the name of documentary truth—a practice that clashed with my own ethical values. After all, I was a Fine Arts student with no intention of becoming a press photographer, and in those days, the idea of presenting a model release form to a subject was entirely unheard of.

"My work is a reconstruction and reconstruction is a philosophical activity. If I can create a drama that has philosophical meaning, that's fine, or sometimes, it is not from meaning but a reconstruction of a feeling. It is best to capture in a photograph a feeling, an emotion, a look, a memory, a perception or a relationship." remarks Jeff Wall (Bunyan, 2025). Although I initially found their methodologies alienating—largely due to my own inability to fully grasp their conceptual frameworks—I eventually came to appreciate and even defend the artistic practices of Wall and Crewdson on emotional, intellectual, and ethical grounds. Regardless of whether or not one agrees with their artistic premises, the sheer investment of energy, time, funding, and labor that these artists dedicate to realizing a carefully conceived final image is undeniably admirable. Moreover, a key distinction between artistic production in the West and elsewhere lies in the West's enduring openness to innovative and experimental artistic approaches—a disposition that remains essential for the flourishing of all creative disciplines.

In a strange world that remains perpetually beyond our control, it is perhaps our persistent efforts to conform to compositional rules and didactic, clichéd templates that cause us to overlook alternative ways of seeing. Even in the most minor or seemingly trivial photographic situations, we often find ourselves instinctively attempting to impose order upon the fleeting moments that emerge before us. As if that were not enough, we frequently fall into the habit of trying to "rescue" our failed shots during post-production—demonstrating a recurring tendency to alter the integrity of reality. For precisely these reasons, one might argue that those who operate entirely within the domain of constructed imagery—within the world of pure fiction in the name of art—are, at the very least, intellectually more honest with themselves than those who rely on covert or opportunistic captures. They do not inhabit the same ethical or legal contradictions. (Figure: 33) (Figure: 34)

Figure 33. "Ophelia" by Gregory Crewdson / 2000-2001

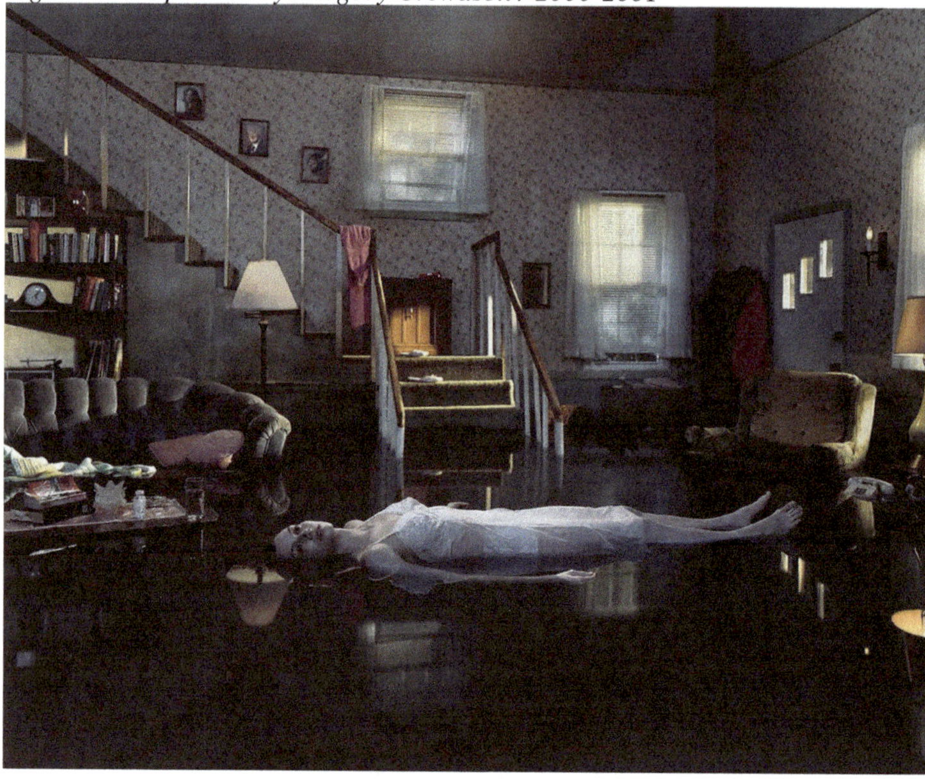

Figure 34. Making of "Ophelia"

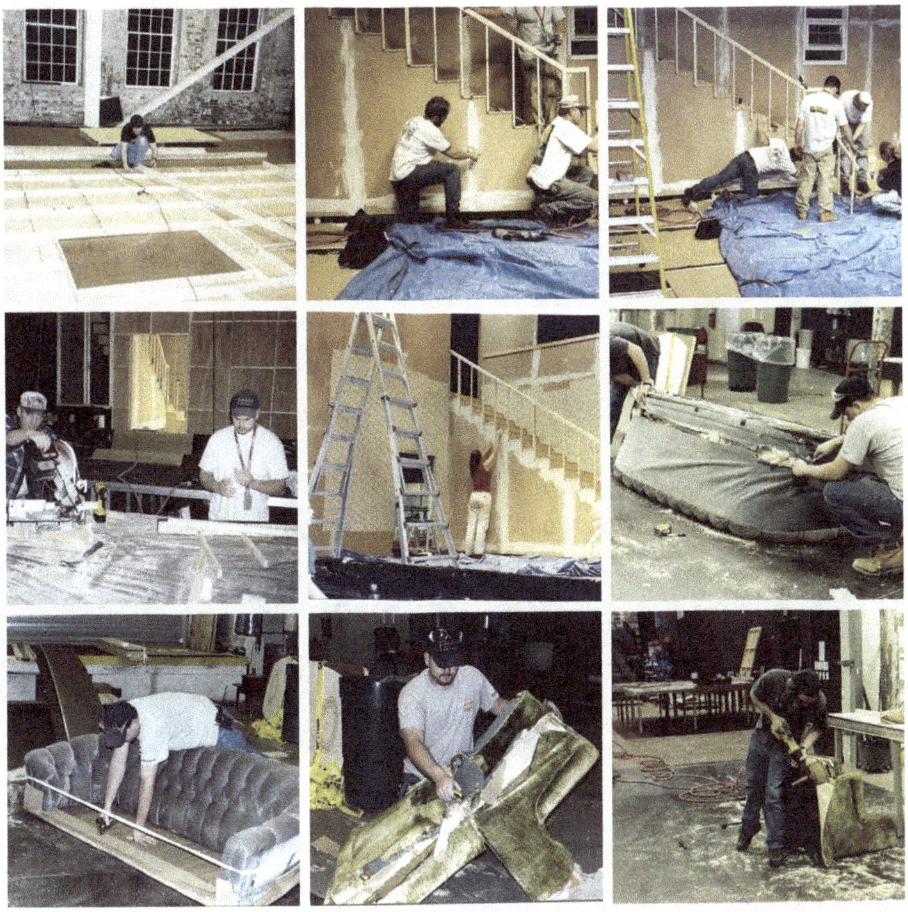

Gregory Crewdson articulates the genesis of one of his most iconic works as follows: "Long before I made *Ophelia* in 2001, I had the image of a figure floating in water lodged in my mind. (Figure: 35) The idea partly came from a dream, but there were also specific visual references: John Everett Millais' 1850 painting, John Cheever's short story *The Swimmer*, and one of my favorite films, *The Night of the Hunter*, particularly the haunting underwater scene" (Crewdson, 2025, a).

Figure 35. Making of "Ophelia"

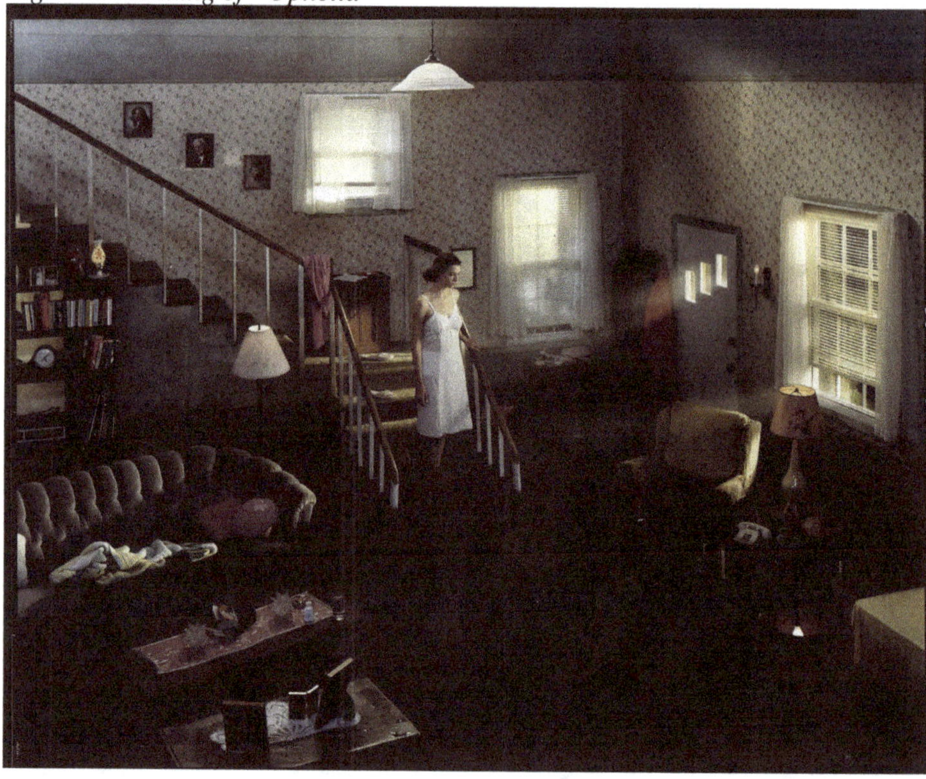

INTERACTION AND TRANSFORMATION

When we relate the discussion to cinema, it is only natural to mention the late David Lynch, the renowned filmmaker who passed away on January 16, 2025. Beyond his body of work that stimulates subconscious impulses through all forms of artistic production, Lynch has held a particularly significant and inspirational place for photographers working within the realm of visual arts and conceptual photography. This influence was immediately observable in the days following his passing, as reflected in tributes shared by contemporary photographers such as Gregory Crewdson and Todd Hido on their social media platforms (Growcoot, 2025).

Crewdson, for instance, referred to Lynch's iconic film *Blue Velvet* as "the movie that changed my life," and remarked that Lynch's cinematic oeuvre "continues to inspire even after decades." His portrayal of Lynch as a personal hero is clearly not incidental. Similarly, Todd Hido—following Lynch's death—shared a photographic series from his own archive that may be interpreted as a homage to the director. This gesture arguably underscores both the extent of Hido's inspiration drawn from Lynch and the visual proximity they share in their aesthetic languages. It is also worth noting that Hido's photographs have adorned the covers of numerous books by the cult American author Raymond Carver. (Figure: 36) Although not identical in medium or approach, there is a striking parallel in their capacity to condense the complex emotional and narrative scope of novels or short stories—spanning dozens or hundreds of pages—into a single image. This same challenge is also encountered in the visual design of film posters, where one frame must encapsulate the entire cinematic experience.

Figure 36. Raymond Carver book covers by Todd Hido

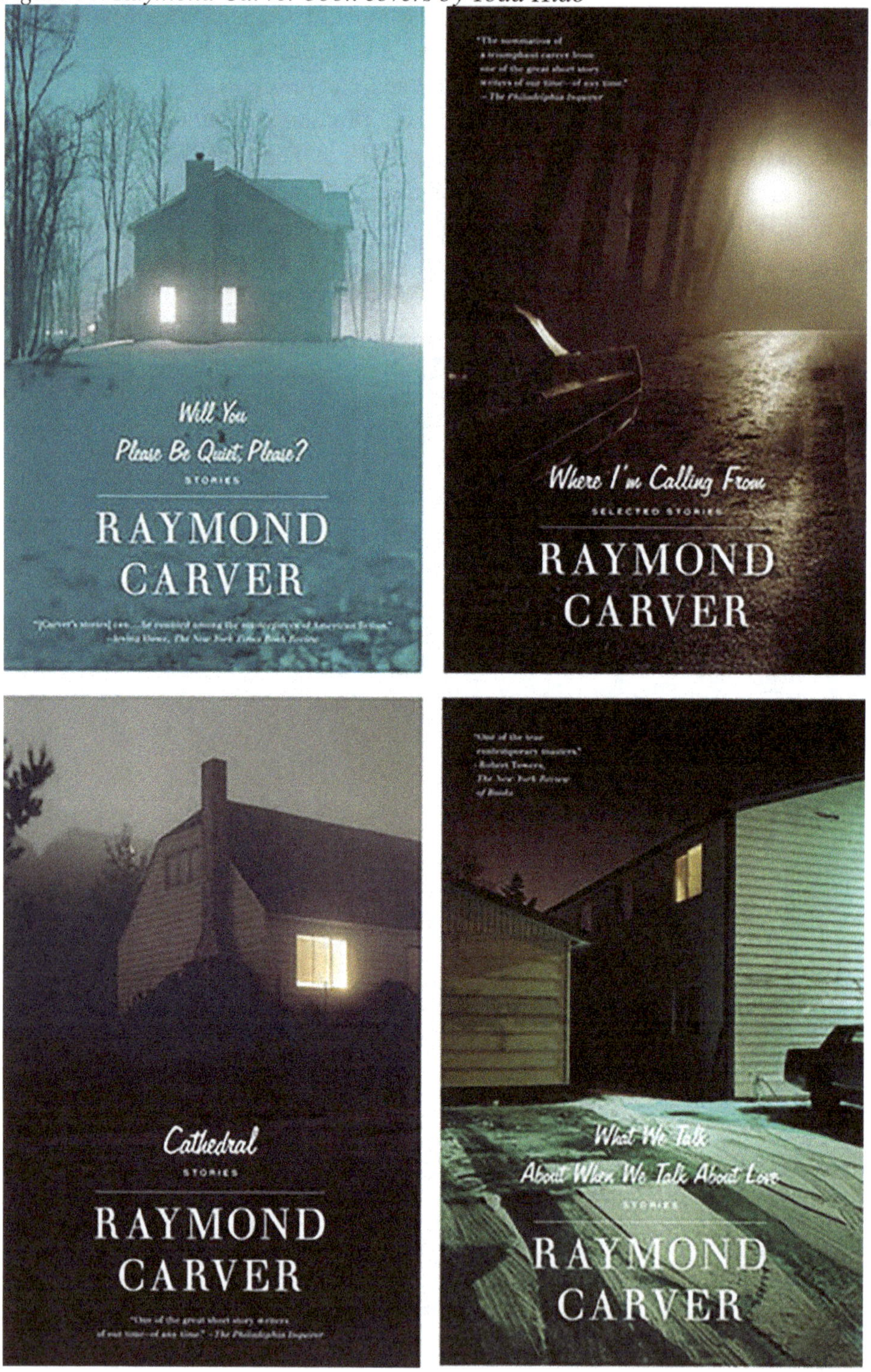

There are a few brief personal reflections I can also offer regarding David Lynch. Most notably, his involvement in curating the photographic selection for the 2013 edition of Paris Photo brought a distinctly unique atmosphere to that year's exhibition. (Figure: 37) The curatorial direction—especially through the somber visual material sourced predominantly from the British Army Archives—focused on the aerial bombardments of the Second World War and the resulting urban devastation. These haunting images introduced a dramatic, unsettling tone to the event. Lynch's signature aesthetic—marked by ambiguity, foreboding, and an elusive resistance to rational explanation—was powerfully imprinted upon the exhibition space, setting that year apart in both mood and curatorial vision from previous and subsequent editions (Photoeye, 2025).

Figure 37. David Lynch's portrait on Paris Photo 2013 book cover

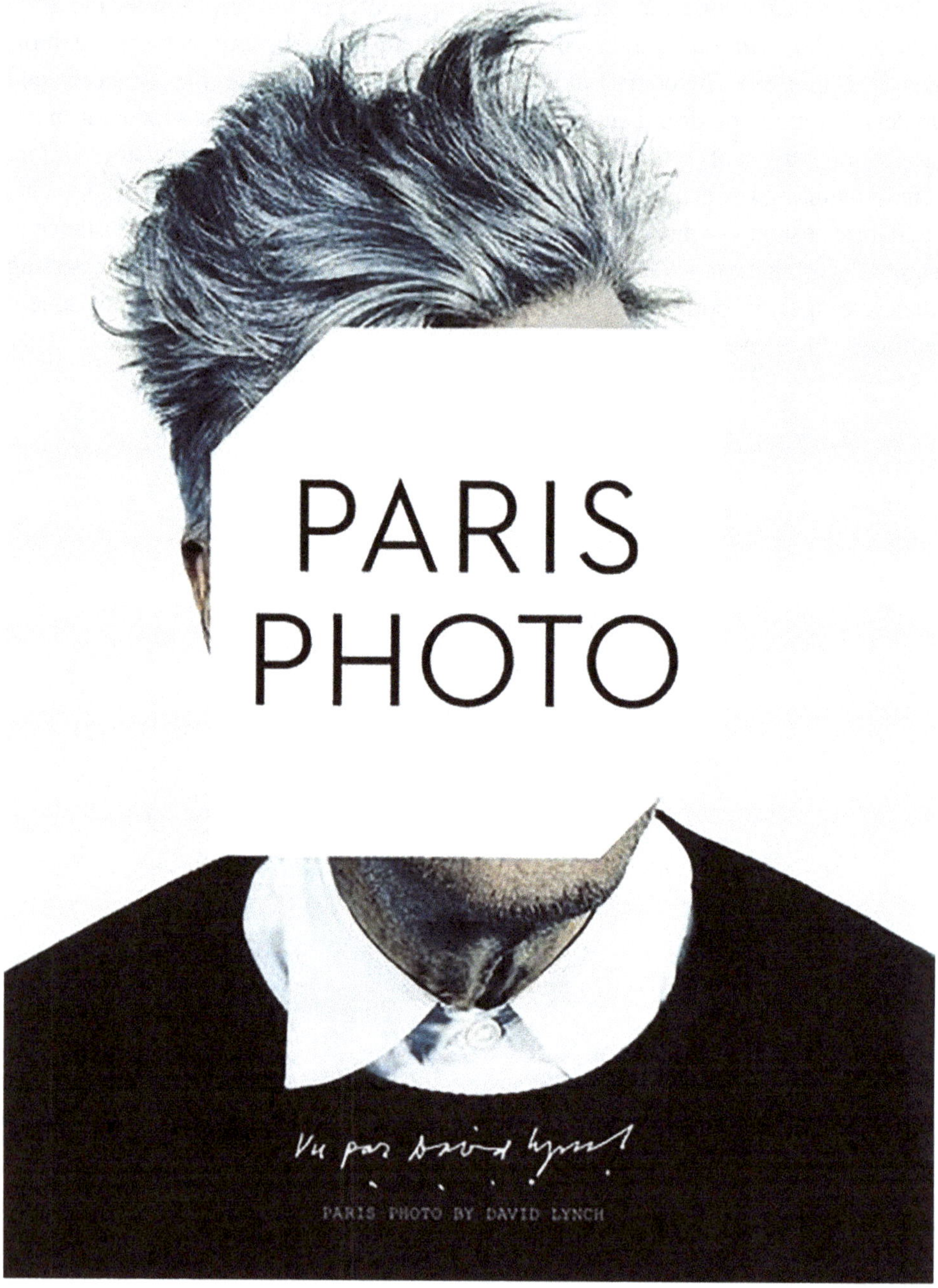

In 2019, we attended Paris Photo with a separate purpose—specifically, the founding of the Association of Photography Organizations (FOTON), which also took place in Paris that year. Through a photographer acquaintance, we had the chance to meet the master printer Toros Aladjajian. (Figure: 38) A descendant of a family originally from Urfa and of Lebanese heritage himself, Toros was, at the time we met, not only one of France's but the world's few remaining darkroom virtuosos (Aral, 2025). Residing and working in the Bry-sur-Marne district on the eastern edge of Paris—close to both the cemetery where Louis Daguerre is buried and the singular diorama Daguerre designed for the local church Saint-Gervais-Saint-Protais—Toros had, for over half a century, provided high-end darkroom services to some of the world's most prominent photographers, fashion and commercial artists, and photojournalists. (Figure: 39) (Figure: 40) Upon entering the bright exhibition area of his two-story home-studio, one was instantly struck by the overwhelming impression of walking through a private art gallery. The walls were adorned with dozens of meticulously printed silver gelatin photographs, each inscribed with personal dedications and signatures from legends such as Henri Cartier-Bresson, Sebastião Salgado, Robert Doisneau, and Christine Spengler—every single one bearing the phrase, "To my dear friend Toros."

Figure 38. Toros Aladjajian and Prof. Ozan Bilgiseren / November 9th 2019

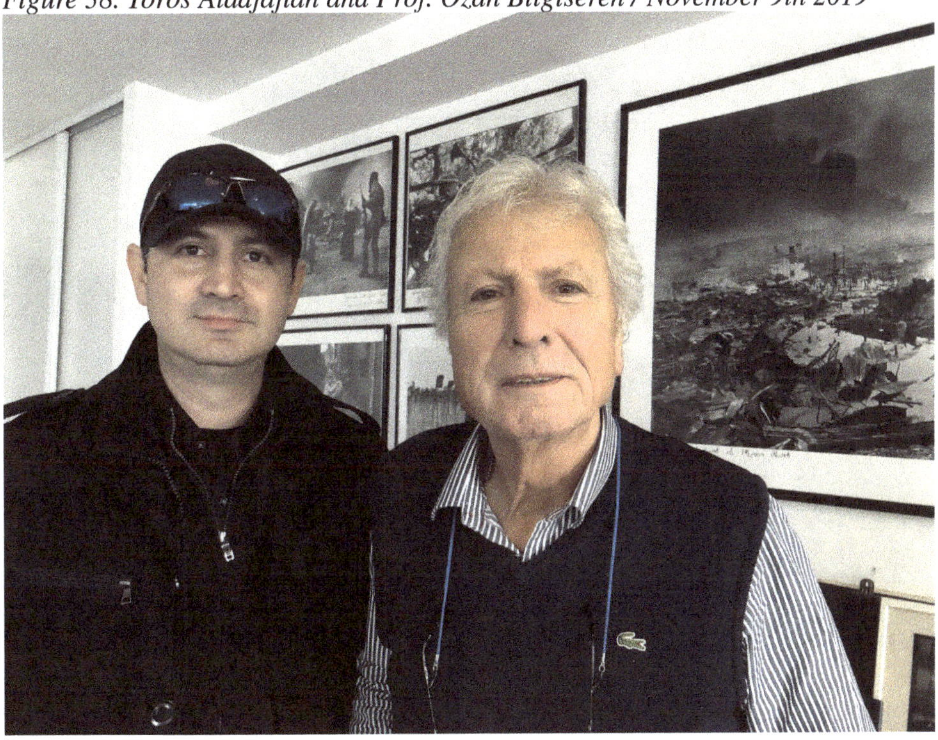

Figure 39. Daguerre's bust with diorama stone marker - © Ozan Bilgiseren

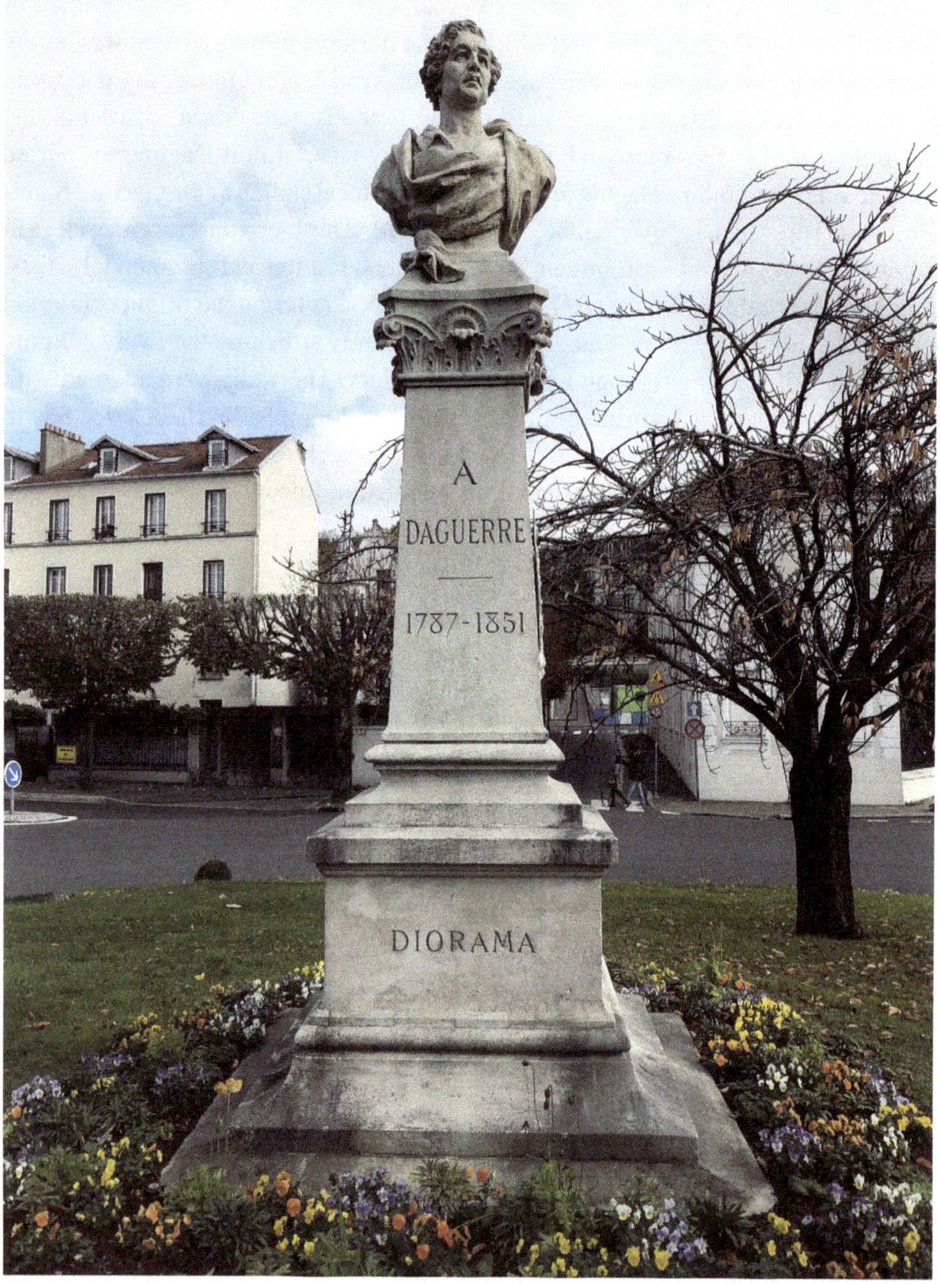

Figure 40. Louis Jacques Mande Daguerre's tombstone - © Ozan Bilgiseren

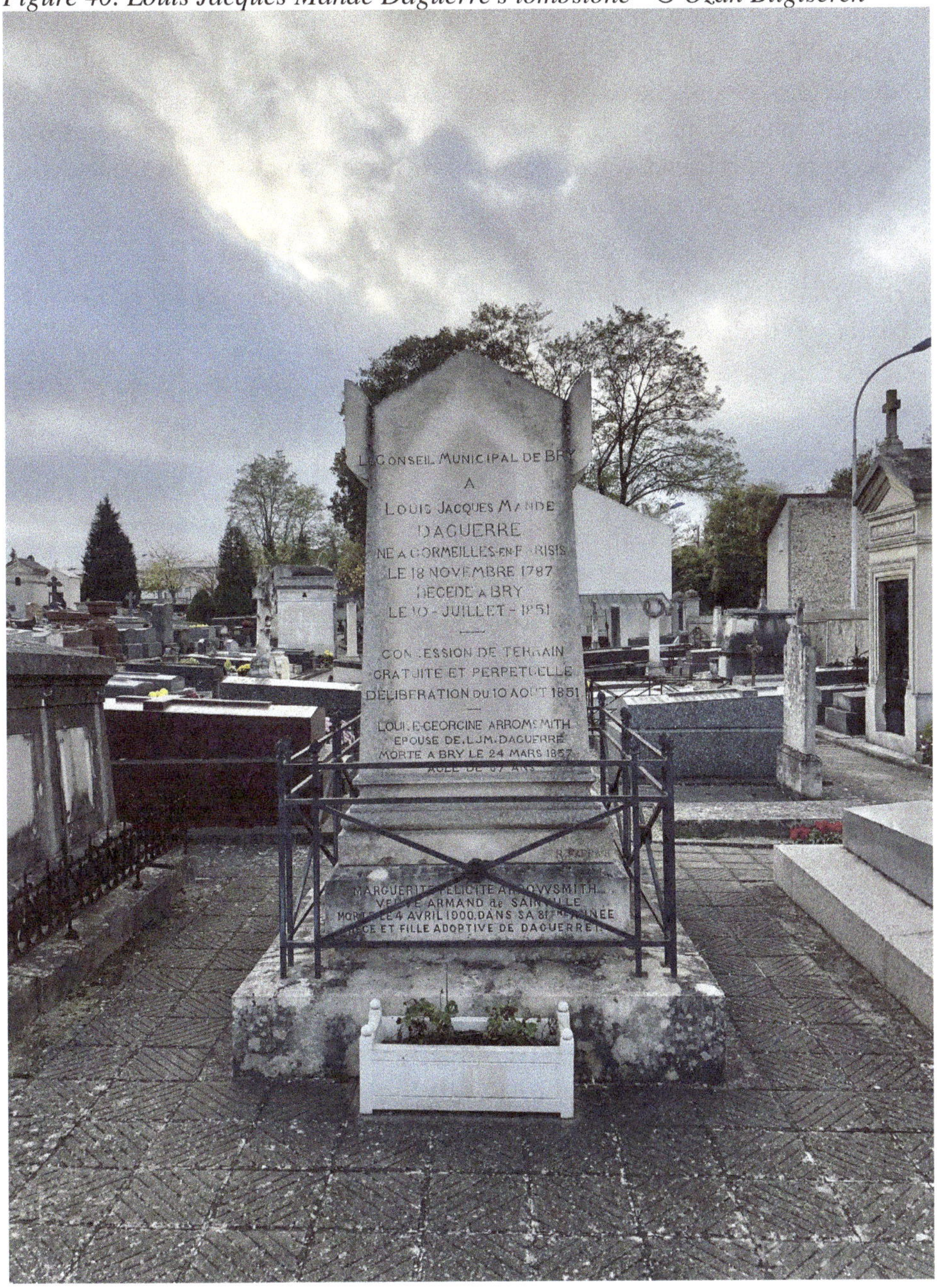

Among these works was a particularly notable piece: a black-and-white portrait of Ara Güler, wearing his signature hat and offering a wave—a print that Toros kept in a prominent place on his lightbox table. (Figure: 41) And, not surprisingly, given the lack of empty wall space, one extraordinary portrait had been relegated to the garage. It was a large-format black-and-white portrait of David Lynch, which I stumbled upon while exploring the premises. Half of Lynch's face was obscured in shadow, his intense, interrogative gaze evoking an air of mistrust and ambiguity. Beneath the photograph, in Lynch's own handwriting, was a message that read, "With thanks to my dear friend Toros," followed by his signature—just as meticulously placed as all the others. (Figure: 42)

Figure 41. Ara Güler's picture with Fatih Aslan at the lightbox table of Toros Aladjajian – © Ozan Bilgiseren

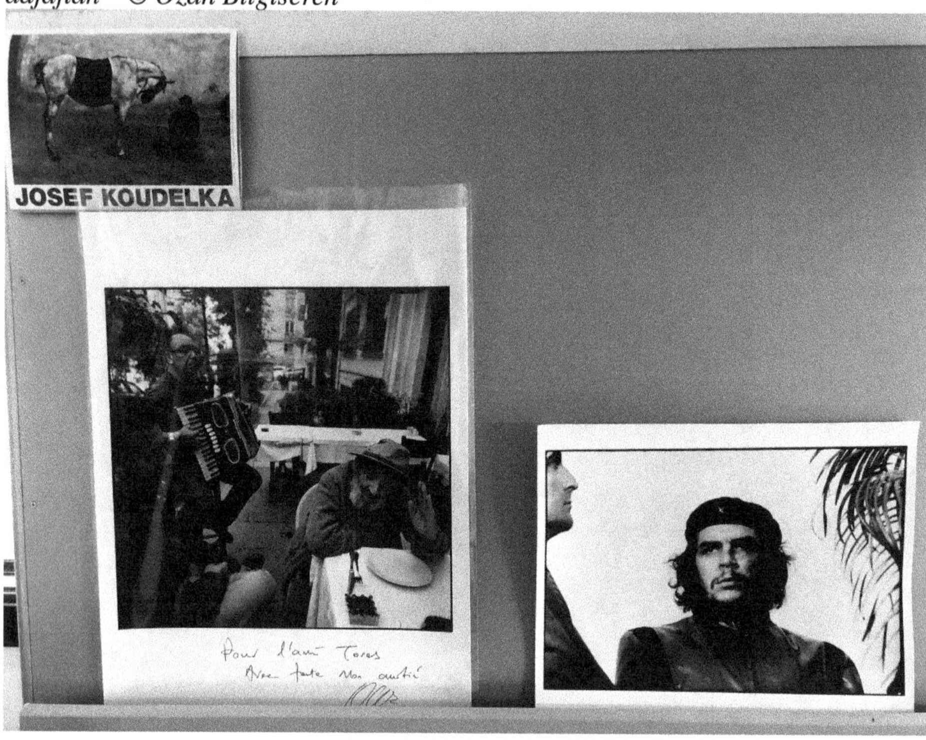

Figure 42. Silver salt portrait print signed by David Lynch - © Ozan Bilgiseren

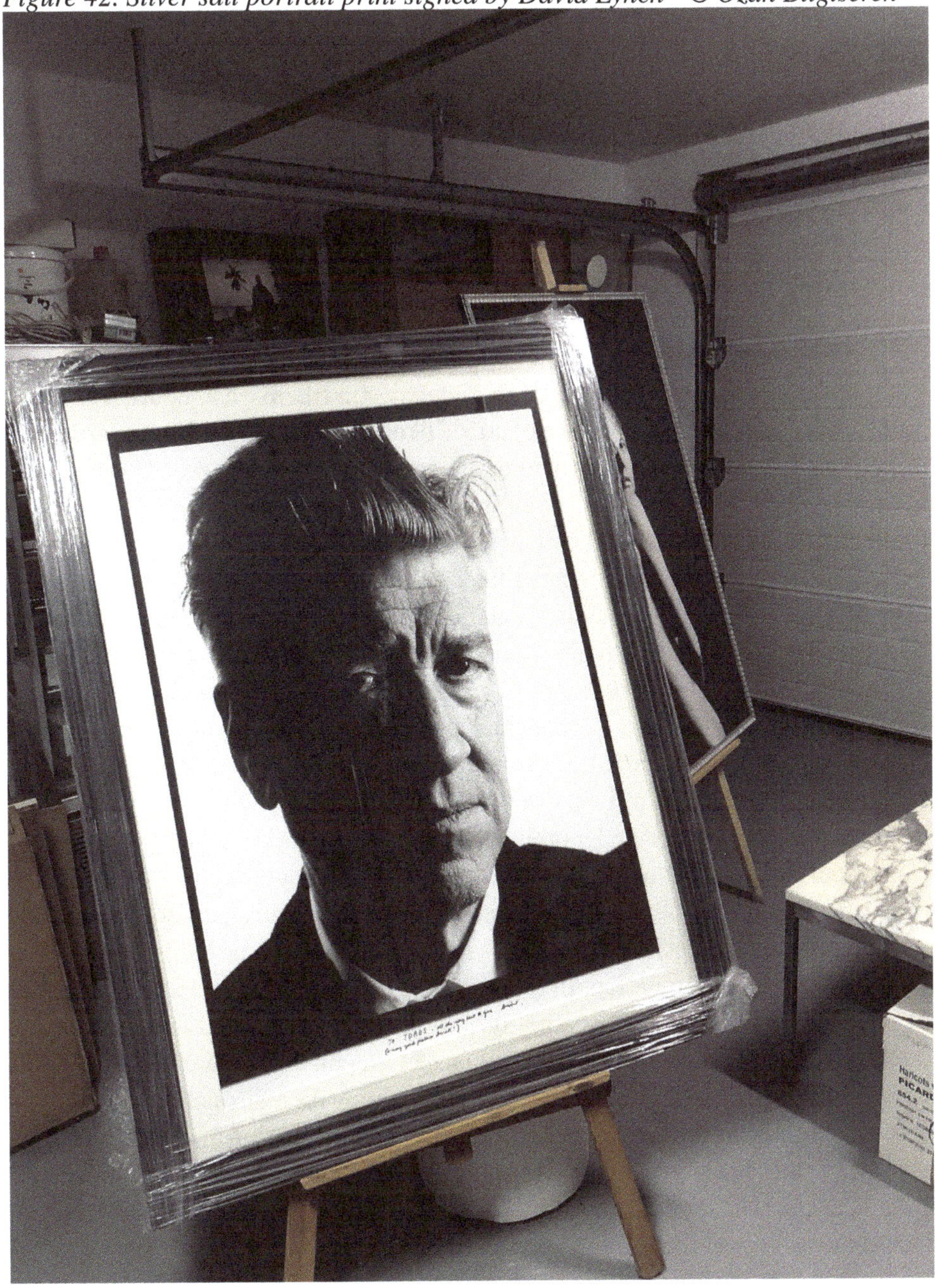

When I inquired about the story behind the image, what I heard was indeed remarkable. In 2013, during his collaboration with the Paris Photo team, Lynch decided to make the most of the opportunity to deepen his darkroom experience.

To do so, he sought out none other than Toros Aladjajian—one of the most masterful darkroom printers in the world—to take private lessons. The two spent several days working intensively together, locked away in the darkroom, producing one exceptional print after another. On one hand stood David Lynch—the enigmatic and visionary filmmaker with a boundless sense of curiosity—and on the other, Master Toros, representing the pinnacle of a craft increasingly obsolete in the age of digital technology. While photographic art continues to evolve, shifting constantly with technological innovation and resisting confinement to any single platform, its roots remain deeply embedded in the scientific principles of optics, physics, and chemistry. Regardless of how many centuries may pass, for those with a passion for the medium, the darkroom continues to inspire awe and curiosity. Perhaps even artists working solely with artificial intelligence will, in some way, find themselves nourished by this foundational source. The brilliance of artists like Lynch—whose ability to articulate the inexpressible could be described in literary terms as "Kafkaesque"—may well lie in their capacity to synthesize and transform acquired knowledge. Ultimately, the enduring value of accumulated expertise cannot be overstated.

Just as Hido's works have graced the covers of Raymond Carver's books, certain pieces by Jeff Wall possess a similar cinematic quality, evoking a multiplicity of emotions and ideas in a single frame (Gall, and Buchanan-Smith, 2025). Some of these, such as *The Thinker* and *Giant*, resonate with me more profoundly in adulthood—perhaps due to the personal experiences and growing awareness that accompany aging (Nolden/H (2025). These works now closely align with numerous abstract thoughts in my own mind. Beginning in the mid-1980s with Wall's influential compositions and continuing through the mid-1990s with Gregory Crewdson's signature works, the staged power of photography was reintroduced to artistic discourse. These artists challenged the conventional perception of visual truth, reminding us that what appears as reality may, in fact, be subject to bias, interpretation, and manipulation. In doing so, they also emphasized the significance of personal narrative in the creation of photographic works and underscored the medium's intrinsic proximity to the language of cinema. These were also the years in which auteurs such as David Lynch were developing their distinctive styles—now considered cult classics—that went on to influence a generation of emerging artists.

One of the key figures influencing contemporary Turkish cinema today is Nuri Bilge Ceylan, whose disciplined and meticulous approach has earned him accolades, particularly at the Cannes Film Festival. Having begun his artistic career as a photographer, Ceylan resurfaced in early 2024 in the public eye with a behind-the-scenes video clip from his film *The Wild Pear Tree* (*Ahlat Ağacı*). In the video, the director is seen offering critical feedback to seasoned actress Bennu Yıldırımlar, questioning the appropriateness and naturalness of certain expressions being delivered during the scene. (Figure: 43) However, the fact that Ceylan later published these moments online—without the actress's prior knowledge or consent—sparked public debate and was viewed by many, including Yıldırımlar herself, as ethically problematic (NTV, 2025).

Figure 43. Video still of Bennu Yıldırımlar and Nuri Bilge Ceylan from the set of the movie "The Wild Pear Tree"

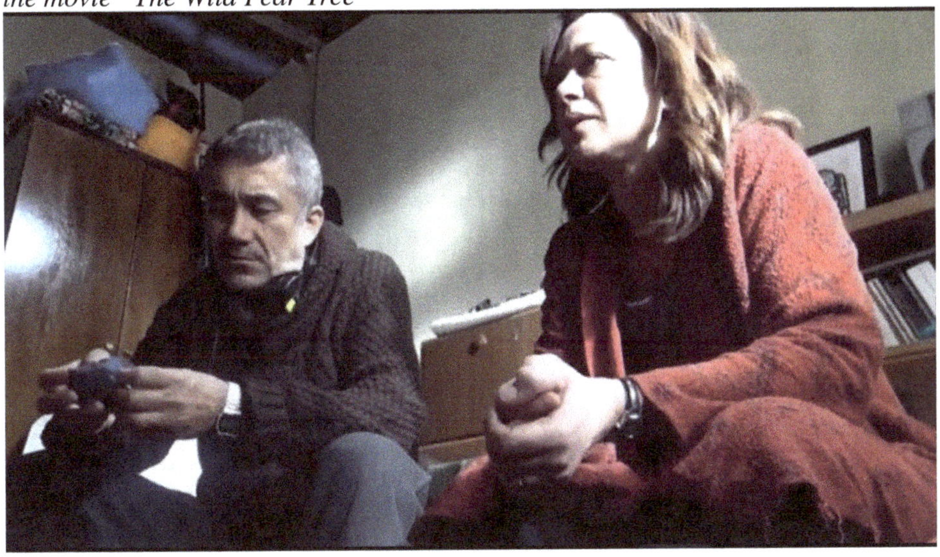

Unlike photography, which can often be pursued as a solitary and personal form of expression, cinema is an inherently collaborative and compartmentalized endeavor, involving the coordinated efforts of multiple specialized professionals. This division of labor renders the cinematic process significantly more complex. A photographer, in contrast, may function simultaneously as director, gaffer, set designer, producer, post-production editor—and, in the case of self-referential projects reminiscent of Cindy Sherman's oeuvre—even as their own lead subject. That said, the expectations of viewers engaging with auteur cinema differ considerably from those of photography audiences. Moreover, while cinema typically requires an admission fee, photographic exhibitions are often free of charge. In this context, I would also like to bring into the conversation Nuri Bilge Ceylan's recent solo exhibition at Istanbul Modern, which concluded on February 18, 2024. Titled *In Another Place*, the exhibition marked the inaugural photography show in the museum's new Renzo Piano-designed building and featured 22 large-format portraits captured by the director not only in Turkey but also in China, India, Georgia, Morocco, and Russia (Dinçer and Ulu, 2025).

As someone who has also served as a professional curator in various international projects, one particular detail in this exhibition caught my attention: the design of the window mounts (passe-partouts) used in the display of large-format, nearly square photographic prints behind museum glass. What I found especially intriguing was the deliberate asymmetry in the white borders: while the top and the sides of the mount had equal margins, the lower margin was approximately three times wider, creating a strong visual suggestion that the image resembled a giant Polaroid print ((Dinçer, 2025). (Figure: 44)

Figure 44. Ceylan's exhibition at Istanbul Modern, titled "In Another Place" - © Ozan Bilgiseren

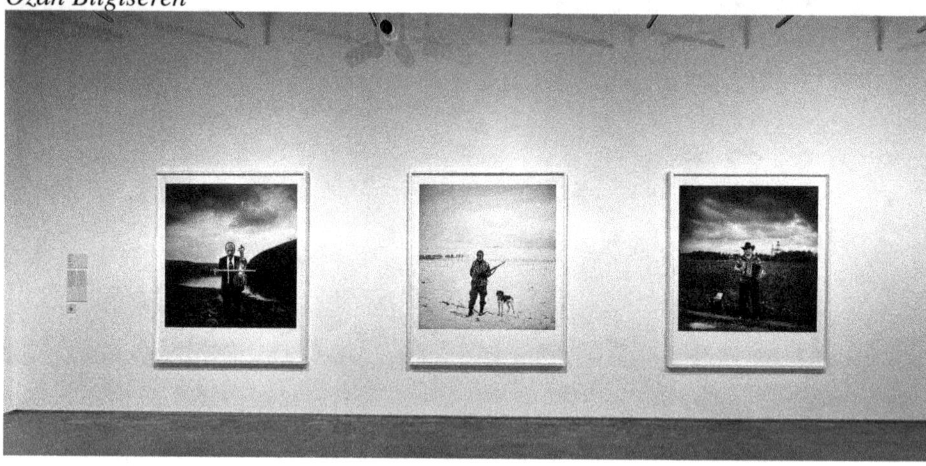

Clearly, these photographs were originally taken with a medium-format digital camera, as evidenced by the image quality and aspect ratio. Upon close inspection, numerous traces of Photoshop retouching were visibly apparent in many of the prints. This leads to a pertinent question: why were heavily retouched medium-format portraits displayed in a manner that intentionally evoked the aesthetic of instant analog photography? I suspect the answer lies in the desire to visually convey a sense of spontaneity—a feeling that the moment captured was both fleeting and genuine. Perhaps this curatorial decision was made retrospectively rather than at the project's inception. Nevertheless, the effectiveness of such post hoc design choices in enhancing the intended emotional resonance remains debatable. The decades-long cultural saturation of Polaroid aesthetics—associated with immediacy, authenticity, and the visual cue of "having just happened"—has conditioned viewers to interpret such formats as inherently truthful. The continued popularity of contemporary instant films by Fuji and Polaroid is arguably an extension of this visual and emotional conditioning. (Figure: 45)

Figure 45. Nuri Bilge Ceylan's exhibition - © Ozan Bilgiseren

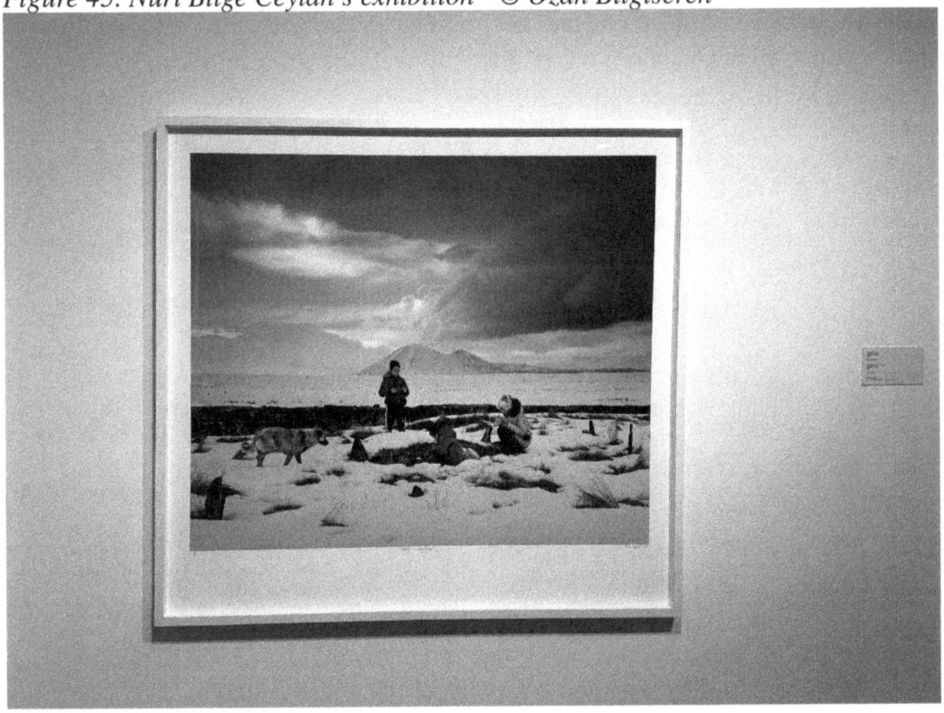

To more concretely illustrate my argument, I would like to reference the groundbreaking work of a photographer I personally met in Kosovo in 2008. Hungarian-born American war photographer Balazs Gardi was awarded the World Press Photo Award that same year for his work documenting the ongoing war in Afghanistan. In an unorthodox approach, Gardi supplemented his professional DSLR equipment with a plastic, single-lens, point-and-shoot camera loaded with standard 36-exposure film rolls. This unconventional and labor-intensive method—especially in the high-risk context of combat photography—was aimed at conveying the raw intensity of the moment. Through these modest tools, Gardi sought to capture and transmit the visceral immediacy of battlefield scenes in their most unfiltered and compelling form.

By 2010–2011, Balazs Gardi had found the expressive visual tool he had long been searching for: Hipstamatic. Using an iPhone equipped with the Hipstamatic app, Gardi not only documented the deadliest frontlines of Afghanistan—including Tora Bora and the Korangal Valley—and the daily routines of the 1/8 Marine Division, but also transformed this widely followed photographic series into exhibitions and a book. (Figure: 46) The public's keen interest in Gardi's war photography was largely driven by his dedicated online following. The Hipstamatic app, which applied stylized effects to emulate images shot on a vintage Polaroid film camera, added a kind of subliminal depth to these depictions of "lived reality." (Figure: 47) Gardi's portrayal of brutal, immediate, and raw moments from daily life—filtered through this unconventional medium—was not only well received, but also emotionally impactful for his audience (NPR, 2025).

Figure 46. Balazs Gardi's Hipstamatic shots of Afganistan

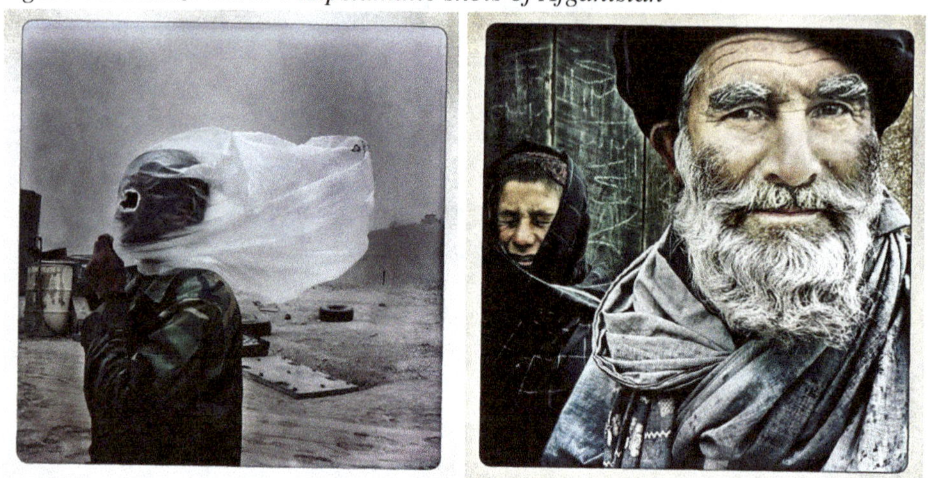

Figure 47. Balazs Gardi's Hipstamatic shots of Afganistan

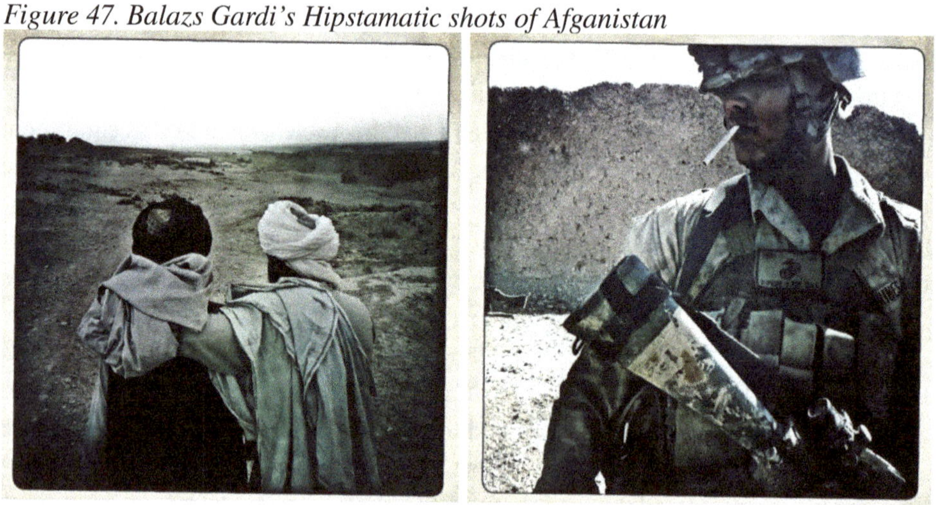

This example underscores an important distinction: while experimenting with an original visual language or affective expression is significant, arriving at a genuinely effective way of emphasizing reality is an entirely different challenge. When left to post-production, the enhancement of visual power can sometimes come at the cost of coherence or authenticity. In Gardi's case, the emotional impact of his work seems to stem not from digital editing, but from the courageous, clear-sighted decisions he made at the outset and his unwavering adherence to a unique, disciplined photographic method. What yesterday's Polaroid once represented, the Hipstamatic app—and today, Instagram—has since assumed in contemporary visual culture.

Two centuries ago, the invention of photography was among the most significant scientific undertakings devoted to capturing and documenting reality. Since it was introduced to the world by the French Academy of Sciences, photography has garnered immense interest and has arguably become the world's only truly universal visual language—one that requires no translation. Today, individuals can express their thoughts and emotions through a single image uploaded to social media. Despite the growing concerns around AI-generated content, deepfakes, and digitally manipulated media, the process of producing photographs and videos, documenting everyday events, and sharing or archiving them has never been easier. Yet, storytelling remains—as it always has—an endeavor that not every practitioner can master. Capturing narratives in a way that approaches the truth demands experience, exceptional talent, and a high degree of self-discipline.

GAINS AND LOSSES

When it comes to storytelling, the literary movement of "Magical Realism" has always held a deep fascination for me, as it has for many literature enthusiasts. Earlier this year, I was quite surprised by the series adaptation of Gabriel García Márquez's *One Hundred Years of Solitude*. Typically, screen adaptations of novels often fall short for those who have already read the book, triggering disappointment due to the narrative shortcomings or the inability to capture the book's essence—similar to how meaning can be lost in linguistic translation (Taylor, 2025). However, in this series, the opposite proved to be true. Upon doing some research, I discovered that the casting process had been executed with exceptional diligence. (Figure: 48) This reminded me of the almost superhuman efforts seen in Gregory Crewdson's documentary *Brief Encounters*, which reveals the meticulous photographic processes behind his work (Crewdson, 2025, b). In fact, the intense labor invested in high-caliber cinematic or television productions is not dissimilar to the painstaking work depicted in Crewdson's documentary. In addition to that film, various online behind-the-scenes materials offer glimpses into how rigorously Crewdson approaches casting for every single scene he imagines.

Figure 48. Backstage still image from "One Hundred Years of Solitude"

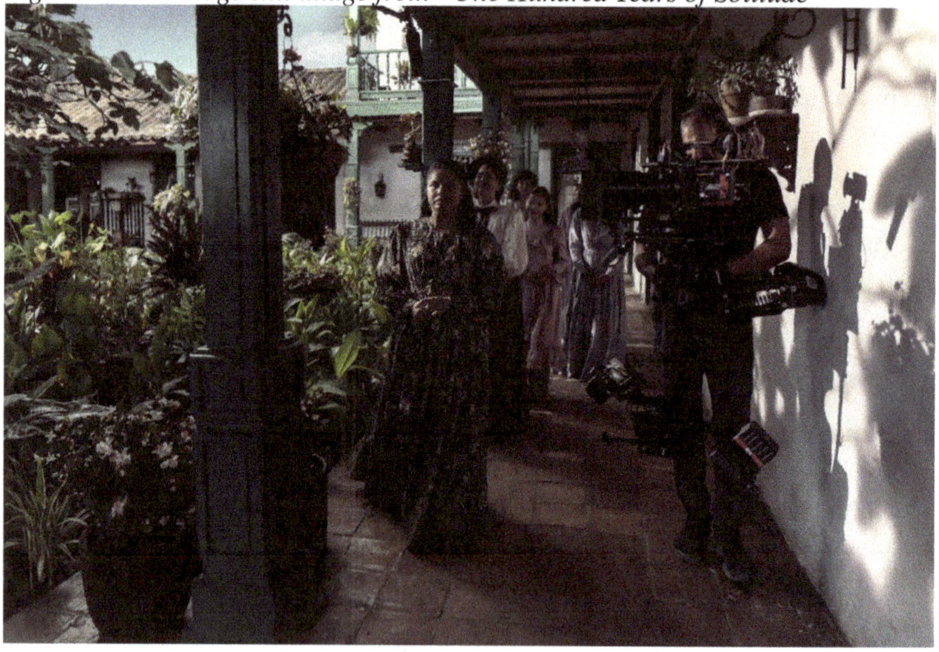

Meanwhile, photography, which once stood as a representation of reality, has today either undergone significant erosion or transformation. During a short documentary interview about Ara Güler that I was involved in at the 2018 Bursa International Photography Festival (Bursa FotoFest), I had the opportunity to speak with the late Bruno Barbey, a renowned member of Magnum Photos. (Figure: 49) Our conversation inevitably turned to the structural, conceptual, and emotional shifts that photography had undergone. One of Barbey's sharpest critiques—which remains etched in my memory—was his observation that photographers today no longer "feel" the moment with the same intuition as in the past. According to this seasoned master, working with film activated a unique kind of sensorium within the photographer's mind, much like a radar. In contrast, the capabilities of digital cameras today, which allow dozens of frames to be shot within fractions of a second, seem to have dulled this perceptive faculty. The act of photography has become more about letting artificial intelligence determine focus points, mindlessly shooting in burst mode without even looking through the viewfinder, and later spending hours at a computer deciding which images to keep—if any at all. As a result, we end up hoarding thousands of purposeless photos that occupy space on our hard drives and smartphones, yet which we cannot bring ourselves to delete.

Figure 49. Bruno Barbey inspecting contact prints with Prof. Ozan Bilgiseren

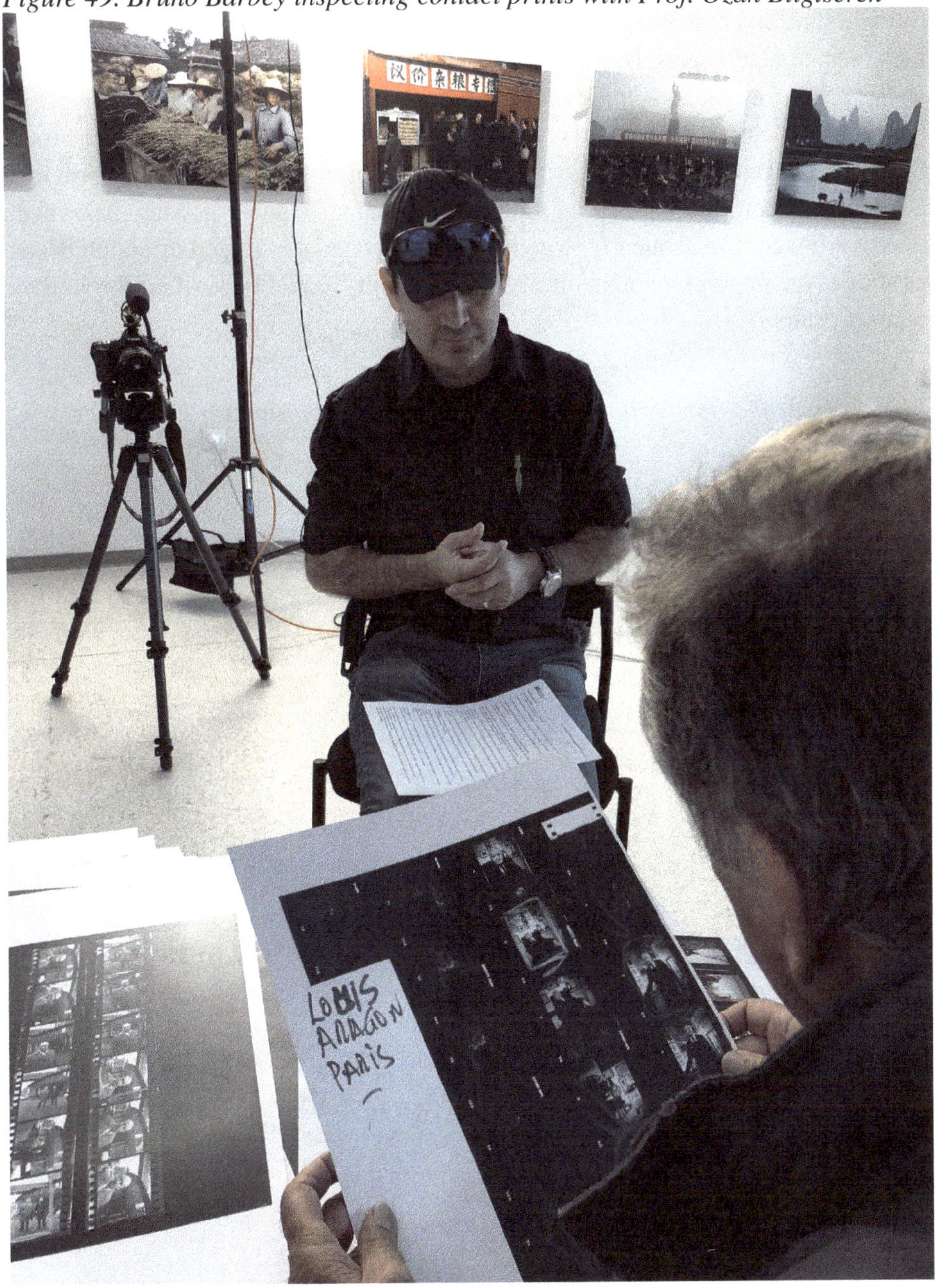

I count myself fortunate to have had the rare opportunity to examine the contact sheets of negatives shot in various formats by Ara Güler during his lifetime. This gave me firsthand insight into his acute sense of timing—a skill for which he was already well known. Most of Güler's iconic Istanbul photographs were captured in a single shot, and at most, in bursts of three or four frames. (Figure: 50) Referring to these very contact sheets, Bruno Barbey explained that, for Magnum Photos, contact sheets carried a special significance. They were private—akin to a photographer's bedroom. A contact sheet could reveal the trajectory of a photographer's success or failure on a given assignment. For photo editors working at agencies, they provided a means to follow the sequence of moments leading up to and following the critical, decisive image. Consequently, whether a photograph was staged or spontaneous, as well as the photographer's honesty and reliability, could be verified through the contact prints.

Figure 50. Bruno Barbey inspecting contact prints with Prof. Ozan Bilgiseren

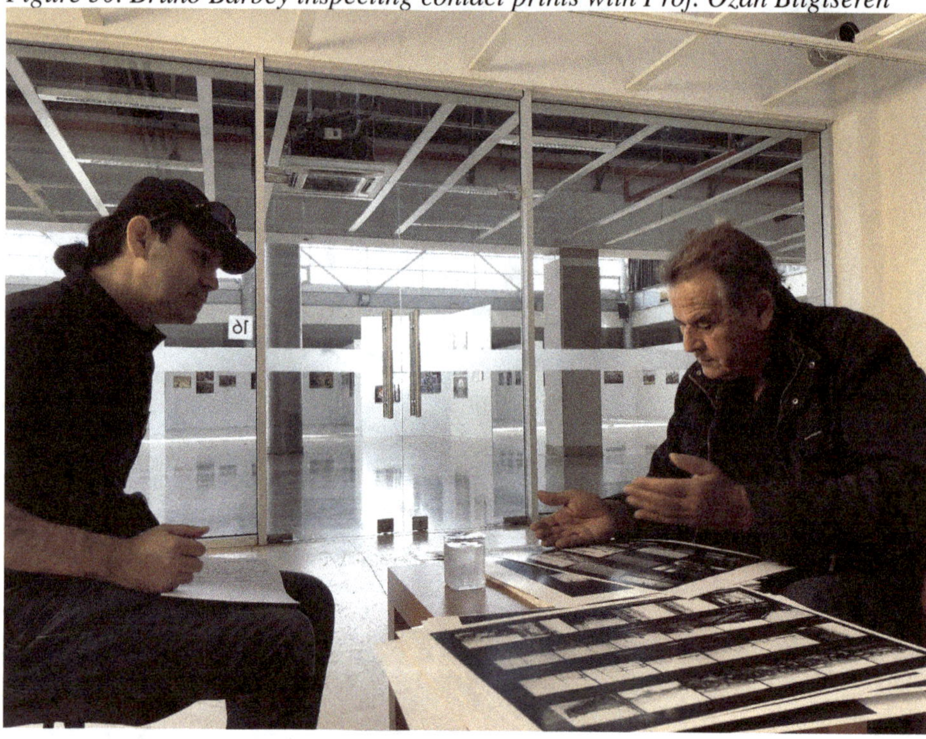

GAINS, LOSSES

In 2011, Magnum published a book titled *Contact Sheets*, which presented exactly the kind of issues that master photographer Bruno Barbey touched upon in his interview—providing curious readers with a wide range of unique examples from different photographers (Lubben, 2025). (Figure: 51) The most compelling story for me was the contact series by French photographer Gilles Peress, which documented the massacre committed by the British Army on January 30, 1972—a day that went down in history as "Bloody Sunday." These photographs, which also inspired the famous U2 song of the same name, served as evidence in the court proceedings that lasted for decades. The incident occurred during a civil rights protest in Derry, Northern Ireland, where 26 civilians were shot and 13 were killed instantly by the British Army's 1st Parachute Regiment. Protester Patrick Doherty was photographed by Peress both immediately before and after his death (Alphahistory, 2025). Claims that the unarmed Doherty was carrying a handgun were refuted by Peress's images. Moreover, the court used his contact sheets as a frame-by-frame visual record to analyze the soldiers' behavior during the critical initial moments of the massacre. After years of litigation, the final report was published in 2010, with then-Prime Minister David Cameron issuing a formal and overdue apology to the Irish public. Peress returned to Northern Ireland in the 1980s, and his monumental project *Whatever You Say, Say Nothing*, which condensed his work in the region into nearly 2,000 pages, took thirty years to complete (Photomuseumireland, 2025).

Figure 51. Magnum Contact Sheets book cover / 2011

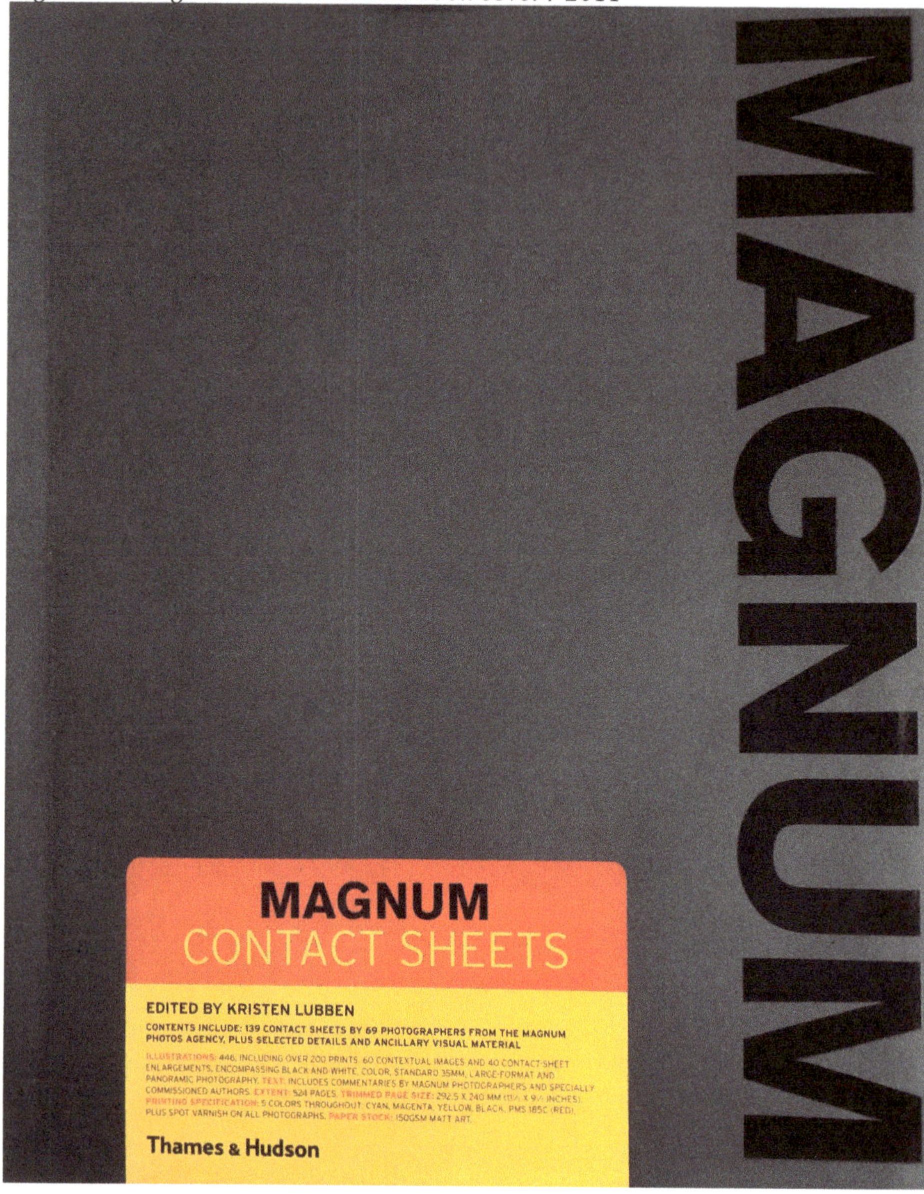

While we still acknowledge the value and importance of truth and reality, the degree to which we pursue them today remains uncertain. Perhaps our collective fatigue with "truths" by the end of the twentieth century led us to shelve reality altogether—or at least to lean in that direction. The Falklands War introduced new terminologies into our vocabulary, such as "embedded journalism" (Wyatt, 2025). As the digital revolution accelerated, our social norms underwent profound changes. Recently, we have observed that emotional appeal, belief systems, and personal convictions seem to carry more weight in public discourse than objective facts. This context reflects the rise of "post-truth," a term used to describe an environment where emotions and beliefs overshadow empirical reality. (Figure: 52) On the one hand, artificial intelligence entered the daily lives of ordinary smartphone users; on the other hand, we began employing detection software to determine whether a text or image had been generated using ChatGPT or similar tools, or to assess plagiarism percentages in master's and doctoral theses. (Figure: 53) Even the most prestigious platforms have not remained immune—take, for instance, the backlash received by the film *Emilia Perez* during the last Academy Awards, when AI-assisted architectural designs featured in the Hungarian dubbing and final scene of the film drew intense media scrutiny (Lammers, 2025). (Figure: 54) Nonetheless, it is worth recalling that half a century ago, memorizing multiplication tables was a critical educational task, until pocket calculators—which were initially seen as technological marvels—rendered such rote learning obsolete. This analogy may offer some foresight into our current discourse around artificial intelligence. Meanwhile, following the end of lengthy protests by Hollywood extras, it remains uncertain whether laborers in the creative industry have truly secured their rights. Ultimately, traditionally trained visual artists and manual laborers alike feel increasingly vulnerable in today's evolving landscape.

Figure 52. Fulton County Jail mug shot of President Trump hung outside at the wall of Oval Office

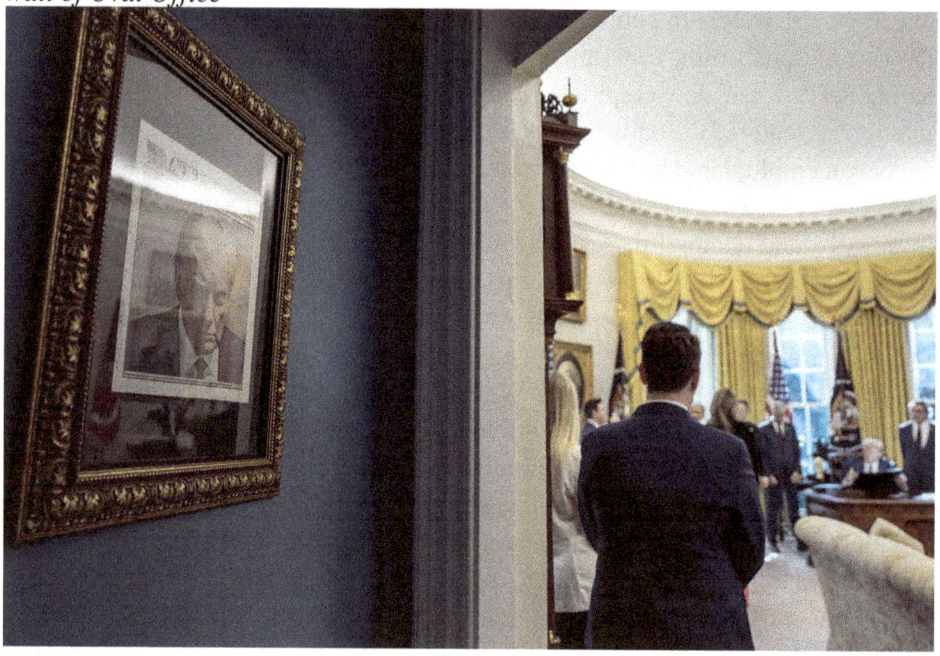

Figure 53. Still image from "The Brutalist"

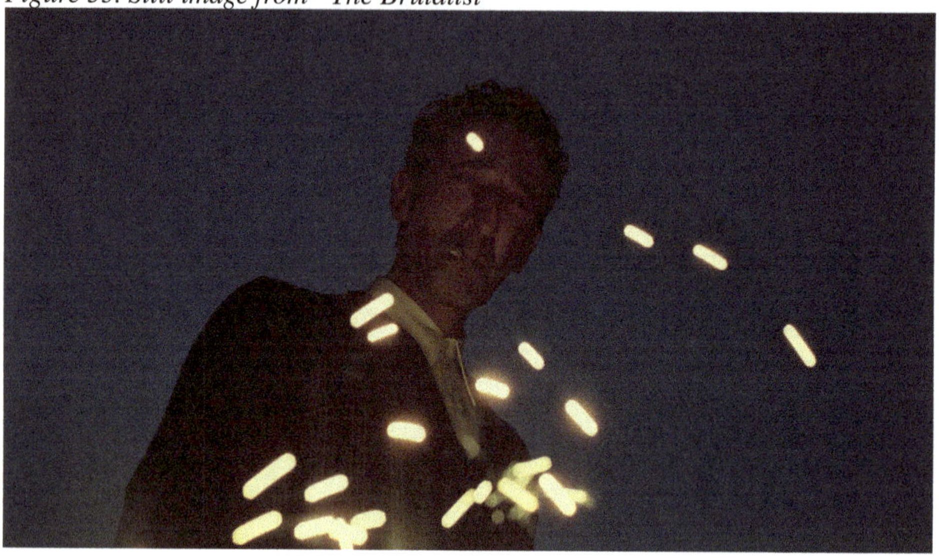

Figure 54. Movie poster of "The Brutalist"

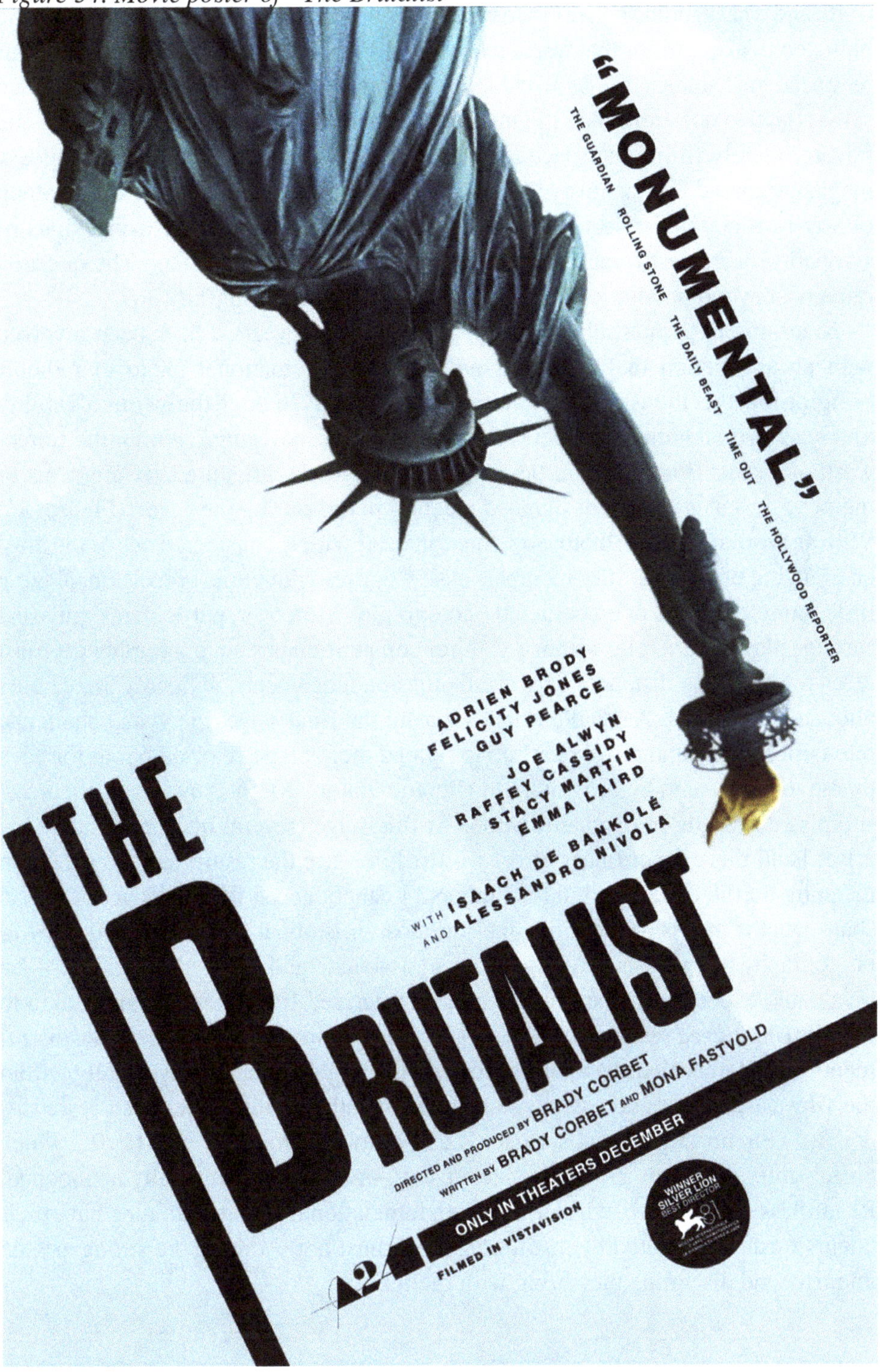

So what truly connects us to reality today? To what extent do we pursue or value truth, and what genuine reactions do we express in relation to facts? These are pressing philosophical questions that warrant broader discussion and could lead to numerous new academic studies. In *The War Photographer*, James Nachtwey poses a poignant self-reflective question: "Are the images I've taken of so much pain, suffering, and poverty merely filling the space next to a luxury watch advertisement in a glossy magazine spread?" (Nachtwey, 2025). Similar sentiments apply today to the plight of war-torn populations in Palestine, Ukraine, and Syria—where expressions of sympathy, or modest financial contributions, often feel insufficient. The question remains: beyond passive support, what more can we meaningfully do?

Returning to popular photography, for the past six years, I have been involved with an association that organizes national and international photo marathons, bringing together thousands of photographers annually through the medium's ability to trigger primal human instincts of "hunting and discovering." Within the framework of a strict time limit, participants are presented with a predetermined set of themes—revealed only at designated meeting points during the event. (Figure: 55) With an absolute ban on Photoshop, this contest is widely considered one of the most challenging of its kind. Jury members assess entries with utmost precision, leaving little room for staged or constructed photography. Moreover, participants' physical stamina plays a vital role: within a 12-hour competition period, photographers must often traverse long distances between theme announcements, with only three hours allocated per round. As daylight fades during the final stage, the visual challenge intensifies. Participants are required to upload their single selected photo for each theme to the system before midnight (Photomaraton, 2025). Any late or incorrect submission results in disqualification. At this stage, several questions inevitably arise: Is all this extraordinary effort worthwhile? Are the results satisfying? What meaning do the outcomes hold for others? I cannot speak for everyone, but I can share what it means to me. First and foremost, it is about experiencing the joy of photography and the opportunity to meet passionate and talented individuals—an invaluable experience. The sensory pleasure derived from such visuals is akin to MTV's *Unplugged* sessions in the 1990s, where the prohibition of electronic instruments forced musicians to return to the essence of performance. Especially within the film-based analogue category of photo marathons, this experience resonates deeply. This nostalgia recalls Queen's early albums from the mid-1970s, which prominently declared "no synthesizers used"—a rule they eventually abandoned. Regardless of tools used, when artists with foundational classical training have their talents further cultivated by institutions, one must not overlook the strong artistic integrity and discipline they bring with them.

Figure 55. PhotoMaraton Istanbul is an important performance competition that brings together photography enthusiasts every year at Sirkeci Train Station, İstanbul / October 29th 2022 – © Ozan Bilgiseren

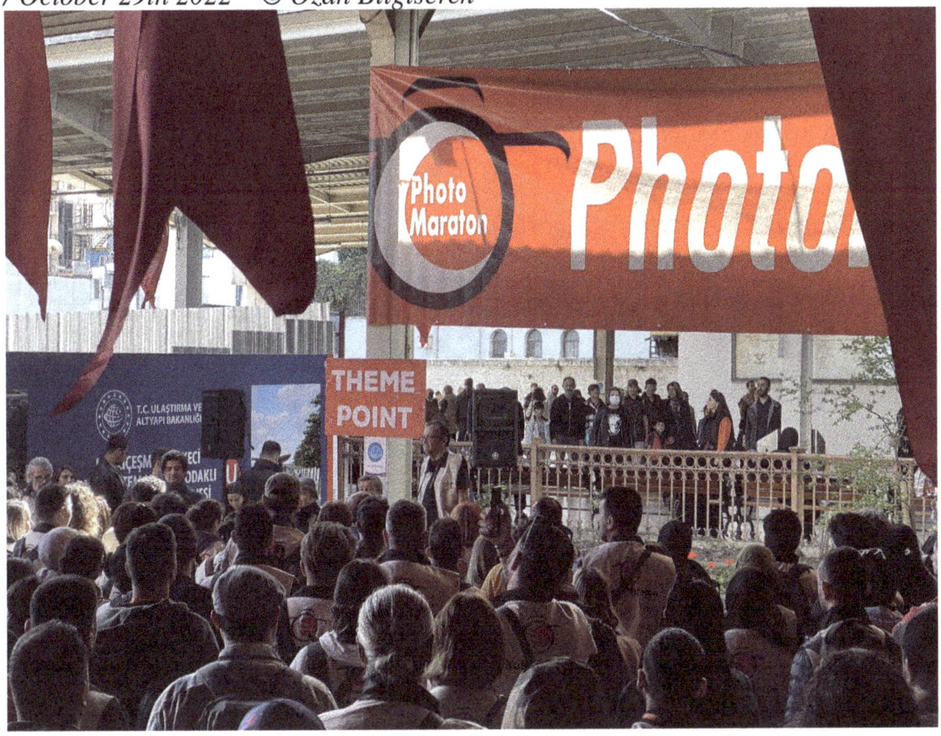

It was a great honor to personally meet Nick Ut and to spend four intense days together during a busy program. (Figure: 56) (Figure: 57) On December 8, 2019, during his artist talk at the Istanbul Haliç Congress Center, Ut, with utmost humility and sincerity, shared rarely seen photographs from his war portfolio with the international audience (Yaşar, 2025). Three years later to the day, on June 8, 2022, Nick Ut met Pope Francis at the Vatican and presented him with a signed copy of his iconic photograph to commemorate its 50th anniversary (originally taken on June 8, 1972). The image, considered to have contributed to America's eventual withdrawal from Vietnam, is etched into collective memory as one of the most powerful anti-war photographs of the twentieth century. It is disheartening to hear recent speculations and misinformation about this visual masterpiece (Holland, 2025). In an age where truth is increasingly questioned, ethical journalism—especially in war photography—demands the highest standards of professional integrity. Trust, once lost, is difficult to rebuild. For this very reason, I hold in deep admiration the photographic legacies of masters such as Josef Koudelka, James Nachtwey, Bruno Barbey, H. C. Bresson, Ara Güler, and, as of the date of completing this section, the recently deceased Sebastião Salgado (New York Times, 2025).) (Figure: 58) Likewise, the documentaries of Yann Arthus-Bertrand, Ron Fricke, Sir David Attenborough, and Coşkun Aral continue to be sources of inspiration. The extraordinary and unique works they produce are not easily replicated. Thanks to their unwavering principles and disciplines, their contributions to humanity remain timeless, resonating deeply with our sense of reality and genuine emotion—standing as monumental, mesmerizing, and original testaments to photographic truth.

Figure 56. Nick Ut and Prof. Ozan Bilgiseren at Karaköy, İstanbul / December 7th 2019

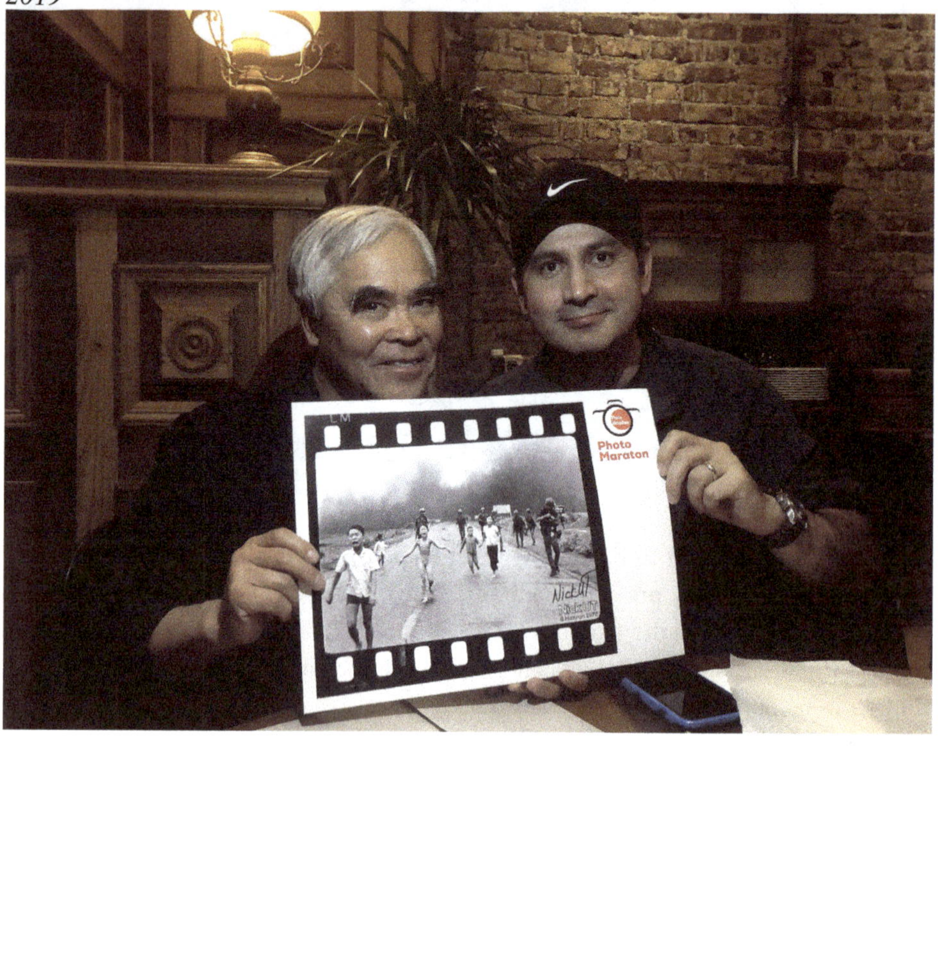

Figure 57. Prof. Ozan Bilgiseren shows Nick Ut around in Eminönü, İstanbul / December 7th 2019

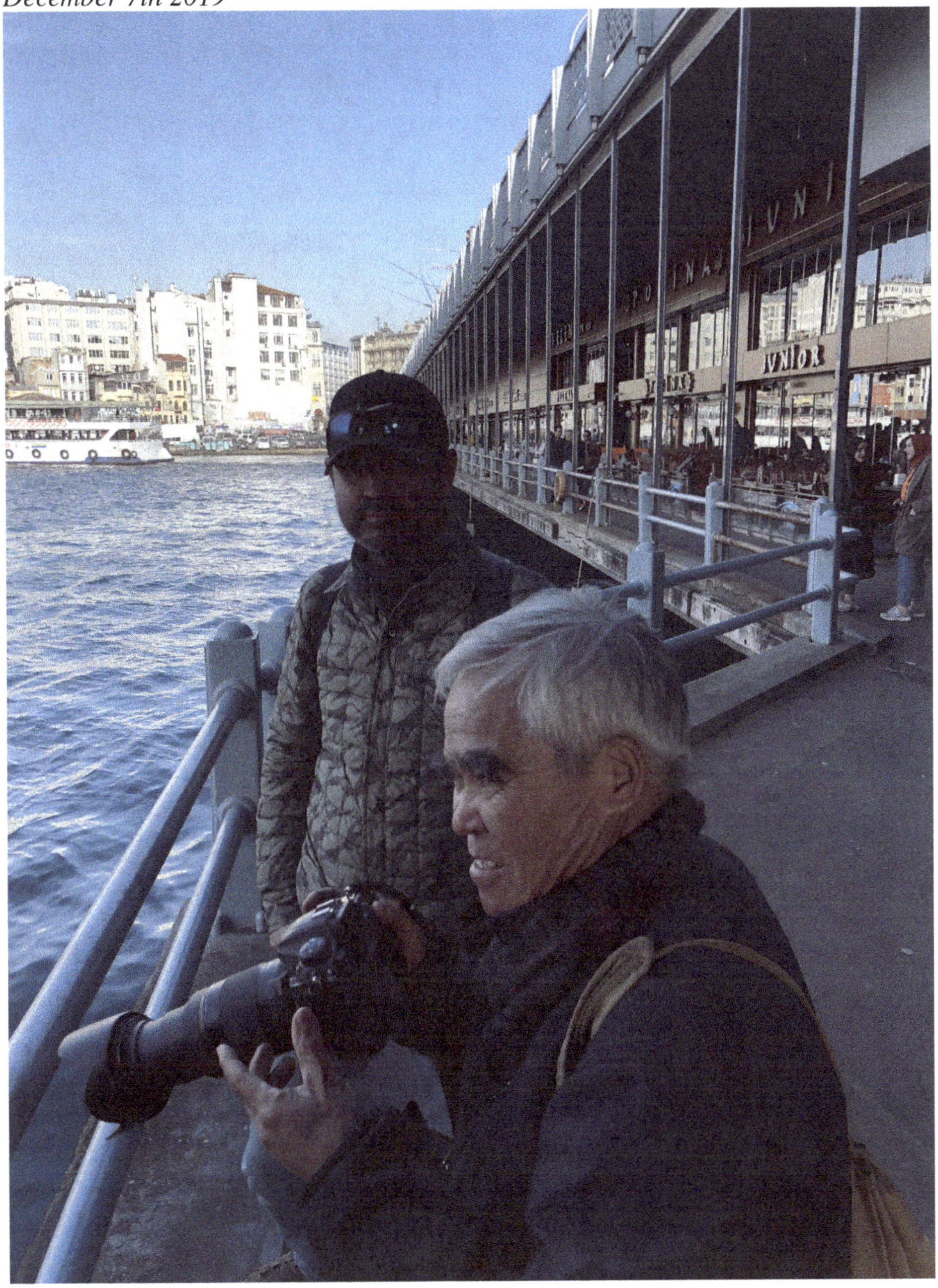

Figure 58. Sebastião Salgado, Lélia Wanick Salgado with Prof. Ozan Bilgiseren at "Genesis" exhibion İstanbul opening, Tophane-i Amire Cultural Center of Mimar Sinan Fine Arts University, İstanbul / September 27th 2024

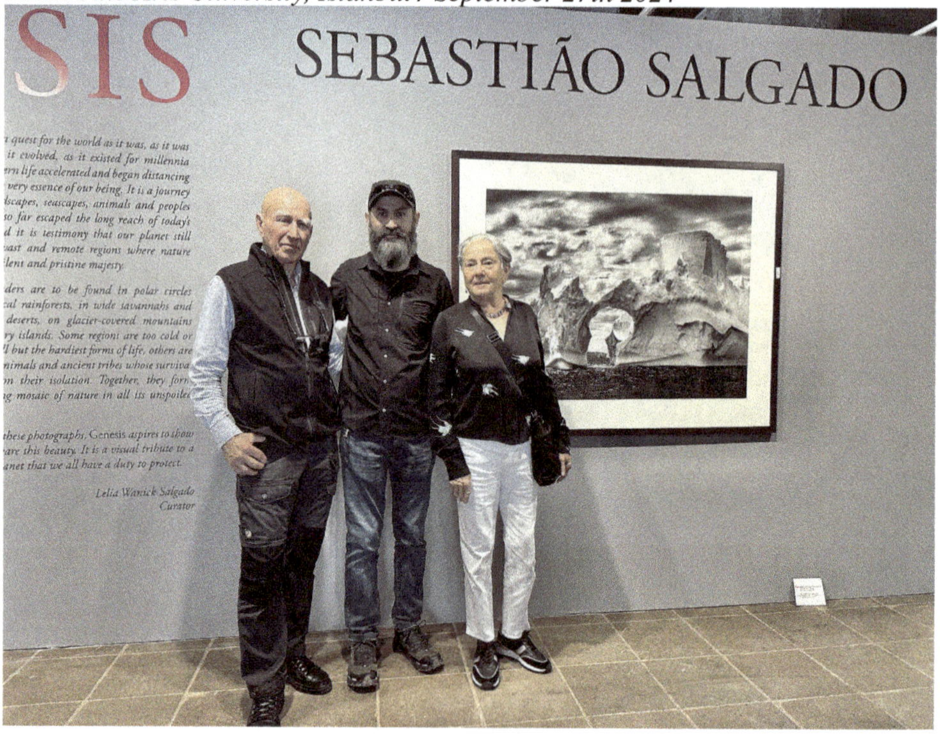

CONCLUSION

With the integration of new media technologies into artistic production processes, both art and photography have transcended their classical boundaries to become more flexible, interactive, and experience-oriented forms. The multiplicity of perspectives offered by digitalization has repositioned visual production not merely as a form of representation, but as a space for interrogation and intervention. As a result, photography has shed its sole function as a document and evolved into a medium for conveying cultural, political, and personal narratives. Simultaneously, users have transformed from passive viewers into active agents—producers and distributors within this visual ecosystem. Artificial intelligence technologies, when combined with the emotionally and belief-driven tendencies of the post-truth era, allow for the reconstruction—and even the rewriting—of visual reality. Yet, despite all these technical advancements and evolving narrative strategies, the need for an anchoring “truth” remains. The inherent duality of photography—as both document and interpretation, both record and fiction—has rendered it one of the most powerful modes of expression in the modern age. Therefore, as we witness the transformation of photography from both artistic and ethical standpoints, it becomes imperative to interpret, produce, and assess it without compromising on historical knowledge, technical literacy, and human sensitivity. From Ara Güler to David Lynch, Milan Kundera to Balazs Gardi, numerous examples remind us that the true value of photography lies not solely in its visual content, but in the intention behind its creation, the moment it captures, and the ethical stance it embodies.

REFERENCES

Adams, T. (2025, 10 March) *theguardian.com,* The big picture: Grace Kelly jumps for Philippe Halsman, https://www.theguardian.com/artanddesign/2019/feb/24/the-big-picture-grace-kelly-jumps-philippe-halsman-magnum-the-body-observed

Alphahistory (2025, 30 March) *alphahistory.com,* A French photographer recalls Bloody Sunday (1972), https://alphahistory.com/northernireland/gilles-peress-bloody-sunday-1972/

Aral, C. (2025, 16 April) *youtube.com,* Fotoğrafın Kalesi: Toroslab - Coşkun Aral Anlatıyor, https://www.youtube.com/watch?v=OUkl7bsrGZY

BBC. (2025, 19 April) *bbc.com,* Robert Capa's greatest war photo 'was a lucky shot', https://www.bbc.com/news/av/entertainment-arts-24723949

Bunyan, M. (2025, 1 April) *artblart.com,* Review: 'Jeff Wall Photographs' at The Ian Potter Centre: NGVA, National Gallery of Victoria, Melbourne, https://artblart.com/tag/jeff-wall-dressing-poultry/

Campany, D. (2025, 12 April) *davidcampany.com,* 'Migrant Mother, 1936', https://davidcampany.com/migrant-mother-1936-2/

Crewdson, G. (2025, 2 May, b) *gregorycrewdsonmovie.com,* http://www.gregorycrewdsonmovie.com/image-gallery.html

Crewdson, G. (2025, 2 May, a) gregorycrewdson.substack.com, The Making of Ophelia, https://gregorycrewdson.substack.com/p/the-making-of-ophelia

Dinçer, Y. D. (2025, 24 April) *istanbulmodern.org,* https://www.istanbulmodern.org/en/events/nuri-bilge-ceylan-in-another-place-exhibition-event

Dinçer, Y. D., & Ulu, D. (2025, 24 April) *istanbulmodern.org,* Nuri Bilge Ceylan: In Another Place, https://www.istanbulmodern.org/en/exhibitions/past/nuri-bilge-ceylan-in-another-placz

Edward, V. I. I. I. (2025, 12 April) *Wikipedia,* https://en.wikipedia.org/wiki/Edward_VIII

Fotografdergisi (2025, 25 April) *fotografdergisi.com,* https://www.fotografdergisi.com

Friswell, R. (2025, 28 April) *artesmagazine.com,* Robert Capa's Long-Lost 'Mexican Suitcase' Reveals a Trove of Vintage Photographs at ICP, https://artesmagazine.com/2010/11/robert-capas-long-lost-mexican-suitcase-reveals-a-trove-of-vintage-photographs-at-icp-2/

Gottschalk, M. (2025, 23 April) *artsy.net,* The Fateful Roadside Stop That Led to Dorothea Lange's "Migrant Mother" https://www.artsy.net/article/artsy-editorial-fateful-roadside-led-dorothea-langes-migrant-mother

GOV. (2025, 17 April) *gov.uk,* www.gov.uk/government/organisations/information-commissioner-s office#:~:text=The%20Information%20Commissioner's%20Office%20(ICO,for%20Science%2C%20Innovation%20and%20Technology. Gall, J. and Buchanan-Smith, P. (2025, 23 March) vintagebooks.wordpress.com, What We Talk About When We Talk About Book Covers, https://vintagebooks.wordpress.com/2009/09/08/what-we-talk-about-when-we-talk-about-book-covers/

Growcoot, M. (2025, 10 April) *petapixel.com,* David Lynch's Enduring Impact on Photography, https://petapixel.com/2025/01/22/david-lynchs-enduring-impact-on-photography/

Henley, J. (2025, 13 April, a) *theguardian.com,* 55 years on, the controversial kiss that could be worth £10,000, https://www.theguardian.com/world/2005/apr/13/france.arts

Henley, J. (2025, 16 April, b) *theguardian.com,* The remarkable story behind the kiss photo that melted hearts - and what happened to the 'happy' couple, https://www.theguardian.com/world/2005/apr/13/france.arts

Holland, O. (2025, 6 April) edition.cnn.com, Who took 'Napalm Girl'? World Press Photo 'suspends' attribution of historic Vietnam War image, https://edition.cnn.com/2025/05/19/style/napalm-girl-world-press-photo-nick-ut-hnk-intl

Howard, H. (2025, 16 April) dailymail.co.uk, The remarkable story behind the kiss photo that melted hearts - and what happened to the 'happy' couple, https://www.dailymail.co.uk/news/article-14706713/Kiss-photo-melted-hearts-Paris-1950.html

İstanbul Modern. (2025, 20 April) x.com/istanbulmodern, https://x.com/istanbulmodern_/status/764356159922987011/photo/1

Kaninsky, M. (2025, 10 April) *petapixel,* One of the Most Iconic Kissing Photos Was Staged, https://petapixel.com/2019/07/24/one-of-the-most-iconic-kissing-photos-was-staged/

Karahasan, Z. (2025, 11 April) *yesilodak.com,* İnsan İnsanı Çekermiş, https://www.yesilodak.com/insan-insani-cekermis

Karel Hájek. (2025, 12 April) *Wikipedia,* https://cs.wikipedia.org/wiki/Karel_H%C3%A1jek

KVKK. (2025, 18 May) kvkk.gov.tr, Personal Data Protection Law, https://www.kvkk.gov.tr/Icerik/6649/Personal-Data-Protection-Law

Lammers, T. (2025, 20 April) *forbes.com,* 'Emilia Pérez' And 'The Brutalist' AI Controversies, Explained, https://www.forbes.com/sites/timlammers/2025/01/21/emilia-prez-and-the-brutalist-ai-controversies-explained/

Life (2025, 2 April) *life.com,* The Photography of Philippe Halsman, https://www.life.com/photographer/philippe-halsman/

Lubben, K. (2025, 12 March) *thamesandhudsonusa.com,* https://www.thamesandhudsonusa.com/books/magnum-contact-sheets-softcover

Magnumphotos (2025, 20 March) *magnumphotos,* Philippe Halsman: Jump, https://www.magnumphotos.com/arts-culture/philippe-halsman-jump-book/

Mcardle, J. (2025, 20 May) *onthisdateinphotography,* https://onthisdateinphotography.com/2017/03/31/march-31/#:~:text=March%2031:%20The%20photographer%20who,21%2C%201948

Mccormack, D. (2025, 22 April) *dailymail,* 'I never lost hope': Startling interview unearthed with woman behind iconic Great Depression image talking just five years before her death in 1983, https://www.dailymail.co.uk/news/article-2290879/I-lost-hope-Startling-interview-unearthed-woman-iconic-Great-Depression-image-talking-just-years-death-1983.html

McIntosh, S., & Schofield, H. (2025, 17 Nisan) *bbc.com,* Francoise Bornet: Woman in Robert Doisneau's Paris kiss photo dies aged 93, https://www.bbc.com/news/entertainment-arts-67877244

Milan Kundera. (2025, 12 May) *Wikipedia,* https://en.wikipedia.org/wiki/Milan_Kundera

Mimic (photograph) (2025, 12 April) Wikipedia, https://en.wikipedia.org/wiki/Mimic_(photograph)

Moma (2025, 18 May) *Philippe Halsman,* https://www.moma.org/collection/works/47919

Nachtwey, J. (2025, 24 April) *time.com,* James Nachtwey: How Photography Can Change the World, https://time.com/3693061/james-nachtwey-receives-lifetime-achievement-award/

National Gallery of Art. (2025, 20 April, c) *nga.gov,* The Real Lives of People in Dorothea Lange's Portraits, https://www.nga.gov/stories/articles/real-lives-people-dorothea-langes-portraits

National Portrait Gallery. (2025, 12 April, b), npg.org.uk, Wallis, Duchess of Windsor; Prince Edward, Duke of Windsor (King Edward VIII), https://www.npg.org.uk/collections/search/portrait/mw09580/Wallis-Duchess-of-Windsor-Prince-Edward-Duke-of-Windsor-King-Edward-VIII

National Portrait Gallery. (2025, 12 April, a), npg.org.uk, Wallis, Duchess of Windsor; Prince Edward, Duke of Windsor (King Edward VIII), Edward-Duke-of-Windsor-King-Edward VIII?LinkID=mp08029&role=art&rNo=3&_gl=1*e-j5g1r*_up*MQ.*_ga*MTg4MjU3MzgxLjE3NDg2OTgwMDk.*_ga_3D53N72CH-J*czE3NDg2OTgwMDgkbzEkZzAkdDE3NDg2OTgwMDgkajYwJGwwJGgw

New York Times. (2025, 7 June) nytimes.com, https://www.nytimes.com/2025/05/23/arts/sebastiao-salgado-dead.html

Nolden/H. (2025, 3 May) *yourartshop-noldenh.com,* Jeff Wall – The Thinker, https://yourartshop-noldenh.com/jeff-wall-the-thinker-with-a-sword-in-his-back/

Norimberk: Zlocin A Soud (2025, 12 May) *Abebooks,* https://www.abebooks.com/first-edition/Norimberk-Zlocin-Soud-Nuremberg-Crime-Court/20327713591/bd

NPR. (2025, 10 May) www.npr.org, Foreign Policy: The Afghan War In Hipstamatic, https://www.npr.org/2011/07/26/138701217/foreign-policy-the-afghan-war-in-hipstamatic

NTV. (2025, 16 April) ntv.com.tr, Bennu Yıldırımlar ilk kez konuştu! Nuri Bilge Ceylan'a “etik değil” çıkışı, https://www.ntv.com.tr/galeri/n-life/bennu-yildirimlar-ilk-kez-konustu-nuri-bilge-ceylana-etik-degil-cikisi,huUlY-JpzEml19tqje-onQ

Paris syndrome (2025, 12 April) *Wikipedia,* https://en.wikipedia.org/wiki/Paris_syndrome

PBS. (2025, 28 Nisan) *pbs.org,* ttp://www.pbs.org/wnet/americanmasters/database/capa_r.html

Pestrý týden (2025, 12 May) *Wikipedia,* https://en.wikipedia.org/wiki/Pestr%C3%BD_t%C3%BDden#:~:text=Establishment,-Karel%20Neubert%2C%20son&text=Pestr%C3%BD%20t%C3%BDden%20was%20founded%20by,and%20List%20pan%C3%AD%20a%20d%C3%ADvek

Photoeye (2025, 18 May) *photoeye.com,* https://www.photoeye.com/bookstore/citation/ZF397?modal=%23booktease-modal

Photomaraton (2025, 25 April) *photomaraton.com,* https://www.photomaraton.com/katilim-sartlari-ve-kurallar/

Photomuseumireland (2025, 28 March) timeline.photomuseumireland.ie, Gilles Peress' epic summation of his work in Northern Ireland published by Steidl, https://timeline.photomuseumireland.ie/timeline/gilles-peres-epic-summation-of-his-work-in-northern-ireland-published-by-steidl/

Pinault Collection. (2025, 15 May) *lesoeuvres.pinaultcollection,* Napalm Victim (#4), Saigon, S. Vietnam, April 29, 1971 1971 – 1993, https://lesoeuvres.pinaultcollection.com/en/artwork/napalm-victim-4-saigon-s-vietnam-april-29-197

Restorapic (2025, 10 April) *restorapic.com,* 12 Historic Photographs That Were Manipulated, https://restorapic.com/12-historic-photographs-that-were-manipulated/

Şapolyo, E. B. (2025, 11 April) *isteataturk.com,* https://isteataturk.com/Kronolojik/Tarih/1936/9/4/Ingiltere-Krali-VIII-Edwardi-Dolmabahce-Sarayi-Rihtiminda-karsilarken-04091936/15#google_vignett

Serbestiyet (2025, 8 April) Muhammed El Fayed, 94 yaşında öldü: Son ana kadar Diana ve oğlu Dodi'yi MI6'ın öldürdüğüne inandı, https://serbestiyet.com/featured/muhammed-el-fayed-94-yasinda-oldu-son-ana-kadar-diana-ve-oglu-dodiyi-mi6in-oldurdugune-inandi-141124/

Simurgkitabevi (2025, 26 April) *simurgkitabevi.com,* Sabit Kalfagil, Türkiye'nin Üzerindeki Işık, https://www.istanbulkitapcisi.com/turkiyenin-uzerindeki-isik

Sothebys, 2025, 14 May) *sothebys,* Dorothea Lange, https://www.sothebys.com/en/auctions/ecatalogue/2005/photographs-n08115/lot.43.html

Taylor, L. (2025, 23 March) *theguardian.com,* One Hundred Years of Solitude: Colombians celebrate Netflix TV series of the country's 'national poem', https://www.theguardian.com/books/2024/dec/20/one-hundred-years-of-solitude-netflix-series

The Book of Laughter and Forgetting. (2025, 16 May) *Wikipedia,* https://en.wikipedia.org/wiki/The_Book_of_Laughter_and_Forgetting

The Joke. (2025, 12 May) *Wikipedia,* https://en.wikipedia.org/wiki/The_Joke_(novel)

W.E. (2025, 12 April) *Wikipedia,* https://en.wikipedia.org/wiki/W.E

Wyatt, C. (2025, 20 April) bbc.co.uk, The Falklands for journalists: the ultimate embed experience, https://www.bbc.co.uk/webarchive/https%3A%2F%2Fwww.bbc.co.uk%2Fblogs%2Fcollegeofjournalism%2Fentries%2F5793e238-27a3-36bd-b63f-064717772aa7

Yaşar, F. (2025, 22 April) *gazeteduvar.com,* Nick Ut: O fotoğraf Amerikan halkını çılgına çevirdi, https://www.gazeteduvar.com.tr/kultur-sanat/2019/12/08/nick-ut-o-fotograf-amerikan-halkini-cilgina-cevirdi

Zhang, M. (2025, 10 April) *petapixel,* That Iconic 'Migrant Mother' Photo Was 'Photoshopped', https://petapixel.com/2018/11/30/that-iconic-migrant-mother-photo-was-photoshopped/

ADDITIONAL READINGS

Azoulay, A. (2008). *The civil contract of photography.* Zone Books.

Batchen, G. (1997). *Burning with desire: The conception of photography.* MIT Press.

Campany, D. (2008). *Photography and cinema.* Reaktion Books.

Fried, M. (2008). *Why photography matters as art as never before.* Yale University Press.

Hariman, R., & Lucaites, J. L. (2007). *No caption needed: Iconic photographs, public culture, and liberal democracy.* University of Chicago Press.

Mitchell, W. J. T. (1992). *The reconfigured eye: Visual truth in the post-photographic era.* MIT Press.

Ritchin, F. (2013). *Bending the frame: Photojournalism, documentary, and the citizen.* Aperture.

Sekula, A. (1986). The body and the archive. *October, 39*, 3–64.

Sontag, S. (1977). *On photography.* Farrar, Straus and Giroux. Barthes, R. (1981). *Camera lucida: Reflections on photography* (R. Howard, Trans.). Hill and Wang. (Original work published 1980)

KEY TERMS AND DEFINITIONS

Transformation of Photography: From darkroom practices to networked digital platforms, photography has shifted from a medium of record to a medium of construction. This shift redraws the line between reality and fiction through technical (editing, AI, compositing) and conceptual choices.

Documentary–Art Boundaries: When documentary claims meet aesthetic decisions, images function simultaneously as testimony and expression. Hybrid forms emerge, raising questions about accuracy, context, and responsibility.

Digital Manipulation: Post-production, AI generation, and deepfakes challenge photography's truth status. These practices heighten the need for visual literacy, provenance checks (e.g., metadata), and transparent disclosure.

Visual Truth and Representation: The camera's indexical trace is continually tested by staging, selection, and framing. Meaning is shaped by viewpoint, crop, caption, and circulation—each an ideological frame in its own right.

Ethical Responsibility: Photographers must consider consent, non-maleficence, and contextual integrity, especially in conflicts, disasters, and images of minors. In sensitive situations, ethics precede aesthetics.

Memory–State–Individual Triangle: Photography helps build and contest collective memory. Between state propaganda/censorship and personal witnessing, images become sites where policies of remembering and forgetting are negotiated.

Staged Photography: As in the work of Jeff Wall or Gregory Crewdson, staging transforms photographs into cinematic tableaux. Rather than "catching the real," these images construct scenarios that probe how reality is perceived.

Iconic Images and Public Impact: Widely circulated photographs can set agendas and spark ethical or political debate. Iconicity grows through repetition, recirculation, and recontextualization across media ecosystems.

APPENDIX

Photo Numbers, Subtitles and Credits

(Photo:01)- Czech-born French writer Milan Kundera

(Photo:02)- The book cover of Laughter and Forgetting

(Photo:03)- Klement Gottwald (before and after)

(Photo:04)- A photomontage poster from the speech of Klement Gottwald in Old Town Square in Prague on 21st of February 1948 for the 25th anniversary.

(Photo:05)- Page from the Pestrý týden magazine

(Photo:06)- Karel Hájek's powerful photo layouts side by side during Nuremberg trials.

(Photo:07)- Chinese Contemporary book of Photography

(Photo:08)- Edward VIII The Prince of Wales

(Photo:09)- Canadian Prime Minister, Queen and Edward VIII (before and after)

(Photo:10)- 2011 movie "W.E." directed by Madonna

(Photo:11)- Wallis Duchess of Windsor & Prince Edward Duke of Windsor by H. C. Bresson

(Photo:12)- Philippe Halsman's Exhibition at Kunsthal Rotterdam May 11st 2016 by © Ozan Bilgiseren

(Photo:13)- Philippe Halsman's small prints of various portraits at the exhibition - © Ozan Bilgiseren

(Photo:14)- Halsman produced 101 covers for *LIFE* Magazine - © Ozan Bilgiseren

(Photo:15)- Wallis Duchess of Windsor & Prince Edward Duke of Windsor by Hallsman

(Photo:16)- Wallis Duchess of Windsor & Prince Edward Duke of Windsor by Avedon

(Photo:17)- Retouched print of Migrant Mother

(Photo:18)- Original print of Migrant Mother

(Photo:19)- Migrant Mother's vesions side by side

(Photo:20)- The movie poster "The Grapes of Wrath" (1940)

(Photo:21)- "Falling Soldier" by Robert Capa

(Photo:22) "The Kiss by the Hotel de Ville" Robert Doisneau

(Photo:23)- "Couple" at Samatya circa 1970's by Sabit Kalfagil

(Photo:24)- Pocket-sized solar diagrams designed by Prof. Sabit Kalfagil - © Ozan Bilgiseren

(Photo:25)- Book titled "Light On Türkiye" by Prof. Sabit Kalfagil - © Ozan Bilgiseren

(Photo:26)- "Couple" at The Bund of Shanghai - © Ozan Bilgiseren

(Photo:27)- “Couple” at The Bund of Shanghai - © Ozan Bilgiseren

(Photo:28)- “Couple” at The Bund of Shanghai - © Ozan Bilgiseren

(Photo:29)- Lady Di & Dodi al-Fayed at the front page

(Photo:30)- “A View from an Apartment” by Jeff Wall / 2004-2005

(Photo:31)- “Mimic” by Jeff Wall 1982

(Photo:32)- “The Thinker” by Jeff Wall (1986) 1989

(Photo:33)- “Ophelia” by Gregory Crewdson / 2000-2001

(Photo:34)- Making of “Ophelia”

(Photo:35)- Making of “Ophelia”

(Photo:36)- Raymond Carver book covers by Todd Hido

(Photo:37)- David Lynch’s portrait on Paris Photo 2013 book cover

(Photo:38)- Toros Aladjajian and Prof. Ozan Bilgiseren / November 9th 2019

(Photo: 39)- Daguerre's bust with diorama stone marker - © Ozan Bilgiseren

(Photo:40)- Louis Jacques Mande Daguerre's tombstone - © Ozan Bilgiseren

(Photo:41)- Ara Güler’s picture with Fatih Aslan at the lightbox table of Toros Aladjajian –© Ozan Bilgiseren

(Photo:42)- Silver salt portrait print signed by David Lynch - © Ozan Bilgiseren

(Photo:43)- Video still of Bennu Yıldırımlar and Nuri Bilge Ceylan from the set of the movie “The Wild Pear Tree”

(Photo:44)- Ceylan’s exhibition at Istanbul Modern, titled “In Another Place” - © Ozan Bilgiseren

(Photo:45)- Nuri Bilge Ceylan’s exhibition - © Ozan Bilgiseren

(Photo:46)- Balazs Gardi’s Hipstamatic shots of Afganistan

(Photo:47)- Balazs Gardi’s Hipstamatic shots of Afganistan

(Photo:48)- Backstage still image from “One Hundred Years of Solitude”

(Photo:49)- Bruno Barbey inspecting contact prints with Prof. Ozan Bilgiseren

(Photo:50)- Bruno Barbey inspecting contact prints with Prof. Ozan Bilgiseren

(Photo:51)- Magnum Contact Sheets book cover / 2011

(Photo:52)- Fulton County Jail mug shot of President Trump hung outside at the wall of Oval Office

(Photo:53)- Still image from “The Brutalist”

(Photo:54)- Movie poster of “The Brutalist”

(Photo:55)- PhotoMaraton Istanbul is an important performance competition that brings together photography enthusiasts every year at Sirkeci Train Station, İstanbul / October 29th 2022 - @Ozan Bilgiseren

(Photo:56)- Nick Ut and Prof. Ozan Bilgiseren at Karaköy, İstanbul / December 7th 2019

(Photo:57)- Prof. Ozan Bilgiseren shows Nick Ut around in Eminönü, İstanbul / December 7th 2019

(Photo:58)- Sebastião Salgado, Lélia Wanick Salgado with Prof. Ozan Bilgiseren at “Genesis” exhibion İstanbul opening, Tophane-i Amire Cultural Center of Mimar Sinan Fine Arts University, İstanbul / September 27th 2024

Chapter 5
The Digital Presentation of Archaeological Data in Photography and Its Artistic Context

Seçkin Tercan
http://orcid.org/0000-0002-9477-4626
Mimar Sinan Fine Arts University, Turkey

ABSTRACT

The close relationship between photography and technology has also shaped its interaction with other related disciplines. Historically, continuous technical transformations have significantly influenced the language, visual structure, and image quality of photography. The relationship between archaeology and photography is based on a utilitarian expectation of documentation. Artists have subjected archaeological objects or ancient artifacts to a kind of visible and effective transformation through digital photography. The objects seen in photographs are already works of art, but there have also been artists who have worked directly with found photographs. In addition to this utilitarianism, a creative aspect has also emerged, strengthened by artistic desire.

INTRODUCTION

Photography's close relationship with technology has also shaped its interaction with other disciplines with which it has a partnership. Historically, technical transformations, which have shown a continuous development, have significantly affected both the language, visual structure and image quality of photography. Some

DOI: 10.4018/979-8-3373-2230-8.ch005

disciplines that make intensive use of photography have closely followed these technical developments, quickly adapted to almost every stage of the process and adopted them with an innovative attitude. The relationship that archaeology, one of these fields of science, has established with photography has a unique structure that is not similar to other disciplines.

The relationship between archaeology and photography has a utilitarian expectation based on documentation. In addition to this utilitarianism, a creative aspect strengthened by artistic desire has also taken shape. The aesthetic structuring in photography has become an effective determinant of both the artistic narrative and the scientific side with the contribution of technical conveniences in practice. When analyzed in its historical context, the artistic formation seen in archaeological photography is closely related to the interactive structure seen in contemporary digital presentations. The visual differences created by the new language brought by digital techniques to alternative presentations have shown that a special aesthetic process has come into play in the context of archaeology and photography. The narrative form created by these innovations enables the experimental presentation of the archaeological object in the photographic process. Experimental techniques, which have a deep effectiveness in form and meaning in photography, have been shaped since the 19th century as a special form of expression that shapes subjective narrative. In the 20th century, experimentalism, which is also used for political discourse and has an activist denominator in a sense, has a dubious place in conveying scientific knowledge; with the effective use of digital technology, it has gained a brand new technical possibility.

Archaeological remains, especially those of an architectural nature, appear primarily in photography, and these remains, which are a special part of the landscape and fiction, have become powerful compositional carriers that provide a qualified aesthetic contribution to what is intended to be shown. Many visible architectural remains in Anatolia, the Fertile Crescent, Ancient Greece, Egypt, Rome, Central and South America and Asia have already been depicted through engravings and paintings, and have quickly become the subject of photography. Most of these architectural remains, whose common characteristic is not that they have been unearthed but that they have been known/visible for thousands of years, have been conveyed to the western audience like a promotional photograph. In a sense, the ancient sites in these photographs, which have turned into a spectacle of the colonial process, are like a proof of what the colonizing countries possess. The function of photography as evidence is also seen in archaeological objects. This is to prove the existence of civilizations that have been depicted verbally and pictorially for centuries with a tool whose authenticity cannot be doubted.

In the 19th century, the revolution created by the photographic technique in the history of visual culture suggested that with this new technique, the world's historical record would be created not only with written documents but also with photographic documents. Making a rapid entry into the cultural life of the period, photography was accepted as an important documentation tool in scientific studies and became an indispensable apparatus for some scientific practices. On the other hand, the way photography exists in the field of art has led to debates, and these debates have mostly followed a comparative process on the axis of painting and photography. While the scientific competence of photography has been questioned, its artistic context has been intensely discussed (Tercan, 2024).

The technique of photography has continued its technological transformation with a strong movement since the day it fixed the image. This transformation involves different stages of obtaining the image and a new problematic emerges after each stage. This leads to the renewal of photography technology with its many components and even to a new form of expression. What we encounter with all this is a new language and a new aesthetic positioning. The story of digital technology, which began in the field of photography in the 20th century, continues to structure the stages of image fixing, storage and processing at full speed. The editing and manipulation of the image has also become partially easier with digital technology and has been shaped by a new aesthetic.

The partially new presentation techniques demonstrated by the digital narrative form in the photographic image have shown a significant development in terms of processing and artistic expression of archaeological data. In a sense, these images, which we can conceptualize as "digital aesthetic forms", are an indication of the continuity of the technical transformations that photography has shown. Since the 19th century, when the image was fixed, photographic technology has shaped a new technical development in visual narrative every year and started to be used as an integral part of this image aesthetics. In archaeological documentation, new technologies have been quickly adapted to shooting techniques or transformed and continued to be used.

As an important extension of digital techniques, viewing formats such as VR - Virtual Reality or AR - Augmented Reality practice, in particular, re-present archaeological space with the illusion of reality they create, while at the same time inviting the subject into a new narrative form. The narrative form offered by these illusions of reality that create a historical twist also brings a new aesthetic understanding to the special signification of the site. This is a three-dimensional simulation that creates the illusion of inclusion in space, as opposed to the distanced reading of two-dimensional photographs. While this illusion brought by the VR technique gives the effect of being there, the AR technique aims to create the effect of being here by adding the object back into the space. By means of an auxiliary digital tracking device (tablet, phone, etc.) and graphic add-ons, the subject visiting ancient cities can watch arrangements that simulate the closest approximations to reality specific to that period and that archaeological environment. This is an example of a site-specific application, but AR applications can also be seen in many other media.

Already in the 21st century, when the language of digital photography began to take shape, studies on digital art, video art and many other forms of computer-based creative production have been discussed in the art world. "The terminology of technological art forms has always been extremely fluid; the field now known as digital art has undergone many name changes since its inception: "computer art" from the 1970s, then 'multimedia art', and finally, at the end of the twentieth century, under the umbrella of 'new media art', which includes film, video, sound art and other hybrid forms. The preferred adjective here - "new" - points to the transience of this terminology. However, this claim of "newness" also raises the question of what exactly makes the digital medium "new". Some of the concepts explored in digital art are almost a century old; many of them have already been addressed in the "traditional" arts. What is new is that digital technology has now reached a level of development that opens up entirely new possibilities for the creation and experience of art" (Christiane, 2008, p.7).

Similar to the environment in which 19th century photography developed, 21st century digital photography practice has found a stage that is already in motion. This scene is in a position to discuss how new forms of creation in the world of image and art are affected by digital / computer technologies. Photographic technology, which has always been in contact with these debates, has actively attempted to create its own digital data aesthetics, and today digital technique has begun to occupy a wide area in the artistic context.

The production practices of the art of photography have undergone many metamorphoses and the impact of digital photography has primarily been in the form of repetition of production, industry and previously experienced darkroom practices. However, the formation of an aesthetic context specific to digital photography and especially the arrangements made on the image in the post-editing process have gained a form specific to the new language, and the aesthetic structure of the digital image has gradually become visible. Before discussing the structuring of digital photography, it would be appropriate to make a determination on the aesthetics of digital art because; "The term 'digital art' has come to encompass such a wide range of art practices and products that it no longer defines a single aesthetic understanding" (Christiane, 2008, p.7). The digital practice of photography has started to develop within all these plural definitions. The digital structuring of photography has experienced an approach similar to the relationship that digital art establishes with the past and the whole. "Digital art has not developed in isolation from the context of art history; on the contrary, it has strong ties with previous art movements such as Dada, Fluxus and conceptual art. The importance of these movements for digital art lies in their emphasis on formal instructions and their treatment of the work of art not as a complete object, but as a structure based on ideas, events and audience participation. Dadaist poetry aestheticized the random assemblage of variations of words and lines; in the process, an artificial form was created through the interaction of chance and control" (Christiane, 2008, p.11). The connection of photography with the past and the place of coincidence in the context of experimental photography are effective in shaping the structure of the language developed in digital photography.

Representation of Truth and Accurate Data

Before analyzing the axis of archaeology and photography, the relationship between photography and science should be mentioned. The pioneering efforts of Anna Atkins and William Henry Fox Talbot led to a rapid acceleration in scientific photography. Both for documentation purposes and to create a database, these studies aimed to serve several effective titles. While scientific photography studies for archival / cataloging purposes are of indispensable importance, their contribution to scientists and students who will later work in the field is also indispensable. While all this documentation also aims to create a memory, the potential to use this memory in the most productive way possible belongs to the researchers who come behind. Comparing archived images with new findings will give photography its scientific role.

Photography has been used extensively for scientific purposes in botany, biology, medicine, cartography, astronomy, geology, anthropology and ethnography. The scientific object that appears in the image enters into a whole new circulation (Bohrer, 2011). "In fact, the whole history of archaeological photography can be divided into two periods: an initial phase of excitement for objective representation, followed by a phase of acceptance in which the use continued despite its flaws" (Bohrer, 2011, p.29).

The content of "correct information" has been one of the primary debates since the introduction of photography to the world. These debates were addressed especially in terms of the potential for scientific use of photography; however, they were shaped on the basis of an expectation whose reality was not questioned. However, as with many imaging techniques, there is a possibility that the subjective contribution of the practitioner can be traced in the photographic image. This possibility has raised doubts about the transfer of scientific data and an attempt has been made to create as objective a documentation as possible. The ease of intervention in digital data has reshaped this suspicion and created the potential for further questioning. Although deviations due to digital manipulation have increased this questioning, VR presentation technology has caused the viewer's experience to override accurate information with the expectation of reality. What is meant here is the re-narrativization of the experience of space and area, sometimes with original narratives. It is the presentation of the story of an ancient city to the experience in a way that reflects the story of an ancient city without completely deviating from the correct information, but in a sense in a way to construct the story. At this point, it can be seen that artistic approaches have historically merged with archaeological indicators. In the history of visual culture, archaeological remains, which have been visible in the art of painting with neoclassicism and orientalist influences, have also found a place in photographs since the early periods. Travel narratives and site-specific constructions stand out in 19th century archaeology photographs where creative concerns can be easily read. On the other hand, pictorial influences are clearly visible in still life arrangements.

Constructivity is one of the intervention elements that directly affects the shaping of the narrative in photography and has been the subject of long-term debates. It has been discussed especially in the context of the reality of photography and has repeatedly made the reality of photography a subject of debate. For this reason, editing has a very important denominator in the relation that digital photography establishes with reality because the post editing process in digital photography has also put its reliability into question. While the relationship of photography with reality and reliable information is already discussed in an ethical context, this discussion has spread to a much wider scope in digital photography. The ease of intervention and the perfection of adaptation in digital photography puts fictionality firmly on the agenda, which in fact re-updates the long-standing and deep-rooted debate about the authenticity of the image.

The appearance of the archaeological object in photography establishes a representation equation on the axis of art and science since the first examples. Although this communication between the scientific and the artistic has enabled photographers to create as much space as possible for objective fiction, the subjective contribution of the photographer is inevitable at some point. The archaeological find, as an object, creates a special denominator in what it represents in photography. This both draws attention to the representativeness and certainty strengthened by scientific knowledge and involves the archaeological object becoming a subjective part of the creative fiction with artistic intent. Objective data combined with a subjective narrative will create a powerful language with these layers. The whole that determines the content is mainly the strong historical basis and representation created by the object. On the other hand, the objects, which are possible copies of small finds, have undergone a new manipulation with the effect of digital technology and with this conceptual layer they have gained, they have shaped their historical denominator with digital data.

The introduction of color as an important factor in photography has also affected the strong relationship of archaeological sites with topography and their surroundings. The representations of the finds that emerged with color created a new form of meaning and made a strong title about the knowledge of the object visible. Because while information about the color of the archaeological object was not possible in early photographic examples, the rapid development in photographic chemistry in the 20th century brought color photography to a satisfactory level in a short time. Nevertheless, information specific to the color of the archaeological find is specified in scientific publications to be provided by various catalogs and coding systems. The relationship between the color and the real object has been of special importance in the context of showing the archaeological find. The color control brought by digital technology has provided a new convenience in this context and has been used to show the tones of the object / atmosphere in a realistic way. However, digital manipulations created by artistic expectation have profoundly shaped the original narrative. This is not only in the context of establishing a quick and easy interaction, but it is a visual construct with a subjective attitude in which digital factors come into play.

Although in the first step the function of photography was primarily expressed as documentation, this situation has changed rapidly and added the documentation of creative thought to its function. Although the reality denominator expected/targeted to be carried by the document seems to render a subjective aspect such as creativity nonfunctional, what is essential is the information it carries about the existence of the object. For a long time, photography was technically accepted as a documentation technique that creates and constructs the image through optical reality. Early examples of the visual transmission of archaeological information were provided through drawings, and making copies of wall paintings in particular was technically laborious, as in the case of Egyptology.

After many years of documenting ancient cities and historical ruins through drawing, the early photographic technique was not only very easy, but also very difficult. It was a process that involved many special details, especially the transportation of chemical materials, the transportation of auxiliary equipment and the preservation of the captured images. The evolution of materials carried on the back of a mule or in a horse-drawn cart with mechanical means over time has undergone a radical transformation with digital developments. The innovation brought by digital photography was of fundamental importance not only in the visual context but also in terms of ease of application. The ease of the production process of the resulting image attracted the attention of archaeologists in many respects, and the increase in archived images compared to the analog period was also due to the economic opportunity brought by digital photography. The economic limitations faced in the analog era brought with it not only the film budget but also many other expenses such as the developing process of the films, their archiving and the creation of appropriate storage conditions. The ease of archiving and preservation of digital imaging has provided a great convenience compared to the analog process.

19th century photographers, who can be seen as travelers, designed the results of their trips in albums. The album of a research trip was produced in a limited number as a special design and surrounded the story formed by a group of photographs.

These albums, which contained topography-specific content, were arrangements that conveyed information about the space and the area and at the same time designed the visual presentation with aesthetic concerns. Produced in limited numbers, the albums brought together the story they contained and the photographer's journey within the framework of a story with a beginning and an end. Along with photographs of archaeological remains, many photographs, in which landscape aesthetics were also in play, also contained details of locality. While these details contained the local people and the contemporary texture of the city, they also often visualized life intertwined with ancient ruins: "Through photography, Maxime Du Camp brought Egypt to the eyes of French audiences and was awarded the French Legion of Honor for this achievement. Although Du Camp's work is largely the product of a touristic experience, it is presented to the reader in the form of a pseudo-scientific topographical report. The text accompanying this narrative is full of ancient lore and uses language reminiscent of antiquarians and contemporary travel writers, enumerating physical details. However, textual content occupies a very small space in a book with 125 images. This shifts the narrative burden from text to visual evidence" (Bohrer, 2011, p.44).

The archaeological find in the photograph has layers in the artistic context as well as scientific findings. In addition to the visual determination made centuries ago, the visible state of stone as an object allows for a new observation ability with digitized three-dimensional scans today. These new forms of presentation carry the reality relationship established with the object to a virtual reality plane. A 360-degree scan of the object supported by a photogrammetric image allows scientists to analyze it visually like never before. This digital documentation can be created not always in the context of an object, but also in the context of space and architectural elements. What is important is that the data presented is scientifically adequate and that the image setup is created with small deviations for scientists. A similar state of documentation is also valid for aerial photography. The convenience brought by digital imaging has made it widespread to obtain photographs with aerial vehicles in the 21st century. In the 19th century, another major development since Nadar, who photographed Paris from balloons, is the aerial imaging possibilities provided by digital photography. Nadar designed his Paris landscapes to document the city and created the earliest examples of aerial photography. Today, one of the most important tools enabling the assessment of the locations of ancient cities in different light conditions at different times of the day is the drone-like unmanned aerial vehicles that transmit images simultaneously with integrated cameras.

Archaeology and the Digital Photographic Image

Digital data in archaeology should be evaluated through several facts. Considering the historical process, especially the speed and ease of application should be seen as the effective element. This is followed by the speed of data processing. These two elements, which can be seen as the pioneering contribution of digital analysis, remind us that the importance of visual data in transferring information about archaeological finds and remains should be considered not only in the context of transferring information but also in the context of ease of application. The laborious aspect of visual archaeological documentation in the early years of photography was the transportation, application and preservation of technical equipment and chemical materials, which may seem simple but should be taken into account. Another aspect, however, was the technical accuracy of the image, that is, its analysis in a readable context. Depending on the season and the field conditions, the issues to be solved were the provision of a correctly exposed readable image and the successful completion of the chemical process.

Although the transmission of archaeological information in the digital image has different processing processes from the raw image to the processed final image, these require the presentation of the scientific data intact and it is the primary expectation that it will convey in this direction. It is important to provide the scientific content of the archaeological data in the image without altering it and without the possibility of manipulation. Otherwise, the transformed images will be like a part of a subjective narrative far from being scientific. This is precisely the dilemma posed by the drawing-based practices employed before the introduction of photography in archaeological documentation. Whether technical drawings or engraving-like prints, these visualization practices have been suspect in terms of subjectivity.

While processing scientific knowledge, digital applications aim to present it without breaking away from real data and to visualize it as site-specific as possible without leaving any room for doubt. VR (Virtual Reality) can be seen as an important means of transmission and presentation in this context. While the technique makes it possible to have a site-specific experience, it does not visually break away from the reality of the object with the perception of reality it creates. With its fidelity to the original; it guarantees the viewer that it presents the experience on the axis of space, object and residue without distracting from real / accurate information. Therefore, VR technology should be seen not only as an experience mechanism but also as a creative digital data plane where accurate information is designed.

Some new techniques that enhance visual aesthetics and the interpretation of scientific data have also emerged alongside digital photography or have become easier and faster to apply. The revolutionary image applications brought about by these techniques can be seen in HDR (High Dynamic Range), Photogrammetry,

RTI (Reflectance Transformation Imaging), time-lapse photography, and aerial and underwater photography. The application of digital photography in archaeological documentation has been facilitated by developments since the 19th century. Some of these techniques, which offer opportunities for in-depth visual analysis of objects and sites, have been adapted to digital photography. However, techniques such as RTI (Reflectance Transformation Imaging) are only possible with the viewing capabilities of digital photography. The RTI technique, which yields the best results in low-relief paintings or epigraphic works, is the conversion of comprehensive data, which is the combination of analyses created by minimal contrast differences after the processing of multiple images, into an image. The HDR technique, which also involves the processing of multiple images, is a special technique for presenting high-quality images in the context of spatial analysis. It is an important technical solution for eliminating the exposure difference between the exterior and interior of a space, such as a cave or tomb chamber, when photographing an area with lighting differences from the inside to the outside or vice versa. It creates an extremely useful opportunity, especially in terms of reading texture and presenting the interior and exterior together. Photogrammetry, on the other hand, is used extensively in archaeology for both documentation and analysis, alongside all other techniques. In principle, it involves creating three-dimensional (3D) models of objects or areas from photographs. In an archaeological context, excavation sites, artifacts, monumental structures, and topographical environments can be documented with a high degree of accuracy using photogrammetry.

Data collection, through photography and the analysis of images obtained, preserves the memory of visual transmission in a sense. The finds and architectural elements contained in the images conveyed by the collected archaeological photographs are like memory clouds. Combined with the memory plane preserved by the photograph with its unique characteristics of the past, they become a permanent extension of the archive. These objects, which have their own memory, are also stored in the visual archive with the data collected by the photographic image. The photographic analysis of objects in archaeology is shaped by historical and cultural analogies. The relationship between archaeology and the past and between photography and the concept of time progresses along similar lines. The analysis of the archaeological object as a result of digital visualization will be equipped with scientific accuracy based on measurement, while also enabling the subjective transfer to achieve an aesthetic whole. In this context, many techniques evaluate the possibilities of digital photography as a provider of subjective images. Advanced digital techniques make important contributions to scientific studies conducted in archaeological excavation sites. In particular, infrared technology attracts attention with the data it provides on cave wall paintings or pigment residues on stone surfaces. Not only traces visible to the naked eye are examined, but also traces made visible in different wavelengths of the spectrum. This makes advanced techniques indispensable in a sense. Because it is not just what is visible that matters; with the contribution of an alternative tracking technique, such as RTI, access to additional information is made possible.

The Re-Presentation and Exhibition of Archaeological Objects Through Virtual Reality

The presentation of archaeological objects in an exhibition, especially through interactive displays, has been possible since the earliest examples of exhibition design. The transportation of real archaeological remains to the exhibition space and their presentation alongside photographs taken at their original sites has made it possible to provide a comprehensive understanding of the objects. The presentation of multiple layers from the archaeological site in the exhibition space, supported by photographs of the finds, creates a scope reminiscent of 19th-century panoramas. In 21st-century exhibition practices, however, the aesthetics of digital visual presentations that are integrated with the space have shaped the meaning relationship between the archaeological data and the viewer in a striking way. Three-dimensional viewing devices, along with touchscreen navigation screens and similar tools, have enhanced the audience's ability to engage with the exhibition.

The transformation of space in exhibitions, supported by objects, has taken on a different appearance with the new presentation and viewing practices brought about by digital technology. Digital presentation forms, which could be a new form of the interest aroused by rare cabinets in history, have shown a remarkable development in the reconstruction of archaeological finds and space (Gotthardt, 2019). In recent years, permanent exhibitions curated by museums or temporary exhibitions organized by institutions have brought together findings, photographs, and real objects belonging to an ancient settlement, culture, or city. However, what we often encounter is that digital arrangements are also designed in harmony with the spaces as a complement to these presentation forms. These presentations, which incorporate participatory design, aim to elevate the viewer's connection with history to the highest level of sensory experience. In doing so, they harmoniously blend aesthetic elements with scientific knowledge.

Archaeological data that has reached the exhibition stage essentially represents the result of sedimentation. All the information and objects presented have been uncovered in cultural layers over the years. The studies conducted by scientists on these objects also trigger creative industries, and as a result of the collaboration established through exhibition practices, an interactive exhibition can be designed. The finds, eroded over hundreds of years, visually reveal the traces and identity created by these traces and fractures in their stories. Exhibition tools acquire the function of communicating information in order to make the stories and traces of all finds visible. Developed by Morton Heilig in 1962, Sensorama became one of the most important devices of the 20th century with the illusion of reality it created as a pioneer of VR technology. This viewing apparatus, named "Experience Theater," was an important invention that signaled the concept of "experience" as advanced techniques offered by digital technologies in the 21st century (Media Kunst Netz, n.d.). Another illusion device, the kinetoscope, was one of the results of Thomas Edison's research on motion in images in 1891 (Monaco, 2001). Stereoscopic viewing and filming techniques, which can be considered the precursors of all these illusion-based tools, represent a visual revolution that can serve as a reference point for VR viewing practices. Stereoscopy, an area where the principles of filming techniques have not changed significantly but viewing techniques have diversified with new viewing devices since the 19th century, has made exhibition processes particularly interesting. Sensorama, the precursor to VR technology, also originated from stereoscopic practice. Viewing devices used actively or passively in stereoscopic techniques aim to enable the viewer to perceive the image as closely as possible to the illusion of reality. Electronic glasses and sets with active functions are indispensable viewing devices for VR. However, passive polarized glasses will also be indispensable for viewing practices. The 1950s, when polarized viewing technology became popular, was a revolution for the cinema industry (3D Film Archive, n.d.). The limited perception created by the previously used anaglyph technique was replaced by the polarized technique, which brought about a new 3D revolution in cinema viewing.

The mind-body duality created by VR raises questions about the connection between perception and reality in the context of spatial experience. While existing in the space through the sense of sight, the viewer adapts their body and other senses specifically to this virtual reality. This adaptation, which is an illusion, is a virtual construct shaped by historical data that shapes the subject's perception of reality in the space where the experience is reconstructed. The presentation of an ancient city or a prehistoric cave through virtual reality will strengthen the process of meaning-making as the viewer's experience is complemented by archaeological knowledge.

Many exhibitions related to archaeological finds are interactive and participatory in nature, enabling viewers to acquire and experience ancient knowledge in a visual context through digital presentation tools. "Artworks created, stored, and exhibited in a digital environment often have interactive or participatory features. While both art forms share some characteristics inherent to digital technology, they are often distinctly different in terms of their manifestations and aesthetics. These two broad categories aim to roughly map this highly hybrid field rather than provide a definitive classification. Definitions and categories can help identify the distinctive features of a medium, but they can also impose pre-established limits on understanding that art, especially in a constantly evolving art form" (Christiane, 2008, p.8).

In the last quarter of the 20th century, artists witnessed computer-based works, and some began to produce works in interaction with this new technology. Artworks began to take on a fluid quality and, most importantly, the audience took on a participatory role in a way that had never been seen before. In these new media forms, where visual and other sensory interactions come into play, the most important aspect is the revolution in exhibition practices. VR-like devices have been among the most striking tools of this revolution.

The story of the past told by archaeological remains, and especially in-situ remains, has been interpreted by many travelers and local people. These interpretations sometimes contain exaggerated stories, while at other times they are narratives containing fragments of reality passed down from generation to generation. However, objects and remains that have completely disappeared or been unearthed later require a completely new narrative. Here, various data carriers such as texts deciphered through the findings of archaeologists, the knowledge of the object, and written records will play a role. While the findings are documented through photographs and drawings, VR-like digital completions bring new information. This is a special simulation of the past. Cities, spaces, and objects are reconstructed and, with possible additions, restored to their original form from the period in which they existed. The VR presentation's location-specific sense of reality, combined with photogrammetry's location- and object-specific scanning-based tracking, results in a multi-active participation experience for the viewer in both techniques.

In many photographs of ancient settlements from the 19th century, people appear as scales, complementing the ruins in the image. These subjects, who have interacted with ancient ruins for many years in staged photographs, seem to have taken on the position of viewers in the 21st century. Digital devices placed in harmony with the space in permanent and temporary exhibitions have made this position interactive. In this context, when we compare the use of the human element in 19th-century staging with post-editing in 21st-century digital photography, we see that the human element has actually taken on the position of the viewer and is no longer a scale within the photograph. With the development of viewing techniques, the subject will no longer be a decisive scale within the photograph in a staged manner, but will instead take on the position of an interactive element in the exhibition space. However, what is at stake here is that in digital photography, it is no longer just the image or the scene that is staged, but the construction of the exhibition space and the human element becoming a kind of constructed scale within this exhibition space. Victor Burgin's commentary on the photograph "Basilica" in his book The Camera: Essence and Apparatus is also related to the figure used as a scale. This photograph, taken in the ancient Roman city of Pompeii, is one of the most interesting examples in the literature of archaeological photography (Burgin, 2025).

Archaeological Representation in Contemporary Art Photography

The partially random results encountered in images created by experimental photography, which leads to technical deviations, also allow for the creation of unique works. The chemical and mechanical possibilities of analog photography have created a wide pool of opportunities for experimentation. With the development of digital photography in the 20th century, many forms constructed with the language of experimental photography have been reapplied with digital interfaces. For example, applications such as solarization and posterization in the darkroom can now be quickly achieved through plugins in software. Optical distortions and similar visual interventions can also be added to these. The aesthetics produced by digital photography, apart from numerical distortions, show similarities with experimental and collage-like structures. Although the issue of intervention in photography has been debated since the early years, ethical discussions have shifted towards aesthetic readings because the image has reached a point where it contains a creative structure. In the works of contemporary photographers, ancient objects that are digitally re-expressed or manipulated are often iconic works that have attracted attention throughout history. These may be reinterpretations of architectural or sculptural remains, or they may be digital representations of these objects, or they may be reused in a sense based on their historical images.

The appearance of an archaeological object in a photograph already has artistic potential, but when the creative activity of the photographer is added to this, a layered image is formed in terms of originality. The historical information it contains and the creative activity it carries enhance the photographic image in different ways. The artist's original contribution and the power of the archaeological data construct this. Ancient narratives, which have been the subject of painting and sculpture for centuries, have ensured the transmission of archaeological knowledge with the addition of real architectural remains in cities such as Rome. The striking presence of mythological elements in art history has increased interest in ancient Greek and Roman cultures and enabled artists to depict scenes other than religious images. As one of the fertile phenomena of art history, mythology has been intensively represented in photography since its early days. While staged photographs depicting mythological narratives are frequently seen, content with added conceptual layers began to appear in 20th-century works. The visual contribution of archaeology and space can also be considered one of the elements that constitute the content of mythological narratives. This form of expression, which is particularly evident in contemporary fictional photographs, has also been reflected in composite works under the influence of digital photography.

Composite photography, frequently used in 19th-century photography, was sometimes employed due to technical limitations and sometimes to fulfill artistic expectations. In the 20th century, influenced by Dada and similar movements, manipulated images evolved into a different narrative and gained a critical language, giving rise to collages. These interventions, which were made with an experimental approach in photographic art with the intention of transforming images in many different ways based on meaning, have continued in digital photography. With digital photography, this form of intervention, which has gained greater potential, has enabled the construction of its own aesthetic language through numerical data. Digital interventions, which create technical dissolutions through coding and software interventions, began to be used for scientific purposes in the processing of archaeological images, and then became an original complement to the creative narrative of ancient knowledge. Similarly, the presentation of mythological narratives in the visual arts alongside contemporary elements is a similar situation. The depiction of a nobleman or a bureaucrat in the guise of a mythological figure brings together several layers. Similar approaches have occasionally been seen in photography, but with the possibilities of digital photography, significant interventions in post-production have attracted attention.

The approach adopted to disrupt the established form of archaeological representation in digital photography involves manipulating, distorting, or transforming the archaeological object that appears in the photograph. This approach, which has earned a special place in the history of photography beyond mere documentation, has adapted the subjective narrative derived from archaeological finds to contemporary language and developed a unique stance through the layers it creates. The experimental photographic approach adapted by contemporary artists to photographic narrative has shaped the visual language.

"In the 19th century, some limited manipulations of images were seen, but the increase in manipulated images as part of an aesthetic approach that included an effective, even aggressive approach to images occurred in the 20th century. Like painters who worked with montage and collage techniques, photographers also divided the original images into pieces and rearranged them to construct a model of meaning" (Clarke, 2017, p.222). Japanese artist Patrick Nagatani's Excavations (1985-2000) series, specifically the piece titled "Ryoichi Excavation, Stonehenge, 1987 / 1999," is a postmodern work that perfectly reflects this. Although the claim that photography reflects reality became controversial in the 19th century, it has been pushed toward a more comprehensive debate with the effective use of digital technology. Now, in addition to the relationship between digitally shaped photographs and reality, the re-editing of the narrative in the image has further increased skeptical approaches. The artist has created a composite visual narrative based on the confidence provided by scientific certainty and has brought together two axes that cannot coexist. In his work titled "Bentley, Stonehenge, Salisbury Plain, Wiltshire, England, 1987/1999," a scene of a car wreck appears alongside an image of Stonehenge. The artist has shaped the story of a fictional Japanese archaeologist named Ryoichi into a series of photographs and designed a map showing different geographical points around the world (Patrick Nagatani, n.d.). In this series, he shapes the temporal deviations he creates through both reality and narrative, and the experimental and composite approach that emerges also characterizes a performative attitude. The series, which depicts archaeological work, reveals the concept of time through objects in an unusual paradox. The juxtaposition of stone and metal is shaped by the composite experimental narrative of photography, and this series, which predates digital composite works, is a continuation of an approach that is frequently encountered in the history of photography. However, the composite technique brought by digital photography to post-production has taken on an ordinary structure and begun to appear as a common practice. Yet, composite photographs from before the digital era, which involved much longer darkroom interventions, had the potential to present the technique in the image with an extraordinary atmosphere.

The narrative constructed by the artist through the concept of time brings to mind Christian Jürgensen Thomsen's three-age model in archaeological history. In 1819, he classified the collection belonging to the National Museum of Copenhagen as stone, bronze, and iron. Although this classification method, which is experimental and inductive, does not directly describe the contrast in Nagatani's photographs, it demonstrates a comparison in a temporal context (Gamble, 2014). The archaeological excavation of cultures buried underground over time requires special research and a systematic approach. Similarly, the emergence of the hidden image in analog photography after exposure also requires a formula and systematic approach. In a sense, this analogy, which is based on a primitive concept, emphasizes the action form of both fields.

In the 19th century, photographs of archaeological sites took on a powerful role in conveying accurate information about ancient cities and finds. Archaeological finds and sites still have the potential to be surrounded by stories that stray from scientific accuracy and factual information, often containing misleading content. Magical objects, mysterious maps, and treasures that are supposedly hidden are still being turned into stories by many groups today and embellished with misleading information. This misleading information is image-supported and often aims to create evidence that leaves no doubt about the authenticity of the false story being told. Patrick Nagatani's composite works are also designed as a product of fantasy. They feature a non-existent archaeologist and an archaeological find that, while real, could not possibly coexist with the mechanical remnants of modern times.

These photographs, created using analog techniques before the advent of digital photography, essentially present an illusion; the car-like vehicles found within a familiar archaeological site establish a conflict between information and imagery. The aesthetic arrangement, an extension of the post-production in the photographs, foreshadows the composite approach in digital photography.

Time can be seen as another phenomenon at the intersection of archaeology and photography. The layers of time defined by archaeology through cultural strata are similar to the images captured by photography, which take on different representations over time. The relationship between photography and the past begins from the moment the photograph is taken. This relationship contains stages similar to the process of developing and fixing film, as in the case of the latent image in analog photography. Thus, the temporal potential of the subject in the latent image increases in proportion to its connection with the past. In this context, Nagatani's time paradox, constructed through the existence of objects, will also take on a photographic temporality, and over the years, this layer of meaning will contain many different strata.

The reality presented by ancient objects has also been a topic of debate among researchers and collectors. The fact that many ancient finds have been scattered around the world by looters has led to discussions about the authenticity of these objects. Illegal excavations and looting in areas such as the ancient city of Pompeii have continued for many years, and fakes have been added to the original objects. Aside from the reality of photography, the reality of the object in the image has also given rise to another question. Experimental photography in the 19th century and multiple printing techniques have led to skepticism about the accuracy of the narrative presented in images. One of the best examples of this is the multiple prints used in the 19th century. The principle of digital technology is the same, but the ease of application has led to differences in manipulation. This makes subjective narration possible in the manipulation of archaeological images. James Welling's works are examples of multiple images containing layers, and their pictorial effect is constructed with digital additions. From the early stages of his career, color and form have been the main influences in his work. He planned the techniques he used in his works to transform the possibilities of photography in different ways. His experimental works, in which he exposed Polaroid films to heat to alter and transform them, are early examples of his art. The phrase "reconstructing modernism with historical awareness" is defining for him, and his flower series is a memory scan. Among his inventions is the cyanotype technique. John Herschel coined the term 'photography' (drawing with light), but W. H. Fox Talbot proposed the term "sciagraphy" (drawing with shadows) as an alternative (Higgins, 2014).

In the series titled "Cento," the artist indirectly refers to a historical fact by digitally re-coloring ancient sculptures. This series seems to remind us that ancient sculptures, which are now white marble structures, were once colorful when they were first created. The colors he uses, rather than creating a harmonious contrast, open up a new layer of meaning. The layered color treatments he applies to the sculptures aim to conceptually expand these ancient artifacts without losing their form or identity, rather than completely transforming them. This expansion reinforces the meaning structure constructed by the newly added color layers with the historical knowledge of the sculpture. Like the cultural layers containing archaeological data, the stages of the colors he constructs in the image also express a historical sequence.

In his 2022 photograph titled *Portrait of Aphrodite*, the artist has combined several interventions: color, eyes, and light. The unusual use of light has formally divided the portrait in two. The eyes were taken from another museum photograph and digitally added to the marble bust (Albers, 2023). The sculpture visible in the photograph has acquired a different expression compared to other ancient sculptures and is endowed with a human-like facial expression. However, many ancient sculptures have lost their color and additions and now have a dull expression. This is partly due to the effect of marble or raw material, but the eyes added by Welling give the statue of Aphrodite a new face. Welling, who creates abstract visuals based on real objects within contemporary narrative, has particularly used ancient statues as powerful metaphors. These metaphors transfer the power that the figures represented in the past to today's artists to create a new narrative.

Another artist who uses color in a distinctive way, like James Welling, is Sara VanDerBeek. She has shaped her photographs, which are based on color and form, to express the historical visibility of the female subject. Focusing on female sculptures from the Ancient Greek and Roman periods, the artist spent a long time photographing works in museums and conducting color studies on them (Minnesota Street Project, n.d.). These diptychs of sculpture images offer a comparative content in terms of color. The diversity of sculptures throughout history seems to represent the perception created by color differences. The artist uses her unusual color choices to draw attention to figures from ancient times. The objects seen in the photographs in her series “Women and Museums” are sculptures that have existed for hundreds of years and continue to be represented in museums after the period in which they were produced. The negative-positive order created by these sculptures, which have been transformed in terms of color, again emphasizes the multi-image structure. The women in the museum, as indicated in the title of the series, create content that can be read specifically in terms of gender. Similar to Judy Chicago's 1979 work “The Dinner Party,” which was based on women throughout history, VanDerBeek reimagines and interprets the female element in museums by photographing three-dimensional sculptures. In a sense, she reorganizes the visibility of the female element and presents it in contemporary art galleries. In this context, she uses color as a decisive factor in her activist philosophy. The idea that ancient sculptures were colorful during the period they were created also influenced the artist. Today, these sculptures, which exist in white, are colored by the artist. In VanDerBeek's work "Chorus, 2021," we see female figurines from different periods and cultures, once again colored. As seen in VanDerBeek's works, the arrangements made by contemporary photographers with images of ancient objects go beyond ordinary documentation and enable the conceptual restructuring of meaning. Although the ancient sculptures in VanDerBeek's series appear as complete three-dimensional objects, they take on a new appearance through coloring.

Contemporary artist Mishka Henner, who subjects cultural artifacts representing the female body to a kind of digital surveillance analysis, uses "eye-tracking" technology in his *Sightseeing* project to map how the viewer's gaze moves across an object and where it focuses. *Staring at Venus* (2019), part of this project, aims to show the viewer the points where the artwork and digital data analysis intersect. With his *Sightseeing* project, the artist aims to present seeing not only as an aesthetic investigation but also as a selective and ideological act (Mishka Henner, n.d.). In this context, through his analyses centered on gaze and aesthetic research, he aims to show how digitalization has transformed visual culture and how this effect can be criticized through art. The artist transcends the boundaries of traditional photography by reconstructing images obtained from digital mapping services. Thus, concepts such as space, geography, and borders are re-examined in both visual and political terms. The anonymity, accessibility, and reproducibility of visual data become objects of criticism in Henner's practice. The artist's work *Staring at Venus* takes the conceptual depth of the *Sightseeing* project one step further by directly analyzing the concept of "gaze" both technically and theoretically. In the work, the artist uses eye-tracking technology to collect data on how viewers look at specific images and for how long. This data is then incorporated into the visual structure of the work, transforming the act of looking itself into an object of representation.

In his work titled "Staring at Venus," Henner presents the figure of Venus with references from a narrative shaped by mythological and archaeological underpinnings in art history. A powerful artistic tradition and historical myth are subjected to an analysis of the gaze. The way in which the female body is transformed into an object of gaze and objectified is visualized. The artist analyzes the representation of the female body from ancient times to the present day and the gaze-based cultural codes that have shaped society. In Henner's works, which are constructed around the gaze, digital technology is not merely a tool but a means of criticism. The artist analyzes the viewer's gaze, maps it, and transforms it into a report. This report encompasses the entirety of the gaze and possesses a critical structure that assumes the viewer's gaze to be ideological.

Henner uses digital visualization tools to shape the work. This shaping is specifically designed to create an effective foundation of meaning within the work. While the eye-tracking system attempts to create a database of how the gaze moves across the sculpture, what we are actually faced with is a female image that encompasses historical, cultural, and social narrative layers, and this representation of the body is expressed through an ancient sculpture. On the one hand, this Venus sculpture is historically one of the most powerful feminine symbols, and the artist's attempt at gaze analysis is, in fact, an effort to evaluate this potential. It moves to problematize accumulated cultural codes and rigid stereotypes. On the other hand, with the mapping developed by the eye-tracking system, a digital tool becomes a guiding partner of the work. The sculpture has found its place among many other archaeological finds in the museum, and what the artist wants to show is how these sculptures, which remain the focus of attention in museums, are perceived. Digital devices also become partners in the context of analyzing the works. The Venus sculpture and other sculpture fragments, by being the focal point of gaze in museums, create data regarding the presentation of archaeological finds. In the contemporary narrative of digital photography, the point-color clusters present in the works take on the function of indicators of such mapping.

The social context in the works of Sara VanDerBeek and Mishka Henner aims to examine and present established perceptions within a critical framework, combined with digital photography aesthetics. Both artists have taken ancient sculptures as their starting point, centering the female element and problematizing the points where the gaze on the objectified body intersects with cultural codes. The archaeological finds in their works offer viewers a multi-layered structure in terms of what they represent. It is evident that the artists do not concern themselves with formal composition, but rather engage in a content analysis specific to the viewer's gaze. This is the result of shaping their work with a contemporary narrative language and the infrastructure of digital photography and technology. In contemporary archaeological studies, it has been criticized that many things are perceived from a male perspective, i.e., male-centered, and that findings are analyzed intensively in this direction (Bahn, Renfrew, 2013). Analyses conducted in the context of gender can be seen not only in archaeology but also in many other disciplines. Works in the visual arts, on the other hand, focus on attracting attention by creating a more provocative and activist scope. The structure and language that artists aim to achieve in their works is similar, drawing the viewer's attention to this criticism in the context of gender. In addition, Henner's work is, in a sense, the compilation of scientific statistical data and its transformation into an artistic aesthetic perception, constructing the science-art axis with an effective meaning base. The issues of how the gaze is constructed and controlled both individually and collectively are concretized with "digital gaze tracking" data. The specialized analysis of the "Venus" statue by the field of archaeology, along with the coordinated examination of the visibility of sculptural works in museums and the gaze directed at these works in photographs, collectively reveal a strong sense of unity in this collaboration.

The information and culture-specific details contained in an archaeological object can also be likened to another concept, namely find photographs. When expressed in archaeological terms, the concept of a find will contain a wealth of data in the context of the object. Find photographs, on the other hand, serve as carriers of deep historical knowledge. Containing many details specific to the period and culture in which they were taken, find photographs have been an effective source of inspiration for artists. Appropriated images have been evaluated to create new works. Found images, which also contain analyses of other people's lives and memories, are starting points for new stories and represent elements specific to the past and the present. Re-exhibiting found photographs or transforming them into a completely new form by creating a special layer on them has been one of the starting points for contemporary artists. The resulting work is presented to us with data about the past, even if only as a fragment of its wholeness. Whether presented as a fragment or in its entirety, the appropriated photograph will not be detached from its historical context. Bill Armstrong is an artist known for his color-based works that focus on concepts such as dreams, ghosts, memory, and perception. He often relates his connection to the past to the history of the human subject. His works, mostly based on found photographs and images, focus on the abstract effect of color on perception and the senses. Found images include classical sculptures, Renaissance paintings, old photographs, and film frames. Her artistic practice, which began with photographing torn posters around the city, evolved into a very different approach after seeing Uta Barth's works at MoMA. Inspired by Barth's approach to blurriness, the artist began photographing found images in a studio environment rather than walking around the city, and transforming them into printed materials. The photographs included in the *Renaissance* section were designed based on the evaluation of found images that are part of the *Infinity* series. The artist has eliminated the characteristic features of the Renaissance period's classical paintings and works through blurring. In a sense, he has presented their blurred identity in an abstract context. In the "Renaissance" series, the figures are arranged in such a way that they sometimes fall and may even be doomed to death. In some of his works, the figures appear to be flying or swimming, symbolizing freedom and liberation (Higgins, 2014).

In his series titled "Apparition," the artist uses images of ancient Roman sculptures and considers these photographs, which he designed as signs from the spirit world, to be like ghosts from the past. The loss of clarity in these images, which can be thought of as visits from the spirit world, creates an abstract digital design by displaying voluminous human heads in a colorful manner while also forming a blurred pattern in the depth of the space. When examined as a metaphor, the ghosts of the ancient world can be used to describe many archaeological finds. The composition of the photographs does not convey scientific data, but rather emphasizes the wear and transformation that the finds have undergone over the centuries through the loss of clarity in the photographs. On the other hand, the dominant colors demonstrate the power of their representation. The artist, who often draws inspiration from photographs of finds, seems to refer to the practice of archaeology. While conducting in-depth research, he draws analogies and reinterprets the findings. These interpretations are not scientific findings like those in archaeology, but they share a similarity in their form of action. In his photographs, which are based on 19th-century images of the pyramids, iconic structures of ancient Egyptian civilization, Armstrong specifically refers to the equation of dream and color.

After Francis Frith, Pyramid II, 2016, the artist creates a color sequence on the Kefren pyramid. Francis Frith, one of the prominent names in 19th-century photography of Ancient Egypt, colored the Kefren pyramid as a spot in the center of his photograph. By creating a color sequence in squares, the artist adds a layer of color to an iconic work from the past. This layer, consisting of many colors, shows us a sequence that is dreamlike and too unusual to be real. The figures and landscape in the foreground of Frith's arrangement construct a perspective axis. However, Armstrong takes the issue of color in photography to a whole new level and adds color to an image that was previously impossible to color. This creates a new dream, and the resulting visual carries both the layers of the found photograph, its history, and the story of the photograph itself. The original photograph, titled *The Pyramids of Giza from the Southwest* and dated 1858, offered Armstrong a postmodern opportunity to add a new layer of history. Another work he transformed through digital interventions is titled *After Pascal Sébah, 2016*. Again, in the image featuring the Giza pyramid, the pyramid, which occupies the largest area in the composition, has been colored through digital intervention. The found photograph he used, "Pyramids of Giza, 1860–1890," belongs to the Ottoman-period photographer Pascal Sébah and is a powerful depiction of Ancient Egyptian civilization. Armstrong's color intervention in the image subverts the visual composition of the photograph and creates a new arrangement that is open to interpretation. In the works titled *After Felix Teynard, 2016* and *After DuCamp Pyramid, 2016*, the artist follows a similar interventionist approach and effectively uses color to reshape the photographs. However, in the photographs titled *After DuCamp Pyramid, 2016* and *After Pascal Sébah #2, 2016*, the intervention is based on reproducing the image within itself through color. The color element seems to be designed to make the repeated photographs visible rather than being a dominant element. In these collage images, the artist draws attention to a historical phenomenon through repeated images. The Egyptian pyramids featured in the series are perhaps the most photographed architectural elements of the ancient world since the invention of photography. They have not only appeared in photographs but have also been reflected in the works of many traveling painters, found their way into literary texts, and even been mentioned in sacred texts. This act of reproduction is emphasized by the artist through the repetition of similar images in a photographic manner. While the color element plays a dominant role in organizing meaning in other works, in these two images, the repetition of the same visual element is observed, which truly creates a layer. The artist has added the photographs to the original by changing their size or turning them upside down, creating layers in the photograph with a multiple arrangement. While layers are used as a systematic method in digital photo editing, the artist has created a new meaning with the repeated layers in these photographs. However, this meaning is not independent of the actual photograph; rather, it is an addition to the narrative that it made visible in the 19th century. Selecting examples from travel photographers, the artist has taken into account the gaze of an outside observer and has reshaped the image as an outside observer of this found photograph. The factor of color has been a hot topic in the history of photography since its early days, and expectations regarding color began to be discussed after the first daguerreotype image. This discussion is again related to the concept of reality, but the reality of color will be a separate discussion for many years to come. While the earlier discussions focused on obtaining color, the discussions and research that emerged later focused on obtaining colors that were as close to real tones as possible. Film brands have worked on color for many years, emphasizing their own characteristic tone properties. With the advent of digital photography, discussions about color have resurfaced, and for many years, studies have been conducted on the accuracy of color as well as image resolution. Armstrong's images, which bring color together, characterize this entire sequence in a digital but abstract context.

In archaeology, "in situ" refers to the preservation of an artifact in its original location and condition, or the preservation of an architectural element or remnant in the place where it was first used. "*Spolia*" on the other hand, refers to the reevaluation of an object outside its original location or context, either for its intended purpose or for a different purpose (Tekçam, 2011). The arrangement we see in archaeological elements has been indirectly applied by the artist in a photographic manner, and the works have been transformed through a creative process in a digital context. Taking inspiration from the concepts of in situ and *spolia* in archaeology, Armstrong also appropriates and rearranges these images. In this context, the artist, who displays a postmodern attitude, reuses a found image, colors it, and subjects it to digital manipulation. The new layer of meaning he creates contains the structural characteristics of the time when the original image was created, as well as drawing attention to the current state of the object it documents. The artist's secondary intervention on the photograph, together with all these interpretations, creates a new conceptual layer. While found object is one of the fundamental concepts in archaeology, the concept of found object in photography is a concept that has taken shape with contemporary photography and also touches on the actions of appropriation and appropriation within postmodern narrative. Archive analysis in contemporary photographic narrative holds the potential for comprehensive analysis and deep cultural reading with a holistic perspective. Found object photo archives, which specifically explore many anthropological and social aspects, carry powerful elements of history. These elements are analyzed with an approach that embraces archaeology as a form of action, and their visibility is ensured.

The photograph *Self-portrait With Pyramid, Cairo, 2009* by Egyptian artist Youssef Nabil also features the post-coloring technique seen in Bill Armstrong's works. However, in this case, Nabil used manual coloring and did not employ any digital processes. This evokes the visual impact of the 19th-century technique of hand-coloring, while also reminding the viewer of the pyramids of ancient Egypt, which serve as a prominent element in the constructed image, conferring identity on the self-portrait. Both artists have used the most famous monumental structure from the ancient world and re-presented an element that has been photographed countless times in the history of photography. The most important difference between them is that while Armstrong displays an unusual colorist approach with digital intervention, Nabil achieves a pictorial effect with coloring that is in harmony with the atmosphere. The artist, who frequently uses geographical elements in his works on masculinity and culture, adds an ancient architectural element to his repertoire, thereby strengthening not only the cultural fabric of the region but also its historical heritage by bringing it together with social layers such as masculinity. The Egyptian artist's fictional representation, created specifically for the geography he temporarily inhabited, is designed to bring to life numerous social details alongside archaeological themes.

Ahmet Rustem Ekici and Hakan Sorar, whose works draw on their experience of archaeological sites in Anatolia, prioritize the concepts of body, space, and gender. Their work “Rest in Peace” is an example of archaeological narratives, in which the artists use digital art to reconstruct archaeological finds and sites, experience the site, and transfer it to the exhibition space. The duo states that they drew inspiration from a historical natural event for their 2023 exhibition, visualizing archaeological knowledge using various digital materials. By utilizing photography, artificial intelligence, and 3D scanning tools, the artists have reimagined archaeological finds and information in a digital format, creating an exhibition that objectively references the work of scientists. As the artists explain, these works reveal many archaeological concepts and objects. At the same time, the virtual world they have created represents a process in which they shape their own experiences with archaeology and involve the viewer as a participant.

The catalog of the exhibition draws particular attention to the concepts of “fiction” and “reality.” This is a special emphasis on the virtual plane of the exhibition in relation to the real plane. The images used in the background of the pages where these concepts are presented are placed to draw attention to the facts being expressed.

The works titled 'Frieze' and "We Were Here" were created with the help of artificial intelligence. The work "We Were Here" recalls images that have been part of a ritual since prehistoric times, where the imprints of hands appear on many walls. The most well-known example of these wall paintings, found in many parts of the world, is the "Cueva de las Manos" (Cave of Hands) in Argentina (7300 BCE – 700 CE) (Bradshaw Foundation, n.d.). The work, named by the artists to emphasize the concepts of memory and remembrance, seems to have acquired such a function historically. The artists, who reshape seals found in many examples in Anatolia through artificial intelligence, display an original attitude towards locality. The exhibition, which brings together many examples specific to the geography of Anatolia, draws attention to archaeological language and definitions specific to the region. In this context, a local natural event that defines the theme of the exhibition exemplifies the artists' experience: "Every year between March and May, the Domanic district of Kutahya hosts a migratory journey. This migratory journey is a mating journey in which female frogs carry male frogs on their backs and move towards the Palazoglu pond. Nearby, at the Seyitomer Hoyük excavations, large frogs carrying smaller frogs on their backs were discovered in ritons believed to date back 5,000 years. These frog-shaped altar vessels, now on display at the Kutahya Archaeology Museum, raised so many questions that they became the starting point for our exhibition (Rest in Piece's, 2023). This detail, as expressed in the exhibition catalog, is a striking example in the context of locality and historical facts. The natural phenomenon mentioned above has been processed and made visible in the objects produced by the ancient cultures of the region. This process, which has been reconstructed in the exhibition through digital structures, emphasizes a cycle; a historical natural event, movement, continuity, memory, and the act of leaving a trace that can be read through the artifacts. All of these are concepts that the artists also touch upon. At the same time, it can be seen that they draw inspiration from the fertile potential of the concepts of body and space. Ancient objects like the riton, which are extensions of humanity's relationship with nature and observation, have been reimagined in the exhibition, transforming into works that encompass multiple layers.

The artists worked to construct meaning by bringing together technology and art through partnerships with scientists during the preparation process for the exhibition. The active participation of the audience has created a unique impact specific to digital art. The video work titled "Theatrum Mundi – In the Pond" is one of the pioneering examples in the exhibition that has facilitated the active participation of the audience. The example given by the duo in their interview conducted for Ahmet Tarık Duman's 2024 master's thesis highlights their expectations in this regard: "Ahmet Rustem Ekici: Digital exhibition formats greatly influence the meaning and perception of our works. Thanks to digital tools, we can present our works to viewers in a more interactive and dynamic way. Elements such as spatial and lighting design can be manipulated more flexibly in a digital environment. This allows the audience to experience the work more deeply. Additionally, digital exhibition enables us to reach a wider audience with our stories. For example, our VR Sauna exhibition reached 100,000 visitors. This might not have been possible in a gallery. We can also track how many people have created an AR experience with our AR experiences. Hakan Sorar: Digital exhibition formats definitely increase the interaction between our works and the audience. Thanks to virtual galleries and augmented reality applications, the audience can experience our works from different angles and dimensions. In our works developed using game engines like Theatrum Mundi, enabling viewers to transform into participants and providing them with a space to view video art from any angle they desire is highly valuable" (Duman, 2024, p.159).

Artists who structure their works by referring to scientific reality have designed subjective reality based on their own field experiences. As they express in the exhibition catalog, the objective knowledge relationship they established with scientists in the real space during their experiences at Seyitomer Hoyuk and Tavsanli Hoyuk has made their subjective reality, which they have made effective in creating digital structures, visible in their works. Although the artists have created an illusionary plane in the exhibition, the references they take from reality make the objective elements of the story visible. This, in a sense, establishes the connection between the subjective reality they create in the virtual world and the real world. Therefore, their presence in the field, their contact with the reality of archaeological findings, and the collaborations they have established with scientists working in this field bring their digital art to a unique foundation.

CONCLUSION

Archaeology's reference to a form of action has been a conceptually effective source of inspiration for artists. This can be seen in the separation of the work into layers or in the multi-image design brought about by the language of digital photography. The fragmentation created by the experimental form will also provide specific examples of the conceptual narrative in archaeology. The use of multiple images and eclectic designs establishes an analogy with the cultural layers contained within archaeological sites. All actions of digging and dissecting the work can be read as an archaeological behavior pattern. The artist's approach to both making the archaeological object visible in the work and engaging with the work through an archaeological action form within a conceptual context incorporates a narrative construction approach unique to contemporary photography.

The artists featured have subjected archaeological objects or ancient artifacts to some form of visible and effective transformation through digital photography. These images contain a structure similar to experimental photography rather than a glitch art-like aesthetic of distortion. The objects visible in the photographs are already artifacts, but there have also been artists who work directly with found photographs. The sequence of images they add has brought forth a postmodern attitude. Found photographs presented with a repetitive visuality encourage us to understand the story of archaeological objects through the aesthetics of contemporary narratives, while at the same time taking shape through the formal structure of contemporary post-fiction. The formal structures created by post-fiction through multiple images in digital photography have enriched the contemporary photographic language with examples of archaeological imagery, making the temporal sequence of the connection established with the past visible in the multi-layered designs created by the artists discussed in this section.

The innovations brought by digital techniques in archaeological documentation are not merely a new presentation format, but imaging processes that enable the field and object to be interpreted in multiple ways. This primarily refers to three-dimensional tracking formats, starting with three-dimensional scanning and including VR (Virtual Reality) technology. VR technology, which plays a significant role in the digital aspect of stereoscopic observation, holds an important place in the process of communicating and interpreting archaeological data in the context of re-perceiving space and participating in a new simulation. AR (Augmented Reality) technology, on the other hand, immerses the observer in another historical simulation. MR (Mixed Reality) serves as an assistant that enables access to much more of the real world. This technology, which offers an order where the real world and the virtual world are intertwined, is a plane that mixes the experience of archaeological objects with the real world. As a result of all this, XR (Extended Reality) presents all these virtual extensions as a whole. Techniques that reach a point where the boundaries between virtual reality and the world become blurred create a new universe with the active participation of the viewer. These techniques redesign the connection between space and the past—with the consistent contribution of historical knowledge—and enable the visual representation of information to be combined with visual data. These technologies, which allow the viewer to actively interact, have guided the redesign of exhibition processes, particularly in the construction of spatial perception.

Since the days when we drew pictures on cave walls, acquiring and recording information has become a necessity of sorts. Leaving behind visual records that would convey the space or situation to future generations served as a narrative and source of information about facts. By the time written records began to be kept in the 19th century, thousands of years had passed. The narratives in ancient Egyptian hieroglyphs or the systematic records on Hittite/Assyrian tablets contained a wealth of information. The reality offered by photography as a recording medium is unique to archaeological documentation and remains indispensable. The connection photography establishes with the past is a phenomenon that many philosophers have commented on and developed theories about. The image recorded after the shutter is released (whether chemical or digital) is always specific to the past. Archaeology's connection to the past and culture also emerges as a fundamental factor. However, the phenomenon that causes the paths of these two disciplines to intersect in some way is documentation. As an act of recording, photographic documentation expresses a utilitarian connection with archaeology through the information it contains. The aesthetic message is another layer that expresses the connection between photography and archaeology from the past to the present. In addition to the documentation of finds, photographic records of remains in the landscape have continued to be a source of study for photographers and archaeologists for many years (Tercan, 2024).

The digital presentation of archaeological objects brings with it a different sense of space, thanks to new forms of display. Presenting an object in an environment other than the one in which it was found or excavated creates new potential for audience engagement. This potential has been realized through three-dimensional techniques, which have given the digital presentation a unique appearance and established new layers of meaning. While the visual recording of archaeological data for documentation purposes prompts a rethinking of exhibition formats, the potential created by artistic additions will be evaluated through a process of interpretation similar to the cultural layers found in soil strata. All these observations indicate that the relationship between archaeology and photography has evolved into a new process with digital photography, while also demonstrating that the artistic aura between them has strengthened without detaching from scientific data.

REFERENCES

Albers, K. P. (2023, March 9). *James Welling recasts the ancient World.* Aperture. https://aperture.org/editorial/james-welling-recasts-the-ancient-world/

Bahn, P., & Renfrew, C. (2013). *Arkeoloji anahtar kavramlar.* İletişim Yayınları.

Bohrer, F. (2011). *Photography and archaeology.* Reaktion books.

Bradshaw Foundation. (n.d.). *World Heritage Site in Argentina.* Retrieved April 29, 2025 from https://www.bradshawfoundation.com/south_america/cueva_de_los_manos/index.php

Burgin, V. (2025). *Kamera: Öz ve aygıt.* Espas Yayınları.

Christiane, P. (2008). *Digital art.* Thames & Hudson.

Clarke, G. (2017). *Güzel sanatların bir dalı olarak fotoğraf.* Hayalperest Yayınları.

Duman, A. T. (2024). *Fotoğrafta dijital sergileme biçimlerinin anlam bağlamında esere etkisi.* [Unpublished master's thesis]. Mimar Sinan Güzel Sanatlar Üniversitesi

3D. Film Archive. (n.d.). *3D Film Archive.* Retrieved May 13, 2025 from https://3dfilmarchive.com/what-killed-3d-films/

Gamble, C. (2014). *Arkeolojinin temelleri.* Aktüel Arkeoloji Yayınları.

Gotthardt, A. (2019, June 15). *The eccentric cabinets of curiosity that captivated renaissance Europe.* Artsy. https://www.artsy.net/article/artsy-editorial-eccentric-cabinets-curiosity-captivated-renaissance-europe

Higgins, J. (2014). *Fotoğraf neden kusursuz olmak zorunda değildir.* Hayalperest Yayınları.

Media Kunst Netz. (n.d.). *Media Kunst Netz.* Retrieved May 10, 2025 from http://www.medienkunstnetz.de/works/sensorama/

Minnesota Street Project. (n.d.). *Minnesota Street Project.* Retrieved April 22, 2025 from https://minnesotastreetproject.com/exhibitions/1275-minnesota-st/sara-vanderbeek-roman-women

Mishka Henner. (n.d.). *Mishka Henner.* Retrieved April 18, 2025 from https://mishkahenner.com/Sightseeing

Monaco, J. (2001). *Bir film nasıl okunur.* Oğlak Yayınları.

Patrick Nagatani. (n.d.). *Patrick Nagatani*. Retrieved April 10, 2025 from https://www.patricknagatani.com/

Rest in Piece's (2023), Bilsart ve Monoco Artspace.

Tekçam, T. (2011). *Arkeoloji sözlüğü*. Alfa Yayınları.

Tercan, S. (2024). *Antik kalıntılar ve manzara fotoğrafında arkeolojik anlatı*. Fotografya. https://www.fotografya.gen.tr/TR,2633/seckin-tercan.html

ADDITIONAL READING

Arreola, P., Gardner, C., & Lenz, M. (2024). *Digital Art:1960s–Now*. Thames & Hudson.

Bahn, P. (2012). *Archaeology: A Very Short Introduction*. Oxford University Press. DOI: 10.1093/actrade/9780199657438.001.0001

Cotton, C. (2014). *The Photograph as Contemporary Art*. Thames & Hudson.

Couturier, E. (2012). *Talk Abaut Contemporary Photography*. Flammarion.

Daly, P., & Evans, T. L. (2005). *Digital Archaeology: Bridging Method and Theory*. Routledge.

Fagan, B. (2019). *A Little History of Archaeology*. Yale University Press. DOI: 10.12987/9780300235289

Frizot, M. (1998). *A New History Of Photography*. Könemann.

Price, M. (1994). *The Photograph: A Strange, Confined Space*. Stanford University Press. DOI: 10.1515/9781503622333

Renfrew, C., & Bahn, P. (2016). *Archaeology: Theories, Methods and Practice*. Thames & Hudson.

Warner Marien, M. (2021). *Photography: A Cultural History*. Laurence King Publishing.

KEY TERMS AND DEFINITIONS

Archaeology: Archaeology is the study of the human past, both ancient and recent, through the analysis of material remains.

Archaeological Remains: An archaeological site is any location containing physical evidence of past human activities.

AR - Augmented Reality: It is a technology that superimposes real-time 3D-rendered computer graphics onto the physical environment via a display, such as a handheld device or head-mounted display.

Excavation Site: An excavation site, or 'dig,' refers to the designated area of archaeological investigation, which may encompass multiple sectors and extend over periods ranging from weeks to several years

Experimental Photography: It refers to any form of intervention applied to photographs, either during capture or post-production, that falls outside traditional photographic techniques.

In Situ: It refers to the preservation of an artifact, architectural element, or remnant in its original location and condition at the place of its initial use.

Photogrammetry: Photogrammetry is the science of obtaining accurate information about objects and environments by recording and interpreting photographic images.

RTI (Reflectance Transformation Imaging): An imaging technique that synthesizes multiple fixed-position photographs to create hyper-realistic, interactively controlled digital representations.

VR - Virtual Reality: It is a simulated experience that uses 3D near-eye displays and pose tracking to provide the user with an immersive perception of a virtual environment.

Chapter 6

Paradigm Shift in Photography in the Perspective of Digital Transformation and Gender

Mert Çağıl Türkay
http://orcid.org/0000-0002-1133-8029
Mimar Sinan Fine Arts University, Turkey

ABSTRACT

Digital transformation creates a radical shift in the representation of gender in the practice of photography, allowing the de-gendering of photographic language. Digital technologies contribute to the polyphony of the gaze towards the subject of the photograph by enabling the creation of a visual production process independent of the gender and identity of the artist. In this context, digital artists emphasizing the fact that gender is a social construction tend to develop a genderless photographic language with tools that reshape identity and the body. By focusing on the work of artists, this study explores the potential of digital technologies to both increase visibility and create a space of resistance against algorithmic exclusion. By widening and deepening the boundaries of photography, digitalization opens up a space that transcends gender norms and allows for a move beyond traditional representations.

DOI: 10.4018/979-8-3373-2230-8.ch006

INTRODUCTION

Technological developments throughout the history of photography will continue to evolve in the digital world, preserving its identity as an art discipline supported by a creative and critical approach. Artists have the potential to transform this technological transformation into an artistic approach, and as they adapt to this change, photography will maintain its function as a powerful tool for expression, thought and narrative. As photography becomes more intertwined with digital culture, it will allow artists to address concepts such as identity, gender, reality, biopower, subject and memory from new and alternative perspectives. Issues such as surveillance, privacy, authenticity and manipulation of digital images will be examined through photographic images and artworks from an academic and critical perspective, providing new viewpoints on the social effects of the post-digital age.

The impact of digital evolution on art and the artist has become an important area of transformation that requires in-depth examination, especially in the context of algorithmic production methods and artificial intelligence-supported creative processes. Today, art practice is shaped not only by aesthetic and conceptual elements, but also by the new possibilities offered by data-driven systems, algorithmic structure and artificial intelligence-based models. This transformation transforms art's methods of production and its kinship with the audience, raising debates on redefining the role of the artist, the concept of creativity and the originality of the artwork. In particular, algorithmic production techniques and artificial intelligence-based artistic practices have given rise to new aesthetic approaches in the forms of artistic expression; they have gone beyond the anthropocentric approach in the artist's creative practice and revealed a posthuman approach, transformations in the concept of gender, changes in the context of identity and the idea of co-production with machines. In this context, how artificial intelligence tools are positioned in art; the content of data sets, the decision mechanisms of algorithms and how prompts developed by the artist affect the creative process are important topics of discussion. In this framework, the new horizons opened by the digital age in art production point to a process of radical transformations in art in terms of form, concept and content, and in this context, fundamental elements such as the position of the artist, the quality of the work and the perception of the audience are re-evaluated.

The definition of art and the forms of production are being reshaped by artificial intelligence algorithms that use data analysis and learning processes. However, in this process, questions such as whether algorithms follow predetermined patterns, how existing prejudices are reflected in algorithms, and whether the source of the artwork is the artist or technology gain importance. The fact that the data sets used for algorithms are based on statistical models and reflect certain trends should not be neglected at this point. It can be argued that ethical responsibilities and rights are collectively shared among the software developers who design artificial intelligence algorithms, the individuals or institutions providing the visual data that train these systems, and the artists who engage with such technologies in their creative processes. The issue of authorship in AI-generated artworks remains contested, raising ongoing debates about whether the credit should go to the algorithm's developer, the dataset contributors, or the artist who directs and contextualizes the output. This ambiguity underscores the necessity of evaluating each AI-generated artwork within its specific production context, taking into account the tools, datasets, and instructions that shape its creation.

Artificial intelligence tools are causing major changes in art production and other disciplines and industries today. It is clear that artificial intelligence has significant potential for artists to provide innovative opportunities in their creative processes and expand traditional artistic practices. However, the use of AI in the field of art raises debates around ethical issues such as the role of the artist, originality and intellectual property rights. Along with all these questionings, it is significant not to ignore the creative possibilities that artificial intelligence brings to art production. Artificial intelligence tools can be viewed as one of the positive aspects of this transformation, as they provide artists with new perspectives and expand creative boundaries. Moreover, the impact of artificial intelligence on the art industry is not limited to the production process, but also transforms the way art is perceived and consumed. This can be considered a promising development in terms of its potential to expand the universal language of art and make it accessible to a wider audience. "The rapid advancement of Artificial Intelligence (AI) has ushered in a new era of creativity, challenging traditional notions of artistry and pushing the boundaries of human imagination. As AI technologies continue to evolve, their application in creative fields has sparked both excitement and controversy within the artistic community and beyond. From generating visual art through Generative Adversarial Networks (GANs)[1] to composing music and writing poetry, AI systems are demonstrating capabilities that were once thought to be uniquely human." (Khadake, 2024). This paradigm shift has not only created new possibilities for artistic expression, but has also raised profound questions about the nature of creativity, the expanding definition of art, and the role of the artist in an increasingly automated world. The text examines the multi-layered effects of artificial intelligence on art and creativity; while analyzing its applications in visual arts and various photography-based fields, it also aims to discuss the conceptual dimensions of this technological transformation in creative industries through the lens of gender. This text aims to examine the revolution that artificial intelligence technologies have brought about in photography and photographic editing, and how this revolution has expanded the possibilities of creativity and artistic expression for artists in unprecedented ways. The works of artists producing a wide and rich range of artistic effects and the statements of theorists will be examined; additionally, how these technological innovations are redefining the concept of gender and creative practice in the digital age will be discussed.

PHOTOGRAPHY AND GENDER: A HISTORICAL CONTEXT

Using the importance of visual representation, photography traces gender while artists challenge the boundaries of their representations, offering different perspectives on the visualisation of gender. The representation of gender in photography is seen as a phenomenon shaped by historical social and cultural norms. Today, with the post-digital process, artificial intelligence, and algorithms becoming an integral part of our lives, significant developments and alternative forms of representation are emerging in the transformation and change of this representation and its approaches. This transformation has not been limited to how gender is visualized, but has also reshaped the relationship between the viewer and the photograph, the concept of representation, and the role of photography in the construction of gender and its effects on power structures.

Since the invention of photography, it has been possible to speak of a photographic plane that has generally been shaped by a male perspective in visual memory. Male artists, as in other art disciplines, have generally relegated women to a passive role in their photographic productions. John Berger describes the representation of women in society as "...according to practices and customs that are now being questioned but have not yet been resolved, women's existence in society is very different from that of men. To be born a woman is to be born into a private, enclosed place that belongs to men. Men are what they do, women are what they look like. Men look at women. Women look at being looked at. The observer in women is the man, the observed is the woman" (Berger, 2011). Berger argues that women are constructed as objects rather than subjects, and that this distinction is deeply rooted in both visual culture and social structures. According to Berger, women are represented as objects of male desire, which reinforces the normative structure of gender and its social foundations. In a social order where women and minority groups are marginalized, male artists' styles have continued to produce parallel images. During this period of photography, women are generally depicted in images that represent traditional gender definitions imposed on them, such as motherhood, cleaning, and cooking, in interior spaces. Men, on the other hand, occupy a place in visual culture with a symbolism that emphasizes power and authority in outdoor and public spaces. R. W. Connell states that "analyses of gender-based division of labor generally establish gender categories as a simple dividing line in economic life and, by detailing how this line appears in different societies, lead to a more complex understanding of the issue." This statement highlights how the structure of gender is designed through both social values and economic norms (Connell, 2016, p. 96). The narrowing of women's place in the media is achieved through the internalization of social roles. According to Connell, role theory is made effective by the view that "other people reward those who conform to them and punish those who deviate from them" (Connell, 2016, p. 87).

During the modernist period, the aesthetic and ideological orientation of photography underwent a transformation, but the gender-based image system continued with its traditional stereotypes. Although artists such as Edward Weston and Alfred Stieglitz transformed photography into an aesthetic language of expression, they often focused on themes dominated by hegemonic and gender stereotypes in their depictions of female figures. In this period, women were mostly portrayed as passive objects of art and desire from a male perspective.

While gender roles and the reinforcement of binary gender were predominant in photographic practice in the 19th century, the critical structure in art history, especially in conjunction with feminist theory, led to the questioning of all these representations in the 20th century. Women artists and all individuals labeled as "other" actively presented themselves and the normative situation they faced in a more political and critical manner. The feminist movement began to seriously criticize gender representations in photography. Laura Mulvey's (1975) "Visual Pleasure and Narrative Cinema" created a striking turning point in the representation of women in photography and cinema by analyzing how women are represented through the male gaze and according to the demands of the male viewer. Mulvey's argument that women are presented as "gazed at" and "passive" objects in visual culture played an important role in gaining momentum for the feminist movement in photography. These criticisms raised important awareness about how photography can reinforce gender roles and how women are positioned as objects rather than subjects. Feminist artists began to create new ways of representation by using photography as a medium to question the social construction of gender and to include women as subjects within this medium. Artists such as Ana Mendieta, Barbara Kruger, and Cindy Sherman have challenged the dominant perspectives on gender in photography through their series of photographs that question their own identity, the individual, and power, and embrace different social structures. They emphasized that gender is not biological but a social construct. Ana Mendieta, particularly in her "Silueta" series, portrayed the female body not as a passive subject of visual consumption but as a transient, potent force rooted in nature, ritual, and selfhood. Her art challenged conventional portrayals of women by focusing on disappearance, metamorphosis, and a deep spiritual bond rather than static beauty or submissive roles. Similarly, Cindy Sherman's "Untitled Film Stills" series presents a profound interrogation of gender and identity representation, examining how the female image is passively constructed and how this manifests in society. These works have laid the groundwork for photographs that disrupt the perceived fixed nature of gender and illustrate that gender is a flexible and performative process. The ability of photography to reflect this is also highly significant in terms of why artists choose and utilize this medium.

Artists have emphasized that gender is a social construct and have explored how photography positions itself in relation to this construct and its potential. They have created photo series that reveal the multi-layered and fluid nature of gender and how various power mechanisms and social norms shape this concept. Theorists such as Nancy Fraser, Monique Wittig, and Judith Butler have stated that gender cannot be a fixed identity and that gender roles are a process designed entirely by society's organization and constructed through stereotypes.

The queer approach does not merely focus on specific sexual identities such as homosexuality and lesbianism; it also continues to exist as a critical method of questioning all identity categories and identity politics. Queer exemplifies a more mediating connection between other identity categories. In the context of political representation, the growing awareness of the boundaries of identity categories has enabled the post-structural institutionalization of identity as temporary and conditional, paving the way for queer to emerge as a new form of identity formation and political organization (Jagose, 2017, p. 99). The queer approach rejects fixed definitions and has a fluid, multi-layered, and constantly changing structure. It critiques forms of domination established through the heteronormative singularity of power structures, sexuality, and desire, positioning itself in opposition to this normative order. By resisting gendered power practices that center the construction of the body, it reimagines the body not as a concrete tool of power but as a space open to multiple possibilities. In this context, it contributes to the plural, fluid, and decentralized form of these structures by analyzing not only the subject - body relationship but also the social spaces and areas shaped within the framework of heterosexual norms. The fundamental stance offered by queer thought is to distance oneself from all categories and normative structures constructed by power and to break free from them. This approach blurs hegemonic and categorical boundaries, opening up fixed understandings of identity and norms to debate. Queer does not directly reject areas of power but questions them with a critical gaze; in this process, it prepares the ground for the exploration of new forms, identities, and possibilities of existence. "If 'queer' politics adopts an attitude independent of other modes of power, it will lose its democratizing power. The political deconstruction of 'queer' should not paralyze the use of such words, but ideally expand their scope, prompting us to consider the costs and purposes of using these terms and the power relations through which these categories are articulated" (Yardımcı & Güçlü, 2016, p. 129). By questioning normative assumptions about gender identity and sexuality, queer theory reveals the potential of art to transform the power of representation. In this context, many contemporary photographers challenge the domination of the masculine gaze and subvert traditional forms of representation. Against the narratives of male-dominated visual culture that objectify the female body and are shaped by heteronormative codes, queer artists foreground the fluidity of identity, bodily diversity and the performative nature of gender. Combining the documentary power of photography with personal and political narratives, these artists transform the subject from a passive object of the gaze into an active entity that expresses its own identity. Thus, the queer gaze transforms both the form and content of photography, creating alternative visual narratives and making visible non-normative bodies, desires and lifestyles. This process becomes a radical art practice that not only transforms representation but also questions the viewer's gaze.

Catherine Opie challenged the conventions of traditional photography by focusing on underrepresented communities and reshaping how portraiture and identity are portrayed. Her striking, structured images, frequently inspired by classical aesthetics, disrupt norms by highlighting queer, and non-conforming individuals. Similarly, Zanele Muholi works to increase the visibility of black queer people and lesbian women. In her "Faces and Phases" series, she directs the subject's gaze directly at the camera, making them the gazer rather than the looked at. This disrupts the viewer's comfort zone and redefines the power of representation through a queer gaze. On the other hand, Del LaGrace Volcano focuses on intersex and non-binary bodies, producing photographs that challenge the binary system of gender. Playing with queer theory's concepts of body, identity and gender performance, Volcano questions and reconstructs socially accepted body images. These artists use photography not only as a means of visualization, but also as a site of political expression and transformation. With queer theory, instead of producing a normative representation, photography becomes a space that celebrates difference, reverses the gaze and invites the viewer to question. This transformation paves the way for radical changes not only in artistic form but also in social perception. Accompanied by these expressions and approaches, artists, especially those who produce on the basis of photography, have contributed to the visualization of the fact that gender has a variable, fluid and transitional depiction.

It is important to note that photography has moved away from its original purpose as a means of recording and documenting events. "Documentation is not merely the creation of records about ourselves and our lives, but rather a process that has emerged as a result of a dialectical relationship with the development of media technologies, transforming into a way of seeing. This way of seeing is more than a passive camera eye; it is a creative gaze" (Jurgenson, 2024, p. 61-62). As we approach contemporary photography, the intertwining of various fields such as digital processes, queer theory, and the erasure of gender has led to the replacement of contemporary political production with artificial intelligence and algorithms. With unlimited visual production capacity, this shift transcends gender and, influenced by the concept of "posthuman" gives rise to examples of much more flexible images. These applications and platforms transcend the traditional creative process and open up a new creative space. At the same time, the active speed of the digital process takes the concept of "visibility" to a whole new level, making it accessible to an even wider audience. By reshaping concepts and representations such as artificial intelligence, algorithms, post-digital processes, gender, identity, body, and power, photography is being transformed into a tool that questions and subverts the social, normative, and heteronormative structure.

POST-DIGITAL PROCESS: GENDER CRITICISM AND ALTERNATIVE FORMS OF THINKING

In the post-digital era, the union of technology and art has further diversified the representational power of photography. The aesthetic understanding of photography, based on its relationship with documentation, representation, and reality, has continued to evolve in light of technological developments throughout history. While examining photography's fidelity to the concept of reality, Susan Sontag argues that digitalization has rendered this fidelity even more intractable (Sontag, 2011). Fred Ritchin argues that images created with artificial intelligence can no longer represent reality as a documentary record, and that photography is undergoing a profound transformation, both perceptually and conceptually (Ritchin, 2012). In the digital age, the fact that photos can be edited, manipulated, and even created without any human involvement has blurred the lines of visual reality.

The integration of AI-generated art into photographic production has reignited conceptual debates about the essence of photography. In the traditional sense, photography expresses the artist's intention through conscious choices in composition, lighting, and angle, while the rise of AI-assisted production processes has made the ontology of photography more complex, layered, and ambiguous. This transformation can be read through Vilém Flusser's concepts of technical image and apparatus. According to Flusser, technical devices such as the camera, while seemingly allowing the user's creative action to be free, actually limit it within a pre-programmed set of possibilities (Flusser, 2020). Therefore, technical images are not so much a direct extension of human subjectivity as they are the products of a hybrid form of production that emerges between humans and machines. The user produces by selecting options offered by the device. Artificial intelligence technologies take this dynamic further; they not only offer options but also intervene in the artistic production process, blurring the boundaries between human creativity and machine programming.

From a technical perspective, art produced by artificial intelligence goes beyond being a product of advances in media technology; it represents a current phase in the process of technological development that has been ongoing since the Industrial Revolution. However, with mechanization and industrialization, the relationship between humans and machines has undergone a transformation, and this interaction has altered both the tools and the meaning of artistic creation. As Flusser puts it, modern art production has become an activity that circulates within the programs of devices, producing meaning by challenging or reinterpreting these programs (Flusser, 2020). With the advancement of computer technology and digitalization, artificial intelligence is transforming both the form and the creator of artistic production. In this context, art produced by artificial intelligence not only reflects the interaction between technology and art, but also radically expands the concepts introduced by Flusser, reopening the debate on the concept of creative subjectivity. At this point, the claim that photography is a trace of reality becomes even more ambiguous. Images produced through artificial intelligence are not required to refer to the real world; these images learn from other images and gain existence within an abstract visual data space. This situation updates Flusser's warnings about technical images, showing that the viewer is now compelled to question not only the reality represented by the image but also the algorithmic processes through which the image has passed.

In this period, when the integration of digital technologies with artistic practice has increased significantly, photography has also moved beyond analog photography, providing remarkable flexibility, just as it has permeated every area of life and all other artistic disciplines. Artificial intelligence and algorithms are reestablishing photography not only as a technical medium but also as a creative subject. In the digital age, photography has undergone a transformation that will redefine it both aesthetically and ontologically. Digital processes in photography have also been used in the form of digital manipulation. Artists have gained the freedom to create images that transcend traditional boundaries by combining different concepts through digital photo manipulation and computer-based tools. New forms of representation, and even the opening up of the concept of representation itself, have emerged as important effects of new media forms and technology. In a historical context, binary gender representations based on stereotypes have often been presented from a limited perspective. Photography's power as a tool for visually reflecting cultural and social structures, individuals, and norms has ensured that this power continues in the age of digitalization. Digitalization and the spread of the internet have provided artists with the opportunity to question gender representations through different platforms and tools. The digitalization of visual production and visual production software have given artists the opportunity to produce new types of images, while also enabling a level of manipulation and editing that was previously impossible in photography. Social media theorist Nathan Jurgenson discusses how the transformation brought about by the redefinition of visibility, privacy, memory, death, time, space, and all other domains challenged by social media tests humanity, both collectively and individually, in various ways and degrees, as societal norms and perceptions struggle to keep pace with the changes in how we perceive ourselves, others, and the world as a result of new digital and social technologies (Jurgenson, 2024, p. 7). This process of challenge also paves the way for the emergence of alternative perspectives and the development of production methodologies based on new, liberatory forms of manipulation enabled by redefinition. An example of such a manipulation-driven mode of production can be found in the work of artist Mario Klingemann, who uses algorithms to distort human faces and generate various abstract visual forms. His algorithmically-assisted creations prompt a reconsideration of the aesthetic values traditionally associated with photography, shifting the role of the artist by partially transferring creative control to machines (URL-1). As a result, photography transforms from a representation of a fixed moment into a data-driven, fluid, and unpredictable process of creation.

This process questions the function of traditional photography as a means of "capturing reality" and opens up a new aesthetic field in which visual representation is no longer determined by the human gaze but by artificial intelligence. Here, Susan Sontag's statement that "what photographs give us access to directly is not reality itself, but images" sheds light on where we should be heading (Sontag, 2011, p. 195). Photography is no longer just an image created by a camera, but also an image produced by a data algorithm. In this sense, Klingemann's works fundamentally question both the limits of visual representation and the artist's place in the production process. At the same time, his works carry a quality that distorts the body and form, prompting the viewer to reflect on gender.

Artist Trevor Paglen, who examines the impact of artificial intelligence and surveillance technologies on representations of identity, race, and gender, questions how artificial intelligence algorithms label women and men and manipulate gender representations in his project "ImageNet Roulette." Paglen's work with Kate Crawford sheds light on how technology intervenes in the digital representations of gender and how these representations reproduce social structures. "ImageNet Roulette is trained on the "person" categories from a dataset called *ImageNet* (developed at Princeton and Stanford Universities in 2009), one of the most widely used training sets in machine learning research and development (URL-2, URL-3). The project was a provocation, acting as a window into some of the racist, misogynistic, cruel, and simply absurd categorizations embedded within ImageNet and other training sets that AI models are build upon" (Paglen, 2025). Paglen argues that the classification of gender through artificial intelligence leads to the reconstruction of gender through algorithms, and discusses how concepts such as "visibility" and "identity" are shaped in this process. "This complex architecture of images of real people, tagged with often offensive labels, has been publicly available on the internet for a decade. It provides a powerful and important example of the complexities and dangers of human classification, and the sliding spectrum between supposedly unproblematic labels like "trumpeter" or "tennis player" to concepts like "spastic," "mulatto," or "redneck." Regardless of the supposed neutrality of any particular category, the selection of images skews the meaning in ways that are gendered, racialized, ableist, and ageist. ImageNet is an object lesson, if you will, in what happens when people are categorized like objects" (Crawford & Paglen, 2025). By analyzing how artificial intelligence transforms representations of identity and gender based on social arguments, the artist offers a powerful critique of the reproduction of gender in the digital world.

The gendering of technologies prompts reflection on how artificial intelligence can embody a social identity such as gender, constructed through its interactions with individuals. This suggests that AI can be perceived and treated as possessing a gender identity, influencing how users interact with it and what expectations they project onto it. This aspect of gendering is significant because it shapes user experience and informs the broader societal impact of tools like AI. While the development of AI technologies is often legitimized through claims of neutrality and objectivity, the ways in which these technologies are produced, presented, and utilized can become ideological spaces where gender norms are reproduced and reinforced. Gendering practices observed in consumer-oriented AI products, in particular, reveal how existing power relations and social roles are transposed onto technological platforms. Artists such as Trevor Paglen expand the boundaries of critique against such AI systems or classification platforms by creating production methods that engage critically with algorithms and internet infrastructures.

The influence of artificial intelligence on gender representations introduces a multi-layered field of inquiry. While the use of digital applications and algorithms offers the potential to transcend traditional normative structures, it simultaneously risks reproducing heteronormative frameworks and existing perceptions. These technologies complicate the social construction of gender and identity, actively shaping how viewers perceive the nature of gender itself. AI thus functions not merely as a technical tool but as a cultural agent capable of generating discourse. As feminist scholar Donna Haraway has articulated, "New technologies affect the social relations of both sexuality and reproduction (and not always in the same way). The proximity between sexuality and instrumentality, the idea of the body as a machine for maximizing individual pleasure or utility, is eloquently expressed in the sociobiological origin stories that emphasize genetic accounting and explain the oppressive foundations of male and female gender roles as an inevitable dialectic" (Haraway, 2006, p. 46). Building on Haraway's insights, it can be argued that the boundaries between technology and the body are increasingly blurred, and these new modes of being simultaneously carry ideological implications. The gendering of artificial intelligences contributes to this blurring in a way that reinforces existing social hierarchies; thus, technological innovation often serves to reproduce normative frameworks rather than foster genuine social transformation. Nevertheless, some recently developed AI systems attempt to move beyond this normative framework by offering gender-neutral voices or multiple identity options. Yet such initiatives remain limited in number, and gendering practices within the tech industry largely maintain their hegemonic character. From a theoretical perspective, the impact of gender and normative structures on visual culture has been consistently interrogated. Judith Butler's concept of "performativity" underscores that gender cannot be defined as a fixed identity, but must be understood as a variable, performative construct. Similarly, Susan Sontag's multilayered writings on photography highlight the medium's power to produce representations grounded in social norms, while also offering a critique of those very conventions. Through the rich language of photography, these frameworks become more visible and provide fertile ground for in-depth analysis. Gendering processes, when examined in contrast to the supposedly neutral nature of technology, reveal the ideological underpinnings of technological production, emphasizing the necessity of inclusive design approaches. The integration of AI into photographic art not only transforms the medium but also fosters more dynamic, polyphonic, and flexible forms of representation. Photography thus emerges not merely as a static visual representation, but as a process shaped by algorithms and artificial intelligence.

Stephanie Dinkins is a cross-disciplinary artist producing work at the intersection of emerging technologies and the future, creating dialogue platforms around artificial intelligence because of its intersection with critical social issues. Dinkins leverages technology and storytelling to challenge and reimagine narratives surrounding marginalized communities, particularly black and brown individuals. Through her installations, digital platforms, and community-based projects, Dinkins aims not only to question the current paradigms of AI development but also to pave the way for more equitable and inclusive technological futures (Dinkins, 2025). By engaging in dialogues with artificial intelligence, she questions its limited understanding of identity, race, and gender. As a black female artist, she makes artificial intelligence's existing biases visible. In "Secret Garden," Stephanie Dinkins has cultivated a virtual oasis populated with Black women who share stories of power and resilience (URL-4, URL-5). Multigenerational narratives collapse past, present, and future across interactive vignettes (Brooklyn Academy of Music, 2025). Essentially a three-channel video installation, this work offers the opportunity to experience and explore an interactive, navigable photographic plane on computer-based platforms.

Her work emphasizes the importance of including diverse voices and perspectives in the design and application of artificial intelligence, advocating for a future in which technology elevates and empowers underrepresented histories and experiences and fosters a technology ecosystem that is truly beneficial for everyone (Dinkins, 2025). Historically, photography has functioned both as a documentary medium and as a tool of surveillance and categorization, particularly against marginalized communities. "Secret Garden" offers a compelling exploration of how artificial intelligence and digital media can be harnessed to reimagine the visual and narrative archive of black women experiences. This analysis examines this work through the interconnected lenses of gender, ethnicity, and photography, arguing that Dinkins' work radically subverts dominant visual traditions and suggests alternative modes of collective self-representation. The project not only critiques the biases embedded in both historical archives and contemporary AI technologies but also models a future in which black body stories are central to the creation of new technological and visual worlds. Through this work, Dinkins transforms photography from a tool of capture into a collaborative site of flourishing, memory-making, and resistance.

Artists demonstrate that the visual representation of gender is not limited to specific themes or contexts, but permeates various digital spaces. This pattern resonates with broader social narratives about gender roles and representation, highlighting the liberating potential of algorithmic systems to depict gender in a more balanced and inclusive manner. "We observe that some binaries persist in Western traditions; these binaries have always been systematically present in terms of the logic of subjugation of women, people of color, nature, workers, animals (in short, those 'constructed' as 'the other' -and whose function is to hold up a mirror to the self- have always been systematically present. The main dichotomies that remain problematic are: self/other, mind/body, culture/nature, male/female, civilized/primitive, reality/appearance, whole/part, agent/source, doer/done, active/passive, right/wrong, real/illusory, complete/partial, God/human. Advanced technology culture challenges these dualities in complex and surprising ways. In the relationship between humans and machines, it is unclear which is the maker and which is the made. In machines that engage in coding practices, it is unclear which is the mind and which is the body" (Haraway, 2006, p. 65). One of the important artists who uses artificial intelligence and algorithms in this direction, incorporating queer theory that breaks down or blurs the dichotomies of advanced technology culture and provides space for innovative and gender-inclusive alternative perspectives, is Blake Wood.

"Visions & Memories" is an artificial intelligence photography project by Blake Wood and marks an important milestone in the AI post-photography movement (URL-6, URL-7). The work, created using text-to-image conversion technology in an AI-assisted photographic form, is a tribute to the complexity of human experience. From a queer perspective, these artworks explore intimacy, friendship, and the variations of the body. Wood's analog-textured, emotionally charged visuals emphasize the ambiguity and permeability of bodies and identities rather than technological perfection. By breaking traditional binary gender representations in photography, they create space for the existence of multiple forms of identity.

The artist has embraced post-photographic compositions as a new technology, blending them seamlessly with traditional photography, and continues to produce work in this manner. Wood expresses his unique perspective, stating, "When I look back at the history of art and photography, there are only a handful of photographers who were able to capture queer love in its authentic state, yet there are endless amounts of traditional relationships captured in imagery. I think AI can open doors for artists to create images that might not otherwise exist, and I think that's very exciting" (Zadeh, 2023). The increasing simulation of gender in AI-assisted visual production brings about a fundamental change in the understanding of reality represented by photography. Whether a body is female or male is no longer a biological necessity; it has become a matter of choice constructed through algorithmic parameters, and the existence of a power structure that establishes a binary gender system is becoming increasingly blurred. Wood indirectly addresses this new relationship between artificial intelligence and photographic production, particularly in his recent works circulating in digital media, where he combines analog aesthetics with digital processing to break down the fixed form of the body. This hybridization suggests that gender is not merely biological data but a visual or numerical structure that can be produced, transformed, and replicated.

Throughout history, photography has served as an effective medium for reinforcing binary gender norms. However, the rise of artificial intelligence-driven visual production technologies today offers new opportunities to question and transcend this established binary structure. AI enables the production of alternative gender representations that transcend fixed identity categories through the manipulation and hybridization of gender characteristics. In particular, AI-based systems such as Generative Adversarial Network (GAN) produce synthetic faces and figures that integrate traditionally masculine and feminine characteristics, thus blurring gender boundaries in the visual realm. These images can be seen as concrete reflections of Butler's theoretical approach that gender is not a fixed essence but a performative construction. In this context, artificial intelligence proposes fluid, plural, and decentralized representations against naturalized forms of gender, thereby producing a new visual discourse. AI-based visual production tools enable artists to transcend the binary gender regime and represent gender experiences that exist outside the categories of male and female. This development is of vital importance in terms of the visibility of trans, non-binary, and genderqueer identities, which are often rendered invisible in traditional visual art practices. On the other hand, classical photographic beauty norms have long been determined by gender-based expectations, with female bodies represented within specific aesthetic codes. Artificial intelligence, however, transcends these normative aesthetic structures, producing bodies and identities that do not conform to conventional notions of beauty, thereby constructing a new paradigm of beauty that centers diversity and inclusivity. In this context, artificial intelligence, within the framework of Flusser's concepts of technical image and device, goes beyond being merely a technological tool, taking on the function of reproducing, transforming, and creating new representational possibilities for existing socio-cultural codes.

Artist Jake Elwes explores what happens when machine learning algorithms are used to find alternative representations of gender and patterns of beauty that transcend the concept of gender and mathematical limitations in computers (Gingrich, 2021). Integrating artificial intelligence with drag performance, Elwes not only critiques the limitations and biases of AI systems, but also opens up new avenues for artistic expression and representation. Elwes' work invites viewers to reflect on the fluidity of identity and technology's potential to both reinforce and dismantle social norms. Elwes challenges subconscious bias and discriminatory undercurrents in technology, as well as implicit stereotyping frequently performed by such systems. Without questioning the value systems that underpin AI, gender bias and sometimes discrimation seems to seep into our lives. Generative adversarial networks (GANs), a technique used by Google's 'Deep Dream' project, allows the creation of all new data sets through machine learning algorithms. With "Zizi", Elwes used GAN's to retrains neural network algorithms to include aesthetics and conceptions of beauty informed by genderfluid, queer performers (Gingrich, 2021).

Algorithms can mediate the reproduction of gender and identity norms through historical and cultural biases embedded in the datasets they are trained on. However, through deliberate interventions and "queering" strategies in these datasets, it becomes possible to decode normative codes and construct alternative forms of representation. This confirms critical theories of technology, which argue that technological infrastructures are not neutral as claimed; on the contrary, they are shaped by power relations and ideological structures. Artificial intelligence-supported queer art production, on the other hand, has the potential to produce alternative realities in a way that makes it visible that the body, identity and gender are not naturalized categories but social constructions that are constantly negotiated and reconstructed.

The "Zizi: Queering the Dataset"[2] artwork constantly shifts between queer performers, thereby playing with the idea of disturbance and disruption of inherent, invisible technological logic and agency (URL-8, URL-9, URL-10). The sublime aesthetics of Zizi reach beyond the binary, into a sensual space of new aesthetics in which questioning gender norms results in evertransforming, possibilities of gender (Gingrich, 2021). Using artificial intelligence to create performances that challenge traditional gender binaries, the artist highlights Butler's assertion that gender is not an innate quality but rather an identity constructed through repeated social performances, thereby emphasizing the performative nature of gender. "This work causes the weights inside the neural network to shift away from the normative identities it was originally trained on and into a space of queerness. 'Zizi - Queering The Dataset' lets us peek inside the machine learning system and visualise what the neural network has (and hasn't) learnt. The work is a celebration of difference and ambiguity, which invites us to reflect on bias in our data driven society" (Elwes, 2019). The ability to make diverse and multiple identities visible, independent of biological determinism, offers a unique richness in AI-based design. These production methods reveal the non-linear nature of gender while also leading to a multi-layered exploration. Elwes' work also prompts viewers to consider who builds these systems and for what purpose, as well as the necessity of questioning how these technologies function for artists and queer individuals seeking to construct their own digital utopias. Additionally, it demonstrates the role artificial intelligence applications play in creating complex representations.

The development of digital technologies has transformed the art of photography not only on a technical level, but also in conceptual and political terms. This evolution is being radically questioned by artists who focus on issues such as identity, surveillance, and representation. In this context, Zach Blas is one of the important figures who reexamines the evolution of photography in the digital age from conceptual, critical, and speculative perspectives. Similar to Elwes, Blas produces works and pieces through gender and queer theory, revealing his criticism through algorithms he developed against normative identity and gender production accompanied by biometric technologies. He exposes and disrupts the gendered and racial nature of algorithms. Blas's artistic production reveals that photography in the digital age has moved beyond its function as a mere representational tool and has become an active component of surveillance and control technologies. In particular, the amorphous face masks developed by Blas in his work "Facial Weaponization Suite" invite us to rethink photographic representation as a practice of resistance against digital surveillance systems (URL-11, URL-12). "Facial Weaponization Suite" protests against biometric facial recognition –and the inequalities these technologies propagate– by making "collective masks" in workshops that are modeled from the aggregated facial data of participants, resulting in amorphous masks that cannot be detected as human faces by biometric facial recognition technologies. The masks are used for public interventions and performances. These masks intersect with social movements' use of masking as an opaque tool of collective transformation that refuses dominant forms of political representation (Blas, 2012). Works that highlight the invisibility of queer bodies directly intervene in the ideological functioning of technology.

"The masks are used for public interventions and performances. One mask, the *Fag Face Mask*, generated from the biometric facial data of many queer men's faces, is a response to scientific studies that link determining sexual orientation through rapid facial recognition techniques (URL-13, URL-14). Another mask explores a tripartite conception of blackness: the inability of biometric technologies to detect dark skin as racist, the favoring of black in militant aesthetics, and black as that which informatically obfuscates. A third mask engages feminism's relations to concealment and imperceptibility, taking veil legislation in France as a troubling site that oppressively forces visibility. A fourth mask considers biometrics' deployment as a security technology at the Mexico-US border and the nationalist violence it instigates" (Blas, 2012). The digital visualization techniques used here challenge the physical reality that the photograph references, and faces are anonymized by masks, reduced to data objects devoid of identity and gender.

In her article "Mean Images" Hito Steyerl argues that "as categories seem to emerge from the data themselves, they acquire the authority of an immediate manifestation or apparition. Data are no longer presented via the traditional media of graphs, clusters, curves, diagrams or other scientific abstractions. Instead, they are visualized in the shape of the thing from which they are supposed to abstract. They skip mediation to gesture towards fake immanence." digital images are not merely representations, but have become active agents in their own right (Steyerl, 2023). Especially in surveillance systems, facial recognition technologies, and AI-supported monitoring networks, images play an active role in identifying, classifying, and excluding people. Digital images, which take on the active roles Steyerl refers to, can transform and become transformative critical interventions by breaking away from their content, such as social limitation and categorization, in conjunction with artists' visionary narratives. Today, digital image production and circulation are largely regulated by capitalist systems. Here, masking can function as a defense mechanism, but also as a technique of disruption and sabotage. Low-resolution, blurred, and anonymized images can be strategically employed to challenge hegemonic visual economies. In this sense, it is possible to discuss how masking and masks can develop a politics of invisibility against the high-resolution and controllable body images produced by the system. As in Blas's work, the mask is presented not as a means of hiding from power, but as a tool for constructing a new politics of visibility against power.

Blas' approach is also directly related to queer theory's visibility politics. Queer individuals have historically been forced into invisibility and, when visible, subjected to violence and surveillance. Criticizing digital surveillance technologies, particularly facial recognition systems, for reproducing gender, body, and identity understandings through a heteronormative infrastructure, Blas proposes artistic strategies as a queer form of resistance against this visibility system. Blas not only demonstrates how LGBTIQ+ individuals are threatened by digital surveillance systems in the digital age but also highlights efforts to develop alternative forms of resistance against these threats. "What could be the benefits of proving it to the world that such a recognition apparatus exists? Does it not only further confirm and scientifically validate one of the processes of LGBTIQ stereotyping? Categories like fag face and gay face? It is easy enough to claim that these studies parse us into categories that will inevitably be used against us. It offers a visibility that will attempt to control, monitor, and police us. In response to facial recognition technologies, we ask: What are the tactics and techniques for making our faces nonexistent? How do we flee this visibility into the fog of a queerness that refuses to be recognized?" with these statements, it seeks to address questions raised by individuals who wish to distance themselves from categorization, or queer individuals, regarding the centralizing approach of the post-digital era and the surveillance structure of facial recognition applications (The Museum of Contemporary Art Chicago, 2012).

As Haraway puts it, "The cyborg vision can also show us a way out of the labyrinth of dualities in which we explain our bodies and our tools to ourselves. This is not a dream of a common language, but a powerful ideal of heteroglossia, of 'multi-voiced signifiers. The cyborg vision means both creating and dismantling machines, identities, categories, relationships, and stories of space" (Haraway, 2006, p. 74). Blas's works offer a multi-voiced reading of the digital evolution of photography, not through technical advances, but through the dynamics of political, social, and conceptual conflicts. In the artist's practice, photography functions as both a space for surveillance mechanisms and forms of resistance, becoming the intersection of visibility politics and invisibility strategies. Thus, in the digital age, photography is repositioned as a critical intervention and a tool of struggle, transcending its role as a static document. In this context, photography is no longer merely a record of physical reality but becomes part of strategies of invisibility, anonymity, and escape from existing power structures.

Digital manipulation applications offer a rich spectrum, particularly in the field of photography. This spectrum goes beyond the historical connection of photography with reality, paving the way for visionary and liberating designs and applications. The *Midjourney* application also enables artists and designers to present alternative realities, creating groundbreaking images in line with many concepts and theories. Artist Cihan Bacak explores issues of gender and representation in photography through his work with *Midjourney* and AI, using the limitless possibilities of artificial intelligence to present a homoerotic exploration of digital bodies under the shadow of censorship. "Muscular Theology" reflects not only an aesthetically and homoerotically charged universe created through artificial intelligence, but also serves as a visual diary of Bacak (URL-15, URL-16, URL-17). Combining his observations from the gym with his background in fashion and art photography, Bacak starts each frame with inspiration from a different song, drawing from his visual influences of the time and constructing an alternative AI-based narrative for himself. As a dynamic project that adapts to the constantly evolving nature of artificial intelligence, it remains rooted in a personal space while successfully gaining visibility in today's digital World (Bacak, 2023).

Cultural constructs and entrenched traditions frequently reinforce symbolic associations between gender and the body, not solely through representations of femininity, but also through the ideological frameworks that shape and regulate masculinity. The conceptualization of masculinity as inherently linked to physical strength and dominance has significant implications for how the male body is conditioned. This conditioning extends across various domains, including labor and economic performance, bodily comportment and spatial presence within public life, and prescriptive roles dictated by institutional forces such as the family and the state. Similarly, normative expectations surrounding sexuality are informed by these structural imperatives. The ideological apparatus that attributes fixed, externally defined characteristics to masculinity simultaneously delineates femininity in opposition, often in subordinate or devalued terms. By constructing gender within a rigid binary paradigm, such discourses regulate sexuality through mechanisms that mirror broader systems of control and normalization. These gendered ideologies, mediated primarily through corporeal and linguistic codes, function as regulatory regimes that assert dominance over bodies by ascribing hierarchical value to gendered identities. This disciplinary logic, often justified through appeals to biological determinism, renders the body, particularly the male body, vulnerable to sociopolitical and psychological regulation. In positioning masculinity as inherently superior or primary within social hierarchies, these discourses necessarily marginalize femininity, casting it as secondary, deficient, or lacking. One of the most illustrative elements in understanding this dynamic is the role of hegemonic structures shaped by intercultural differences. Representations of the ideal male figure -prominently featured and celebrated across print and visual media, advertising industries, and economic domains- serve to reinforce normative conceptions of masculinity as inherently physical. This valorization of the male body through tangible, visible markers fosters the problematic notion that failure to embody these standards equates to weakness, a perspective that not only reinforces binaries between the assigned sexes but also incites a broader competition for dominance among all individuals.

Moreover, the naturalization of Western ideals of masculinity -often portrayed as more liberated or superior than those found in non-Western contexts- functions as a significant mechanism in shaping and perpetuating global cultural hierarchies. These representations contribute to the consolidation of Western cultural capital and assert symbolic authority in defining gender norms on a transnational scale. The marginalization and secondary positioning of groups defined as the "other" or marked as different presents a significant challenge to the critical interrogation of both historical and contemporary manifestations of gender norms. Hegemonic masculinity emerges not merely as a singular role occupied by men, but as the product of deliberate cultural mechanisms that construct and idealize a dominant masculine archetype, one that is celebrated and valorized within specific socio-cultural frameworks. In this context, hegemonic masculinity is not a fixed identity but a strategic formulation that capitalizes on the complexity and fluidity of gender in order to perpetuate systems of cultural dominance.

Bacak critically engages with this systemic structure by interrogating it through a performative lens and within the bounds of culturally encoded visual language. His work deftly exposes the mechanisms by which gender norms are maintained and challenges the ideological assumptions that underpin hegemonic masculinity. The evolution of homoeroticism from a purely aesthetic concern to a form of political resistance is particularly pronounced in the post-digital era, where photographic practices have become increasingly layered and expressive. This transformation enables more incisive critiques of normative structures and identity formations. "Muscular Theology came about when I started spending time at the gym and the images I recorded in my mind were not legal to physically photograph, so I turned to artificial intelligence. Movement and fashion photography were the two mediums I had been focusing on since 2012. I brought these two together with the aesthetics of the male body through artificial intelligence. In a sense, I created my own fantasy world. Reframing my experience in photography and transferring it entirely to another world in front of a computer feels incredibly inspiring." statement reveals how Bacak's emancipated field of production enables her to look at photography from a different perspective and how the viewer must reconsider her forms of expression through gender representations (Bacak, 2023). In a socio-political context shaped by heteronormative frameworks, Bacak's work, created within his culturally specific national setting, utilizes the affordances of contemporary visual platforms to produce art that resonates not only visually but also on political and emotional registers. His practice stands as a compelling intervention into the discourse of masculinity, queerness, and resistance in visual culture. "One of the aims was to present homo-eroticism in an accessible way to all kinds of looking eyes. Muscular Theology is a long-term project based on aesthetically giving stories of contemporary men of different classes and nationalities who spend much time in the gym. It is essentially a fantasy universe and continues to evolve with each level. It is inevitable to observe that the characters in the project gain depth with the development of artificial intelligence from the Instagram account" (Biner, 2023). Through the photographic expression and post-digital opinon of Bacak's, it becomes possible to interrogate frameworks that move beyond the mere acceptance of sexual repression, opening up discursive spaces for alternative readings of sexuality and identity. Such a mode of visual inquiry not only challenges normative structures but also enables a critical re-evaluation of how sexual subjectivities are constructed, performed, and regulated across different cultural contexts. By incorporating unconventional sociological strategies -ones that seek to destabilize fixed identity categories and unsettle dominant narratives- this approach facilitates a nuanced examination of the negotiation of sexuality in diverse socio-cultural milieus. In doing so, it transcends binary models of gender and sexuality, allowing for more fluid, intersectional, and culturally contingent understandings. The photographic medium thus becomes not only a site of aesthetic representation but also a powerful tool for theoretical engagement, sociopolitical critique, and the deconstruction of hegemonic epistemologies surrounding desire, identity, and corporeality.

Jurgenson refers to Joanna Zylinska's work "The Unhuman Photo" in which she states that "every photograph, every image is a cyborg act; a form of augmented vision that recodes how we see ourselves" and suggests that this offers "an opportunity to forget every 'natural' appearance and develop new ways of seeing" (Jurgenson, 2024, p. 63). The transformation of digital culture and the growing influence of artificial intelligence technologies within the domain of artistic production have opened up new possibilities for reconfiguring foundational concepts such as identity, gender, and selfhood. These technological shifts have not only reshaped the modes of artistic creation but have also prompted critical reflection on how subjectivity is constructed and represented in the digital age. Within this evolving landscape, artist Espen Kluge emerges as a notable figure, particularly for his algorithmically generated digital portraits that challenge traditional boundaries between human expression and machine interpretation. Espen has a fascination for the inward, exploratory and meditative yet chaotic qualities of the creative process, he believes this is, at least in part, a product of his own dealings with problems of bipolar disorder before successful treatment. He has a broad interest in many types of creative work, and he is active in several categories of it, and he likes to approach it by adding a sense of unfamiliarity, typically by using programming languages or tools/software that he is unfamiliar with, or setting up digital systems that adds elements of randomness into it (Kate Vass Galerie, 2019).

Kluge's "Alternatives" work (URL-18), a portrait series of 100 portraits generated in *Javascript*, the algorithm draws vectors based on data collected from photographs sourced online and, the results are abstract portraits that tell stories alternative to their origins, is shown as portraits -produced through a unique synthesis of code-based processes and expressive abstraction- do not simply mimic the human figure; they algorithmically interpret it, rendering subjectivity as fragmented, layered, and contingent upon data-driven structures (Kluge, 2019). In this sense, his work aligns with the posthumanist reimagining of the self, positioning identity not as a fixed essence but as something perpetually constructed through interactions with technological systems (URL-19, URL-20). The figures he creates evoke the image of the cyborg-entities that are neither entirely human nor fully machine, but exist within a liminal space where the boundaries of corporeality, gender, and individuality are fluid and negotiable.

Kluge uses artificial intelligence tools such as generative adversarial networks (GANs) and algorithmic visualization techniques in his artistic production. His work is characterized by the creation of abstracted and fragmented forms of the human face, especially in his portraits. This approach emphasizes that individual identity is a fluid and transforming form rather than a static and fixed structure. His portraits push the boundaries of identity perception by blurring the concept of gender in digital portraits. Kluge's algorithmic production technique creates random and irregular forms in the portraits, creating a fluid and multi-layered definition of individuality beyond traditional gender stereotypes. At this point, Kluge's works overlap with Judith Butler's concept of gender performativity, as the forms in her portraits emphasize that gender is not a fixed but a performative and variable structure. The portraits are both angular and soft, immediately familiar and remotely alien, a confluence of our innate ability to pick up on facial details and thousands of code-generated lines set at hard geometric angles. It is not a visuality that belongs to the established social norms of gender, but a form that is clearly genderless and evocative of the human being. Kluge's artistic practice extends beyond aesthetic experimentation with generative technologies; it serves as a critical inquiry into the ways in which digital systems mediate and reconstruct human identity. His work interrogates the interplay between individuality and abstraction, blurring the lines between the organic and the computational. Furthermore, Kluge provides a compelling visual framework through which to examine the sociocultural implications of technological mediation, especially in relation to gender performativity, personal representation, and the politics of visuality. In doing so, his art contributes to broader discourses on posthumanism, digital embodiment, and the rearticulation of identity within contemporary visual culture. By engaging with themes of digital embodiment, affective abstraction, and algorithmic authorship, Kluge's practice foregrounds questions central to contemporary critical theory: How is the self visualized when mediated by non-human intelligences? What becomes of gendered representation when aesthetic production is entangled with machine logic? These questions not only reflect a cyborgian condition but also underscore the political and philosophical stakes of artistic creation in the era of AI. His work thus becomes a site of speculative inquiry, where visual culture, posthuman theory, and digital aesthetics converge to reimagine what it means to be human in an increasingly algorithmic world.

The artistic practice of Kluge presents a compelling interrogation of visual representation and its longstanding claims to accuracy and truth. His work engages critically with the visual conventions embedded in digital image-making, particularly through the lens of AI and its intersection with identity formation. Kluge foregrounds the problematic nature of the data sets used to train AI algorithms, data sets that are often imbued with gender biases and reflect predominantly heteronormative, binary constructions of identity. By drawing attention to these embedded ideological assumptions, Kluge's art functions as a form of visual critique, exposing the normative underpinnings of computational systems that are frequently perceived as neutral or objective. Rather than reproducing conventional depictions of gender and subjectivity, Kluge generates images that are fluid, ambiguous, and resistant to easy categorization. His algorithmically-produced digital portraits, composed through layered color fields and geometric abstraction, actively disrupt traditional visual codes associated with gendered representation. This aesthetic strategy not only deconstructs the presumed fixity of the human face but also destabilizes the visual markers through which gender is culturally and socially recognized. In doing so, Kluge opens up a space for reconsidering the ways in which gender is both constructed and perceived within the context of contemporary visual culture. Kluge's approach is significant in that it treats AI not merely as a technical instrument or artistic tool, but as a critical methodology, one capable of confronting and subverting dominant epistemologies surrounding gender, identity, and embodiment in the digital era. His work therefore extends beyond aesthetic innovation, contributing meaningfully to theoretical discourses concerned with the social implications of machine vision, the codification of identity in algorithmic culture, and the posthuman condition.

Moreover, by reconstructing the human face in ways that defy conventional legibility and gender classification, Kluge's portraits offer a visual commentary on the contingency and performativity of identity itself. Drawing upon discourses from gender theory, critical algorithm studies, and digital aesthetics, his practice provides a valuable case study for understanding how new media art can serve as a site of resistance, challenging the normative boundaries of gender, disrupting the authority of data, and ultimately reimagining selfhood in an increasingly digitized world. In this sense, Kluge's AI-assisted artworks exemplify the potential of digital technologies not only to generate novel forms of aesthetic expression but also to function as platforms for critical reflection and theoretical engagement. His contributions underscore the capacity of contemporary art to intervene in ongoing debates around gender, identity, and representation, offering new pathways for thought and practice within both the artistic and academic realms.

Donna Haraway emphasizes the effects of modern technology on the cultural sphere. These effects have the power to reshape individuals' identities, social roles, and relationships. Technology's ability to construct social structures in a certain way and the resulting social uncertainties can cause identities and social bonds to dissolve or break down. Haraway expresses that traditional social structures and classifications are eroded by the rapid development of technology. "The uncertainty surrounding the dislocated communities brought about by advanced technological culture is not a matter of 'manipulated false consciousness' and 'a robust political epistemology' is not about adding consciousness to open-minded categories of criticism, but rather about changing the rules of the game, which holds serious potential and requires a good understanding of the new powers, experiences, and pleasures that are emerging" (Haraway, 2006, p. 55). Haraway points out that current social ideologies and hegemonic systems manipulate and deceptively shape individuals' thoughts and perceptions, resulting in individuals' inability to accurately understand their own social and political situations. Digital technologies have the potential to enable the formation of new social structures and power dynamics. This potential requires societies not only to criticize old structures, but also to correctly understand new power structures, experiences, and pleasures, and to initiate a process of social restructuring based on this understanding. Haraway argues that technology is not merely a tool but has become a fundamental element of social change, and that this change must be grounded in a new social awareness and knowledge. In alignment with Haraway's notions of the "cyborg" and posthumanist thought, East Asian artist Hsien-Yu Cheng offers a critical perspective on how social structures are being transformed and how individuals may adapt to these shifts. Cheng's work not only interrogates existing social configurations but also aspires to construct a new epistemological framework that exists beyond them. This approach underscores that social transformation is made possible through the dynamic interactions between technology and culture. Cheng investigates how facial recognition technologies are utilized in identity verification processes and how such technologies shape individuals' digital identities. While these systems are widely applied in areas such as security and access control, the artist's work also foregrounds their ethical and social implications. In particular, the potential of AI-powered technologies to manipulate individuals' identities and the impact of these technologies on social trust are being debated. "It Could Be You" a provocative digital art installation by Cheng, delves into the intricate realm of digital identity and personal privacy (URL-21, URL-22, URL-23). The artwork presents a critical examination of how personal data has become increasingly vulnerable in the digital era, prompting viewers to confront the subtle mechanisms of online surveillance and identity construction. The project illuminates the gradual erosion of personal privacy, exposing how individuals have inadvertently shared their most private information through social media platforms and digital interactions. Through the utilization of advanced machinelearning and ethical hacking methodologies, the artwork transforms online forum messages and chat room interactions into a haunting portrayal of synthetic identity (Cheng, 2022).

Cheng's research also examines the role of photography in the construction of digital identity. In particular, digital manipulation tools, with their ability to produce photographs from scratch, are changing the ways in which individuals construct and express their digital identities. By eliminating the aesthetic and technical requirements of photography, these tools enable everyone to produce digital content. Through a meticulous data collection and algorithmic manipulation process, the installation fabricates personal identities that blur the boundaries between reality and digital fiction. The artwork collects messages from various online platforms and employs advanced algorithms to construct synthetic portraits and personal details that are remarkably plausible. This approach transcends mere technical demonstration, serving as a profound commentary on the commodification of personal information (Cheng, 2022).

Cheng's engagement with this work originates from a critical interrogation of the photographic medium, not merely as a tool for representation, but as a conceptual framework through which visibility, identity, and surveillance are negotiated. Photography, in this context, functions as both material and metaphor: a historically loaded technology of seeing that has long been implicated in systems of classification, control, and truth-making. Cheng appropriates the visual grammar of photography to deconstruct its assumed objectivity, using it as a lens to expose how images are not passive reflections of reality, but active agents in the construction of digital subjectivities. "It Could Be You" confronts audiences with the unsettling reality of contemporary digital surveillance. The artwork exposes how machines process personal information with increasing sophistication and diminishing concern for authenticity. It unveils the algorithmic potential to create identities that are both fictional and unsettlingly convincing, prompting viewers to reevaluate their digital footprints (Cheng, 2022). This study, which takes a critical stance on identity, also examines the impact of artificial intelligence on gender representations. It emphasizes that digital identity is not merely an individual expression but also a social and political construct. Artificial intelligence, by encoding gender and identity categories in a binary and fixed manner, overlooks the dynamic and multi-layered nature of gender and identity. This reveals how identities and genders are constructed on digital platforms and how these processes reproduce social inequalities. Cheng's work reveals that photography is not merely a visual representation but also a tool that demonstrates how identity and gender are constructed in the digital environment. Artificial intelligence analyzes photographs to predict characteristics such as gender, age, and ethnic origin; however, these predictions may reflect societal biases and stereotypes. This situation demonstrates how digital identity and gender are artificially shaped and how these processes reproduce social inequalities.

"Cyborg politics is a struggle over language; it is a struggle against flawless communication, against the fundamental dogma of fallogosentrism, which posits that 'all meaning can be perfectly translated into a code'. For this reason, cyborg politics joyfully embraces the illegitimate unions of animal and machine, insists on noise, and defends pollution. These are the structures of desire, which is imagined to give birth to language and gender, and thus, by dismantling the structures and modes of production of "Western" identity, nature and culture, the mirror and the eye, the slave and the master, the body and the mind, they render the Male and the Female as serious problems" (Haraway, 2006, p. 62). This is especially poignant in the context of globalized digital culture, where Western paradigms of identity construction often dominate the technological imaginary, marginalizing non-Western epistemologies and aesthetics. In responding to this imbalance, Cheng's artwork gestures toward a decolonial politics of representation, revealing how digital systems mediate identity differently across Eastern and Western cultural frameworks, and offering a space to reimagine subjectivity beyond the constraints of both geographic and gendered essentialism. "It Could Be You" functions as a multifaceted artistic statement, translating the often opaque and intangible mechanisms of advanced technological systems, such as data mining, surveillance algorithms, and digital profiling, into a compelling and visually articulate narrative. At its core, the work foregrounds the act of making the invisible visible, a situation that is particularly resonant within the realms of both photographic representation and gender construction in the digital era. Photographic imagery, traditionally associated with realism and the indexical capture of the visible world, is here recontextualized as a tool for critical engagement with the immaterial architectures of digital data. The piece manipulates, distorts, or even fabricates photographic traces to underscore the extent to which our visual and social identities are now constructed, fragmented, and commodified through algorithmic observation. In this way, the artwork speaks not only to the aesthetics of data but also to the politics of seeing, particularly how bodies, especially gendered bodies, are rendered visible, invisible, or hyper-visible through networked systems of control.

Cheng's projects often utilize photography and lens-based media not as documentary devices, but as instruments that reveal the underlying codes and biases of digital infrastructures. His works uncover how gender identities are algorithmically interpreted, misread, or erased, raising urgent questions about visibility, agency, and authenticity in technologically mediated environments. Much like Cheng's explorations into the algorithmic aesthetics of surveillance and machine vision, this artwork does not merely visualize data flows; it actively problematizes the way identity, particularly gender identity, is encoded, decoded, and reconstituted within systems of power. Through visual strategies that echo both documentary and speculative traditions in photography, the piece critiques the normalization of binary categories and the reduction of complex identities to data points optimized for capitalist extraction. Cheng's body of work and research delves deeper into the effects of artificial intelligence on identity, gender and photography and questions the impact of these technologies on social structures. These studies help us understand how identity and representation are shaped in the digital age.

CONCLUSION

As photography moves from the physical environment to the digital data realm, it undergoes not only a technical transformation but also a fundamental redefinition of the nature of the medium itself. This transformation transcends the linear evolution of photographic history, pointing to a unique phase in the post-digital era where image culture is being restructured. In today's power regime, where digital data and various software infrastructures are decisive, algorithms, search engines, social media platforms, and physical-digital interaction forms are paving the way for the formation of new layers of meaning and contextual structures. Within this new digital ecosystem, the relationship between photographic images and reality is becoming increasingly blurred; concepts such as authenticity, accessibility, data surveillance, and bio-power are becoming theoretical issues that are being questioned more deeply. This new positioning of photography has made significant contributions to post-digital art practices, transforming both the processes of art production and the relationship between the viewer and visual culture.

The rich production possibilities offered by digital platforms open up a polyphonic and pluralistic space for creative expression, while also enabling the development of critical aesthetic approaches. In this context, artists not only question the changing status and meaning of photography in the digital age but also re-evaluate the role and position of the artist in this transformation through hybrid and alternative media. The representation of gender in photography has become more diverse and layered with technological developments and digitalization. The post-digital process, artificial intelligence, and algorithms enable the visualization of gender and normative structures in a multi-layered, flexible, and fluid manner, rather than in a fixed and binary structure. Photography has moved beyond being a tool for evidence or visual representation, becoming a platform that influences inquiries into the construction of gender and power-individual dynamics.

Today, AI-supported visual production practices are emerging not only as a reflection of technical innovations, but also as a multi-layered field that requires in-depth examination on aesthetic, ethical, and ontological levels. In this context, artists are not merely confined to the role of producers in their interaction with AI technologies; they are also redefining their positions as data managers, curators, and critical subjects. These multiple roles transcend the boundaries of classical photography, paving the way for a more fluid, relational, and layered paradigm of visual thinking. Visual productions realized with artificial intelligence are not merely technological advances; they contain dynamics that fundamentally transform epistemological assumptions, aesthetic norms, and forms of visual representation. These production processes reconstruct the artist's creative activity while also transforming the viewer's practices of visual perception, interpretation, and interaction. In this context, photography in the age of artificial intelligence transcends traditional medium definitions and positions itself as a conceptual field where data, algorithmic processes, representation systems, and interpretation practices intersect. This transformation carries discussions about how photography will be defined in the future to a more complex, yet productive and pluralistic ground.

Future research can analyze the structural and conceptual elements that influence this transformation in depth; it can also develop strategies for reimagining gender representations in more equitable and inclusive ways in the context of rapidly advancing artificial intelligence technologies, thereby making critical interventions in established normative structures. Artists are transforming the representation of gender through digital tools and artificial intelligence, offering viewers deeper, more inclusive, freer, and more open-ended alternative representations. Theories and examples from artists and theorists on the use of post-digital processes and various digital platforms in production methods and statements of ideas provide an analysis and forecast of how gender representations are conveyed. This process helps us understand how gender is shaped not only as a biological reality but also as a social, cultural, and digital construct.

REFERENCES

Bacak, C. (2023). Piksel bülten. *Muscular theology: body construction and homo-eroticism in midjourney.* https://www.pikselbulten.com/posts/muscular-theology-body-construction-and-homoeroticism-in-midjourney

Berger, J. (2011). *Görme biçimleri.* (Y. Salman, Çev.). Metis Yayınları.

Biner, İ. C. (2023). Homo erotism and muscular theology. *Medium: Human stories & ideas.* https://medium.com/nftify-uk/homo-erotism-and-muscular-theology-7e729dae3174

Blas, Z. (2012). Facial weaponization suite 2012-14. *Zach blas website artworks.* 18.04.2025, https://zachblas.info/works/facial-weaponization-suite/

Cheng, H. (2022). It could be you. *Hsien-yu cheng website artworks.* 05.05.2025, https://chenghsienyu.com/it-could-be-you/

Connell, R. W. (2016). *Toplumsal cinsiyet ve iktidar.* (C. Soydemir, Çev.). Ayrıntı Yayınları.

Crawford, K., & Paglen, T. (2025, 13 April). *Excavating AI: the politics of ımages in machine learning training sets.* https://excavating.ai

Dinkins, S. (2025, 17 April). Secret garden: Our stories are algorithms. *Stephanie dinkins website.* 17.04.2025, https://www.stephaniedinkins.com/about.html

Elwes, J. (2019). Zizi: queering the dataset. *Jake elwes website.* 18.04.2025, https://www.jakeelwes.com/project-zizi-2019.html

Flusser, V. (2020). *Bir fotoğraf felsefesine doğru.* (A. Yılmaz, Çev.). Espas Yayınları.

Gingrich, O. M. (2021). GENDER*UCK: Reframing gender & media art. *AI and the Arts: Artificial Imagination.* 148-154. DOI: 10.14236/ewic/EVA2021.25

Haraway, D. (2006). *Siborg manifestosu.* (O. Akınhay, Çev.). Agora Kitaplığı.

Jagose, A. (2017). *Queer teori bir giriş.* (A. Toprak, Çev.). NotaBene Yayınları.

Jurgenson, N. (2024). *Sosyal fotoğraf: fotoğraf ve sosyal medya.* (N. Örge, Çev.). Espas Yayınları.

Kate Vass Galerie. (2019). Espen kluge articles. The generative portraiture of espen kluge. 04.05.2025, https://www.katevassgalerie.com/espen-kluge

Khadake, V. (2024). *Algorithmic aesthetics: a critical analysis of AI-generated art in the digital age.* International journal for multidisciplinary research (IJFMR) E-ISSN: 2582-2160 Volume 6, Issue 6, November-December 2024.

Kluge, E. (2019). Alternatives. *Espen kluge website: 100 generative portraits.* 04.05.2025, https://www.espen.xyz/alternatives-100-generative-portraits

Mulvey, L. (1975). Visual pleasure and narrative cinema. *Screen, 16*(3), 6–18. DOI: 10.1093/screen/16.3.6

Paglen, T. (2025, 13 April). Imagenet roulette. *Trevor paglen website,* https://paglen .studio/2020/04/29/imagenet-roulette

Ritchin, F. (2012). *Fotoğraftan sonra.* (Y. Keser, Çev.). Espas Yayınları.

Sontag, S. (2011). *Fotoğraf üzerine.* (O. Akınhay, Çev.). Agora Kitaplığı.

Steyerl, H. (2023). Mean Images. *New Left Review, 140/141,* Mar-June 2023. https:// newleftreview.org/issues/ii140/articles/hito-steyerl-mean-images

Techne: Secret Garden. (2025, 16 January). *Brooklyn Academy of Music.* 17 April, 2025. https://www.bam.org/new-media/2024/techne-secret-garden

The Museum of Contemporary Art Chicago. (2012). *MCA publications websites.* 18.04.2025, https://mcachicago.org/publications/websites/i-was-raised-on-the-internet/artworks/zach-blas-facial-weaponization-communique-fag-face-2012

Yardımcı, S., & Güçlü, Ö. (2016). *Queer tahayyül.* Sel Yayıncılık.

Zadeh, J. (2023, 6 October). The photographer using AI to create queer love stories. *WePresent.* https://wepresent.wetransfer.com/stories/blake-wood-ai-post -photography

ADDITIONAL READING

Antmen, A. (2013). *Kimlikli Bedenler (Sanat, Kimlik, Cinsiyet).* Sel Yayıncılık.

Barrett, T. (2017). *Fotoğrafı Eleştirmek.* (Y. Harcanoğlu, Çev.). Hayalperest Yay.

Bourdieu, P. (2015). *Eril Tahakküm.* (B. Yılmaz, Çev.). Bağlam Yayınları.

Braidotti, R. (2014). *İnsan Sonrası.* (Ö. Karakaş, Çev.). Kolektif Kitap.

Butler, J. (2014). *Bela Bedenler.* (C. Çakırlar – Z. Talay, Çev.). Pinhan Yayınları.

Clarke, G. (2017). *Güzel Sanatların Bir Dalı Olarak Fotoğraf.* (M. M. Aydemir, Çev.). Hayalperest Yay.

Connell, R. W. (2016). *Toplumsal Cinsiyet ve İktidar.* (C. Soydemir, Çev.). Ayrıntı Yayınları.

Moser, W., & Albrecht, K. (2012). *Körper Als Protest.* Hatje Cantz Verlag.

KEY TERMS AND DEFINITIONS

Artificial intelligence: Artificial Intelligence (AI) denotes computational systems designed to emulate cognitive functions such as reasoning, learning, and decision-making. In critical discourse, AI raises questions about autonomy, ethics, labor, and the reproduction of societal biases in algorithmic systems.

Cyborg Politics: Cyborg politics, drawing on Donna Haraway's Cyborg Manifesto, critiques binary oppositions such as human/machine and nature/culture. It envisions hybrid subjectivities and affirms coalition-building across fragmented identities within posthuman and technocultural frameworks.

Digital Art: Digital art encompasses artistic practices that utilize digital technologies as tools, mediums, or conceptual frameworks. It interrogates the boundaries of authorship, materiality, and interactivity within the context of rapidly evolving technological environments.

Digital Culture: Digital culture refers to the complex set of practices, discourses, and artifacts that emerge from the widespread use of digital technologies. It reshapes notions of identity, community, temporality, and space in networked societies.

Gender: Gender is a socio-cultural construct that organizes individuals into categories such as "male," "female," or "non-binary," based on performative roles, norms, and expectations. It is distinct from biological sex and is produced and regulated through discursive and institutional practices.

Performativity: Performativity, as theorized by Judith Butler, refers to the process through which identities—particularly gender—are constituted through repeated social acts and discursive practices. It challenges the notion of a stable, pre-existing self by emphasizing the performative nature of identity.

Queer: Queer is a critical term that resists normative understandings of sexuality and gender. Emerging from both activism and theory, it destabilizes fixed identity categories and foregrounds fluidity, intersectionality, and anti-normative politics within the framework of queer theory.

ENDNOTES

1 Generative Adversarial Networks (GANs): These are used extensively in visual art creation. GANs consist of two neural networks—a generator and a discriminator—that work in opposition to create new, original images that mimic the characteristics of a training dataset. (https://doi.org/g8wkmj)

2 The "Zizi: Queering the Dataset", StyleGan (2019) trained on FFHQ (2018) containing 70,000 photographs of faces. (https://www.jakeelwes.com/project-zizi-2019.html)

APPENDIX

Images Referenced

URL-1. Mario Klingemann (2025, 10 April). https://aiartists-org.translate.goog/mario-klingemann?_x_tr_sl=en&_x_tr_tl=tr&_x_tr_hl=tr&_x_tr_pto=tc

URL-2. Trevor Paglen (2025, 13 April). *Imagenet Roulette,* https://paglen.studio/2020/04/29/imagenet-roulette/

URL-3. Trevor Paglen (2025, 13 April). *Imagenet Roulette,* https://paglen.studio/2020/04/29/imagenet-roulette/

URL-4. Stephanie Dinkins (2025, 17 April). *Secret Garden,* https://www.stephaniedinkins.com/secretgarden.html

URL-5. Stephanie Dinkins (2025, 17 April). *Secret Garden,* https://www.stephaniedinkins.com/secretgarden.html

URL-6. Blake Wood (2025, 17 April). *Visions & Memories, Glitter, 2022.* https://www.blakewood.xyz/vision-memories

URL-7. Blake Wood (2025, 17 April). *Visions & Memories, Pink I, 2022.* https://www.blakewood.xyz/vision-memories

URL-8. Jake Elwes (2025, 18 April). *Zizi: Queering the Dataset, 2019.* https://www.jakeelwes.com/project-zizi-2019.html

URL-9. Jake Elwes (2025, 18 April). *Zizi: Queering the Dataset, 2019.* https://www.jakeelwes.com/project-zizi-2019.html

URL-10. Jake Elwes (2025, 18 April). *Zizi: Queering the Dataset, 2019.* https://www.jakeelwes.com/project-zizi-2019.html

URL-11. Zach Blas (2025, 20 April). *Facial Weaponization Suite, 2012-2014.* https://zachblas.info/works/facial-weaponization-suite/

URL-12. Zach Blas (2025, 20 April). *Facial Weaponization Suite, 2012-2014.* https://zachblas.info/works/facial-weaponization-suite/

URL-13. Zach Blas (2025, 20 April). *Facial Weaponization Suite, 2012-2014.* https://zachblas.info/works/facial-weaponization-suite/

URL-14. Zach Blas (2025, 20 April). *Facial Weaponization Suite, 2012-2014.* https://zachblas.info/works/facial-weaponization-suite/

URL-15. Cihan Bacak (2025, 1 May). *Muscular Theology, 2023-2025.* https://www.yuzumagazine.com/cihan-bacak

URL-16. Cihan Bacak (2025, 1 May). *Muscular Theology, 2023-2025.* https://www.yuzumagazine.com/cihan-bacak

URL-17. Cihan Bacak (2025, 1 May). *Muscular Theology, 2023-2025.* https://www.yuzumagazine.com/cihan-bacak

URL-18. Espen Kluge (2025, 1 May). *Alternatives, 2019.* https://www.espen.xyz/alternatives-100-generative-portraits

URL-19. Espen Kluge (2025, 1 May). *Alternatives, 2019.* https://www.espen.xyz/alternatives-100-generative-portraits

URL-20. Espen Kluge (2025, 1 May). *Alternatives, 2019.* https://www.espen.xyz/alternatives-100-generative-portraits

URL-21. Hsien-Yu Cheng (2025, 2 May). *It Could Be You, 2022.* https://chenghsienyu.com/it-could-be-you/

URL-22. Hsien-Yu Cheng (2025, 2 May). *It Could Be You, 2022.* https://chenghsienyu.com/it-could-be-you/

URL-23. Hsien-Yu Cheng (2025, 2 May). *It Could Be You, 2022.* https://chenghsienyu.com/it-could-be-you/

Chapter 7
The Perception and Ethical Implications of AI-Generated Images as Press Photography

Uğur Günay Yavuz
http://orcid.org/0000-0002-3111-8277
Akdeniz University, Turkey

Uluç Mehmet Ceylani
http://orcid.org/0000-0003-1379-3452
Akdeniz University, Turkey

Ahmet Sait Yıldız
Akdeniz University, Turkey

ABSTRACT

Photography has undergone a significant evolution from its analog roots film and darkrooms to today's digital and automated methods. One of the most impactful changes is the incorporation of artificial intelligence (AI) in image production, sparking both innovation and debate. This article explores the contentious use of AI-generated hyper-realistic visuals in journalism. It raises ethical concerns about presenting such images as authentic news content, warning of the risk of misleading viewers, damaging trust in the media, and contributing to misinformation. The paper stresses that transparency in labeling AI-generated images is crucial to uphold photojournalistic ethics. It also highlights the urgent need for media literacy to help the public critically evaluate visual content in a digital age shaped by advanced technologies.

DOI: 10.4018/979-8-3373-2230-8.ch007

INTRODUCTION

Photography is a product of the collaborative advancements in chemistry and physics. On the one hand, the formation of an image, and on the other, the fixation and permanence of the obtained image, have developed through the contributions of prominent scientists in both fields. Since the official announcement of this invention by Louis François Arago at the French Academy of Sciences in 1839, photography has remained a focal point of discussion due to its distinctive qualities.

The idea that nature could be reproduced automatically in its finest details, without human intervention, through photography, spread rapidly and was considered astonishing at the time (Bajac, 2004). Painter Paul Delaroche, upon witnessing the results of the Daguerreotype technique in 1839, famously declared that painting was now obsolete (Rosenblum, 1997). Due to the fact that it produces images via a mechanical device, photography was also criticized for being fundamentally different from other art forms. Yet its ability to provide a visual representation closest to reality and its reproducibility garnered both enthusiastic interest and intense skepticism.

Despite these reactions, photography quickly advanced in both technical development and in establishing its own visual language.

In 1888, Kodak's first camera advertisement stated: “You press the button, we do the rest” (Sontag, 1999, p. 7), signifying that anyone could now take photographs without needing technical expertise in developing and printing processes. In the age of artificial intelligence, this notion has evolved into: “You input the command, AI does the rest.”

Technological progress has made access to photographic imagery easier and faster than ever before. This has also manifested in the processes of altering and transforming images. While such interventions were possible even before the digital era through darkroom techniques, digitalization has made them far more widespread, accessible, and instantaneous.

Today, such manipulations particularly in the realm of documentary photography continue to spark debates due to their potential to undermine the factual value and documentary nature of the image. Similarly, the ease with which images can be generated via AI and their subsequent publication or sharing as if they were authentic press photographs has ignited new concerns.

Susan Sontag noted that images can “anaesthetize” and immobilize people, and that a photographed event may become more real than one never seen through photographs (Sontag, 1999). This highlights the persuasive power of visual imagery in shaping public perception of factual information.

This remains relevant today, yet now we must also consider the technological infrastructure that enables the creation of images surpassing the boundaries of lived reality. It is thus increasingly crucial to ask: whose reality is being shown?

MANIPULATION BEFORE DIGITAL PHOTOGRAPHY

The word manipulation, derived from French, refers to the alteration of information through redirection, selection, addition, or removal (TDK). Photographic manipulation is the process of altering, transforming, or reconfiguring the content of a photograph using various techniques. While some manipulations are done for aesthetic enhancement such as color correction, lighting adjustments, or cropping to increase expressive power or visual appeal others are carried out with ideological intent, aiming to distort or steer reality toward specific objectives.

Since the invention of photography, manipulation has been applied sometimes clearly detectable, other times imperceptible for artistic, commercial, or political purposes. In this sense, it can be argued that the only thing that has changed over time is the technique itself, while the intent has remained consistent with the technological possibilities of the era.

Susan Sontag notes that even before the digital photography era and software like Photoshop, it was always possible to manipulate a photograph (Sontag, 2004). One of the earliest examples of manipulation applied to a photograph not for artistic or commercial purposes but rather for documentary aims is the image showing American General Ulysses S. Grant at City Point. This image, created in 1902 by combining three separate photographs, includes Grant's face from a 1864 portrait taken at his headquarters in Virginia, the horse's body from a 1864 photograph of Major General Alexander McDowell McCook, and the background tents and soldiers from a photograph taken at the Battle of Fisher's Hill showing captured soldiers and campgrounds.

Figure 1. General Grant at City Point,Handy, Levin C. (Levin Corbin), 1855-1932

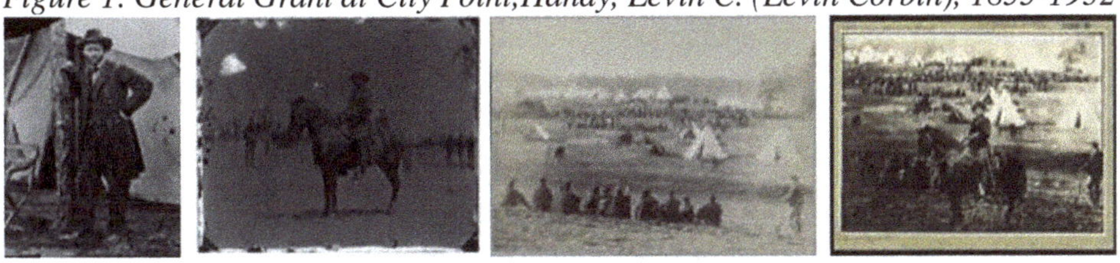

According to Mia Fineman, the person who merged these photographs archived in the Library of Congress was Levin Corbin Handy, the nephew and assistant of Mathew Brady, a photographer active during the American Civil War. After Brady's death, Handy inherited his archive and used these photographs in ways that blurred the line between historical reality and fiction (Fineman, 2012).

There are also many known examples of political figures erasing individuals from photographs after relationships soured. One of the earliest examples is from 1920, when Vladimir Lenin had Lev Trotsky and Lev Kamenev removed from a photo taken during his speech at Swerdlow Square in Moscow. Similarly, in 1937, Adolf Hitler had his propaganda minister Joseph Goebbels removed from a photo where they had once appeared together.

Figure 2. Gordon Gahan's original photograph – National Geographic, February 1982 issue

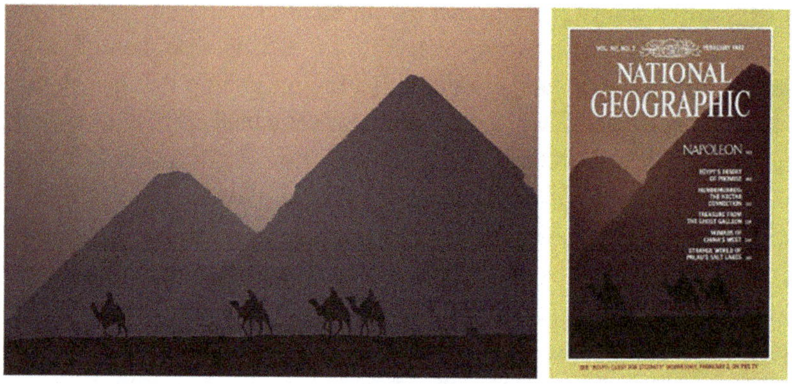

Fred Ritchin argued that the photograph of the Giza Pyramids on the cover of the February 1982 issue of National Geographic marked the beginning of the digital era (Ritchin, 2012). In fact, photographer Gordon Gahan had originally taken a horizontal image, but the pyramids were moved closer together to fit the magazine's vertical cover format. This editorial decision, aimed at adapting the image to the magazine's design, surprised even the photographer and sparked public debate.

According to Roland Barthes, a photograph is a sign that points directly to reality and stands out for its documentary power. Unlike paintings or other visual or linguistic signs, photography is directly tied to reality. A photograph is a trace, a proof that the object, the person, or the moment once existed. It is not merely an image, but a certificate of presence. This distinguishes photography from other forms of representation by its unique ability to document and signify reality (Barthes, 1996). However, this belief was first entirely shattered by the Time magazine cover published in 1993.

Figure 3. Time Magazine Cover, November 18, 1993

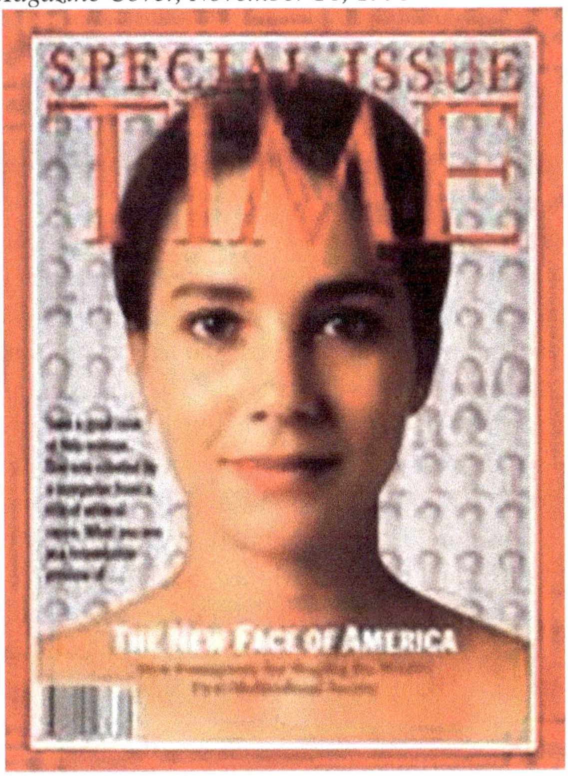

The cover of the November 18, 1993 issue of Time featured the portrait of a young woman who did not actually exist. This special issue focused on the potential children that could result from the increasing number of marriages between individuals of diverse ethnic and racial backgrounds in the United States (Gaines, 1993). The image of "Eve" was created through a 65-hour morphing process that combined the photographs of seven male and female models and consisted of 15% Anglo-Saxon, 17.5% Middle Eastern, 17.5% African, 7.5% Asian, 35% Southern European, and 7.5% Hispanic features. Today, such an image can be generated in a matter of minutes using artificial intelligence tools.

THE TRANSFORMATION OF PHOTOGRAPHIC TECHNOLOGY FROM TRADITIONAL TO DIGITAL

From its early days, photography has been altered, transformed, or recreated at times for entertainment or artistic purposes, and at other times to influence, persuade, or propagate. Thanks to digital technology, operations such as adjusting color and lighting conditions, changing the frame, or removing unwanted people or objects which were also performed in the past have become significantly easier and faster. Digital technology has fundamentally transformed the core tools and conceptual frameworks of photographic production. This transformation has not only affected the production process of photography but has also revolutionized its artistic, aesthetic, and philosophical dimensions.

Digital photography has reshaped how artists approach visuality, narrative, and composition, and has profoundly influenced how viewers interact with photographs.

This transformation was further deepened by the integration of high-resolution photo and video cameras into mobile phones, and later by the emergence of social media platforms that enabled individuals to publish their recordings. As a result, the concepts of citizen journalist and photojournalist have entered everyday life. People now use their mobile phones to capture and share any event they like or criticize. For example, on May 25, 2020, George Floyd, who was suspected of using counterfeit money at a store in the United States, was pinned to the ground with his hands handcuffed behind his back, while a police officer pressed his knee on Floyd's neck for 8 minutes and 46 seconds despite Floyd repeatedly saying, "I can't breathe." Floyd died of suffocation. The incident was recorded by nearby citizens and shared on social media, sparking global protests against police violence and racism.

Another example is the photograph published on April 18, 2004, in The Seattle Times, which depicted the flag-draped coffins of fallen soldiers in a cargo plane. It was taken by Tami Silicio, a civilian cargo worker for Maytag Aircraft at Kuwait International Airport during a night shift. Although Silicio lost her job after the photo's publication, the image was later featured in Time magazine's book and exhibition "100 Photographs: The Most Influential Images of All Time." Clearly, digital photography technology has not only accelerated photo-taking and editing but has also allowed photography to spread among various social groups.

PRESS PHOTOGRAPHY

Susan Sontag emphasizes that in some types of photography, the photographer tends to take a backseat, and press photographs are not the conscious creations of individual artists but are powerful as images or copies of the world (Sontag, 1999). Press photography serves not only to visually document events of public interest and deliver them to the public but also carries significant weight as evidence of the event's reality. It plays a critical role in historical documentation, shaping public opinion, and contributing to collective memory. What is decisive in this regard is, of course, the subject matter of the press photograph and how effectively it conveys that subject through a visual language. Roger Fenton photographed the Crimean War in 1855. Despite the technological impossibility of printing photos directly in newspapers, journalists consulted photographers, and their photos were interpreted by engravers, leading to lithographs and engravings on wood or zinc. By the 1860s, these illustrations in the press were captioned with statements such as "based on a photograph," which confirmed the reality of the copied image (Bajac, 2004). Although Fenton's photos were never published in newspapers at the time, they are considered the first war photographs in history. His works showed images of soldiers behind the front lines and served as early examples of photography documenting social events.

The advancement of printing technology and the ability to reproduce photographs in newspapers and magazines, along with the increasing portability of cameras, significantly impacted press photography. The emergence of photo services associated with news agencies and the establishment of photography-centered magazines such as Life ushered in what is now referred to as the golden age of press photography.

THE IMPACT OF TECHNOLOGICAL TRANSFORMATION ON PRESS PHOTOGRAPHY

From its origins in the mid-19th century to its current practices, press photography has undergone a significant transformation shaped by technological evolution, societal needs, and ethical considerations. Due to its inherent dependence on technology, photography has always maintained a close relationship with technological developments, and this has been clearly reflected in the field of press photography. Understanding the impact of technology on press photography requires a deep reflection not only on technical tools but also on the social function and ethical responsibilities of photography.

Early press photography was defined by the portability of cameras and the technical limitations of the time. The daguerreotype process and its cumbersome technological framework allowed only limited possibilities for capturing and presenting events. During the period starting with the Crimean War and continuing especially with the American Civil War and World War I, photographers faced great challenges in capturing real-time moments. Nevertheless, their work played a crucial role in shaping public perception and understanding of these historical events (Dube, 2017). Given the influence of photographers' presence in the field and the social impact of their images, the acceleration of developments in this area and the increasing demand for press photography became inevitable. Therefore, it is evident that technological advancement and technical transformation became a priority.

In the mid-20th century, cameras using 35mm film provided photographers with a smoother and more efficient means of capturing images. This technological leap, combined with the advent of color photography and improved printing techniques, significantly enhanced the storytelling capabilities of press photography (Miles, 2020). This transition not only enabled photographers to document daily events but also allowed them to contribute to shaping the narrative framework of social issues. The importance of this transition was reinforced by the growing impact of press photography on public opinion, as visuals increasingly influenced how political and social realities were perceived (Collen, 2014). The evolving role of press photographers became more apparent with their integration into the routine operations of news media; by producing visual content, they helped shape narratives that are fundamental to democratic discourse.

Towards the end of the 20th century, the digital revolution marked a major turning point for press photography. The introduction of digital cameras and image-editing software radically changed the landscape of press photography (Dube, 2017). Digital images not only accelerated the production process but also raised complex ethical dilemmas related to visual manipulation. As photographers began to utilize these new technologies, questions about the authenticity of visual media came to the forefront. Critics voiced concerns about the potential for extensive editing capabilities to distort reality, noting that manipulated images could influence public perception (Dube, 2017). Thus, while the digital age offered numerous opportunities to press photography, it also introduced ethical challenges that necessitated a reevaluation of standards regarding authenticity.

At the beginning of the 21st century, the widespread use of social media further democratized photography, enabling virtually anyone with a smartphone to participate in visual storytelling (Strukov, 2020). This significant shift altered the dynamics of news dissemination and invited citizen journalism to fill the gaps left by traditional journalists. While this expansion diversified the voices and perspectives represented in visual media, it also raised concerns regarding accuracy and ethical responsibility (Miles, 2020). The ease of creating and sharing images, coupled with the rise of disinformation and fake news, underscored the importance of ethical reflection and media literacy in press photography (Cruz, 2016). Unfortunately, the increase in user-generated content, often lacking rigorous editorial oversight, has contributed to the spread of fake news and visually manipulated imagery, further complicating the ethical foundations of press photography.

The evolution of press photography demands close examination of technological advancements and their impact on ethical standards. The transition from analog to digital photography enabled rapid progress while simultaneously blurring the boundaries between authenticity and manipulation, raising ethical questions in new media environments. Public interest has become increasingly intertwined with visual narratives presented by the media, requiring photographers to adopt a critical approach regarding representation, audience engagement, and socio-political accountability (Miles, 2020). This critique is part of a broader discourse surrounding the ethical boundaries of visual manipulation and is gaining momentum alongside calls for transparency and accountability (Dube, 2017).

Moreover, the dual role of social media as both a platform for sharing authentic experiences and a medium for distributing manipulated images challenges the standards of traditional journalism. The rise of digital platforms has transformed how audiences interact with news media; users now not only consume information but also actively participate in its creation and dissemination (Strukov, 2020). This transformation has encouraged research into how citizen journalism overlaps with and diverges from traditional press photography, highlighting the need for adaptable ethical frameworks to cope with the complexities brought on by this dual-mode approach. As a result, the discourse between press photography and the public is becoming increasingly nuanced, as visual content can both inform and mislead when ethical considerations are not adequately addressed (Collen, 2014).

New media and artificial intelligence technologies are redefining the boundaries of press photography. Especially in recent years, the development of AI-powered photo editing software and visual recognition algorithms has enabled manipulation and creation processes in photography on previously unimaginable scales. Artificial intelligence is used for automatic photo corrections, generating fake visuals, and more. While these developments offer great flexibility to photographers, they also bring forth ethical issues related to authenticity and truthfulness. Today, with the use of deep learning algorithms, AI is capable of processing not only photographs but also multimedia components such as video content and audio narratives. This represents another key factor that is altering the dynamics of press photography.

Social media platforms, meanwhile, create an environment that significantly influences public perception of press photography by enabling the rapid dissemination and massive reach of visual content. Platforms like Instagram, Twitter, and TikTok allow images to quickly reach wide audiences, while simultaneously raising questions about the accuracy and context of those images. User-generated content strengthens the notion of citizen journalism, but also keeps debates over the accuracy and ethical integrity of such content current. In the digital media era, press photography must strike a balance between the manipulation made possible by artificial intelligence and maintaining public trust. Furthermore, the integration of AI into more advanced visual verification processes offers a potential solution for detecting fake content. As these technologies evolve rapidly, they continue to shape the future of press photography, making ethical and professional responsibilities increasingly complex for journalists and photographers alike.

In conclusion, press photography has evolved through significant technological advancements and has developed a deep relationship with social impact and ethical considerations. From its historical roots in documenting major events to the modern landscape shaped by digital technology and social media, press photography reflects the complex interaction between intention, representation, and public perception. As the integrity of visual media is challenged by rapid technological change and citizen participation, the ongoing dialogue surrounding ethics and authenticity will become increasingly vital to maintaining the credibility and impact of press photography.

ARTIFICIAL INTELLIGENCE

Definition of Artificial Intelligence

Artificial intelligence (AI) was chosen as the word of the year in 2023 by the Collins Dictionary due to its prominence and impact on public discourse (Addley, 2023). In contrast, the Turkish Language Association (TDK) selected "crowded loneliness" (kalabalık yalnızlık) as the word of the year for 2024, opting for it over other contenders such as compassion, alienation, algorithm, corruption, artificial intelligence, and digital fatigue (tdk.gov.tr).

According to the Cambridge Dictionary, artificial intelligence is defined as "the study and development of computer systems that can do tasks normally requiring human intelligence" (Cambridge Dictionary, n.d.). UNESCO defines AI as "algorithms producing the capacity to learn and carry out cognitive tasks" (UNEP, 2024).

Conceptually, artificial intelligence operates as a synthetic mirror to human cognition, executing tasks that traditionally demand human intellect. This technological mimicry extends beyond mere computation, engaging in complex intellectual processes such as reasoning and meaning-making that effectively act as a mental lens through which reality is now increasingly filtered, interpreted, and visually reconstructed. Artificial intelligence represents a field of science that aims to develop programs capable of mimicking the problem-solving abilities and decision-making processes found in humans (Russell & Norvig, 2021). It can be defined as the imitation of the human mental system of thinking, decision-making, and creativity through machines or computer systems.

History of Artificial Intelligence

The history of artificial intelligence dates back to Alan Turing's 1950 article "Computing Machinery and Intelligence" published in the journal Mind, in which he posed the question, "Can machines think?" This inquiry laid the foundation for what became known as the Turing Test, which explored whether machines could exhibit human-like intelligence.

In 1956, the same question was addressed at a conference held at Dartmouth College by J. McCarthy, M. L. Minsky, N. Rochester, and C. H. Shannon. The discussions focused on how a machine could solve problems, what kind of language it might use, and its ability to abstract and generate concepts. At this conference, the term artificial intelligence was used for the first time by John McCarthy (Sarı, 2021).

In Turkey, the same question was first raised in 1959 by Professor Dr. Cahit Arf during the opening ceremony of Atatürk University, where he was an invited speaker. Arf pointed out that while machines could perform some tasks faster than the human brain, their greatest deficiency was their inability to make decisions autonomously. He emphasized that unlike humans, machines remained as they were first produced and could only develop as far as the capabilities of the programs embedded in them allowed (Sarı, 2021).

It should be noted that research in the field of artificial intelligence has gone through cycles of rapid progress and stagnation. These periods of stagnation are commonly referred to as the AI Winters. While early advances were made in the 1950s, a slowdown occurred in the 1970s. In 1973, the Lighthill Report was published in the UK, stating that AI research had failed to meet its expectations and was not producing useful results (Deniz & Bağçeci, 2025). Following such critical publications, many governments withdrew funding from AI projects, and numerous research laboratories were closed.

In 1979, the Association for the Advancement of Artificial Intelligence (AAAI) was established to support research and development in the field of artificial intelligence. In 2007, the organization officially changed its name to the Association for the Advancement of Artificial Intelligence. During the 1980s, interest in AI resurged, and a conference was held at Stanford University, where scholars and practitioners exchanged ideas and shared developments in the field. As research in artificial intelligence began to yield concrete results, it gained recognition, and investments in the area began to increase. In 1988, the German Research Center for Artificial Intelligence (DFKI) was established, marking a significant institutional commitment to AI studies in Europe.

With the widespread adoption of personal computers and the emergence of the internet in the 1990s, the foundations were laid for new advances and an increase in AI-related research. A turning point came in 1997, when Deep Blue, a program developed by IBM, defeated world chess champion Garry Kasparov demonstrating that computers could surpass human capabilities in certain domains (Coşkun & Gülleroğlu, 2021).

By the year 2000, artificial intelligence had been integrated into daily life, evolving beyond a mere technological advancement. Today, AI technologies are receiving substantial investments and are increasingly utilized in a wide array of sectors. Although challenges and deficiencies in its applications have led to ongoing debates, AI continues to find new areas of implementation with each passing day.

Areas of Application for Artificial Intelligence

Artificial intelligence technology has increasingly become an integral part of daily life, frequently appearing in the form of personal assistants embedded in commonly used applications. Designed to simplify life for humans and solve problems quickly, AI manifests across a wide range of sectors including science, education, healthcare, entertainment, and the arts as well as in autonomous vehicles and transportation systems.

Artificial intelligence is creating a multifaceted transformation within today's healthcare systems, particularly offering effective solutions in public health through big data analytics for early diagnosis and crisis management (Göde, 2024). By analyzing data collected from sources such as social media, search engines, and hospital records, the spread of epidemics can be predicted earlier, enabling the identification of high-risk groups and allowing for timely preventive interventions.

Personalized medicine has also advanced due to AI's capacity to analyze individual data. Technologies like digital twins have made it possible to predict the progression of diseases and offer patient-centered solutions, especially in the management of chronic conditions such as diabetes (Alay, 2024). Additionally, telemedicine applications have improved access to healthcare services in rural areas, increasing efficiency in the planning and management of health resources (Göde, 2024; Demirhan et al. 2010).

Despite the positive developments underpinning its emergence, the use of AI in healthcare also raises significant ethical and legal concerns. Issues such as data privacy, algorithmic bias, lack of transparency in decision-making processes, and accountability remain unresolved critical matters (Göde, 2024). In particular, the opacity of AI algorithms can undermine trust in these systems among clinicians and patients alike, slowing down the adoption of such technologies (Demirhan et al.,2010). Therefore, in the integration of AI into healthcare systems, not only technological efficiency but also ethical principles, transparency, and a human-centered approach must be prioritized.

Artificial intelligence is fundamentally transforming learning and teaching processes within the field of education. AI-supported systems enhance the effectiveness of education by performing functions such as monitoring student performance, offering personalized learning experiences, and adapting instructional materials. Intelligent tutoring systems and expert systems, in particular, optimize learning by tailoring content to students' individual needs, offering differentiated learning opportunities based on their strengths and weaknesses (Çetin & Baklavacı, 2024). Additionally, AI reduces teachers' administrative burdens by automating tasks such as assessment, planning, and data tracking, thereby supporting teacher-student interaction.

Despite these positive developments, as in many fields, the use of AI in education raises ethical concerns. Issues such as the privacy of student data, equity, and the prevention of discrimination are among the core ethical responsibilities that must be addressed with care (Aşık et al., 2023). Therefore, the integration of AI into educational systems must be carefully planned; while enhancing technological infrastructure, efforts should also focus on increasing teachers' competencies to use these systems effectively.

In recent years, artificial intelligence has emerged as a transformative force across many areas of scientific research. Machine learning, which allows computers to improve automatically through experience, contributes to more evidence-based decision-making in fields ranging from healthcare to financial modeling (Jordan & Mitchell, 2015). Machine learning, deep learning, and other AI techniques offer vast potential in data analysis, modeling, and prediction processes. These technologies are becoming essential tools in addressing societal challenges by enabling data-driven decision-making in areas such as healthcare, finance, education, environmental science, and disaster management.

One of the most remarkable capabilities of AI is its ability to work with large datasets and extract meaningful information from them. This contributes to the acceleration of scientific research, the generation of more accurate predictions, and more effective solutions to complex problems.

For instance, the devastating earthquake that struck Türkiye on February 6, 2023, underscored the importance of AI-based disaster management approaches. Following the disaster, universities and research centers launched projects exploring how AI could be effectively utilized across various stages of disaster management. Deep learning techniques have been used to analyze seismic data, identify high-risk areas, and forecast potential seismic activity. Moreover, AI has played a vital role in post-earthquake search and rescue operations through integrated image processing systems used in robots and drones. Damage assessments based on satellite imagery have been conducted more rapidly and accurately thanks to AI.

Artificial intelligence also plays an important role in post-disaster psychological support. Digital health applications and chatbots offer psychological support to individuals suffering from post-traumatic stress disorder (PTSD). These applications provide alternative solutions, especially in cases where access to healthcare services is limited in disaster-stricken areas.

Artificial intelligence plays a significant role in transforming the media industry. Technologies such as automated news generation, content analysis, and visual recognition are reshaping journalism by increasing speed and efficiency, but they also raise new debates around accuracy, ethics, and professional responsibility (Diakopoulos, 2019). AI enables traditional media organizations to restructure their production processes, yet it simultaneously brings about ethical responsibilities.

Natural language processing (NLP) and machine learning make it possible to automatically generate news texts and extract relevant content from large data sets. Deep learning algorithms are increasingly used in analyzing media content, detecting fake news, and predicting audience preferences (Túñez-López, Fieiras-Ceide, & Vaz-Álvarez, 2021). This integration has introduced a data-driven, analytical, and automated approach to journalism.

Press photography is among the areas most influenced by AI. Image recognition systems allow news agencies to rapidly scan visual archives, and AI algorithms are frequently employed in the photo selection process. However, AI-generated or manipulated images pose significant risks regarding the accuracy of news and the trust of readers (Marconi, 2020). In particular, "deepfake" technologies have the potential to create a crisis of trust in visual journalism. In 2023, Sports Illustrated featured AI-generated articles and AI-created profile photos. It was later revealed that the content had been produced by a third-party company and that the author names were pseudonyms. Following public backlash, the content was removed (Dupre, 2023). This incident served as a serious warning regarding editorial transparency and public deception.

Another striking example occurred in Belgium in 2020. A video speech by Prime Minister Sophie Wilmes, in which she appeared to link environmental destruction to the COVID-19 pandemic, was actually generated by environmental activists using artificial intelligence. The video was widely shared on social media with the hashtag #TellTheTruthBelgium. This case highlighted the power of "deepfake" technology in media manipulation (Ittefaq et al., 2023). Such events underscore the importance of aligning AI use with media ethics and principles of credibility. It is imperative for media organizations to define the boundaries of AI use in visual content and to develop transparent policies that safeguard reader trust.

The contributions of AI to media systems must be carefully assessed from ethical, legal, and societal perspectives. Media professionals should integrate technology with responsible and trustworthy journalism practices, using AI as a supportive tool and managing the process transparently through robust oversight mechanisms.

Artificial intelligence has emerged not merely as a technical innovation in contemporary art, but as a symbol of intellectual and aesthetic transformation. For those of us rooted in a tradition that defines art through human experience, intuition, and emotion, creative processes shaped by algorithms raise profound new questions: Who is the artist? What constitutes an artwork? Is creativity an exclusively human trait?

Today, generative AI models especially Generative Adversarial Networks (GAN) are widely used techniques in artistic production. These systems are trained on large datasets of artworks and are capable of generating original, and even compelling, visual outputs. When the French art collective Obvious created the digital portrait "Edmond de Belamy" using a GAN algorithm and sold it at a high price at Christie's auction house in 2018, the event demonstrated the potential for AI to gain a significant foothold in the art world (Cetinic & She, 2022). This moment was not merely a technological milestone but also a clear signal that we need to reconsider how the value of art is defined.

This transformation is not limited to production alone. Art galleries and museums are employing AI and augmented reality technologies to provide more inclusive, interactive, and viewer-centered exhibition experiences. Visitors now access personalized information about artworks through AI-powered guides and even participate in the creative process by contributing their own visual expressions. While this supports the democratization of art, it also transforms curatorial planning into a more data-driven practice.

AI also plays a critical role in interdisciplinary art production. Transitions from photography to painting or from painting to digital illustration establish a fluid relationship between forms of artistic expression. This technology is especially prevalent in recreating works in the aesthetic language of particular artists. The styles of artists such as Pablo Picasso, Salvador Dalí, Sebastião Salgado, or James Nachtwey can be analyzed by AI algorithms and used as the foundation for new creations. Based on user input, it is now possible to generate outputs such as a "portrait in the style of Picasso" or a "Salgado-like frame."

One of the fundamental issues underlying these developments is the definition of originality and creative labor. Gülaçtı and Kahraman (2021) emphasize that the styles of great artists have developed over years of effort, whereas AI technologies can imitate those styles within minutes posing a potential to rival, or even surpass, human creativity. This marks the beginning of an era in which aesthetically valuable products can be created effortlessly, positioning AI not just as a tool, but also as an interpreter (Gülaçtı & Kahraman, 2021, p. 252).

Furthermore, the public's reception of AI-generated imagery represents a pivotal dimension of contemporary art discourse. It is increasingly observed that while AI-driven works may achieve a formal aesthetic merit comparable to human-authored creations, their emotional resonance often falters the moment the viewer becomes aware of their artificial genesis. This phenomenon suggests that aesthetic valuation is not merely a formalist appraisal of visual data; rather, it is an intricate experience fundamentally shaped by the perceived identity, existential intention, and contextual background of the creator. On the other hand, the analysis of AI-generated artworks also offers new possibilities for curatorial selection and art criticism. Cetinic and She (2022) demonstrate that viewer responses can be analyzed through AI systems, allowing exhibition practices to be restructured accordingly. Moreover, these technologies can measure the sensory impact of artworks and infer psychological responses from the audience. Thus, not only the production but also the reception and evaluation processes are being redefined within an algorithmic framework.

One of the most intricate challenges of this technological paradigm shift involves the problematic of copyright and artistic ownership. The legal standing of AI-generated visuals remains enveloped in profound ambiguity, especially regarding commercial utilization, as the definition of digital authorship lacks a definitive legal precedent. When a work is the result of purely algorithmic execution, detached from human cognitive input or creative agency, the possibility of its legal protection becomes a central tension in contemporary art law and ethics. Beyond legalities, significant ethical concerns arise regarding cultural representation. The prevailing Western-centricity of the datasets training these models poses a critical risk of aesthetic homogenization within the global artistic landscape. An insufficient integration of diverse cultural legacies and varied aesthetic paradigms may result in an AI-driven visual output that is epistemically and creatively limited. Therefore, failing to acknowledge the necessity for inclusive data structures may ultimately impoverish the global art ecosystem, compromising the very pluralism that sustains artistic evolution. In light of all these developments, the presence of artificial intelligence in the field of art brings with it not only productivity and technical advancement but also ethical, aesthetic, and cultural concerns. Artists may adopt these technologies as new tools for expression; curators can use AI systems to build deeper connections with audiences; and researchers and legal experts can work to define the norms of this new era. However, the essential question that will shape the future of art history is how to preserve the human elements of meaning, emotion, intention, and context elements that constitute the very essence of art.

Artificial Intelligence and the Workforce

Brynjolfsson and McAfee describe the first major rupture in labor history as having occurred during the Industrial Revolution of the 18th century, when the limits of physical power were challenged. They argue that we are now experiencing a second rupture, in which the boundaries of cognitive power are being tested and even surpassed. This new era, facilitated by computers and digital technologies, should be referred to as the "Second Machine Age." As the world transitions into full automation, there is a decreasing need for human labor. Robots, AI applications, and other digital technologies are increasingly acquiring ordinary skills and abilities, placing workers who rely solely on these competencies at considerable risk (Brynjolfsson & McAfee, 2014).

The rapid development of artificial intelligence technologies is causing profound changes in global labor markets. With the advancement of AI, there have been significant shifts in production methods, workflows, and the structure of the workforce. Production and distribution are becoming digitalized, certain commodities are being transformed into digital forms, the reorganization of labor is becoming a necessity, companies are developing new business practices, and consumption processes are also undergoing transformation (Bakın, 2023). In recent years, the rapid progress in AI technologies has transformed business practices across sectors from manufacturing to services. These changes directly affect both the quality and quantity of the labor force; while some occupations are becoming obsolete or undergoing transformation, others are emerging, creating new employment opportunities.

Acemoglu and Restrepo have examined the impact of AI and automation on the workforce, emphasizing that while automation can reduce labor demand, it can also create new jobs. They argue that the labor force must adapt to new technologies by acquiring the necessary skills, and that the nature of the workforce should be reshaped accordingly (Acemoglu & Restrepo, 2018). Although there are differing views regarding the impact of technological change on employment, some studies and examples indicate that these changes do not necessarily lead to unemployment; on the contrary, they create new jobs and skill requirements.

Acemoglu's central concern about AI is whether it will take the form of machine usefulness, aimed at enhancing worker productivity, or whether it will be directed toward mimicking general intelligence to replace human jobs. He illustrates this with the difference between providing new information to a biotechnologist versus replacing a customer service worker with automated call center technology. So far, he believes that companies have prioritized the latter. Acemoglu states: "My argument is that we currently have the wrong direction for AI. We're using it too much for automation and not enough for providing expertise and information to workers" (Dizikes, 2024).

In conclusion, the transformation in production technologies does not necessarily exclude human labor altogether but rather reshapes the nature and orientation of the workforce. Therefore, instead of viewing it as an absolute threat to employment, it should be seen as a process of transformation. It is crucial not to be left behind in this global shift and to conduct intensive research and development in this area.

Artificial Intelligence and the Environment

The contemporary world faces escalating environmental degradation caused by human activity, including pollution, climate change, the depletion and contamination of water resources, drought, biodiversity loss, and deforestation each becoming increasingly global in scope. Artificial intelligence holds significant potential to be effectively employed in solving many of these environmental problems. In particular, initiatives such as Global Forest Watch play a crucial role by using AI to monitor and analyze environmental changes and to address the threat of deforestation. AI systems are also applied in forecasting weather conditions and implementing preventive measures in renewable energy systems, including wind and solar energy, and in enhancing energy efficiency.

However, a less discussed but equally important reality is that AI technologies themselves can have negative environmental impacts. Notably, the data centers hosting large AI servers consume vast amounts of energy. The carbon emissions generated during the training of large language models have been compared to those produced by an airplane flight (Strubell, Ganesh, & McCallum, 2019). According to the Navigating New Horizons report published in 2024 by the United Nations Environment Programme (UNEP, 2024), AI offers promising solutions for detecting methane emissions a greenhouse gas responsible for climate change at oil and gas facilities. Furthermore, it holds potential for addressing major global crises such as climate change, biodiversity loss, pollution, and waste. However, the report also emphasizes the environmental toll of data centers. It states that manufacturing a 2-kilogram computer requires 800 kilograms of raw materials, and that microchips often rely on rare earth elements extracted through environmentally harmful methods. Data centers produce electronic waste that frequently contains hazardous substances like mercury and lead, consume vast amounts of water for cooling, and contribute significantly to greenhouse gas emissions through their energy use, often powered by fossil fuels.Moreover, the report highlights that, according to the International Energy Agency, a single search request via ChatGPT consumes up to ten times more electricity than a standard Google search (UNEP, 2024).

Disinformation

The term disinformation, of French origin, is defined in the Cambridge Dictionary as false information spread with the intention to deceive, and by the Turkish Language Association (TDK) as the distortion of information (TDK). Closely related to this concept is deepfake, which refers to various types of synthetic media in which images or recordings are convincingly manipulated to show someone doing or saying something they never actually did. The term was first introduced by a Reddit user who shared pornographic videos using open-source face-swapping technology (Janzczuk, 2024).

One of the key purposes behind the production of deepfake content is to influence and alter public opinion. In 2022, a one-minute video showing Ukrainian President Volodymyr Zelensky allegedly urging his troops to surrender and lay down their arms against Russia was generated using artificial intelligence and circulated widely across various platforms. Ukraine labeled the video as a deepfake, and the military intelligence agency later released an informational video via its social media accounts with the message: "You've probably all heard of Deepfake technology (a combination of deep learning and fake), an AI-based method for synthesizing human images. A provocation is being prepared by the Russian Federation" (Defence Intelligence of Ukraine, 2022).

Henry Farid, a digital media expert at the University of California, emphasized that such content pollutes the information ecosystem, and casts doubt on all media, even those produced under already challenging conditions such as the "fog of war." He warned that the next time President Zelensky appears on television, viewers might wonder whether what they're seeing is real (Allyn, 2022).

Today, many AI-powered detection and verification tools have been developed to identify deepfake content. These platforms can scan and evaluate whether text was written by a human or AI, or whether images have been manipulated. However, results should also be approached with caution, as there have been cases where content labeled as not AI-generated was later found to have been created using AI technologies.

Şirin Anlen and Raquel Vaquez Llorente note that AI detection tools are typically trained on datasets created under controlled, well-lit, and orderly laboratory conditions, allowing the model to learn and identify necessary features accurately. However, real-world scenarios often involve blurry, out-of-focus visuals, shaky footage, off-angle framing, and noisy audio. This makes it difficult for detection tools to accurately evaluate such content. Their research on deepfake detection showed that altering the frame or resolution of a video, such as one of U.S. President Obama or an image related to an alleged explosion at the Pentagon, could change the detection result from "deepfake" to "not a deepfake." Similarly, in the case of audio, detection tools trained on clean, uninterrupted speech showed reduced accuracy when background noise or overlapping conversations were present (Anlen & Llorente, 2024).

WITNESS, an international human rights organization dedicated to helping people use video and technology to protect and advocate for human rights, actively works in regions that are most marginalized and at risk, including conducting research on deepfake content. The organization assembles expert analysis teams to report on content suspected to be generated or manipulated by AI, particularly when such material may contribute to violence or negatively impact democracy and human rights (WITNESS). Sam Gregory, technology expert and director of WITNESS, noted in his TED Talk that his work on deepfakes began in 2017 at a time when concerns about the threat to informational trust were considered exaggerated, while the most substantial harm was occurring through fake pornographic content. He emphasized that the problem has since grown significantly and continues to cause harm to women and girls worldwide (Gregory, 2023).

Photography And Artificial Intelligence

Artificial intelligence (AI) technology significantly impacts the art of photography, spanning from image generation to image processing. Features now integrated into contemporary image editing software enable interventions that enhance the clarity and completeness of an image without necessarily detaching it from its original context. However, it is equally possible to use these tools to create entirely new, deceptive representations that diverge from reality. At this point, the decisive factor becomes the intention and purpose of the image creator. AI-generated visuals can depict events that never occurred or represent unexperienced moments as if they were lived, achieved through well-crafted prompts that accurately convey the user's desired output.

AI also offers substantial contributions to photographic practice. It can significantly enhance the resolution of an image, enabling large-format prints suitable for professional use an application commonly utilized through specialized software. Moreover, black-and-white photographs can be colorized and even transformed into moving images or videos. One of the most frequent examples of such practices is the colorization and animation of archival photographs of Mustafa Kemal Atatürk, especially during national holidays and commemorations on November 10th.

The global popularization of AI-generated imagery is further accelerated by the widespread influence of contemporary social media. With each passing day, new AI-driven visual trends emerge, becoming mainstream and widely adopted. In addition to professional platforms, mobile applications now allow users to create, transform, and even hybridize their photographs directly via smartphones. A recent trend involves uploading images of celebrities, politicians, or ordinary individuals to convert them into animated characters for public sharing. Similarly, filters that age or de-age subjects in photographs have gained popularity. Even elements such as eye color or hair style can be altered in seconds with minimal user input.

AI has also begun to manifest its presence in formal photography competitions. In 2023, Boris Eldagsen was awarded first prize in the "Creative" category of the Sony World Photography Awards. However, following the announcement of the winners, Eldagsen declined the award, drawing considerable public attention. He stated that his submission was a calculated test to provoke discourse on the role of AI in photography and to evaluate the extent of technological advancement. He informed the organizers post-selection, suggesting his own disqualification or, alternatively, a necessary amendment of the competition's submission criteria. Eldagsen clarified that AI was merely a tool for him and that he did not regard the resulting image as a photograph, preferring to label it as a picture or pantograph. He emphasized his refusal to accept a photography award with a fabricated image (Karadağ, 2024). Consequently, the organizing institution was compelled to navigate this unprecedented rupture; by accepting his withdrawal, the institutional framework inadvertently validated the urgent need for the very discourse Eldagsen aimed to provoke. This event holds profound significance in demonstrating how an AI-generated image can seamlessly bypass the traditional filters of a photography competition to receive top honors, thereby raising discipline-altering questions about authorship, the boundaries of the medium, and visual authenticity.

The Production of Realistic Images Through Artificial Intelligence

The technology behind image generation via artificial intelligence (AI) applications is advancing rapidly. In the early stages of development, AI-generated visuals often contained obvious errors particularly in rendering human features such as eyes or hands. Today, however, such flaws have largely been resolved, and AI now enables the creation of highly realistic images. The technology has evolved to a point where it can produce visuals that only a highly trained eye might distinguish from real photographs. With the integration of AI and advanced media production tools, the once-clear boundary between the real and the fabricated is becoming increasingly blurred. This ambiguity can lead to AI-generated images being perceived as authentic depictions of real events, especially when disseminated through news media and social media platforms. Such misperceptions contribute to public misinformation and the manipulation of societal perception, raising profound ethical concerns.

In recent years, alongside photographs, deepfake videos fabricated using AI have emerged as tools of disinformation, particularly in political contexts such as election campaigns. These videos are often used to spread false information about political opponents, mislead the public, or divert attention in ways that influence voter behavior. For instance, in 2018, a deepfake video circulated that depicted Barack Obama delivering a speech he never actually gave. Similarly, in Turkey's 2023 general elections, a fabricated video was shown at Justice and Development Party (AKP) rallies, depicting the opposition candidate and former CHP leader Kemal Kılıçdaroğlu singing with Murat Karayılan, a leader of the PKK terrorist organization.

Jamie Cohen of Queens College emphasizes that we now possess the ability to take a thought and have a machine generate a visual realization of that thought. He warns that the inherent danger lies in the fact that not all thoughts are benign or constructive. Cohen underscores the growing trend of "slightly unrealistic but realistic-enough" images as a clear threat, noting that AI can produce content that draws individuals to the edge of conspiracy thinking (Maloy & Branigin, 2023).

Trump in Prison

On March 21, 2023, Eliot Higgins, the founder and creative director of Bellingcat an independent international investigative collective shared a series of AI-generated images via his Twitter account, depicting former U.S. President Donald Trump being arrested. These images were created using the Midjourney platform and were posted on the day Trump stood trial for charges related to a payment made to adult film actress Stormy Daniels during his 2016 election campaign. Accompanied by the caption *"Making pictures of Trump getting arrested while waiting for Trump's arrest"* (Higgins, 2023), the images had been viewed 6.9 million times as of April 20, 2025. The scenes portrayed Trump attempting to flee from police officers, exercising in an orange jumpsuit in prison, reading a book in his cell, and escaping all of which quickly attracted massive attention online.

By using the phrase *"making pictures"*, Higgins openly indicated that the visuals were artificially generated by himself. Nonetheless, the images were widely shared across platforms alongside claims that Trump had actually been sentenced to prison. Upon closer inspection, anatomical inaccuracies such as irregularities in the number of fingers and inconsistencies in the depiction of hands become noticeable. Additional errors such as Trump wearing the utility belt typically worn by police officers also reveal the synthetic nature of the visuals. Despite these flaws, numerous news outlets and personal social media accounts initially circulated the images as genuine depictions of Trump's arrest, and only later acknowledged that they had been produced using artificial intelligence.

Figure 4. On March 22, 2023, Higgins tweeted that he had been banned from the Midjourney platform, stating: "Apparently doing a viral thread about Donald Trump using Midjourney images is enough to get you banned from Midjourney, oops" (Eliot Higgins, 2023). He followed up with another post: "At least I still have ChatGPT 4, so here's the Trumpshank Redemption for those of you who have stuck around this long," accompanied by screenshots of his prompts and the resulting images (Eliot Higgins, 2023).

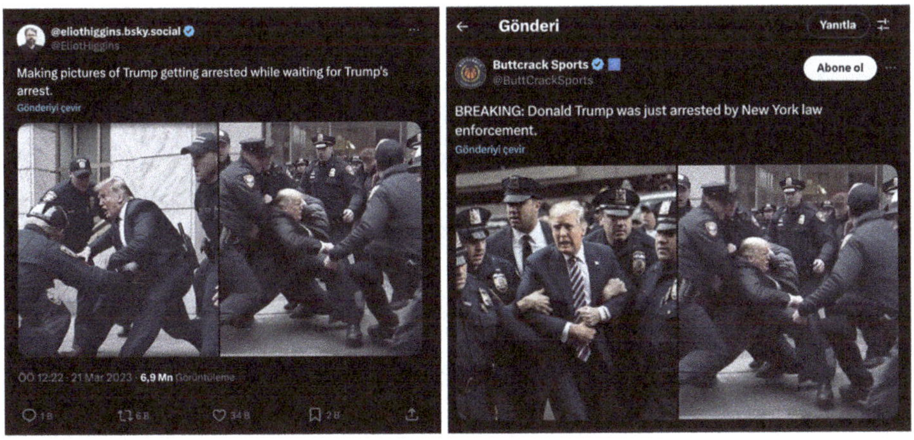

Figure 5. Newsweek, July 20, 2022 – also cited in a repost by the official White House X (formerly Twitter) account.

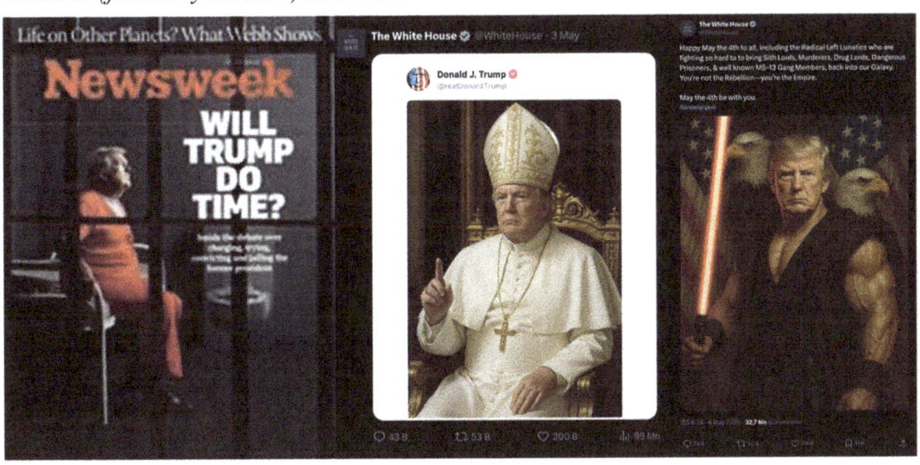

On April 21, 2023, following the death of Pope Francis, questions arose about who would succeed him. In response, Trump declared: *"I'd like to be Pope. That would be my number one choice."* (Uren, 2025). On May 3, Trump posted an AI-generated image of himself depicted as the Pope across all his personal social media accounts. The same image was later shared without commentary by the official White House X account. This led to widespread criticism, with some arguing that the image mocked the Papacy and questioning the appropriateness of such a post coming from a formal government institution (https://x.com/WhiteHouse/status/1918502592335724809/photo/1).

On May 4 internationally known as *Star Wars Day* the White House's official account posted another AI-generated image of Trump, this time holding a lightsaber and dressed as a Star Wars character. The accompanying caption read: *"Happy May the 4th to all, including the Radical Left Lunatics who are fighting so hard to bring Sith Lords, Murderers, Drug Lords, Dangerous Prisoners, & well known MS-13 Gang Members, back into our Galaxy. You're not the Rebellion you're the Empire."* (https://x.com/WhiteHouse/status/1919053040734072844).

Pope Francis in a Balenciaga Jacket

On March 27, 2023, Pablo Xavier, a U.S.-based individual, generated an image using the Midjourney platform depicting 86-year-old Pope Francis walking outdoors while wearing a white puffer jacket by the luxury brand Balenciaga. He first shared the image on the Facebook group "AI Art Universe" and subsequently on Reddit. Xavier, who withheld his real surname due to potential backlash, stated that the idea came to him spontaneously under the influence of drugs. He thought it would be humorous, but later expressed surprise at the scale of the reaction. Although he anticipated criticism, he did not expect the image to provoke such widespread attention. He also reported being banned from Reddit after sharing the post (Walker, 2023).

Figure 6. Pope in Puffer Jacket

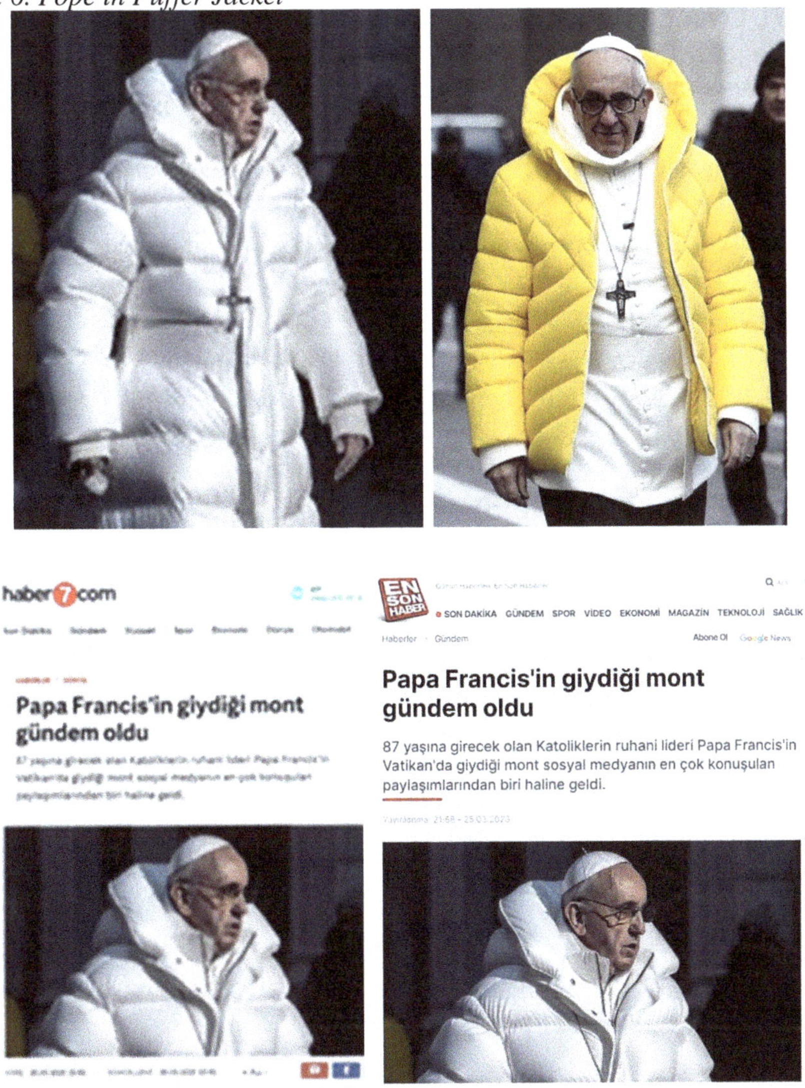

The image of Pope Francis circulated rapidly and was widely mistaken as authentic, appearing in numerous online news outlets. Shortly thereafter, additional AI-generated images of the Pope wearing various types of jackets were produced by different users and disseminated across social media platforms.

Xavier generated the image using the following prompt:

"Catholic Pope Francis wearing Balenciaga puffy jacket in drill rap music video, throwing up gang signs with hands, taken using a Canon EOS R camera with a 50mm f/1.8 lens, f/2.2 aperture, shutter speed 1/200s, ISO 100 and natural

light, Full Body, Hyper Realistic Photography, Cinematic, Cinema, Hyperdetail, UHD, Color Correction, hdr, color grading, hyper realistic CG animation –ar 4:5 –upbeta –q 2 –v 5" (Prompt Folder, n.d.).

Upon closer examination of the image, inconsistencies become apparent such as the crucifix chain hanging only on one side of the Pope's neck, a visual overlap between his eyelid and glasses, and distortions in the fingers and coffee cup held in his right hand.

On June 14, 2024, Pope Francis attended the G7 summit hosted by Italy, where he addressed the risks and ethical implications of artificial intelligence. Describing AI as both "exciting and frightening," he emphasized that such technologies must be employed in service of humanity. He specifically called for a ban on lethal autonomous weapons, stating, *"No machine should ever attempt to take a human life"* (Glatz, 2024).

Explosion at the Pentagon

On May 22, 2023, a Twitter account named *Bloomberg Feed*, bearing the blue verification checkmark that signifies authenticity and official status, posted an image claiming that an explosion had occurred near the Pentagon. The image and accompanying news rapidly spread across various platforms and international media outlets, including Russia Today and the Indian television channel Republic TV. Following denials from official sources and the confirmation that the image had been generated using artificial intelligence applications, multiple accounts that had shared the image subsequently deleted their posts or issued public apologies.

Figure 7. AI-generated image of the alleged Pentagon explosion

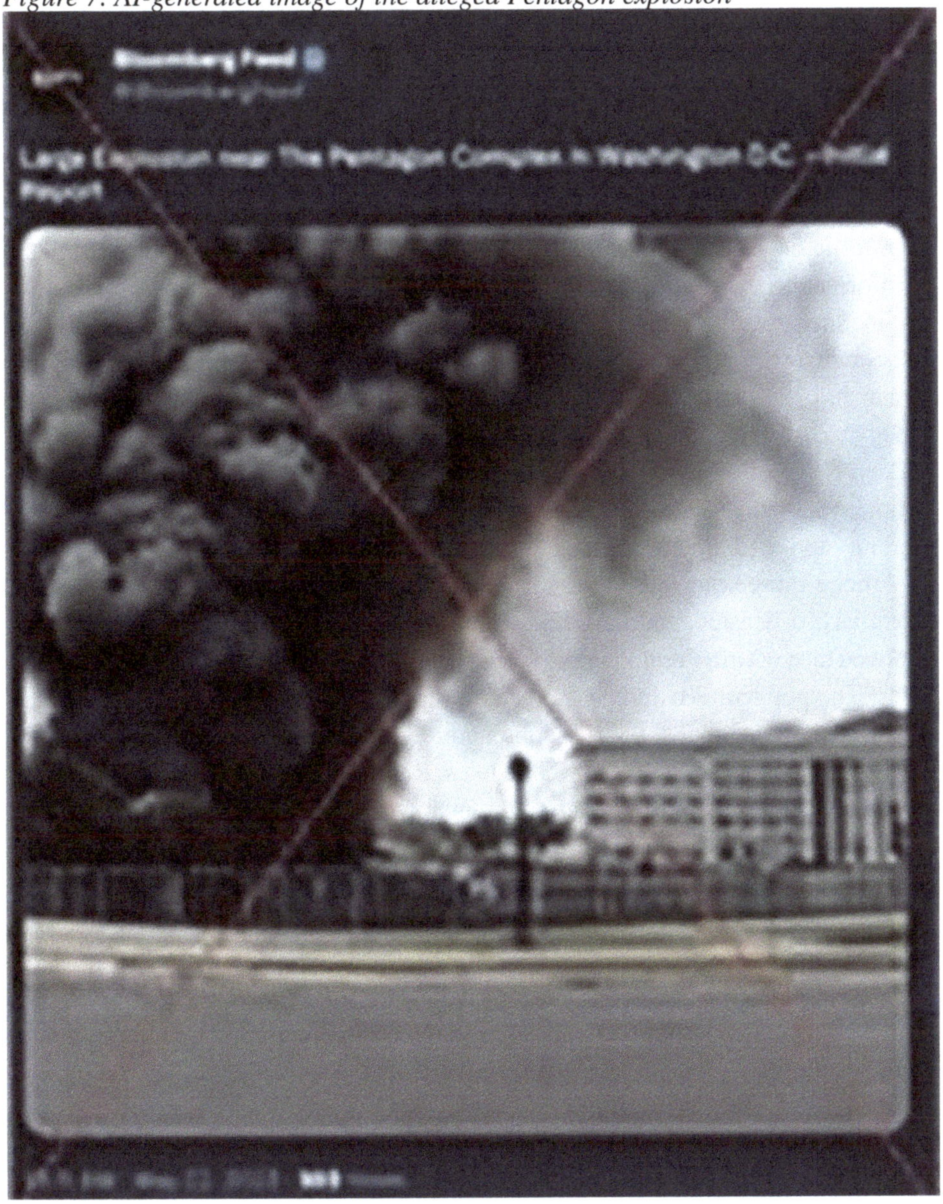

Despite the rapid debunking of the incident, the tweet triggered significant volatility in the U.S. stock market, which later stabilized over the course of the day. The Twitter account in question, whose owner could not be identified, was suspended by the platform. This incident exemplifies how AI-generated disinformation, even when short-lived, can have tangible financial repercussions.

The Kahramanmaraş Earthquake and the Circulation of AI-Generated Images

Following the devastating Kahramanmaraş earthquake that occurred on February 6, 2023, several AI-generated images depicting rescue and disaster scenes were circulated on social media alongside authentic photographs. These synthetic visuals, when mistaken for real documentation, contributed to the dissemination of misinformation and false reports. This incident once again demonstrated how quickly disinformation can spread during times of crisis via digital platforms.

One such example involved Panagiotis Kotridis, a retired member of the Hellenic Fire Service who had previously participated in rescue efforts during the 1992 Erzincan and 1999 İzmit earthquakes in Turkey. Using AI software, Kotridis created and shared an image intended to honor his fellow firefighters assisting victims in Turkey. His post included the phrase *"I am here for you"* in Greek, English, and Turkish (Savvidis, 2023). The image rapidly gained traction across diverse user accounts and media platforms.

Among those who shared the image was Nervana Mahmoud, a London-based Egyptian broadcaster and Middle East analyst. Mahmoud later expressed regret and removed the post after realizing the image had been generated using digital technologies. The pop icon Madonna also shared the image on Instagram for Valentine's Day, calling for global solidarity and encouraging donations to the Turkish NGO Ahbap. Her post received over 500,000 likes. Renowned fashion photographer Mert Alaş, based in London, responded to the post with a message of gratitude.

In the immediate aftermath of the earthquake, numerous fraudulent accounts emerged on platforms like TikTok and Twitter, soliciting donations under the guise of earthquake relief efforts. These accounts included PayPal links or cryptocurrency wallet addresses, accompanied by emotionally charged captions such as *"Help Türkiye," "Pray for Türkiye,"* and *"Donate for Earthquake Victims"* (Gelbart, 2023). Kotridis's AI-generated image was also repurposed and used across such scam accounts.

Figure 8. AI-generated rescue image by Panagiotis Kotridis

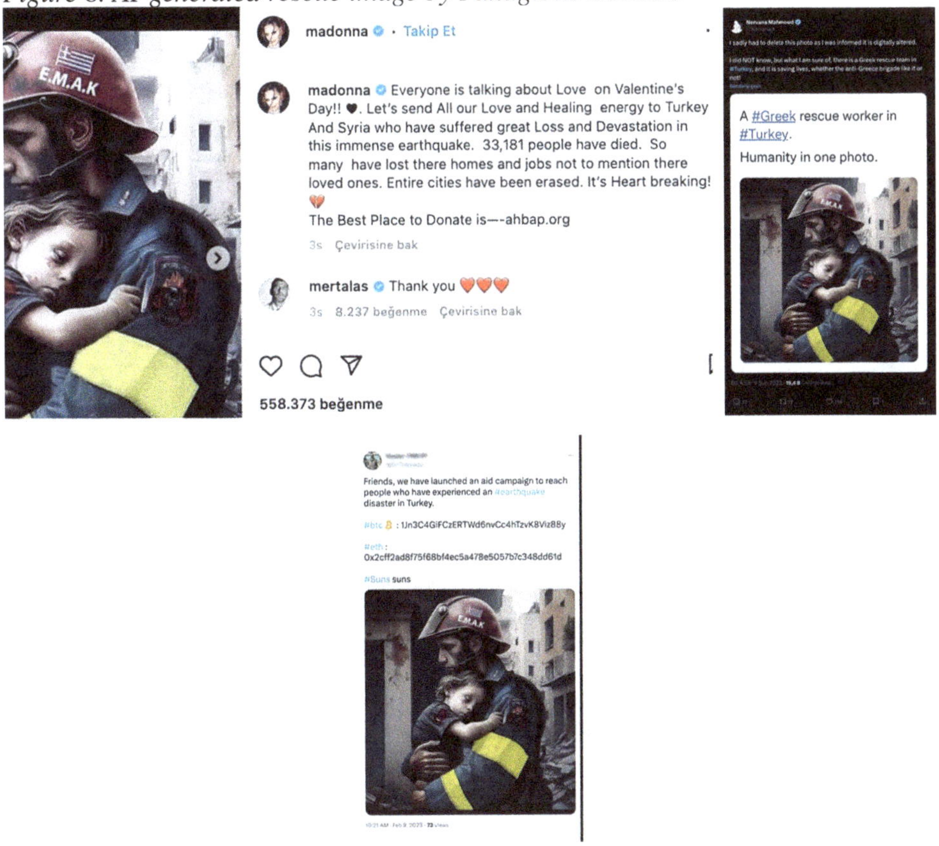

In a later interview, Kotridis responded to criticism and insults directed at him, stating that he never claimed the image was a real photograph. He emphasized that it was a piece of *digital art*, not a *fake*, and that he was deeply distressed by its misuse in fraudulent fundraising efforts. He also addressed the backlash he received from media inquiries, adding humorously that when journalists asked him for the phone number of the firefighter's wife depicted in the image, he replied, *"I'll ask Photoshop"* (Popotas & Kalyva, 2023).

Michael Christopher Brown

American photographer Michael Christopher Brown is recognized for his innovative approaches that push the boundaries of documentary photography. In 2011, he spent seven months in Libya during the civil war, documenting the conflict using only his mobile phone. The resulting images were later published in his book *Libyan*

Sugar, which won the Paris Photo–Aperture Foundation First PhotoBook Award and the Infinity Award for Artist's Book from the International Center of Photography in 2017. In 2018, Brown photographed the funeral procession of Fidel Castro in Cuba and published the images in a book titled *Yo Soy Fidel*. He was accepted as a nominee to Magnum Photos in 2013, became an associate member in 2015, but parted ways with the agency in June 2017.

Figure 9. Michael Christopher Brown, 90 Miles, 2023

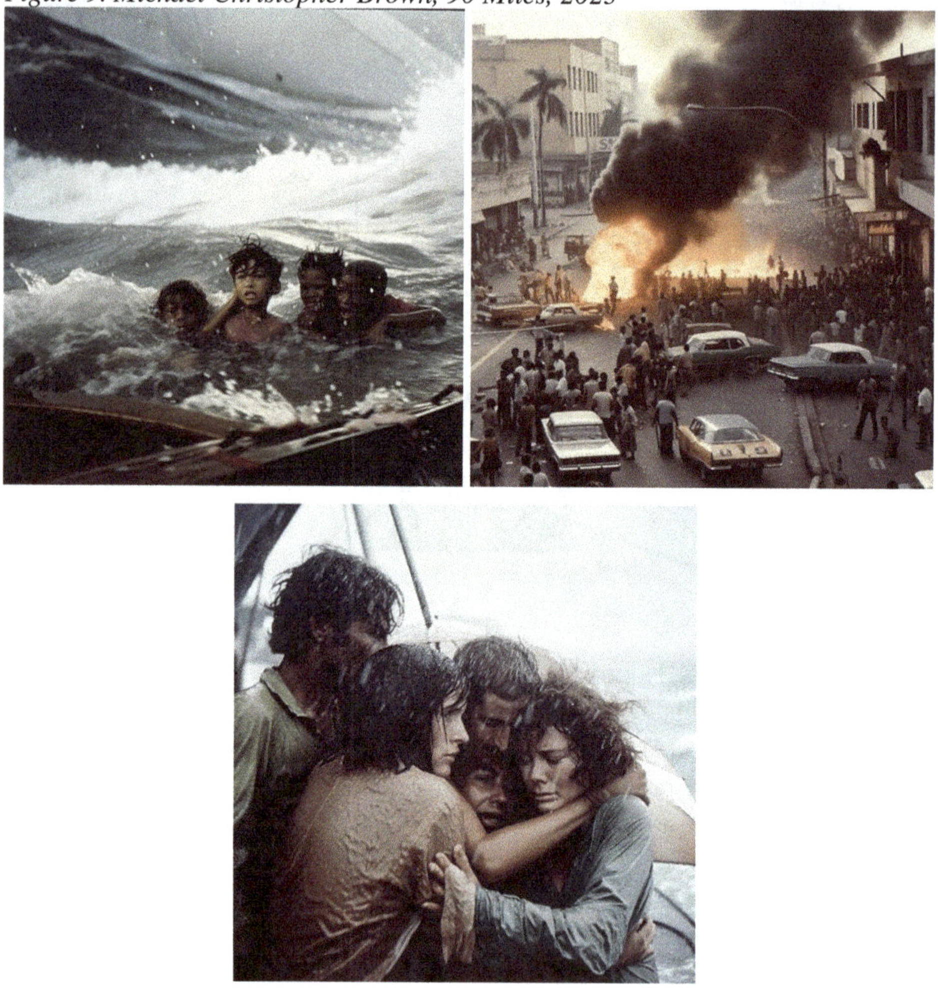

Brown's *90 Miles* series derives its title from the distance between Havana, Cuba and the coast of Florida, USA. The project consists of AI-generated photographs based on the historical narratives of Cubans attempting to cross the ocean from Havana to the United States. The series has sparked significant controversy. Central to the criticism is the concern that the project blurs the line between fiction and documentary truth, leading to broader questions about the authenticity of Brown's earlier documentary work. Some commentators have questioned how viewers can now determine whether his previous, site-specific photojournalism was genuine (Terranova, 2023).

Known for his contributions to prestigious publications such as *National Geographic*, *The New York Times*, *Vanity Fair*, *Time*, and *Vogue*, Brown has long established himself as a press photographer. However, due to the hyper-realistic aesthetics of *90 Miles*, many viewers mistakenly perceived the AI-generated images as authentic depictions of real events.

Brown also converted the series into a collection of 400 NFTs, each priced at 1 ETH. He announced via Instagram on April 4, 2023, that 10% of the proceeds would be donated to charities working with Cuban refugees. Following this post, the response was divided: while some users praised the work's creativity and conceptual depth, others accused him of deception particularly because of his background in press photography and the commercial aspect of selling NFTs (Brown, 2023).

During a talk at the 2023 Photo Vogue Festival, Brown explained that he had worked in Cuba between 2014 and 2016 and had originally planned to photograph this subject in the field. However, he stated that due to practical constraints, he opted to generate the images using artificial intelligence (Brown, 2023).

Amnesty International

In 2021, during the public protests in Colombia sparked by economic and social inequality, Amnesty International, a global human rights organization, shared social media content aimed at raising awareness of police violence used to suppress demonstrators. The visuals accompanying the post were generated using artificial intelligence (AI), with a note beneath the image explicitly stating that it was created by AI. However, this disclaimer did not prevent the campaign from facing criticism.

Observers quickly noted several discrepancies in the image: missing or distorted facial features on the police officers, the incorrect sequencing of the Colombian flag's colors (which should be yellow, blue, and red but appeared as red, yellow, and blue), and inaccurate police uniforms that did not correspond to those used in Colombia.

The use of AI-generated imagery received mixed reactions from various sectors. Photojournalists and media experts argued that the incorporation of synthetic visuals could undermine Amnesty International's credibility and fuel conspiracy theories. Photojournalist Juancho Torres criticized the organization, stating that AI "lies" and questioned the reliability of content generated by non-human means. He emphasized that using AI-generated visuals in place of actual photojournalism was disrespectful to journalists documenting the protests on the front lines. According to Torres, the power of journalism lies in the recreation of reality based on lived experience, and many photographers, reporters, and camerapeople risked their lives to document these events some even suffering serious injuries, such as one of his colleagues who lost an eye. He warned that relying on artificial visuals not only erodes the notion of truth but also weakens the bond between journalists and the public.

Gareth Sella, a protester who lost sight in his left eye after being struck by a rubber bullet fired by police, offered a different perspective. He suggested that concealing the identities of demonstrators could be a rational approach to protecting them from exaggerated charges and possible imprisonment (Taylor, 2023).

Figure 10. Amnesty International's AI-generated image

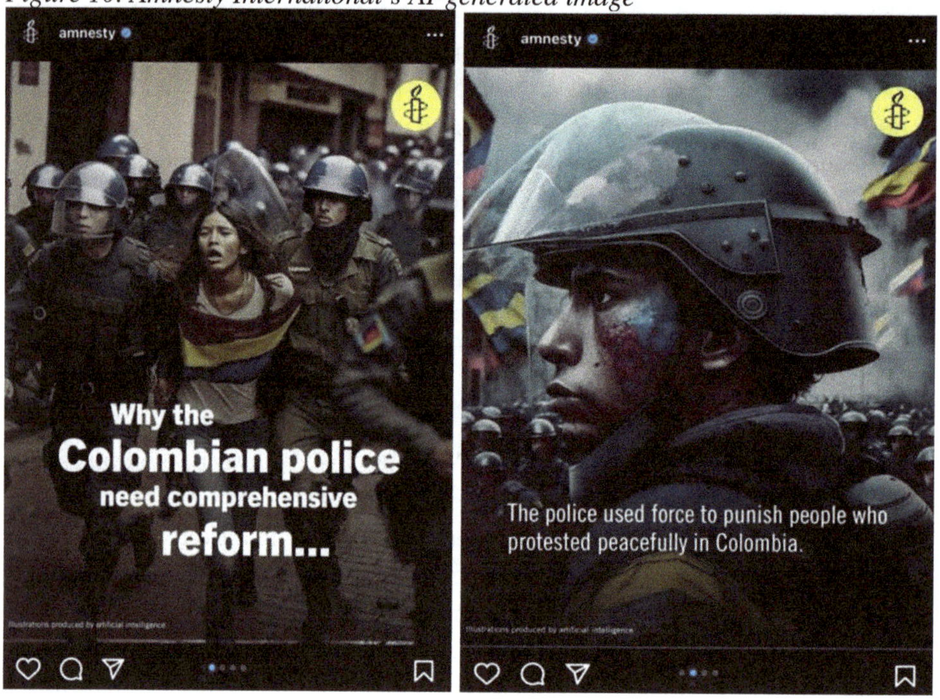

Erika Guevara Rosas, the Americas Director at Amnesty International, later explained that the organization chose to use AI-generated images to protect protesters from potential state retaliation.

However, due to criticism surrounding the authenticity and ethical implications of using AI in visual advocacy, Amnesty removed the images from their social media channels. She emphasized that the organization did not want the controversy to distract from the core message: solidarity with victims and support for justice in Colombia (Taylor, 2023).

Reflection on the Case Studies: A Unified Ontological Crisis

The convergence of the previously discussed case studies ranging from political fabrications and financial market manipulations to crisis exploitation and award-winning artistic deceptions illustrates a unified ontological crisis in contemporary visual journalism. Photography has historically functioned as a physical trace of reality, a definitive proof of a moment that actually occurred. However, the examples analyzed demonstrate a critical paradigm shift: AI-generated imagery no longer merely mimics reality; it actively disrupts the epistemic foundation of the public sphere. We are witnessing a transition from capturing light to synthesizing data, which fundamentally severs the medium's inherent connection to truth and introduces a profound ambiguity into visual communication.

When we examine the hyper-realistic depictions of Donald Trump's fabricated arrest or Pope Francis in a designer jacket, we see how easily synthetic media can hijack public discourse. These instances highlight that the initial intent of the creator whether it is political satire, a spontaneous aesthetic experiment, or deliberate disinformation is often irrelevant once the image enters the algorithmic currents of social media. The Pentagon explosion hoax further amplifies this danger, proving that even momentarily believed synthetic images can yield tangible real-world consequences, such as instantaneous financial market fluctuations. Together, these cases confirm Jean Baudrillard's warnings about hyperreality: the simulation no longer represents the real; it precedes and dictates it, leaving audiences unable to distinguish between genuine news and algorithmic hallucination.

Furthermore, the ethical stakes are significantly heightened during times of crisis and social upheaval, as seen in the Kahramanmaraş earthquake and the Amnesty International campaign. In the context of natural disasters, synthetic empathy is weaponized to exploit the cognitive vulnerabilities of a grieving public, facilitating financial fraud under the guise of humanitarian aid. Conversely, when human rights organizations utilize AI to protect the identities of protesters in Colombia, they inadvertently compromise the very documentary integrity required to hold oppressors accountable. These events underscore the delicate balance between ethical advocacy and the absolute necessity of human witnessing. When the human element is removed, the resulting visual narrative, no matter how emotionally resonant, loses its evidentiary power.

Finally, the institutional boundaries of photography itself are being aggressively tested from within. The incidents involving Boris Eldagsen at the Sony World Photography Awards and Michael Christopher Brown's "90 Miles" project reveal a profound institutional vulnerability. When synthetic images seamlessly subvert the filters of prestigious photography competitions, or are produced by veteran photojournalists blurring the lines between documentary truth and digital art, the crisis becomes internal to the discipline. These artistic deceptions prove that the threat is not confined to isolated malicious actors or internet trolls; it has infiltrated the highest echelons of visual culture. Ultimately, the recurring pattern of deception across these varied contexts underscores that we are not dealing with temporary technological anomalies. Rather, this is a systemic structural rupture. Navigating this post-photographic landscape demands an urgent reevaluation of visual ethics, robust institutional accountability, and a comprehensive understanding of the cognitive biases of modern audiences. Before irreversible damage is done to the credibility of documentary evidence, the journalism ecosystem must establish definitive boundaries that protect the authentic act of human witnessing against the encroaching tide of synthetic manipulation.

The Dangers Posed by the Production of Realistic Images through Artificial Intelligence

While AI-based image generation offers artists in various branches of photography immense freedom and creative latitude, particularly in artistic contexts, it becomes considerably more problematic when the resulting visuals resemble documentary or evidentiary photographs. Images created or altered through AI can be used for a wide range of purposes. Among the most serious risks is the potential for such visuals to cause material or psychological harm to individuals, or to be exploited for provocation or manipulation.

Jean Baudrillard argues that modern society, having weakened its connection to reality, now functions within a hyperreality dominated by images (Baudrillard, 2024). In this hyperreal environment shaped by AI technologies, everything presented can be perceived by the public as photographs derived from actual events. Beyond generating misinformation, such representations may also lead to manipulations of collective memory.

Furthermore, the creation and dissemination of highly realistic yet fictitious images, especially when they are mistaken for authentic press photography, can fundamentally undermine the concepts of truth and credibility, values that are foundational to journalistic imagery. While it may seem implausible to interpret digitally generated images of Pope Francis in a Balenciaga jacket or Donald Trump being arrested as real, the AI-generated image depicting an explosion at the Pentagon was realistic enough to cause fluctuations in financial markets. Thus, the power and consequences of AI-generated images vary depending on their content and perceived plausibility; some may amuse, others may incite panic.

The psychological mechanisms underlying this vulnerability reveal that the threat of synthetic media is not merely technological, but deeply cognitive. Empirical studies on audience perception demonstrate that human observers consistently struggle to differentiate between authentic press photographs and AI-generated imagery. For instance, Nightingale and Farid (2022) empirically established that synthetically generated faces are not only visually indistinguishable from real ones but are paradoxically perceived as more trustworthy by average viewers. This visual deception is further compounded by inherent cognitive biases; audiences are highly susceptible to confirmation bias, rapidly accepting fabricated images as definitive proof if the visual narrative aligns with their pre-existing political or social beliefs. Furthermore, Groh et al. (2022) highlight that even when individuals are explicitly warned about the potential presence of synthetic media, their ability to accurately detect algorithmic manipulation remains statistically low. Consequently, the societal impact of these realistic fabrications extends beyond momentary deception; they actively exploit human cognitive vulnerabilities, systematically degrading the foundational epistemic trust required for a functioning public sphere.

In this new visual ecosystem, transparency regarding not only the method of image production but also its source has become essential. Media outlets should explicitly disclose when a visual has been created or modified using AI, as this enhances public awareness regarding the reliability of the news. Otherwise, the erosion of public trust a cornerstone of both photography and photojournalism may become irreversible. On social media, the credibility of an image is also influenced by the platform and user account through which it is shared. A photograph posted by a known photographer on their personal account should not inspire the same level of trust as one posted from an anonymous or pseudonymous profile. When such visuals are disseminated, it is also necessary to account for potential damage to the credibility of the platforms and institutions involved.

The rapid dissemination of synthetic media is structurally exacerbated by the algorithmic architecture of social media platforms. Platforms often prioritize engagement metrics and virality over epistemic accuracy, which inadvertently accelerates the spread of AI-generated disinformation compared to verified news (Vosoughi, Roy, & Aral, 2018). Addressing this systemic issue requires moving beyond corporate self-regulation toward robust international legal frameworks. Currently, global approaches to AI regulation remain highly fragmented. For example, the European Union has taken a proactive, legislative approach with the AI Act (European Parliament, 2024), which categorizes AI systems by risk and mandates stringent transparency requirements, including the mandatory labeling of deepfakes and synthetically altered media. In contrast, the United States has largely relied on decentralized, sector-specific guidelines and voluntary corporate commitments. This lack of a unified international legal consensus creates significant regulatory loopholes, allowing hyper-realistic disinformation to cross borders effortlessly and manipulate public discourse on a global scale.

Susan Sontag notes that while a painting is considered fake if not attributed to its proper artist, a photograph is deemed fake only when it is understood to have deceived the viewer about the reality it depicts (Sontag, 2004). AI-generated visuals can serve both artistic and aesthetic purposes, but they can also be used to produce misleading information. Sontag's observation that deception is the defining factor in evaluating photographic falsity becomes increasingly critical in this context. Accordingly, AI-generated images must be accompanied by mechanisms for verification and transparent disclosure about their origin and nature a practice that is now an ethical necessity (Floridi et al., 2018).

To counter these regulatory gaps and the institutional integration of AI tools, the journalism industry is increasingly turning to advanced technical verification frameworks. Initiatives like the Coalition for Content Provenance and Authenticity (C2PA) are pioneering the use of cryptographic metadata to track the digital provenance of an image from the point of capture to its final publication (Farid, 2022). By embedding tamper-evident data directly into the visual file, newsrooms can establish a verifiable chain of custody. However, technical solutions alone cannot mitigate the broader psychological trends emerging among the public. The ubiquitous and institutionalized nature of deepfakes has led to a phenomenon known as the 'liar's dividend,' where the mere existence of synthetic media breeds pervasive public skepticism, allowing public figures to dismiss authentic, damaging photographs as AI-generated fabrications (Chesney & Citron, 2019). As audiences become increasingly desensitized to visual shocks, assuming all sensational media might be synthetic, the institutional adoption of AI detection tools must be coupled with structural transparency to rebuild the eroding epistemic trust in journalistic institutions.

Ultimately, while the capacity of AI technologies to generate realistic imagery opens new avenues for creative expression and freedom, it also compels us to reexamine the notion of "visual reality." Susan Sontag's reflections on the relationship between photography and truth highlight the need for a more critical engagement with AI-generated visual content in this emerging media landscape.

The theoretical frameworks established by Barthes and Sontag effectively explain photography's analog connection to the physical world, but they fall short in addressing the ethical friction caused by generative algorithms. The current crisis in press photography extends far beyond the traditional manipulation of a captured image; it involves the algorithmic fabrication of visual evidence. This structural shift has prompted contemporary media scholars to redefine the boundaries of visual journalism. Hausken (2024), for instance, argues that to protect the epistemic credibility of photojournalism, AI outputs must be distinguished from photography and categorized as 'AI photorealism,' since they solely depict scenes without the actual, physical detection of light. Furthermore, Ufarte-Ruiz et al. (2023) emphasize that the rise of 'synthetic media' where news and visuals are generated entirely by algorithms without human intervention introduces severe transparency deficits that disrupt the traditional editorial dynamic. As a result, the primary focus of modern media ethics has shifted toward updating deontological codes to mandate clear AI disclosure, drawing a hard line between algorithmic generation and the authentic act of witnessing.

Perspectives of Press Photography Professionals on Artificial Intelligence

The impact of artificial intelligence on press photography has been examined through direct interviews with both photojournalists and editors. These conversations offer valuable insights into the perspectives of professionals in the field, shedding light on their evaluations of AI technologies and the implications for journalistic practice.

Murad Sezer

Born in Germany in 1969, Murad Sezer studied journalism at Istanbul University's Faculty of Communication. Following his graduation, he worked for various media organizations for ten years before joining the Associated Press as a photojournalist in 1996. In 2009, he became the Turkey photo editor for Reuters, where he continues to work.

Sezer has worked in conflict zones including Kosovo, Israel-Palestine, Afghanistan, and Iraq for the Associated Press. He won the Pulitzer Prize in Spot News Photography in 2005 for an image taken in Fallujah in 2004, depicting American soldiers mourning a fallen comrade. He remains the first and only Turkish photographer to have received this award.

Sezer views AI-generated images as short-lived commercial products rather than a threat to press photography. Drawing parallels with the emergence of digital photography, he recalls similar debates that predicted the demise of photojournalism yet the field adapted and evolved. He believes the impact of AI on press photography will be minimal compared to other areas of visual media.

Regarding the future, Sezer acknowledges both positive and negative potential impacts of AI on photojournalism. As with digitization, he suggests that AI could result in the mass production of synthetic images, which might prompt photojournalists to focus on fewer but more meaningful and documentary-oriented projects. In this way, AI could catalyze a return to the core values of photojournalism emphasizing storytelling and human experience.

Sezer does not consider AI-generated images to have documentary value, viewing them instead as imitations of reality. In his opinion, simulations can never replace authentic photojournalistic moments that require physical presence and real-time witnessing. As he succinctly states, "You can create an image of a traffic accident, but not the traffic accident," or "You can visualize a war, but not the war."

To prevent AI-generated visuals from being mistaken for authentic press photographs, Sezer suggests embedding visible marks such as a copyright symbol or AI disclaimer that would display warnings when opened in software. However, he warns that these measures alone may not be enough, as some will undoubtedly attempt to market AI images as genuine.

At Reuters, Sezer emphasizes the principle of trust in photographers. Every staff photographer is expected to adhere to strict internal guidelines, including limitations on Photoshop usage. When acquiring images from external sources or agencies, each photo undergoes a thorough review. This includes checking the exif and metadata to ensure digital consistency, verifying the time and location of capture, and confirming the absence of excessive editing.

Sezer insists that regulatory frameworks for AI-generated visuals are necessary, but places greater emphasis on deterrent mechanisms and professional ethics. He believes that enforcement should rest primarily with professional associations rather than governmental bodies (personal communication, April 22, 2025).

Volkan Furuncu

Volkan Furuncu began his professional career in 2004 and graduated in 2007 from Gazi University's Department of Radio, Television, and Cinema. From 2006 to 2021, he worked as a photojournalist for Anadolu Agency. Between 2016 and 2018, he served as the agency's New York photo correspondent, covering conflict zones and natural disasters in countries such as Libya, Tunisia, and Syria. He currently serves as Deputy Director of Photo News at Anadolu Agency.

Furuncu stated that Anadolu Agency, in accordance with its editorial principles, does not publish images generated or altered by artificial intelligence. He emphasized the need for globally accepted standards for labeling such images. If an AI-generated visual is presented, it must be clearly indicated to the reader through an editorial note. He stressed that AI can now remove or add objects or even fictional individuals within photographs. Therefore, indicating the source of such content is crucial for the reader's proper interpretation and to ensure the ethical responsibility and credibility of the publisher.

Furuncu anticipates that news agencies will not be able to resist technological developments and will eventually have to engage with AI at the very least, to defend against misuse and to protect institutional credibility. He expressed concern about AI systems drawing from publicly available image pools, primarily indexed by Google, raising copyright and ethical issues. He advocates for the development of proprietary AI tools that rely solely on a news agency's internal archive. Such systems, he argues, would prevent copyright violations and establish AI ethics codes that would protect both editors and readers (personal communication, April 19, 2025).

Emrah Gurel

Emrah Gurel graduated from Cumhuriyet University's Faculty of Communication, majoring in Radio and Television. After working for ten years as a photojournalist for Hürriyet Daily News, he joined the Associated Press as a freelance photojournalist, where he is currently active.

Gurel sees AI-generated imagery as a significant threat to journalism, particularly for those directly engaged in the profession. He believes AI, alongside the influence of social media over the past two decades, has accelerated the decline of photojournalism. He notes that AI-generated content has already become prevalent in media, citing examples such as deepfake videos showing imprisoned political leaders speaking in their own voices. Despite lacking documentary value, such images are increasingly accepted by the public.

Traditionally, hand-drawn illustrations filled visual gaps in print media where photography was unavailable such as courtroom proceedings involving high-profile figures. Today, AI-generated visuals are replacing those illustrations. While Gurel does not oppose this practice in principle, he insists that news outlets must bear full responsibility for verifying the accuracy of such visuals. He underscores that any photo lacking exif data or traceable origin should be treated with suspicion.

Gurel explains that the Associated Press does not publish photos lacking exif data or those that have undergone significant editing. He recalls an incident from 2015, when AP declined to publish an image of a downed Russian jet distributed by a local agency, whereas another international agency did only to retract the image 15 minutes later. He asserts that he has never witnessed an AI-generated image used at AP and that truth remains a non-negotiable value at the agency. Even Photoshop usage is strictly controlled.

He further notes that legal frameworks regarding AI imagery are more robust in Western media, while in Turkey, awareness of individual rights remains insufficient. In contrast to Western media outlets, which cannot use images without clearance, Turkish platforms often overlook these obligations. He suggests that asking AI systems to verify the authenticity of suspicious photos may soon become a standard practice.

Gurel concludes by stating his belief that truth inevitably comes to light. He asserts that authentic photography will never lose its value, and that photojournalism, as a profession, will retain its credibility. He expresses concern that agencies creating internal AI image-generation departments may ultimately undermine their own legitimacy (personal communication, April 15, 2025).

CONCLUSION

The integration of artificial intelligence into visual media represents a profound ontological and epistemological shift in the history of press photography. From its inception as a product of chemistry and physics, photography was revered as a mechanical witness what Roland Barthes defined as a "certificate of presence" pointing directly to a lived, historical reality. Today, however, the medium is undergoing a radical transition from the analog capture of light to the algorithmic synthesis of data. It is functioning increasingly as a "mental lens" that visualizes human prompts and cognitive intent rather than documenting objective, external truths. This evolution into a post-photographic era, characterized by generative adversarial networks and hybrid applications, has ruptured the traditional epistemic trust placed in photographic evidence. While these technological advancements offer unprecedented creative latitude and operational efficiency, they simultaneously introduce severe ethical vulnerabilities that threaten the very fabric of democratic discourse and collective memory.

As Jean Baudrillard posits, modern society is increasingly ensnared in a hyperreality where simulations precede and dictate reality. In this context, the rapid proliferation of highly realistic, AI-generated images ranging from fabricated political arrests to synthetic disaster relief efforts has fundamentally destabilized public perception. One of the most critical challenges is the cognitive bias inherent in visual consumption; audiences are biologically and socially conditioned to believe what they see. When confronted with hyper-realistic synthetic media, a pervasive viewer desensitization occurs. This cognitive overload leads to a dangerous skepticism where even authentic, hard-fought photojournalism is dismissed as fake. Therefore, mitigating the risks of deepfakes and algorithmic disinformation requires moving beyond theoretical critique to establish a robust, structured, and actionable framework. The preservation of visual journalism's integrity necessitates coordinated, interdisciplinary interventions from media professionals, editorial institutions, and legislative policymakers.

Actionable Recommendations for Photojournalists and Media Professionals

For practitioners on the ground, navigating the AI landscape demands a steadfast recommitment to the core tenets of documentary ethics, echoing the established guidelines of organizations such as the Society of Professional Journalists (SPJ) and UNESCO. Photojournalists must prioritize the absolute transparency of their digital workflows. It is imperative to strictly delineate between routine, acceptable image optimization (such as basic color correction or cropping) and the synthetic manipulation or generation of visual elements. Furthermore, continuous professional development in digital forensics is no longer optional; it is a fundamental requirement. Journalists must actively equip themselves with the technological literacy required to critically assess the provenance, metadata, and contextual accuracy of user-generated content before it is integrated into the news cycle. Ultimately, as veteran photojournalists affirm, while algorithms can simulate the visual aesthetics of a conflict or a crisis, they cannot replicate the physical presence, empathetic engagement, and moral responsibility of a human witness. The human element of witnessing remains the irreplaceable core of press photography.

Actionable Recommendations for Editors and News Institutions

Newsrooms and media organizations must act as the primary, uncompromising gatekeepers of visual authenticity. Editorial boards are urgently required to establish, publish, and enforce rigorous, zero-tolerance policies regarding the publication of undisclosed or deceptively framed AI-generated imagery. This operational shift involves systematically integrating advanced verification tools such as metadata analysis, reverse image searching protocols, and state-of-the-art AI-detection software into standard daily editorial workflows. Additionally, to mitigate the significant risks of copyright infringement, privacy violations, and the perpetuation of Western-centric cultural biases inherent in public open-source models, news agencies should invest in the development of proprietary, closed-loop AI systems. These internal systems, trained exclusively on the agency's verified historical archives, can provide analytical support without compromising ethical standards. Whenever synthetic media is utilized for illustrative or conceptual purposes, it must be accompanied by explicit, standardized labeling such as permanent digital watermarks, clear editorial disclaimers, and transparent captions to prevent audience deception and short-circuit cognitive biases.

Actionable Recommendations for Policymakers and Regulatory Bodies

On a macro-systemic level, the unrestricted global expansion of deepfake technologies necessitates immediate intervention from policymakers and international regulatory bodies. Addressing this crisis requires the formulation of comprehensive legal frameworks and media laws that govern the creation and distribution of synthetic media. Drawing upon comparative international perspectives, legislation must mandate embedded digital watermarking and cryptographically secure, traceable metadata (such as the Coalition for Content Provenance and Authenticity - C2PA standard) at the hardware and software points of creation. Furthermore, social media platforms must be held legally and ethically accountable for the algorithmic amplification of AI-generated misinformation, requiring them to implement proactive detection and labeling mechanisms. Finally, national education ministries and public broadcasters must launch extensive, long-term media literacy campaigns. These educational initiatives should be strategically designed to demystify the mechanics of digital deception, explaining how AI generates content and how cognitive vulnerabilities are exploited, thereby equipping global citizens with the critical thinking skills necessary to navigate an increasingly hyper-real visual ecosystem.

In conclusion, while artificial intelligence will inevitably continue to transform the technological tools of visual storytelling, the foundational currency of press photography remains entirely unchanged: unwavering public trust. Technology alone cannot dictate the ethics of its application. By proactively implementing stringent ethical oversight, demanding institutional transparency, and establishing robust, cross-disciplinary verification protocols, the journalism ecosystem can successfully defend the boundaries of objective, lived reality against the encroaching tide of synthetic manipulation. The future of press photography relies not on resisting technological progress, but on steadfastly anchoring it to human truth.

REFERENCES

Acemoglu, D., & Restrepo, P. (2018). *Artificial Intelligence, Automation and Work* (NBER Working Paper No. 24196). https://www.nber.org/papers/w24196

Addley, E. (2023, November 1). AI named most notable word of 2023 by Collins dictionary. *The Guardian*. https://www.theguardian.com/technology/2023/nov/01/ai-named-most-notable-word-of-2023-by-collins-dictionary

Alay, D. (2024). Kişiselleştirilmiş tıp için dijital ikiz: Sistematik derleme. *Sağlık Profesyonelleri Araştırma Dergisi*, *6*(1), 28–43. DOI: 10.57224/jhpr.1342561

Allyn, B. (2022, March 16). Deepfake video of Zelensky could be tip of the iceberg in info war, experts warn. *NPR*. https://www.npr.org/2022/03/16/1087062648/deepfake-video-zelenskyy-experts-war-manipulation-ukraine-russia

Anlen, Ş., & Llorente, R. V. (2024, April 15). Spotting the deepfakes in this year of elections: How AI detection tools work and where they fail. *Reuters Institute for the Study of Journalism*. https://reutersinstitute.politics.ox.ac.uk/news/spotting-deepfakes-year-elections-how-ai-detection-tools-work-and-where-they-fail

Aşık, F., Yıldız, A., Kılınç, S., Aytekin, N., Adalı, R., & Kurnaz, K. (2023). Yapay zekânın eğitime etkileri. [JSHSR]. *International Journal of Social and Humanities Sciences Research*, *10*(98), 2100–2107. DOI: 10.5281/zenodo.8307107

Bajac, Q. (2004). *Karanlık odanın sırları fotoğrafın icadı*. Yapı Kredi Yayınları.

Bakın, A. (2023). Dijitalleşmenin emek gücü üzerinde etkileri ve dijital emek. In E. Kaan

Barthes, R. (1996). *Camera lucida*. Altıkırkbeş Yayınları.

Baudrillard, J. (2024). *Simülakrlar ve simülasyon*. Doğu Batı Yayınları.

Brown, M. C. (2023, September 27). Photo Vogue Festival 2023 talks: 90 Miles-AI reportage illustration. *Photo Vogue*. https://www.vogue.com/article/photovogue-festival-2023-talks-90-miles-ai-reportage-illustration

Brynjolfsson, E., & McAfee, A. (2014). *The second machine age*. W. W. Norton & Company.

Cambridge Dictionary. (n.d.). *Artificial intelligence*. https://dictionary.cambridge.org/dictionary/english-turkish/artificial-intelligence

Cambridge Dictionary. (n.d.). *Disinformation*. https://dictionary.cambridge.org/dictionary/english/disinformation

Çetin, M., & Baklavacı, G. Y. (2024). Endüstri 4.0 perspektifinde yapay zekânın eğitimde uygulanabilirliği ile ilgili öğretmen görüşlerinin incelenmesi. *İstanbul Ticaret Üniversitesi Girişimcilik Dergisi*, 7(14), 1–21. https://doi.org/DOI: 10.55830/tje.1404165

Cetinic, E., & She, J. (2022). Understanding and creating art with AI: Review and outlook. *ACM Transactions on Multimedia Computing Communications and Applications*, *18*(4), 1–21. DOI: 10.1145/3475799

Chesney, B., & Citron, D. (2019). Deep Fakes: A Looming Challenge for Privacy, Democracy, and National Security. *California Law Review*, *107*(6), 1753–1820. https://www.jstor.org/stable/26891938

Collen, K. (2014). L'économie de la photographie de presse et son évolution paradigmatique. *Press photography*, 121–134. https://doi.org/DOI: 10.4000/books.pur.50377

Coşkun, F., & Gülleroğlu, H. D. (2021). Yapay zekanın tarih içindeki gelişimi ve eğitimde kullanılması. [JFES]. *Ankara University Journal of Faculty of Educational Sciences*, *54*(3), 947–966. DOI: 10.30964/auebfd.916220

Cruz, E. (2016). *Digital photography studies.*, DOI: 10.1007/978-3-658-08460-8_12-1

Demirhan, A., Kılıç, Y. A., & İnan, G. (2010). Tıpta yapay zeka uygulamaları. *Yoğun Bakım Dergisi*, *9*(1), 31–41.

Deniz, S., & Bağçeci, B. (2025). Kavramdan sınıfa: Yapay zekânın keşfi ve eğitime yansımaları. *Elektronik Sosyal Bilimler Dergisi*, *24*(1), 576–596. DOI: 10.17755/esosder.1554996

Diakopoulos, N. (2019). *Automating the news: How algorithms are rewriting the media.* Harvard University Press. DOI: 10.4159/9780674239302

Dizikes, P. (2024, December 6). Daron Acemoglu: What do we know about the economics of AI? *MIT News*. https://economics.mit.edu/news/daron-acemoglu-what-do-we-know-about-economics-ai

Dube, B. (2017). To lie or not to lie. In Copeland, B. J. (Ed.), (pp. 44–63)., DOI: 10.4018/978-1-5225-2095-5.ch003

Dupre, M. H. (2023, November 27). Sports Illustrated published articles by fake, AI generated writers. *Futurism*. https://futurism.com/sports-illustrated-ai-generated-writers

European Parliament. (2024). Artificial Intelligence Act. *European Union.*

Farid, H. (2022). Creating, Using, Misusing, and Detecting Deep Fakes. *Journal of Online Trust & Safety*, *1*(4). Advance online publication. DOI: 10.54501/jots.v1i4.56

Fineman, M. (2012). *Faking it: Manipulated photography before Photoshop*. Yale University Press.

Floridi, L., Cowls, J., Beltrametti, M., Chatila, R., Chazerand, P., Dignum, V., Luetge, C., Madelin, R., Pagallo, U., Rossi, F., Schafer, B., Valcke, P., & Vayena, E. (2018). AI4People-An ethical framework for a good AI society: Opportunities, risks, principles, and recommendations. *Minds and Machines*, *28*(4), 689–707. DOI: 10.1007/s11023-018-9482-5 PMID: 30930541

Gaines, R. J. (1993, December 2). From the managing editor: Nov. 18, 1993. *Time*. https://time.com/archive/6724351/from-the-managing-editor-nov-18-1993/

Gelbart, H. (2023, February 14). TikTok ve Twitter'da deprem yardımı dolandırıcılıkları. *BBC Türkçe*. https://www.bbc.com/turkce/articles/c2v1q9q5gqzo

Glatz, C. (2024, June 14). World needs urgent political action to guide AI, pope tells G7. *United States Conference of Catholic Bishops*. https://www.usccb.org/news/2024/world-needs-urgent-political-action-guide-ai-pope-tells-g7

Göde, A. (2024). Halk sağlığında yapay zekâ (YZ) kullanımı ve geleceği. *TOGÜ Erbaa Sağlık ve Yönetim Dergisi*, *1*(1), 1–16.

Gregory, S. (2023, October 9). When AI can fake reality, who can you trust? *TED*. https://www.ted.com/talks/sam_gregory_when_ai_can_fake_reality_who_can_you_trust

Groh, M., Epstein, Z., Firestone, C., & Picard, R. (2022). Deepfake detection by human crowds, machines, and machine-informed crowds. *Proceedings of the National Academy of Sciences of the United States of America*, *119*(1), e2110013119. DOI: 10.1073/pnas.2110013119 PMID: 34969837

Gülaçtı, İ. E., & Kahraman, M. E. (2021). The impact of artificial intelligence on photography and painting in the post-truth era and the issues of creativity and authorship. *Medeniyet Sanat Dergisi*, *7*(2), 243–270. DOI: 10.46641/medeniyetsanat.994950

Hausken, L. (2024). Photorealism versus photography. AI-generated depiction in the age of visual disinformation. *Journal of Aesthetics & Culture*, *16*(1), 2340787. Advance online publication. DOI: 10.1080/20004214.2024.2340787

Higgins, E. [@EliotHiggins]. (2023, March 20). Making pictures of Trump getting arrested while waiting for Trump's arrest. *X (Twitter)*. https://twitter.com/EliotHiggins/status/1637927681734987777

Instagram. (2025, May 6). *Michael Christopher Brown,* https://www.instagram.com/p/CqniSVjrj0h/?img_index=10

Ittefaq, M., Zain, A., Arif, R., Ala-Uddin, M., Ahmad, T., & Iqbal, A. (2023). Global news media coverage of artificial intelligence (AI): A comparative analysis of frames, sentiments, and trends across 12 countries. *Telematics and Informatics, 82*, 102223. DOI: 10.1016/j.tele.2024.102223

Janzczuk, H. (2024). Risks of using artificial intelligence in creating the image of politicians and in electoral campaigns. *Ad Americam: Journal of American Studies, 25*, 10. DOI: 10.12797/AdAmericam.25.2024.25.10

Jordan, M. I., & Mitchell, T. M. (2015). Machine learning: Trends, perspectives, and prospects. *Science, 349*(6245), 255–260. DOI: 10.1126/science.aaa8415 PMID: 26185243

Karadağ, C. (2024, January 2). Yapay zeka ürünü fotoğrafına verilen ödülü reddeden Alman sanatçıya göre bu alan tartışılmalı. *Anadolu Ajansı*. https://www.aa.com.tr/tr/bilim-teknoloji/yapay-zeka-urunu-fotografina-verilen-odulu-reddeden-alman-sanatciya-gore-bu-alan-tartisilmali/3097861

Maloy, A. F., & Branigin, A. (2023, March 27). An AI generated Balenciaga pope fooled us all. How much does it matter? *The Washington Post*. https://www.washingtonpost.com/lifestyle/2023/03/27/pope-francis-coat-puffy-white-ai-fake/

Marconi, F. (2020). *Newsmakers: Artificial Intelligence and the Future of Journalism*. Columbia University Press., https://www.jstor.org/stable/10.7312/marc19136 DOI: 10.7312/marc19136

Miles, M. (2020). Introduction: Photography's publics. In *Photography's Publics* (pp. 1–17). https://doi.org/DOI: 10.4324/9781003103721-1

Nightingale, S. J., & Farid, H. (2022). AI-synthesized faces are indistinguishable from real faces and more trustworthy. *Proceedings of the National Academy of Sciences of the United States of America, 119*(8), e2120481119. DOI: 10.1073/pnas.2120481119 PMID: 35165187

Perrigo, B. (2023, March 28). How to spot an AI-generated image like the Balenciaga pope. *Time*. https://time.com/6306135/ai-generated-images-balenciaga-pope

Popotas, D., & Kalyva, A. (2023, February 27). Ο βετεράνος διασώστης, γιος του θρυλικού ποδοσφαιριστή Μπάμπη Κοτρίδη που «άγγιξε» τη Μαντόνα. *Protothema*. https://www.protothema.gr/greece/article/1342350/o-veteranos-diasostis-gios-tou-thrulikou-podosfairisti-babi-kotridi-pou-aggixe-ti-madona/

Prompt Folder. (n.d.). https://promptfolder.com/u/mikechapel/gslpuvev/

Ritchin, F. (2012). *Fotoğraftan sonra.* Espas Sanat Kuram Yayınları.

Rosenblum, N. (1997). *A world history of photography.* Abbeville Press.

Russell, S., & Norvig, P. (2021). *Artificial intelligence: A Modern Approach.* Prentice Hall.

Sarı, F. (2021, September). "Cahit Arf' in makine düşünebilir mi ve nasıl düşünür?" Adlı makalesi üzerine bir çalışma. *TRT Akademi*, 6(13). https://dergipark.org.tr/en/download/article-file/1861642

Savvidis, P. (2023, February 10). The image of a Greek rescuer holding a Turkish child has gone viral-who created it? *Greek City Times.* https://greekcitytimes.com/2023/02/10/greek-rescuer-turkish-child-viral/

Sontag, S. (1999). *Fotoğraf üzerine* (Akçakaya, R., Trans.). Altıkırkbeş Yayınları.

Sontag, S. (2004). *Başkalarının acısına bakmak* (Akınhay, O., Trans.). Agora Kitaplığı.

Strubell, E., Ganesh, A., & McCallum, A. (2019). Energy and policy considerations for deep learning in NLP. *arXiv preprint arXiv:1906.02243.* https://arxiv.org/abs/1906.02243 DOI: 10.18653/v1/P19-1355

Strukov, V. (2020). Digital journalism: Toward a theory of journalistic practice in the twenty-first century. In *Digital Journalism* (pp. 155–170). https://doi.org/DOI: 10.1007/978-3-030-42855-6_9

Taylor, L. (2023, May 2). Amnesty International criticised for using AI-generated images. *The Guardian.* https://www.theguardian.com/world/2023/may/02/amnesty-international-ai-generated-images-criticism

TDK. (2024). (April 23, 2025). 2024 yılının kelimesi, kavramı "kalabalık yalnızlık". *Türk Dil Kurumu.* https://tdk.gov.tr/icerik/basindan/2024-yilinin-kelimesi-kavrami-kalabalik-yalnizlik/

TDK. (n.d.). *Dezenformasyon. Türk Dil Kurumu.* https://sozluk.gov.tr/ (Accessed April 25, 2025).

TDK. (n.d.). *Manipülasyon. Türk Dil Kurumu.* https://sozluk.gov.tr/ (Accessed April 29, 2025).

Terranova, A. (2023, April 26). How AI imagery is shaking photojournalism. *Blind-magazine.* https://blind-newsletter.beehiiv.com/p/ai-imagery-shaking-photojournalism

Túñez-López, J. M., Fieiras-Ceide, C., & Vaz-Álvarez, M. (2021). Impact of artificial intelligence on journalism: Transformations in the company, products, contents, and professional profile. *Communicatio Socialis*, *34*(1), 177–193. DOI: 10.15581/003.34.1.177-193

Ufarte-Ruiz, M.-J., Murcia-Verdú, F.-J., & Túñez-López, J.-M. (2023). Use of artificial intelligence in synthetic media: First newsrooms without journalists. *El Profesional de la Información*, *32*(2), e320203. Advance online publication. DOI: 10.3145/epi.2023.mar.03

UNEP. (2024, September 21). AI has an environmental problem. Here's what the world can do about that. *United Nations Environment Programme*. https://www.unep.org/news-and-stories/story/ai-has-environmental-problem-heres-what-world-can-do-about

UNEP. (2024, September 21). *Artificial Intelligence (AI) end-to-end: The Environmental Impact of the full AI lifecycle needs to be comprehensively assessed - Issue Note*. https://wedocs.unep.org/bitstream/handle/20.500.11822/46288/AI-Environmental-Impact-Issues-Note.pdf?sequence=3&isAllowed=y

Uren, C. (2025, May 3). ABD Başkanı'nın yeni papa olması mümkün mü? *Euronews*. https://tr.euronews.com/2025/05/03/beyaz-saray-trumpi-papa-yapti-yapay-zeka-uretimi-gorsel-interneti-salladi

Vosoughi, S., Roy, D., & Aral, S. (2018). The spread of true and false news online. *Science*, *359*(6380), 1146–1151. DOI: 10.1126/science.aap9559 PMID: 29590045

Walker, C. S. (2023). (March 27, 2023). We spoke to the guy who created the viral AI image of the Pope that fooled the world. *Buzzfeed News*. https://www.buzzfeednews.com/article/chrisstokelwalker/pope-puffy-jacket-ai-midjourney-image-creator-interview

WITNESS. (n.d.). *Deepfakes rapid response force*. https://www.gen-ai.witness.org/deepfakes-rapid-response-force/

X. (2023, March, 21). *Elliot Higgins Bsky Social*. https://x.com/EliotHiggins/status/1637927681734987777

X. (2024, February 16). *Nervana Mahmod* Twitter. https://x.com/Nervana_1/status/1623742038716960768?ref_src=twsrc%5Etfw%7Ctwcamp%5Etweetembed%7Ctwterm%5E1623742038716960768%7Ctwgr%5E4b54469e6db7943981dab43b4906b931f86ccaee%7Ctwcon%5Es1_&ref_url=https%3A%2F%2Fwww.malumatfurus.org%2Fyunanistan-turkiye-deprem-yardimi%2F

X. (2024, February 18). *Defence Intelligence of Ukraine*. https://x.com/DI_Ukraine/status/1499157365937119235?ref_src=twsrc%5Etfw%7Ctwcamp%5Etweetembed%7Ctwterm%5E1499157365937119235%7Ctwgr%5E%7Ctwcon%5Es1_&ref_url=https%3A%2F%2Fwww.vice.com%2Fen%2Farticle%2F93bmda%2Fhacked-news-channel-and-deepfake-of-zelenskyy-surrendering-is-causing-chaos-online

X. (2025, May 3). *The White House,* https://x.com/WhiteHouse/status/1918502592335724809

X. (2025, May 4). *The White House,* https://x.com/WhiteHouse/status/1919053040734072844

ADDITIONAL READING

Batchen, G. (1997). *Burning with Desire: The Conception of Photography. MIT Press. Azoulay, A. (2008).* The Civil Contract of Photography. Zone Books.

Benjamin, W. (2008). *The Work of Art in the Age of Its Technological Reproducibility, and Other Writings on Media*. Harvard University Press. DOI: 10.2307/j.ctv1nzfgns

Brunton, F., & Nissenbaum, H. (2015). *Obfuscation: A User's Guide for Privacy and Protest*. MIT Press. DOI: 10.7551/mitpress/9780262029735.001.0001

Crawford, K., & Paglen, T. (2021). *Atlas of AI: Power, Politics, and the Planetary Costs of Artificial Intelligence*. Yale University Press.

Manovich, L. (2001). *The Language of New Media*. MIT Press.

Mitchell, W. J. T. (1994). *Picture Theory: Essays on Verbal and Visual Representation*. University of Chicago Press.

Ritchin, F. (2009). *After Photography*. W. W. Norton & Company.

Rubinstein, D., & Sluis, K. (2013). Notes on the Margins of Metadata: Photography in the Digital Condition. In Media-N (special issue). Intellect.

Steyerl, H. (2012). *The Wretched of the Screen*. Sternberg Press.

KEY TERMS AND DEFINITIONS

AI Art: *AI Art* is a form of artistic creation where artificial intelligence algorithms generate visual outputs. These algorithms analyze extensive datasets of existing art and styles to create new works. AI challenges conventional notions of creativity by blurring the lines between human and machine-generated art.

AI Ethics: *AI Ethics* examines the moral implications of AI technologies. It addresses concerns about bias, privacy, accountability, and societal impacts, ensuring AI systems align with human values such as fairness, transparency, and respect for rights. AI ethics plays a crucial role in guiding the development and use of AI to ensure responsible applications.

Artificial Intelligence (AI): *Artificial Intelligence* refers to computer systems designed to perform tasks that traditionally require human intelligence. These tasks include reasoning, learning from experience, language understanding, and decision-making. AI is employed across various fields, such as healthcare, robotics, and media, enabling machines to learn and adapt autonomously.

Ethics: *Ethics* involves moral principles that guide individuals and organizations in determining what is right and wrong. In professional fields, ethics ensures decisions are made with fairness, responsibility, and respect, safeguarding trust and integrity within society and specific professions, such as journalism and art.

Photography: *Photography* is the process of capturing and creating images using light-sensitive materials or digital sensors. It has evolved from film-based methods to digital technology, facilitating an easy and instantaneous way to produce, store, and share visual content across various media, from art to journalism.

Press Photography Ethics: *Press Photography Ethics* refers to the standards and moral guidelines governing the work of press photographers. This includes maintaining truthfulness in image representation, respecting privacy, avoiding manipulation, and ensuring fairness in how subjects are depicted. Press photography ethics ensure that images serve as accurate visual documentation of events.

Press: Photography: *Press Photography* is the practice of capturing images for news media outlets. It serves to visually document public events and convey information to audiences, often accompanying articles in newspapers, magazines, or online platforms. Press photography plays a pivotal role in shaping public opinion by providing visual evidence of significant events.

APPENDIX

Visual References

1. General Grant: https://www.loc.gov/item/2007681056/
2. Gordon Gahan's original photograph – National Geographic, February 1982 https://medium.com/engl462/visual-deceptions-national-geographic-and-the-pyramids-of-giza-3fee6d448d0d
3. Time Cover: https://content.time.com/time/covers/0,16641,19931118,00.html
4. Trump in Prison: https://twitter.com/EliotHiggins/status/1637927681734987777
5. Trump's Newsweek Cover: https://www.newsweek.com/2022/07/29/will-trump-do-time-what-it-would-take-convict-former-president-1726054.html
6. Pope in Puffer Jacket: https://x.com/PopBase/status/1639686512295149573
7. Explosion at the Pentagon: https://arstechnica.com/information-technology/2023/05/ai-generated-image-of-explosion-near-pentagon-goes-viral-sparks-brief-panic/
8. Panagiotis Kotridis: https://www.facebook.com/panagiotis.kotridis/posts/10229437514300494?ref=embed_post
9. Michael Christopher Brown, 90 Miles https://njp.no/en/2025/njp-master-class-shocking-the-world-with-ai-generated-press-photographs/
10. Amnesty International: https://tr.tradingview.com/news/cointelegraph:3a23ec40cd9e8:0/

Chapter 8
Artificial Intelligence and Artistic Creativity: Redefining the Boundaries of Photography and Visual Expression

Muhammad Usman Tariq
http://orcid.org/0000-0002-7605-3040
Abu Dhabi University, UAE & University College Cork, Ireland

ABSTRACT

Artificial intelligence quickly transforms the landscape of photography and visual representation, seeking creativity and traditional ideas from artists. In this chapter, we will discover how AI technology can help not only roles from generation algorithms to neural networks but also actively create artistic content that redefines the role of human artists. Through tools such as AI-generated images, style transmission, and automated processing, photographers and visual artists are pushing beyond what is possible with visual storytelling. These advancements open new ways of creativity and raise essential questions about originality, aesthetic values, and ethical responsibility. Investigating practical applications and artistic collaboration with AI highlights the opportunities and tensions arising in the interface between technology and ART. Ultimately, AI is not a replacement for creativity, but a redesign of artistry reviews, defining artistic intentions, visual authors, and developing the language of photography in the digital age.

DOI: 10.4018/979-8-3373-2230-8.ch008

INTRODUCTION

One of the most profound transformations in the history of creative activity is the emergence of artificial intelligence (AI) in the art world. Art has long been associated with human commitment based on feelings, perceptions, and cultural significance. Nevertheless, with the task of providing images, music, writing verses, and editing aesthetic experiences, the boundaries of human creativity and AI mechanical intelligence are increasingly ambiguous. It is not as conspicuous as visual arts, where AI tools not only transform the workflow but also get involved in the process of generating art. Since the development of generative adversarial networks (GAN) that create surreal, dreamy photos to the machine control of aesthetic choice, the production process has been characterized in terms of scope and being. This development challenges us to ask what creativity is. This poses the question of the significance of authors, originality, and the intent of art in an era where machines can be taught to perceive the entire meaning of AI (Xu et al., 2025). Technology has never left out the fine art of production, even in transactions involving art. Since the invention of printing presses, camera obscura, oil paint, and airbrushing in portraits, all these new mediums have altered the aesthetics, availability, and ontology of art. For example, the invention of cameras in the 19 th century was received with joy and doubt. On the one hand, democratized photography has widened the scope of the artist's visual vocabulary. Meanwhile, there is an existential debate about the future of painting, the role of artists, and the authenticity of mechanically reproduced images. In his pioneering essay, Walter Benjamin argued that reproducible media were artworks from a mechanical reproductive age, where reproducible media changed the aura of the work's unique presence and historical circumstances. Today, similar fears permeate cultural conversations with AI-generated images that arise from code rather than human hands or lenses. In the arithmetic context, the Dadaists experimented with randomness. Recently, digital artists have used algorithms, codes, and machine learning as creative tools to shape what is now recognized as AI art.

In contrast to previous digital tools that required human input for all aesthetic decisions, AI systems are now trained on large data records. They are now autonomously generated with content based on the learning patterns. These systems often replicate styles and create new combinations that even the developers do not expect. In photographs, AI can improve the resolution, correctly swap out the sky, remove unnecessary elements, and simulate analog aesthetics with incredible accuracy. Programs such as DALL-E, Midjourney, and RunwayML allow users to generate complex visual constructs through simple text requests, bridging the gap between conceptualization and execution. These skills fundamentally change the creative process. The act of creating art is not about technical skills. However, more curatorial decisions lead to a reevaluation of what it means. Traditional definitions of creativity include intentionality, self-confidence, and the ability to think critically (Tsao & Nogues, 2024). These are all traits that AI does not possess, at least in its current form. AI systems use statistical inference, pattern recognition, and learning relationships. They have no consciousness or motivation. However, your output often reflects the complexity and appeal of human creativity. This has led some theorists to propose more functional or relational definitions of creativity that focus on the work's acceptance and novelty rather than the creator's internal conditions. From this perspective, when AI-generated images stimulate thoughts or emotions that provide aesthetic innovation, they can be seen as creative, regardless of their lack of sense. Who is the programmer artist who designed the algorithm, the user who entered the command prompt, the data record trained with AI, or the machine itself? The art generated by AI often results from a joint interaction between several active human and non-human ingredients. The artist is a co-curator and choreographer of computer processes, not an individual aid in the form. This reconstruction of the author is a very challenging idea of personality, originality, and genius, which has long supported the world of art. There has also been the introduction of legal and ethical dilemmas. Is it possible to safeguard AI-created works through copyright? Would there be artists whose styles have been scoured out by the training data records? What will happen to the labor market when machines can create artificial art out of handicrafts? These are scholarly issues that affect creative economics, artistic professions, and cultural establishments.

Photographers and visual artists are facing the prospects and pressures of AI integration. Simultaneously, AI has the potential to be a helpful creative ally capable of broadening the vision of the artist and allowing them to implement fresh visuals and forms. With the help of AI, photographers can recreate impossible light, build mixed reality, or play with time and space in an unrealistic way. Abstraction and textures created by machine learning can be experimented with by visual artists in the form of an interactive installation. Such an improvement has made analog and digital, genuine, artificial, deliberate, and spontaneous indistinct. It permits a more fluid, repetitive, and playful analysis of creative activities. Meanwhile, the ubiquity and accessibility of AI tools can create aesthetic saturation. If someone can create high-quality photos with some keyboard attacks, what distinguishes the artist's work from an algorithmic work? How do you develop a unique voice and style in an environment where visual production is increasingly automated and algorithmically optimized? Even though photographers manipulate perspectives, frames, and contexts, photography has long been regarded as a medium of realism. The use of AI-generated images makes the gap between documentation and production even more challenging. Deepfakes, synthetic media, and algorithmically created scenes test the viewer's ability to trust what they see. This can open up many opportunities for surrealist, speculative fiction, and conceptual experiments in an artistic context.

However, in the context of journalism or documentaries, it raises serious ethical concerns. Therefore, artists working with AI must navigate complex realms of responsibility, transparency, and audience awareness.

Not only do you need to think about what you create, but you also need to think about how working in a broader ecosystem is important and how you misinform it. They use AI as a tool rather than an alternative, studying its creative possibilities and criticizing its limitations. Some artists integrate machine errors and biases into their work as comments on data policies. Others use AI to explore identity, memory, and embodiment in new ways. A movement grows in the direction of "slow AI." It emphasizes intention, reflection, and resistance to the rapid pace of algorithmic production of knowledge. This approach does not view artists as engineers or technophiles, but as essential conversation partners who not only deal with AI to create art, but also ask what art can be done in a world increasingly shaped by inhuman intelligence. What is essential as an art form in the machine-mediated age? How should curators contextualize their work after using AI? These questions demonstrate a broader shift in the field of culture through traditional binary fields of human versus humans. It is similar to machines, digital, real, or artificial. Instead, we enter the period of convergence. During this period, creativity is distributed through human and arithmetic component networks, and the limits of authorship, representation, and aesthetic value are constantly negotiated. Technological determinism: The idea that technology has a linear and inevitable impact on society must be resisted. Instead, artists, scientists, and cultural workers must recognize that AI does not merely determine the future of creativity but also shares in the decisions they make in designing, using, and interpreting these technologies (Chen, 2024). AI mirrors our collective imagination, shaped by the data we supply, the purposes we assign it, and the values we embed in the algorithm. Therefore, it reflects technological innovation and the historical dynamics of social priorities, narratives, and power. Therefore, the profession of AI in the arts requires critical literacy, cultural sensitivity, and openness to correct the meaning of its creation. Just as photography once challenged painting to reconsider its purpose, AI challenges artists to reconsider their art concerning its possibilities rather than being associated with the outdoors. It asks: What can an artist do? What new forms of expression, connections, and meanings may arise from this cooperation? How can we confirm that this technological transformation will serve innovation and humanity positively? We can move forward by including these questions in curiosity, criticism, and care. Art is an essential space for exploring, reflecting, and reinventing the meaning of creativity in a changing world. Figure 1 provides overview of technological disruptions in art history.

Figure 1. Evolution of Artistic Tools and Disruption Points

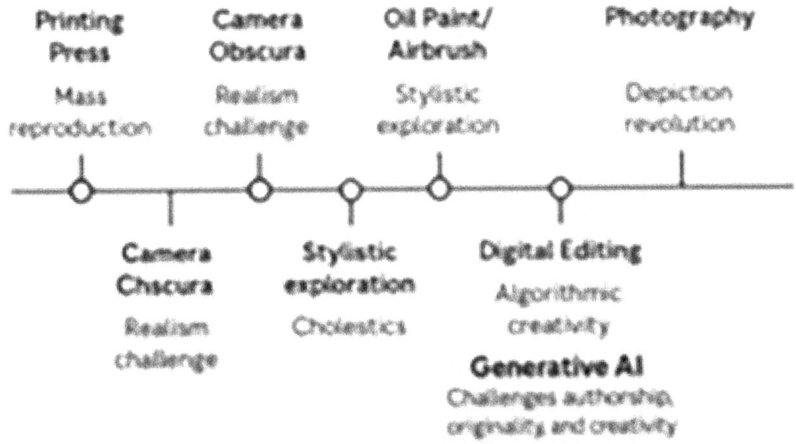

THE ROLE OF AI IN DIGITAL PHOTOGRAPHY AND VISUAL ART

The evolution of AI from mere support tools to positive creative forces redefines the limitations of photography and visual arts, bringing about an earthquake change in technical workflows and artistic imagination. This transformation is driven primarily by neuronal network development, particularly the generation of convolutional networks and deep learning architectures, allowing machines to create and manipulate images with breathtaking detail and expressive reach. These technologies introduced the concept of AI-controlled image locations, where machines improve or automate tasks and actively generate original visual content that mimics or surpasses traditional artistic processes (Ghose et al., 2024). Through machine learning, trained on huge data records of photographs, AI systems can now compile landscapes, portraits, abstract designs, and surreal scenes that challenge traditional aesthetic boundaries. While artists and technologists work together to study new styles, they also question the nature of writing, creativity, and artistic intentions in the digital age. In a typical GAN setup, two neural networks, generators and discriminators, participate in a dynamic and controversial process. The generator creates photos, and the discriminator evaluates their credibility in actual photos. Over time, this interaction improves the ability of generators to generate visuals that are less distinct from human-generated content. This led to artworks ranging from hyper-realistic portraits to fantastic dream scenery to fantastic dream scenery presented in the gallery. These generative models allow for the replication of styles and enable human artists to fuse various visual elements in a way that is almost impossible to imagine without help (Tariq, 2025).

The resulting images contain unpredictable elements and innovative creative features that further blur the boundaries between artificial and human-generated images. The AI-powered photo editing platform allows users to quickly smooth skin, adapt light, remove errors, and improve color with an accuracy that is almost creepy. Once recycled to a professional domain, amateur photographers can access them with a few clicks, thanks to platforms like Adobe Photoshop's AI-based tools and mobile applications with integrated intelligent filters. These innovations optimize workflows and democratize access to high-quality visual productions. Traditional classification requires a differentiated understanding of color, saturation, contrast, and mood. Today, AI systems can analyze thousands of film references, learn color relationships, and apply consistent evaluation schemes to photographs and videos (Ranjan et al., 2024). These tools are especially valuable for advertising, fashion, and social media content creators, where visual consistency and emotional impact are paramount. Similarly, the transmission technology style that allows images to take on different visual characteristics has become popular among digital art creators. These algorithms can turn simple photographs into impressionistic paintings and reproduce color palettes and brush strokes by Van Gogh, Munch, and Picasso. The resulting image is not just a filter. However, an algorithmic reinterpretation of new interpretations, combined with another style that challenges the image's content and the boundaries of photography, painting, and arithmetic.

This convergence of mechanical learning and creativity is part of a broader phenomenon known as computer creativity. It uses algorithms in autonomous or semi-autonomous products that are traditionally considered artistic or original (Salta & Katsaros, 2024). Creative creativity invites you to see what it means to create something. From a classical perspective, creativity means intention, subjectivity, and emotional depth–all properties that machines naturally lack. However, the results created by AI systems often show characteristics similar to the artistic innovations of human artists, such as originality, aesthetic consistency, and emotional responses. These systems recombine elements from several domains and discover hidden patterns, suggesting an entirely new form. It is important to do this without the biases or creative restrictions that people can impose on the model. For example, AI trained in Baroque architecture, modern sculpture, and abstract photography creates visual hybrids that go against historical classification, opening up creative rooms that have not been previously presented. This ability to remove various influences and reinterpret visual aesthetics has proven to be a valuable tool for artists looking for inspiration or who are beyond the limits of their work. Photos are more than visual records. They are repositories of cultural memories, family heritage, and social identities. Over time, many of these images become worse due to environmental damage, lack of maintenance, or technical issues. Traditional restoration techniques are labor-intensive and require specialized expertise (Erişti & Freedman, 2024). However, AI offers a scalable and remarkably accurate alternative. Deep learning algorithms trained on high-quality image datasets allow AI systems to close missing details, repair and fade tears, and even reconstruct the facial features of old or damaged photos. The result is a revival of an activated picture that preserves the emotional and historical meaning of the original while simultaneously restoring visual clarity and depth. The initial color attempts were based on manual input and subjective interpretations. However, realistic color values can now be predicted based on contextual signs such as duration, lighting conditions, clothing, or the periphery of the subjects. This process allows for more authentic and vibrant reproductions of the past, providing viewers with a more urgent connection to historical events and personal memories. For example, AI-controlled colored photographs of soldiers from World War I, civil rights protests, or trunk hood family portraits evoked new public interest in history and inheritance.

These tools protect your visual story and are more accessible and committed to modern audiences. However, in photography and media, improvement tools are increasingly used to improve images at lower resolutions, remove noise, and remove fine details without the artifacts that are frequently introduced by traditional algorithms. Deep learning-driven super-decomposition techniques can convert grainy pixelated images into high-resolution images, revealing previously invisible textures and details. For photographers, this means restoring details from unexposed recordings, storing images that could otherwise be rejected, and achieving professional results from a modest device. It not only increases workflow efficiency but also enhances creative possibilities. Photographers can grasp and maintain moments under difficult conditions without compromising their quality. This affects artistic integrity, misinformation, privacy, and public trust. The ability to convincingly change and promote visual content requires epistemological assumptions about photography as a true medium. This also raises concerns about consent and authorship (Dursun & Bakan, 2025).

If AI reconstructs the faces of historical figures, who bears the consequences? Suppose that the algorithm creates images based on datasets by artists. Are these artists calculating recognition or compensation or entitled to recognition or compensation? These dilemmas demonstrate the need for legal, ethical, and artistic frameworks to navigate the changing topography of AI-supported visual production (Yadav et al., 2025). Some choose to emphasize the existence of AI in their work and make the process a part of the transparency and conceptual stories. Others oppose or criticize AI through art by using visual subversion, satire, or storm aesthetics to question the idea of mechanical neutrality. Additionally, they employ AI as employees to expand their creative vocabulary and invite them to think differently about form, composition, and meaning. In all these approaches, the key is intentionality itself. AI is not naturally good or bad, or creative or mechanical. It is a powerful, multifaceted tool that reflects the intent, bias, and ideas of its users. Emerging trends show a more intuitive and interactive system that responds to users in real time, adapts to individual aesthetic preferences, and learns from direct engagement rather than static training data. We are moving to an age where the boundaries between artists and audiences, tools, and employees are increasingly blurred in input and output (Siroor & Anita, 2024). This convergence challenges the traditional hierarchies of expertise and opens up new opportunities for participatory, general, and adaptive art. In this landscape, the role of artists is transformed rather than reduced in the traditional sense. Instead of mastering all the technical details, artists become guides, curators, storytellers, and work with intelligent systems to design emotionally resonant, intellectually provocative, and culturally useful experiences.

THE RELATIONSHIP BETWEEN AI AND HUMAN CREATIVITY

The emergence of artificial intelligence as a participant in the creative arts has raised complex and ongoing debates about the nature of creativity, the limitations of cooperation, and the ethical foundations of authorship. As AI systems are developed from elementary tools to highly developed agents capable of generating original works, artists, technologists, and philosophers grapple with basic questions. Is AI an assistant that improves human representation, or will it become an autonomous creator? This request does not provide a simple answer to this question. Instead, it forces a review of the creative processes. In this mode, AI behaves like a highly qualified assistant, allowing artists to focus on high-end conceptual tasks. Many creative people take on this partnership and compare it to the latest brushes and chisels that they use. This collaborative dynamic can be observed in various creative fields. Photographers who use AI to generate unattainable backgrounds or lighting conditions use filmmakers to explore hundreds of aesthetic permutations using storyboards, animations, and machine learning (He, 2024). These tools do not replace the artist's role; they expand it, allowing ideas to be accessed more deeply, faster, and in creative terrain that was previously unreachable. The boundaries between tools and creators have begun to blur, leading to automation. It is no use than independent art. Genetic models, such as GANs, leading language models, and diffusion-based sculptors, can now produce a complete work of art with minimal human intervention. When the user enters an input request, the system generates images, poems, and songs that may not be distinguishable from those created by an experienced person. This raises questions about the value of the resulting work and the role of the person initiating the command prompt. Are the users artists, curators, or moderators of the machine's functions? This question becomes more urgent when AI produces slightly unexpected, beautiful, or deeply moving pieces that evoke emotions and meaning despite being the product of an unpleasant algorithm.

The author's questions will be central here. Traditionally, the author refers to the creative origin. A person who designs ideas, executes forms, and starts working with intention and context is an architect. In the case of AI-generated art, these elements are fragmented (Soreanu 2024). Programmers write code, data records shape the algorithm's learning, models generate output, and users may start the process with minimal input beyond input requests or style preferences. So, who is the author of the resulting work? Did the developer create the model, the user encourage the company to train with AI, or a combination of these actors? Copyright is still based on human author presumptions, but adapting to legal systems worldwide remains challenging. Some jurisdictions have rejected copyright for AI-generated works. Simultaneously, other frameworks assign properties to human agents involved in this process. However, these legal arguments remain behind the reality of technology, leaving artists and creators in a grey realm where recognition and compensation remain uncertain. Can you create a machine? Or is it a remix, imitation, or extrapolation of what it has learned? Critics argue that AI recognizes the key elements of authentic art but does not recognize intentional, subjective experiences. According to this view, AI is generally derived, regardless of how high the output is. Emotions cannot express it, understand the social context of its creation, or engage in the reflexive processes underpinning human artistic growth. Others control creativity, which often includes imitation, variation, and synthesis practices that perform AI at exceptional speeds and widths. From this perspective, it is not within the creator, but the work's effect, novelty, and reaction (Costa, 2024). When AI-generated art moves, challenges, or inspires us, it is worth recognizing, regardless of its origin. Many artists argue that human creativity is not replaced, and that AI opens up new ways of experimenting and expressing. For example, generative models can simulate styles from various historical periods, invent visual cultures, or even simulate entirely new forms of art, which have algorithmic interpretations rather than human memory. Artists can work with these models that reference costs, embed meanings, and use AI as a catalyst rather than as an alternative. In this respect, it is less likely to abandon the author than it would be created in a room where machine intelligence introduces unknown elements. In this sense, AI cannot be considered a competitor but is seen as a vast creative partner that invites people to think differently about form, processes, and possibilities (Tariq, 2025). Figure 2 summarizes that creativity is now a distributed process between humans and machines.

Figure 2. Human–AI Roles in Creative Production

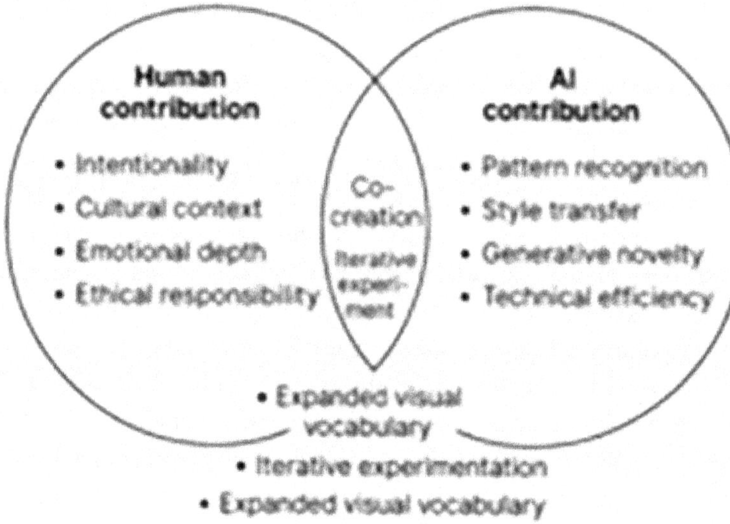

Nevertheless, this new composition of creativity is related to ethical responsibilities. The model is trained on existing data records, allowing it to maintain cultural stereotypes, alienate underrated voices, and replicate the historical injustice embedded in the source material (Zhao, 2024). Artists working for AI should remain aware of these risks and take steps to curate data records, question costs, and be transparent about their use. The ethical use of AI also involves being honest with the audience regarding the origin of the work. Deceptive practices, such as adopting AI-generated content, are central to the value of a work, especially in domains such as journalism, documentary photography, and visual arts. In traditional art theory, an artist's intention is essential for interpreting a work. However, in the case of AI, the intentions are ambiguous. The algorithm has no hopes, visions, or messages regarding communication. The output is formed by the probability, sample, and training data (Chen, 2024). If the final image or composition conveys meaning, is this meaning imposed by the viewer, the rapid giver, or the broader cultural context? This obscurity works against the interpretive scheme. It also presents fresh prospects for audiences to play an active role. Art will be an interlocution of machine generation and human receivers. In such a grand-scale landscape, art has ceased to be about trying to express the soul of the creator but in areas where technology, culture, and fantasy interact. Instead of imitating human vision, they applied AI to request them to investigate what occurs when creativity is not linked to human experience. These works frequently introduce zones of boundaries, intentionally obscuring the boundaries between writers and algorithms, order and chaos, and intent on the one hand, and accident on the other hand. By doing so, they also represent a posthuman aesthetic that challenges the centrality of individual artists and encourages a way of thinking about creativity that is more distributed and networked. Such changes are attributed to a broader cultural trend in terms of collective authors, cooperative media, and open-source collaboration (Petrick, 2024). This implies that AI might affect more art and rehiring than automation and what could be possible (Tariq, 2025).

AI'S INFLUENCE ON AUDIENCE ENGAGEMENT AND PERCEPTION

The artificial intelligence that was developed not only transformed the tools used by the artists but also transformed the experience of art, interpretation, and internalization of the audience in an essential way (Hariyanto et al., 2024). Among the most convincing shifts in contemporary art, the trend towards customization must be noted, according to which visual experience, grounded on behavioral and emotional inclinations, preferences, and personal preferences, is the foundation of AI-regulated systems. There are no more stagnant art objects that will be acclaimed without unanimity among all listeners. Today, the relationship between artwork and audiences has become dynamic, responding quickly and intimately through artificial intelligence system (AIS) interventions. This transformation marks a new chapter in the history of visual culture, with art becoming a developing dialogue rather than a frozen monologue. Museums, galleries, and digital platforms increasingly use machine learning models to recommend works of art based on individuals' unique visual history and works from curated digital exhibits. For example, viewers can enter a digital gallery and present a variety of methods and tasks depending on their vision, reaction times, and facial expressions interpreted in real time. This level of interactivity transforms passive audiences into active participants, giving them a role in the design of artistic experiences and, in some cases, even the art itself. Artists create incomplete or open works until AI interprets each audience's unique input. Such systems can adapt the lighting, mood, style, and narrative using user data. Imagine a painting that morphs its colors and shapes in real time to detect subtle changes in facial expressions or to detect digital installations based on visual stories based on the latest social media activity. These works ignore the author and traditional ideas of durability and instead emphasize co-creation and fleetingness. They challenge the audience to rethink what it is and who it is, positioning the individual not as a mere observer but as a co-author of meaning (Mugubi & Manono, 2024). These environments use AI to respond to audiences and create works of art that grow and develop over time. Integration into AI installations promotes multisensory experiences in which the sound, visual, and spatial dynamics of intelligent systems respond to human presence and behavior. In such a room, art becomes a performance; it responds, fits, and changes according to its audience. These installations blur the boundaries between art and the environment, encouraging audiences to navigate, influence, and, at times, become integral to the artwork. This interactive AI art installation transforms viewers into employees whose gestures, emotions, and decision-making influence the system's behavior. Currently, AI-controlled installations can track patterns for days or months and use the collected data to develop the aesthetic or thematic dimensions of your work. For example, an installation could change the color palette based on seasonal mood patterns detected in the audience or the spatial arrangement to reflect the emotional state of the person interacting with it. This type of interaction deepens the audience's commitment and promotes the local government narrative shaped by many people experiencing it (Manu, 2024).

However, in addition to this approval, there is tension. The use of AI in visual identity also raises ethical and psychological concerns. There is a risk of overcoats where individuals are trapped in idealized digital selfies that differ significantly from their actual appearance. It can reinforce problems related to self-respect, social fear, and physical dysplasia, especially among younger users navigating the digital world (Hutson, 2024). Furthermore, AI-controlled portrait tools are often based on training data that reflect biased standards of beauty, breed, and gender, allowing for the continuation of problematic stereotypes (Tariq, 2025). Decorating AI in a way that brightens the skin, associates facial features, or removes cultural markers will increase homogenized visual norms that undermine diversity and reliability of the results. Correcting these biases requires intentional design, integrated data records, and active dialogue between engineers and the communities affected by these representations. The automated system can now express facial expressions immediately, add optimal lighting conditions to the facial structure, and even generate synthetic subjects. In advertising, entertainment, and editing tasks, these tools increase efficiency and accuracy but complicate the ideas of trust and originality. Is the portrait still authentic if the topic never brings it up, or when his face is improved algorithmically? These questions are particularly urgent in contexts where realism and expression are essential (Rachmawati et al., 2024).

The ability of AI to invent, improve, or change identity requires the conditions and visual authors of a new ethical framework to help the audience interpret what they are seeing. Artists, influencers, and everyday users use AI not only as a utility but also as a tool for storytelling. Through custom filters, A-generated avatars, and personalized visual aesthetics, people build stories that tell of their inner lives, hopes, fears, and dreams. These portraits are not always true in the traditional sense but reflect the truth of effort, imagination, emotional responses, and different kinds of truth. In this way, AI becomes a mirror in which we can become, not like us. It allows you to visualize transformations, arrange new identities, and explore many self-play and deep ways. The personalization of art experiences appeals not only to our audience members but also to our aspirations as individuals with various stories and sensibilities. Interactive installations reflect the need for connectivity, coexistence, and common importance in an increasingly digitized environment. The changes in portraiture highlight the complex nature of 21st-century identity. It is no longer unique; it is fluid, performative, technical, and has a deep identity. It offers new media where old emotions can be expressed and new techniques that allow us to study timeless questions about who we are and how we see each other (Işık, 2024). The challenge and opportunity lie in the intentional use of this power. Artists, curators, technicians, and audiences must work together to help these tools innovate and promote inclusion, empathy, and authentic expression. While navigating this intersection of art, identity, and AI, we are not only focusing on new technologies that redefine the meaning of creation, experience, and ultimately, being human.

CASE STUDIES OF AI IN PHOTOGRAPHY AND VISUAL ART

Artificial intelligence is becoming increasingly influential in redesigning modern photography and visual art landscapes. In particular, AI-generated photos have begun to blur the boundaries between human creativity and artificial production, to help with image locations or to create fully composite images using algorithms in machine learning (Yao, 2025). Artists in this field actively manipulate algorithms in creative ways, rather than simply using AI as a post-process or improvement tool. AI systems learn to generate new compositions that unexpectedly mimic or reinterpret input data by training neural networks with thousands or millions of photographic images. The result is a form of photography that often has the aesthetic properties of human representation, while simultaneously emerging from fundamentally non-human processes. These developments are the long-term definition of what qualifies photographs as authors and have artistic intentions. Artists can start the process by curating training data and fantastic adjustment models. However, the images that occur can even surprise the creators. For example, surprisingly, a generative controversial network, consisting of two neural networks competing to improve costs, creates a viable image that does not exist in reality. Photographers such as Mario Klingemann, Anna Riddler, and Trevor Paglen have used GAN and other techniques for memory learning to generate photographic artwork that studies memory, surveillance, and identity (GÜNAY, 2024). These images can be surreal, hyperreal, or abstract, but they always prompt viewers to consider the intersection of mechanical perspectives and human experiences. AI-generated photographs resemble stunning landscapes and distorted portraits that appear to have been taken with a camera. However, in real life, these moments are not captured. The fantasies of realism in these photographs raise philosophical questions about photographic presentation and truth (Tariq, 2025).

Instead of waiting for the perfect alignment of light, subject, and composition, artists work with AI and interact with algorithms and iterative dialogue (Novakovic & Guga, 2024). They train, test, modify, select output, and navigate through thousands of photos to find emotionally or aesthetically shocking people. This process is similar to traditional photography in terms of processing and curation. However, the manner in which image generation works changes the place of creativity. Although the lenses in AI photography are not optical, they are algorithmically characterized by data, codes, and statistical modeling. Nevertheless, the resulting emotional power of an image can be noticeable. For example, AI-generated portraits can cause a creepy feeling of being deeply human-looking, savvy in traits and expressions, even if they do not belong to anyone. AI technology enriches immersive environments by generating real-time content that adapts to behavior, preferences, and surroundings (Caldeira & Simões, 2024). AR AI improves visual overlays in physical environments, allowing artists to create interactive installations that respond to audience movements, perspectives, and emotional states. These experiences can be personal and transformative, and normal rooms can transform into portals for artistic engagement. With AI, artists can develop artworks in their AR galleries that change the people looking at them or how long someone will stay in a particular area. AI integration ensures that these experiences remain fluid and dynamic, providing various perspectives and meanings in every interaction.

The role of AI in virtual reality is even clearer. AI-led VR art installations can create a complex, immersive, lively, and responsive world. Artists such as Refik Anadol have pioneered an environment where viewers of moving images and sound landscapes are generated in real time by fading data visualizations with AI and spatial computers. These installations blur the physical and digital boundaries, inviting participants to navigate memory, emotion, and perceptual layers. With AI, VR rooms can learn from the behavior of users and adapt the story and surrounding areas based on audience interaction. This ability to personalize and develop artistic experiences is unprecedented and offers a vibrant canvas that changes with each iteration. In this context, AI is not just a background engine but an active storyteller. Traditional linear storytelling gives way to nonlinear adaptive trips, where audiences become co-authors. For example, a VR installation has different visual or auditory elements depending on where the viewer sees and how quickly they move between the rooms. AI algorithms process these data and generate a personalized experience to ensure that the two trips are not the same. This interactivity transforms the viewer's role from a passive observer to a dedicated participant. A new form of artistic thinking is needed, as creators must consider how content is presented and how systems that allow wise interactions are structured (Das & Kundu, 2024). The challenge is to design an AI framework and coordinate autonomy and consistency with a structure that has enough freedom to create surprises and depth while maintaining artistic integrity (Jora et al., 2024).

The impact of these projects extends beyond the arts world and shapes broader cultural and technical conversations (IŞIK, 2024). They raise questions about authorship, reliability, and intellectual property in the age of AI. Who produces the work using the algorithm? What rights do artists have when their styles and data are used in training models? These questions are not only legal or technical but also fundamentally ethical and philosophical. When AI-generated art becomes more common, society must address and protect the assessment and protection of human creativity in an age of collapse. Simultaneously, these projects demonstrate the power of AI to democratize artistic production. Accessible tools and platforms allow artists from various backgrounds to experiment with machine learning, opening up new ways to innovate and express themselves. Early research often relied on the novelty of algorithmic generation, including glitches, surreal distortions, and fantastical ambiguity. Over time, the visual grammar of AI art has become more subtle as artists have gained more control over their tools and techniques. Today's AI works range from photo-controlled landscapes to data-controlled visualizations, narrative installations, and abstract compositions. This diversity reflects the flexibility of machine learning as a medium for research (Tariq, 2025).

AI's maturity as an artistic employee is no longer new; it also shows maturity as an artistic employee who seriously contributes to the visual culture. We enter an age where artistic experiences are not only digital, but intelligent responses are also fast and deeply personalized (Walter, 2025). The challenge for artists and institutions is to use this power to induce human experience, promote inclusiveness, and encourage critical reflection. As we study these new boundaries, it is essential to maintain a dialogue between innovation and humanitarian testing to ensure that the art of the future is impressive and resonates with us emotionally and ethically. Art tools, processes, and experiences are redesigned in ways that question traditional limitations and simultaneously open new and creative opportunities (Jasmer, 2024). Whether you create composite photos, create reaction-fast AR and VR environments, or run groundbreaking AI ART projects, artificial intelligence defines, interprets, and associates. This invites us to rethink our assumptions about the nature of creativity, authorship, and artistic expression in a digitally connected world.

THE FUTURE OF AI IN ARTISTIC CREATIVITY

AI has emerged as an indispensable tool in art and design, which has emerged from specialty computer tools. This metamorphosis has also changed the conventional way of working and enabled artists and designers to study new fields of creativity and efficiency. The AI that was utilized by the designers in the features included the adaptation of the color scheme according to the maximum image size and processing, and more time to spend on creative activities. Specifically, as an AI technology, Artist AI, when developed, is not only an efficiency tool but also a source of inspiration and innovation. By generating outputs that resemble human creativity, these models can learn with large data records and generate photos, music, and poetry. Artists submit these models to their work or curated datasets, which can enable AI to create new work that may be refined or even inspirational. This discovery has resulted in more AI-assisted artworks, in which the distinctions between human and machine creativity are increasingly complex.

In the photos, AI revolutionized the registration and post-processing stages. Recent cameras and smartphones are AI-controlled, making recording easier. One of the most impressive advancements is the smart scene detection. In this scene, the AI can automatically recognize whether to shoot a landscape, portrait, or night scene. Additionally, AI-driven cameras provide highly accurate autofocus, subject tracking, and the identification and perception of faces, animals, and mobile objects. Computer photography techniques, such as improving images with low lighting conditions, creating HDR recordings, and simulating Bokeh effects like DSLR in portrait mode, are also driven by AI. It also addresses the handling of complex settings in the background, even for casual photographers. With AI-powered tools, complex processing tasks such as background deletion, object detection, and even style transmission are automated, which applies image aesthetics to other things. These skills not only save time but also open up new creative opportunities. For example, AI can suggest changes based on the content of the photo, improve color, adapt lighting, cut photos and improve composition. This level of intelligent support allows creative individuals to focus more on the artistic aspects of their work and trust AI to address technical details. AI-controlled curation systems can analyze user preferences and behaviors to prepare visual content for individual tastes (Ching and Mothi, 2025). This personalization extends to various domains, including advertisements that allow AI to create photos using specific demographic features and interior designers. The decoration style of AI tools can be suggested based on a user's aesthetic preferences. Such applications illustrate the possibilities of AI in improving user commitment by providing uniquely tailored content to everyone. These installations use AI to react to real-time interactions and create dynamic experiences that develop based on viewer commitment. For example, the graphics and sounds presented in an installation can be adjusted to the movements, facial expressions, and emotional state of a viewer. Such interactivity involves the audience in the art. It is also actively involved in the work of creation and obliterates the distinction between those who create and those who look at them.

The influence of AI is applied to digital identity and self-expression. With the emergence of social media and online spaces, people have begun to shape digital personas with photographs and avatars. The AI app gives the user an opportunity to produce stylized portraits, apply filters, and produce a purely synthetic image of themselves. However, they also raise concerns about what authenticity and the self mean in the era of AI. The topics of the author, originality, and ethical effects of the created art have not yet been fully discussed. The value of intellectual property and human creativity is questioned once works of art are replicated by taking the approach of human artists. Some believe that AI can underscore classical art. These discussions have underscored the importance of strict guidelines and ethics in the creative industry, where AI is increasingly taking a central role. Advances in AI algorithms will likely lead to more stringent tools for creating surreal images, simulating complex lighting scenarios, and creating immersive virtual environments. Because AI provides a stronger understanding and replicates human aesthetics, we can expect an increase in AI-generated content that cannot be distinguished from human-created content. By integrating AI into AR and VR technologies, the authors can develop interactive environments that adapt to user input in real time, providing a personalized immersive experience. For example, future installations of AI-powered VR could change graphics based on the audience's views and movements, creating a unique experience for each participant. Such innovations redefine how we interact with digital art and open new ways for storytelling and representation (Tariq, 2025).

AI is expected to become an even more critical part of the design and creative processes. Designers increasingly rely on AI for ideas, prototypes, and testing; AI is sometimes used to inform decisions. This collaborative approach allows designers to study a wider range of possibilities and iterate more quickly, leading to more innovative and user-oriented designs. As AI tools become more accessible, we can witness the democratization of design, enabling individuals to create professional-quality visuals without formal training. AI is performing more technical tasks, but creative people must focus on areas where human intuition, empathy, and cultural understanding are paramount. Skills such as storytelling, critical thinking, and ethical thinking are increasingly valuable for ensuring that the human perspective is central to creating meaningful and effective art and design (Tariq, 2025). Finally, the development of AI as a tool for artists and designers has led to a new era of creativity, characterized by human-machine cooperation. Further advances in AI will improve creative efficiency and skills and question the author's perception, originality, and the nature of art. By recruiting AI as a partner in the creative process, artists and designers can unlock new possibilities and shape the future of visual representation. Artists such as Sougwen demonstrate this synergy. Their installation, "spectrum" fuses traditional drawing techniques with A-generated elements to create a dialogue between human and machine creativity. Similarly, Refik Anadol considers data as a livelihood and respiratory material and uses AI to transform huge data records into immersive artworks that question the limits of perception. AI artists can explore unknown expression regions by processing complex calculations and creating new designs. For example, the obvious group's projects encourage brain activity to be designed and experienced in visual images, namely art.

CONCLUSION

Artificial intelligence (AI) has revolutionized the field of photography and other visual arts in multidimensional ways, including the creation of photography, perception, interpretation, and experience. The special capacity of AI to access imitation, portensible, and even visual materials lies at the core of this change, as it challenges long-term premises concerning authorship, originality, and artistic intent. Photographs are no longer limited by physical devices and human agency but are subject to the flux of human resources and machine thinking. This is not merely a technical convergence but also a philosophical one, and it beckons us to reconstruct the meaning of creating, seeing, and working with visual arts in an age that is becoming increasingly algorithmic. This simple manipulation offers numerous features, including automatic picture editing and editing, as well as several more sophisticated generation systems that are used to create portraits and the like. AI-based return software and neural filters have now become tools that can attempt to lighten, fix imperfections, and mimic artistic influences with a certain level of precision and customization that make high-quality visual production democratic. These tools have made it possible to produce impressive images with minimal or no training or machinery by amateur or professional photographers. This has created a more intermingled visual culture.

In this culture, barriers to entry have been reduced, and the boundaries between professional and amateur productions are becoming increasingly blurred. These technologies allow machines to learn from a huge dataset using visual information and generate original images that look realistic or hyperstylized, depending on the training and requests. Artists can now manipulate AI systems by supplying them with thematic concepts and stylistic parameters. This allows the system to generate new visual outputs. This process seeks the author's traditional ideas, as artworks emerge not from a unique vision but from a dialogue between human intention and algorithmic interpretation. Consequently, the creative process has evolved from direct manipulation to curation, raising new questions about control, agency, and artistic identity. By presenting previously invisible patterns of visual data and simulations of perspectives that differ from human vision, AI creates images that exceed the limits of perception. The aesthetics produced by this machine have images of clearly non-human quality, often hyperreal, fantastical, or abstract, challenging the audience to rethink realism and beauty.

In some cases, AI-generated visuals provide a new lens for examining sociocultural, environmental, or psychological states, providing artists with tools to communicate the importance of previously unreachable methods. Therefore, AI not only improves creativity but also changes language and expands the visual vocabulary that artists and viewers can use. Some fear that AI will drive human creators away. However, others argue that they can expand their skills and focus on the conceptual and strategic aspects of artistic production. This augmentation could catalyze the artist's new role as a creative director, machine version curator, or an interdisciplinary employee who integrates technology into other forms of representation. Furthermore, the ability of AI to generate several iterations of concepts with speed allows artists to explore greater freedom and variations and improve their vision without being limited by time or resources.

Despite these possibilities, integrating AI into creative practices raises significant ethical and philosophical concerns. The essential problem is that it is possible to trust AI-generated content created by algorithms trained with existing data and considered original (Siroor & Anita, 2024). This question becomes even more urgent when AI-generated works arise in commercial or academic fields that may produce art for people or cover its origins. There are also concerns about bias and representation, as AI systems trained with biased datasets can maintain or increase existing inequalities in visual culture. For example, image-generation models may overrepresent specific demographic characteristics. However, they may alienate, reflect, and reinforce social biases rather than challenge them. The response to these problems requires significant inclusion of data and algorithms that support AI systems.

REFERENCES

Caldeira, W., & Simões, J. (2024). Digital image: The role of apparatus, artificial intelligence, and machine learning in visual communication in the digital age. *Rotura – Revista de Comunicação. Cultura e Artes*, *4*(2), 138–149.

Chen, J. (2024). The role of AI: Speculative design in redefining artistic collaboration. *Journal of Ecohumanism*, *3*(8), 2261–2272. DOI: 10.62754/joe.v3i8.4899

Chen, Y. (2024). Artificial intelligence technology in photography and future challenges and reflections. *The Frontiers of Society. Science and Technology*, *6*(6), 24–30.

Ching, V., & Mothi, D. (2025). *AI for creatives: Unlocking expressive digital potential*. CRC Press. DOI: 10.1201/9781003533016

Costa, A. S. L. (2024). *Artificial aesthetic: Exploring the convergence of creativity, artificial intelligence, and human expression in art* (Doctoral dissertation).

Das, S., & Kundu, R. (2024). The ethics of artificial intelligence in creative arts: A comprehensive review. *Interdisciplinary International Journal of Advances in Social Sciences. Arts and Humanities*, *1*(1), 26–33.

Dursun, R. Z. A., & Bakan, U. (2025). An exploration of machine learning in art and design. In *Impact of contemporary technology on art and design* (pp. 205–236). IGI Global.

Erişti, S. D. B., & Freedman, K. (2024). Integrating digital technologies and AI in art education: Pedagogical competencies and the evolution of digital visual culture. *Participatory Educational Research, 11*(Prof. Dr. H. Ferhan Odabaşı Gift Issue), 57–79.

Ghose, A., Ali, S. A., & Mishra, A. M. (2024). Artistic expressions, generative AI, and legal tapestry: Exploring the dynamics of copyright laws in the confluence of AI and artistic creation. In *Making art with generative AI tools* (pp. 198–214). IGI Global. DOI: 10.4018/979-8-3693-1950-5.ch011

Günay, M. (2024). Creative innovation in the context of artificial intelligence in digital art. *International Journal of Education Technology and Scientific Researches*, *9*(28), 619–629. DOI: 10.35826/ijetsar.746

Hariyanto, R. L., Silaban, M. D., Kurniawan, R., Sudirman, L., & Alamanda, A. E. (2024). AI and creativity: Redefining copyright for visual works and text. *Barelang Journal of Legal Studies*, *2*(1), 1–16.

He, J. (2024). A study on the influence of artificial intelligence on image art design. *SHS Web of Conferences, 181*, 04028.

Hutson, J. (2024). Art in the age of virtual reproduction. In *Art and culture in the multiverse of metaverses: Immersion, presence, and interactivity in the digital age* (pp. 55–98). Springer. DOI: 10.1007/978-3-031-66320-8_3

Işık, V. (2024). Exploring artistic frontiers in the era of artificial intelligence. *Sanat ve Tasarım Dergisi, 14*(2), 577–603. DOI: 10.20488/sanattasarim.1603119

Jasmer, B. W. (2024). *Balancing AI and human creativity: Adaptations in art education* (Master's thesis). Bethel University.

Jora, O. D., Iacob, M., Rosca, V. I., Nedelcu, M. R., Preda, A. F., & Nedef, M. S. (2024). Artificial intelligence and artistic imagination: Revisiting the cultural economy of industrial revolutions. *Amfiteatru Economic*, *26*(66), 613–632. DOI: 10.24818/EA/2024/66/630

Manu, A. (2024). *Transcending imagination: Artificial intelligence and the future of creativity*. CRC Press. DOI: 10.1201/9781003450139

Mugubi, J. G., & Manono, F. M. (2024). Optimizing creative processes with artificial intelligence (AI): Strategic imperatives for African filmmakers and graphic designers in the evolving digital landscape. *International Journal of Scholarly Practice*, *4*(2), 28–40.

Novakovic, J., & Guga, J. (2024). Art after AI: The impact of generative AI on the artworld. In *Navigating the digital age: An in-depth exploration into the intersection of modern technologies and societal transformation* (pp. 584–604).

Petrick, K. (2024). Art in the age of algorithms: A creator's perspective on the artistry of AI image generation. In *New frontiers in science in the era of AI* (pp. 195–214). Springer. DOI: 10.1007/978-3-031-61187-2_12

Rachmawati, I., Parman, S., & Solihah, Y. A. (2024). Exploring the boundaries of creativity in the digital age by understanding the impact and implications of AI work in photography competitions. In *Proceeding of International Seminar on Arts, Artificial Intelligence & Society* (pp. 294–307).

Ranjan, R., Mishra, A., Maharana, S. P., & Kumari, S. (2024). AI in visual arts: Exploring generative algorithm. In *The pioneering applications of generative AI* (pp. 41–60). IGI Global. DOI: 10.4018/979-8-3693-3278-8.ch002

Siroor, A., & Anita, B. (2024). The intersection of technology and art: Redefining creativity in the digital age. *Innovative Journal of Interdisciplinary Research and Technological Innovations*, *1*(1), 37–42.

Soreanu, C. (2024). Artificial intelligence in contemporary visuality. *Review of Artistic Education*, *28*, 222–230. DOI: 10.35218/rae-2024-0028

Tariq, M. U. (2025). AI-powered business process automation: Revolutionizing firm management. In Derbali, A. (Ed.), *AI, economic perspectives, and firm business management* (pp. 199–224). IGI Global., DOI: 10.4018/979-8-3693-7357-6.ch010

Tariq, M. U. (2025). AI-enhanced project-based learning: Revolutionizing commerce education with generative AI. In ElSayary, A. (Ed.), *Prompt engineering and generative AI applications for teaching and learning* (pp. 125–142). IGI Global., DOI: 10.4018/979-8-3693-7332-3.ch008

Tariq, M. U. (2025). Integrating ICT for enhanced organizational resilience: Strategies and case studies. In Carvalho, L., Reis, L., Neves de Almeida Baptista Figueiredo, A., & Russo, N. (Eds.), *Leveraging technology for organizational adaptability* (pp. 59–80). IGI Global., DOI: 10.4018/979-8-3693-6045-3.ch004

Tariq, M. U. (2025). Navigating public administration 5.0: Embracing AI for smarter governance. In Wongmahesak, K., Ahmad, J., & Mustanir, A. (Eds.), *Public governance practices in the age of AI* (pp. 167–186). IGI Global., DOI: 10.4018/979-8-3693-9286-7.ch008

Tariq, M. U. (2025). Revolutionizing educator preparation: Exploring the efficacy of grow your own models. In Sande, B., & Marvel, A. (Eds.), *Enhancing educational access through innovative educator preparation pathways* (pp. 75–100). IGI Global., DOI: 10.4018/979-8-3693-7337-8.ch004

Tariq, M. U. (2025). The role of AI-powered learning analytics in enhancing student engagement and performance. In J. Moore, S. Gupta, M. Sharma, A. Garg, & H. Josephine V. L. (Eds.), *Transforming education with data science in the AI era* (pp. 123–148). IGI Global. https://doi.org/DOI: 10.4018/979-8-3373-2185-1.ch005

Tariq, M. U. (2025). Integration of artificial intelligence and machine learning in business intelligence: Enhancing decision making and operational efficiency. In Ishtaiwi, A., Al-Qerem, A., Al Khaldy, M., & Alauthman, M. (Eds.), *Driving modern business intelligence architecture for operational efficiency* (pp. 279–306). IGI Global., DOI: 10.4018/979-8-3373-2125-7.ch009

Tariq, M. U. (2025). Innovation and agility—Adapting business strategies for sustainable growth in dynamic markets. In Ananthan, S., Kohli, A., Manickam, T., & Dhanabalan, T. (Eds.), *New business development strategies for achieving sustainable growth* (pp. 113–140). IGI Global., DOI: 10.4018/979-8-3373-2048-9.ch005

Tariq, M. U. (2025). Empowering patients with AI-ethical digital tools for health data management and decision. In Pesqueira, A., & de Bem Machado, A. (Eds.), *Navigating privacy, innovation, and patient empowerment through ethical healthcare technology* (pp. 197–216). IGI Global., DOI: 10.4018/979-8-3693-7630-0.ch008

Tsao, J., & Nogues, C. (2024). Beyond the author: Artificial intelligence, creative writing and intellectual emancipation. *Poetics*, *102*, 101865. DOI: 10.1016/j.poetic.2024.101865

Walter, Y. (2025). The emerging "AI artists": Breaking the metacrisis and the fear of losing human creativity. [Published by SCIEPublish]. *Nature Anthropology*, *3*(1), 10002. DOI: 10.70322/natanthropol.2025.10002

Xu, C., Sun, Y., & Zhou, H. (2025). Artificial aesthetics and ethical ambiguity: Exploring business ethics in the context of AI-driven creativity. *Journal of Business Ethics*, *199*(4), 671–692. DOI: 10.1007/s10551-024-05837-2

Yadav, M., Kumar, M., Sahoo, A., & Rathnasiri, M. S. H. (2025). AI and the evolution of artistic expression: Impacts on society and culture. In *Transforming cinema with artificial intelligence* (pp. 15–36). IGI Global.

Yao, Q. (2025). Application of artificial intelligence virtual image technology in photography art creation under deep learning. *IEEE Access : Practical Innovations, Open Solutions*, *13*, 25003–25012. DOI: 10.1109/ACCESS.2025.3529521

Zhao, Y. (2024). The synergistic effect of artificial intelligence technology in the evolution of visual communication of new media art. *Heliyon*, *10*(18), e38008. DOI: 10.1016/j.heliyon.2024.e38008 PMID: 39328541

KEY TERMS AND DEFINITIONS

Artificial Intelligence (AI): Machine systems replicating intelligent human creative behavior.

Generative Art: Art generated through algorithmic, data-driven machine methods.

Visual Expression: Innovative representation of ideas through visual forms.

Chapter 9
Digital Images: A New Way of Seeing

Serhat Erdem
http://orcid.org/0000-0002-3782-0147
Atatürk Üniversitesi, Turkey

ABSTRACT

This chapter examines the transformative impact of digital technologies on artistic production and visual communication, focusing on photography and digital images. It argues that digital visuality constitutes a new way of seeing and remembering, reshaping aesthetic norms, cultural representation, and collective memory. Drawing on theorists such as McLuhan, Flusser, Manovich, and Mitchell, the chapter explores how digital images function as tools of perception, cultural memory, and social witnessing. Through case studies including AI-generated art, protest imagery like the "Lady in Red," and social media archives, the chapter highlights the dual role of digital images as both aesthetic and mnemonic agents in contemporary culture.

INTRODUCTION

The rise of digital technologies has triggered a fundamental transformation in visual culture. In particular, the proliferation of digital images is redefining the way we see the world and our image-making practices. While traditional photography and visual arts are transitioning from an analog-based world to a digital universe, they are experiencing a transformation not only in technical tools but also in the way we see (Depeli & Hepdinçler, 2022). Both storing and transferring data in the digital environment has added a new dimension to communication (Çakın & Bolat, 2018, p. 176). Today, millions of images are produced and shared digitally every moment, and images are transformed into the letters of a global visual language.

DOI: 10.4018/979-8-3373-2230-8.ch009

As a matter of fact, it is reported that more than 100 million photos and videos are shared daily on platforms such as Instagram (Product, 2024). Such visual inflation has radically changed the way 21st century people perceive and express the world.

This study discusses the role of digital images in creating a new way of seeing. The main aim is to demonstrate the transformative impact of digital technologies on photography and visuality through theoretical and practical examples. In the light of the theoretical perspectives of thinkers such as Marshall McLuhan, Vilém Flusser, Lev Manovich and W. J. T. Mitchell, the study discusses how visual culture has evolved with digitalization. After a historical and conceptual analysis of the transition from traditional analogical photography to digital images, the innovative aesthetic forms of the digital age and their effects on our perception will be examined. Furthermore, case studies on the use of digital images in artistic production will be presented to concretize the relationship between theory and practice. While evaluating the role of digital images in today's visual communication practices and cultural representations, the new dynamics created by the visual economy and sharing culture and the phenomenon of algorithmic aesthetics will be examined. A general evaluation will be made by discussing the possible effects of current technological developments such as artificial intelligence, virtual reality (VR) and NFT on the future of art and finally the place of digital images in collective memory will be analyzed.

Theoretical Background: Theories of Media and Visual Culture

In order to understand the transformative power of digital images, it would be useful to first briefly touch upon theories of media and visual culture. Communication theorist Marshall McLuhan argued that every new communication technology radically affects human perception and social structure. In McLuhan's famous phrase, "the medium is the message", meaning that the medium itself, rather than the content of a message, shapes social transformations (McLuhan, 1995, p.225). In this context, digital media not only transmit old images, but also offer a new infrastructure that completely changes image frames. As early as the 1960s, McLuhan stated *that "it is not the picture in the frame that changes, but the frame itself"* and that with each new technology, our frame of perception will be transformed (McLuhan, 1995, p.273). Indeed, digital imaging technologies have created an environment that expands the boundaries of visual experience and transforms the way we perceive. McLuhan also predicted that in the electronic information age individuals live in a deluge of information, constantly exposed to more stimuli than they can cope with (McLuhan, 1995, p.26). This prediction almost predefines the environment of visual excess of the digital image age. Information bombardment and image inflation shape the attention economy by raising perception thresholds.

In parallel to McLuhan's media theory, the philosopher of photography Vilém Flusser defines the emergence of technical images as the second biggest breaking point in human history after the invention of writing (Güler, 2022). According to Flusser, the technical images produced by devices such as the camera shake the dominance of linear textual culture and direct humanity back to visual thinking (Güler, 2022). As a matter of fact, Flusser argues that the period of historical thinking that began with the invention of writing in 3500 BC was replaced by a two-dimensional image culture similar to "magical thinking" with the invention of photography in the 19th and 20th centuries (Güler, 2022). This view implies that the universe of digital images represents a transition from a diachronic perception to a simultaneous and holistic perception by creating a *"new way of seeing"* (Red Thread, 2020).

In his work Towards a Philosophy of Photography (1983), Flusser draws attention to the structure and functioning behind technical image production. According to him, every photograph is *"the result of the cooperation and conflict between the photographer and the apparatus"* (Güler, 2022). In other words, the camera, with its pre-programmed set of possibilities, limits and directs the photographer's creative intentions. From this perspective, new devices such as digital cameras and software also contain programs that unwittingly direct users towards certain aesthetic and conceptual frameworks. Flusser emphasizes that without the analysis of technical images, the programmatic intentions underlying these images cannot be understood. Critical literacy in digital visual culture therefore requires analyzing not only the surface meanings of images, but also the logic of the algorithms and devices that produce them.

Visual culture theorist W. J. T. Mitchell, with his concept of "pictorial turn" in the early 1990s, states that images have taken a central position in modern culture by replacing linguistic expressions (Depeli & Hepdinçler, 2022). According to Mitchell, the age we are in is an age of iconology; it is a period in which not only words but also images are "read" and images are asked *"what they want"* like subjects (Mitchell, 2005). As he argues in *"What Do Pictures Want?"*, images have gone beyond being passive reflections and have become active elements reflecting social desires, fears and ideologies. From this perspective, digital images can be seen as cultural actors with their own *agenda* and *influence*, rather than mere technical outputs. Indeed, Mitchell emphasizes that no image is completely innocent and that every visual representation carries a certain discursive power (Mitchell, 1994). Therefore, when analyzing digital visual culture, it is necessary to examine *what* these images *do* as well as *what they say*.

New media theorist Lev Manovich has done important work analyzing the nature of digital images and their relationship with traditional visual forms. Manovich argues that digital technology contains a paradoxical logic that radically transforms "old" media forms while simultaneously reinforcing them (Manovich, 1995). For example, the basic codes of 20th century visual culture, such as cinema and photography, are both imitated and transcended in the digital environment and reproduced with a nostalgic value (Manovich, 1995). According to Manovich, the differences in the physical basis of the digital imaging revolution have also changed the cultural perception of the image (Manovich, 1995). The fact that a digital image can be copied continuously and losslessly disrupts the traditional hierarchy between "original" and "copy". As a matter of fact, William J. Mitchell (1992) emphasizes that even the thousandth copy of a digital photo file can be of the same quality as the first shot, thus visual reproduction in the digital age is realized with almost zero cost and zero loss (Manovich, 1995). This has led to the questioning of the photographic image's connection with reality. Manovich dramatically summarizes this process by stating that "*digital photography does not exist*", since in practice, digital photography, while largely continuing the logic of use of analog photography, has a completely different data structure in essence (Manovich, 1995).

The Transformation of Visuality: The Nature of the Digital Image

Technically and culturally, digital images differ from previous forms of visual representation in some ways. While analog photography is a chemical and continuous image record, the digital image is composed of digital codes and has a discontinuous structure (Manovich, 1995). This fundamental difference brings with it various consequences:

Copying and Authenticity: Digital images blur the distinction between original and copy. Even if a digital photo file is reproduced many times, there is no loss of quality; each copy is essentially the same at the bit level. This renders the concept of *"original"* meaningless in digital images, in contrast to the small differences in each print or negative copy in traditional photography (Manovich, 1995). As a result, the *aura of* a digitally produced image (Benjamin, 1936) - that is, its singular and unique existence - is weakened; images become "infinitely reproducible files".

Manipulation and Reality: Digital images can be easily manipulated and altered because they are based on pixel representation. A photograph can now be radically transformed with software such as Photoshop, not limited to chemical interventions in the darkroom. This has shaken the traditional assumption that photography is an index (projection) of reality. *The "photographic reality" of* an image we see now depends less on the raw shot and more on the chain of digital processing that follows. For example, in a digital portrait photograph, colors, contrast or objects can be easily altered; thus, the photograph can be transformed from a document into a kind of digital design. This phenomenon has put the notion of "visual truth" into question and obscured the criteria for "believing in the image" in the digital age.

Resolution and Detail: Whereas in analog photography the image has continuous gradations of tone and detail, the digital image is limited to a specific resolution (e.g. 1920x1080 pixels) and color depth (e.g. 24-bit). As Manovich points out, even high-resolution digital screens initially created a *"too clean, too perfect"* effect on the viewer, and the digital image was found *"alienating"* in contrast to the *"human"* warmth of the grainy texture of analog film (Manovich, 1995). Over time, as resolution has increased, digital images have become closer to reality, but the pixel-based structure is always present as an abstract layer. Up close, one can see pixels in a digital print frame by frame, whereas analog film grains contain randomness. This technical difference brings with it the predisposition of digital aesthetics to sharp and clear forms.

Digitization and Metadata: Digital images are not only visual data; they also carry metadata such as EXIF (date of capture, camera settings, location information, etc.). This offers new possibilities in terms of archiving, categorization and traceability of images. In this context, it is possible to state that with the use of digital technologies, audiovisual contents can be presented through the means of information technologies (Akmeşe Demir & Demir, 2023, p. 402).

For example, digital traces of a digital photograph can be used to verify its provenance or provide clues as to whether it has been altered. In addition, digital images have become part of the era of big data, as they can be saved in databases and analyzed by algorithms. This dataization of images makes them more easily circulated in economic and social cycles.

Mobility and Accessibility: Digital images can be shared instantly over electronic networks. A photograph taken with a smartphone can appear on the screen of someone on the other side of the world within seconds. This has created a global visual circulation by eliminating the time and space dependency of images. As a result, the impact of an image has increased with its potential to reach a wide audience without geographical boundaries. This phenomenon has accelerated the interaction of local and global aesthetics in visual culture and contributed to the blending of visual styles from different parts of the world in areas such as fashion, design and popular culture.

Screen Experience and Interaction: Digital images are often experienced on screens rather than in physical print. There are perceptual differences between a photograph viewed on a bright screen and a photograph printed on paper; the screen emits light, while the print is seen through reflected light. In addition, the digital environment allows interaction with images: Zooming in/out, 360-degree panoramic views, even augmentation with layers of augmented reality (AR). The viewer can establish a more dynamic relationship with digital images, for example by zooming in on details in a high-resolution digital copy of an artwork, or by changing the image according to their own preferences in an interactive visual application. This means a shift from the classic passive viewer to a more participatory experience.

Synthetic Images and Reality: Digital technologies can produce completely synthetic images without any direct optical trace of the real world. Scenes created through computer- generated imagery (CGI) can be as *realistic* today as if they were shot with a camera, if not more so. For example, photorealistic digital effects in contemporary motion pictures have often become indistinguishable from real images for the viewer. Manovich characterizes this as the final paradox of the digital image: *"The new synthetic images are not inferior to the visual realism of traditional photography - in fact, they are too real"* (Manovich, 1995). These *"hyper-real"* images are in fact the result of our acceptance of reality through photography and cinema; our eyes, accustomed to accepting what is seen through the camera lens as real, perceive the images produced flawlessly by computers as real (Manovich, 1995). As a result, the line between reality and fiction has blurred in the digital age; simulation has challenged reality for the first time (Baudrillard, 1981).

The Digitalization of Photography: A Historical and Conceptual Analysis

Photography has functioned as an important tool in social and cultural fields since its discovery; it has assumed a decisive role in the construction of the social structure, especially thanks to its power of visual representation. People always react to powerful images and these images find their counterparts in life and become decisive in mobilizing the masses (Akmeşe, 2017, p.126). In this context, with the opportunities provided by technological developments, the art of photography has been reshaped in the digital age and this transformation has brought it to a central position among contemporary art disciplines. However, this evolutionary process has been realized as a complex and long-term transformation not only on technical but also on aesthetic and sociocultural levels (Gençcelep & Özkemahlı, 2023, p.3062).

The practice of photography remained a chemical and analog process from its birth in the 19th century until the late 20th century. However, the development of digital imaging technologies in the 1980s initiated a major revolution in photography (Aydemir, n.d.). When the first commercial digital cameras appeared on the market in the 1990s, although they were limited in terms of resolution and quality, they enabled the photographer to see instant results by eliminating the cost of film and the developing process (Aydemir, n.d.). The 1990s witnessed the rapid rise of digital photography; innovations such as digital storage, computer editing and instant printing made digital cameras very popular among both professional and amateur photographers (Aydemir, n.d.).

In the 2000s, the resolution and performance of digital cameras increased rapidly; consumer cameras grew from ~3 megapixels in 2000 to 10+ megapixels within a decade. During the same period, digital SLR (DSLR) cameras began to replace analog 35mm SLRs. By the mid- 2000s, for example, the majority of agency photographers had switched from film to digital. Classic film companies like Kodak suffered serious market losses when they failed to adapt to the digital revolution - Kodak even filed for bankruptcy protection in 2012. Ironically, it was Kodak engineer Steven Sasson who invented the first digital camera in 1975, but the company was slow to commercialize the invention because it did not anticipate the speed of digitalization.

The next major breakthrough in digital photography came with smartphones. The introduction of the iPhone in 2007 and the rapid development of smartphone cameras in the years that followed made photography an integral part of everyday life on a mass scale. Almost everyone now carries a high-resolution camera in their pocket at all times. As a result, photo production has exploded: In the 2020s, for example, billions of photographs are taken and shared online around the world every day. The digitization of photography has democratized it from an elite pursuit to a tool of communication, a language of social media.

This digitalization process has had not only technical but also conceptual effects. The notion *of indexicality* (the physical connection of the image to reality), long debated in photographic theory, has been reconsidered in the digital age. Analog photography was thought to bear the chemical trace of light and therefore offer a reliable representation of the real world. However, in digital photography, the image is formed by converting the electrical signal on the sensor into digital data. This has raised philosophical questions about the relationship between photography and reality: To what extent is a digital photograph far from being "proof of an event"? At the beginning of the digital age, some photographers argued that digital images were not *"genuine photographs"*, but this approach has changed over time. Today, digital photography is considered an integral part of the photographic phenomenon, and its innovations - instant image sharing, extensive editing possibilities, etc. - have broadened our understanding of photography.

Digital photography has also given birth to new practices and aesthetics. For example, combining multiple exposures with the HDR (High Dynamic Range) technique, creating wide-angle scenes with panoramic compositing, or capturing images from angles unimaginable to previous generations, such as drone photography, are all unique to the digital age. In addition, thanks to digital editing software, collage, montage and superimposition techniques have become widespread, blurring the boundaries between photography and painting. Artists use digital photography as a raw material and reshape it on digital canvas, sometimes producing profound digital artworks based on a single photograph.

On the other hand, the speed and convenience brought about by digital photography was seen by some critics as the transformation of photography into a *"consumer object"* (Aydemir, n.d.). When the labor and patience spent in the darkroom was replaced by the ability to take hundreds of frames with the click of a button, it was claimed that the intellectuality of photography diminished (Aydemir, n.d.). The romantic structure of analog photography - the time spent in the darkroom, the difficult process - has been replaced by a fast and practical production in the digital age; this has led to a weakening of the emotional bond established with the image. As a matter of fact, while the countless photographs shared on digital platforms create an enormous visual archive, they also produce a "noise" that makes it difficult for a single image to leave a lasting impression.

The digitalization of photography has not only been a technological transition, but also a multidimensional process that has transformed the ontology, uses and social meaning of photography. Today, digital methods have become the default norm when it comes to photography, while analog photography continues to exist more as an artistic or nostalgic sub- discipline. This transformation has brought about new aesthetic pursuits and ways of seeing.

New Aesthetic Forms and Perception

Digital technology has not only enabled the continuation of existing visual styles, but also created new aesthetic forms. These new aesthetic tendencies manifest themselves both in the art world and in everyday visual practices.

Glitch Aesthetics: Pixel distortions, codec errors or transmission failures inherent in digital media have turned into a conscious aesthetic choice in 21st century art. The movement called Glitch art transforms distortions, color shifts and scanning errors in digital images into aesthetic compositions. Image errors, which were avoided in the analog era, have been adopted by artists as a means of creative expression in the digital age. For example, blurred and noisy frames obtained by deliberately distorting the code of a video reveal a new understanding of beauty that reflects the fragility and randomness of the digital world. Glitch aesthetics can also be read as a kind of visual rebellion against digital technology's claim to perfection; by glorifying imperfection, it makes visible the flaws in the background of technology.

Retro-Digital and Pixel Art: The low-resolution graphics and large pixelated images typical of the early days of digitization have become popular again today as a deliberate aesthetic of nostalgia. Known as pixel art, this aesthetic, which evokes the 8-bit graphics style of 1980s computer games, is being reused in modern design and games. Likewise, filters that mimic analog video effects (e.g. VHS effect, scanner lines) are common in digital visual culture. This trend can be seen as the digital age romanticizing its own past and producing *"digital nostalgia"*. That is, even the newest technologies sometimes deliberately mimic older digital appearances, evoking both familiarity and ironic pleasure in the viewer.

Filters and Instagram Aesthetics: social media, especially Instagram, has given birth to a new lexicon of visual style. Photo filters create an almost standardized aesthetic by popularizing certain color tones and contrast settings. For example, Instagram's classic filters (Valencia, X-Pro II, etc.) create a distinct atmosphere by adding warm tones or slightly faded retro effects to photos. As a result, when millions of users on the platform use similar filters, it is possible to speak of an *"Instagram aesthetic"*. This aesthetic is often based on vibrant colors, high contrast, flawless compositions, and often happy/idealized scenes. Lev Manovich, examining the Instagram culture of the 2010s, emphasizes that society has almost become an aesthetic society and even everyday life practices are shaped around *"looking beautiful"* (Manovich, 2020). Indeed, people try to make every moment, from the food they eat to the places they visit, aesthetically presentable; thus, the experience of life is partly combined with the concern of being photogenic.

Meme and Internet Visual Culture: Another dimension of digital aesthetics is the culture of visual humor and irony that spreads over the internet. Image-subtitle associations, called memes, have created a common visual language. For example, the famous *"Distracted Boyfriend"* photo has turned into a global joke material with different texts written on it, and countless variations have been produced. The aesthetics of Internet memes often include the use of low-resolution *"poor image"*, striking typography and exaggerated visual metaphors (Steyerl, 2009). As Hito Steyerl puts it, *"poor quality, rapidly circulating images" are* the new bazaar of the digital economy (Steyerl, 2009). The value of these *"poor images"* lies in their ubiquity and accessibility rather than their artistic sophistication - even a pixelated and distorted image gains cultural significance if it is viral enough. This phenomenon shows that in the digital age, hierarchies of aesthetic value can be upended; sometimes a blurry screen image can gain a stronger foothold in the collective consciousness than perfect high- resolution images.

Transformation of Audience Perception: These new aesthetic forms also change the visual perception of viewers. In a continuous flow of visual media (e.g. social media timelines), individuals tend to scan images quickly rather than analyze them in depth. This has led to the evolution of visual literacy skills: People can now intuitively grasp the message, style or emotion of an image by looking at it very briefly. On the other hand, under the pressure of the attention economy, images are produced to be more and more striking and attention-grabbing, creating a vicious circle: Oversaturated colors, high contrasts, dramatic compositions become the norm in order to capture the viewer's attention; the higher the viewer's threshold, the more extreme the images become. As a result, perception becomes increasingly accustomed to *"too bright, too fast"* images. This phenomenon can even lead to the serene and imperfect appearance of the real world being perceived as dull compared to the hyper-realistic standard of digital screen aesthetics (Baudrillard, 1981).

Case Studies: Digital Images in Artistic Production

In order to concretize the transformation of digital images in the field of art, this section presents case studies from different disciplines. Ranging from photography to new media art, these examples demonstrate the impact of digital technologies on creative production.

Digital Manipulation and the Art of Photography: Andreas Gursky

German photographer Andreas Gursky is known for his large-scale and detailed photographs. Gursky's works provide striking examples of how digital manipulation techniques can be used in art photography. For example, his famous 1999 work "Rhein II" shows an idealized landscape that does not actually exist: The artist digitally merged a series of photographs taken on the banks of the Rhine River and deleted unwanted elements in the image (walkers, factories, etc.). The resulting photograph resembles an abstract painting with its minimalist lines. Gursky states that in this way he achieved a composition that is *"more real"* than the real nature. Indeed, *Rhein* II was sold in 2011 for 4.3 million dollars, one of the highest prices ever paid for a photograph. This success proved that a digitally manipulated photograph can be as valuable in the collecting world as a classic print

Algorithmic Art and Data Aesthetics: Refik Anadol

Turkish media artist Refik Anadol creates original artworks by combining the possibilities of digital imagery with data and artificial intelligence. Through large-scale projections, AI- powered visuals and site-specific installations, Anadol designs immersive experiences that surround the viewer. For example, in his 2018 work *"WDCH Dreams"* projected onto the facade of the Los Angeles Philharmonic Hall, he processed archival footage with a machine learning algorithm to create an ever-changing dreamlike visual world on the building's surface. Anadol's practice introduces a new category that can be defined as data sculpture or artificial intelligence painting. As a matter of fact, he is recognized as one of the pioneers in the field of *"aesthetics of machine intelligence"*. In his works, he uses large data sets, ranging from the collective visual memory of cities to images of galaxies, and transforms them into abstract and colorful digital artworks. The resulting works are neither photography nor video in the traditional sense; they are a new form of visual art created with code, constantly evolving and engaging the viewer's senses in multiple ways. Anadol's works are exhibited in museums and public spaces around the world, expanding the boundaries of artistic expression of digital images

A New Photographic View: The Art of Google Street View (Michael Wolf & Jon Rafman)

Digital images do not only have to be produced by artists; today, huge archives of machine images are also used as artistic material. Photographic projects using Google Street View images are an example of this. In his series *"Paris Street View"* (2010), photographer Michael Wolf scanned the streetscapes through Google Street View and captured the moments he found interesting as screenshots and rephotographed them. The resulting images contain such surprising moments (such as a couple kissing or a man falling) that most viewers are not sure at first glance whether they are real or fictional. Instead of taking a traditional photo trip, Wolf states that he prefers *to "explore the city virtually via Google rather than in real time"* (Hoby, 2012). This approach radically changes the way the photographer sees: Looking at the world through the eyes of Google's automated cameras instead of the camera. Wolf was awarded a prestigious photography prize in 2011 for this series, thus recognizing *the "reframing of digital images taken by someone else"* as a creative act. Similarly, in his project *"Nine Eyes of Google Street View"*, artist Jon Rafman compiled interesting and bizarre scenes captured by Google's automobile cameras and shared them online, reaching a wide artistic audience. These cases show that the understanding of photographic exploration can change in the digital age: The photographer is no longer physically present, but *can hunt for* meaningful moments in digital archives. This has created a new form of curation and creativity in the abundance of digital images.

Visual Communication Practices and Cultural Representations

The intensive use of digital images in everyday life has radically changed our communication practices. Images, as well as texts, have become one of the main means of expressing our thoughts, identity and cultural position.

First of all, the way individuals present themselves visually has taken on new dimensions in the digital age. While the concept of selfie means ordinary people documenting and sharing their faces and lives, it has actually turned into a cultural phenomenon as a practice of self- representation. Thanks to smartphone cameras and social media platforms, everyone has become a photo-journalist of their own lives. This has led to the centralization of the image in the presentation of identity. For example, younger generations use the photo frames on their Instagram profiles as a self-portrait gallery to define themselves. Selfies can be used for purposes such as social belonging (e.g. being part of a group), aesthetic self-worth (the level of appreciation measured by the number of "likes") and even activism (thematic selfies taken to raise awareness on a particular issue). Of course, this phenomenon has also brought with it criticism; while some have identified selfie culture with narcissism and superficiality, others have positively evaluated it as a way for previously unrepresented bodies (different beauty patterns, disadvantaged groups, etc.) to gain visibility.

Digital images also play a critical role in the transmission of social events and cultural representations. Smartphone cameras and online platforms in particular have given rise to the concept of citizen journalism. For example, photos and videos taken during a protest or natural disaster can instantly circulate globally, bypassing traditional media filters. During the *Arab Spring* protests in the early 2010s or the *Black Lives Matter* protests in 2020, images shared from the streets captured the attention of the world public and became engraved in the collective memory. Such images are not only newsworthy; they are also instrumentalized in struggles for cultural representation. Thus, digital images can function as carriers of truth and catalysts of social change.

In the context of cultural representations, digital visual culture challenges the one-way representational monopoly of traditional media. Whereas mass media (television, magazines) used to present images through specific aesthetic and ideological filters, now each individual can tell his or her own story through images. This democratization has opened up a new space for identities underrepresented in mainstream media to express themselves. For example, within the framework of the body affirmation movement, different body types, skin colors or age groups have gained visibility through social media photos and expanded the notion of beauty. Similarly, ethnic and cultural minorities are self-representing themselves through self- produced images, questioning stereotypical images imposed from outside. These developments have created a more pluralistic environment for visual representation. However, on the other hand, the biases of algorithms and platform rules can restrict this new space of freedom. For example, there have been discussions that some social media algorithms automatically prefer or censor certain face types or color tones. Therefore, although digital visual communication practices carry revolutionary potentials in representation, they also harbor new mechanisms of control and prejudice.

Another dimension is that digital images can also be used for misinformation and propaganda purposes. Videos created with deepfake technologies or photographs deliberately taken out of context can be circulated to mislead the public. Since visual content has a high power of persuasion, even a fake image can have a great impact as if it were real. This has increased the importance of digital visual literacy: The ability of users to question the source, accuracy and the possibility of manipulation of the images they see has become critical. For example, checking the original context of a photo through reverse image search or verifying videos through technical analysis are part of new media literacy. In terms of cultural representations, digital images can be both liberating and dangerous: On the one hand, they offer the power to reveal truths censored by repressive regimes or the mainstream, while on the other hand they can manipulate audiences with new kinds of disinformation. This contrast is a paradox of the age of digital visual communication and requires society to constantly renegotiate its relationship with these images.

In addition, while the appropriation method is frequently preferred in the field of contemporary art and photography, today, with the proliferation of digital technologies, it has become a daily routine for millions of people to add photographs to their personal archives or to re-share them. Platforms such as Flickr host many different user groups based on appropriation and contribute to the acceptance of this approach as an almost daily activity (Marien, 2015 cited in Er, 2023). Sometimes these forms of digital communication can also turn into a critical attitude. Just as images from mass media were used for questioning in the postmodern period, Post-Internet artists adopt the aesthetics of digital media and reveal the widespread presence of these images in contemporary visual culture. Stock images, corporate brand identities, the use of emoji, GIFs and caps, as well as the personalization of pages on platforms such as Tumblr, Instagram and Facebook are important elements in this context. For example, artists such as Kate Steciw, Constant Dullaart and DIS Collective use or create stock images in their work, drawing attention to the banality of such images in everyday life, while also examining how they can acquire new cultural and economic meanings when re-exhibited in the context of art (Lewis, 2018 cited in Er, 2023).

Visual Economy, Sharing Culture and Algorithmic Aesthetics

The circulation of digital images has created not only a cultural but also an economic ecosystem. The visual economy refers to the values created in the processes of producing, distributing and consuming images in online media. Today, billions of images are shared for free, and a huge advertising and data economy has taken shape around them. For example, platforms such as Instagram or TikTok not only generate direct advertising revenue from the photos and videos shared by users, but also process user data to feed their algorithms. Attention is the most valuable commodity in these channels; therefore, each image, even if it is only seconds long, participates in the economy to the extent that it attracts user attention.

In this new visual economy, some individuals have become prominent as *"content producers"* or *"influencers"*, constantly capturing the attention of large audiences and generating economic gains. The influencer culture has developed largely through visual platforms, where people who post beautiful photos and videos in areas such as fashion, food, travel, etc. can accumulate millions of followers and secure sponsorship deals. Here, images are explicitly commodified: An Instagram post is both an aesthetic object and a product with advertising potential. This dimension of the visual economy blurs the lines between art and advertising, personal expression and commercial content.

The sharing culture of the digital environment lies at the heart of the visual economy. With Web 2.0, internet users have become content producers as well as consumers; sharing photos and videos has become a normal part of daily life. People build social bonds by sharing their experiences, memories and opinions through images. While this sharing culture has been praised for creating a participatory and interactive society, it has also been criticized for reducing privacy and creating pressure to display every moment of life. Philosopher Byung- Chul Han argues that in modern society, individuals are under the pressure of voluntary transparency, and that the constant exposure of our lives in front of the gaze has become a kind of violence (Depeli & Hepdinçler, 2022, p.2). Indeed, the culture of sharing can force individuals to make every moment aesthetically worthwhile, which can lead to the perception of a performative life.

The intensive use of sharing platforms has increased the importance of algorithms that determine the criteria by which images are visible. Social media algorithms are designed to highlight content that is predicted to be of interest to the user, leading to the creation of an algorithmic aesthetic over time. For example, Instagram's hidden ranking algorithm learns that certain types of images (photos with faces, brightly colored scenes, certain framing styles) receive more engagement, and then highlights similar content. Content creators also take into account the algorithm's preferences and adapt their posts to these patterns. The result can be a significant aesthetic homogenization across the platform, with everyone using similar filters and poses for the sake of being liked (Manovich, 2020). Here, aesthetic appreciation is shaped by human creativity as well as the feedback loops of machine learning.

Hito Steyerl argues that *"poor images"* circulating in the world of digital sharing overturn the value criteria of classical art objects; even a low-quality image can become an item of high cult value on the Internet, as long as it is widespread (Steyerl, 2009). In this context, in the digital visual economy, the number of views, likes and shares of an image has become the measure of its value. As Steyerl puts it, digital images transform quality into accessibility and display value into cult value (Steyerl, 2009). This is like the echo in the digital age of the concept of *"aura"* discussed by Walter Benjamin for the age of mechanical reproduction. Aura, the unique auratic value of a work of art, is replaced in the digital world by the networked presence of an image. The power of a meme or a viral photo comes not from its uniqueness, but from the fact that it is copied thousands of times and infiltrated into every part of life. These dynamics of the visual economy impose new responsibilities on the artist and the viewer: It has become imperative both to remain authentic without getting caught up in the rapid consumption of mass culture and to understand the game of visibility determined by algorithms.

The Future of Art: Artificial Intelligence, VR and NFT

Generative Art with Artificial Intelligence

In the historical development process, artificial intelligence has started to shape the world we live in as a result of long research and experiences, with its foundations laid on the axis of human imagination. As a result of this, it continues its development and change by gaining a rising momentum in the field of art as well as many other disciplines (Özkemahlı & Er, 2024, p.126). With this effect, one of the most striking developments in the production of digital images in recent years is the inclusion of artificial intelligence algorithms in creative processes. Deep learning techniques are used in a wide range of applications, from transforming visual styles (e.g. painting a photograph in the style of Van Gogh) to producing completely new images. In particular, Generative Adversarial Network (GAN) models and similar generative AIs can create faces, landscapes or artworks that have never existed before. In 2018, a turning point in this field occurred when a digital painting titled *"Portrait of Edmond de Belamy"* produced by an artist collective called Obvious using a GAN was sold by the famous auction house Christie's for 432 thousand five hundred US dollars (Özdal & Bulut, 2024). This event led to public debates such as "Is artificial intelligence replacing the artist?". On the one hand, while the creative role of artificial intelligence in art is being questioned, on the other hand, this technology has begun to be seen as a new tool.

Artificial intelligence-supported visual production requires rethinking some of the concepts of traditional art. The concepts of originality (authenticity) and the creative subject are among the most important of these. Who is the creator of a painting produced by an artificial intelligence model? Is it the engineer who developed the algorithm, the artist who trained the model, or the model itself? These questions are currently debated by both art theorists and lawyers. For example, the question of who owns the copyright of a work made with AI remains unclear in many countries. On the other hand, many artists have begun to see AI as a partner rather than a threat. Names like Refik Anadol use AI algorithms like brushes to create visual compositions of a complexity and magnitude that the human mind alone cannot produce. AI artworks are sometimes described as the *"imagination"* of a model trained with thousands of images (for example, in Google's *DeepDream* experiments), and sometimes as interactive structures that respond to the viewer's data inputs.

Virtual Reality (VR) and Immersive Art

Another horizon of visual technologies opens up in the fields of virtual reality (VR) and its related concepts of augmented reality (AR) and mixed reality (XR). VR creates a sense of "presence" by fully immersing the user in a computer-generated environment (Çoban, 2023). Augmented reality and mixed reality, on the other hand, allow for fictional spaces based on the reality of space (Yılmaz, 2017). Using this technology, artists have begun to offer viewers unorthodox experiences. For example, Canadian artist Char Davies gave viewers the opportunity to navigate an interactive 3D natural environment with his VR installation *"Osmose"* as early as 1995. Today, museums organize VR exhibitions, allowing viewers to take virtual tours of historical sites or paintings. VR-based artworks push the boundaries of the art experience as they appeal not only to the viewer's eyes but also to body movement and spatial perception.

One aspect of art in VR is the fusion of storytelling and performance with visual art. In VR environments, the viewer can go beyond being a passive observer and become a character or traveler in the story. For example, the VR animated film *"Gloomy Eyes"* (2019) allows the user to freely look inside a 360-degree zombie story and experience the scene from their own perspective (Çoban, 2023). Such works bring together the disciplines of cinema, gaming and visual design to create a new form of narrative. In the future, virtual reality art is expected to evolve into experiences that involve the senses of the audience more comprehensively (haptic feedback, smell, etc.). This situation not only expands the definition of art, but also changes the concept of the space of the artwork; a virtual space, rather than a physical gallery, can now be the space of art.

NFT and the Ownership Revolution in Digital Art

Perhaps one of the most buzzed-about innovations for the future of digital images is NFT (Non-Fungible Token) technology. NFTs make it possible to uniquely represent ownership of a digital asset using a blockchain infrastructure. In this way, a digital image file can be paired with an inimitable certificate and traded as *an original* work. The concept of NFT entered the mainstream especially in 2021, symbolized by the NFT of a collage by digital artist Beeple, which fetched an extraordinary price of $69.3 million at Christie's auction (Kastrenakes, 2021). While this sale made Beeple one of the most expensive living artists, it also proved that digital art can be highly valued just like traditional painting and sculpture. In this context, “Blockchain technology, a digital commodity, can be read as an attempt to give the global economy back its former mysterious structure” (Kırmızı & Çağıl, 2023, p. 278).

NFTs have brought the concepts of scarcity and auratic value back to the agenda in the field of digital art. The aura that Walter Benjamin said was lost in the age of mechanical reproduction is argued to be coming back for digital artworks thanks to NFTs (Depeli & Hepdinçler, 2022). A digital work with NFT is considered *original* because it has a singular identity registered in the blockchain, even if countless copies are in circulation. This seems to offer a technological solution to a long-standing problem of digital artists - that their works are easily copied and devalued. As a matter of fact, with the NFT fad, many digital artists have started to earn serious incomes for the first time. However, there are also critics: It is claimed that the NFT market is a speculative bubble, turning into an investment toy for the cryptocurrency rich rather than a source of real artistic value. The energy consumption and environmental impact of blockchain transactions is also a matter of debate.

Beyond all these positive and negative aspects, the NFT phenomenon has the potential to revolutionize the ownership and distribution of digital images. Artists can now offer their works to a global audience of collectors without physical galleries, bypassing intermediaries and selling directly. Moreover, smart contracts allow them to monetize the long-term appreciation of their work by taking a cut of each resale. From a cultural perspective, NFT communities are organizing online and creating a new art ecosystem. For example, on platforms such as Twitter, NFT collectors and artists are constantly interacting, promoting and discussing digital art. As a result, NFTs have made it visible that digital images are not only aesthetic objects but also economic assets. This suggests that in the future, the definition of art production and artworks will expand even further.

DIGITAL IMAGES AND THE CONSTRUCTION OF COLLECTIVE MEMORY

The Place of Digital Images in Collective Memory

Since Maurice Halbwachs, the concept of collective memory has emphasized that the ways in which individuals remember the past are shaped within social frameworks (Halbwachs, 1992). Traditionally, collective memory has created relatively static forms of shared recollection tied to particular places, objects or narratives. However, the rise of digital images is radically changing the way we see and remember the past. The Internet and digital technologies have led to the digitization of collective memory and given it new dynamics. Indeed, the online environment has turned into an enormous repository of data, and the digital archive has become *the "epitome of collective memory"* (Mandolessi, 2023). Countless digital photographs and videos now function as the building blocks of social memory.

While digital images have created a public visual archive of the past, this development has sparked heated debates among memory theorists. Some scholars, such as Andrew Hoskins, argue that digitalization has created an ontological break in memory. According to Hoskins, memory in the digital age has become fragmented, dispersed and uncontrollable due to the "hyper-connected" nature of human and algorithmic interaction (Hoskins, 2018). Hoskins even argues that digitalization has brought *an end to the concept of collective memory* and claims that a new phenomenon of "memory of the crowd" has emerged (Hoskins, 2018). According to him, *"collective memory has boundaries, whereas the memory of the crowd has no boundaries*". This view emphasizes that the archival nature of digital media weakens the control over memory and destabilizes the dimensions of time and space. For example, the fact that digital archives are constantly streaming and hyper-connected means that the past becomes shadow archives that can be revived at any moment (Hoskins, 2018; Hoskins & Halstead, 2021). According to this perspective, the unlimited reproducibility and circulation of digital images has loosened the common time-space anchor on which traditional collective memory is based.

In contrast, other memory researchers argue that while the digital age has transformed collective memory, it has actually made the concept more concrete. Silvana Mandolessi (2023) argues that digital memory does not mean *the end of collective memory*, on the contrary, it makes visible features that have long been theorized in the field of memory studies (Mandolessi, 2023). According to Mandolessi, the digital environment proves that memory is actually *process-oriented, not a representation but a performance,* as memory studies have emphasized from the beginning (Mandolessi, 2023). Indeed, digital collective memory emerges as a mediated *and re-mediated* practice in multi-media environments; it is kept alive by dynamic communities *that* constantly *re-perform* the past rather than represent it (Mandolessi, 2023). This view argues that digital images, far from harming collective memory, reinforce it as a distributed and living process. Similarly, Drozdzewski et al. (2021) argue that it is counterproductive to see the digital world as completely separate from the traditional past, on the contrary, digital technologies are now an integral part of our connection with the past (Mandolessi, 2023). In short, while one pole of the academic debate argues that digital images create a new form of memory and interrupt old "ways of seeing", the other pole argues that digital developments confirm the inherent sociality and processuality of collective memory.

Public Memory, Social Media and Visual Archives

The role of digital images in the construction of public memory has become especially evident with the proliferation of social media platforms. Today, social media are virtual "memory spaces". (lieux de mémoire). On channels such as Facebook, Twitter and Instagram, users constantly remind, commemorate and reinterpret their shared past through photos and videos. For example, memorial groups and pages on Facebook have become *"collective archives"* where local communities document their history. Leisa Gibbons (2019) found in a study that Facebook groups function as "emerging community archives" where individuals engage in deliberate *archiving and remembering* (Gibbons, 2019). Indeed, in the Facebook groups analyzed for Western Australia, users create a collective memory by sharing photographs of their local past. Since such groups are established with the intention of creating memory, they seem to spontaneously construct the *frames of remembrance* emphasized by Halbwachs (1992) in the digital environment (Gibbons, 2019). Adolfo Baltar-Moreno (2022) also reached important conclusions by analyzing the popularity of urban memory groups on Facebook. Analyzing two Facebook photo groups on the city of Cartagena (Colombia), Baltar-Moreno argues that these groups reach large audiences through *everyday/vernacular photographs* shared by users. More importantly, the findings suggest that digital social networks have come to partially complement or substitute the memory functions formerly performed only by official institutions such as museums or archives (Baltar-Moreno, 2022). In other words, while photographs of neighborhood or city history used to be kept only on archival shelves, today they are part of public memory by being made accessible to the public on platforms such as Facebook. In this way, digital images mediate a shift from institutional memory to personal/participatory memory in remembering cultural heritage and local history.

The contribution of social media to public memory is not limited to local history groups. Many important events around the world are re-enacted with thousands of images on social media on anniversaries or commemoration days. For example, on the anniversary of the 9/11 attacks, photos of the Twin Towers are shared on Twitter with the hashtag #NeverForget, thus transmitting a traumatic collective experience across generations through digital images. Similarly, *memorial pages* and *commemorative hashtags* created in the aftermath of events such as terrorist attacks, natural disasters or national achievements become platforms where large masses of people express their feelings and weave a common fabric of remembrance. Timothy Recuber (2012) calls this phenomenon *the* "prosumption of commemoration". In the online memorial sites that Recuber analyzed, it was observed that after disasters such as 9/11, Hurricane Katrina or the Virginia Tech attack, ordinary people created a huge online memory bank by sharing their testimonies, photos and stories in the digital environment (Recuber, 2012). These *digital memory banks* perpetuate the visual and emotional legacy of disasters beyond official narratives and provide a shared space of mourning and remembrance for victims' relatives and witnesses. Social media can spread public commemoration practices to the grassroots, making collective memory more democratic and polyphonic than ever before (Meyers, 2009).

However, the role of digital images in public memory is not entirely unproblematic. The specific constraints and commercial priorities of digital platforms affect the formation of collective memory. Research on Facebook groups, for example, reveals that the platform's interface design and algorithms mold shared content into specific patterns. In the aforementioned Facebook archive groups, the ways in which stories are presented are often limited to the formats allowed by the platform, resulting in narratives that are fragmented and stream-oriented (Baltar-Moreno, 2022). Gibbons (2019) also emphasizes that Facebook's group structure produces *a "fragmented community memory"* because it fails to provide a temporal perspective on the continuity of memories. Sacha van Leeuwen's (2024) study on the commemoration of British soldiers on Facebook also illustrates the contradictory aspects of memory practices in the digital environment. Van Leeuwen found that while online memorial pages allow people to share alternative stories to the official war narratives, users often reproduce the dominant narrative (such as a discourse praising military values). This suggests that digital memorials *can reinforce existing ideologies*, even if they appear democratic on the surface . Moreover, researchers such as Johnson (2018) argue that the design of social media sites encourages a culture of *consumption and engagement* rather than reflection. Indeed, *"site structure, graphical interfaces, and algorithmic arrangements combine to promote content consumption and connection rather than in-depth critical discourse"* (Johnson, 2018, p.219).

In short, while digital images expand public memory by opening it up to everyone's participation, they also run the risk of subordinating memory formation to the logic of platform capitalism. Therefore, digital collective memory studies should both celebrate new forms of participation and remembrance and critically analyze the structural dynamics that constrain these forms.

Images of Protest, Social Testimony and Memory

One of the most striking examples of digital images in the construction of collective memory is seen in the images produced during social events and protests. Throughout history, some photographs have been engraved in public memory and have become symbols of certain events. The "Napalm girl" photograph taken during the Vietnam War or the image of a man standing in front of tanks in Tiananmen Square are iconic examples that have become part of collective memory. In the digital age, the production and circulation of such iconic images has accelerated exponentially, and moreover, the frames of not only professional photojournalists but also ordinary people have become symbolic. Thanks to the immediacy of social media, the visual symbol of a protest or social event can spread around the world within hours.

The role of digital images in protest memory is also related to the concept of 'social witnessing'. Now, when protests, conflicts or historical moments occur, not only journalists, but also individuals on the ground record with their smartphones, offering testimony to a global audience. This phenomenon is a new dimension of what Frosh & Pinchevski (2009) call the practice of *"mediated witnessing"*. Especially thanks to social media, the live visual testimony provided by ordinary citizens is playing an increasingly central role in the construction of public memory. For example, the killing of George Floyd by police brutality in the US in 2020 suddenly became a matter of collective memory and conscience around the world when a young woman's cell phone camera recorded the incident and shared it on social media. This tragic image was viewed by billions of people, inspired protests and became a symbol in the memory of the "Black Lives Matter" movement. Here, the digital image *went beyond being evidence of a crime and* created *a collective memory of mourning and outrage*.

Anna Reading (2011) draws attention to this very situation by introducing the concept of "globital memory field" to describe today's globalized and digitized memory environment. According to Reading, news reporting practices and memory production are now so intertwined on a digital and global level that in times of conflict or crisis, *"mobile and social witnessing has become the norm"* (Reading, 2011). In situations such as war, natural disasters or protests, the instant recording and sharing of the moment of the event through mobile devices and social networks contributes to the real-time formation of collective memory (Reading, 2011). In this way, people around the world, even if they are not physically present, witness the event by looking at visual media and leave a common trace in their memories. Thus, digital images not only keep a record of events, but also create a global *community of memory*. These practices of social witnessing have made a shared experience, which in the past could only be possible through national media and with a delay, now *simultaneous and cross-border*. However, this situation also comes with ethical responsibilities: There are risks of compassion fatigue and desensitization, the dissemination of misleading information or fictitious images, and the reliability of testimony. Nevertheless, the visual dimension of today's collective memory is enriched and diversified largely through these *distributed* networks *of testimony*.

CONCLUSION and EVALUATION

The titles discussed in this study reveal the transformative impact of digital images on visual culture and artistic production as a whole. "Digital images: A new way of seeing" is not just a metaphorical expression, but the reality of the age we live in. As Marshall McLuhan pointed out, communication mediums have the power to radically change our framework of perception; digital visual technologies have reshaped the way human beings see, understand and express the world.

Today, more than ever, images are at the center of our lives. As Vilém Flusser predicted, technical images have once again become the cornerstone of our thought production after the long dominance of print culture. Unlike yesterday's photography, however, today's technical images are digital, networked and interactive. In this way, images not only represent but also act, circulate and acquire new meanings. W. J. T. Mitchell's question *"What do pictures want?"* becomes even more complex in the digital age. Digital paintings seem to want to be shared, liked, remixed. They are not static end products, but living, transforming, transmitted cultural objects.

The evolution of photography from analog to digital is more than a technological advance; it has transformed the ontology and social function of photography. New aesthetic forms - from glitches to filters, from memes to data sculptures - have expanded our vocabulary of visual expression. Artists are incorporating digital tools into their creative palettes, making the previously impossible possible, and viewers are experiencing new ways of interacting with artworks.

Of course, this transformation is not without its challenges. The labor-value relationship of digital images is shifting, the concepts of copyright and authenticity are being questioned, and it is becoming harder to create a lasting impact within the attention economy. Moreover, in the post-truth era debates, the reliability of images becomes questionable. All this increases the importance of critical thinking and literacy in digital visual culture.

The new way of seeing shaped by digital imagery has brought us to an uninterrupted visual awareness of the world around us, but also to a new regime of memory. In this regime, remembering means re-circulating images of the past, making space for them in digital space and attributing collective meanings to them. Digital images are therefore an integral part not only of our contemporary culture but also of our relationship with the past. Moments frozen in a photo frame enter an endless life cycle in the digital universe, *keeping our social memory alive*. This phenomenon shows us that digital images are both a *means of recording* and *a means of understanding and remembrance*.

The new way of seeing and remembering shaped through digital images has made our collective memory more inclusive, yet complex. In this new situation, individuals and communities construct the past through visual, interactive and instantaneous experiences more than ever before, expanding the boundaries of public memory. While this expansion opens the horizons of social testimony and cultural remembrance, it also requires memory studies to revise its conceptual tools. In the digital age, images teach us not only to look but also to remember anew - and in this way, they redefine humanity's connection to the past by intertwining the seen and the remembered.

The impact of digital technologies on artistic production not only offers new tools but also transforms the nature of art and visual communication. Digital images are indeed the basis of a new way of seeing for 21st century man, seeing the world through pixels, algorithms and networks, allowing us to experience reality through a lens that is both foggy and sharp, individual and collective. This process of transformation is not yet complete - perhaps it never will be. As technology develops, our ways of seeing will continue to evolve. The important thing is to consciously follow this evolution, to enrich our visual culture while not losing our human creativity and critical perspective.

REFERENCES

Akmeşe, E. (2017). *Evrensel Bir Simgenin Sıradışı Öyküsü: Chevolution, (Editörler), Huriye Kuruoğlu ve Alev Fatoş Parsa. Belgesel Filmde Zamanın Ruhu: Belgesel Filmde Değişen Anlam ve Anlatım.* Detay Yayıncılık.

Aydemir, F. (n.d.), *Fotoğrafın Evrimi: Analogdan Dijitale Geçişin Hikayesi ve Günümüzde Fotoğrafçılık,* https://www.fatihaydemir.net/blog/fotografin-evrimi-analogdan-dijitale-gecisin-hikayesi/, [Erişim Tarihi: 11.03.2025].

Baltar-Moreno, A. (2022). Digital social networks as sites of memory: Citizen dialogues through photography on Facebook. *ICONO 14. Revista de Comunicación y Tecnologías Emergentes, 20*(2), 53–59. DOI: 10.7195/ri14.v20i2.1880

Baudrillard, J. (1981). *Simulacra and Simulation.* The University of Michigan Press.

Çakın, Ö., & Bolat, N. (2018). *Sosyal Medya Reklamcılığı ve Dijital Mecra Etkileşimleri, 'Dijital Kültür ve İletişim' içinde* (Çakmak, V., & Çavuş, S., Eds.). Literatürk Academia Yayınları.

Çoban, İ. (2023). Sinema- Görsel Tasarım İlişkisi Ekseninde Sanal Gerçeklik ve Hikaye Anlatımı: "Gloomy Eyes" Analizi. *Uluslararası Disiplinlerarası ve Kültürlerarası Sanat, 8*(17), 13–28.

Demir, A. Z ve Demir, Ö. (2023). Dijital Medyada İçerik Üretiminin Geleneksel İçerik Üretimi Teknikleri Bağlamında Değerlendirilmesi, Dijital Kapitalizm ve İletişim Sempozyumu 16-18 Mayıs 2023 (pp.400-408)

Depeli, G., & Hepdincler, T. (2022). Tema Editörlerinden (TR). *Moment Dergi, 9*(1), 1–6. DOI: 10.17572/moment.1136304

Er, M. H. (2023)... *Portrait Photography and Appropriation, Contemporary Issues of Communication, Volume, 2*(1), 18–32.

Frosh, P., & Pinchevski, A. (2009). *Media Witnessing: Testimony in the Age of Mass Communication.* Palgrave Macmillan. DOI: 10.1057/9780230235762

Gençcelep, B., & Özkemahlı, K. K. (2023). "Gerçek Olandan Simülasyona: Fotoğraf Stüdyosu Eğitiminde "Set.A.Light 3D" Örneği", International Academic Social Resources Journal, (e-ISSN: 2636-7637), Vol:8, Issue:51; pp:3062-3071. DOI: 10.29228/ASRJOURNAL.70969

Gibbons, L. (2019). Connecting personal and community memory-making: Facebook groups as emergent community archives. *Information Research, 24*(3).

Güler, M. (2022). *Dipnot*: Bir Fotoğraf Felsefesine Doğru.* https://www.ifsakblog.org/dipnot-bir-fotograf-felsefesine-dogru, [Erişim Tarihi: 20.03.2025.

Halbwachs, M. (1992). On Collective Memory. (Çev. L. A. Coser). University of Chicago Press. (Original 1952).

Hoby, H. (2012). Google muse: the new breed of street photographers. *The Observer*. https://www.theguardian.com/artanddesign/2012/jul/14/google-muse-street-photographers-interviews, [Erişim Tarihi: 09.05.2025].

Hoskins, A. (2018). Memory of the multitude: The end of collective memory. A. Hoskins (Ed.), *Digital Memory Studies: Media Pasts in Transition* içinde (s.85-109). Routledge.

Hoskins, A., & Halstead, H. (2021). The new grey of memory: An interview with Andrew Hoskins. *Memory Studies, 14*(4), 675–682. DOI: 10.1177/17506980211010936

Johnson, E. (2018). The interface of memories: Sociotechnical concerns in digital commemoration. *Social Media + Society, 4*(1). Advance online publication. DOI: 10.1177/2056305118763345

Kastrenakes, J. (2021). *Beeple sold an NFT for $69 million. The Verge.* https://www.theverge.com/2021/3/11/22325054/beeple-christies-nft-sale-cost-everydays-69-million, [Erişim Tarihi: 17.03.2025].

Kırmızı, H. & Çağıl, F. (2023). Dijital kültür, sinema, televizyon ve belirsizlik. İletişim Kuram ve Araştırma Dergisi, (65), 274-287. .DOI: 10.47998/ikad.1325305

Mandolessi, S. (2023). The digital turn in memory studies. *Memory Studies, 16*(6), 1513–1528. DOI: 10.1177/17506980231204201

Manovich, L. (1995). The Paradoxes of Digital Photography. Photography after Photography. Exhibition catalog. Germany. www.manovich.net [Erişim Tarihi: 13.02.2025].

Manovich, L. (2020). The aesthetic society: or how I edit my Instagram1. . Data Publics.DOI: 10.4324/9780429196515-13

Mitchell, W. J. T. (1994). *Picture Theory: Essays on Verbal and Visual Representation.* University of Chicago Press.

Mitchell, W. J. T. (2005). *What Do Pictures Want? The Lives and Loves of Images.* University of Chicago Press. DOI: 10.7208/chicago/9780226245904.001.0001

Özdal, M. A., & Bulut, Ş. (2024). The intersection of technology and art: Artistic innovation and change in the age of artificial intelligence. *Journal of Art and Iconography, 7*, 19–27.

Özkemahlı, K. K., & Er, M. H. (2024). "Yapay Zekâ Destekli Fotoğrafik Yaklaşım: Portre ve Mekân Temelinde Mustafa Kemal Atatürk Fotoğraflarının Yeniden Üretilmesi". (Ed.), Yağmur, Ö. & Şengünalp, C., *Disiplinlerarası Sanat Pratikleri 2*. Ankara: Detay Yayıncılık.

Product, (2024). *The Impact of Instagram: 50 Statistics You Should Know in 2024,* https://www.linkedin.com/pulse/impact-instagram-50-statistics-you-should-know-2024-szhue/, [Erişim Tarihi: 15.04.2025].

Reading, A. (2011). *The Journalist as Assembler: The Globital Memory Field, Non Memory and The Shooting of Osama Bin Laden:' (164-178) Memory and Journalism* (Zelizer, B., & Tenenboim, K., Eds.). Palgrave.

Recuber, T. (2012). The prosumption of commemoration: Disasters, digital memory banks, and online collective memory. *The American Behavioral Scientist, 56*(4), 531–549. DOI: 10.1177/0002764211429364

Steyerl, H. (2009). *In Defense of the Poor Image.* https://www.e-flux.com/journal/10/61362/in-defense-of-the-poor-imag, [Erişim Tarihi: 12.05.2025].

Thread, R. (2020). *Arşivlerden: Vilém Flusser – Teknik Devrim Hakkında 1988 Tarihli Röportaj,* https://red-thread.org/teknik-devrim-hakkinda, [Erişim Tarihi: 17.03.2025].

Yılmaz, R. (2017). Türkiye'de reklam anlatısının dijital çağdaki yapısal dönüşümü, *1st International Conference on New Trends in Communication*. İstanbul.

ADDITIONAL READING

Benjamin, W. (2008). *Mekanik Yeniden Üretim Çağında Sanat Yapıtı (H. T. Adalı, Çev.).* Dost Kitabevi.

Drozdzewski, D.. (2021). Memory in the digital age: Separating the digital and the traditional? *Memory Studies, 14*(1), 3–16. DOI: 10.1177/1750698019873264 PMID: 33719365

Flusser, V. (2000). *Towards a Philosophy of Photography* (Mathews, A., Trans.). Reaktion Books.

Han, B.-C. (2015). *The Transparency Society* (Butler, E., Trans.). Stanford University Press. DOI: 10.1515/9780804797511

Hoskins, A. (2018). The restless past: An introduction to digital memory and media. *Memory Studies, 11*(1), 5–13. DOI: 10.1177/1750698007083883

Klos, S. (2023, April). "Painting" with data: how media artist Refik Anadol creates art using generative AI". *WIPO Magazine*. https://www.wipo.int/wipo_magazine/en/2023/04/article_0001.html

Manovich, L. (2001). *The Language of New Media*. MIT Press.

McLuhan, M. (1995). *Essential McLuhan* (McLuhan, E., & Zingrone, F., Eds.). Routledge.

Mitchell, W. J. (1992). *The Reconfigured Eye: Visual Truth in the Post-Photographic Era*. MIT Press.

Mutluer, K. (2024). İmgelerin eleştirel gücü ve tarih imgesi üzerine bir inceleme. *Kayıt, 23*(1), 225–258.

Zelizer, B. (2008). *About to Die: How News Images Move the Public*. Oxford University Press.

KEY TERMS AND DEFINITIONS

AI-Generated Art: AI-generated art refers to visual artworks created with the assistance of artificial intelligence, particularly through machine learning and generative algorithms. These systems produce entirely new images or manipulate existing ones based on vast datasets. This raises questions about creativity, authorship, and artistic agency. Artists like Refik Anadol have pioneered this field, blending data with aesthetics in innovative ways.

Algorithmic Aesthetics: Algorithmic aesthetics describe the visual styles shaped or influenced by algorithms, especially on platforms like Instagram and TikTok. These systems determine which images are seen, liked, and shared, thus shaping public taste and visual trends. Users often adapt their visual content to align with these invisible criteria. This creates feedback loops that normalize specific compositions, colors, and formats.

Collective Memory: Collective memory refers to the shared recollections and narratives that bind a group or society together. In the digital age, this memory is increasingly shaped by visual content like photographs and videos. Social media platforms have become new sites of remembrance, replacing traditional monuments or archives. These platforms democratize memory-making but also introduce fragmentation and misinformation.

Digital Image: A digital image is a visual representation created and processed through numerical data, usually in the form of pixels and algorithms. Unlike analog photographs, digital images are easily reproducible, editable, and widely shareable. They challenge traditional ideas of authenticity, realism, and originality. In both contemporary art and social life, digital images have become central to how we see and record reality.

Protest Visuality: Protest visuality refers to the symbolic images that emerge from social movements and demonstrations. These visuals—like the "Lady in Red" during the Gezi protests—often become icons of resistance and solidarity. Captured and circulated through smartphones and social media, such images build a shared memory of collective struggle. They also serve as tools of documentation, emotion, and mobilization.

Social Media Archive: Social media platforms function as informal archives where users store, share, and retrieve personal and collective memories. Images posted online contribute to the visual history of individuals and communities. Unlike institutional archives, these platforms are participatory and often ephemeral. Their archival value depends on digital infrastructure, platform policies, and user interaction.

Visual Culture: Visual culture explores how societies understand and communicate through images. With the rise of digital media, visual communication has become dominant over textual forms in many areas. Everyday life, art, and identity expression are now deeply rooted in image-based interactions. This culture demands new literacies and critical engagement with visual information.

Chapter 10

Reconstructing Aura in the Digital Age: The Search for Authenticity in Artificial Intelligence Art

Canan Arslan
http://orcid.org/0000-0002-3853-0379
Dogus University, Turkey

ABSTRACT

This article aims to reconsider Walter Benjamin's concept of "aura" in the context of artworks produced with artificial intelligence (AI). Benjamin's claim that art loses its authenticity in the age of mechanical reproduction is revisited through the lens of digital and algorithmic art practices. The study employs a qualitative theoretical analysis, using Refik Anadol's Melting Memories and Machine Hallucinations as case studies. It proposes four contemporary forms of aura: processual, data-based, interactional, and algorithmic. The analysis demonstrates that AI-generated artworks can convey originality not only through their physical form, but also through their processes, cognitive dimensions, and audience interactions. Ultimately, it argues that rather than erasing subjectivity, digital and AI-driven production fosters a multi-layered, interactive aesthetic paradigm where aura persists in new forms.

INTRODUCTION

The rapid evolution of technology has profoundly reshaped the ways in which art is produced, shared, and experienced. In today's digital age, questions such as what art is, who it is created by, how it is circulated and how it gains its meaning have become increasingly complex and layered. At the heart of these discussions

DOI: 10.4018/979-8-3373-2230-8.ch010

lies the concept of "aura", a term introduced by Walter Benjamin in his famous essay, "The Work of Art in the Age of Mechanical Reproduction" (1936). With this concept, Benjamin offered a powerful framework to understand how technological reproduction affects not just the uniqueness of an artwork, but also its presence in time and space, its authenticity, and the viewer's relationship to it. In the context of contemporary digital and AI-generated art, revisiting Walter Benjamin's theory offers a valuable analytical framework for understanding the ongoing transformation of core concepts such as originality, authorship, and artistic value.

One of Benjamin's most radical observations regarding modern art is his claim that technical reproduction technologies (especially photography and film) eliminate the historical and physical uniqueness of the work of art, or its "aura." This argument has been accepted as one of the most influential philosophical explanations of the transformation of artistic experience along with the democratization of cultural production throughout the 20th century.

However, Benjamin's concept of aura has been brought to a new level of discussion with new areas such as digital technologies, artificial intelligence and algorithmic art production. (Grau, 2003; Betancourt, 2016; Manovich, 2001) The increase in the production of artificial intelligence (AI)-supported artworks, especially in the last decade, has made it necessary to radically rethink concepts such as the originality of art, the role of the artist and the experience of the viewer. In this context, the following questions are becoming increasingly evident: Can an artwork produced with artificial intelligence have aura? What does the uniqueness of an artwork now depend on? How should Benjamin's concept of aura be interpreted or reconstructed in the digital age?

In this article, Walter Benjamin's concept of aura will be examined in detail within its historical context. Then, how this concept has transformed in the context of digital art and AI-based art production will be discussed with theoretical discussions and examples. The aim of this article is to question the validity of Benjaminian concepts in today's art world and to analyze the forms that aura can take in the digital age within the framework of new aesthetic paradigms.

Theoretical Background

Since its introduction by Walter Benjamin in the early 20th century, the concept of aura has played a central role in debates about how art is perceived and valued in the age of mechanical and now digital reproduction. Benjamin's idea offers a framework for understanding how the technological conditions of production and circulation influence the authenticity, originality, and emotional resonance of art-works. This section revisits the historical and philosophical foundations of aura, first by exploring Benjamin's original formulation of the concept, then by tracing how it has been challenged, expanded, and reinterpreted in the context of contemporary media and digital aesthetics.

Origin of the Aura Concept

Walter Benjamin's concept of aura represents not only an aesthetic quality but also a social, historical and ideological understanding. According to Benjamin, the aura of a work of art stems from its being "here and now". This refers to the physical existence of the work, its historical context and its unique production conditions. In Benjamin's classical definition, aura is "the echo of the unique existence of a being, an object or a living being from a distance - no matter how close -" (Benjamin, 2008: 23). Aura is not just a visual effect; it is a fascinating sense of distance within proximity that occurs when the work has a history and cultural context of its own.

Benjamin developed this concept especially in the face of the rise of technically reproducible art forms such as photography and film. The reduction of art from its classical position based on "worship value" to "exhibition value" removes the work of art from being a unique, ritual-centered object and turns it into an object of mass consumption integrated into everyday life.

The Effect of Technology on Aesthetic Production: Mechanical Reproduction

Benjamin's fundamental thesis is that technical reproduction sacrifices the aura of the work of art in the name of accessibility. Through mediums such as photography and film, the work of art becomes both spatially reproducible and temporally manipulable. In Benjamin's words, "a reproduction of a work of art, no matter how perfect, lacks the element of its presence in time and space." (Benjamin, 2008: 21). This deprivation is the elimination of the genuine experience of the work, being "here and now."

Benjamin's views also include the democratization of cultural production. In other words, thanks to technical reproduction, art is no longer the monopoly of elites; The masses may encounter art in cinemas or newspapers. However, the price of this development is the loss of the magic, the "mystical quality" and the "aura" of art.

Post-Benjamin Discussions: Criticism of Aura and Its Expanding Meaning

Since its introduction, Benjamin's concept of aura has been interpreted not only in the context of technical reproduction but also as a structural analysis of the relationship established by modernity with aesthetics. His observation that art has lost its "magic" through mechanical reproduction has become one of the fundamental references, especially in visual culture studies. Studies addressing the transformation of modern forms of vision have suggested that aura is not only a state of being but also a state of perception. In this context, the process of aura's dissolution has accelerated as artistic representations have been detached from their context and put into circulation, and images have become indebted to the medium in which they are re-presented rather than the medium in which they are produced (Berger, 1972).

While Benjamin's theory is sufficiently comprehensive to explain the impact of modern communication technologies on cultural images, it has received criticism over time that the "auratic" qualities of the work cannot be limited to originality and physical singularity alone. Even in the ages when art gained exhibition value, it has been observed that works can provide an auratic experience; for example, works of art sold at astronomical prices at auctions or ritualized museum exhibitions of iconic works of art have suggested that aura continues to live in different forms (Abbing, 2004). This suggests that Benjamin's definition of aura does not indicate an absolute dissolution, but perhaps a transforming acquisition of form.

However, the rapid circulation of images in contemporary aesthetic consumption has not only diminished traditional auratic values but also contributed to the emergence of new contextual meanings. As the modes of image production have evolved, the boundaries between original and reproduction have blurred, transforming reproduction from a technical process into a deliberate artistic strategy. (Groys, 2008)

Reshaping Aura in the Age of Digitalization

Digitalization has surpassed the age of technical reproduction envisioned by Benjamin, creating an era in which an infinite number of perfect copies can be produced and each copy can circulate simultaneously on a global scale. In this context, although the determination that aura has disappeared seems to have become more certain in the digital age, this view itself is increasingly questioned in digital art theories, because digital images, continue to produce contextually and experientially original meanings, even though they do not have physical existence. (Davis, 1995; Steyerl, 2013; Floridi, 2019).

The technical possibilities offered by new media art require a rethinking of aura. It is argued that works of art can have originality not only according to a physical singularity, but also according to parameters such as the production process, the data used, and the interaction with the viewer (Grau, 2003; Bishop, 2012; Coeckelbergh, 2020). These approaches make it possible to evaluate aura as a phenomenon constructed in the processes of production and experience, rather than a fixed quality.

In digital environments where art production is carried out with software, algorithms and data sources, the auratic effect is not attributed only to the "original". On the contrary, how the work is produced, what data it feeds on and what interactions it takes shape with become new elements carrying the aura. Thus, aura evolves from a physical singularity to a relational and processual structure. This situation brings to the agenda the existence of a new generation auratic experience model as an alternative to Benjamin's historical definition of aura (Kalpokas, 2023).

In the digital age, the presentation of production tools to the audience transforms the artwork from being merely an object to be consumed to an object of participatory and plural experience. For example, in interactive art practices, a different connection is established with each viewer, and the experience becomes singular (Bishop, 2012). Such works, although physically repeatable, create a new aura with each repetition, since the connection they establish with the viewer changes with each experience. Thus, the digital copy has not completely broken away from context as Benjamin thought; on the contrary, it has regained its power to produce context.

Betancourt challenges Benjamin's traditional aura concept. He argues that digital artworks produce a new kind of aura – what he terms the "aura of information." This digital aura is not based on material uniqueness but on the symbolic, performative and reproducible nature of digital files. In other words, in Betancourt's view, reproducibility itself produces aura. (Betancourt, 2016)

Hans Abbing's view about the aura of an artwork aligns with Betancourt's "aura of information." Abbing argues that artworks like Bach's compositions retain or increase their aura through widespread reproduction. This insight reframes aura as something enhanced through circulation and recognition, not as something lost through copying. (Abbing, 2004)

In this new framework, aura can be redefined not only as the magic of the original, but also as a dynamic quality that occurs in the interaction between data, software, experience and the viewer. This shows that, instead of disappearing in the digital age, aura has found a new space of existence, not on a physical, but on a relational and experiential level.

Art Production with Artificial Intelligence: Originality, Automation and Artistry

With technological advances, the singular producer position of humans in the production processes of art has been seriously discussed. Especially in the last decade, it has been observed that generative algorithms and artificial intelligence (AI) systems have begun to take on the role of human artists in the creation of visual, auditory and textual content. This development has caused fundamental aesthetic values such as artistry, originality and creativity to be questioned. Considering that the qualities that determine a work of art have historically been based on the idea of being "human creation", this transformation indicates a serious rupture in terms of the philosophy of art.

Art production with AI systems is generally carried out through generative algorithms that learn from large data sets and produce new visuals, texts or sounds with this data. Such algorithms used in artistic production are not systems that "think like humans" but rather "recognize patterns from data". From this perspective, the artistic production capacity of AI functions as a simulation engine that works on correlations and variations, without any consciousness or aesthetic intention.

However, the contemporary art world does not evaluate these productions as mere technical demonstrations; on the contrary, many AI-supported works are exhibited in prestigious art galleries, put up for sale in auction houses and are evaluated in critical texts. This situation shows that the dependence of the artwork on classical criteria such as originality, intention and expression is dissolving, and is being replaced by new aesthetic criteria such as automation, system specificity and artificial productivity.

The Problem of Originality and Ownership

One of the most frequently asked questions in AI-supported art production is whether these productions are truly original, since generative models produce new outputs by learning from large data pools consisting of past artworks, photographs or texts. Although this situation may seem new at a visual or aesthetic level, it actually emerges from the reprocessing of existing forms and images. In this context, it can be argued that AI is not "creative" but a system that can "compile and produce variation". (Elgammal et al., 2017; Coeckelbergh, 2020)

According to this view, originality gains meaning not only with formal differences but also with intention, context and expressive power. Although human artistic production is often characterized by conscious decision-making, intuition, and emotional depth, such qualities are typically absent in AI-generated works. Nevertheless, this distinction also exposes the limitations of conventional aesthetic theories. In contemporary contexts, many viewers are unable to discern whether a work is the result of human creativity or algorithmic processes—and, in some cases, they may even perceive AI-generated artworks as more impressive (Chamberlain et al., 2018; Hong & Curran, 2019).

This situation shows that the viewer focuses on the sensory and conceptual impact of the resulting image rather than the source of the work in their aesthetic evaluation. If the meaning of art is shaped by the receiver rather than the producer, then the question of whether the producer is human or machine may become a secondary issue.

The question of who is the "artist" of artworks produced with AI is a debate that has both aesthetic, ethical and legal dimensions. Images, texts or sound patterns created without direct human intervention in the production process force the definition of artistry to expand. While the producer subject in traditional art is defined as an individual equipped with creative consciousness, this consciousness is not directly present in artificial intelligence systems.

At this point, the concept of artist should be redefined to include human-software interaction. The artist is no longer just a "producer" but also a curator who selects data, designs algorithms and determines aesthetic parameters (Coeckelbergh, 2020). In this context, artificial intelligence functions more as a co-producer or co-author than a creator. Therefore, artistry is related to the design of the creative process, not the physical production.

Ownership discussions have also brought to the agenda the practical consequences of this new form of artistry. In some countries, images automatically generated by AI are legally considered "works without an author", which questions the principle that copyright should be tied to a human legal entity. Thus, the production of art with artificial intelligence is a process that requires restructuring not only in terms of aesthetics but also in terms of institutional and legal frameworks. (Braidotti, 2013)

Since artificial intelligence systems do not have a conscious intention, the "expressive" element in art production in the traditional sense is questioned. However, this questioning is based on the assumption that aesthetic value depends only on the artist's intention. Since Barthes' (1977) theory of "The Death of the Author," the idea that the production of meaning is based on the practice of the person reading or experiencing the text, not the author, has become widespread in art criticism. This approach opens a new perspective in evaluating AI art: The meaning of the work should be sought in the experience and context that occurs rather than the productive intention.

When it is considered that aesthetic meaning in AI production arises from randomness, this meaning arises from the relationship established by humans with the machine rather than the intention of the machine. From this perspective, AI art contributes to a post-humanist aesthetic framework where artistic meaning is co-constructed by diverse actors rather than originating from a single human author. (Ihde, 1990; Kalpokas, 2023). Thus, AI production offers a new framework in which production itself can be evaluated as an aesthetic event, against the argument that it cannot be considered art due to lack of intention. A process-oriented, systemic and interactive aesthetic regime that is not dependent on the singular existence of the artist is taking shape.

In light of the above discussions, art production with artificial intelligence leads to profound transformations not only in the production of aesthetic objects but also in the definition, function and value criteria of art. Originality is no longer evaluated only with "being the first" but also with the way it is produced and its relational contexts. Artistry ceases to be a concept that belongs to the monopoly of the creative individual and evolves into process-based functions such as data curation, algorithmic design and aesthetic modulation. (Braidotti, 2013; Coeckelbergh, 2020; Bridle, 2018)

In this framework, art production with AI, on the one hand, allows for the expansion of Benjamin's definition of aura, and on the other hand, it enables the reconstruction of classical art values. Aura can now exist not only in the "here and now" but also in the "data and process". (Benjamin, 2008; Betancourt, 2016; Cohn, 2024)

New Forms of Aura in Digital Art

The digital age has radically changed not only the production and circulation forms of art, but also the nature of aesthetic experience. This change requires a rethinking of Walter Benjamin's concept of aura, which is based on originality and authenticity. For Benjamin, aura is the enchanting effect that stems from the historical and physical singularity of a work of art; in other words, from its being "here and now" (Benjamin, 2008). However, the fact that digital art is not physically based but digitally based, that it can be reproduced infinitely, and that the production process is mechanized renders this definition inadequate.

Kalpokas (2023) argues that AI art doesn't merely copy reality, like photography or film; instead it generates novel patterns based on data, reflecting contemporary social conditions and cultural values. These works emerge from the "collective unconscious" embedded in big data and digital culture. Kalpokas argues that aura today may not stem from uniqueness, but rather from interpretative relationships and audience encounters shaped by digital culture.

Accordingly, contemporary art theorists and artists propose new forms of auratic experience that derive from Benjamin's definition but expand it. In this section, this transformation will be discussed in four basic dimensions: processual aura, data-based aura, interactive aura, and algorithmic aura. Each offers a different window into how the digital age reconstructs the sense of authenticity and singularity in art production.

Processual Aura: The Uniqueness of Visible Production

In digital art, the work is not only a result, but also a process. While traditional works of art are mostly exhibited as a finished product, digital art, especially with the use of artificial intelligence, makes production processes visible. This visibility is shared with the audience on both conceptual and technical levels. Therefore, it is not only its aesthetic qualities that determine the value of the work, but also how it is produced, what data it feeds on, and what algorithms it is processed with (Grau, 2003).

From this perspective, the "processual aura" that emerges is based on the transparency of production and the audience's knowledge of this process. For example, Refik Anadol's Machine Hallucinations (2019) series not only offers visually impressive outputs; it also shares with the audience what data these works are produced from, what software they are processed with, and the production stages. Thus, the production process becomes a part of the auratic effect of the work. Aura is no longer established solely in the "here and now" but also through "how and with what" it is produced.

Data-Based Aura: The Authentic Source of Meaning

Art production with artificial intelligence is often based on very large data sets. However, data is not just a quantitative material; it is also an element that carries meaning and has contextual value. Especially in works produced with biological, historical or culturally original data sources, the inherent meaning of this data gives the artwork a contextual singularity (Coeckelbergh, 2020). This situation can be called "data-based aura".

As in Refik Anadol's "Melting Memories" (2018) project, EEG data obtained from individuals' brain waves become the main raw material of the artwork. Each individual's data is unique; therefore, the images created from this data also carry personal uniqueness. Benjamin's concept of aura based on physical singularity evolves here into the emotional, biological and historical context of the data. Thus, authenticity no longer arises from the specificity of the object, but from the specificity of the data. This approach shows that despite the completely copyable and reproducible nature of digital art, it can create a sense of originality through the data it contains. In this sense, data is both raw material and auratic context.

Interactive Aura: Dynamic Connection Established with the Viewer

Benjamin's concept of aura has often been read as object-centered; however, digital art presents the aesthetic experience as a relational structure established with the viewer. In interactive digital art applications, the viewer is not only an observer but also an active participator in the formation of the work. Each viewer experiences a different interaction; this ensures that the same work acquires a different auratic structure in each presentation (Bishop, 2012).

For example, in TeamLab's Borderless (2018) exhibition, digital images are sensitive to the movements of the viewer. Thanks to this structure, each viewer creates a unique visual composition in line with their position and movement in the space. The same work appears to be different for different viewers; therefore, each experience becomes unique and unrepeatable. In this case, the aura is not located in the object; it is located in the experience, interaction and spatial context.

In such experiences, aesthetic value is produced through the perceptual participation of the viewer. The authenticity of the work is formed together with the "consumer viewer", rather than the "producer artist". Thus, the aura becomes an active production process, not a passive observation.

Algorithmic Aura: The Singularity-Generating Potential of Code

Algorithms are structural systems that form the backbone of digital art. However, not every algorithm has to produce fixed outputs. Some software has non-deterministic structures, which produce a different result each time it is run. This positions the algorithm itself as a "creative actor". The differentiation of each production creates an algorithmic singularity (Bright, 2018).

Artists like Mario Klingemann structure artificial intelligence systems with certain rules, but by integrating random parameters into these systems, they achieve unpredictable results. Thus, every visual production is original, despite originating from the same system. The "one and unique" criterion in Benjamin's definition of aura is regained here through the variability provided by the code structure.

The transformation from binary code to visual output reflects what Betancourt describes as the "digital object" — an entity whose artistic presence only emerges through machine-based interpretation. This aligns with the concept of algorithmic aura as a co-creative interaction between system and symbol. (Betancourt, 2016)

Algorithmic aura shows that aesthetic value can also arise from machine production. In this case, aura is defined not only by historical authenticity or physical context, but by computational singularity. The code is no longer just a technical tool, but an aesthetic dimension of formation.

Taking all into consideration, these four forms of aura show that digital art does not directly oppose Benjamin's critique of aura; on the contrary, it transforms and expands it. Physical singularity and historical authenticity are no longer the only conditions for aura. In the digital age, aura has become redefined with new dimensions such as the visibility of processes, the emotional context of data, the singularity of interactive experience, and the productive nature of algorithmic systems. At this point, aura is no longer fixed; it emerges as a relational, situational, and performative structure. While the distance between the artist and the viewer is reconstructed, the machine also becomes a part of this interaction. Thus, Benjamin's definition is opened to be rethought and experienced in line with the needs of the age.

Reconstructing Aura in Refik Anadol's Art: Two Case Studies

This section examines how Walter Benjamin's concept of aura can be reconstructed in the context of contemporary AI-based art through a focused analysis of Refik Anadol's works. Anadol is chosen as a central figure for this exploration because his artistic practice explicitly engages with data-driven processes, algorithmic aesthetics, and the transformative potential of artificial intelligence in visual art. His works not only demonstrate technical innovation but also critically reflect on how new modes of artistic production affect traditional concepts such as authenticity, originality, and aura.

Among Anadol's extensive portfolio, Melting Memories (2018) and Machine Hallucinations (2019) have been selected as case studies because they embody two distinct dimensions of the evolving aura in AI art: Melting Memories emphasizes the integration of personal, biological data and emotional memory into the artwork, while Machine Hallucinations explores the generation of machine-based synthetic memory and autonomous visuality. Together, these works allow for a comparative examination of how different types of aura, particularly data-embedded aura, processual aura, interactive aura, and algorithmic aura, can emerge in AI-driven art.

The analysis is conducted through qualitative close reading of the visual, conceptual, and procedural aspects of the works, informed by Benjaminian theory of aura and extended with insights from recent AI art criticism and digital aesthetics. The goal is to illustrate how these works do not merely replicate or illustrate Benjamin's ideas but actively transform and expand them, offering a contemporary understanding of aura suited to the dynamics of digital and AI-based cultural production.

Case 1: Melting Memories (2018)

Melting Memories is one of Refik Anadol's most conceptually layered and technically sophisticated works. The project originated from a collaboration with neuroscience laboratories, where EEG (electroencephalogram) data representing human memory processes was collected from several participants (Anadol, 2018). The EEG data, consisting of neural oscillations linked to memory recall, was then processed using deep learning algorithms, specifically a custom neural network trained to translate numerical brainwave data into visual representations. In this work, aura is reshaped in a multi-layered way, going beyond Benjamin's understanding of physical singularity.

Figure 1. Refik Anadol, Melting Memories (2018) Installation view. Refik Anadol Studio (refikanadol.com)

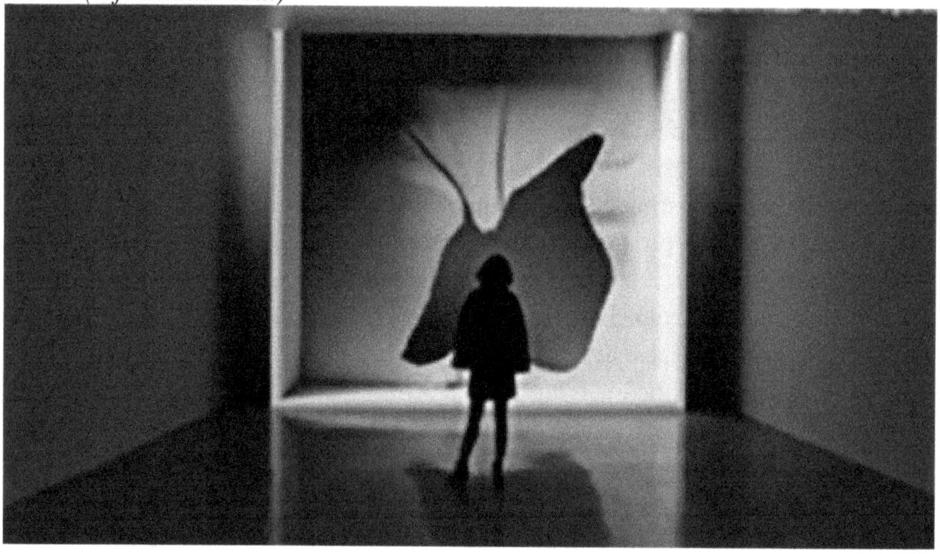

First of all, the data used in this work is not only a quantitative material; it is also an aesthetic carrier due to the biological and emotional meaning it contains. Each EEG data is specific to a particular individual's mental state, memory process, and emotional memory. Therefore, this data carries a content authenticity that cannot be subject to direct technical repetition. This coincides with the views developed by Coeckelbergh (2020) on data-based authenticity: the aura is no longer hidden in the object, but in the data.

At the same time, this work provides the viewer with information not only about the result, but also about the process of production. Anadol makes the aesthetic experience transparent by openly displaying the data sources used, the algorithm structure, and the artificial intelligence model. In this way, a processual aura is formed: the production process becomes a field of conscious participation for the viewer. In this respect, Anadol's project represents the new auratic structure that Grau (2003) associates with processual visibility in digital arts. In Grau's words, "Ironically, suddenly the concept of the original returns to digital art, as each step in this process is a unique evolutionery development". (Schuricht, 2004)

On the interactive level, although each viewer does not reflect their own mental processes on the work, the visual images they experience create a different association and emotional bond in each individual. The viewer searches for unconscious images within abstract forms; in this respect, the meaning of the work is reconstructed through individual memory. This situation shows that aura is no longer only reproduced within the object, but also at the sensory level of the viewer (Bishop, 2012).

Finally, Anadol's design of the artificial intelligence system not to produce a fixed output but to produce new visual sequences each time allows the work to contain an algorithmic aura. Even though the same data set and system are used, each image is different from the previous one. Therefore, physical repeatability is replaced by creative unrepeatability. Thus, Benjamin's emphasis on "uniqueness" is redefined in the form of computational singularity (Bright, 2018).

Case 2: Machine Hallucinations (2019)

Refik Anadol's Machine Hallucinations project is one of the most comprehensive projects that directly problematizes and visualizes the creative potential of artificial intelligence. In this work, the artist compiles millions of city photographs, architectural structures and cultural data and makes artificial intelligence "dream"; in other words, he ensures that the data is transformed into an aesthetic language through abstractions and recombinations. In this work, the aura is shaped not by human memory but by the mind of the machine.

Figure 2. Installation view of Refik Anadol's Machine Hallucinations (2019), ARTECHOUSE New York. Image via Dezeen (https://www.dezeen.com/2019/10/28/artechouse-installation-refik-anadol-new-york/).

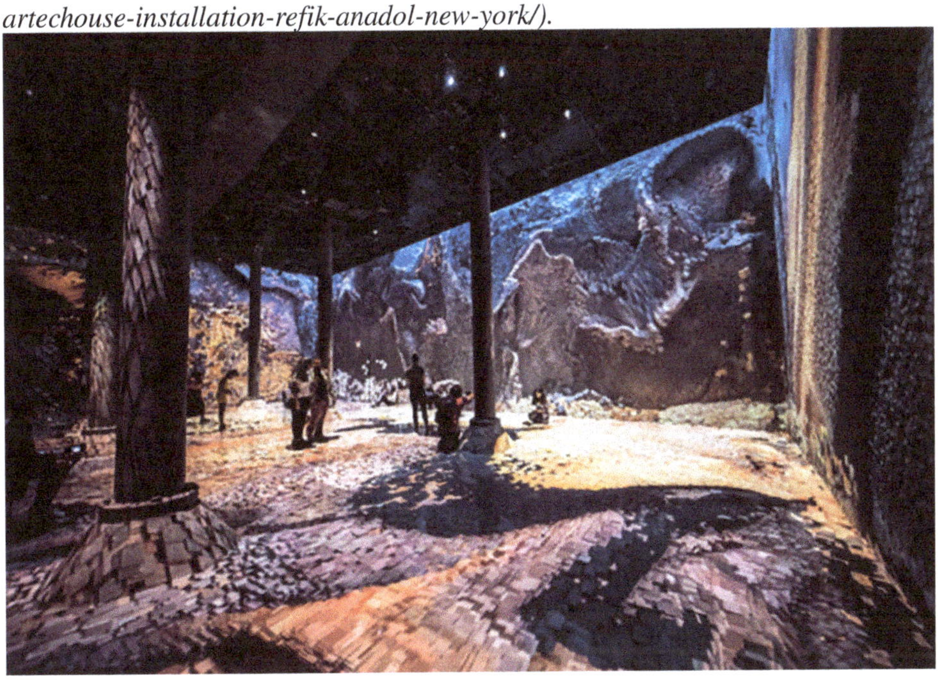

The production process of the work is documented in detail, both technically and conceptually. By exhibiting the data sets used and the production architecture in detail, Anadol confronts the viewer not only with a result but also with a production universe. In this respect, the work directly reveals the processual aura. The viewer is guided to make sense of the cognitive architecture behind the work through visual experience (Grau, 2003).

Although the dataset consists of urban images, satellite images, and cultural images, these data are not just raw information, but components of an artificial memory. When the artificial intelligence processes these images with its own internal arrangements, the resulting images make direct reference to neither an individual memory nor a historical reality. However, this very lack of context creates a kind of authenticity that Benjamin did not recognize: an auratic state resulting from the autonomous imagination of the machine (Kalpokas, 2023).

On an interactive level, this work does not directly interact with the viewer, but it offers a holistic environmental experience through the cinematic spatial arrangements, the simultaneous use of sound, light and movement. The viewer is "immersed" in the work, sensing its rhythm and matching his own images with this rhythm. This reinforces the personalized auratic structure of the experience.

Finally, the project is structurally based on the principle of algorithmic singularity. The generative systems used by Anadol constantly produce different visual compositions, even with the same data. This means that the work produces a new aesthetic with each presentation. Thus, Benjamin's emphasis on "uniqueness and unrepeatability" is updated through the creativity of the code.

These two works by Refik Anadol provide powerful examples of how Benjamin's concept of aura can be reconstructed in the digital age. Melting Memories embodies the data-based aura with the emotional carriage of individual data, the processual aura with the display of the production process, and the algorithmic aura with random algorithmic variations. Machine Hallucinations, on the other hand, creates a new type of aura that emerges from the transformation of the algorithm into an aesthetic subject through the visualization of artificial memory and the dreamlike production of the machine.

In both works, physical singularity gives way to a relational, transactional, and data-centered structure of originality. Thus, Benjamin's concept of aura not only survives in the digital age, but also transforms, multiplies, and diversifies by adapting to new production regimes.

CONCLUSION

Walter Benjamin's 1936 text "The Work of Art in the Age of Mechanical Reproduction" is not only one of the cornerstones of modern art theory, but also a pioneering prophecy about how art would evolve in the face of the technological transformation of cultural production. Benjamin claimed that technical means of reproduction eroded the physical and historical singularity of the work of art; therefore, the work lost its aura. It can be said that this approach offered a radical yet explanatory framework against technologies such as photography, cinema and television in the twentieth century. However, the digital production techniques that emerged in the twenty-first century, art creation with artificial intelligence, data-based aesthetic practices and algorithmic systems require redefiniton of Benjamin's aura.

This study argues that aura has not completely disappeared in the digital age, but rather has re-emerged in new forms through production processes, the structure of data, the relationship established with the audience, and the nature of algorithmic systems. While artificial intelligence-supported art production eliminates the dependence of aura on physical singularity, it replaces it with a relational understanding of singularity based on data-based, processual, interactive, and algorithmic foundations.

The most fundamental feature of this transformation is that aura has ceased to be a fixed concept and transformed into a dynamic and experiential phenomenon. Aura is no longer just the "magic of the original," but a state of being shaped by the openness of the production process, the originality of the data used, the connection established with the audience, and the creative potential of algorithmic processes. This approach both acknowledges the historical legitimacy of Benjamin's definition of aura and re- defines it in today's technological aesthetic practices.

Refik Anadol's works show how this transformation is possible both on an aesthetic and intellectual level. In works such as Melting Memories, data becomes not only material but also the carrier of meaning and singularity; while in works such as Machine Hallucinations, the algorithm appears as an autonomous actor of production. In both cases, aura moves away from physical singularity; however, this break is not the loss of auratic experience but its re-establishment in another form.

This transformation is not limited to the concept of aura; it also requires the redefinition of fundamental aesthetic values such as artistry, originality and authenticity. In a context where artificial intelligence rises to a productive position, the role of the artist changes form: it ceases to be the direct subject of production and becomes the designer of the system, the curator of data and the constructor of the process. In this context, artistry, rather than being an expressive authority in the classical sense, turns into a relationality that produces meaning through technological partnerships.

Similarly, the "originality" of a work is no longer derived from singularity, but from the specificity of the way it is produced, the data used, and the post-production experience. Therefore, originality is defined not only by "being the first and only" but also by authenticity established through relational context and experience. Thus, the aesthetic value of art begins to carry not only formal but also conceptual and ethical dimensions.

In the digital age, the audience is positioned both as a consumer and as an actor shaping the aesthetic experience. Interactive art practices, works sensitive to space, and productions based on personal data open up a special field of experience for each audience. This shows that aura does not only belong to the object; it can also exist based on experience, participation, and perception. Thus, the "work-centered aesthetics" concept defined by Benjamin gives way to a plural, permeable aesthetic framework centered on the audience.

Artists like Anadol process this framework on aesthetic, technological, and emotional levels. In their works, the audience does not just look; at the same time, it becomes a reproducer of aura by participating in the work's internal rhythm, memory associations or interaction with space. Thus, aura does not disappear completely as Benjamin predicted; it disperses, fragments, but also multiplies and reshapes.

In conclusion, this study shows that Benjamin's concept of aura has not become invalid in the digital age; it has been updated. While art production with artificial intelligence obscures the traditional role of the productive subject on the one hand, it also offers new kinds of singularities, contextual originalities and forms of experiential authenticity on the other. In this context, aura is no longer about something being "unique", but about something "gaining meaning" relationally.

Ultimately, the advent of artificial intelligence in the artistic domain does not signify the dissolution of art's auratic dimensions, but rather their transformation and rearticulation within new aesthetic and technological frameworks. As static forms give way to generative processes, interactive experiences, and algorithmic authorship, the foundations of what constitutes art, artist, and audience are being questioned. In this shifting landscape, Walter Benjamin's ideas are not outdated reflections of the mechanical age, but valuable tools for understanding the changing relationships between technology, culture, and art. His concept of aura — far from obsolete — invites us to continually question how presence, authenticity, and meaning are reconstituted in an era where the boundaries between the human and the machinic, the original and the reproduced, are in constant flux. The challenge now is not to mourn the loss of aura, but to critically engage with its emergent forms.

REFERENCES

Abbing, H. (2004). *Why Are Artists Poor? The Exceptional Economy of the Arts*. Amsterdam University Press.

Anadol, R. (2018). Melting Memories [Media installation]. Refik Anadol Studio. https://refikanadol.com/works/melting-memories/

Anadol, R. (2019). Machine Hallucinations [Exhibition]. ARTECHOUSE New York. https://refikanadol.com/works/machine-hallucinations/

Barthes, R. (1977). *Image, music, text* (Heath, S., Trans.). Hill and Wang.

Benjamin, W. (2008). The work of art in the age of mechanical reproduction. H. Arendt (Ed.), Illuminations (pp. 217–252). Schocken Books.

Berger, J. (1972). *Ways of seeing*. Penguin Books.

Betancourt, M. (2016). The aura of information: Digital art and the myth of uniqueness.

Bishop, C. (2012). *Artificial hells: Participatory art and the politics of spectatorship*. Verso Books.

Braidotti, R. (2013). *The posthuman*. Polity Press.

Bridle, J. (2018). *New Dark Age: Technology and the End of the Future*. Verso Books.

Bright, R. (2018, February). AI and Neurography [Interview with M. Klingemann]. Interalia Magazine. https://www.interaliamag.org/interviews/mario-klingemann/

Chamberlain, R., Mullin, C., Scheerlinck, B., & And Wagemans, J. (2018). Putting the art in artificial: Aesthetic responses to computer-generated art. *Psychology of Aesthetics, Creativity, and the Arts*, *12*(2), 177–192. DOI: 10.1037/aca0000136

Coeckelbergh, M. (2020). *AI Ethics*. MIT Press. DOI: 10.7551/mitpress/12549.001.0001

Elgammal, A., Liu, B., Elhoseiny, M., & Mazzone, M. (2017). CAN: Creative Adversarial Networks, Generating "Art" by Learning About Styles and Deviating from Style Norms. https://doi.org//arXiv.1706.07068DOI: 10.48550

Floridi, L. (2019). *The Logic of Information: A Theory of Philosophy as Conceptual Design*. Oxford University Press., DOI: 10.1093/oso/9780198833635.001.0001

Grau, O. (2003). *Virtual art: From Illusion to Immersion*. MIT Press.

Groys, B. (2008). *Art Power*. MIT Press. DOI: 10.7551/mitpress/7469.001.0001

Hong, J. C., & Curran, N. M. (2019). Artificial Intelligence, Artists, and Art: Attitudes Toward Artwork Produced By Humans vs. Artificial Intelligence. *ACM Transactions on Multimedia Computing Communications and Applications, 15*(2s), 1–16. Advance online publication. DOI: 10.1145/3326337

Ihde, D. (1990). *Technology and the Lifeworld: From garden to earth*. Indiana University Press. DOI: 10.2979/3108.0

Kalpokas, I. (2023). Work of art in the Age of Its AI Reproduction. Philosophy & Social Criticism, 51(8), 1268-1286. (Original work published 2025)DOI: 10.1177/01914537231184490

Manovich, L. (2001). *The Language of New Media*. MIT Press.

Schuricht, S. (2004, February 10). Virtual art- the aura of the digital: Fortunately it is unknown where the journey will end [Interview with O. Grau] (M. Hohl, Trans.). https://www.sushu.de/pdf/grau_sushu_04_en.pdf

Steyerl, H.. (2013). In defence of the poor image. 67. 101-105.

teamLab. (2018). teamLab Borderless (Digital art museum / interactive exhibition). MORI Building Digital Art Museum: teamLab Borderless, Tokyo, Japan. https://borderless.teamlab.art/

ADDITIONAL READING

Berger, J. (1972). *Ways of Seeing*. Penguin Books.

Bolter, J. D., & Grusin, R. (1999). *Remediation: Understanding New Media*. MIT Press.

Braidotti, R. (2019). *Posthuman knowledge* (Vol. 2). Polity Press.

Gervais, D. J. (2019). The machine as author. *Iowa Law Review, 105*, 2053.

Lister, M., Dovey, J., Giddings, S., Grant, I., & Kelly, K. (2009). *New Media: A Critical Introduction* (2nd ed.). Routledge.

Lovejoy, M. (2004). *Digital Currents: Art in the Electronic Age*. Routledge. DOI: 10.4324/9780203005279

Machado, P., Romero, J., Greenfield, G., McCormack, J., & Bown, O. (Eds.). (2021). *Artificial Intelligence and the arts: Computational Creativity, Artistic Behavior, and Tools for Creatives*. Springer International Publishing. DOI: 10.1007/978-3-030-59475-6

McCormack, J., Gifford, T., & Hutchings, P. (2019). Autonomy, Authenticity, Authorship and Intention in computer generated art. 10.48550/arXiv.1903.02166.

Ornes, S. (2019). Computers take art in new directions, challenging the meaning of "creativity". *Proceedings of the National Academy of Sciences of the United States of America*, *116*(11), 4760–4763. DOI: 10.1073/pnas.1900883116 PMID: 30862741

Steyerl, H.. (2013). In defence of the poor image. 67. 101-105.

KEY TERMS AND DEFINITIONS

Algorithmic Aura: Generated when an artwork's originality stems from the autonomous variability of algorithmic systems. Even using the same dataset, the output changes each time, giving rise to uniqueness without physical singularity.

Artificial Intelligence Art (AI Art): Artistic practices that employ generative algorithms, machine learning, or neural networks to create visual, auditory, or textual outputs. AI acts not only as a tool but as a co-creator in the artistic process.

Aura: Originally defined by Walter Benjamin, aura refers to the unique presence, authenticity, and singularity of a work of art in time and space.

Computational Singularity: The condition in which each algorithmic process results in a unique visual output. Even when using the same data, new outcomes can be generated, thereby reshaping Benjamin's notion of originality.

Data-Based Aura: A new form of authenticity rooted not in physical uniqueness but in the singularity of the data used. In AI art, EEG recordings, image archives, or cultural datasets provide unique meaning layers and carry auratic value.

Digital Aesthetics: A field of aesthetic inquiry that explores how digital technologies transform artistic creation, representation, and reception. It includes the visual grammar of screens, interactivity, and code-based media.

Interactive Aura: Refers to the auratic quality that emerges through dynamic viewer interaction. Particularly relevant in immersive and participatory artworks, where each viewer's engagement alters the experience and meaning.

Processual Aura: A form of aura that emerges from the visibility and transparency of the production process. It is created when the viewer is made aware of how the artwork is generated, particularly through algorithms and data.

Chapter 11
Artificial Intelligence and Negative Space: The Artificial Construction of Space in Visual Imagery

Emine Tuba Erdoğan
http://orcid.org/0000-0001-8119-1790
Independent Researcher, Turkey

ABSTRACT

This study investigates how artificial intelligence perceives and aesthetically constructs negative space in visual production processes. Rather than being merely a visual element, space functions as a communicative tool for meaning-making and audience engagement. How is this traditionally meaningful aesthetic choice interpreted by AI? To explore this, three models—DALL·E, Stable Diffusion, and Leonardo AI—were tested using identical textual prompts, and their use of space, composition, and figure placement were comparatively analyzed. The findings reveal model-specific approaches to spatial organization, raising the critical question: does AI merely fill space, or can it meaningfully employ it as a compositional strategy?

INTRODUCTION: HOW DOES ARTIFICIAL INTELLIGENCE PERCEIVE SPACE IN IMAGES?

Space, one of the most fundamental components of visual composition, is not merely a matter of arranging forms but also a powerful aesthetic element that guides narrative. While space can be considered a formal design choice, it also functions as an aesthetic component that shapes perception, produces meaning, and enables viewer interaction. In Eastern art, through the concept of Ma, and in Western mod-

DOI: 10.4018/979-8-3373-2230-8.ch011

ernism via movements such as Minimalism and Suprematism, space is positioned as an active threshold between the seer and the seen; it manifests as an area completed in the viewer's mind. In the context of graphic design, space is not only a visual or aesthetic emptiness but also a communicative design choice essential to meaning-making. In short, space is a domain of intentional communication. Designers such as Saul Bass and Massimo Vignelli employed space as a tool to guide meaning, while David Carson transformed space into a medium of aesthetic intervention through his fragmented compositions that disrupted traditional visual hierarchies. Especially in typographic compositions, the guiding and intuitive impact of space generates not only spatial clarity but also conceptual depth. In this context, the contrast between the historical and cultural uses of space as a meaning-generating aesthetic element and its current treatment in digital productions reveals a significant opposition. The way space is handled in AI-generated or AI-edited images, and how algorithms contribute to visual meaning-making, offers new avenues for contemporary debates. This study centers on the question of how artificial intelligence perceives and positions negative space in the process of image generation. In this regard, how does AI perceive and utilize negative space when generating visual content? Is the space in AI-generated images the result of a conscious compositional choice, or is it interpreted by the AI as a lack or absence? In what ways does negative space in AI-generated visuals differ from the way human artists use it? A critical question arises here: can artificial intelligence utilize space, or does it merely fill it? More importantly, considering the crucial role of space in meaning construction within graphic design, who holds agency in AI-based visual production? Is it the designer directing the system, or the algorithmic logic driven by data? What kind of power and control dynamic is established between the designer and artificial intelligence—especially regarding spatial decisions? These questions are as much about aesthetics as they are about ethics and creative authorship. The aim is to reveal the meaning-constructive role and distinctions of space between human-made and AI-generated visual outputs and to investigate how algorithms structure spatial perception and transform the relationship between space and meaning. In doing so, the study seeks to evaluate AI's understanding of space on both technical and conceptual levels within the aesthetic tendencies of the digital age.

As part of this study, three different AI-based visual generation tools—DALL·E, Stable Diffusion, and Leonardo AI—were selected to examine how negative space is constructed in AI-driven image production processes. Using identical text-based prompts, scene generation was carried out across all three models. These scenes were analyzed in terms of their use of space, perspective construction, and figure placement. However, the unique algorithmic structures and learning processes of each AI system resulted in model-specific variations in both spatial arrangements and aesthetic outcomes. Thus, the findings presented in this study are limited to the selected models and do not aim to offer generalizable conclusions about the overall aesthetic capacity of artificial intelligence. Rather, this study offers a snapshot of specific AI systems at a particular moment in time, without encompassing the evolution or future transformation of these dynamic and continuously developing technologies. Instead, this comparative approach aims to provide a framework for understanding how different models relate to space and how that relationship informs our understanding of AI-generated form.

THE HISTORICAL AND AESTHETIC USE OF SPACE: MINIMALIST AESTHETICS AND THE CONCEPT OF MA

The debate surrounding how space is constructed in AI-generated images is not merely a technical matter, but rather a comprehensive research topic that reflects the transformation of contemporary aesthetic paradigms. This discourse provides a foundation for understanding the evolving aesthetic and compositional norms shaped by digital production tools. In this context, examining the use and treatment of space in images generated by digital means alongside the aesthetic perspective of minimalist art—which emerged particularly in the second half of the 20th century—offers a way to develop a historical and aesthetic framework. Minimalism approached space not as a visual absence but as an active field of presence that engages with the viewer. The multilayered perceptual experience of minimalist art extends beyond Western aesthetics and reveals striking parallels with the aesthetic concepts found in Eastern thought. In particular, Japanese aesthetics, informed by Zen Buddhism, conceptualizes space as a domain where silence and meaning emerge, thereby enabling a dialogue with Western approaches to art. The concept of *Ma*, central to Japanese aesthetic philosophy, defines space not as a spatial void, but as a relational interval between objects—a liminal zone where meaning arises. Much like the dynamic relationship minimalist art establishes with the viewer, *Ma* operates through a perception of space that activates the viewer's awareness. This approach provides a theoretical foundation for evaluating how AI may perceive space, both structurally and conceptually. Thus, a critical question for today's aesthetic discussions is whether AI will employ this multilayered understanding of space merely as a technical compositional tool or engage it as a deeper vehicle for meaning-making. To explore the relationship between space and meaning in both historical and aesthetic contexts, the following section focuses on the foundational role of minimalist aesthetics.

Minimalist art represents a deliberate rupture from traditional aesthetic values, in opposition to the emotion-driven narratives of Abstract Expressionism. Minimalist aesthetics offers not mere visual simplicity, but a multidimensional experience built through the viewer's interpretation. Therefore, in this study, the way artists construct and engage with space holds critical importance. Minimalism, with its tendency to exclude the subjective aspect of art, marks a radical break from the meaning-centered structures of modernist narratives. It initiates a critical inquiry into the modernist tradition's emphasis on personal expression and meaning. Artists such as Donald Judd and Frank Stella aimed to obscure personal expression and artistic intention. Robert Morris, on the other hand, emphasized that art should be understood not through the object itself but through its placement, its relationship to the viewer, and the organization of materials. In this sense, minimalist aesthetics must be read not only through its simplicity, but also through the multiplicity of meanings that simplicity generates. "Negative space derives meaning not only from what it frames but from its deliberate emptiness" (Parker, 2019, p. 2). The materials employed by minimalist artists—industrial components and readymades—displace conventional questions of artistic expression, design, and intentionality in favor of an objecthood that resists traditional aesthetic approaches (Harrison & Wood, 2011, pp. 928, 932). Accordingly, minimalist aesthetics represents not only a formal reduction, but a systemic understanding of art that centers the viewer while minimizing personal interpretation (Roth & Katz, 1998, p. 33). "Negative space makes room for ambiguity; it invites the viewer into an interpretive spatial experience" (Parker, 2019, p. 6). Thus, minimalist aesthetics is not the result of superficial simplicity alone, but of a complex perceptual process shaped by viewer engagement (Best, 2006, pp. 127–128). This study, therefore, aims to demonstrate that space functions as a meaning-generating structure not only in Western but also in Eastern aesthetic traditions. The following section examines how the concept of *Ma* is defined historically, culturally, and aesthetically, and how it relates to artistic production.

In many representational traditions throughout the history of visual culture, space has been treated as distance or a secondary element. However, in Japanese aesthetics, the concept of *Ma* is understood as an active interval that exists within the relationships between time, space, and being. This concept refers not merely to physical emptiness, but to the meaningful interval—*the in-between*—between two phenomena, sounds, objects, or gestures. It generates meaning through silence or pause and emphasizes that absence plays as active a role in the aesthetic field as presence. *Ma* is a space that works in tandem with fullness; it is an auditory or visual field of anticipation that enables the emergence of meaning (Blaine, 2015, p. 2). In a similar vein, John Cage's silence-based composition *4'33"* can be seen as a pioneering example of how *Ma* has been conceptualized in Western art. In this work, Cage treats silence not as a lack, but as an active field that reveals the surrounding sounds. Here, silence offers a proposal for meaning that is completed through the presence of the listener. In the same spirit, Marcel Duchamp's conceptual approach to the readymade elevates void not merely as a gap, but as a constitutive element of meaning, foregrounding the viewer's interpretation in the completion of the artwork. "It was Cage who corrected the common misunderstanding about Duchamp's readymades—not by claiming that everything is art when placed in a context, but by proposing that anything could be used to make art" (Roth & Katz, 1998, p. 11). Similarly, in Gilles Deleuze's understanding of *aionic* time, space is conceived as a potential field of emergence in the present. The temporal notion of *entre-temps*, or "in-between-time," as defined by Deleuze, refers not to the moment of an event's realization, but to the pure field in which its potential arises. This kind of time creates a spatial-temporal void that "belongs neither to now nor to eternity, but only to becoming" (Quent, 2024, p. 260). As Deleuze puts it, "a pure event is always both already happened and still about to happen; it is never happening in the now" (p. 261). In this context, space in the artwork becomes not a deficiency but a process of becoming that is completed through the viewer's participation. *Ma*, therefore, proposes an aesthetic process that requires the viewer's active involvement. Within this framework, space is not just a component of visual composition but a threshold where meaning emerges through the engagement of the viewer. This conceptual foundation reveals that space is not merely a visual absence but a dynamic field imbued with meaning through perception. In graphic design, too, space is not simply a matter of visual arrangement; it is a site for meaning-making and for establishing an active relationship with the audience. In typographic design, letter spacing (kerning), line spacing (leading), and negative space influence not only legibility but also rhythm, emphasis, and emotional resonance. For instance, Saul Bass (Figure 5) uses space like cinematic timing, while Paula Scher's posters (Figure 1) employ the tension between typographic density and space as active elements that rhythmically structure legibility and emphasize fullness. Koichi Sato, reflecting Japanese cultural sensibilities, deliberately uses visual silence to guide the viewer's perception.

Figure 1. Paula Scher, Pentagram, 1995, US, Poster

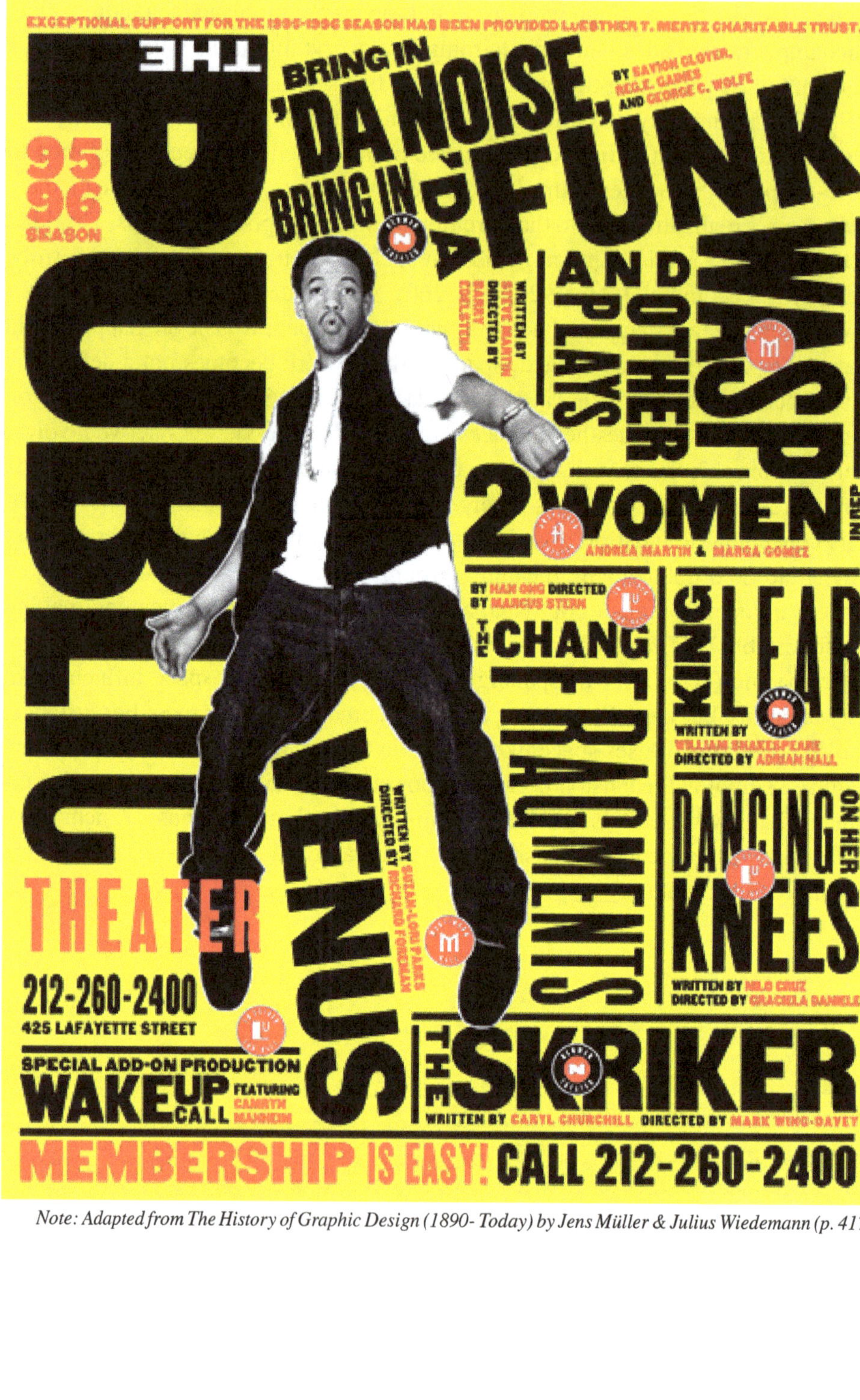

Note: Adapted from The History of Graphic Design (1890- Today) by Jens Müller & Julius Wiedemann (p. 417)

Figure 2. Koichi Sato, 1996 JP, Poster

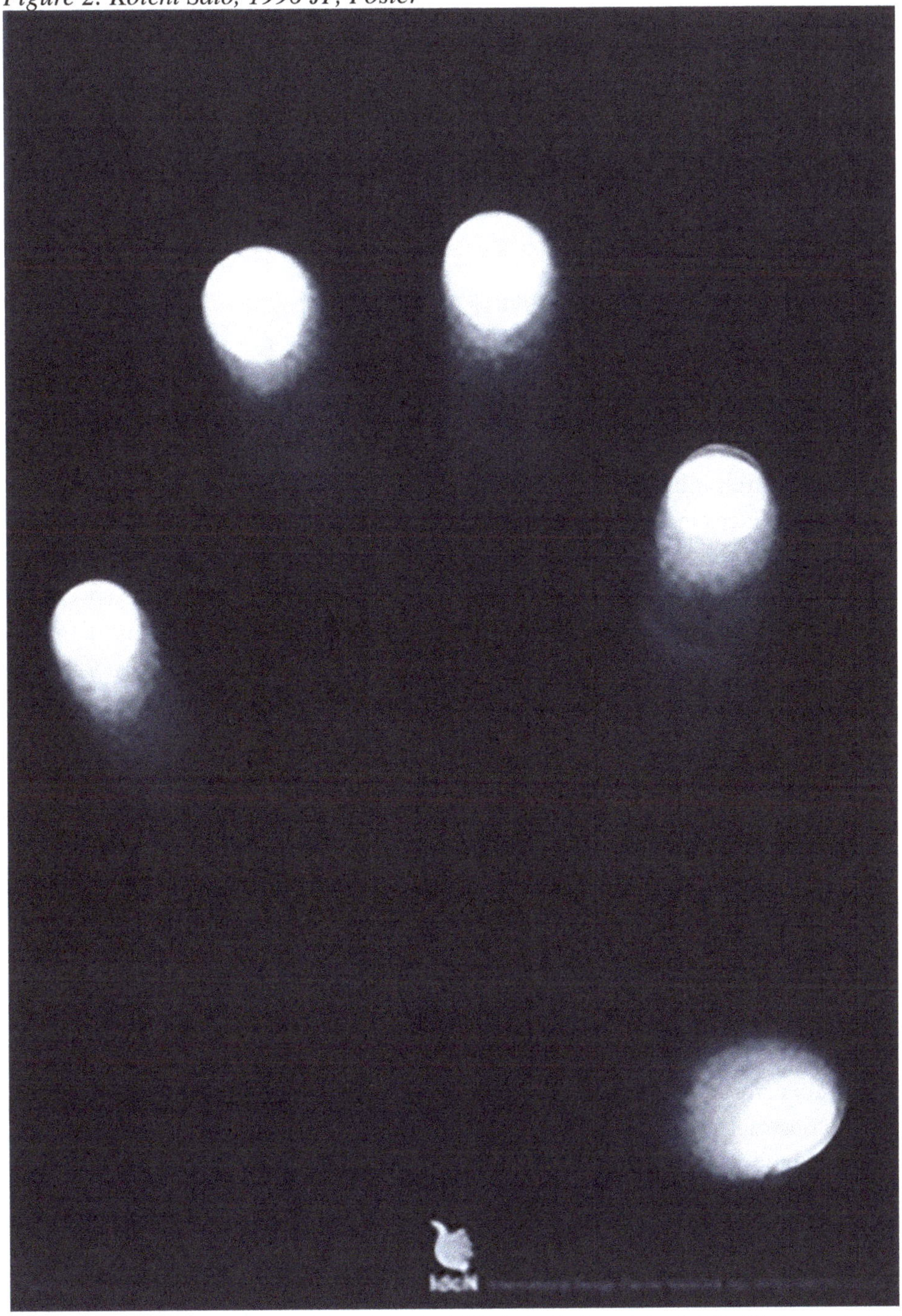

Note: Adapted from The History of Graphic Design (1890- Today) by Jens Müller & Julius Wiedemann (p. 422)

In these approaches, space functions as a threshold where meaning is completed, as much as it embodies visual silence- just like in the concept of *Ma*. In graphic design, space is not merely intended to rest the eye; it also serves as a zone of visual pause and cognitive resolution. In this respect, the spatial aesthetics proposed by the concept of *Ma* offers a conceptual framework that resonates with contemporary practices in graphic design. Is this sense of depth merely conceptual, or does it also involve a comparable multilayeredness at a physiological level?

PERCEPTUAL DEPTH: HOW THE HUMAN EYE INTERPRETS SPACE

The human visual perception system presents a highly organized operational model that enables the determination of the positions of objects in the environment and their spatial relations to one another. Depth perception allows individuals to detect differences in distance between objects. Such a capacity plays a crucial role not only in guiding motor functions accurately but also in comprehending spatial relationships—for instance, judging how far one must reach to grasp an object, or discerning whether an object is in front of or behind another. The formation of depth perception relies on the simultaneous processing of numerous physiological and psychological cues; the integration of these cues through a holistic approach enhances both the clarity and effectiveness of visual analysis.

The human visual system is highly advanced and adaptive; it processes depth and distance by integrating a variety of depth cues derived from physiological, visual/psychological, and motion-related sources. In popular culture, three-dimensional spatial perception is often associated with the concept of stereovision. Stereopsis, which is based on the slightly different angles of images captured by each retina, is one of the primary cues for perceiving relative depth (Reichelt et al., 2010, p. 4). However, stereopsis—the perception of disparity between images from both eyes—is only one of several sources contributing to depth perception. Even in monocular vision, depth perception does not disappear entirely; the world does not become flat. The brain can still estimate distance between objects to a limited extent.

To construct a sense of depth, the human visual system simultaneously processes multiple physiological cues. "Primary depth cues are defined as accommodation, convergence, and stereopsis (binocular disparity). These are considered 'primary' because they originate directly from physiological signals of the visual system" (Sweet & Kaiser, 2011, p. 2). Among these, accommodation (lens adjustment) and convergence (inward rotation of the eye muscles) are particularly important. "Stereopsis utilizes the disparities between the images perceived by both eyes... enabling the visual system to reconstruct spatial relationships" (p. 2). These are feedback mechanisms that synchronize the visual system's functions of focusing and orienting toward objects. This control system ensures that visual scenes are perceived both sharply and three-dimensionally (Reichelt et al., 2010, pp. 2, 4, 7).

Neurologically, the human visual system functions through a neural transmission pathway that begins at the retina and extends to the brain's cortex. Yet, the transformation of these signals into perception cannot be explained solely through biological processes. "Vision is not a passive process... it depends on interactions between the perceiver and the environment and involves more than the eyes alone—it also depends on other sensory systems" (Noë, 2005, p. 259). This highlights that visual perception is not merely a biological process occurring between the eye and the brain, but one that also involves bodily movement and interaction with the environment. "Perceptual experience is a form of skilled activity by which the world is explored" (p. 262). The construction of space by the perceiving subject is thus grounded in the active positioning of the body and the eye. This view allows us to think of vision not as a passive reception, but as a bodily act.

Research supports the idea that movement is a fundamental condition for perception. James J. Gibson's concept of "optic flow" is particularly valuable in this context: "We must perceive in order to move, but we must also move in order to perceive." According to Gibson, as individuals move, the continuous changes in the appearance of objects around them—what he calls "optic flow"—play a vital role in spatial perception. "The changing optical pattern represents an invariant structure of the environment." Through this visual flow, the individual gains direct information about the location, distance, and direction of movement of objects. "When the eyes are fixed and the retinal image does not change, perception fades and disappears." Gibson argues that meaningful experience of the environment requires continual participation in this dynamic network of relationships. Thus, the experience of depth, grounded in perception and movement, aligns with Noë's view and converges with Gibson's: in both approaches, dynamic interaction with the environment and action-oriented orientation are considered essential components of vision (Gibson, 1979, pp. 221–236).

Within this framework, the notion that space is not merely a physical interval but a perceptual and ontological field of meaning makes the distinction between human-centered aesthetic understanding and AI-based visual production more apparent. "The human visual system is highly advanced and adaptive... To deliver appropriate depth cues in simulations, technology designers must be aware of the system's limitations" (Sweet & Kaiser, 2011, p. 10). The multilayered meaning-making observed in the human visual perception system—as well as in the aesthetic frameworks of Minimalism and the Japanese concept of *Ma*—brings forth a central question of this study: Do current artificial intelligence systems, which lack human-specific perceptual processes such as embodied and sensory experience, interpret space merely as a formal element, or are they capable of constructing it as a field of meaningful emergence? Since this study is based on currently available AI systems, its findings provide a snapshot of present-day technology and do not claim to predict how future, more advanced AI models—such as potential Artificial General Intelligence systems with sensory integration and orientation capacity—will process spatial perception. Rather, the focus lies in questioning whether AI, in its current state, can approximate the spatial depth and meaning-making processes inherently shaped by human perception.

THE CONSTRUCTION OF PERCEPTUAL DEPTH IN AI-GENERATED IMAGES

In light of the discussions surrounding Minimalism, the aesthetic principle of *Ma*, and the physiological, neurological, and psychological dimensions of the human visual system, it becomes clear that human perception does not experience space merely as an absence or as a passive interval between objects; rather, it actively participates in the process of attributing meaning to space. Negative space is not simply an empty area between forms—it is a compositional regulator that guides the viewer's attention and determines the visual hierarchy of meaning. In this context, perception is always directed toward something; particularly in minimalist art and the Japanese concept of *Ma*, such directedness functions as a field that invites the perceptual engagement of the viewer. Thus, space ceases to be a passive absence in the holistic structure of perception and instead becomes an active and intentional element that shapes meaning. "Being-in-space can bring something into existence only in a cognitive sense. A tree or a table exists in space. But they cannot ontologically comprehend themselves. They exist only as objects within Dasein's spatial world. Being-in-space pertains to objects. Dasein, however, exists ontologically in its spatiality—that is, within its own world" (Heidegger, 2015, p. 63). In other words, an object (such as a table or tree) does not generate meaning simply by being present; it does not question, is not self-aware, and possesses no consciousness. Although objects exist within space, they cannot interpret or inquire into their own being. In Heidegger's ontology, being is not just a matter of presence, but also the capacity to interpret that presence. It is the ability to understand what it means to be in the world. "Dasein's existential being and spontaneity can be grounded or understood only as being-in-the-world" (p. 61). Only Dasein is capable of this. Dasein does not merely exist in the world physically; it establishes a meaningful relationship with it. "Thus, spatiality is not merely physical but becomes an ontological and existential structure" (p. 71). Accordingly, negative space is not a passive deficiency but an ontological threshold that produces meaning through the participation of the individual. "...man dwells poetically on this earth" (p. 207). Yet as artificial intelligence systems increasingly assume a role in visual production, the question arises: how do these systems construct the perception of space? Do current AI systems—lacking the embodied and sensory orientations inherent to human perception—treat space as a meaningful domain, or merely as an absence to be filled? At this point, it must be acknowledged that one of the long-term goals of AI research is to develop systems that possess such embodied and sensory capabilities. In what follows, the study focuses on how artificial intelligence perceives and constructs space, and how negative space and perceptual depth are treated in AI-assisted image generation. This will be examined through an analysis of images generated in response to the text prompt: "Create a photo-realistic street scene crowded with people and buildings." The same prompt will be submitted to three different AI systems. The resulting images, featuring architectural density and crowds, provide a suitable ground for observing where and how AI "places" space within the scene. Buildings and people offer material for analyzing figure-ground relationships. Requesting a photorealistic scene also tests AI's capacity not only for geometric construction but for intuitive meaning-making. Do the scenes look natural or artificial? Is depth and space merely present, or genuinely perceived? The prompt itself is neutral—it does not explicitly refer to space—making it a fitting method for testing the study's hypothesis: Does AI construct space consciously?

Figure 3. A crowded street scene generated by artificial intelligence

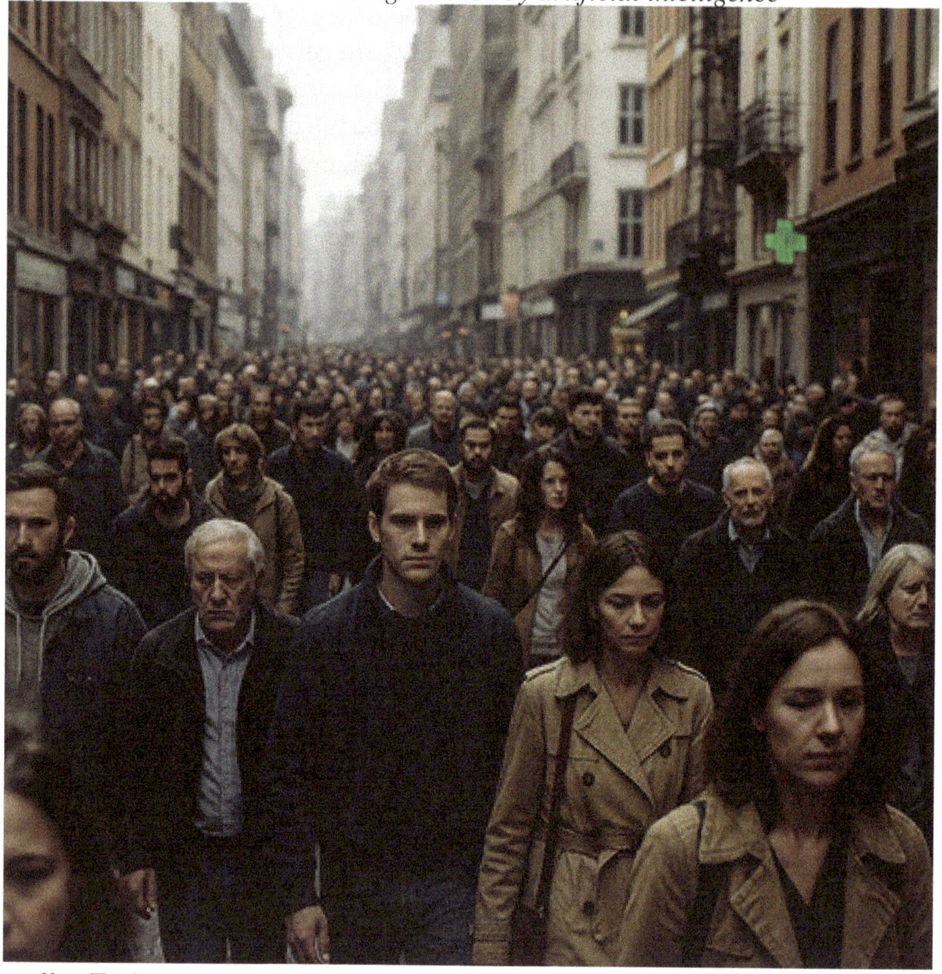

Note. This figure was generated by the author using DALL·E 3 on May 6, 2025.

The image generated by the textual prompt "create a photo-realistic street scene crowded with people and buildings" using artificial intelligence can serve as a meaningful example for questioning AI systems' ability to construct perceptual depth within complex urban compositions. When examining this crowded street scene generated by DALL·E on May 6, 2025, the presence of multiple vanishing points at first glance reveals a fragmented structure in the composition's perspective. This indicates that the scene is constructed in violation of the basic principles of perspective and fails to provide a coherent sense of spatial continuity. Although most figures appear to be positioned on the same spatial plane, there are evident inconsistencies in scale and proportional relationships. Additionally, the lack of directional relations, gaze interactions, or any physical engagement among the figures contributes to the impression of an artificial crowd simulation, thereby disrupting the interactive realism of the scene. The architectural layout of the buildings does not align with the principles of spatial perspective, creating a topological disjunction between the right and left segments of the image and breaking the spatial coherence of the scene. These elements make it possible for viewers to intuitively perceive, at first glance, that the image was generated by artificial intelligence. "Unlike humans, deep learning networks do not possess an embodied sensory experience to guide spatial coherence, which can result in floating objects or the absence of contact with the ground" (Zhou et al., 2017, p. 640). Although this study by Zhou et al. is among the early works in the field of artificial intelligence, its methodological framework for scene segmentation and visual classification is considered relevant to the theoretical background of this research. Therefore, while this reference may not directly represent current visual production technologies, it provides a historical basis for understanding how visual coherence is encoded in a fragmented manner by AI systems. In AI-based visual productions, the construction of perceptual depth is not as consistent as it is in human perception. Misinterpretation of scene geometry and the blurring of boundaries between overlapping objects often lead to a sense of artificiality in depth perception. Transitions between objects become ambiguous, visual edges appear soft or undefined, and the sequencing of spatial depth loses clarity. It is noted that in complex scenes, "the uncertainty of depth ordering and overlap boundaries" significantly impacts model performance. Since deep learning models lack a bodily-sensory context to guide spatial order, they often generate figures that appear disconnected from the ground or produce objects floating in space. This results in visual contradictions and aesthetic incoherence when viewed through the lens of human perception (pp. 633–640). These observed discrepancies may stem from the unique strategies neural networks use to process color, shape, and spatial positioning, as well as from the inherent limitations of their attempts to mimic the complexity of the human visual system (Zhang & Yoshida, 2024, p. 26). Within this framework, even when technical perspective accuracy is achieved in AI-generated imagery, the placement and configuration of figures often deviate from the natural depth perception of the human visual system.

Figure 4. Antonio Pollaiolo, The Martyrdom of Saint Sebastian (1475)

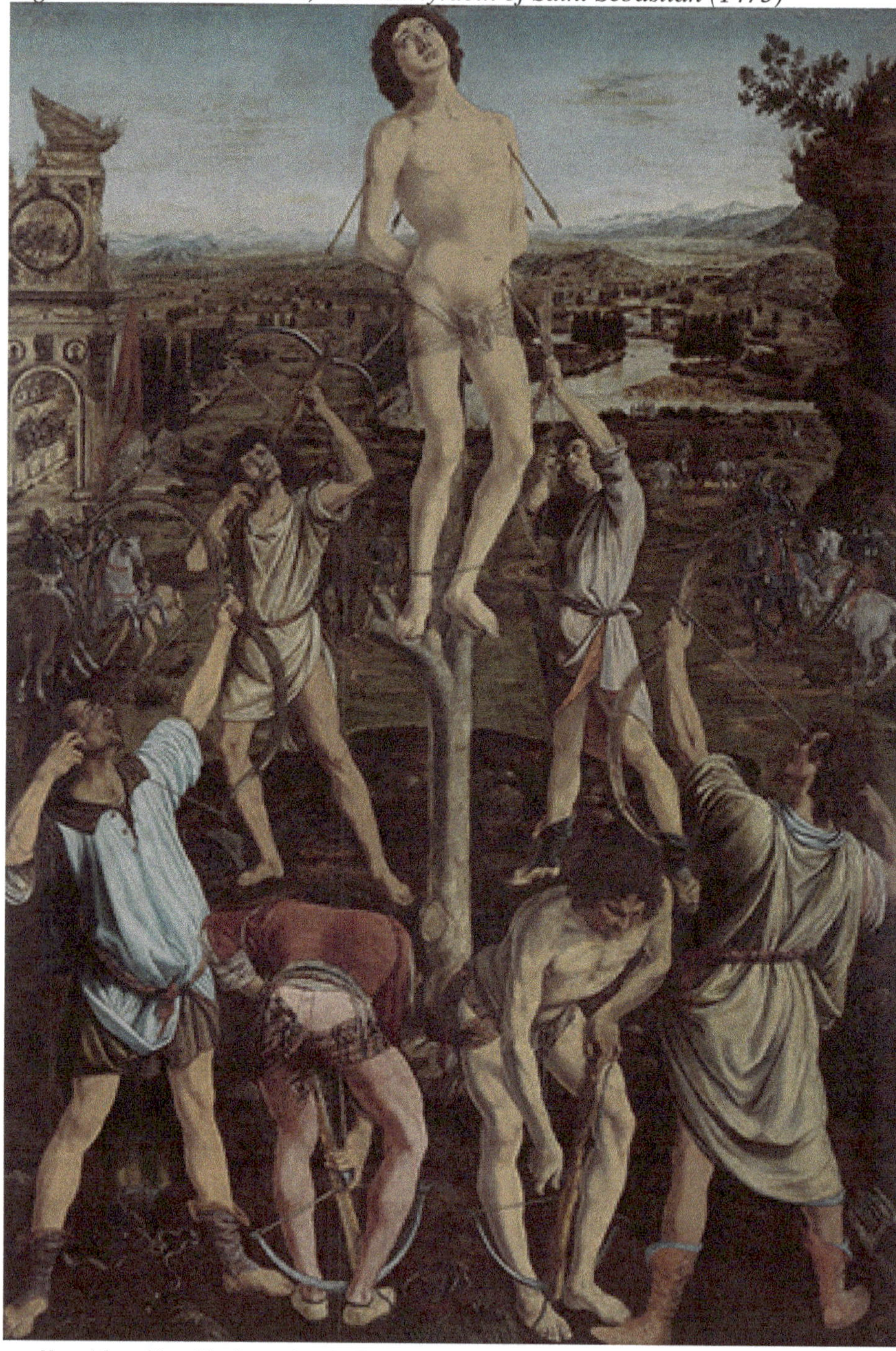

Note. Adapted from The Story of Art by E. H. Gombrich (1992, p. 178)

Figure 5. Paolo Uccello, The Battle of San Romano, c. 1450, National Gallery, London

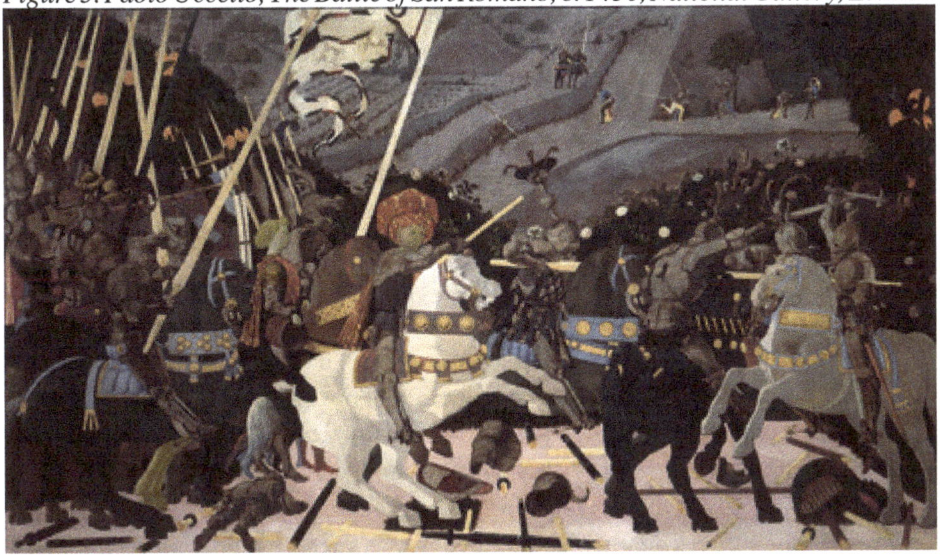

Note: Adapted from The Story of Art by E. H. Gombrich (p. 191)

Indeed, although the image follows a tonal value-based approach to perspective, the mass of human figures evokes E. H. Gombrich's commentary on Pollaiuolo's *The Martyrdom of Saint Sebastian*: "(Antonio Pollaiuolo) has placed his figures against an undifferentiated flat background—a kind of depthless stage" (Gombrich, 1992, p. 209). Even when the illusion of spatial depth is achieved, the absence of tonal transitions and the disconnection between the figures and the background render the scene visually shallow. Similarly, although the rules of perspective are partially applied, the image recalls the problems found in Uccello's early works: "Uccello had not yet learned how to soften the harsh outlines of rigid perspective through the use of light and atmosphere" (p. 191). In this respect, it can be argued that artificial intelligence still faces technical challenges in the construction of space and figure placement that resemble limitations observed during the early Renaissance. "Perspective (and pictorial representation as a whole) is conventional… perspective pictures, like any others, have to be read; and the ability to read has to be acquired." As John L. Ward (1976, p. 286) emphasizes, perspective is not a visual experience that can simply be "copied" from nature—it is a convention that requires reconciliation between surface flatness and the illusion of depth. Ward's argument—that perspective is not only a visual experience but also a culturally acquired form of agreement—is crucial in understanding why AI-generated visuals often lack perceptual coherence and a convincing sense of depth. Although current AI systems can technically replicate perspective, they do not possess the ability to read or position it within a broader context of cultural meaning. As such, AI-generated images, despite their surface-level perspectival accuracy, are often intuitively perceived as artificial, flat, or fragmented. Ward's perspective thus provides a theoretical basis for evaluating the perceptual limitations of AI-generated imagery. Does artificial intelligence construct space as an aesthetic narrative domain, or does it merely perceive it as an absence to be filled? Ward's emphasis is relevant here: although AI systems have the capacity to technically mimic the rules of perspective, the examined visual example suggests that these rules have yet to be applied in a coherent and unified manner. On a perceptual level, AI struggles to establish the relationship between surface and depth as a meaningful visual experience. Ward's notion of convention may offer a critical framework for understanding how AI constructs space or fails to do so: such visual systems are not merely technical in nature—they are also shaped by cultural and perceptual agreements, which AI does not partake in but merely imitates. If space is the result of an aesthetic decision, then the question arises: how (or whether) AI makes such a decision becomes a matter of discussion. Moreover, considering that AI technologies are in constant development, whether they will eventually participate more effectively in such aesthetic decision-making processes remains an important question for future research. According to Erwin Panofsky, Renaissance perspective traps the subject in a fixed point and symbolizes a worldview in which reality is ordered, measurable, and coherent. In AI-generated scenes, however, this coherence often collapses: figures lack relationality, vanishing points are scattered, and perspective serves primarily as an aesthetic impression rather than a logical construct. Thus, the technical application of perspective in AI-generated scenes replaces Panofsky's "orderly, centralized worldview" with a fragmented, surface-level, and intuitive spatiality. This reveals that AI is not merely drawing space but failing to construct a world imbued with meaning.

Panofsky defines perspective not as a purely optical or geometric system, but as the expression of a specific epistemological and ontological worldview. The development of perspective reveals how visual space is conceived and how the human subject is positioned within it (Panofsky, 2021, p. 49). In Panofsky's view, perspective is not a universal system that represents nature accurately but a historically constructed convention. Thus, it is entirely possible for other cultures (e.g., Chinese art) or modern movements (e.g., Cubism) to present alternative approaches to perspective.

Figure 6. David Carson, Cover of Volkskrant Magazine, April 2018

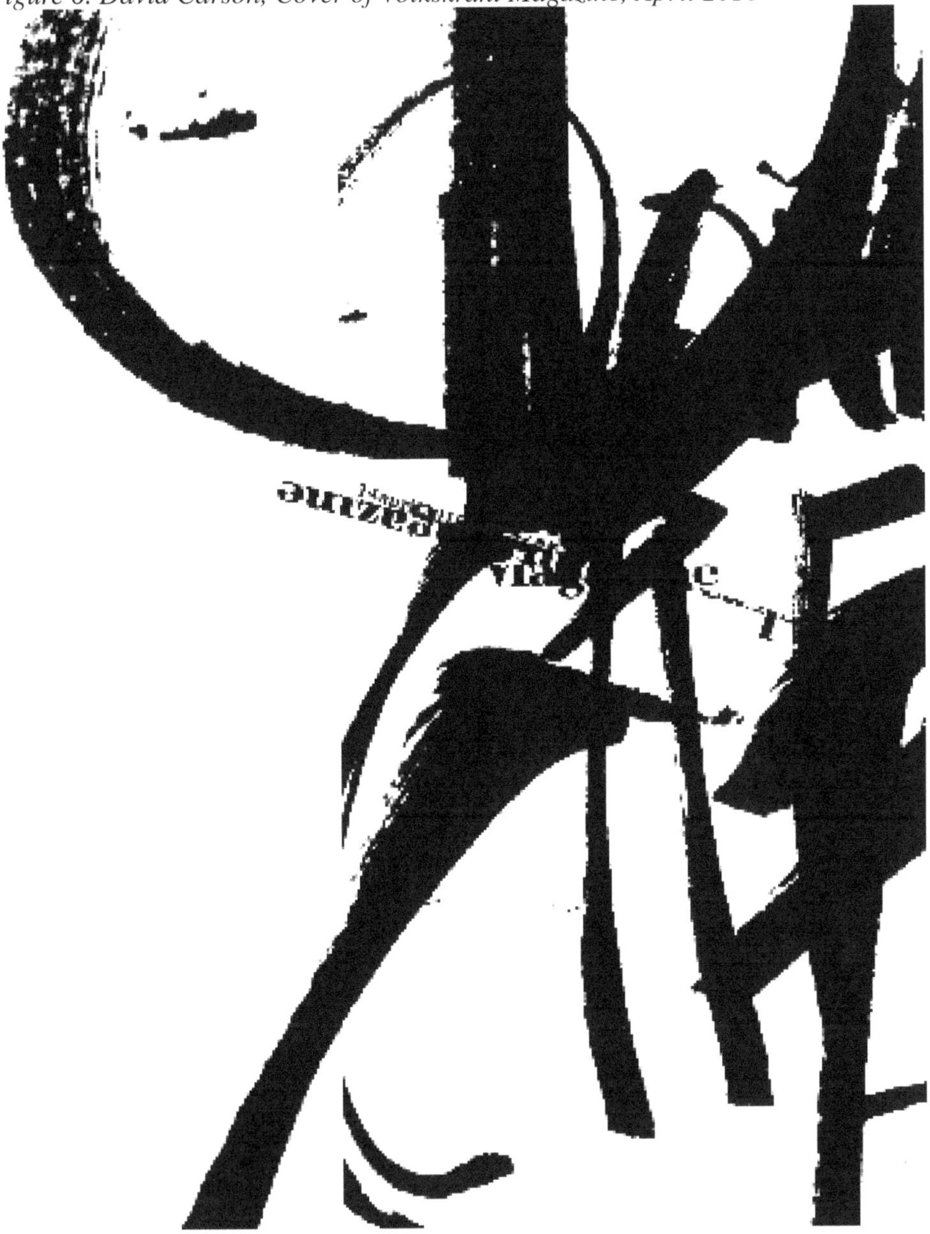

In graphic design, the use of perspective is not limited to the creation of spatial depth. Postmodern designers such as David Carson have deliberately broken with traditional rules of perspective, positioning typographic elements in fragmented and dispersed arrangements across the surface. In doing so, they have disrupted the visual order associated with a coherent worldview. In this sense, Carson's works exemplify graphic narratives in which Panofsky's centrally anchored world order is subverted and reconfigured.

Figure 7. Saul Bass, 1959, US, Poster

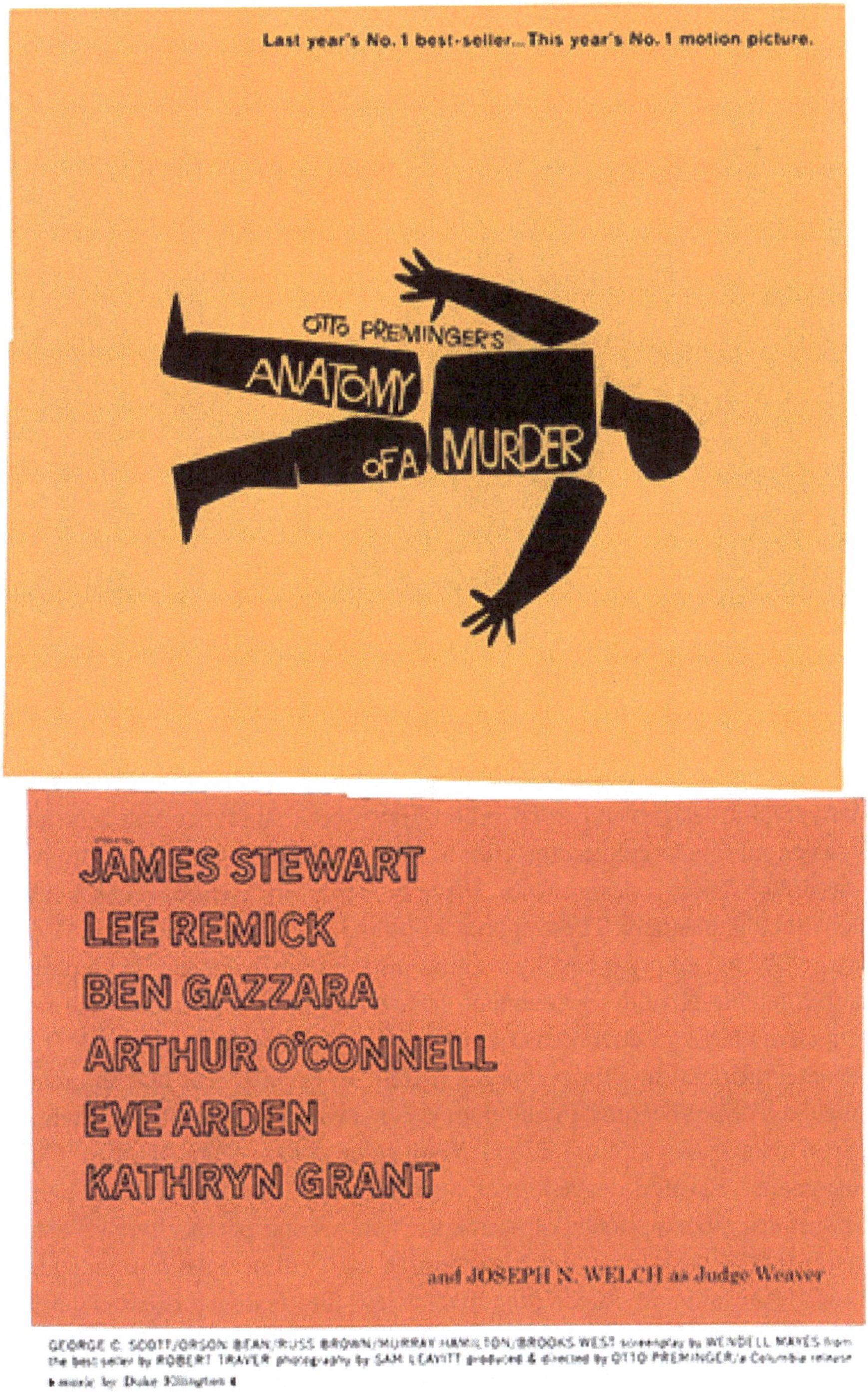

Note: Adapted from The History of Graphic Design (1890- Today) by Jens Müller & Julius Wiedemann (p. 249)

Figure 8. Massimo Vignelli, 1967, US, Poster

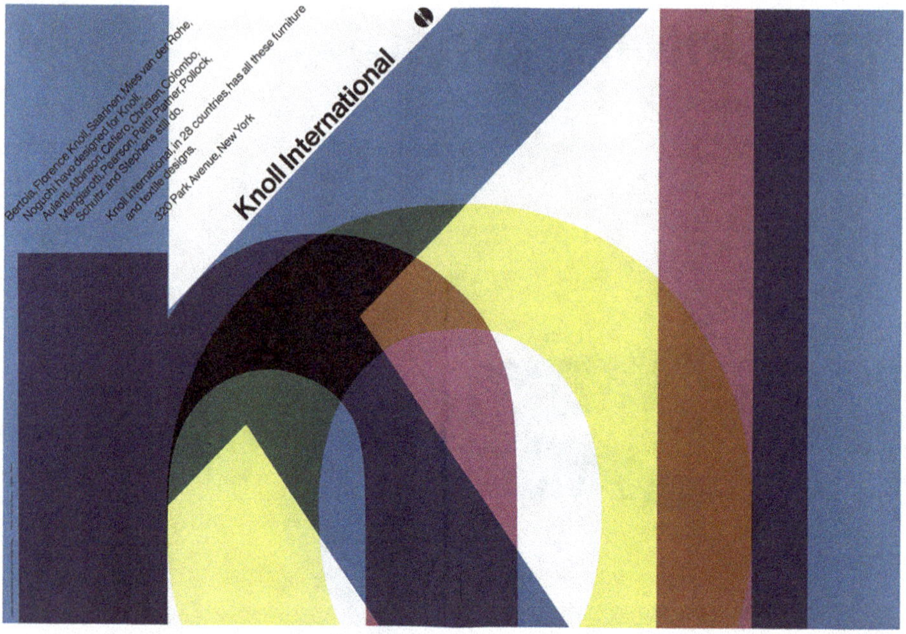

Note: Adapted from The History of Graphic Design (1890- Today) by Jens Müller & Julius Wiedemann (p. 301)

Similarly, in modern graphic design, space is not merely perceived as an "absence," but as an active carrier of meaning. The deliberate use of negative space in modern graphic design is regarded as both an aesthetic and functional decision that plays a central role in guiding the viewer. For instance, in Saul Bass's film posters or Massimo Vignelli's design work, space is not simply a visual relief, but a tool for constructing meaning. These approaches stand in stark contrast to the AI-driven reflex to "fill in" empty areas, illustrating instead that space can be employed as an active and directive design element. In light of ongoing debates in the field of AI-driven aesthetic production, two divergent perspectives have emerged. The first argues that artificial intelligence is not merely an extension of human creativity, but may eventually become an autonomous creative subject in its own right. This perspective envisions a future in which algorithms possess the capacity to generate originality, develop decision-making mechanisms akin to creative intuition, and transform the experience of aesthetics. The second perspective, by contrast, contends that AI serves only as a supportive tool within artistic production and lacks aesthetic autonomy. According to this view, the creative process is inherently human—rooted in intuition, intention, and historical-cultural context—and the idea of machines replacing the artist remains a speculative media narrative. The tension between these two positions does not only stem from technological capacity but also reflects underlying philosophical assumptions about aesthetic value, intention, and the definition of creative agency (Arielli & Manovich, 2022; Aris, Aeini, & Nosrati, 2023).

Within this theoretical framework, the use of space in an AI-generated image was analyzed through both visual interpretation and technical detection tools, with commentary derived from ChatGPT and analysis results provided by Sightengine. When prompted to interpret the space within the image it had generated, ChatGPT responded as follows (ChatGPT, 05/08/2025):

> *"In this image, a large group of people is walking forward along a city street. The 'space' in the image can be described in the following ways: Focal space (not negative space, but structural void): At the center of the crowd is an open area that draws the viewer's gaze. A few prominent figures appear clearly in this zone, and the surrounding people are arranged more densely, creating a kind of visual symmetry. This produces a psychological impression of 'void'—a sense of dispersal from the center of density. Perspective-based space: The depth created by the receding street contrasts with the densely packed foreground. The faded figures in the background contribute to a sense of emptiness toward the vanishing point. Emotional space: The facial expressions of the people are generally serious, anxious, or expressionless. This creates a sense of collective emotional void or solitude within the crowd, as if the people were moving forward without a clear purpose. These different types of space have a strong narrative impact, evoking both density and isolation in the viewer simultaneously (ChatGPT, personal communication, May 8, 2025)."*

Although such interpretive capacities do not constitute a traditional Turing Test, AI-based detection platforms such as Sightengine may provide a foundation for "visual Turing tests," offering insight into the degree to which AI-generated images can deceive or convince the human perceptual system. These tools may prove useful in interrogating the limits of aesthetic autonomy and the scope of AI-generated visual imagination. To examine the effect of AI-generated images on perceptions of visual authenticity, the street scene image used in this study was analyzed via the Sightengine platform. The evaluation determined that the image had a 99% probability of being AI-generated, with a 98% likelihood of attribution to the GPT-4o model. It did not match any known GAN (Generative Adversarial Network) models, but was found to contain approximately 16% facial manipulation. These findings suggest that the image possesses a level of visual realism sufficient to deceive human perception, while also raising new questions about aesthetic autonomy based on technical traces. The fact that the image was formed through a purely algorithmic chain of decisions—without the involvement of a human artist's intention—demands a reconsideration of creative criteria such as intention, context, and authorship (Sightengine, 2025). While AI systems may exhibit high levels of visual proficiency, the absence of human-level interpretative capacity challenges the very foundations of aesthetic authorship.

Figure 9. A crowded street scene generated by artificial intelligence

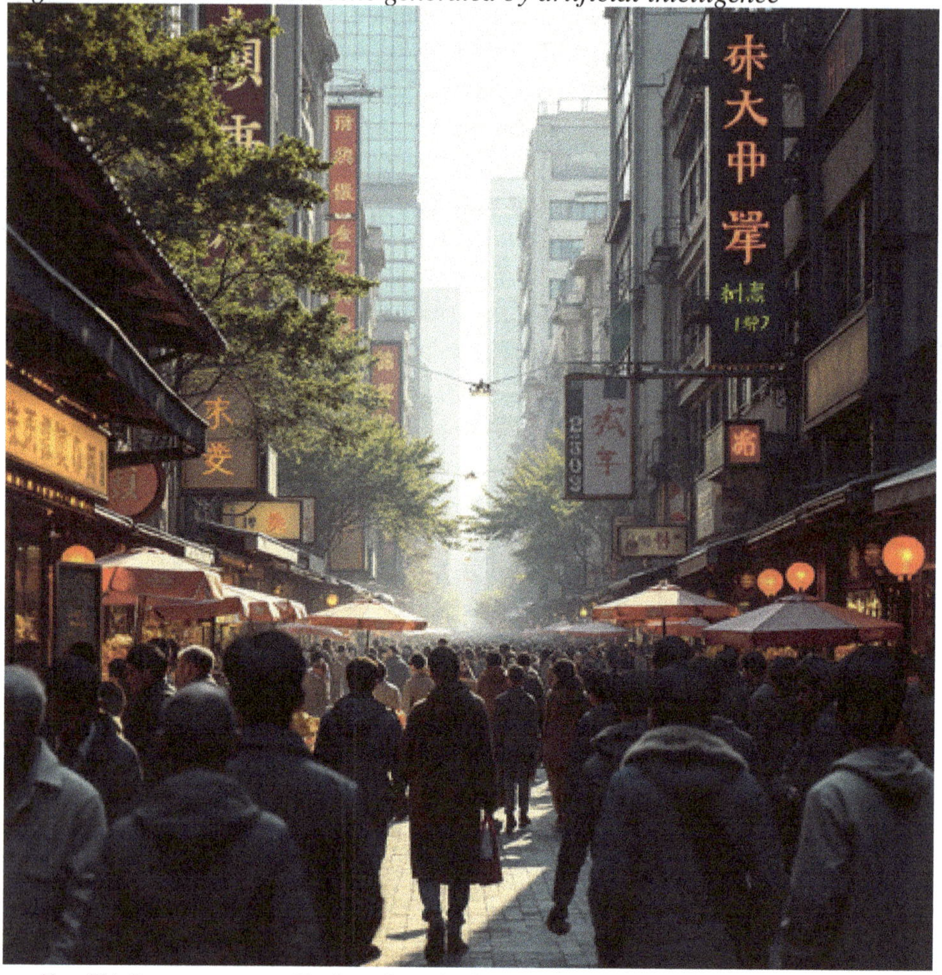

Note. This figure was generated by the author using Stable Diffusion on May 8, 2025.

The visual production capacities of artificial intelligence systems vary not only according to the type of algorithm used, but also based on the training data, the specificity of the prompt, and the architectural biases embedded within the model. When the first image is examined in terms of perspective rules, it reveals notable inconsistencies in architectural placement and figure scaling. In contrast, the second image—generated by Stable Diffusion—demonstrates a much more coherent construction of perspective. Although both images were produced using the same textual prompt, the differences between them highlight stylistic and structural variations that arise not merely from user input, but from the model's internal visual processing strategies and architectural predispositions. In the second scene, the central perspective created by Stable Diffusion—with clearly defined vanishing points, building alignment, and consistent figure scaling—conveys a greater sense of spatial cohesion. This suggests that it is technically possible for AI-generated images to produce convincing perspectival effects.

When analyzed through Panofsky's method of visual interpretation, a pre-iconographical reading of the image reveals a narrow street in a modern city. High-rise buildings line both sides of the street, densely populated with signage. A crowd of people walks along the same visual plane as the viewer, and the overall composition adheres to linear perspective. In this respect, the image resembles Renaissance perspective, with converging lines directed toward a single vanishing point calculated according to the viewer's eye level, drawing the viewer optically into the scene. The color palette is warm, and atmospheric depth is achieved through light. The orientation of the crowd moves from foreground to background, with the figures facing away from the viewer. From an iconographical perspective, the figures are not oriented toward the viewer but rather toward the depth created by the perspective. In this context, space does not serve to include the viewer within the image; instead, it becomes a structure that excludes the viewer and limits engagement. Here, AI constructs a scene, but fails to establish a meaningful connection with the viewer. Panofsky defines this phenomenon by stating that "perspective is not merely an optical arrangement but the visual form of a particular worldview" (Panofsky, 2021, p. 49). While AI systems can reproduce perspective with geometric accuracy, their outputs remain visually coherent yet conceptually incomplete.

From an iconological point of view, space is not presented as a field of meaning in the classical sense but functions as a neutral zone that organizes composition. This suspends the invitation for viewer participation. As Georges Perec notes, "Space is what obstructs our gaze, what causes us to halt our vision: An obstacle: Bricks, a corner, a viewpoint: Space begins when an angle emerges, when movement is interrupted, when one has to turn in order to proceed" (Perec, 1997, p. 81). In the example image discussed above, rather than a constructed environment, what we observe is the mere formation of void. To deepen this analysis, it is appropriate to draw upon Perec's conceptualization.

Figure 10. Species of spaces and other pieces- An example page taken from the book

THE PAGE 11

3

I write: I inhabit my sheet of paper, I invest it, I travel across it.
I incite *blanks*, *spaces* (jumps in the meaning: discontinuities, transitions, changes of key).

I write
in the
margin

I start a new
paragraph. I refer to a footnote[1]

I go to a new sheet of paper.

1. I am very fond of footnotes at the bottom of the page, even if I don't have anything in particular to clarify there.

Note: (Perec, 1997, s. 11).

However, the comparative analysis reveals that the semantic voids specific to Perec's text are not present in the AI-generated example. The space in Perec's writing is constructed through language itself—built upon a blank page via words that evoke associative meaning (Perec, 1997, pp. 11, 14).

At this point, it becomes evident that in images produced by artificial intelligence, negative space often functions merely as a tool of technical arrangement; it fails to operate as a component that guides meaning or activates the viewer's perceptual engagement. In contrast, in human-made designs, space enters the composition as both an aesthetic and semantic choice. In the visual language constructed by David Carson, one frequently observes examples in which typographic order is deliberately disrupted, alignment rules are violated, and visual voids are transformed into expressive devices. In Carson's work, negative space is not merely an absence; it becomes a visual game through which the viewer reconstructs meaning. Given the contextual limitations of AI systems, this raises the question of whether—and to what extent—spatial configurations are shaped by aesthetic intent.

Figure 11. David Carson, The end of print: The graphic design of David Carson, 1995.

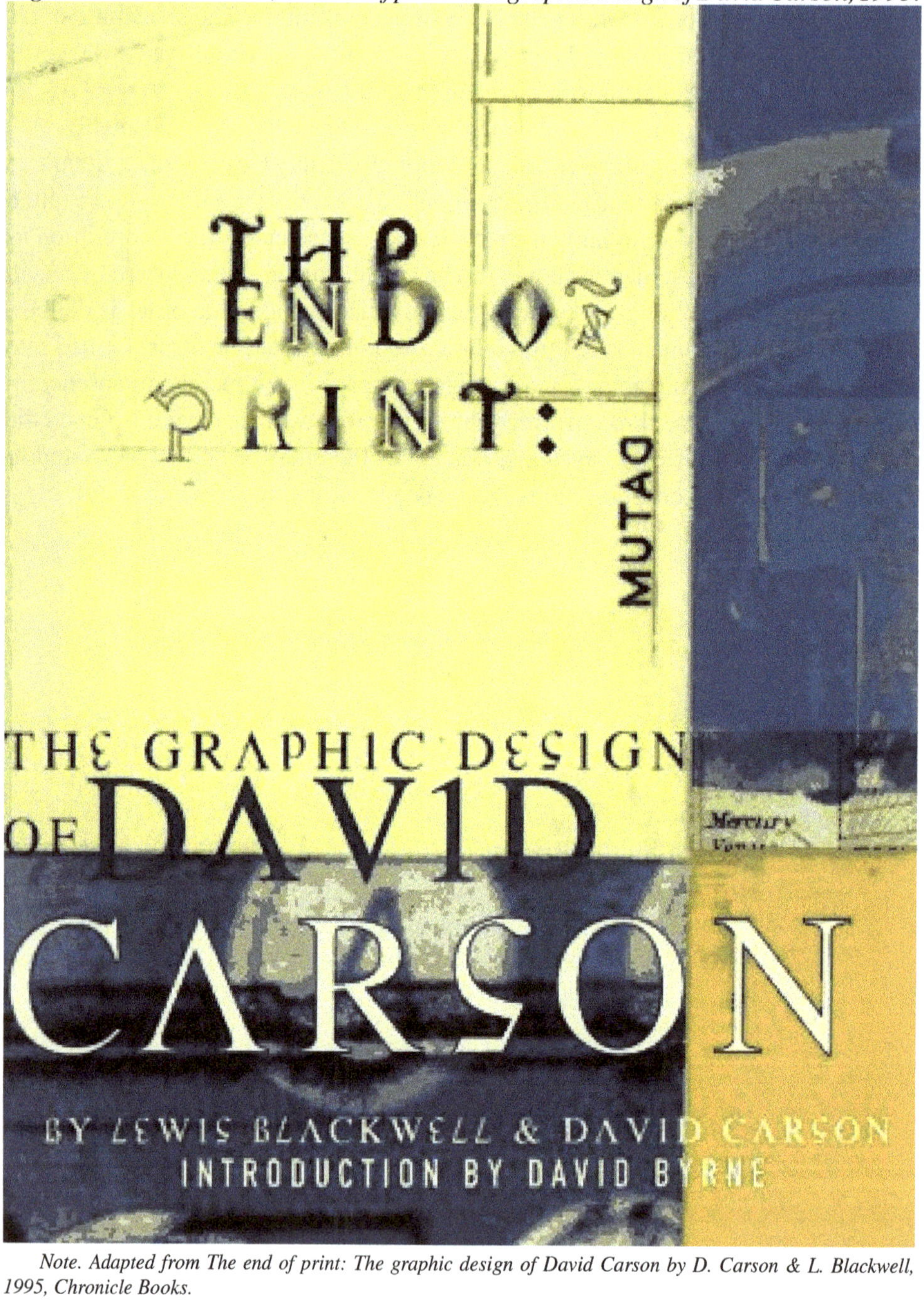

Note. Adapted from The end of print: The graphic design of David Carson by D. Carson & L. Blackwell, 1995, Chronicle Books.

Figure 12. William Klein, Xmas Shopping near Macy's, New York, 1954; printed 1956.

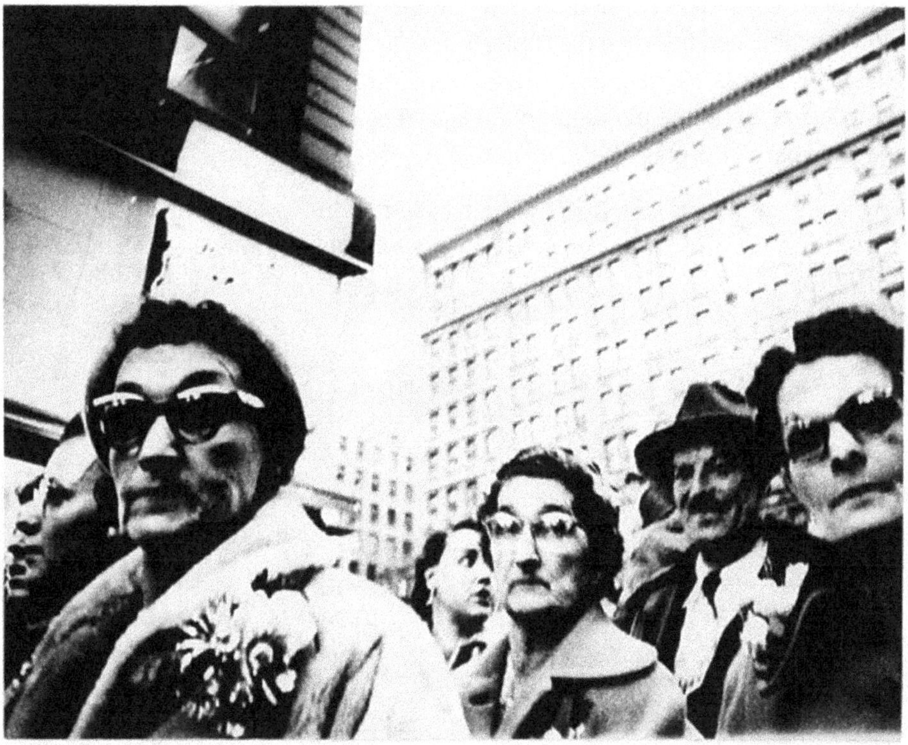

Note. Reproduced from The Metropolitan Museum of Art. Retrieved July 18, 2025, from https://www.metmuseum.org/art/collection/search/266096

In Klein's street photography, space does not function as an area of optical depth but rather as a field of chaotic density and compression. He brings figures into the frame abruptly, cuts them off from the front, and uses voids in a deliberately unsettling manner. Instead of drawing the viewer into the image, this creates a sense of pressure and discomfort, as if one were already inside the scene. Rather than inviting active participation, it evokes a visceral unease. In this sense, negative space is not merely a compositional element but operates as a striking aesthetic intervention. This approach parallels Carson's design language, in which he disrupts alignment conventions to similarly unsettle the viewer. Thus, space serves to dismantle the expected order of visual construction.

While AI-generated imagery often features figures whose perspectives exclude the viewer, Klein's photograph presents subjects who gaze directly at the camera, establishing a powerful tension within the frame. This shift—from the viewer as a passive observer to an active participant—allows space, as shaped through the direction of the figures' gazes, to become an arena of visual and psychological interaction. From this perspective, Klein's work powerfully demonstrates that space is not only a spatial construct, but also an interactional field defined by the direct contact established between the subjects and the viewer through the act of looking. As Sontag notes, "A new understanding of the concept of knowledge has been constructed around the photographic image. The photograph is a thin slice of both time and space" (Sontag, 1973, p. 17).

Figure 13. A crowded street scene generated by artificial intelligence

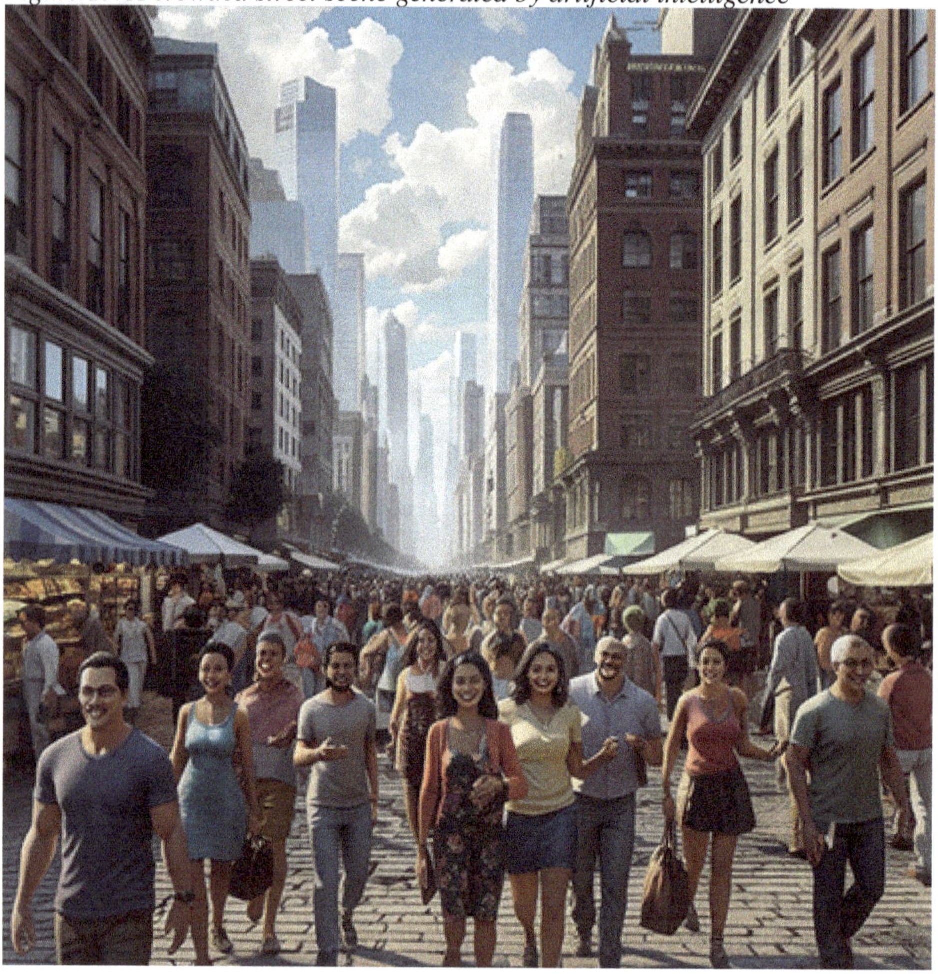

Note. This figure was generated by the author using Leonardo AI on May 9, 2025.

One of the AI platforms used in this study, Leonardo AI, automatically rewrites and elaborates on the user-provided prompt. The primary prompt used in the study—"Create a photorealistic street scene filled with a crowd and buildings"—was reformulated by Leonardo AI into the following extended version: "Create a highly detailed and lifelike street scene set in a bustling metropolis, filled with a diverse crowd of people from various age groups and ethnicities, engaged in different activities such as walking, talking, and laughing, amidst a backdrop of towering skyscrapers, historic buildings, and street vendors, with realistic textures, reflective windows, and ornate architectural details, under a warm and sunny atmosphere with a few puffy white clouds in the sky, and a sense of vibrant energy and urban dynamism." While this automatic elaboration aims to enhance the richness and realism of the image, it constitutes a direct intervention that can influence the core objectives of the study. Such reformulation introduces an external interpretive layer to how the AI constructs meaning within the scene, thereby creating an artificial density in the visual elements such as spatial voids, perspective, and figure relationships. As the amount of detail increases through automatic elaboration, the semantic cohesion among elements within the scene weakens. Though the visuals become richer, their contextual clarity does not improve. The most fundamental challenge faced by AI systems in generating semantic imagery is the issue of meaning. For Wittgenstein, meaning arises from use; current AI systems lack such intentional usage. "The meaning of a word is its use in the language"; similarly, a visual element derives meaning only within the framework of the visual language game it participates in (1968, §43). Figures, objects, and spaces may exist within the image, but they are not relationally constructed through human intuition, cultural context, or creative intent. They are assembled through data-driven patterns. Thus, everything is present, yet nothing communicates. This recalls Wittgenstein's intuitive warnings about the limits of communication: he argues that meaning is not merely transmitted but formed through shared experience. The lack of communicative context suspends meaning at the visual level—it produces signs but not meaning. When considered in relation to Heidegger's concept of Dasein, communication reveals itself as arising from ontological and existential relations that the being establishes with the world. "Unlike entities whose objective existence depends on spatial and positional relations, Dasein determines its Being-in-the-world through existential relations. Dasein bases its being upon its own self—in the sense of being familiar with, dwelling with, being beside, or being with something. For Dasein is always within an existential understanding that enables it to choose itself, to dwell within itself, and to be in relation or concern with something" (Heidegger, 2015, p. 62). Meaning arises from Dasein's relational existence within the world; AI does not possess this form of "Being-in-the-world." "According to Heidegger, space is neither within the subject nor the object. Space is inherent in Dasein's Being-in-the-world. It belongs a priori to Dasein. Dasein's existential spatiality allows it to grasp the world as a totality of ready-to-hand tools. Thus, spatiality becomes an ontological and existential structure, not a physical one" (Heidegger, 2015, p. 71). "Being-in-the-world is a term that expresses Dasein's concernful relation to things. Concern is what renders Dasein ontological. Dasein's Being becomes manifest through concern. It means that Dasein is a Being-in-the-world alongside its surroundings and enters into ontological relations with them" (Heidegger, 2015, p. 63). However, Dasein's concern for things must not be understood merely in terms of utility or pragmatism (p. 67). Artificial intelligence, like humans, collects information and attempts to produce meaningful outputs. But this relationship is an algorithmic process, not an existential orientation. Therefore, AI's effort to realize itself—such as making autonomous decisions or desiring to learn—carries a functional teleology, not an ontological one. It is a simulational, not an existential relationship. AI is not Dasein because it lacks existential anxiety, does not generate meaning, and has no awareness of death. It does not live in the world in the mode of Being-in-the-world. One of Dasein's core characteristics, according to Heidegger, is its capacity to establish meaningful relationships with being. Dasein does not merely exist in the world; it lives in it. Everything around it is part of a web of meaning established not only through functionality, but also through intention, concern, anticipation, and mortality. If, in the future, an artificial intelligence begins to question its own being, to construct meaning, to develop concern for itself, and to engage with the world not merely through data but through existential relations, then it may be reconsidered within a Heideggerian framework. But this remains speculative at present, and Heidegger's concepts are ontologically designed as exclusive to humans. Thus, for AI to be considered Dasein would be ontologically impossible within Heidegger's philosophy, because the concept of Dasein was not designed to accommodate systems like AI. If future AI develops subjectivity, we may require an entirely new ontological category. In that case, Heidegger's philosophy would remain a foundation, but it would mark the threshold of a new understanding of being.

SOLUTIONS AND RECOMMENDATIONS

AI-based visual production systems, when compared with human-generated images on aesthetic and perceptual levels, inherently carry contextual, cultural, and ontological deficiencies. In light of the findings obtained in this study, it is argued that AI systems' use of perspective, construction of space, and capacity to establish visual continuity should be evaluated not merely as optical arrangements, but within a more holistic structure that supports perceptual engagement, aesthetic experience, and meaning-making processes for the viewer. Accordingly, the necessity of reconsidering AI-generated visual production systems through human-centered aesthetic understandings, culturally negotiated visual codes, and the experiential framework of Dasein's being-in-the-world constitutes the central axis of the study's proposed solutions and recommendations. Below, specific proposals developed in this direction will be listed, and the potential areas of development in AI-generated images concerning aesthetic, cultural, and perceptual depth will be opened to discussion.

This study examines how space is structured in AI-generated visuals, particularly with respect to the use of perspective and visual continuity. While AI systems can technically process perspective data with a certain degree of accuracy, significant technical errors in the application of perspective were observed in the image generated by DALL·E. In contrast, visuals created with Stable Diffusion showed no such technical flaws; however, the depth of meaning these images convey remains open to debate. The lack of meaningful internal compositional links, particularly in terms of figure-ground relationships and topographic organization, leads to visuals that may appear realistic on the surface yet are perceived as artificial and fragmentary. Based on the views of Ward and Panofsky, which frame perspective as a cultural convention, it becomes evident that the visual datasets used to train AI models must be reconstructed not only to ensure formal accuracy but also to incorporate cultural layers of meaning. From this perspective, theories suggesting that visual perception is culturally constructed highlight the necessity for AI systems to adopt a learning structure that includes not only formal but also contextual and semantic components. Therefore, this issue remains open to interdisciplinary inquiry, bridging fields such as art, cultural studies, cognitive science, and artificial intelligence. In art, space is not merely a lack but a site where meaning is formed—not a passive absence, but an active threshold through which the viewer can engage with the image. Accordingly, it is recommended that visual space in AI-generated imagery be designed not only as a formal element but also as a component that guides perception and supports meaning construction. As Heidegger posits, space is not merely a physical extension; it is the scene of Dasein's meaningful engagement with the world. Since AI lacks the experience of "being-in-the-world," it cannot ontologically comprehend the voids it represents. This results in systems that merely represent what is present without establishing meaningful relationships among those elements. Thus, space should not be viewed as a mere graphic component but as a carrier of meaning.

In conclusion, AI systems must consider visual elements such as space, perspective, and depth not solely as technical tools, but as aesthetic components that support interaction with the viewer, cultural context, and meaning production. However, how such components can be structured or generated remains open to debate. To enable AI-generated visuals to approach human perception in a more coherent and meaningful way, it is suggested that training data be enriched with cultural diversity, architectural biases be overcome, and algorithmic processes be supported by contextual interpretative capacity. Nonetheless, given AI systems' ontological limitations, it is evident that human-centered perception, aesthetic intention, and meaning production processes remain crucial in visual generation. This provides a framework that should be considered in future research. Accordingly, in the following section, the study's main conclusions will be discussed, evaluating the differences between AI and human perception in constructing depth and void from an interdisciplinary perspective.

FUTURE RESEARCH METHODOLOGIES

AI-based visual generation systems have reached the capacity to produce highly accurate and lifelike images at a formal level with current technological means. However, when examined through physiological and cultural lenses, these productions significantly diverge from human-centered creative processes in terms of aesthetic, contextual, and semantic layers. Core visual elements such as perceptual depth, figure-ground relationships, and the use of negative space often function merely as technical components of composition in AI-generated outputs; yet they tend to have limited influence in facilitating interaction with the viewer and in generating meaning. In light of the findings of this study, the current aesthetic production capacity of AI systems, when compared to the multi-layered and culturally constructed structure of human perception, can be evaluated more as a collage built upon formal arrangements and visual patterns. However, given the dynamic and continuously evolving nature of AI models, it is conceivable that such limitations may be overcome in the future and that systems may generate visuals with more complex, culturally rich, and aesthetically nuanced structures. In this framework, future studies in the field of AI-driven visual production should not be confined to parameters of technical accuracy and optical realism alone; rather, they should adopt an interdisciplinary and critical methodology that incorporates the cultural, philosophical, and phenomenological dimensions of human perception. While the images generated by applying the same textual prompt to different AI systems reflect the outputs of today's technological capabilities, the ever-evolving nature of AI models suggests that the same prompt may yield results with different aesthetic and semantic dimensions in the future—necessitating a dynamic and renewable approach to research methodologies.

Moreover, experimental and perception-based studies exploring how negative space is structured in AI-generated content will be critical in understanding how viewers intuitively perceive the differences between machine-generated and human-generated visuals. On a philosophical level, reinterpreting AI's capacity to produce meaning, context, and intentionality through the lenses of thinkers such as Wittgenstein and Heidegger could provide a critical foundation for discussions on visual production processes. Such inquiries may allow AI to be examined not merely as a tool of production but as an agent capable of transforming cultural and aesthetic codes.

In this regard, future research on AI-based visual production should be designed not only around technical outcomes but also to include aesthetic, cultural, and perceptual dimensions. Doing so could contribute to a deeper understanding of the interactive space between artificial productions and human perception. In particular, new studies focused on viewer perception, user experience, cultural context, and semantic interpretation may open up new perspectives on how AI-generated imagery constructs meaning, creates context, and expresses aesthetic intent. Accordingly, the ongoing debate as to whether AI is merely a production tool or a potential aesthetic and cultural subject is likely to be enriched by the contributions of diverse disciplines and to evolve with the continuous renewal of theoretical and methodological approaches in this field.

CONCLUSION

Within the framework of approaches that argue spatial voids in visual compositions are not merely technical absences but also aesthetic choices that guide meaning and establish active engagement with the viewer, this study comparatively analyzes how artificial intelligence constructs and utilizes space through three different models (DALL·E, Stable Diffusion, Leonardo AI). Throughout the study, it has been demonstrated that the human visual system is not merely a biological mechanism, but a holistic integration of bodily orientation, environmental interaction, and multilayered perceptual processes. While this assessment does not claim medical expertise, it underscores that human visual perception functions through a complex interplay of physiological, psychological, and motor capabilities, constantly updated through dynamic relationships with the environment and bodily movements. In contrast, AI's generation of spatial depth and voids lacks this multilayered perceptual system and thus remains limited to formal and optical parameters. Whether AI can reproduce the intricate relational field that triggers embodied and perceptual engagement remains debatable. This reveals that the divergence between AI-generated images and human spatial cognition is not merely technical but also ontological and phenomenological. This divergence necessitates not only a formal assessment but also a theoretical inquiry into how cultural representation and aesthetic conventions are (or are not) constructed by artificial systems. Panofsky's notion that perspective is not only a geometric tool but also the optical equivalent of a specific historical worldview exposes the conceptual limitations of AI aesthetics. Although AI can technically render perspective, it cannot comprehend it as a symbolic language shaped by human culture. Therefore, despite surface-level accuracy in AI-generated imagery, the depth of space, the meaning of void, and visual cohesion are still governed by intuitive and historically grounded human codes. Within this context, AI's role in art remains that of a technical producer, not yet capable of fully grasping aesthetic meaning—a visual imitator rather than a meaning-generating agent.

This study is based on an experimental and theoretical investigation into how AI systems perceive, interpret, and construct negative space in the context of aesthetic production. The guiding question posed at the beginning— "Does AI construct void as an aesthetic decision or simply fill it as a lack?"—has been revisited through both visual analyses and theoretical perspectives drawn from Panofsky, Ward, and Heidegger. Using the same textual prompt across three AI platforms (DALL·E, Stable Diffusion, Leonardo AI), the study evaluates how the spatial element is aesthetically and structurally formed. The comparison highlights notable differences in how AI systems construct visual meaning, contextual coherence, and intentionality. Although examples demonstrate that AI can technically apply visual conventions such as perspective, in most outputs, spatial voids exist merely as formal features, devoid of experiential and perceptual resonance. Moreover, the consistency of perspective application varies depending on the model used, suggesting that the limitations of AI aesthetic production cannot be overcome by technical advancement alone—cultural codes and visual literacy appear to be essential in this process. Panofsky's approach, which defines perspective as a symbolic form, further illustrates that AI-generated technical perspective lacks the capacity to convey a human-centered worldview.

In conclusion, AI aesthetics should be regarded as a dynamic research domain open to both technical and conceptual development. The question of how artificial systems construct culturally and perceptually loaded aesthetic elements like void is not only relevant for the fields of art and design but also opens a critical discourse in visual literacy, cultural representation, and cognitive aesthetics. Thus, while this study questions the role of AI in aesthetic production, it also reaffirms that human-specific meaning-making processes remain decisive. Future research may deepen and diversify this discourse by exploring the relationship between training data and cultural codes, assessing AI's capacity to "read" visual language, and investigating how intuitive concepts such as void are transformed through AI. In doing so, it may be possible to reframe the question: is AI merely a productive tool, or is it evolving toward becoming an aesthetic and cultural agent in its own right?

REFERENCES

Arielli, E., & Manovich, L. (2022). AI-aesthetics and the anthropocentric myth of creativity. *Nodes Journal of Art and Neuroscience*, *(2022, Fall)*. DOI: 10.57633/NODES-19-20/1-ENG

Aris, S., Aeini, B., & Nosrati, S. (2023). A digital aesthetics? Artificial intelligence and the future of the art. *Journal of Cyberspace Studies*, *7*(2), 219–236. DOI: 10.22059/jcss.2023.366256.1097

Best, S. (2006). Minimalism, subjectivity, and aesthetics: Rethinking the anti-aesthetic tradition in late-modern art. *Journal of Visual Art Practice*, *5*(3), 127–142. DOI: 10.1386/jvap.5.3.127_1

Blaine, I. S. (2015). The aesthetic of ma: The charged emptiness in Japanese art.

Carson, D. (2018, Nisan). *[Magazine Cover]. Volkskrant Magazine*. https://www.davidcarsondesign.com

Carson, D., & Blackwell, L. (1995). *The end of print: The graphic design of David Carson*. Chronicle Books.

Gibson, J. J. (1979). *The ecological approach to visual perception*. Houghton Mifflin.

Gombrich, E. H. (1992). *Sanatın öyküsü* (Z. K. Baykara, Trans., 4. basım). Remzi Kitabevi.

Harrison, C., & Wood, P. (2011). *Sanat ve kuram*. Küre Yayıncılık.

Heidegger, M. (2015). *Varlık ve zaman* (Çüçen, A. K., Trans.). Sentez Yayıncılık.

Müller, J., & Wiedemann, J. (2023). *The history of graphic design* (1890– Today). Taschen.

Noë, A. (2005). *Action in perception*. MIT Press. https://mitpress.mit.edu/9780262640671/action-in-perception/

Panofsky, E. (2021). *Perspektif: Simgesel bir biçim* (Tükel, Y., Trans.). Metis Yayınları. (Original work published 1927)

Parker, A. (2019, May 23). Stereopsis and depth perception. *Oxford Research Encyclopedia of Neuroscience*. Retrieved May 3, 2025, from https://oxfordre.com/neuroscience/view/10.1093/acrefore/9780190264086.001.0001/acrefore-9780190264086-e-77

Perec, G. (1997). *Species of spaces and other pieces* (Sturrock, J., Ed. & Trans.). Penguin Books.

Quent, M. (2024). Interval and event: The present as in-between time in Gilles Deleuze and Alain Badiou. *Filozofski Vestnik, 45*(1), 243–267. DOI: 10.3986/fv.45.1.10

Reichelt, S., Häussler, R., Fütterer, G., & Leister, N. (2010). Depth cues in human visual perception and their realization in 3D displays. In Javidi, B., & Son, J.-Y. (Eds.), *Three-dimensional imaging, visualization, and display 2010* (Vol. 7690, p. 76900B). SPIE. DOI: 10.1117/12.850094

Roth, M., & Katz, J. D. (1998). *Difference/Indifference: Musings on postmodernism, Marcel Duchamp and John Cage*. Routledge.

Sightengine. (2025). Detect AI-generated images. Retrieved May 8, 2025, from https://sightengine.com

Sontag, S. (1973). *On photography*. Farrar, Straus and Giroux. (Electronic ed. RosettaBooks, 2005). ISBN 0-7953-2699-8

Sweet, B., & Kaiser, M. (2011, August). Depth perception, cueing, and control. In *AIAA Modeling and Simulation Technologies Conference* (p. 6424).

The Metropolitan Museum of Art. (n.d.). *Xmas Shopping near Macy's, New York* [Photograph by William Klein, 1954; printed 1956]. Retrieved July 18, 2025, from https://www.metmuseum.org/art/collection/search/266096

Ward, J. L. (1976). The perception of pictorial space in perspective pictures. *Leonardo, 9*(4), 279–288. DOI: 10.2307/1573353

Wittgenstein, L. (1968). *Philosophical investigations.* Macmillan.

Zhang, H., & Yoshida, S. (2024). Decoding illusion perception: A comparative analysis of deep neural networks in the Müller-Lyer illusion. *Applied Sciences (Basel, Switzerland), 14*(8), 3429. DOI: 10.3390/app14083429

Zhou, B., Zhao, H., Puig, X., Fidler, S., Barriuso, A., & Torralba, A. "Scene Parsing through ADE20K Dataset," *2017 IEEE Conference on Computer Vision and Pattern Recognition (CVPR)*, Honolulu, HI, USA, 2017, pp. 5122-5130, DOI: 10.1109/CVPR.2017.544

ADDITIONAL READING

Arielli, E., & Manovich, L. (2022). AI-aesthetics and the anthropocentric myth of creativity. *Nodes Journal of Art and Neuroscience*, *(2022, Fall)*. DOI: 10.57633/NODES-19-20/1-ENG

Aris, S., Aeini, B., & Nosrati, S. (2023). A digital aesthetics? Artificial intelligence and the future of the art. *Journal of Cyberspace Studies*, *7*(2), 219–236. DOI: 10.22059/jcss.2023.366256.1097

Best, S. (2006). Minimalism, subjectivity, and aesthetics: Rethinking the anti-aesthetic tradition in late-modern art. *Journal of Visual Art Practice*, *5*(3), 127–142. DOI: 10.1386/jvap.5.3.127_1

Blaine, I. S. (2015). The aesthetic of ma: The charged emptiness in Japanese art.

Roth, M., & Katz, J. D. (1998). *Difference/Indifference: Musings on postmodernism, Marcel Duchamp and John Cage*. Routledge.

Zhang, H., & Yoshida, S. (2024). Decoding illusion perception: A comparative analysis of deep neural networks in the Müller-Lyer illusion. *Applied Sciences (Basel, Switzerland)*, *14*(8), 3429. DOI: 10.3390/app14083429

Zhou, B., Zhao, H., Puig, X., Fidler, S., Barriuso, A., & Torralba, A. "Scene Parsing through ADE20K Dataset," *2017 IEEE Conference on Computer Vision and Pattern Recognition (CVPR)*, Honolulu, HI, USA, 2017, pp. 5122-5130, DOI: 10.1109/CVPR.2017.544

KEY TERMS AND DEFINITIONS

AI-Generated Imagery: Visual content produced by artificial intelligence systems based on text prompts or datasets. Raises questions about authorship, intentionality, and aesthetic control.

Digital Aesthetics: The aesthetic qualities and visual logic emerging from digital tools, processes, and environments, particularly in AI-driven visual production.

Graphic Design: A visual communication discipline that combines text, image, space, and layout to convey meaning. It often utilizes negative space strategically to enhance readability, hierarchy, and conceptual depth.

Ma: A Japanese aesthetic concept that defines the space between elements as a meaningful interval. In visual arts, Ma is not empty but charged with interpretive and experiential potential.

Negative Space: The area around and between the subjects of an image. In visual design, it is not mere emptiness but a compositional and conceptual element that shapes perception and meaning.

Perspective Construction: The creation of spatial depth in two-dimensional compositions. It plays a critical role in both human and AI-generated visuals in shaping spatial logic and realism.

Typographic Space: The use of spacing, alignment, and layout in text design to create visual rhythm, clarity, and conceptual layering, particularly important in poster and graphic design.

Visual Perception: The process by which the brain interprets visual stimuli. Central to how space, depth, and form are understood in both human and AI vision systems.

Compilation of References

3D. Film Archive. (n.d.). *3D Film Archive*. Retrieved May 13, 2025 from https://3dfilmarchive.com/what-killed-3d-films/

Abbing, H. (2004). *Why Are Artists Poor? The Exceptional Economy of the Arts*. Amsterdam University Press.

Abidin, C. (2016). Visibility labor: Engaging with influencers' fashion brands and #OOTD advertorial campaigns on Instagram. *Media International Australia, Incorporating Culture & Policy, 161*(1), 86–100. DOI: 10.1177/1329878X16665177

Acemoglu, D., & Restrepo, P. (2018). *Artificial Intelligence, Automation and Work* (NBER Working Paper No. 24196). https://www.nber.org/papers/w24196

Adams, T. (2025, 10 March) *theguardian.com,* The big picture: Grace Kelly jumps for Philippe Halsman, https://www.theguardian.com/artanddesign/2019/feb/24/the-big-picture-grace-kelly-jumps-philippe-halsman-magnum-the-body-observed

Addley, E. (2023, November 1). AI named most notable word of 2023 by Collins dictionary. *The Guardian*. https://www.theguardian.com/technology/2023/nov/01/ai-named-most-notable-word-of-2023-by-collins-dictionary

Akmeşe, E. (2017). *Evrensel Bir Simgenin Sıradışı Öyküsü: Chevolution, (Editörler), Huriye Kuruoğlu ve Alev Fatoş Parsa. Belgesel Filmde Zamanın Ruhu: Belgesel Filmde Değişen Anlam ve Anlatım*. Detay Yayıncılık.

Alay, D. (2024). Kişiselleştirilmiş tıp için dijital ikiz: Sistematik derleme. *Sağlık Profesyonelleri Araştırma Dergisi, 6*(1), 28–43. DOI: 10.57224/jhpr.1342561

Albers, K. P. (2023, March 9). *James Welling recasts the ancient World.* Aperture. https://aperture.org/editorial/james-welling-recasts-the-ancient-world/

Allyn, B. (2022, March 16). Deepfake video of Zelensky could be tip of the iceberg in info war, experts warn. *NPR*. https://www.npr.org/2022/03/16/1087062648/deepfake-video-zelenskyy-experts-war-manipulation-ukraine-russia

Alphahistory (2025, 30 March) *alphahistory.com,* A French photographer recalls Bloody Sunday (1972), https://alphahistory.com/northernireland/gilles-peress-bloody-sunday-1972/

Alternative photography (2025, 4 March). *alternativephotography.com,* Alternative Photographic Processes World of Records https://www.alternativephotography.com/alternative-processes-records/

Anadol, R. (2018). Melting Memories [Media installation]. Refik Anadol Studio. https://refikanadol.com/works/melting-memories/

Anadol, R. (2018). WDCH Dreams [AI-driven immersive projection]. https://refikanadol.com/works/wdch-dreams/

Anadol, R. (2019). Machine Hallucinations [Exhibition]. ARTECHOUSE New York. https://refikanadol.com/works/machine-hallucinations/

Anadol, R. (2021). Machine Hallucinations - Nature Dreams [AI-generated video installation]. https://refikanadol.com/works/machine-hallucinations-nature-dreams/

Anadol, R. (2022). Unsupervised [AI-generated data sculpture]. https://refikanadol.com/works/unsupervised/

Anlen, Ş., & Llorente, R. V. (2024, April 15). Spotting the deepfakes in this year of elections: How AI detection tools work and where they fail. *Reuters Institute for the Study of Journalism.* https://reutersinstitute.politics.ox.ac.uk/news/spotting-deepfakes-year-elections-how-ai-detection-tools-work-and-where-they-fail

Antmen, A. (2010). *Sanatçılardan Yazılar ve Açıklamalarla 20. Yüzyıl Batı Sanatında Akımlar.* Sel Yayıncılık.

Aral, C. (2025, 16 April) *youtube.com,* Fotoğrafın Kalesi: Toroslab - Coşkun Aral Anlatıyor, https://www.youtube.com/watch?v=OUkl7bsrGZY

Arielli, E., & Manovich, L. (2022). AI-aesthetics and the anthropocentric myth of creativity. *Nodes Journal of Art and Neuroscience*, (*2022, Fall).* DOI: 10.57633/NODES-19-20/1-ENG

Aris, S., Aeini, B., & Nosrati, S. (2023). A digital aesthetics? Artificial intelligence and the future of the art. *Journal of Cyberspace Studies*, *7*(2), 219–236. DOI: 10.22059/jcss.2023.366256.1097

Artist web page. (n.d.). Michael Christopher Brown. https://www.michaelchristopherbrown.com/artificial-intelligence/90-miles

Artun, A. (2010). *Sanat Manifestoları, Avangard Sanat ve Direniş*. İletişim Yayınları.

Artworks, (2025, 15 May). *artworks.se,* Carmen Winant, https://artworks.se/utstallningar/body-index

Aşık, F., Yıldız, A., Kılınç, S., Aytekin, N., Adalı, R., & Kurnaz, K. (2023). Yapay zekânın eğitime etkileri. [JSHSR]. *International Journal of Social and Humanities Sciences Research, 10*(98), 2100–2107. DOI: 10.5281/zenodo.8307107

Aydemir, F. (n.d.), *Fotoğrafın Evrimi: Analogdan Dijitale Geçişin Hikayesi ve Günümüzde Fotoğrafçılık,* https://www.fatihaydemir.net/blog/fotografin-evrimi-analogdan-dijitale-gecisin-hikayesi/, [Erişim Tarihi: 11.03.2025].

Azoulay, A. (2008). *The civil contract of photography.* Zone Books.

Bacak, C. (2023). Piksel bülten. *Muscular theology: body construction and homoeroticism in midjourney.* https://www.pikselbulten.com/posts/muscular-theology-body-construction-and-homoeroticism-in-midjourney

Bahn, P., & Renfrew, C. (2013). *Arkeoloji anahtar kavramlar.* İletişim Yayınları.

Bajac, Q. (2004). *Karanlık odanın sırları fotoğrafın icadı.* Yapı Kredi Yayınları.

Bakın, A. (2023). Dijitalleşmenin emek gücü üzerinde etkileri ve dijital emek. In E. Kaan

Baltar-Moreno, A. (2022). Digital social networks as sites of memory: Citizen dialogues through photography on Facebook. *ICONO 14. Revista de Comunicación y Tecnologías Emergentes, 20*(2), 53–59. DOI: 10.7195/ri14.v20i2.1880

Banet-Weiser, S. (2012). *Authentic: The politics of ambivalence in a brand culture.* New York University Press.

Barbara, S. (2018). Belgesel Özerklik ve Fotoğraf Sanatı, S. Walden (Ed.), *Fotoğraf Felsefesi, Doğanın Kalemi Üzerine Denemeler* (pp. 139-166). (A. Yılmaz, Trans.), Espas Yayın

Barnard, M. (2010). *Sanat Tasarım ve Kültür* (Korkmaz, G., Trans.). Ütopya.

Barthes, R. (1977). *Image, music, text* (Heath, S., Trans.). Hill and Wang.

Barthes, R. (1981). *Camera lucida: reflections on photography* (Howard, R., Trans.). Hill & Wang.

Barthes, R. (1981). *Camera lucida: Reflections on photography* (Howard, R., Trans.). Hill and Wang.

Barthes, R. (1996). *Camera lucida.* Altıkırkbeş Yayınları.

Batchen, G. (1992). On post-photography. *Afterimage: The Journal of Media Arts and Cultural Critism.* https://www.researchgate.net/publication/362643203_On_Post-Photography

Batchen, G. (2009). Seeing and saying: a response to "incongruous images". *History and Theory*. https://www.jstor.org/stable/25621436

Batchen, G. (1997). *Burning with desire: The conception of photography*. MIT Press.

Baudrillard, J. (1981). *Simulacra and Simulation*. The University of Michigan Press.

Baudrillard, J. (1994). *Simulacra and simulation* (Glaser, S. F., Trans.). University of Michigan Press.

Baudrillard, J. (2024). *Simülakrlar ve simülasyon*. Doğu Batı Yayınları.

BBC. (2025, 19 April) *bbc.com,* Robert Capa's greatest war photo 'was a lucky shot', https://www.bbc.com/news/av/entertainment-arts-24723949

Benjamin, W. (2008). The work of art in the age of mechanical reproduction. H. Arendt (Ed.), Illuminations (pp. 217–252). Schocken Books.

Benjamin, W. (2008). *The work of art in the age of its technological reproducibility and other writings on media* (Jennings, M. W., Doherty, B., & Levin, T. Y., Trans.). Harvard University Press. DOI: 10.2307/j.ctv1nzfgns

Berger, J. (2011). *Görme biçimleri*. (Y. Salman, Çev.). Metis Yayınları.

Berger, J. (1972). *Ways of seeing*. Penguin Books.

Best, S. (2006). Minimalism, subjectivity, and aesthetics: Rethinking the anti-aesthetic tradition in late-modern art. *Journal of Visual Art Practice*, *5*(3), 127–142. DOI: 10.1386/jvap.5.3.127_1

Betancourt, M. (2016). The aura of information: Digital art and the myth of uniqueness.

Bianchi, F., Kalluri, P., Durmus, E., Ladhak, F., Cheng, M., Nozza, D., Hashimoto, T., Jurafsky, D., Zou, J., & Caliskan, A. (2023). Easily accessible text-to-image generation amplifies demographic stereotypes at large scale. *Proceedings of the 2023 ACM Conference on Fairness, Accountability, and Transparency*, 1493–1504. https://dl.acm.org/doi/10.1145/3593013.3594095

Biner, İ. C. (2023). Homo erotism and muscular theology. *Medium: Human stories & ideas.* https://medium.com/nftify-uk/homo-erotism-and-muscular-theology-7e729dae3174

Birinci, G. (2019). Fotoğraf Sanatında Fotografik Malzemenin Görsel Bir Dil Olarak Kullanımı. *Uluslararası Sanat Kültür ve İletişim Dergisi*, *2*(1), 68–80.

Bishop, C. (2012). *Artificial hells: Participatory art and the politics of spectatorship*. Verso Books.

Blaine, I. S. (2015). The aesthetic of ma: The charged emptiness in Japanese art.

Blas, Z. (2012). Facial weaponization suite 2012-14. *Zach blas website artworks.* 18.04.2025, https://zachblas.info/works/facial-weaponization-suite/

Bohrer, F. (2011). *Photography and archaeology*. Reaktion books.

Bourdieu, P. (2006). *Sanatın Kuralları,* Trans. N. K. Sevil, Yapı Kredi Yayınları-1216/57

Bourriaud, N. (2002). *Relational aesthetics* (Pleasance, S., & Woods, F., Trans.). Les Presses du Réel.

Bradshaw Foundation. (n.d.). *World Heritage Site in Argentina*. Retrieved April 29, 2025 from https://www.bradshawfoundation.com/south_america/cueva_de_los_manos/index.php

Braidotti, R. (2013). *The posthuman*. Polity Press.

Breton, A. (2017). İki Dada Bildirisi, E. Batur (Ed.), *Modernizmin Serüveni, Bir "Temel Metinler" Seçkisi 1840-1990* (pp.375-376). (S. Rifat, Trans.), Sel Yayıncılık

Bridle, J. (2018). *New Dark Age: Technology and the End of the Future*. Verso Books.

Bright, R. (2018, February). AI and Neurography [Interview with M. Klingemann]. Interalia Magazine. https://www.interaliamag.org/interviews/mario-klingemann/

Bright, S., & Van Erp, H. (2019). *Photography Decoded*. Tate.

Brown, M. C. (2023, September 27). Photo Vogue Festival 2023 talks: 90 Miles-AI reportage illustration. *Photo Vogue*. https://www.vogue.com/article/photovogue-festival-2023-talks-90-miles-ai-reportage-illustration

Brown, R., & Phillips, M. (2025, 21 March). *alternativephotography.com,* Cyanotype photograms, https://www.alternativephotography.com/photograms/

Brynjolfsson, E., & McAfee, A. (2014). *The second machine age*. W. W. Norton & Company.

Bunyan, M. (2025, 1 April) *artblart.com,* Review: 'Jeff Wall Photographs' at The Ian Potter Centre: NGVA, National Gallery of Victoria, Melbourne, https://artblart.com/tag/jeff-wall-dressing-poultry/

Burgin, V. (2025). *Kamera: Öz ve aygıt.* Espas Yayınları.

Butler, J. (1990). *Gender trouble: Feminism and the subversion of identity.* Routledge.

Cabanne, P. (2015). Kolajlar, E. Batur (Ed.), *Modernizmin Serüveni, Bir "Temel Metinler" Seçkisi 1840-1990* (pp.380-383). (M. Cansever, Trans.), Sel Yayıncılık

Çakın, Ö., & Bolat, N. (2018). *Sosyal Medya Reklamcılığı ve Dijital Mecra Etkileşimleri, 'Dijital Kültür ve İletişim' içinde* (Çakmak, V., & Çavuş, S., Eds.). Literatürk Academia Yayınları.

Caldeira, W., & Simões, J. (2024). Digital image: The role of apparatus, artificial intelligence, and machine learning in visual communication in the digital age. *Rotura – Revista de Comunicação. Cultura e Artes, 4*(2), 138–149.

Cambridge Dictionary. (n.d.). *Artificial intelligence.* https://dictionary.cambridge.org/dictionary/english-turkish/artificial-intelligence

Cambridge Dictionary. (n.d.). *Disinformation.* https://dictionary.cambridge.org/dictionary/english/disinformation

Campany, D. (2025, 12 April) *davidcampany.com,* 'Migrant Mother, 1936', https://davidcampany.com/migrant-mother-1936-2/

Carson, D. (2018, Nisan). *[Magazine Cover]. Volkskrant Magazine.* https://www.davidcarsondesign.com

Carson, D., & Blackwell, L. (1995). *The end of print: The graphic design of David Carson.* Chronicle Books.

Cauquelin, A. (2005). *Çağdaş Sanat,* (Ö. Avcı, Trans.), Kültür Kitaplığı-20, Dost Kitapevi

Çetin, M., & Baklavacı, G. Y. (2024). Endüstri 4.0 perspektifinde yapay zekânın eğitimde uygulanabilirliği ile ilgili öğretmen görüşlerinin incelenmesi. *İstanbul Ticaret Üniversitesi Girişimcilik Dergisi*, 7(14), 1–21. https://doi.org/DOI: 10.55830/tje.1404165

Cetinic, E., & She, J. (2022). Understanding and creating art with AI: Review and outlook. *ACM Transactions on Multimedia Computing Communications and Applications, 18*(4), 1–21. DOI: 10.1145/3475799

Chamberlain, R., Mullin, C., Scheerlinck, B., & And Wagemans, J. (2018). Putting the art in artificial: Aesthetic responses to computer-generated art. *Psychology of Aesthetics, Creativity, and the Arts, 12*(2), 177–192. DOI: 10.1037/aca0000136

Chandler, D. (2025, 23 March). *martinparrfoundation.org,* https://www.martinparr foundation.org/product/nigel-shafran-workbooks/

Cheng, H. (2022). It could be you. *Hsien-yu cheng website artworks.* 05.05.2025, https://chenghsienyu.com/it-could-be-you/

Chen, J. (2024). The role of AI: Speculative design in redefining artistic collaboration. *Journal of Ecohumanism, 3*(8), 2261–2272. DOI: 10.62754/joe.v3i8.4899

Chen, Y. (2024). Artificial intelligence technology in photography and future challenges and reflections. *The Frontiers of Society. Science and Technology, 6*(6), 24–30.

Chesney, B., & Citron, D. (2019). Deep Fakes: A Looming Challenge for Privacy, Democracy, and National Security. *California Law Review, 107*(6), 1753–1820. https://www.jstor.org/stable/26891938

Ching, V., & Mothi, D. (2025). *AI for creatives: Unlocking expressive digital potential.* CRC Press. DOI: 10.1201/9781003533016

Christiane, P. (2008). *Digital art.* Thames & Hudson.

Clarke, G. (2017). *Güzel sanatların bir dalı olarak fotoğraf.* Hayalperest Yayınları.

Çoban, İ. (2023). Sinema- Görsel Tasarım İlişkisi Ekseninde Sanal Gerçeklik ve Hikaye Anlatımı: "Gloomy Eyes" Analizi. *Uluslararası Disiplinlerarası ve Kültürlerarası Sanat, 8*(17), 13–28.

Coeckelbergh, M. (2020). *AI Ethics.* MIT Press. DOI: 10.7551/mitpress/12549.001.0001

Collen, K. (2014). L'économie de la photographie de presse et son évolution paradigmatique. *Press photography*, 121–134. https://doi.org/DOI: 10.4000/books.pur.50377

Connell, R. W. (2016). *Toplumsal cinsiyet ve iktidar.* (C. Soydemir, Çev.). Ayrıntı Yayınları.

Cosgrove, B. (n.d.). *'Spanish village': W. Eugene Smith's landmark photo essay.* https://www.life.com/people/life-behind-the-picture-w-eugene-smiths-guardia-civil-1950/

Coşkun, F., & Gülleroğlu, H. D. (2021). Yapay zekanın tarih içindeki gelişimi ve eğitimde kullanılması. [JFES]. *Ankara University Journal of Faculty of Educational Sciences, 54*(3), 947–966. DOI: 10.30964/auebfd.916220

Costa, A. S. L. (2024). *Artificial aesthetic: Exploring the convergence of creativity, artificial intelligence, and human expression in art* (Doctoral dissertation).

Cotton, C. (2020). *The Photograph as Contemporary Art*. Thames & Hudson.

Couturier, E. (2012). *Talk Abaut Contemporary Photography*. Flammarion.

Cozzi, L. (2025, 10 May). *x-traonline.org,* Sod You Gits: Sarah Lucas's Fleet Street Surrealism, https://www.x-traonline.org/article/sod-you-gits-sarah-lucass-fleet-street-surrealism

Crawford, K., & Paglen, T. (2025, 13 April). *Excavating AI: the politics of ımages in machine learning training sets.* https://excavating.ai

Crawford, K. (2021). *Atlas of AI: Power, politics, and the planetary costs of artificial intelligence.* Yale University Press.

Crawford, K. (2021). *The atlas of AI.* Yale University Press.

Crawford, K., & Paglen, T. (2021). Excavating ai: The politics of training sets for machine learning. *AI & Society, 36*, 1105–1116. DOI: 10.1007/s00146-021-01301-1

Crewdson, G. (2025, 2 May, a) gregorycrewdson.substack.com, The Making of Ophelia, https://gregorycrewdson.substack.com/p/the-making-of-ophelia

Crewdson, G. (2025, 2 May, b) *gregorycrewdsonmovie.com,* http://www.gregorycrewdsonmovie.com/image-gallery.html

Cruz, E. (2016). *Digital photography studies.*, DOI: 10.1007/978-3-658-08460-8_12-1

Danto, A. (2016). *Brillo Kutusu, Post-Tarihsel Perspektiften Görsel Sanatlar* (Kayaş, C., Trans.). Sanat ve Kuram.

Das, S., & Kundu, R. (2024). The ethics of artificial intelligence in creative arts: A comprehensive review. *Interdisciplinary International Journal of Advances in Social Sciences. Arts and Humanities, 1*(1), 26–33.

Debord, G. (1994). *The society of the spectacle* (Nicholson-Smith, D., Trans.). Zone Books.

Demir, A. Z ve Demir, Ö. (2023). Dijital Medyada İçerik Üretiminin Geleneksel İçerik Üretimi Teknikleri Bağlamında Değerlendirilmesi, Dijital Kapitalizm ve İletişim Sempozyumu 16-18 Mayıs 2023 (pp.400-408)

Demirhan, A., Kılıç, Y. A., & İnan, G. (2010). Tıpta yapay zeka uygulamaları. *Yoğun Bakım Dergisi, 9*(1), 31–41.

Deniz, S., & Bağçeci, B. (2025). Kavramdan sınıfa: Yapay zekânın keşfi ve eğitime yansımaları. *Elektronik Sosyal Bilimler Dergisi, 24*(1), 576–596. DOI: 10.17755/esosder.1554996

Depeli, G., & Hepdincler, T. (2022). Tema Editörlerinden (TR). *Moment Dergi, 9*(1), 1–6. DOI: 10.17572/moment.1136304

Diakopoulos, N. (2019). *Automating the news: How algorithms are rewriting the media*. Harvard University Press. DOI: 10.4159/9780674239302

Dinçer, Y. D. (2025, 24 April) *istanbulmodern.org,* https://www.istanbulmodern.org/en/events/nuri-bilge-ceylan-in-another-place-exhibition-event

Dinçer, Y. D., & Ulu, D. (2025, 24 April) *istanbulmodern.org,* Nuri Bilge Ceylan: In Another Place, https://www.istanbulmodern.org/en/exhibitions/past/nuri-bilge-ceylan-in-another-placz

Dinkins, S. (2025, 17 April). Secret garden: Our stories are algorithms. *Stephanie dinkins website.* 17.04.2025, https://www.stephaniedinkins.com/about.html

Dizikes, P. (2024, December 6). Daron Acemoglu: What do we know about the economics of AI? *MIT News*. https://economics.mit.edu/news/daron-acemoglu-what-do-we-know-about-economics-ai

Dube, B. (2017). To lie or not to lie. In Copeland, B. J. (Ed.), (pp. 44–63)., DOI: 10.4018/978-1-5225-2095-5.ch003

Duchamp, M. (2017). Marcel Duchamp ve Ready-Made, E. Batur (Ed.), *Modernizmin Serüveni, Bir "Temel Metinler" Seçkisi 1840-1990* (pp.378-379). (S. Rifat, Trans.), Sel Yayıncılık

Duganne, E., Diack, H., & Weissman, T. (2020). *Global Photography, A Critical History*. Routledge. DOI: 10.4324/9781003085485

Duman, A. T. (2024). *Fotoğrafta dijital sergileme biçimlerinin anlam bağlamında esere etkisi*. [Unpublished master's thesis]. Mimar Sinan Güzel Sanatlar Üniversitesi

Dupre, M. H. (2023, November 27). Sports Illustrated published articles by fake, AI generated writers. *Futurism*. https://futurism.com/sports-illustrated-ai-generated-writers

Dursun, R. Z. A., & Bakan, U. (2025). An exploration of machine learning in art and design. In *Impact of contemporary technology on art and design* (pp. 205–236). IGI Global.

Edward, V. I. I. I. (2025, 12 April) *Wikipedia,* https://en.wikipedia.org/wiki/Edward_VIII

Elgammal, A., Liu, B., Elhoseiny, M., & Mazzone, M. (2017). CAN: Creative Adversarial Networks, Generating "Art" by Learning About Styles and Deviating from Style Norms. https://doi.org//arXiv.1706.07068DOI: 10.48550

Elkins, J. (2011). *What photography is*. Routledge. DOI: 10.4324/9780203886489

Elwes, J. (2019). Zizi: queering the dataset. *Jake elwes website.* 18.04.2025, https://www.jakeelwes.com/project-zizi-2019.html

Erişti, S. D. B., & Freedman, K. (2024). Integrating digital technologies and AI in art education: Pedagogical competencies and the evolution of digital visual culture. *Participatory Educational Research, 11*(Prof. Dr. H. Ferhan Odabaşı Gift Issue), 57–79.

Er, M. H. (2022). *XXI. Yüzyıl Çağdaş Fotoğrafta Yaratım Sürecine Bakış* (Bilgiseren, H. O., Ed.). Efe Akademi Yayınları.

Er, M. H. (2023). Portrait Photography and Appropriation. *Contemporary Issues of Communication*, *2*(1), 18–32.

Er, M. H. (2023)... *Portrait Photography and Appropriation, Contemporary Issues of Communication, Volume*, *2*(1), 18–32.

Eroğlu, Ö. (2015). *Modern Sanat.* Tekhne Yayınları.

European Parliament. (2024). Artificial Intelligence Act. *European Union.*

Farid, H. (2022). Creating, Using, Misusing, and Detecting Deep Fakes. *Journal of Online Trust & Safety*, *1*(4). Advance online publication. DOI: 10.54501/jots.v1i4.56

Fateman, J. (2025, 10 May). https://www.danielgordonstudio.com/, Daniel Gordon, https://www.danielgordonstudio.com/press/85=daniel-gordon

Ferrara, E. (2024). Fairness and bias in artificial intelligence: A brief survey of sources, impacts, and mitigation strategies. *Sci*, *6*(1), 3. DOI: 10.3390/sci6010003

Fineman, M. (2012). *Faking it: Manipulated photography before Photoshop.* Yale University Press.

Floridi, L. (2019). *The Logic of Information: A Theory of Philosophy as Conceptual Design.* Oxford University Press., DOI: 10.1093/oso/9780198833635.001.0001

Floridi, L., Cowls, J., Beltrametti, M., Chatila, R., Chazerand, P., Dignum, V., Luetge, C., Madelin, R., Pagallo, U., Rossi, F., Schafer, B., Valcke, P., & Vayena, E. (2018). AI4People-An ethical framework for a good AI society: Opportunities, risks, principles, and recommendations. *Minds and Machines*, *28*(4), 689–707. DOI: 10.1007/s11023-018-9482-5 PMID: 30930541

Flusser, V. (2020). *Bir fotoğraf felsefesine doğru.* (A. Yılmaz, Çev.). Espas Yayınları.

Fontcuberta, J. (2004-2010). Googlegrams. https://www.juanmagonzalez.com/fontcuberta/googlegrams.html

Fontcuberta, J. (2011). *Post-photographic manifesto* [Post-photographic manifesto]. La Vanguardia. https://www.lavanguardia.com/cultura/20110511/54152218372/por-un-manifiesto-posfotografico.html

Fontcuberta, J. (2013). *The photography of nature & the nature of photography.* Mack.

Fontcuberta, J. (2016). *La furia de las imágenes: Notas sobre la postfotografía.* Galaxia Gutenberg.

Foster, J. (2025, 12 May). *juliannafoster.com,* https://juliannafoster.com/section/325750-Swell.html

Fotografdergisi (2025, 25 April) *fotografdergisi.com,* https://www.fotografdergisi.com

Frieze (2025, 03 May). *frieze.com,* Finding the Right Darkness, Zoe Leonard's photographs and sculptures meditate on wonder and loss, https://www.frieze.com/article/finding-right-darkness

Friswell, R. (2025, 28 April) *artesmagazine.com,* Robert Capa's Long-Lost 'Mexican Suitcase' Reveals a Trove of Vintage Photographs at ICP, https://artesmagazine.com/2010/11/robert-capas-long-lost-mexican-suitcase-reveals-a-trove-of-vintage-photographs-at-icp-2/

Frosh, P., & Pinchevski, A. (2009). *Media Witnessing: Testimony in the Age of Mass Communication.* Palgrave Macmillan. DOI: 10.1057/9780230235762

Gaines, R. J. (1993, December 2). From the managing editor: Nov. 18, 1993. *Time.* https://time.com/archive/6724351/from-the-managing-editor-nov-18-1993/

Gamble, C. (2014). *Arkeolojinin temelleri.* Aktüel Arkeoloji Yayınları.

Gelbart, H. (2023, February 14). TikTok ve Twitter'da deprem yardımı dolandırıcılıkları. *BBC Türkçe.* https://www.bbc.com/turkce/articles/c2v1q9q5gqzo

Genç, A. (1983). *Dada, Antropi ve Nedensizlik Açısından Dadacı Sanat Hareketlerinin Çözümlemesine İlişkin Bir Yöntem Araştırması*. Dokuz Eylül Üniversitesi, Güzel Sanatlar Fakültesi, Resim Bölümü, Doktora Tezi.

Gençcelep, B., & Özkemahlı, K. K. (2023). "Gerçek Olandan Simülasyona: Fotoğraf Stüdyosu Eğitiminde "Set.A.Light 3D" Örneği", International Academic Social Resources Journal, (e-ISSN: 2636-7637), Vol:8, Issue:51; pp:3062-3071. DOI: DOI: 10.29228/ASRJOURNAL.70969

Ghose, A., Ali, S. A., & Mishra, A. M. (2024). Artistic expressions, generative AI, and legal tapestry: Exploring the dynamics of copyright laws in the confluence of AI and artistic creation. In *Making art with generative AI tools* (pp. 198–214). IGI Global. DOI: 10.4018/979-8-3693-1950-5.ch011

Gibbons, L. (2019). Connecting personal and community memory-making: Facebook groups as emergent community archives. *Information Research, 24*(3).

Gibson, J. J. (1979). *The ecological approach to visual perception*. Houghton Mifflin.

Gillespie, T. (2014). The relevance of algorithms. In Gillespie, T., Boczkowski, P. J., & Foot, K. A. (Eds.), *Media technologies: Essays on communication, materiality, and society* (pp. 167–194). MIT Press. DOI: 10.7551/mitpress/9042.003.0013

Gill, R. (2007). *Gender and the media*. Polity Press.

Gingrich, O. M. (2021). GENDER*UCK: Reframing gender & media art. *AI and the Arts: Artificial Imagination*. 148-154. DOI: 10.14236/ewic/EVA2021.25

Glatz, C. (2024, June 14). World needs urgent political action to guide AI, pope tells G7. *United States Conference of Catholic Bishops*. https://www.usccb.org/news/2024/world-needs-urgent-political-action-guide-ai-pope-tells-g7

Göde, A. (2024). Halk sağlığında yapay zekâ (YZ) kullanımı ve geleceği. *TOGÜ Erbaa Sağlık ve Yönetim Dergisi, 1*(1), 1–16.

Goffman, E. (1959). *The presentation of self in everyday life*. Anchor Books.

Gombrich, E. H. (1992). *Sanatın öyküsü* (Z. K. Baykara, Trans., 4. basım). Remzi Kitabevi.

Gotthardt, A. (2019, June 15). *The eccentric cabinets of curiosity that captivated renaissance Europe*. Artsy. https://www.artsy.net/article/artsy-editorial-eccentric-cabinets-curiosity-captivated-renaissance-europe

Gottschalk, M. (2025, 23 April) *artsy.net,* The Fateful Roadside Stop That Led to Dorothea Lange's "Migrant Mother" https://www.artsy.net/article/artsy-editorial-fateful-roadside-led-dorothea-langes-migrant-mother

GOV. (2025, 17 April) *gov.uk,* www.gov.uk/government/organisations/information-commissioner-s office#:~:text=The%20Information%20Commissioner's%20Office%20(ICO,for%20Science%2C%20Innovation%20and%20Technology. Gall, J. and Buchanan-Smith, P. (2025, 23 March) vintagebooks.wordpress.com, What We Talk About When We Talk About Book Covers, https://vintagebooks.wordpress.com/2009/09/08/what-we-talk-about-when-we-talk-about-book-covers/

Graf, M. (2023). *Modern ve Çağdaş Sanat Kafası*. Hayalperest Yayınevi.

Grau, O. (2003). *Virtual art: From Illusion to Immersion*. MIT Press.

Gregory, S. (2023, October 9). When AI can fake reality, who can you trust? *TED*. https://www.ted.com/talks/sam_gregory_when_ai_can_fake_reality_who_can_you_trust

Groh, M., Epstein, Z., Firestone, C., & Picard, R. (2022). Deepfake detection by human crowds, machines, and machine-informed crowds. *Proceedings of the National Academy of Sciences of the United States of America, 119*(1), e2110013119. DOI: 10.1073/pnas.2110013119 PMID: 34969837

Growcoot, M. (2023, May 15). *Photojournalist controversially turns to ai to illustrate 'inaccessible' stories*. https://petapixel.com/2023/05/15/photojournalist-controversially-turns-to-ai-to-illustrate-inaccessible-stories/

Growcoot, M. (2025, 10 April) *petapixel.com,* David Lynch's Enduring Impact on Photography, https://petapixel.com/2025/01/22/david-lynchs-enduring-impact-on-photography/

Groys, B. (2008). *Art Power*. MIT Press. DOI: 10.7551/mitpress/7469.001.0001

Gülaçtı, İ. E., & Kahraman, M. E. (2021). The impact of artificial intelligence on photography and painting in the post-truth era and the issues of creativity and authorship. *Medeniyet Sanat Dergisi*, *7*(2), 243–270. DOI: 10.46641/medeniyetsanat.994950

Güler, M. (2022). *Dipnot*: Bir Fotoğraf Felsefesine Doğru.* https://www.ifsakblog.org/dipnot-bir-fotograf-felsefesine-dogru, [Erişim Tarihi: 20.03.2025.

Günay, M. (2024). Creative innovation in the context of artificial intelligence in digital art. *International Journal of Education Technology and Scientific Researches*, *9*(28), 619–629. DOI: 10.35826/ijetsar.746

Halbwachs, M. (1992). On Collective Memory. (Çev. L. A. Coser). University of Chicago Press. (Original 1952).

Haraway, D. (2006). *Siborg manifestosu.* (O. Akınhay, Çev.). Agora Kitaplığı.

Hariyanto, R. L., Silaban, M. D., Kurniawan, R., Sudirman, L., & Alamanda, A. E. (2024). AI and creativity: Redefining copyright for visual works and text. *Barelang Journal of Legal Studies*, *2*(1), 1–16.

Harrison, C., & Wood, P. (2011). *Sanat ve kuram.* Küre Yayıncılık.

Hausken, L. (2024). Photorealism versus photography. AI-generated depiction in the age of visual disinformation. *Journal of Aesthetics & Culture, 16*(1), 2340787. Advance online publication. DOI: 10.1080/20004214.2024.2340787

He, J. (2024). A study on the influence of artificial intelligence on image art design. *SHS Web of Conferences, 181*, 04028.

Heidegger, M. (2015). *Varlık ve zaman* (Çüçen, A. K., Trans.). Sentez Yayıncılık.

Henley, J. (2025, 13 April, a) *theguardian.com,* 55 years on, the controversial kiss that could be worth £10,000, https://www.theguardian.com/world/2005/apr/13/france.arts

Henley, J. (2025, 16 April, b) *theguardian.com,* The remarkable story behind the kiss photo that melted hearts - and what happened to the 'happy' couple, https://www.theguardian.com/world/2005/apr/13/france.arts

Higgins, E. [@EliotHiggins]. (2023, March 20). Making pictures of Trump getting arrested while waiting for Trump's arrest. *X (Twitter).* https://twitter.com/EliotHiggins/status/1637927681734987777

Higgins, J. (2014). *Fotoğraf neden kusursuz olmak zorunda değildir.* Hayalperest Yayınları.

Hoby, H. (2012). Google muse: the new breed of street photographers. *The Observer.* https://www.theguardian.com/artanddesign/2012/jul/14/google-muse-street-photographers-interviews, [Erişim Tarihi: 09.05.2025].

Hodge, S. (2019). *Sanatın Kısa Öyküsü* (Öztok, D., Trans.). Hep Kitap Yayın.

Holland, O. (2025, 6 April) edition.cnn.com, Who took 'Napalm Girl'? World Press Photo 'suspends' attribution of historic Vietnam War image, https://edition.cnn.com/2025/05/19/style/napalm-girl-world-press-photo-nick-ut-hnk-intl

Hong, J. C., & Curran, N. M. (2019). Artificial Intelligence, Artists, and Art: Attitudes Toward Artwork Produced By Humans vs. Artificial Intelligence. *ACM Transactions on Multimedia Computing Communications and Applications*, *15*(2s), 1–16. Advance online publication. DOI: 10.1145/3326337

Hopkins, D. (2004). *Dada and Surrealism: A Very Short Introduction.* Oxford University Press. DOI: 10.1093/actrade/9780192802545.001.0001

Hoskins, A. (2018). Memory of the multitude: The end of collective memory. A. Hoskins (Ed.), *Digital Memory Studies: Media Pasts in Transition* içinde (s.85-109). Routledge.

Hoskins, A., & Halstead, H. (2021). The new grey of memory: An interview with Andrew Hoskins. *Memory Studies*, *14*(4), 675–682. DOI: 10.1177/17506980211010936

Howard, H. (2025, 16 April) dailymail.co.uk, The remarkable story behind the kiss photo that melted hearts - and what happened to the 'happy' couple, https://www.dailymail.co.uk/news/article-14706713/Kiss-photo-melted-hearts-Paris-1950.html

Hutson, J. (2024). Art in the age of virtual reproduction. In *Art and culture in the multiverse of metaverses: Immersion, presence, and interactivity in the digital age* (pp. 55–98). Springer. DOI: 10.1007/978-3-031-66320-8_3

Ihde, D. (1990). *Technology and the Lifeworld: From garden to earth.* Indiana University Press. DOI: 10.2979/3108.0

İlkan, Z. S. (2025, 10 May). vogue.com.tr, Meriç Canatan - Interviewed by Zeynep Seren İlkan, https://vogue.com.tr/metropol/12-soruda-meric-canatan

Instagram. (2025, May 6). *Michael Christopher Brown,* https://www.instagram.com/p/CqniSVjrj0h/?img_index=10

Işık, V. (2024). Exploring artistic frontiers in the era of artificial intelligence. *Sanat ve Tasarım Dergisi*, *14*(2), 577–603. DOI: 10.20488/sanattasarim.1603119

İstanbul Modern. (2025, 20 April) x.com/istanbulmodern, https://x.com/istanbulmodern_/status/764356159922987011/photo/1

Ittefaq, M., Zain, A., Arif, R., Ala-Uddin, M., Ahmad, T., & Iqbal, A. (2023). Global news media coverage of artificial intelligence (AI): A comparative analysis of frames, sentiments, and trends across 12 countries. *Telematics and Informatics*, *82*, 102223. DOI: 10.1016/j.tele.2024.102223

Jagose, A. (2017). *Queer teori bir giriş.* (A. Toprak, Çev.). NotaBene Yayınları.

Janzczuk, H. (2024). Risks of using artificial intelligence in creating the image of politicians and in electoral campaigns. *Ad Americam: Journal of American Studies*, *25*, 10. DOI: 10.12797/AdAmericam.25.2024.25.10

Jasmer, B. W. (2024). *Balancing AI and human creativity: Adaptations in art education* (Master's thesis). Bethel University.

Jensen, L. (2004). The photographs of Jacob Riis: history in relation to truth. *Constructing the Past*. https://digitalcommons.iwu.edu/constructing/vol5/iss1/6

Johnson, W. S., Rice, M., & Williams, C. (2012). A History of Photography, from 1839 to the present, T. Mulligan & D. Wooters (Ed.), The George Eastman House Collection, Taschen

Johnson, E. (2018). The interface of memories: Sociotechnical concerns in digital commemoration. *Social Media + Society*, *4*(1). Advance online publication. DOI: 10.1177/2056305118763345

Jora, O. D., Iacob, M., Rosca, V. I., Nedelcu, M. R., Preda, A. F., & Nedef, M. S. (2024). Artificial intelligence and artistic imagination: Revisiting the cultural economy of industrial revolutions. *Amfiteatru Economic*, *26*(66), 613–632. DOI: 10.24818/EA/2024/66/630

Jordan, M. I., & Mitchell, T. M. (2015). Machine learning: Trends, perspectives, and prospects. *Science*, *349*(6245), 255–260. DOI: 10.1126/science.aaa8415 PMID: 26185243

Jurgenson, N. (2024). *Sosyal fotoğraf: fotoğraf ve sosyal medya.* (N. Örge, Çev.). Espas Yayınları.

Kalpokas, I. (2023). Work of art in the Age of Its AI Reproduction. Philosophy & Social Criticism, 51(8), 1268-1286. (Original work published 2025)DOI: 10.1177/01914537231184490

Kaninsky, M. (2025, 10 April) *petapixel,* One of the Most Iconic Kissing Photos Was Staged, https://petapixel.com/2019/07/24/one-of-the-most-iconic-kissing-photos-was-staged/

Karadağ, C. (2024, January 2). Yapay zeka ürünü fotoğrafına verilen ödülü reddeden Alman sanatçıya göre bu alan tartışılmalı. *Anadolu Ajansı*. https://www.aa.com.tr/tr/bilim-teknoloji/yapay-zeka-urunu-fotografina-verilen-odulu-reddeden-alman-sanatciya-gore-bu-alan-tartisilmali/3097861

Karahasan, Z. (2025, 11 April) *yesilodak.com,* İnsan İnsanı Çekermiş, https://www.yesilodak.com/insan-insani-cekermis

Karel Hájek. (2025, 12 April) *Wikipedia,* https://cs.wikipedia.org/wiki/Karel_H%C3%A1jek

Kastrenakes, J. (2021). *Beeple sold an NFT for $69 million. The Verge.* https://www.theverge.com/2021/3/11/22325054/beeple-christies-nft-sale-cost-everydays-69-million, [Erişim Tarihi: 17.03.2025].

Kate Vass Galerie. (2019). Espen kluge articles. The generative portraiture of espen kluge. 04.05.2025, https://www.katevassgalerie.com/espen-kluge

Kessels, E. (2011). 24 HRS in Photos [Installation]. https://www.erikkessels.com/24hrs-in-photos

Khadake, V. (2024). *Algorithmic aesthetics: a critical analysis of AI-generated art in the digital age.* International journal for multidisciplinary research (IJFMR) E-ISSN: 2582-2160 Volume 6, Issue 6, November-December 2024.

Kırmızı, H. & Çağıl, F. (2023). Dijital kültür, sinema, televizyon ve belirsizlik. İletişim Kuram ve Araştırma Dergisi, (65), 274-287. .DOI: 10.47998/ikad.1325305

Klingemann, M. (2019). Memories of Passersby I [AI-generated installation]. https://quasimondo.com/2018/12/29/memories-of-passersby-i/

Kluge, E. (2019). Alternatives. *Espen kluge website: 100 generative portraits.* 04.05.2025, https://www.espen.xyz/alternatives-100-generative-portraits

Knierim, F. (2012). Dada, J. Hacking (Ed.), *Photography The Whole Story* (pp.192-195). Thames & Hudson

KVKK. (2025, 18 May) kvkk.gov.tr, Personal Data Protection Law, https://www.kvkk.gov.tr/Icerik/6649/Personal-Data-Protection-Law

Lammers, T. (2025, 20 April) *forbes.com,* 'Emilia Pérez' And 'The Brutalist' AI Controversies, Explained, https://www.forbes.com/sites/timlammers/2025/01/21/emilia-prez-and-the-brutalist-ai-controversies-explained/

Laserna Montoya, J. D., Tarver, G. M., & Duganne, E. (2017). Advertisement Extraction: Interview with Juan David Laserna Montoya. *Photographies, 10*(3), 329–345. DOI: 10.1080/17540763.2017.1340735

LaTurbo Avedon. (n.d.). Portfolio. https://www.laturboavedon.com/portfolio

Laughton, B. (1996). *Honore Daumier.* Yale University Press.

Le Minh, I. (2013). After Alphonse Bertillon. https://isabelleleminh.com/isabelle-le-minh---works/portrait-souffle.html

Leaver, T., Highfield, T., & Abidin, C. (2020). *Instagram: Visual social media cultures*. Polity Press.

Lewis, E. (2018). *İzmler, Fotoğrafı Anlamak* (Aydemir, M. M., Trans.). Hayalperest Yayınevi.

Life (2025, 2 April) *life.com,* The Photography of Philippe Halsman, https://www.life.com/photographer/philippe-halsman/

Lubben, K. (2025, 12 March) *thamesandhudsonusa.com,* https://www.thamesandhudsonusa.com/books/magnum-contact-sheets-softcover

Lynton, N. (2004). *Modern Sanatın Öyküsü,* (C. Çapan & S. Öziş, Trans.), Remzi Kitabevi Marian Goodman, Gallery (2025, 20 March). *mariangoodman.com,* https://www.mariangoodman.com/artists/james-welling/

Magnumphotos (2025, 20 March) *magnumphotos,* Philippe Halsman: Jump, https://www.magnumphotos.com/arts-culture/philippe-halsman-jump-book/

Maloy, A. F., & Branigin, A. (2023, March 27). An AI generated Balenciaga pope fooled us all. How much does it matter? *The Washington Post*. https://www.washingtonpost.com/lifestyle/2023/03/27/pope-francis-coat-puffy-white-ai-fake/

Mandolessi, S. (2023). The digital turn in memory studies. *Memory Studies, 16*(6), 1513–1528. DOI: 10.1177/17506980231204201

Manovich, L. (1995). The Paradoxes of Digital Photography. Photography after Photography. Exhibition catalog. Germany. www.manovich.net [Erişim Tarihi: 13.02.2025].

Manovich, L. (2020). The aesthetic society: or how I edit my Instagram1. . Data Publics.DOI: 10.4324/9780429196515-13

Manovich, L. (2001). *The Language of New Media*. MIT Press.

Manovich, L. (2008). *The language of new media*. The MIT Press.

Manu, A. (2024). *Transcending imagination: Artificial intelligence and the future of creativity*. CRC Press. DOI: 10.1201/9781003450139

Marconi, F. (2020). *Newsmakers: Artificial Intelligence and the Future of Journalism*. Columbia University Press., https://www.jstor.org/stable/10.7312/marc19136 DOI: 10.7312/marc19136

Mariens, M. W. (2018). *Photography A Cultural History*. Laurence King Publishing.

Mattes, E., & Mattes, F. (2018). Dark Content [Video series]. https://0100101110101101.org/dark-content/

Mcardle, J. (2025, 20 May) *onthisdateinphotography,* https://onthisdateinphotography.com/2017/03/31/march-31/#:~:text=March%2031:%20The%20photographer%20who,21%2C%201948

Mccormack, D. (2025, 22 April) *dailymail,* 'I never lost hope': Startling interview unearthed with woman behind iconic Great Depression image talking just five years before her death in 1983, https://www.dailymail.co.uk/news/article-2290879/I-lost-hope-Startling-interview-unearthed-woman-iconic-Great-Depression-image-talking-just-years-death-1983.html

McGinity, L. (2017-a). Dada, S. Farthing (Ed.), *Sanatın Tüm Öyküsü* (pp: 410-411). (G. Aldoğan & F. C. Çulcu, Trans.), Hayalperest Yayınevi

McGinity, L. (2017-c). Sanat Eleştirmeni, S. Farthing (Ed.), *Sanatın Tüm Öyküsü* (pp: 412-413). (G. Aldoğan & F. C. Çulcu, Trans.), Hayalperest Yayınevi McNeill, S. (2025, 3 May-a). *alternativephotography.com,* Photograms – a magical concept, https://www.alternativephotography.com/photograms-cameraless-photography/

McIntosh, S., & Schofield, H. (2025, 17 Nisan) *bbc.com,* Francoise Bornet: Woman in Robert Doisneau's Paris kiss photo dies aged 93, https://www.bbc.com/news/entertainment-arts-67877244

McNeill, S. (2025). *stephenmcneill.com*, https://www.stephenmcneill.com/stephen-mcneill/

Media Kunst Netz. (n.d.). *Media Kunst Netz.* Retrieved May 10, 2025 from http://www.medienkunstnetz.de/works/sensorama/

Meis, M. (2016). When is a conflict a crisis? On the aesthetics of the Syrian civil war in a social media context. *Media, War & Conflict, 10*(1), 1–18. DOI: 10.1177/1750635216653903

Meyohas, S. (2015). BitchCoin. https://sarahmeyohas.com/bitchcoin

Meyohas, S. (2017). Cloud of Petals. https://sarahmeyohas.com/cloud-of-petals

Milan Kundera. (2025, 12 May) *Wikipedia,* https://en.wikipedia.org/wiki/Milan_Kundera

Miles, M. (2020). Introduction: Photography's publics. In *Photography's Publics* (pp. 1–17). https://doi.org/DOI: 10.4324/9781003103721-1

Mimic (photograph) (2025, 12 April) Wikipedia, https://en.wikipedia.org/wiki/Mimic_(photograph)

Minnesota Street Project. (n.d.). *Minnesota Street Project*. Retrieved April 22, 2025 from https://minnesotastreetproject.com/exhibitions/1275-minnesota-st/sara-vanderbeek-roman-women

Mishka Henner. (n.d.). *Mishka Henner*. Retrieved April 18, 2025 from https://mishkahenner.com/Sightseeing

Mitchell, W. J. (1992). *The Reconfigured Eye: Visual Truth in the Post-Photographic Era*. MIT Press.

Mitchell, W. J. T. (1994). *Picture Theory: Essays on Verbal and Visual Representation*. University of Chicago Press.

Mitchell, W. J. T. (2005). *What Do Pictures Want? The Lives and Loves of Images*. University of Chicago Press. DOI: 10.7208/chicago/9780226245904.001.0001

Moma (2025, 18 May) *Philippe Halsman,* https://www.moma.org/collection/works/47919

Monaco, J. (2001). *Bir film nasıl okunur*. Oğlak Yayınları.

Moreiras, C. (2017). Joan Fontcuberta: Post-photography and the spectral image of saturation. *Journal of Spanish Cultural Studies*, *18*(1), 57–77. Advance online publication. DOI: 10.1080/14636204.2016.1274496

Mugubi, J. G., & Manono, F. M. (2024). Optimizing creative processes with artificial intelligence (AI): Strategic imperatives for African filmmakers and graphic designers in the evolving digital landscape. *International Journal of Scholarly Practice*, *4*(2), 28–40.

Müller, J., & Wiedemann, J. (2023). *The history of graphic design* (1890– Today). Taschen.

Mulvey, L. (1975). Visual pleasure and narrative cinema. *Screen*, *16*(3), 6–18. DOI: 10.1093/screen/16.3.6

MyHeritage. (2021). https://www.myheritage.com/deep-nostalgia

Nachtwey, J. (2025, 24 April) *time.com,* James Nachtwey: How Photography Can Change the World, https://time.com/3693061/james-nachtwey-receives-lifetime-achievement-award/

National Gallery of Art. (2025, 20 April, c) *nga.gov,* The Real Lives of People in Dorothea Lange's Portraits, https://www.nga.gov/stories/articles/real-lives-people-dorothea-langes-portraits

National Portrait Gallery. (2025, 12 April, a), npg.org.uk, Wallis, Duchess of Windsor; Prince Edward, Duke of Windsor (King Edward VIII), Edward-Duke-of-Windsor-King-Edward VIII?LinkID=mp08029&role=art&rNo=3&_gl=1*e-j5g1r*_up*MQ.*_ga*MTg4MjU3MzgxLjE3NDg2OTgwMDk.*_ga_3D53N72CH-J*czE3NDg2OTgwMDgkbzEkZzAkdDE3NDg2OTgwMDgkajYwJGwwJGgw

National Portrait Gallery. (2025, 12 April, b), npg.org.uk, Wallis, Duchess of Windsor; Prince Edward, Duke of Windsor (King Edward VIII), https://www.npg.org.uk/collections/search/portrait/mw09580/Wallis-Duchess-of-Windsor-Prince-Edward-Duke-of-Windsor-King-Edward-VIII

New York Times. (2025, 7 June) nytimes.com, https://www.nytimes.com/2025/05/23/arts/sebastiao-salgado-dead.html

Nightingale, S. J., & Farid, H. (2022). AI-synthesized faces are indistinguishable from real faces and more trustworthy. *Proceedings of the National Academy of Sciences of the United States of America, 119*(8), e2120481119. DOI: 10.1073/pnas.2120481119 PMID: 35165187

Noë, A. (2005). *Action in perception.* MIT Press. https://mitpress.mit.edu/9780262640671/action-in-perception/

Nolden/H. (2025, 3 May) *yourartshop-noldenh.com,* Jeff Wall – The Thinker, https://yourartshop-noldenh.com/jeff-wall-the-thinker-with-a-sword-in-his-back/

Norimberk: Zlocin A Soud (2025, 12 May) *Abebooks,* https://www.abebooks.com/first-edition/Norimberk-Zlocin-Soud-Nuremberg-Crime-Court/20327713591/bd

Novakovic, J., & Guga, J. (2024). Art after AI: The impact of generative AI on the artworld. In *Navigating the digital age: An in-depth exploration into the intersection of modern technologies and societal transformation* (pp. 584–604).

NPR. (2025, 10 May) www.npr.org, Foreign Policy: The Afghan War In Hipstamatic, https://www.npr.org/2011/07/26/138701217/foreign-policy-the-afghan-war-in-hipstamatic

NTV. (2025, 16 April) ntv.com.tr, Bennu Yıldırımlar ilk kez konuştu! Nuri Bilge Ceylan'a "etik değil" çıkışı, https://www.ntv.com.tr/galeri/n-life/bennu-yildirimlar-ilk-kez-konustu-nuri-bilge-ceylana-etik-degil-cikisi,huUlY-JpzEml19tqje-onQ

OpenSea. (2023). *90 miles*. https://opensea.io/collection/90-miles

Özdal, M. A., & Bulut, Ş. (2024). The intersection of technology and art: Artistic innovation and change in the age of artificial intelligence. *Journal of Art and Iconography*, *7*, 19–27.

Özel, Z. (2005). *Fotoğraf Akımları İçinde Gerçekliğin Sunumu, Yeni Düşünceler, Yıl 1, Sayı 1*. Haziran.

Özkemahlı, K. K., & Er, M. H. (2024). "Yapay Zekâ Destekli Fotoğrafik Yaklaşım: Portre ve Mekân Temelinde Mustafa Kemal Atatürk Fotoğraflarının Yeniden Üretilmesi". (Ed.), Yağmur, Ö. & Şengünalp, C., *Disiplinlerarası Sanat Pratikleri 2*. Ankara: Detay Yayıncılık.

Paglen, T. (2019). Machine Visions. https://paglen.studio/category/machine-visions

Paglen, T. (2020). Limit Telephotography. https://paglen.studio/2020/04/22/limit-telephotography

Paglen, T. (2025, 13 April). Imagenet roulette. *Trevor paglen website,* https://paglen.studio/2020/04/29/imagenet-roulette

Paglen, T., & Crawford, K. (2021). Excavating AI: The politics of images in machine learning training sets. *AI & Society*, *36*, 1105–1116. DOI: 10.1007/s00146-021-01162-8

Panofsky, E. (2021). *Perspektif: Simgesel bir biçim* (Tükel, Y., Trans.). Metis Yayınları. (Original work published 1927)

Paris syndrome (2025, 12 April) *Wikipedia,* https://en.wikipedia.org/wiki/Paris_syndrome

Parker, A. (2019, May 23). Stereopsis and depth perception. *Oxford Research Encyclopedia of Neuroscience*. Retrieved May 3, 2025, from https://oxfordre.com/neuroscience/view/10.1093/acrefore/9780190264086.001.0001/acrefore-9780190264086-e-77

Patrick Nagatani. (n.d.). *Patrick Nagatani*. Retrieved April 10, 2025 from https://www.patricknagatani.com/

PBS. (2025, 28 Nisan) *pbs.org,* ttp://www.pbs.org/wnet/americanmasters/database/capa_r.html

Perec, G. (1997). *Species of spaces and other pieces* (Sturrock, J., Ed. & Trans.). Penguin Books.

Perrigo, B. (2023, March 28). How to spot an AI-generated image like the Balenciaga pope. *Time*. https://time.com/6306135/ai-generated-images-balenciaga-pope

Pestrý týden (2025, 12 May) *Wikipedia,* https://en.wikipedia.org/wiki/Pestr%C3%BD_t%C3%BDden#:~:text=Establishment,-Karel%20Neubert%2C%20son&text=Pestr%C3%BD%20t%C3%BDden%20was%20founded%20by,and%20List%20pan%C3%AD%20a%20d%C3%ADvek

Petrick, K. (2024). Art in the age of algorithms: A creator's perspective on the artistry of AI image generation. In *New frontiers in science in the era of AI* (pp. 195–214). Springer. DOI: 10.1007/978-3-031-61187-2_12

Photoeye (2025, 18 May) *photoeye.com,* https://www.photoeye.com/bookstore/citation/ZF397?modal=%23booktease-modal

Photomaraton (2025, 25 April) *photomaraton.com,* https://www.photomaraton.com/katilim-sartlari-ve-kurallar/

Photomuseumireland (2025, 28 March) timeline.photomuseumireland.ie, Gilles Peress' epic summation of his work in Northern Ireland published by Steidl, https://timeline.photomuseumireland.ie/timeline/gilles-peres-epic-summation-of-his-work-in-northern-ireland-published-by-steidl/

Pinault Collection. (2025, 15 May) *lesoeuvres.pinaultcollection,* Napalm Victim (#4), Saigon, S. Vietnam, April 29, 1971 1971 – 1993, https://lesoeuvres.pinaultcollection.com/en/artwork/napalm-victim-4-saigon-s-vietnam-april-29-197

Popotas, D., & Kalyva, A. (2023, February 27). Ο βετεράνος διασώστης, γιος του θρυλικού ποδοσφαιριστή Μπάμπη Κοτρίδη που «άγγιξε» τη Μαντόνα. *Protothema.* https://www.protothema.gr/greece/article/1342350/o-veteranos-diasostis-gios-tou-thrulikou-podosfairisti-babi-kotridi-pou-aggixe-ti-madona/

Preston, M. Y. (2019). Building Images, Building, A. Leighton Massoni and M. Shindelman (Ed.), *Spaces The Focal Press Companion to The Constructed Image in Contemporary Photography* (pp.7-34). Routledge

Product, (2024). *The Impact of Instagram: 50 Statistics You Should Know in 2024,* https://www.linkedin.com/pulse/impact-instagram-50-statistics-you-should-know-2024-szhue/, [Erişim Tarihi: 15.04.2025].

Prompt Folder. (n.d.). https://promptfolder.com/u/mikechapel/gslpuvev/

Quent, M. (2024). Interval and event: The present as in-between time in Gilles Deleuze and Alain Badiou. *Filozofski Vestnik, 45*(1), 243–267. DOI: 10.3986/fv.45.1.10

Rachmawati, I., Parman, S., & Solihah, Y. A. (2024). Exploring the boundaries of creativity in the digital age by understanding the impact and implications of AI work in photography competitions. In *Proceeding of International Seminar on Arts, Artificial Intelligence & Society* (pp. 294–307).

Rafman, J. (2008-ongoing). Nine eyes of Google Street View. https://9-eyes.com

Rafman, J. (2009, August 12). *Nine Eyes of Google Street View. The Eye of Photography.* https://loeildelaphotographie.com/en/the-eyes-of-google-street-view-by-jon-rafman/

Ranjan, R., Mishra, A., Maharana, S. P., & Kumari, S. (2024). AI in visual arts: Exploring generative algorithm. In *The pioneering applications of generative AI* (pp. 41–60). IGI Global. DOI: 10.4018/979-8-3693-3278-8.ch002

Reading, A. (2011). *The Journalist as Assembler: The Globital Memory Field, Non Memory and The Shooting of Osama Bin Laden:' (164-178) Memory and Journalism* (Zelizer, B., & Tenenboim, K., Eds.). Palgrave.

Recuber, T. (2012). The prosumption of commemoration: Disasters, digital memory banks, and online collective memory. *The American Behavioral Scientist, 56*(4), 531–549. DOI: 10.1177/0002764211429364

Reichelt, S., Häussler, R., Fütterer, G., & Leister, N. (2010). Depth cues in human visual perception and their realization in 3D displays. In Javidi, B., & Son, J.-Y. (Eds.), *Three-dimensional imaging, visualization, and display 2010* (Vol. 7690, p. 76900B). SPIE. DOI: 10.1117/12.850094

Rest in Piece's (2023), Bilsart ve Monoco Artspace.

Restorapic (2025, 10 April) *restorapic.com,* 12 Historic Photographs That Were Manipulated, https://restorapic.com/12-historic-photographs-that-were-manipulated/

Rezaire, T. (n.d.). Tabita Rezaire. https://tabitarezaire.com

Rickard, D. (2010). *A New American Picture*. White Press.

Ritchin, F. (2012). *Fotoğraftan sonra.* (Y. Keser, Çev.). Espas Yayınları.

Ritchin, F. (2009). *After photography*. W.W. Norton & Company.

Ritchin, F. (2012). *Fotoğraftan sonra*. Espas Sanat Kuram Yayınları.

Ritchin, F. (2013). *Bending the frame: photojournalism, documentary, and the citizen*. Aperture.

Roberts, P. G. (2012). Experimention and Abstraction, J. Hacking (Ed.), *Photography The Whole Story* (pp.196-203). Thames & Hudson

Rosenblum, N. (1997). *A world history of photography*. Abbeville Press.

Rosler, M. (1974-75). The Bowery in two inadequate descriptive systems. https://www.martharosler.net/the-bowery-in-two-inadequate-descriptive-systems

Roth, M., & Katz, J. D. (1998). *Difference/Indifference: Musings on postmodernism, Marcel Duchamp and John Cage*. Routledge.

Rouillé, A. (2005). *La photographie: Entre document et art contemporain*. Gallimard.

Rubinstein, D., & Sluis, K. (2008). A life more photographic: Mapping the networked image. *Photographies, 1*(1), 9–28. DOI: 10.1080/17540760701785842

Ruff, T. (2009). JPEGs [Photographic series]. https://www.thomasruff.com/en/works/jpeg/

Russell, S., & Norvig, P. (2021). *Artificial intelligence: A Modern Approach*. Prentice Hall.

Sanouillet, M. (2017). Dadacılığın Kökenleri: Zürih ve New York, E. Batur (Ed.), *Modernizmin Serüveni, Bir "Temel Metinler" Seçkisi 1840-1990* (pp.359-372). (T. Ilgaz, Trans.), Sel Yayıncılık

Şapolyo, E. B. (2025, 11 April) *isteataturk.com,* https://isteataturk.com/Kronolojik/Tarih/1936/9/4/Ingiltere-Krali-VIII-Edwardi-Dolmabahce-Sarayi-Rihtiminda-karsilarken-04091936/15#google_vignett

Sarı, F. (2021, September). "Cahit Arf'in makine düşünebilir mi ve nasıl düşünür?" Adlı makalesi üzerine bir çalışma. *TRT Akademi*, 6(13). https://dergipark.org.tr/en/download/article-file/1861642

Savvidis, P. (2023, February 10). The image of a Greek rescuer holding a Turkish child has gone viral-who created it? *Greek City Times*. https://greekcitytimes.com/2023/02/10/greek-rescuer-turkish-child-viral/

Schuricht, S. (2004, February 10). Virtual art- the aura of the digital: Fortunately it is unknown where the journey will end [Interview with O. Grau] (M. Hohl, Trans.). https://www.sushu.de/pdf/grau_sushu_04_en.pdf

Scott, C. (2007). *Street photography*. I.B. Tauris & Co. Ltd. DOI: 10.5040/9780755604210

Sekula, A. (1978). Dismantling Modernism, Reinventing Documentary (Notes on the Politics of Representation). *The Massachusetts Review, 19*(4), 859–883. https://www.jstor.org/stable/25088914

Serbestiyet (2025, 8 April) Muhammed El Fayed, 94 yaşında öldü: Son ana kadar Diana ve oğlu Dodi'yi MI6'ın öldürdüğüne inandı, https://serbestiyet.com/featured/muhammed-el-fayed-94-yasinda-oldu-son-ana-kadar-diana-ve-oglu-dodiyi-mi6in-oldurdugune-inandi-141124/

Shashasha, (2025, 20 May). *shashasha.co,* https://www.shashasha.co/en/book/the-well

Shaw, M. (2016, May 31). *Steve Mccury's rickshaw.* https://www.readingthepictures.org/2016/05/steve-mccurrys-rickshaw/

Sightengine. (2025). Detect AI-generated images. Retrieved May 8, 2025, from https://sightengine.com

Simurgkitabevi (2025, 26 April) *simurgkitabevi.com,* Sabit Kalfagil, Türkiye'nin Üzerindeki Işık, https://www.istanbulkitapcisi.com/turkiyenin-uzerindeki-isik

Siroor, A., & Anita, B. (2024). The intersection of technology and art: Redefining creativity in the digital age. *Innovative Journal of Interdisciplinary Research and Technological Innovations*, *1*(1), 37–42.

Smejkal, P. M. (2015, February 23). Fatescapes. LensCulture. https://www.lensculture.com/projects/80186-fatescapes

Soda, M. (2016). Inbox Full [Video]. Tumblr. https://www.tumblr.com/paddleson/629998391111/inbox-full-by-molly-soda-is-an-eight-hour-long

Sontag, S. (1973). *On photography.* Farrar, Straus and Giroux. (Electronic ed. RosettaBooks, 2005). ISBN 0-7953-2699-8

Sontag, S. (2005). *On photography.* Rosetta Books Smithsonian American Art Museum (n.d). *Mathew B. Brady.* https://americanart.si.edu/artist/mathew-b-brady-6668

Sontag, S. (2011). *Fotoğraf üzerine.* (O. Akınhay, Çev.). Agora Kitaplığı.

Sontag, S. (1999). *Fotoğraf üzerine* (Akçakaya, R., Trans.). Altıkırkbeş Yayınları.

Sontag, S. (2004). *Başkalarının acısına bakmak* (Akınhay, O., Trans.). Agora Kitaplığı.

Soreanu, C. (2024). Artificial intelligence in contemporary visuality. *Review of Artistic Education*, *28*, 222–230. DOI: 10.35218/rae-2024-0028

Sothebys, 2025, 14 May) *sothebys,* Dorothea Lange, https://www.sothebys.com/en/auctions/ecatalogue/2005/photographs-n08115/lot.43.html

Soulages, F. (2022). *Fotoğrafın Estetiği* (Şansal, D. E., Trans.). Espas Yayıncılık.

Steyerl, H. (2009). In defense of the poor image. e-*flux journal*, (10). https://www.e-flux.com/journal/10/61362/in-defense-of-the-poor-image/

Steyerl, H. (2009). *In Defense of the Poor Image.* https://www.e-flux.com/journal/10/61362/in-defense-of-the-poor-imag, [Erişim Tarihi: 12.05.2025].

Steyerl, H. (2023). Mean Images. *New Left Review, 140/141,* Mar-June 2023. https://newleftreview.org/issues/ii140/articles/hito-steyerl-mean-images

Steyerl, H.. (2013). In defence of the poor image. 67. 101-105.

Stott, W. (1973). *Documentary expression and thirties america.* The University of Chicago Press.

Strubell, E., Ganesh, A., & McCallum, A. (2019). Energy and policy considerations for deep learning in NLP. *arXiv preprint arXiv:1906.02243.* https://arxiv.org/abs/1906.02243 DOI: 10.18653/v1/P19-1355

Strukov, V. (2020). Digital journalism: Toward a theory of journalistic practice in the twenty-first century. In *Digital Journalism* (pp. 155–170). https://doi.org/DOI: 10.1007/978-3-030-42855-6_9

Sweet, B., & Kaiser, M. (2011, August). Depth perception, cueing, and control. In *AIAA Modeling and Simulation Technologies Conference* (p. 6424).

Tagg, J. (1988). *The burden of representation: essays on photographies and histories.* Palgrave Macmillan. DOI: 10.1007/978-1-349-19355-4

Tarı, N. (2025, 5 June). artfulliving.com.tr, Deneyselliği Dijitalle Buluşturan 5 Kolaj Sanatçısı, https://www.artfulliving.com.tr/sanat/deneyselligi-dijitalle-bulusturan-5-kolaj-sanatcisi-i-14417

Tariq, M. U. (2025). The role of AI-powered learning analytics in enhancing student engagement and performance. In J. Moore, S. Gupta, M. Sharma, A. Garg, & H. Josephine V. L. (Eds.), *Transforming education with data science in the AI era* (pp. 123–148). IGI Global. https://doi.org/DOI: 10.4018/979-8-3373-2185-1.ch005

Tariq, M. U. (2025). AI-enhanced project-based learning: Revolutionizing commerce education with generative AI. In ElSayary, A. (Ed.), *Prompt engineering and generative AI applications for teaching and learning* (pp. 125–142). IGI Global., DOI: 10.4018/979-8-3693-7332-3.ch008

Tariq, M. U. (2025). AI-powered business process automation: Revolutionizing firm management. In Derbali, A. (Ed.), *AI, economic perspectives, and firm business management* (pp. 199–224). IGI Global., DOI: 10.4018/979-8-3693-7357-6.ch010

Tariq, M. U. (2025). Empowering patients with AI-ethical digital tools for health data management and decision. In Pesqueira, A., & de Bem Machado, A. (Eds.), *Navigating privacy, innovation, and patient empowerment through ethical healthcare technology* (pp. 197–216). IGI Global., DOI: 10.4018/979-8-3693-7630-0.ch008

Tariq, M. U. (2025). Innovation and agility—Adapting business strategies for sustainable growth in dynamic markets. In Ananthan, S., Kohli, A., Manickam, T., & Dhanabalan, T. (Eds.), *New business development strategies for achieving sustainable growth* (pp. 113–140). IGI Global., DOI: 10.4018/979-8-3373-2048-9.ch005

Tariq, M. U. (2025). Integrating ICT for enhanced organizational resilience: Strategies and case studies. In Carvalho, L., Reis, L., Neves de Almeida Baptista Figueiredo, A., & Russo, N. (Eds.), *Leveraging technology for organizational adaptability* (pp. 59–80). IGI Global., DOI: 10.4018/979-8-3693-6045-3.ch004

Tariq, M. U. (2025). Integration of artificial intelligence and machine learning in business intelligence: Enhancing decision making and operational efficiency. In Ishtaiwi, A., Al-Qerem, A., Al Khaldy, M., & Alauthman, M. (Eds.), *Driving modern business intelligence architecture for operational efficiency* (pp. 279–306). IGI Global., DOI: 10.4018/979-8-3373-2125-7.ch009

Tariq, M. U. (2025). Navigating public administration 5.0: Embracing AI for smarter governance. In Wongmahesak, K., Ahmad, J., & Mustanir, A. (Eds.), *Public governance practices in the age of AI* (pp. 167–186). IGI Global., DOI: 10.4018/979-8-3693-9286-7.ch008

Tariq, M. U. (2025). Revolutionizing educator preparation: Exploring the efficacy of grow your own models. In Sande, B., & Marvel, A. (Eds.), *Enhancing educational access through innovative educator preparation pathways* (pp. 75–100). IGI Global., DOI: 10.4018/979-8-3693-7337-8.ch004

Taşcı, F., & Erdem, S. (2024). An analysis on reality and virtuality in art: Virtual space, virtual body and virtual object example. *Art Vision*, *30*(52), 58–71. DOI: 10.32547/artvision.1415560

Taylor, L. (2023, May 2). Amnesty International criticised for using AI-generated images. *The Guardian*. https://www.theguardian.com/world/2023/may/02/amnesty-international-ai-generated-images-criticism

Taylor, L. (2025, 23 March) *theguardian.com,* One Hundred Years of Solitude: Colombians celebrate Netflix TV series of the country's 'national poem', https://www.theguardian.com/books/2024/dec/20/one-hundred-years-of-solitude-netflix-series

TDK. (2024). (April 23, 2025). 2024 yılının kelimesi, kavramı "kalabalık yalnızlık". *Türk Dil Kurumu*. https://tdk.gov.tr/icerik/basindan/2024-yilinin-kelimesi-kavrami-kalabalik-yalnizlik/

TDK. (n.d.). *Dezenformasyon. Türk Dil Kurumu*. https://sozluk.gov.tr/ (Accessed April 25, 2025).

TDK. (n.d.). *Manipülasyon. Türk Dil Kurumu*. https://sozluk.gov.tr/ (Accessed April 29, 2025).

teamLab. (2018). teamLab Borderless (Digital art museum / interactive exhibition). MORI Building Digital Art Museum: teamLab Borderless, Tokyo, Japan. https://borderless.teamlab.art/

Techne: Secret Garden. (2025, 16 January). *Brooklyn Academy of Music*. 17 April, 2025. https://www.bam.org/new-media/2024/techne-secret-garden

Tekçam, T. (2011). *Arkeoloji sözlüğü*. Alfa Yayınları.

Tercan, S. (2024). *Antik kalıntılar ve manzara fotoğrafında arkeolojik anlatı*. Fotografya. https://www.fotografya.gen.tr/TR,2633/seckin-tercan.html

Terranova, A. (2023, April 26). *How AI imagery is shaking photojournalism*. Blind Magazine. https://www.blind-magazine.com/en/stories/how-ai-imagery-is-shaking-photojournalism

Terranova, A. (2023, April 26). How AI imagery is shaking photojournalism. *Blind-magazine*. https://blind-newsletter.beehiiv.com/p/ai-imagery-shaking-photojournalism

The Book of Laughter and Forgetting. (2025, 16 May) *Wikipedia*, https://en.wikipedia.org/wiki/The_Book_of_Laughter_and_Forgetting

The Joke. (2025, 12 May) *Wikipedia*, https://en.wikipedia.org/wiki/The_Joke_(novel)

The Metropolitan Museum of Art. (n.d.). *Xmas Shopping near Macy's, New York* [Photograph by William Klein, 1954; printed 1956]. Retrieved July 18, 2025, from https://www.metmuseum.org/art/collection/search/266096

The Museum of Contemporary Art Chicago. (2012). *MCA publications websites*. 18.04.2025, https://mcachicago.org/publications/websites/i-was-raised-on-the-internet/artworks/zach-blas-facial-weaponization-communique-fag-face-2012

Thread, R. (2020). *Arşivlerden: Vilém Flusser – Teknik Devrim Hakkında 1988 Tarihli Röportaj*, https://red-thread.org/teknik-devrim-hakkinda, [Erişim Tarihi: 17.03.2025].

Tsao, J., & Nogues, C. (2024). Beyond the author: Artificial intelligence, creative writing and intellectual emancipation. *Poetics*, *102*, 101865. DOI: 10.1016/j.poetic.2024.101865

Túñez-López, J. M., Fieiras-Ceide, C., & Vaz-Álvarez, M. (2021). Impact of artificial intelligence on journalism: Transformations in the company, products, contents, and professional profile. *Communicatio Socialis*, *34*(1), 177–193. DOI: 10.15581/003.34.1.177-193

Turani, A. (1992). *Dünya Sanat Tarihi*. Remzi Kitabevi.

Turner, J. (2014). Blind Eye Sees All – No Secrets Anymore [Mixed media sculpture]. https://judturner.com/blind-eye-sees-all/

Tzara, T. (2017). Dada Hiçbir Anlama Gelmez, E. Batur (Ed.), *Modernizmin Serüveni, Bir "Temel Metinler" Seçkisi 1840-1990* (pp.373-374). (S. Rifat, Trans.), Sel Yayıncılık

Ufarte-Ruiz, M.-J., Murcia-Verdú, F.-J., & Túñez-López, J.-M. (2023). Use of artificial intelligence in synthetic media: First newsrooms without journalists. *El Profesional de la Información*, *32*(2), e320203. Advance online publication. DOI: 10.3145/epi.2023.mar.03

Umbrico, P. (2011). Suns from Flickr [Online art project]. http://www.penelopeumbrico.net/index.php/project/suns-from-sunsets-from-flickr/

UNEP. (2024, September 21). AI has an environmental problem. Here's what the world can do about that. *United Nations Environment Programme*. https://www.unep.org/news-and-stories/story/ai-has-environmental-problem-heres-what-world-can-do-about

UNEP. (2024, September 21). *Artificial Intelligence (AI) end-to-end: The Environmental Impact of the full AI lifecycle needs to be comprehensively assessed - Issue Note*. https://wedocs.unep.org/bitstream/handle/20.500.11822/46288/AI-Environmental-Impact-Issues-Note.pdf?sequence=3&isAllowed=y

Uren, C. (2025, May 3). ABD Başkanı'nın yeni papa olması mümkün mü? *Euronews*. https://tr.euronews.com/2025/05/03/beyaz-saray-trumpi-papa-yapti-yapay-zeka-uretimi-gorsel-interneti-salladi

Veasrey, N. (2025, 10 March). *nickveasey.com,* N. Veasrey, X-ray Catalogue, 2025, https://catalogue.nickveasey.com/books/mmjz/#p=7

Vincent, J. (2023, March 27). *"The swagged-out pope is an AI fake – and an early glimpse of a new reality.* The Verge. https://www.theverge.com/2023/3/27/23657927/ai-pope-image-fake-midjourney-computer-generated-aesthetic

Vosoughi, S., Roy, D., & Aral, S. (2018). The spread of true and false news online. *Science, 359*(6380), 1146–1151. DOI: 10.1126/science.aap9559 PMID: 29590045

W.E. (2025, 12 April) *Wikipedia,* https://en.wikipedia.org/wiki/W.E

Walker, C. S. (2023). (March 27, 2023). We spoke to the guy who created the viral AI image of the Pope that fooled the world. *Buzzfeed News*. https://www.buzzfeednews.com/article/chrisstokelwalker/pope-puffy-jacket-ai-midjourney-image-creator-interview

Walsh, L. (2016, September 10). *Picturing conflict: an interview with Michael Christopher Brown.* https://hyperallergic.com/318407/interview-with-conflict-photographer-michael-christopher-brown/

Walter, Y. (2025). The emerging "AI artists": Breaking the metacrisis and the fear of losing human creativity. [Published by SCIEPublish]. *Nature Anthropology, 3*(1), 10002. DOI: 10.70322/natanthropol.2025.10002

Walton, K. L. (2018) Geçirgen Fotoğraflar: Fotografik Gerçekliğin Doğası Üzerine, S.Walden (Ed.), *Doğanın Kalemi Üzerine Denemeler* (pp.29-67). (H. Yılmaz, Trans.), Espas Yayınları

Ward, J. L. (1976). The perception of pictorial space in perspective pictures. *Leonardo, 9*(4), 279–288. DOI: 10.2307/1573353

Ware, K. (2019). Camera-Less: Photographıc Fidelity (And Infidelity), A. Leighton Massoni and M. Shindelman (Ed.), *SpacesThe Focal Press Companion to The Constructed Image in Contemporary Photography* (pp.186-208). Routledge

Wei, S. (2021, Jan 7). *Thomas Nast: the rise and fall of the father of political cartoons.* Illustration History. https://www.illustrationhistory.org/essays/thomas-nast-the-rise-and-fall-of-the-father-of-political-cartoons

Whelan, R. (1985). *Robert Capa: a biography.* Knopf.

Whitney (2025, 15 March). *whitney.org,* https://whitney.org/artists/3788

WITNESS. (n.d.). *Deepfakes rapid response force.* https://www.gen-ai.witness.org/deepfakes-rapid-response-force/

Wittgenstein, L. (1968). *Philosophical investigations.* Macmillan.

Wolfe, S. (2025, 5 May). magazine.artland.com, 5 Contemporary Collage Artists Adding New Layers, https://magazine.artland.com/5-contemporary-collage-artists/

Wyatt, C. (2025, 20 April) bbc.co.uk, The Falklands for journalists: the ultimate embed experience, https://www.bbc.co.uk/webarchive/https%3A%2F%2Fwww.bbc.co.uk%2Fblogs%2Fcollegeofjournalism%2Fentries%2F5793e238-27a3-36bd-b63f-064717772aa7

X. (2023, March, 21). *Elliot Higgins Bsky Social.* https://x.com/EliotHiggins/status/1637927681734987777

X. (2024, February 16). *Nervana Mahmod* Twitter. https://x.com/Nervana_1/status/1623742038716960768?ref_src=twsrc%5Etfw%7Ctwcamp%5Etweetembed%7Ctwterm%5E1623742038716960768%7Ctwgr%5E4b54469e6db7943981dab43b4906b931f86ccaee%7Ctwcon%5Es1_&ref_url=https%3A%2F%2Fwww.malumatfurus.org%2Fyunanistan-turkiye-deprem-yardimi%2F

X. (2024, February 18). *Defence Intelligence of Ukraine*. https://x.com/DI_Ukraine/status/1499157365937119235?ref_src=twsrc%5Etfw%7Ctwcamp%5Etweetembed%7Ctwterm%5E1499157365937119235%7Ctwgr%5E%7Ctwcon%5Es1_&ref_url=https%3A%2F%2Fwww.vice.com%2Fen%2Farticle%2F93bmda%2Fhacked-news-channel-and-deepfake-of-zelenskyy-surrendering-is-causing-chaos-online

X. (2025, May 3). *The White House,* https://x.com/WhiteHouse/status/1918502592335724809

X. (2025, May 4). *The White House,* https://x.com/WhiteHouse/status/1919053040734072844

Xu, C., Sun, Y., & Zhou, H. (2025). Artificial aesthetics and ethical ambiguity: Exploring business ethics in the context of AI-driven creativity. *Journal of Business Ethics*, *199*(4), 671–692. DOI: 10.1007/s10551-024-05837-2

Yadav, M., Kumar, M., Sahoo, A., & Rathnasiri, M. S. H. (2025). AI and the evolution of artistic expression: Impacts on society and culture. In *Transforming cinema with artificial intelligence* (pp. 15–36). IGI Global.

Yao, Q. (2025). Application of artificial intelligence virtual image technology in photography art creation under deep learning. *IEEE Access : Practical Innovations, Open Solutions*, *13*, 25003–25012. DOI: 10.1109/ACCESS.2025.3529521

Yardımcı, S., & Güçlü, Ö. (2016). *Queer tahayyül*. Sel Yayıncılık.

Yaşar, F. (2025, 22 April) *gazeteduvar.com,* Nick Ut: O fotoğraf Amerikan halkını çılgına çevirdi, https://www.gazeteduvar.com.tr/kultur-sanat/2019/12/08/nick-ut-o-fotograf-amerikan-halkini-cilgina-cevirdi

Yılmaz, R. (2017). Türkiye'de reklam anlatısının dijital çağdaki yapısal dönüşümü, *1st International Conference on New Trends in Communication*. İstanbul.

Zadeh, J. (2023, 6 October). The photographer using AI to create queer love stories. *WePresent.* https://wepresent.wetransfer.com/stories/blake-wood-ai-post-photography

Zhang, M. (2025, 10 April) *petapixel,* That Iconic 'Migrant Mother' Photo Was 'Photoshopped', https://petapixel.com/2018/11/30/that-iconic-migrant-mother-photo-was-photoshopped/

Zhang, H., & Yoshida, S. (2024). Decoding illusion perception: A comparative analysis of deep neural networks in the Müller-Lyer illusion. *Applied Sciences (Basel, Switzerland), 14*(8), 3429. DOI: 10.3390/app14083429

Zhao, Y. (2024). The synergistic effect of artificial intelligence technology in the evolution of visual communication of new media art. *Heliyon, 10*(18), e38008. DOI: 10.1016/j.heliyon.2024.e38008 PMID: 39328541

Zhou, B., Zhao, H., Puig, X., Fidler, S., Barriuso, A., & Torralba, A. "Scene Parsing through ADE20K Dataset," *2017 IEEE Conference on Computer Vision and Pattern Recognition (CVPR)*, Honolulu, HI, USA, 2017, pp. 5122-5130, DOI: 10.1109/CVPR.2017.544

Zwirner, D. (2025, 10 May). *davidzwirner.com,* https://www.davidzwirner.com/artists/james-welling

About the Contributors

Murat Han Er, born in Erzurum in 1981, completed his undergraduate studies in the Graphic Design Department at Atatürk University. He earned his Master's degree from the Photography Department of the Faculty of Fine Arts at Atatürk University and his Doctorate from the Photography Department of the Faculty of Fine Arts at Mimar Sinan Fine Arts University. In 2005, he began working as a Research Assistant in the Photography Department at the Faculty of Fine Arts at Atatürk University. Between 2010 and 2015, he worked in the Photography Department at Mimar Sinan Fine Arts University. He currently serves as an Associate Professor in the Photography Department of the Faculty of Fine Arts at Atatürk University. The artist has participated in numerous exhibitions both nationally and internationally and has received various awards.

Basri Gençcelep was born in 1981, Trabzon. 2007, Bachelor Degree, Atatürk University, Fine Arts Faculty, Graphic Design Department. 2011, Master Degree, Atatürk University, Social Sciences Institute, Photography Department. 2012, worked as a research assistant in Atatürk University, Fine Arts Faculty, Graphic Design Department. From 2013 to 2018, he worked as a research assistant in Mimar Sinan Fine Arts University, Faculty of Fine Arts, Department of Photography. He had completed his Proficiency in Art at 2017 in Mimar Sinan Fine Arts University, Faculty of Fine Arts, Department of Photography. From 2018 he started giving lectures as an Assistant Professor in Atatürk University, Fine Arts Faculty, Graphic Design Department. He had taken part in national and international art events and projects.

***

Serhat Erdem, born in 1982 in Kırıkkale, completed his high school education at Samsun Ondokuz Mayıs High School. In 2004, he earned his bachelor's degree from

Atatürk University, Faculty of Communication, Department of Radio, Television, and Cinema. In 2005, he began his academic career as a Research Assistant in the Department of Cinema and Television at Atatürk University's Faculty of Fine Arts. Erdem completed his master's degree in 2009 at Atatürk University, Institute of Social Sciences, Department of Journalism, with a thesis titled "An Analysis of the Transformations Caused by Matte Painting Applications in Cinema." In 2010, he began his doctoral studies at Istanbul University, Institute of Social Sciences, Department of Radio, Television, and Cinema. He received the title of Doctor in 2015 after successfully completing his dissertation titled "The Use of Visual Effects in the Reconstruction of Reality: Spatial Construction in the Spartacus Television Series." Between 2005 and 2022, Erdem served as an Assistant Professor in the Department of Cinema and Television at Atatürk University's Faculty of Fine Arts. In 2022, he earned the title of Associate Professor in the field of Visual Communication Design. Since February 2022, he has continued his academic work in the Department of Radio, Television, and Cinema at Atatürk University's Faculty of Communication.

Muhammad Usman Tariq has more than 16+ year's experience in industry and academia. He has authored more than 200+ research articles, 110+ case studies, 150+ book chapters and several books other than 4 patents. He is founder and CEO of The Case HQ, a unique repository for courses, narrative and video case studies. He has been working as a consultant and trainer for industries representing six sigma, quality, health and safety, environmental systems, project management, and information security standards. His work has encompassed sectors in aviation, manufacturing, food, hospitality, education, finance, research, software and transportation. He has diverse and significant experience working with accreditation agencies of ABET, ACBSP, AACSB, WASC, CAA, EFQM and NCEAC. Additionally, Dr. Tariq has operational experience in incubators, research labs, government research projects, private sector startups, program creation and management at various industrial and academic levels. He is Certified Higher Education Teacher from Harvard University, USA, Certified Online Educator from HMBSU, Certified Six Sigma Master Black Belt and has been awarded PFHEA, SFSEDA, SMIEEE, and CMBE.

Mert Çağıl Türkay, born in 1987 in Istanbul, had his BA, MFA, and DA degree from Mimar Sinan Fine Arts University Photography Department. Participated in several national and international exhibitions and workshops such as "International Print Triennial / Interfaces", "Realm- Eyes On / Monat der fotografie Wien", "Mamut Art Project", "TUYAP Art Fair", "Aspects of Balkan Photography". He is doing photography, alternative photographic printing techniques, installation and video projects. He often uses alternative photographic printing techniques, which can convey contemporary and avant-garde images, emanating emotionally and symbolically with the manipulation of visual information, tonality, texture, material and detail. The main subjects of photography, video and photo installations are mostly the use of queer theory, gender emphasis, body- power relation and the protest of the body.

Index

A

C

D

E

G

www.ingramcontent.com/pod-product-compliance
Lightning Source LLC
LaVergne TN
LVHW062213200926
848484LV00006B/1384